The Handbook of Artificial Intelligence

Volume IV

The Handbook of Artificial Intelligence

Volume IV

edited by

Avron Barr

Paul R. Cohen

and

Edward A. Feigenbaum

ADDISON-WESLEY PUBLISHING COMPANY, INC.
Reading, Massachusetts   Menlo Park, California   New York
Don Mills, Ontario   Wokingham, England   Amsterdam   Bonn
Sydney   Singapore   Tokyo   Madrid   San Juan

Many of the designations used by manufacturers and sellers to distinguish their products are claimed as trademarks. Where those designations appear in this book and Addison-Wesley was aware of a trademark claim, the designations have been printed in initial capital letters.

Library of Congress Cataloging-in-Publication Data
(Revised for volume 4)

The Handbook of artificial intelligence.

Includes bibliographies and indexes.
Vol. 4 edited by Avron Barr, Paul R. Cohen, and
Edward A. Feigenbaum.
Vol.   has imprint: Reading, Mass.: Addison-Wesley Pub. Co.
   I. Artificial intelligence.   I. Barr, Avron, 1949–   .
II. Feigenbaum, Edward A.   III. Cohen, Paul R.
Q335.H36   006.3   80-28621

ISBN 0-201-51819-8 (hrd.)
ISBN 0-201-51731-0 (pbk.)

Cover design by Copenhaver Cumpston
Text design by Dianne Kanerva
Set in 10-point Century Schoolbook by DEKR Corporation

ABCDEFGHIJ-DO-89
First printing, December, 1989

To the memory of our good friend
Dianne Kanerva
(Technical Editor, *The Handbook of Artificial Intelligence*
Volumes I–III)

Editors

Avron Barr
Paul R. Cohen
Edward A. Feigenbaum

Contributors

H. Penny Nii

Edmund H. Durfee
Victor R. Lesser
Daniel D. Corkill

Bruce G. Buchanan
Reid G. Smith

James Allen

Michael R. Lowry
Raul Duran

Yumi Iwasaki

Alfred Round

Robert M. Haralick
Alan K. Mackworth
Steven L. Tanimoto

CONTENTS OF VOLUME IV

Acknowledgments

The editors and authors thank the following individuals.

Michael B. Albers	Herve Lambert
Mohamed Bachiri	G. E. Light
David Barstow	Virginia G. Lowry
Ross Beveridge	Mitchell Lubars
Inderpal Bhandari	Roy Maxion
Harold Brown	Ian Miller
Jim Daniell	Steven Painter
Clive Dym	Derek Partridge
Bob Engelmore	Liam Peyton
Larry Eshelman	Thomas Pressburger
Allen Goldberg	Eric Schoen
Cordell Green	Jos Schreinemakers
David Hammock	Linda Shapiro
Mehdi Harandi	Jay Showalter
Neil Iscoe	Douglas Smith
Yoshiteru Ishida	David Steier
Peter Jackson	Marilyn Stelzner
Philip Johnson	Eswaran Subramanian
Laura Jones	Bob Woodham
Richard Jullig	Robert Young

PREFACE

The Handbook of Artificial Intelligence began as a seminar directed by Edward Feigenbaum at Stanford University in the Spring of 1975. The idea was that if each student wrote eight or ten short articles, this would be sufficient to cover much of the field. Like many early AI projects, the *Handbook* had big goals but was somewhat naive about what it would take to achieve them. Ultimately it took more than one hundred graduate students and researchers, roughly 1500 pages, and seven years to represent most of AI at a level of detail that was accessible but not superficial. And we almost missed the boat: The early 1980s were certainly the last opportunity to survey the whole field with a successful balance of breadth, accessibility, and depth. By then, AI was already growing rapidly, like our ubiquitous search trees, getting wider and deeper as scientists extended the field and specialized areas within it. On the commercial front, AI was making front page news.

If we have any illusions that the *Handbook* project was finished in 1982, they were quickly dispelled. First, the books were remarkably successful, which convinced us that they filled a niche. Second, Addison-Wesley took over the *Handbook* and encouraged us to continue the project. Finally, the books had a surprisingly long life given the rapid progress of AI research. It became clear that by the mid-1980s, people were reading the *Handbook* to get a snapshot of the state of AI circa 1980. This convinced us that future volumes of the *Handbook* should not attempt to revise earlier volumes, but should instead summarize the field as we now understand it, circa 1990.

For this reason, we stress that although several chapters in this volume cover topics discussed in previous volumes, they are not revisions of the previous chapters. Computer vision, for example, was covered at length in Volume III by Takeo Kanade and his colleagues. But vision is a huge area of research and the chapter in this volume, by Robert Haralick, Alan Mackworth and Steven Tanimoto, offers a different perspective. Similarly, new distinctions and perspectives underlie the chapter by Michael Lowry and Raul Duran; in Volume II, the topic was called Automatic Programming, here it is Knowledge-based Software Engineering.

Two other chapters synthesize recent work in new frameworks. In his chapter on Natural Language Understanding, James Allen integrates work on unification grammars, semantic processing, contextual

knowledge, and discourse analysis. Some of the most dramatic changes
since the original volumes have happened in the area of Expert Systems.
The original volumes organized the discussions of expert systems not in
terms of architectures, or knowledge representations, or any other underlying principles, but in terms of three applications areas: science, medicine, and education. The new chapter, by Bruce Buchanan and Reid
Smith, offers a framework of fundamental principles and issues, within
which specific expert systems serve as illustrations.

This volume also includes four chapters on topics that were nascent
or nonexistent when we published the previous volumes. Yumi Iwasaki
has written a broad, analytical survey of work in Qualitative Physics,
an area that is becoming increasingly important as AI systems begin to
interact with physical devices in real environments. Alfred Round's chapter on Simulation has similar concerns but a different orientation. It
describes efforts to integrate numerical simulation and AI techniques.
This work is representative of many research ventures that are forging
new technologies at the intersections of AI and other fields.

Edmund Durfee, Victor Lesser, and Daniel Corkill discuss the problem of Cooperative, Distributed AI systems. Researchers in this challenging new area are trying to develop coordinated collections of spatially
and functionally distributed agents that work simultaneously on problems that are too large for individual systems to solve efficiently.
H. Penny Nii's chapter on Blackboard Systems should perhaps be on
everyone's list of basic readings, so pervasive are blackboard architectures in AI today (e.g., most of the systems described in Durfee, Lesser,
and Corkill's chapter are based on blackboards).

In the early days of the *Handbook* project, individual articles were
contributed by graduate students and assembled into chapters by the
editors. Often the editors rewrote the articles, making us de facto
authors. By the time the third volume was being compiled, however, we
had stopped soliciting individual articles. Nearly all the chapters in
Volume III were produced by one or two experts. This gave us longer,
more integrated chapters, although the basic form continued to be one
or more overview articles followed by discussions of individual systems.

In Volume IV, we went one step further and commissioned signed
chapters by some of the best people in the field. We asked them to describe
the state of the art, the significant developments and the open questions
in their areas. We bid authors to strive for breadth (albeit within one
area of AI) and depth, although we secretly believed they would have to
sacrifice breadth for depth. Remarkably, this didn't happen. Instead,
many sacrificed the "Handbook format" of the first three volumes. To see
why this is significant, recall the structure of previous *Handbook* chapters: an introductory section was often followed by an "issue" section,
and then by several sections—the bulk of every chapter—describing

systems. In this volume, in contrast, the bulk of every chapter is devoted to issues, principles, and theory. Although systems still figure prominently, much more text is given to their analysis. It reflects a significant maturation of AI that this volume of the *Handbook* is less concerned with the systems we build than with what we have learned and have still to learn by building them.

Avron Barr
Paul Cohen
Ed Feigenbaum

Chapter XVI

Blackboard Systems

H. Penny Nii—Stanford University

CHAPTER XVI: BLACKBOARD SYSTEMS

A. OVERVIEW

HISTORICALLY THE BLACKBOARD MODEL arose from abstracting features of the HEARSAY-II (Erman et al., 1980) speech-understanding system developed between 1971 and 1976. HEARSAY-II was able to respond to spoken commands and queries about computer science abstracts stored in a database. From an informal summary description of the HEARSAY-II program, the HASP system was designed and implemented between 1973 and 1975. The domain of HASP was ocean surveillance, and its task was the interpretation of continuous passive sonar data. (*Domain* refers to a particular area of discourse, for example, chemistry. *Task* refers to a goal-oriented activity within the domain, for example, to analyze the molecular composition of a compound.) HASP, as the second example of a blackboard system, not only added credibility to the claim that a blackboard approach to problem solving was general, but it also demonstrated that it could be abstracted into a robust model of problem solving. Subsequently many application programs have been implemented whose solutions were formulated using the blackboard model. Because the characteristics of the application problems differed and the interpretation of the blackboard model varied, the design of these programs differed considerably. However, the blackboard model of problem solving has not undergone any substantial changes in the last fifteen years.

B.   BLACKBOARD MODEL OF PROBLEM SOLVING

A *problem-solving model* is a scheme for organizing reasoning steps and domain knowledge to construct a solution to a problem. *Reasoning* refers to a computational process whereby needed information is inferred from what is already known.

For example, in a *backward-reasoning model*, problem solving begins by reasoning backward from a goal to be achieved toward an initial state (data). More specifically, in a *rule-based backward-reasoning model*, knowledge is organized as if-then rules and modus ponens inference steps are applied to the rules from a goal rule back to an "initial-state rule" (a rule whose premise clause matches input data; see Article III.C4, in Vol. I). An excellent example of this approach to problem solving is the MYCIN program (Shortliffe, 1976; see Article VIII.B1, in Vol. II). In a *forward-reasoning model*, however, the inference steps are applied from an initial state toward a goal. The OPS system exemplifies such a reasoning model (Forgy and McDermott, 1977). In an *opportunistic reasoning model,* pieces of knowledge are applied either backward or forward at the most "opportune" time (see Article XI.C, Vol. III).

Put another way, the central issue of problem solving is the question: "What pieces of knowledge should be applied when and how?" A problem-solving model provides a conceptual framework for organizing knowledge and a strategy for applying that knowledge.

B1.   The Blackboard Model

THE BLACKBOARD MODEL of problem solving is a highly structured, special case of opportunistic problem solving. In addition to opportunistic reasoning as a knowledge-application strategy, the blackboard model prescribes the organization of the domain knowledge and all the input and intermediate and partial solutions needed to solve the problem. We refer to all possible partial and full solutions to a problem as its *solution space* (see Article II.A, Vol. I).

In the blackboard model, the solution space is organized into one or more application-dependent hierarchies. (The hierarchy may be an abstraction hierarchy, a part-of hierarchy, or any other type of hierarchy appropriate for solving the problem.) Information at each level in the hierarchy represents partial solutions and is represented by a unique vocabulary that describes the information. The domain knowledge is partitioned into independent modules of knowledge that transform information on one level of the hierarchy, possibly using information at other levels, into information on the same or other levels. The knowledge modules perform the transformation using algorithmic procedures or heuristic rules that generate actual or hypothetical transformations. Opportunistic reasoning is applied within this overall organization of the solution-space and task-specific knowledge; that is, which module of knowledge to apply is determined dynamically, one step at a time, resulting in the incremental generation of partial solutions. The choice of a knowledge module is based on the solution state (particularly the latest additions and modifications to the data structure containing pieces of the solution) and on the existence of knowledge modules capable of improving the current state of the solution.

At each step of knowledge application, either forward- or backward-reasoning methods may be applied. There are various other ways of categorizing reasoning methods, for example, event driven, goal driven, model driven, expectation driven, and so forth. Without getting into the subtle differences between these methods, it is safe to say that any one of these reasoning methods can be applied at each step in the problem-solving process.

The blackboard model is usually described as consisting of three major components, as shown in Figure B–1:

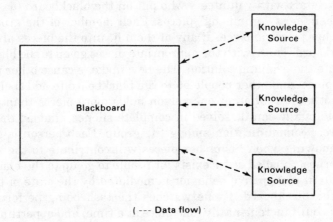

(--- Data flow)

Figure B–1.   The blackboard model.

1. *The knowledge sources*—The knowledge needed to solve the problem is partitioned into *knowledge sources*, which are kept separate and independent.

2. *The blackboard data structure*—The problem-solving state data are kept in a global data store, the *blackboard*. Knowledge sources produce changes to the blackboard, which lead incrementally to a solution to the problem. Communication and interaction among the knowledge sources take place solely through the blackboard.

3. *Control*—The knowledge sources *respond opportunistically to changes* in the blackboard.

Although the structure of the control is left open, the *scheduler*, as will be described shortly, implements the *control strategy*. The actual locus of control can be in the knowledge sources, on the blackboard, in a separate module, or in some combination of the three.

The difficulty with this description of the blackboard model is that it only outlines the organizational principles. For those interested in building a blackboard system, the model does not specify how it is to be realized as a computational entity—the blackboard model is a conceptual entity, not a computational specification. Given a problem to be solved, the blackboard model provides enough guidelines for sketching a solution, but a sketch is a long way from a working system. To design and build a system, a detailed model is needed. Before moving on to add details to the blackboard model, we explore the implied behavior of this abstract model.

Let us consider a hypothetical problem of a group of people trying to put together a jigsaw puzzle (Figure B–2). Imagine a room with a large blackboard and around it a group of people each holding oversized jigsaw pieces. We start with volunteers who put on the blackboard (assume it's sticky) their most "promising" pieces. Each member of the group looks at his or her pieces and sees if any of them fit into the pieces already on the blackboard. Those with the appropriate pieces go up to the blackboard and update the evolving solution. The new updates cause other pieces to fall into place, and other people go to the blackboard to add their pieces. It does not matter whether one person holds more pieces than another. The whole puzzle can be solved in complete silence; that is, there need be no direct communication among the group. Each person is self-activating, knowing when his or her pieces will contribute to the solution. No a priori established order exists for people to go up to the blackboard. The apparent cooperative behavior is mediated by the state of the solution on the blackboard. If one watches the task being performed, the solution is built incrementally (one piece at a time) and opportunistically (as an opportunity for adding a piece arises), as opposed to starting, say, systematically from the left top corner and trying each piece.

Figure B–2.   Solving jigsaw puzzles.

This analogy illustrates quite well the blackboard problem-solving behavior implied in the model. Now, let's change the layout of the room in such a way that there is only one center aisle wide enough for one person to get through to the blackboard. Now, no more than one person can go up to the blackboard at one time, and a monitor is needed, someone who can see the group and can choose the order in which a person is to go up to the blackboard. The monitor can ask all people who have pieces to add to raise their hands. The monitor can then choose one person from those with their hands raised. To select one person, criteria for making the choice are needed; for example, the person who raises a hand first, the person with a piece that bridges two solution islands (that is, two clusters of completed pieces), and so forth. The monitor needs a strategy or a set of strategies for solving the puzzle. The monitor can establish a strategy before the puzzle solving begins or can develop strategies as the solution begins to unfold. In any case, note that the monitor has broad executive power. The monitor has so much power that it could, for example, force the puzzle to be solved systematically from left to right; that is, the monitor has the power to violate one essential characteristic of the original blackboard model, that of opportunistic problem solving.

This analogy, though slightly removed from the original one, in which multiple people could work at the blackboard simultaneously, is useful for computer programmers interested in building blackboard systems. Given the serial nature of most current computers, the conceptual distance between the original analogy and a running blackboard system is a bit far, and the mapping from the analogy to a system is prone to misinterpretation. By adding the constraint that solution building physically occurs one step at a time, in some order determined by the monitor (when multiple steps are possible and desirable), the blackboard model is brought closer to the realities inherent in serial computing environments.

Although the analogy to jigsaw puzzle solving gives us additional clues to the nature of the behavior of blackboard systems, it is not a very good example for illustrating the organization of the blackboard or the partitioning of appropriate knowledge into knowledge sources. To illustrate these aspects of the model, we need another example. This time let us consider another hypothetical problem, that of finding koalas in a eucalyptus forest (Figure B–3).

Imagine yourself in Australia. One of the musts if you are a tourist is to go and look for koalas in their natural habitat. So, you go to a koala preserve and start looking for them among the branches of the eucalyptus trees. You find none. You know that they are rather small, grayish creatures that look like bears. (More details at this descriptive level would be considered factual knowledge and can be used as a part of a prototypical model of koalas.) The forest is dense, however, and the combination of rustling leaves and the sunlight reflecting on the leaves adds to the difficulty of finding these creatures, whose coloring is similar to their environment. (The signal-to-noise ratio is low.)

You finally give up and ask a ranger how you can find them. He gives you the following story about koalas: "Koalas usually live in groups

Figure B–3.   Finding koalas (photo by Ron Garrison,
Zoological Society of San Diego).

and seasonally migrate to different parts of the forest, but they should be around the northwest area of the preserve now. They usually sit on the crook of branches and move up and down the tree during the day to get just the right amount of sun. (This is knowledge about the prototypical behavior patterns of koalas. The ranger suggests a highly model-driven approach to finding koalas.) If you are not sure whether you have spotted one, watch it for a while; it will move around, though slowly. (This is a method of detection as well as confirmation.)" Armed with the new knowledge, you go back to the forest with a visual image of exactly where and what to look for. You focus your eyes at about 30 feet with no luck, but you try again, and this time focus your eyes at 50 feet, and suddenly you do find one. Not only one, but a whole colony of them.

Let's consider one way of formulating this problem along the lines of the blackboard model. Many kinds of knowledge can be brought to bear on the problem: the color and shape of koalas, the general color and texture of the environment (the noise characteristics), the behavior of the koalas, effects of season and time of the day, and so on. Some of the knowledge can be found in hypothetical books, such as a *Handbook of Koala Sizes and Color* or *Geography of the Forest*. Some knowledge is informal—the most likely places to find koalas at any given time or their favorite resting places. How can these diverse sources of knowledge be used effectively? First, we need to decide what constitutes a solution to the problem. Then, we can consider what kinds of information are in the data, what can be inferred from them, and what knowledge might be brought to bear to achieve the goal of finding the koalas.

Think of the solution to this problem as a set of markings on a series of snapshots of the forest. The markings might say, "This is certainly a koala because it has a head, body, and limbs and because it has changed its position since the last snapshot;" or "This might be a koala, because it has a blob that looks like a head;" or "These might be koalas because they are close to the one we know is a koala and the blobs could be heads, legs, or torsos." The important characteristics of the solution are that the solution consists of bits and pieces of information and that it is a reasoned solution with supporting evidence and supporting lines of reasoning.

Having decided that the solution would consist of partial and hypothetical identifications, as well as complete identifications constructed from partial ones, we need a solution-space organization that can hold descriptions of bits and pieces of the koalas. One such descriptive framework is a part-of hierarchy. For each koala, the highest level of description is the koala itself, which is described on the next level by head and body; the head is described on the next level by ears, nose, and eyes; the body is described by torso, legs, and arms; and so on. Each level has descriptors appropriate for that level; size, gender, and height on the koala level, for example. Each primitive body part might be described on the lower levels in terms of geometric features, such as shapes and line segments. Each shape has color and texture associated with it as well as its geometric descriptions (see Figure B–4). To identify a part of the snapshot as a koala, we need to mark the picture with line segments and regions. The regions and pieces of lines must eventually be combined, or synthesized, in such a way that the description of the constructed object can be construed as parts of a koala or a koala itself. For example, a small, black circular blob could be an eye, but it must be surrounded by a bigger, lighter head blob. The more pieces of information we can find that fit the koala description, the more confident we can be. In addition to the body parts that support the existence of a koala, if the hypothesized koala is at about 30 to 50 feet above ground, we would be more confident than if we found the same object at 5 feet.

The knowledge needed to fill in the koala descriptions falls into place with the decision to organize the solution space as a part-of abstraction hierarchy. We would need a color specialist, a shape specialist, a body-part specialist, a habitat specialist, and so forth. No one source of knowledge can solve the problem; the solution to the problem depends on the combined contributions of many specialists. The knowledge held by these specialists is logically independent. Thus a color specialist can determine the color of a region without knowing how the shape specialist determined the shape of the region. However, the solution of the problem depends on both of them. The torso specialist does not have to know whether the arm specialist checked if an arm had paws or not (the torso

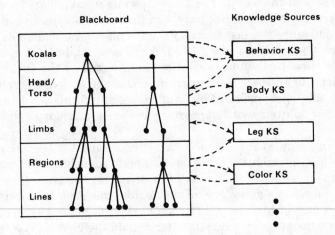

Figure B–4. Koalas: Blackboard structure and knowledge sources.

specialist probably doesn't even know about paws), but each specialist must rely on the others to supply the information each needs. Cooperation is achieved by assuming that whatever information is needed is supplied by someone else.

The jigsaw puzzle and the koala problems illustrate the organization of information on the blackboard data structure, the partitioning of domain knowledge into specialized sources of knowledge, and some of the characteristic problem-solving behavior associated with the blackboard model. Neither of these, however, answers the questions of how the knowledge is to be represented, or what the mechanisms are for determining and activating appropriate pieces of knowledge. As mentioned earlier, problem-solving models are conceptual frameworks for formulating solutions to problems. The models do not address the details of designing and building operational systems. How a piece of knowledge is represented, as rules, objects, or procedures, is an engineering decision. It involves such pragmatic considerations as "naturalness," availability of a knowledge representation language, and the skill of the implementers, among others. What control mechanisms are needed depends on the complexity and the nature of the application task. We can, however, attempt to narrow the gap between the model and operational systems by adding more details to the three primary components in terms of their structures, functions, and behaviors.

B2.   The Blackboard Framework

APPLICATIONS ARE IMPLEMENTED with different combinations of knowledge representations, reasoning schemes, and control mechanisms. The variability in the design of blackboard systems is due to many factors, the most influential being the nature of the application problem itself. It can be seen, however, that blackboard architectures underlying the application programs have many similar features and constructs. (Some of the better known applications are discussed in Section D, and architectural alternatives are described in Section E.)

The *blackboard framework* is created by abstracting these constructs. (An implicit assumption is made that systems can be described at various levels of abstraction. Thus the description of the framework is more detailed than the model and less detailed than a specification, a description from which a system can be constructed. Here, they are called the model, framework, and specification levels.) The blackboard framework, therefore, contains descriptions of the blackboard system components that are grounded in actual computational constructs.

The purpose of the framework is to provide design guidelines appropriate for blackboard systems in serial computing environments. We can view the blackboard framework as prescriptive; that is, it prescribes what must be in a blackboard system specification. However, note that application problems often demand extensions to the framework, as can be seen in the sample systems in Section D. Figure B–5 shows some modifications to Figure A–1 to reflect the addition of system-oriented details.

The knowledge sources.   The domain knowledge needed to solve a problem is partitioned into *knowledge sources* that are kept separate and independent. The objective of each knowledge source is to contribute information that will lead to a solution to the problem. A knowledge source takes a subset of current information on the blackboard and updates it as encoded in its specialized knowledge.

> Each knowledge source is responsible for knowing the conditions under which it can contribute to a solution. Each knowledge source has *preconditions* that indicate the condition that must exist on the blackboard before the body of the knowledge source is *activated*.

> The knowledge sources are represented as procedures, sets of rules, or logic assertions. To date most of the knowledge sources have been represented as either procedures or as sets of rules. Systems that deal with signal processing either make liberal use of procedures in their rules or use procedurally encoded knowledge sources.

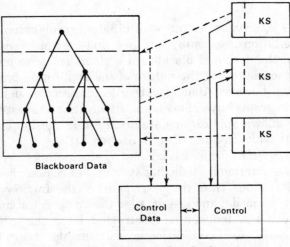

(— Control flow; --- Data flow)

Figure B–5.   The blackboard framework.

The knowledge sources modify only the blackboard or control data structures (which will be described shortly), and only the knowledge sources modify the blackboard. All modifications to the solution states are explicit and visible.

We can view a knowledge source as a large rule. The major difference between a rule and a knowledge source is the granularity of the knowledge each holds. The condition part of this large rule is often called the *knowledge source precondition,* and the action part is called the *knowledge source body.*

The blackboard data structure. The problem-solving state data are kept in a global data store, the *blackboard.* Knowledge sources produce changes to the blackboard that lead incrementally to a solution, or a set of acceptable solutions, to the problem. Interaction among the knowledge sources takes place solely through changes on the blackboard.

The blackboard consists of objects from the solution space. These objects can be input data, partial solutions, alternatives, and final solutions (and, possibly, control data). The design of the blackboard structure reflects the basic plan for how the problem is to be solved. The objects on the blackboard are hierarchically organized into levels of analysis. Information associated with objects (that is, their properties) on one level serves as input to a set of knowledge sources, which, in turn, place new information on the same or other levels.

The objects and their properties define the vocabulary of the solution space. The properties are represented as attribute-value pairs. Each level uses a distinct subset of the vocabulary. (Many times, the names of the attributes on different levels are the same, for example, "type." Often these are shorthand notations for "type-of-x-object" or "type-of-y-object." Sometimes they are duplications of the same attribute for convenience.)

The relationships between the objects are denoted by named links. The relationship can be between objects on different levels, such as "part-of" or "in-support-of," or between objects on the same level, such as "next-to" or "follows."

The blackboard can have multiple blackboard panels; that is, a solution space can be partitioned into multiple hierarchies.

Control. The knowledge sources *respond opportunistically to changes* on the blackboard.

A set of control modules monitors the changes on the blackboard, and a scheduler decides what actions to take next.

Various kinds of information are made globally available to the control modules. The information can be on the blackboard or kept separately.

The control information is used by the control modules to determine the *focus of attention*.

The focus of attention indicates the next thing to be processed. It can be either the knowledge sources (that is, which knowledge sources to activate next) or the blackboard objects (which solution islands to pursue next), or a combination of both (which knowledge sources to apply to which intermediate solutions).

The solution is built one step at a time. Any type of reasoning step (data driven, goal driven, expectation driven, and so on) can be applied at each stage of solution formation. As a result, the sequence of knowledge source invocations is dynamic and opportunistic rather than fixed and preprogrammed.

Pieces of problem-solving activities occur in the following iterative sequence:

1. A knowledge source makes change(s) to blackboard object(s). As these changes are made, a record is kept in a global data structure that holds the control information.

2. Each knowledge source indicates the contribution it can make to the new solution state. (This can be defined a priori for an application, or dynamically determined.)

3. Using the information from points 1 and 2, a scheduler selects a focus of attention.

4. Depending on the information contained in the focus of attention, an appropriate control module prepares it for execution as follows:
   a. If the focus of attention is a knowledge source, a blackboard object (or sometimes, a set of blackboard objects) is chosen to serve as its context (knowledge-centered scheduling).
   b. If the focus of attention is a blackboard object, a knowledge source to process that object is chosen and instantiated with the object as its context (event-centered scheduling).
   c. If the focus of attention is a knowledge source and an object, an instance of that knowledge source is made ready for execution with the object as its context.

Termination criteria.   Criteria are provided to determine when to terminate the problem-solving process. Usually, one of the knowledge sources indicates when the problem-solving process is terminated, either because an acceptable solution has been found or because the system cannot continue further for lack of knowledge or data.

Problem-Solving Behavior and Knowledge Application

The problem-solving behavior of a system is determined by the knowledge-application strategy encoded in the control modules. The choice of the most appropriate knowledge-application strategy depends on the characteristics of the application task and on the quality and quantity of domain knowledge available to the task.

It might be said that this is a hedge, that there should be a knowledge-application strategy or a set of strategies built into the framework to reflect different problem-solving behaviors. It is precisely this lack of doctrine that makes the blackboard framework powerful and useful. If an application task calls for two forward-reasoning steps followed by three backward-reasoning steps at some particular point, the framework allows for this. This is not to say that a system with built-in strategies cannot be designed and built. If there is a knowledge-application strategy "generic" to a class of applications, it might be worthwhile to build a skeletal system with that particular strategy. See Section D4 for an example.

Basically the acts of choosing a particular blackboard region and choosing a particular knowledge source to operate on that region determine the problem-solving behavior. Generally a knowledge source uses information on one level as its input and produces output information on another level. Thus, if the input level of a particular knowledge source is on the level lower (closer to data) than its output level, the application of this knowledge source results in bottom-up forward reasoning.

Conversely, a commitment to a particular type of reasoning step is a commitment to a particular knowledge-application method. For example, if we are interested in applying a data-directed, forward-reasoning step, we would select a knowledge source whose input level is lower than its output level. If we are interested in goal-directed reasoning, we would select a knowledge source that put the information needed to satisfy a goal on a lower level. Using the constructs in the control component, we can make any type of reasoning step happen at each step of knowledge application.

How a piece of knowledge is stated often presupposes how it is to be used. Given a piece of knowledge about a relationship between information on two levels, that knowledge can be expressed in top-down or bottom-up application forms. These can further be refined. The top-down form can be written as a goal, an expectation, or as an abstract model of the lower level information. For example, a piece of knowledge can be expressed as a conjunction of information on a lower level needed to generate a hypothesis at a higher level (a goal), or it can be expressed as information on a lower level needed to confirm a hypothesis at a higher level (an expectation), and so on. The framework does not presuppose nor does it prescribe the knowledge-application, or reasoning, methods. It merely provides constructs within which any reasoning methods can be implemented. The control component of the framework is extensible in many directions. In the PROTEAN system described in Section D4, the control problem is viewed as a planning problem. Knowledge sources are applied according to a problem-solving plan in affect. The creation of a problem-solving plan is treated as another problem to be solved using the blackboard approach.

B3. Perspectives

THE ORGANIZATIONAL UNDERPINNINGS of blackboard systems have been our primary focus. The blackboard framework is a system-oriented interpretation of the blackboard model. It is a mechanistic formulation intended to serve as a foundation for system specifications. In describing problem-solving programs, we are usually interested in their performance and problem-solving behavior, not their organization. We have found, however, that some classes of complex problems become manageable when they are formulated and organized along the lines of the blackboard model. Also, interesting problem-solving behavior can be programmed using the blackboard organization as a foundation.

Even though the blackboard framework still falls short of being a computational specification, given an application task and the necessary task domain knowledge, it provides enough information so that a suitable blackboard system can be designed, specified, and built. Some examples of complex problems with interesting problem-solving behavior are discussed in Section D. The examples show that new constructs can be added to the blackboard framework as the application problems demand, without violating its guidelines.

There are other perspectives on the blackboard model. It is sometimes viewed as a model of general problem solving (Hayes-Roth, 1983). It has been used to structure cognitive models (McClelland, 1981, and Rumelhart and McClelland, 1982). The OPM system (Hayes-Roth et al., 1979) simulates the human planning process (see Article XI.C, Vol. III). Sometimes the blackboard model is used as an organizing principle for large, complex systems built by many programmers. The ALVan project (Stentz and Shafer, 1985) takes this approach.

B4. Summary

THE BASIC APPROACH to problem solving in the blackboard framework is to divide the problem into loosely coupled subtasks. These subtasks roughly correspond to areas of specialization within the task. For a particular application, the designer organizes the solution space and knowledge needed to find the solution. The solution space is divided into analysis levels of intermediate solutions, and the knowledge is partitioned into knowledge sources that perform the subtasks of finding the intermediate solutions. The intermediate solutions are globally accessible on the blackboard, making it a medium of interaction between the knowledge sources. Generally a knowledge source uses information on one level of analysis as its input and produces output information on another level. The decision to employ a particular knowledge source is made dynamically using the latest information on the blackboard. This particular approach to problem decomposition and knowledge application is very flexible and works well in diverse application domains. One caveat, however: How the problem is partitioned into subtasks makes a great deal of difference to the clarity of the approach, the speed with which solutions are found, the resources required, and even the ability to solve the problem at all.

C. EVOLUTION OF BLACKBOARD ARCHITECTURES

Metaphorically we can think of a set of workers, all looking at the same blackboard: each is able to read everything that is on it, and to judge when he has something worthwhile to add to it. This conception is just that of Selfridge's Pandemonium (Selfridge, 1959): a set of demons, each independently looking at the total situation and shrieking in proportion to what they see that fits their natures. (Allen Newell, 1962)

C1. Prehistory

THE PRECEDING QUOTATION is the first reference to the term *blackboard* in the AI literature. Newell was concerned with the organizational problems of programs that existed at the time (for example, checker-playing programs, chess-playing programs, and theorem-proving programs), most of which were organized along a generate-and-test search model. (Newell, 1969) (See Article II, Volume I of the *Handbook*.) The major difficulty in these programs was rigidity. Newell notes:

> . . . a program can operate only in terms of what it knows. This knowledge can come from only two sources. It can come from assumptions [or] it can come from executing processes . . . either by direct modification of the data structure or by testing . . . but executing processes take time and space [whereas] assumed information does not have to be stored or generated. Therefore the temptation in creating efficient programs is always to minimize the amount of generated information, and hence to maximize the amount of stipulated information. It is the latter that underlies most of the rigidities.

In one example, Newell discusses an organization to synthesize complex processes by means of sequential flow of control and hierarchically organized, closed subroutines. Even though this organization had many advantages (isolation of tasks, space saving by coding nearly identical tasks once, and so on), it also had difficulties. First, conventions required for communication among the subroutines often forced the subroutines to work with impoverished information. Second, the ordered subroutine calls fostered the need for doing things sequentially. Third, and most importantly, it encouraged programmers to think of the total program in terms of only one thing going on at a time. In problem solving, however, many things often can be processed at any given time (for example, exploring various branches of a search tree), and relatively weak and scattered information is necessary to guide the exploration for a solution (for example, observations noticed while going down one branch of a search tree could be used when going down another branch). The primary difficulties with this organization, then, were inflexible control and restricted data accessibility. It is within this context that Newell notes that the difficulties "might be alleviated by maintaining the isolation of routines, but allowing all the subroutines to make use of a common data structure." He uses the blackboard metaphor to describe such a system.

The blackboard solution proposed by Newell eventually became the production system (Newell and Simon, 1972), which in turn led to the development of the OPS system (Forgy and McDermott, 1977). In OPS, the "subroutines" are represented as *condition-action rules*, and the data are globally available in the *working memory*. (See Davis and King, 1977; and Article III.C4, Vol. I, for an overview of production systems.) One of the many "shrieking demons" (those rules whose "condition sides" are satisfied) is selected through a *conflict-resolution* process. This emulates the selection of one of the loudest demons, for example, one that addresses the most specific situation. Although not a blackboard system, OPS does reflect the blackboard concept as stated by Newell and provides for flexibility of control and global accessibility to data. The blackboard systems as we know them today took a slightly more circuitous route before coming into being.

In a paper first published in 1966 (later published in Simon, (1977)), Simon mentions the term blackboard in a slightly different context from Newell. The discussion is within the framework of an information processing theory about discovery and incubation of ideas:

> In the typical organization of a problem-solving program, the solution efforts are guided and controlled by a hierarchy or tree of goals and subgoals. Thus the subject starts out with the goal of solving the original problem. In trying to reach this goal, he generates a subgoal. If the subgoal is achieved, he may then turn to the now-modified original goal. If difficulties arise in achieving the subgoal, sub-subgoals may be created to deal with them . . . we would specify that the goal tree be held in some kind of temporary memory, since it is a dynamic structure, whose function is to guide search, and it is not needed when the problem solution has been found. . . . In addition, the problem solver is noticing various features of the problem environment and is storing some of

these in memory. . . . What use is made of [a feature] at the time it is noted depends on what subgoal is directing attention at that moment . . . over the longer run, this information influences the growth of the subgoal tree. . . . I will call the information about the task environment that is noticed in the course of problem solution and fixated in permanent (or relatively long-term) memory the 'blackboard.'

Although Newell's and Simon's concerns appear within different contexts, the problem-solving method they were using was the goal-directed, generate-and-test search method. They encountered two common difficulties: the need for previously generated information during problem solving and flexible control. It was Simon who proposed the blackboard ideas to Raj Reddy and Lee Erman for the HEARSAY project.[1]

Although the blackboard metaphor was suggested by Simon to the HEARSAY designers, the final design of the system, as might be expected, evolved out of the needs of the speech-understanding task. Such system characteristics as hierarchically organized analysis levels on the blackboard and opportunistic reasoning, which we now accept as integral parts of blackboard systems, were derived from needs and constraints that were different from Newell's and Simon's. Analysis levels were especially important because they permitted the use and integration of different "vocabularies" in problem solving. In most problem-solving programs of the time such as game-playing and theorem-proving programs, the problem space had a homogeneous vocabulary. In the speech-understanding problem, there was a need to integrate concepts and vocabularies used in describing grammars, words, phones, and so on.

Two interesting observations are to be made from early history. First, the early allusions to a blackboard are closely tied to search methodologies, and, not surprisingly, the use of generate-and-test search is evident in HEARSAY-II. Second, although the HEARSAY-II blackboard system was designed independently from the OPS system, there are, as we might expect, some conceptual similarities. For example, the *scheduler* in HEARSAY-II is philosophically and functionally very similar to the *conflict-resolution* module in OPS, which, in turn, is a way of selecting one of the shrieking demons.

C2.   The HEARSAY Project

THE FIRST ARTICLE on the HEARSAY system appeared in the *IEEE Transactions on Audio and Electroacoustics* in 1973 (Reddy et al., 1973a).[2]

---

[1] These historical notes are communications from Herbert Simon.
[2] The manuscript was delivered to IEEE on April 30, 1972.

There, the authors described the limitations of extant speech-recognition systems and proposed a model that would overcome them. The article stated that although the importance of context, syntax, semantics, and phonological rules in the recognition of speech was accepted, no system had been built that incorporated these ill-defined sources of knowledge. At the same time, the authors' previous work indicated:

1. The limitation of syntax-directed methods of parsing from left to right had to be overcome.

2. Parsing should proceed both forward and backward from anchor points.

3. Because of the lack of feedback in a simple part-of hierarchical structure, the magnitude of errors on the lower level propagated multiplicatively up the hierarchy; that is, minor errors in the signal level, for example, became major errors on a sentence level.

The system architecture described in the Reddy article, later to be known as the HEARSAY-I architecture, was based on a model that addressed the following requirements:

1. The contribution of each source of knowledge (syntax, semantics, context, and so on) to the recognition of speech had to be measurable.

2. The absence of one or more knowledge sources should not have a crippling effect on the overall performance.

3. More knowledge sources should improve the performance.

4. The system must permit graceful error recovery.

5. Changes in performance requirements such as increased vocabulary size or modifications to the syntax or semantics should not require major modifications to the model.

The functional diagram of the HEARSAY-I architecture is shown in Figure C–1, and the system behavior is summarized as follows:

The EAR module accepts speech input, extracts parameters, and performs some preliminary segmentation, feature extraction, and labeling, generating a 'partial symbolic utterance description.' The recognition overlord (ROVER) controls the recognition process and coordinates the hypothesis generation and verification phases of various cooperating parallel processes. The TASK provides the interface between the task being performed and the speech recognition and generation (SPEAK-EASY) parts of the system. The system overlord (SOL) provides the overall control for the system.

From Figure C–2 illustrating the recognition process, we can glean the beginnings of an organization of a blackboard system. Note how the recognition overlord (ROVER) controlled the invocation of processes, just

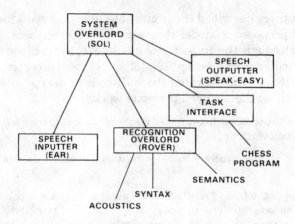

Figure C–1.   Overview of the HEARSAY-I system (from Reddy, 1973a).

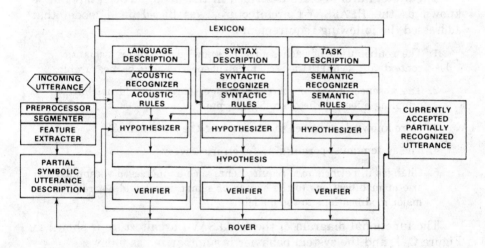

Figure C–2.   Details of the recognition process (from Reddy, 1973a).

as later in HEARSAY-II, the scheduler controlled the invocation of the knowledge sources.

Since the different recognizers are independent, the recognition overlord needs to synchronize the hypothesis generation and verification phases of various processes. . . . Several strategies are available for deciding which subset of the processes generates the hypotheses and which verifies. At present this is done by polling the processes to decide which process is most confident about generating the correct hypothesis. In voice chess, [The task domain for HEARSAY-I was chess moves.] where the semantic source of knowledge is dominant, that module usually generates the hypotheses. These are then verified by the syntactic and acoustic recognizers. However, when robust acoustic cues are present in the incoming utterance, the roles are reversed with the acoustic recognizer generating the hypotheses.

Knowledge sources are activated in a lock-step sequence consisting of three phases: poll, hypothesize, and test. During the polling phase, the recognition overlord queries the knowledge sources to determine which ones have something to contribute to that region of the sentence hypothesis that is "in focus" and with what level of "confidence." In the hypothesizing phase, the most promising knowledge source is activated to make its contribution. Finally, in the testing phase, knowledge sources evaluate the new hypotheses.

Some of the difficulties encountered in HEARSAY-I can be attributed to the way in which the solution to the application task was formulated, and other difficulties arose from the design of the system. The problem was formulated to use the hypothesize-and-test paradigm only on the word level, that is, the blackboard only contained a description at the word level. This meant that all communication among the knowledge sources was limited to sharing information at the word level. This formulation caused two major difficulties. First, it becomes difficult to add nonword knowledge sources and to evaluate their contributions. Second, the inability to share information contributed by nonword knowledge sources caused the information to be recomputed by each knowledge source that needed it. The difficulty lay in trying to force the use of a single vocabulary (that is, from the word level) when multiple vocabularies (for example, on the acoustic level) were needed.

The architectural weaknesses of HEARSAY-I, as stated by its designers, lay in the lock-step control sequence that limited parallelism,[3] the lack of provision to express relationships among alternative sentence hypotheses, and the built-in problem-solving strategy that made modifications awkward and comparisons of different strategies impossible (Lesser et al., 1974). To overcome these difficulties, information (in the multiple vocabularies needed to understand utterances) used by all the knowledge sources was uniformly represented and made globally accessible on the blackboard in HEARSAY-II. In addition, a scheduler dynamically selected and activated the appropriate knowledge sources. The design of the HEARSAY-II system is described in detail in Section D1.

---

[3] The term "parallelism" was used quite early in the project even though at that time the system ran on uniprocessors. Later (ca. 1976), experiments with parallel executions were conducted on the C.mmp system (Fennell and Lesser, 1977).

During the time that HEARSAY-II was being developed, the staff of the HASP project was looking for an approach to solve its application problem. The search for a new methodology came about because the plan-generate-and-test problem-solving method that was successful for interpreting mass-spectrometry data in the DENDRAL program (Lindsay et al., 1980; see Article VII.C, Vol. II) was found to be inappropriate for the problem of interpreting passive sonar signals. In the history of blackboard systems, HASP represents a branching point in the philosophy underlying the design of blackboard systems. Generally later systems can be thought of as modifications of, or extensions, to either the HEARSAY-like or HASP-like designs.

C3. The HASP Project

THE TASK OF HASP was to interpret continuous sonar signals passively collected by hydrophone arrays monitoring an area of the ocean. Signals are received from multiple arrays, each consisting of multiple hydrophones. Each array has some directional resolution. Imagine a large room full of plotters, each recording digitized signals from the hydrophones. Now, imagine an analyst going from one plotter to the next trying to discern what each one is hearing, and then integrating the information from all the plots in order to discern the current activity in the region under surveillance. This interpretation and analysis activity goes on continuously day in and day out. The primary objective of this activity is to detect enemy submarines.

The objective of the HASP project was to write a program that "emulated" the human analysts, that is, to incorporate, in a computer program, the expertise of the analysts, especially their ability to detect submarines. (This was in 1973 before the term "expert system" was coined. The HASP problem was chosen because it appeared to be similar to the DENDRAL problem, a signal interpretation problem for which there were experts who could do the job (see Article VII.C, Vol. II). The system designers were confident that the problem-solving approach taken in DENDRAL would work for HASP. What was DENDRAL's task, and what was its approach? To quote from Feigenbaum (1977), the task was:

> to enumerate plausible structures (atom-bond graphs) for organic molecules, given two kinds of information: analytic instrument data from a mass spectrometer and a nuclear magnetic resonance spectrometer; and

user-supplied constraints on the answers, derived from any other sources of knowledge (instrumental or contextual) available to the user.

DENDRAL's inference procedure is a heuristic search that takes place in three stages, without feedback: *plan-generate-and-test.*

Plan produces direct (i.e., not chained) inference about likely substructures in the molecule from patterns in the data that are indicative of the presence of the substructure. In other words, *Plan* worked with combinatorially reduced abstracted sets to guide the search in a generally fruitful direction.

Generate is a generation process for plausible structures. Its foundation is a combinatorial algorithm that can produce all the topologically legal candidate structures. Constraints supplied by the user or by the *Plan* process prune and steer the generation to produce the plausible set and not the enormous legal set.

Test refines the evaluation of plausibility, discarding less worthy candidates and rank-ordering the remainder for examination by the user. . . . It evaluates the worth of each candidate by comparing its predicted data with the actual input data. . . . Thus, *test* selects the "best" explanation of the data.

If some of the words in this description were replaced, the plan-generate-and-test approach seemed appropriate for the HASP tasks:

Plan by selecting types of ships that could be in the region of interest. The Plan phase would use intelligence reports, shipping logs, and so on.

Generate plausible ship candidates and their signal characteristics.

Test by comparing the predicted signals with the real signals.

The system designers had already talked with the analysts and had read their training manuals. They knew that the necessary knowledge could be represented as rules. Difficulties were encountered immediately; some of these were:

1. The input data arrived in a continuous stream, as opposed to being batched like in DENDRAL. The problem of a continuous data stream was solved by processing data in time-framed batches.

2. The analysis of the activities in the ocean had to be tracked and updated over time. Most importantly, past activities played an important role in the analysis of current activities.

3. Numerous types of information seemed relevant but remote from the interpretation process, for example, the average speeds of ships.

To address the second problem, it was immediately clear that a data structure was needed that was equivalent to a "situation board" used by the analysts; the data structure was called the *current best hypothesis* (CBH). CBH reflected the most recent hypothesis about the situation at any given point in time. This could serve as the basis for generating a "plan;" that is, the CBH could be used as a basis for predicting the situation to be encountered in the next time frame. The prediction process could also use and integrate the variety of information mentioned in item 3. The predicted CBH would then be used to verify that the interpretation from the previous time frame was correct, to reduce the number of alternatives generated during past time frames, and to reduce the number of new signals not accounted for in the predicted CBH that needed to be analyzed in full. CBH was thought of as a cognitive "fly-wheel" that maintained the continuous activities in a region of ocean between time frames.

Then there came the bad news: There was no plausible generator of the solution space, nor any simulator to generate the signals of hypothesized platforms. The bad news had a common root; given a platform, there was a continuum of possible headings, speeds, and aspects relative to an array. Each parameter, in addition to variations in the water temperature, depth, and so on, uniquely affected the signals "heard" at an array. Consequently there was a continuum of possibilities in the solution space, and for the simulator to simulate. The designers tried to limit the number of possibilities, for example, by measuring the headings by unit degrees, but this still left an enormous search space. Moreover, there was insufficient pruning knowledge to make the generate-and-test method practical. The DENDRAL approach was abandoned. Then the designers learned of the HEARSAY-II approach. HEARSAY-II in fact had solution space generators and used them. It was the idea of fusing uncertain and partial solutions to construct solutions, combined with "island driving," that intrigued HASP's designers (see Article V.C1, Vol. I, for a description of "island driving"). The design of the HASP system is described in detail in Section D2.

D. BLACKBOARD APPLICATION SYSTEMS

The APPLICATION SYSTEMS described here are presented in chronological order. The designs of many of the systems are similar because of similarities in the application tasks, propagation of ideas, or involvement of the same designers. Figure D–1 shows a general chronology and intellectual lineage of the various application and skeletal systems. The figure includes some of the better known and better documented systems. Only a few of the many application systems are described here. They are research programs and were selected because they illustrate different designs and because they contributed new ideas and features to the repertoire of blackboard system architectures. For each application, the task and domain characteristics are described. The task description is followed by a summary of the system design in four parts: the blackboard structure, the knowledge source organization, the control component, and the knowledge application strategy employed. Unique features in the system are pointed out and discussed within the context of either the application task or its history.

D1. HEARSAY-II

MOST OF THE BACKGROUND information on HEARSAY-II was covered in Section C2 and is not repeated here. One additional item of historical context is worth noting, however. Various continuous speech-understanding projects were brought under one umbrella in the Defense Advanced Research Projects Agency (DARPA) Speech Understanding Project, a five-year project that began in 1971. The goals of the Speech Understanding Project were to design and implement systems that "accept continuous speech from many cooperative speakers of the general American dialect in a quiet room over a good quality microphone, allowing a slight tuning of the system per speaker, by requiring only natural adaptation by the user, permitting a slightly selected vocabulary of 1000 words, with a highly artificial syntax . . . in a few times real time . . ." (Newell et al., 1973). Hearsay-II was developed at Carnegie-Mellon University for the Speech Understanding Project and successfully met most of these goals.

27

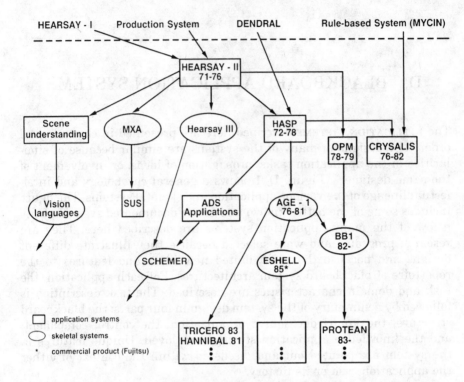

Figure D–1.   Influences among blackboard systems. References: HEAR-
SAY-I (Reddy et al., 1973b); Production system (Newell
and Simon, 1972, and David and King, 1977); DENDRAL
(Lindsay et al., 1980); MYCIN (Shortliffe, 1976); HEAR-
SAY-II (Erman et al., 1980); Scene understanding (Nagao
and Matsuyama, 1980) Vision language (Shafer et al.,
1986); MXA (Lakin and Miles, 1984); SUS (Lakin and
Miles, 1984); HEARSAY-III (Erman et al., 1981); HASP
(Nii et al., 1982); ADS (Advanced Decision Systems Inc.)
applications (Spain, 1983, and McCune and Drazovich,
1983); AGE-1 (Nii and Aiello, 1979); CRYSALIS (Terry,
1983); OPM (Hayes-Roth et al., 1979); BB1 (Hayes-Roth,
1985); TRICERO (Williams et al., 1984); HANNIBAL
(Brown et al., 1982); PROTEAN (Hayes-Roth et al., 1987);
ESHELL (Fujitsu Labs, 1987).

The Task

The goal of the HEARSAY-II system was to understand speech utterances. To prove that it understood a sentence, it performed the spoken commands. In the earlier HEARSAY-I period, the domain of discourse was chess (for example, "Bishop moves to king knight five"). In the HEARSAY-II era, the task was to answer queries about, and to retrieve documents from, a collection of computer science abstracts in the area of artificial intelligence. For example, the system understood the following types of command:

Which abstracts refer to the theory of computation?

List those articles.

What has McCarthy written since nineteen seventy-four?

The HEARSAY-II system was not restricted to any particular task domain. "Given the syntax and the vocabulary of a language and the semantics of the task, it attempts recognition of the utterance in that language" (Reddy et al., 1973b). The vocabulary for the document retrieval task consisted of 1,011 words in which each extended form of a root (for example, the plural of a noun) was counted separately. The grammar defining a legal sentence was context-free, and it included recursion, embedded semantics, and pragmatic constraints. For example, in the place of noun in conventional grammars, this grammar included such non-terminals as topic, author, year, and publisher. The grammar allowed each word to be followed, on the average, by seventeen other words in the vocabulary.

The problem of speech understanding is characterized by error and variability in both the input and the knowledge. "The first source of error is due to deviation between ideal and spoken messages due to inexact production [input], and the second source of error is due to imprecise rules of comprehension [knowledge]" (Erman et al., 1980). Because of these uncertainties, a direct mapping between the speech signals and a sequence of words making up the uttered sentence is not possible. The HEARSAY designers structured the understanding problem as a search in a space consisting of complete and partial interpretations. These interpretations were organized within an abstraction hierarchy containing signal parameters, segments, phones, phonemes, syllables, words, phrases, and sentence levels. This approach required the use of a diverse set of knowledge that produced large numbers of partial solutions on the many levels. Furthermore, the uncertainties in the knowledge generated many competing, alternative hypothetical interpretations.

To avoid a combinatorial explosion, the knowledge sources had to construct partial interpretations by applying constraints at each level of abstraction. For example, one kind of constraint is imposed when an adjacent word is predicted, and the prediction is used to limit subsequent search. The constraints also had to be added in such a way that their accrual reduced the uncertainty inherent in the data and the knowledge sources.

To control the combinatorial explosion and to meet the requirement for near "real-time" understanding, the interpretation process had to be selective in exploiting the most promising hypotheses, both in terms of combining them (for example, combining syllables into words) and in terms of predicting neighboring hypotheses around them (for example, a possible adjective to precede a noun). Thus the need for incremental problem solving and flexible, opportunistic control were inherent in HEARSAY's task.

The Blackboard Structure

The blackboard was partitioned into six to eight (depending on the configuration) levels of analysis corresponding to the intermediate levels of the decoding process. (See Lesser and Erman (1977) for a comprehensive discussion on the results of experiments conducted with two different blackboard configurations.) These levels formed a hierarchy in which the solution-space elements on each level could be described loosely as forming an abstraction of information on its adjacent lower level. One such hierarchy was composed of, from the lowest to the highest level: parametric, segmental, phonetic, phonemic, syllabic, word, word sequence, phrasal, and conceptual levels (see Figures D–2 and D–3). Each blackboard element represented a hypothesis. An element at the lexical level, for example, represented a hypothesized word whose validity was supported by a group of syllables on the syllable class level. The blackboard could be viewed as a three-dimensional problem space with time (utterance sequence) on the x-axis, information levels containing a hypothesized solution on the y-axis, and alternative solutions on the z-axis (Lesser et al., 1974).

Each hypothesis, no matter which level it belonged to, was constructed using a uniform structure of attribute-value pairs. Some attributes, such as its level name, were required for all levels. The attributes included a validity rating and an estimate of the "truth" of the hypothesis represented as some integer value. The relationships among the hypotheses on different levels were represented by links, forming an AND/OR tree over the entire hierarchy. Alternative solutions were formed by expanding along the OR paths. Because of the uncertainty of the knowledge sources that generated the hypotheses, the blackboard had a potential for containing a large number of alternative hypotheses.

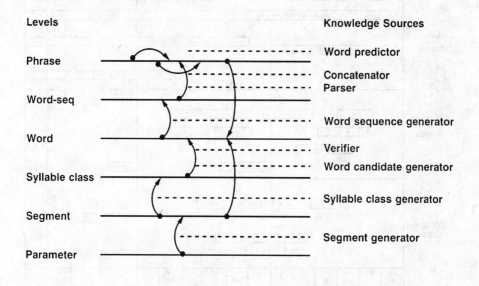

Figure D–2.   HEARSAY-II blackboard and knowledge sources.

The Knowledge Source Structure

Each knowledge source had two major components: a condition part (often referred to as a *precondition*) and an action part. Both the condition and the action parts were written as arbitrary SAIL procedures (see Article VI.C2–5, Vol. II). "The condition component prescribed the situations in which the knowledge sources may contribute to the problem-solving activity, and the action component specified what that contribution was and how to integrate it into the current situation" (Erman et al., 1980). When executed, the condition part searched the blackboard for hypotheses that were of interest to its corresponding action part. In addition, the condition part produced a simple description of the kinds of hypotheses the action part would generate if it were to be activated. That is, the condition part served as a look-ahead in a search process.

Upon activation, the action part performed the generation for all the contexts (the hypotheses) passed to it. For example, the condition part of the Word-Sequence-Generator might produce a description consisting of the lengths of word sequences that the action part would generate. The action part of this knowledge source, if activated, generated the actual sequences of words. The tasks of the knowledge sources ranged from classification (classifying acoustic segments into phonetic classes),

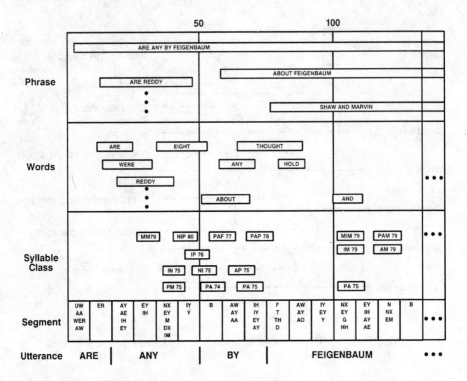

Figure D–3.　A Blackboard state in HEARSAY-II. (From Erman et al., 1980. Copyright, Association for Computer Machinery, Inc. Reprinted by permission.)

to recognition (recognizing words), to generation and evaluation of predictions.

Control

The control component consisted of a blackboard monitor and a scheduler (see Figure D–4). The monitor kept an account of each change made to the blackboard, its primitive change type, and any new hypotheses. Based on the change types and declarative information provided about the condition part of the knowledge sources, the monitor placed pointers to those condition parts, which potentially could be executed, on a scheduling queue.[4] In addition to the condition parts ready for execution, the scheduling queue held a list of pointers to any action parts ready for

[4] In Figure D–4, the "focus-of-control database" contained a table of primitive change types and the condition parts that could process each change type. The primitive change types possible within the system were predefined and consisted of such items as "new syllable" and "new word created bottom up." This paragraph is based on discussions with Lee Erman.

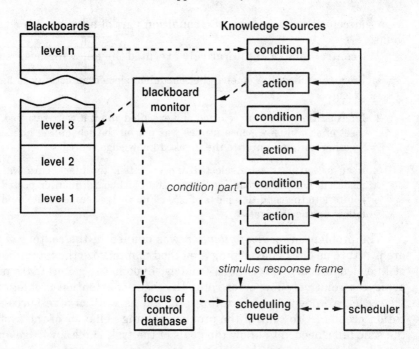

Figure D–4.   Schematic of HEARSAY-II architecture.

execution. These actions parts were called the *invoked knowledge sources*. A knowledge source became invoked when its condition part was successful. The condition parts and the invoked knowledge sources on the scheduling queue were called *activities*. The scheduler calculated a priority for each activity at the start of each system cycle and executed the activity with the highest rating.

To select the most productive activity (the most important and promising with the least amount of processing and memory requirements), the scheduler used experimentally derived heuristics to calculate priorities for each activity. These heuristics were represented as embedded procedures within the scheduler. As described earlier, the look-ahead information needed by the scheduler was provided in part by the condition part of each knowledge source. The condition part produced a *stimulus frame*, a set of hypotheses that satisfied the condition; and a *response frame*, a stylized description of the blackboard changes the knowledge source action part might produce upon execution. For example, the stimulus frame might indicate a specific set of syllables, and the response frame would indicate an action that would produce a word. The scheduler used the stimulus-response frames and other information on the blackboard to select the next thing, either the execution of an invoked knowledge source or the evaluation of a condition part of a knowledge source, to do.

The control component iteratively executed the following basic steps:

1. From the scheduling queue, the scheduler selected an activity to be executed.

2. If a condition part were selected and executed and if it were satisfied, a set of stimulus-response frames was put on the scheduling queue together with a pointer to the invoked knowledge source.

3. If an action part were selected and executed, the blackboard was modified. On the scheduling queue, the blackboard monitor posted pointers to the condition parts of other knowledge sources that could follow up the change.

The problem of *focus of attention* was defined in the context of this architecture as one of developing a method to minimize the total number of knowledge source executions (that is, hypotheses generated) and to achieve a relatively low error rate. The focus-of-attention problem was viewed as a knowledge-scheduling problem as well as a resource-allocation problem.[5] To control the problem-solving behavior of the system, the scheduler needed to know the goals of the task and knowledge application strategies to be able to evaluate the next best move. Although various general solutions have been suggested (Hayes-Roth and Lesser, 1976), it appears that ultimately we need a knowledge-based scheduler to effectively control the combinatoric search and for the effective use of the knowledge sources.

Knowledge-Application Strategy

Within the system framework described earlier, HEARSAY-II employed two problem-solving strategies. The first was a *bottom-up* strategy whereby interpretations were synthesized directly from the data, working up the abstraction hierarchy. For example, a word hypothesis was synthesized from a sequence of phones. The second was a *top-down* strategy in which alternative sentences were produced from a sentential concept, alternative sequences of words from each sentence, alternative sequences of phones from each word, and so on. The goal of this recursive generation process was to produce a sequence on the parametric level that was consistent with the input data (that is, to generate a hypothetical solution and to test it against the data). Both approaches have the

---

[5] If we compare the HEARSAY-II control constructs with those of the blackboard framework discussed in Section B2, they are basically the same. Some aspects of the control in HEARSAY are emphasized more (for example, scheduling) than others.

potential for generating a vast number of alternative hypotheses and with it a combinatorially explosive number of knowledge source activations. Problem-solving activity was, therefore, constrained by selecting only a limited subset of invoked knowledge sources for execution. The scheduling module thus played a crucial role within the HEARSAY-II system.

Orthogonal to the top-down and bottom-up approaches, HEARSAY-II employed a general hypothesize-and-test search strategy. A knowledge source would generate hypotheses, and their validity would be evaluated by some other knowledge source. A hypothesis could be generated by a top-down analytic or a bottom-up synthetic approach. Often a knowledge source generated or tested hypotheses by matching its input data against a "matching prototype" in its knowledge base. For example, a sequence of hypothesized phones on the phone level was matched against a table containing prototypical patterns of phones for each word in the vocabulary. A word whose phones satisfied a matching criterion became a word hypothesis for the phones. The validation process involved assigning credibility to the hypothesis based on the consistency of interpretation with the hypotheses on an adjacent level. See Figure D–3 for what a solution state looked like in HEARSAY-II.

At each problem-solving step, any one of the many problem-solving strategies could be initiated—bottom-up synthesis, top-down goal generation, island driving, hypothesis generation, and so on. The decision about whether a knowledge source could contribute to a solution was local to the knowledge source (the condition part). The decision about which knowledge source should be executed in which one of many contexts was global to the solution state (the blackboard), and the decision was made by a global scheduler. The scheduler was opportunistic in choosing the next step, and the solution was created one step at a time.

Additional Notes

The condition parts of the knowledge sources were complex, CPU-intensive procedures that needed to search large areas of the blackboard. Each knowledge source needed to determine what changes had been made since the last time it viewed the blackboard. To keep from firing the condition parts continually, each condition part declared a priori the kinds of blackboard changes in which it was interested. The condition part, when executed, looked only at the relevant changes since the last cycle. All the changes that could be processed by the action part were passed to it to avoid repetitive executions of the action part. Thus the focus was not on a particular hypothesis on the blackboard, but on the *type* of hypotheses.

The HEARSAY-II system maintained alternative hypotheses. However, the maintenance and the processing of alternatives are always complex and expensive, especially when the system does not provide general support for this. In HEARSAY-II, the problem was aggravated by an inadequate network structure that did not allow the shared network to be viewed from different perspectives. In the current jargon, it did not have good mechanisms for processing multiple worlds. Currently there are better techniques for processing and maintaining alternative worlds.

The evidence to support a hypothesis at a given level can be found on lower levels or on higher levels. For example, given a word hypothesis, its validity could be supported by a sequence of syllables or by grammatical constraints. The evidential support is represented by directional links from the evidence to the hypothesis it supports. The link that goes from a higher level to a lower level hypothesis represents a "support from above" (that is, the justification for the hypothesis can be found at a higher level). A link that goes in the opposite direction represents support from below (that is, the reason for the hypothesis can be found at a lower level). Although the names of the support mechanisms were first coined in HASP (Nii and Feigenbaum, 1978), the bidirectional reasoning mechanisms were first used in the HEARSAY-II system.

In HEARSAY-II the confidence in a hypothesis generated by a knowledge source was represented by an integer between 1 and 100. The overall confidence in the hypothesis was accumulated by simple addition of the confidence attached to the evidence (that is, supporting hypotheses). When the confidence in a hypothesis was changed, the change was propagated up (if the support was from below) and down (if the support was from above) the entire structure.

D2. HASP/SIAP

THE HASP PROJECT began in 1972 under the sponsorship of the DARPA. It was terminated in 1975 but was reinstated in 1976 under the name SIAP. At the time, the computational resources needed to maintain a major ocean surveillance system of sensors with conventional methods of statistical signal processing seemed economically unfeasible. It was also a time when artificial intelligence techniques were first being applied to the problem of signal interpretation. The DENDRAL program (Lindsay et al., 1980) was achieving significant success, and the Speech Understanding Project, of which the HEARSAY Project was a part, was under way. The major objectives of the HASP project were to demonstrate that artificial intelligence techniques could contribute significantly in addressing the surveillance problem and, further, that the task could be accomplished with reasonable computing resources. HASP was successful in meeting both these objectives.

The Task

The task of the HASP/SIAP system was to develop and maintain a situation board that reflected the activities of platforms (surface ships and submarines) in a region under surveillance. The situation board was developed by interpreting multiple, continuous streams of acoustic signals produced by objects in the region and by integrating intelligence reports with the interpretation.

The acoustic input to the system comes in the form of digitized data from multiple hydrophone arrays, each monitoring a part of the region. Each array has multiple hydrophones with some directional resolution. The major sources of acoustic radiation are rotating shafts and propellers and reciprocating machinery on board a platform. The *signature*, or sound spectrum, of a platform under steady operation contains persistent fundamental narrow-band frequencies and some of their harmonics. The front-end signal-processing hardware and software detect energy peaks appearing at various spectral frequencies and follow these peaks over time. On an analyst's sonograms, the peaks appeared as a collection of dark vertical stripes (see Figure D–5). Under ideal conditions, a hydrophone picks up sound energy near its axis. In practice, the terrain of the ocean floor, water temperature, and other platforms interfere, producing

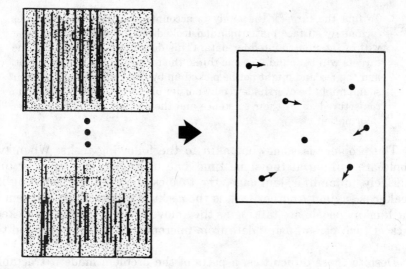

Figure D–5.   HASP/SIAP task.

signals with very low signal-to-noise ratios. That is, the stripes in the sonogram appear against a very fuzzy background.

During the first phase of the project, the acoustic input consisted of segments that described signal events. For example, a piece of input might have contained a frequency and indicated it as a beginning of a frequency shift (called a *knee*). Later, five-minute segments produced by a signal-processing front-end system were used as the input data.

In addition to the acoustic data, intelligence reports were available to HASP. The reports contained information about movements of friendly and hostile platforms with varying degrees of confidence. Routine information on commercial shipping activities was also included in these reports.

As in the speech understanding problem, the sonar signal-understanding problem is characterized by a large solution space, a low signal-to-noise ratio, and uncertain knowledge. Unlike the speech problem, the semantics and the syntax are ill defined in the sonar problem. That is, the targets of highest priority, the enemy submarines, are not likely to be well known and, at the same time, are trying their best to go undetected. The implications are these:

1. There is no "legal move generator" for the solution space except at the highest level of abstraction. (It is assumed that different types of platform, including enemy submarines and their general characteristics, are known.)

2. We must rely heavily on the analysts' methods and heuristics in detecting and classifying enemy submarines.

3. To find the targets, the analysts accounted for all known entities (primarily surface platforms) and looked for the targets of interest within the unaccounted-for data. (This does not guarantee that the targets will be found. For one thing, the targets might be very quiet, and their sound might not be picked up by the hydrophones, or their sound might be overshadowed by noisier platforms. The HASP system conjectured about their existence and their whereabouts from other information.)

The problem is somewhat akin to the following tasks: When two people are talking at the same time, one in English and another in a relatively unfamiliar language, try to pick up what the non-English speaker is saying. Another task is the cocktail conversation problem in which many people are talking as they move around; the task is to keep track of each person using data from microphones scattered around the room.

Despite these difficulties, aspects of the problem made it tractable. The situation unfolded over a relatively long time period because the platforms moved rather slowly, but the data collection was relatively frequent and from many different locations. This meant that the system was given many chances to interpret the situation with data sets containing slightly different information. For example, two hydrophones might pick up incomplete harmonic sets attributable to the same platform, but they might be fractured in different ways. When combined, they provided more information than from each one separately. There were also many different kinds of knowledge that could be used, bits and pieces, such as in the koala problem discussed in Section B1. The general strategy employed was to accumulate both positive and negative evidence for hypothesis elements.

The Blackboard Structure

The data structure on the blackboard represented the best understanding of the situation at any given point in time. It was a dynamic entity that evolved over time. Referred to as the *current best hypothesis* (CBH), it was partitioned into an abstraction hierarchy consisting of input segments, lines, harmonic sets, acoustic sources, platforms, and fleet levels (see Figures D–6 and D–7). The signal data arrived on the segments level, and the report data arrived on either the fleets level or the platforms level, depending on the content of the report.

Unlike the HEARSAY-II system in which the "answer" to the problem was the hypothesized sentence on the highest level, HASP's "answer"

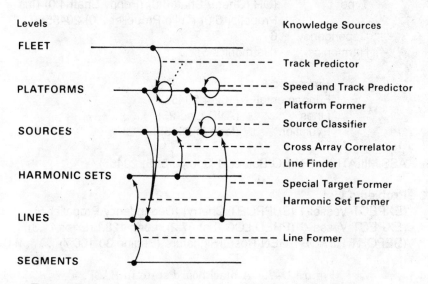

Figure D–6.   HASP/SIAP blackboard and knowledge sources.

The Current Best Hypothesis at Time 20455

Vessel-1
Class   (OR (Cherry 8.4) (Iris 6.9) (Tulip 6.2) (Poppy 4.8)
             20455 . . .)
Location   ((Lat 37.3) (Long 123.1) (Error 37))
Speed   15.7
Course   135.9
Sources   (AND Source-1 Source-5)

Source-1
Type   (OR (Cherry Propeller 5.5) Poppy Shaft 2.5)
                 (Poppy Propeller 2.0) (Cherry Shaft 2.5)
                 20455 . . .)
Dependency   Unknown
Regain   (20230)
Harmonics   (Harmonic-1)

Harmonic-1
Fundamental   (224.5 20520)
Evolution   (fade-in 20230 fade-out 20210 . . .)

Lines   (AND Line-1 Line-2 Line-6 Line-12)

Source-5
Type   (OR (Cherry Shaft 6.0) (Poppy Shaft 4.0) (Iris
                 Propeller 5.0) (Tulip Propeller 2.0) 20455)
Dependency   6
Harmonics   (Harmonics-5)

Harmonic-5
Fundamental   (162.4 20455)
Lines   (AND Line-25)
Evolution   (fade-in 20455)

ASSIMILATION (RATIO Source-1 Source-5 .5) 20455)

Problems List
(EXPECT Vessel-1 (SUPPORT Cherry) (Dependency Propeller 5))
(EXPECT Vessel-1 (PRED.LOC (Lat 37.2) (Long 123.) (Error 41.3))
(REPORT REPORT-GEN Rose (Signature (Engine 30 166.7) ....))

Figure D–7.   A blackboard state in HASP.

was the network of partial solutions that spanned the entire blackboard. In other words, partial solutions were considered acceptable, if not desirable. For example, a partial solution of the form "There's something out there producing these lines" was acceptable, even though a preferable solution was, "There is a platform of type x, whose engine is accounted for by the following harmonics and whose propeller seems to be producing the following lines, and no shaft data are currently being received."

The nodes on the blackboard were called *hypothesis elements* rather than "hypotheses" as they were in HEARSAY-II. The hypothesis elements formed a network, each element representing a meaningful aggregation of lower level hypothesis elements. No attempt was made to maintain uniformity of attributes across the levels (see Figure D–7). Each knowledge source knew the relevant vocabulary (*attributes*) associated with those levels in which it was interested. The lines level and the harmonic-sets level used a descriptive vocabulary that dealt primarily with signal characteristics, and the sources level used vocabulary dealing primarily with machinery. The signal-to-symbol transformation can be said to have occurred between the harmonic-sets level and the sources level. Signal information in a hypothesis element on the harmonic-sets level was translated into machinery information in a hypothesis element on the sources level; that is, there was an element-for-element transformation between the two levels.

In contrast to HEARSAY-II, each hypothesis element could have alternative values for its attributes but no alternative links. The hierarchy was organized as an AND tree, with a possibility for local alternatives. Although this approach reduced the possibilities of combinatoric explosion, and consequently computational time and space, it was awkward for the system to "change its mind" about the solution. In a HEARSAY-like blackboard structure, a change of mind only involves focusing on an alternative substructure. In HASP, either the affected hypothesis elements had to be reanalyzed (which could result in reorganizing the whole CBH), or the past analyses dealing with the elements in question had to be forgotten and the analysis restarted from the point of departure. The latter approach was used in HASP because the human analysts tended to behave in a similar manner. (In the human system, there are analysts whose task is to do offline postanalyses. What they learn from the postanalyses is often added to the pool of knowledge about the task. HASP had no counterpart to this activity.)

In addition to the blackboard, HASP had other globally accessible information generated directly or indirectly by the knowledge sources (refer to Figure D–8). This global information was used primarily by the control modules:

Event list. All changes made to the blackboard, together with the types of these changes, were posted on the event list. Each event had a

Blackboards   **Knowledge Sources**

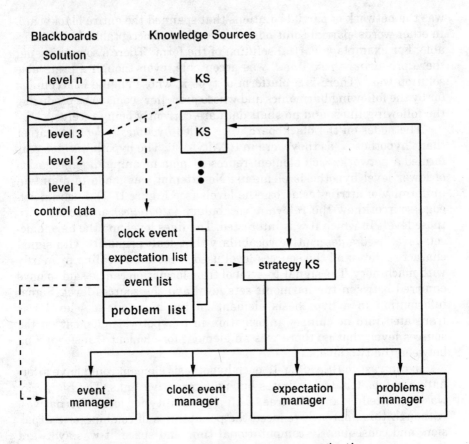

Figure D–8.   HASP/SIAP system organization.

generic "change type" associated with it. It also had associated with it a blackboard node (hypothesis element). An event in the event list was selected by a control module to become a focus of attention. The focus of attention then had two components: a change type and a blackboard node that served as context for subsequent knowledge sources. (This will be discussed in more detail later in the section on Control.)

Expectation list.   The expectation list contained events expected to occur in the future. For example, acoustic signature of platforms reported by an intelligence report to be in a particular region was posted on the expectation list. The canonical acoustic signatures of all the known platforms were stored in a static knowledge base.[6] Periodically the expectation list was searched to see if expected data had arrived.

---

[6] In the entire discussion of blackboard systems, the role and the form of the static, or passive,

Problem list. This list contained descriptions of the various problems the knowledge sources encountered. For example, when no rule fired during the execution of a knowledge source, it might have meant, "I should know, but don't." Such information was useful to the programmers. The most important use of this list, however, was for posting missing or desired information. A knowledge source could post pieces of information that, if available, would increase the confidence in its hypothesis. For example, a knowledge source might indicate that if the dependency relationship was known for a given set of lines, it might be able to identify the platform (see Figure D–7). In such a case, an operator might provide the information if it were known, or a goal might be set up by a control module to find the information.

Clock-event list. A clock event consisted of a time and associated rules. The rules were to be executed at the designated time. Because behaviors at various levels were known for some types of platforms, knowledge sources tracked the expected and actual behavior by this mechanism. The types of behavior known to the system ranged from the temporal characteristics of the sonograms to the physical movement of the platforms.

History list. All the processed events and their context (for example, a modified blackboard node, its values, and the bindings in a rule that made the change) were kept on this list. The history list was used to recount the knowledge-application steps and their contexts that led to the generation of the CBH. (Because the program processed events in a breadth-first order and humans had difficulties in following this processing order, the history list was used to construct a text that made it appear as though the processing had been in depth-first order.) This list was also used by the programmers to ensure that solutions were arrived at by an expected line of reasoning. Of special interest was the occurrence of right answers for wrong reasons.

The Knowledge Source Structure

Each knowledge source consisted of a condition part (called a *precondition*) and an action part. In contrast to the HEARSAY-II knowledge source organization, the precondition part and the action part were contained in one module. The precondition part consisted of a list of pairs of tokens; the pair consisted of a name of an event type and its modifier (new, old, or modified). The modifier indicated the status of the hypothesis element; for example, modified hypothesis element. When an event

---

knowledge base have been omitted. It is assumed that taxonomies, facts, and definitions are represented in some form. This type of knowledge is awkward to represent as rules and is usually represented as tables, records, property lists, or frames. (See Article XVII in this Volume.)

became "focused" (that is, selected by a control module), knowledge sources whose precondition contained the event type of the focused event were executed. An event type was one of several predefined categories of changes that could be made in the system. The action part of a knowledge source consisted of a set of rules. In this organization, the precondition can be viewed as a simple context-independent trigger for a set of rules. The detailed test for applicability of knowledge were in the condition parts of the rules. The knowledge source could create bindings local to it that remained valid for the duration of its execution. The bindings served to "freeze" the context until all the rules in a knowledge source were evaluated.

Control

The control modules in HASP were in the same form as the domain knowledge sources, that is, sets of rules. The knowledge sources formed a simple control hierarchy consisting of strategy knowledge source and event managers (see Figure D–8). Although the control knowledge sources were logically independent, they were executed in a predefined order. The strategy knowledge source decided which categories of state change, or events, (clock-event, problem, expectation, or blackboard events) to process next, based on priorities as encoded in its knowledge base. An appropriate event-management knowledge source was executed based on this decision.

Once activated, an event manager, in turn, decided which specific event to focus on. The basis of this decision varied with the event manager. For example, the clock-event manager selected events that needed to be processed at a given time, and within those events the priority rested with events dealing with enemy platforms. The knowledge sources associated with the focused event were then executed in some predefined order. The node associated with the focused event served as the context for the knowledge source's execution.

Section C3 mentioned that the scheduling module and the focus-of-attention mechanisms were simpler in HASP than in HEARSAY-II. This is because it was known what blackboard changes were significant for making progress toward a solution, so the HASP programmer decided what blackboard changes were to be called *events*. That is, only certain changes to the blackboard were called events. For each such change, it was also known what knowledge sources were available for following up on the new information. By making the precondition of a knowledge source the occurrence of specific types of blackboard changes, the selection of knowledge sources for a given event became a very simple matter. For example, a table of change types and applicable knowledge sources could be used. (In HASP, a set of rules was used. The condition side contained event types and a few other simple conditions, and the action side contained a sequence of knowledge sources to be executed.)

In this scheme, however, the process of selecting the most promising event (a blackboard change and the node on which the change was made) became a major issue. The selection of an event is really the selection of a node, which, in turn, is really a selection of a solution island. The focus-of-attention problem in HASP was primarily a problem of determining which solution island to work on next, rather than a problem of which part of which knowledge source to apply next (that is, generate new alternatives or pursue existing ones), as in HEARSAY-II. In HASP the hierarchical control knowledge sources were all biased toward the selection of a solution island that would have the highest payoff in subsequent processing cycles.

The basic actions of the control component were iterations of the following:

1. The strategy knowledge source decided which event category to focus on, that is, clock events, expectations, problems, or blackboard events.

2. The manager of the chosen event category selected a specific event from that category to process next. The event information contained the name of a node to which a change was made and a specific change type (for example, "new-platform-found") associated with that change. The node name and the change type constituted the focus of attention.

3. Based on the change type of the focus-of-attention node, knowledge sources associated with the change type were executed in some predefined order. Information in the node associated with the focus of attention served as the context for the activated knowledge sources.

4. The executing knowledge sources produced changes to the blackboard, and the changes were recorded in the appropriate event category.

To summarize, in HASP there were four categories of events: expectation, clock, problems, and blackboard. Each category of events contained a predetermined set of event types (that is, a set of expectation event types, a set of blackboard-change event types, and so on). For each event type, the knowledge sources that could process an instance of the event type were also predetermined. The system was open-ended in that new event types and new knowledge sources could be added without perturbing the existing ones. The major task for the control mechanism was to select the next solution island to be processed.

Knowledge-Application Strategy

As in HEARSAY-II, HASP used a mixed reasoning strategy. Instead of using a *legal move generator* as in HEARSAY-II where the space of legal solutions was known from the grammar and vocabulary, HASP used a *plausible hypotheses generator* based on the heuristics used by the analysts. The construction of higher level partial solutions from lower level partial solutions, the determination of their properties, the generation of expectations, and so on were driven by empirical association rules obtained from an analyst.

Most of the fifty knowledge sources in HASP were engaged in bottom-up processing. Several pieces of data from a lower level were combined to form or update information on a higher level (for example, lines into harmonic sets). Similarly, information on one level was translated into a different vocabulary on another level (for example, harmonic sets into mechanical parts). The data were processed breadth first. That is, all the harmonic sets were formed from lines, and all sources were assigned to harmonic sets, and so on, in a pipeline fashion up the hierarchy.

The most powerful reasoning strategy used in HASP was the top-down, model-driven strategy. The assumption underlying model-driven reasoning is that when interpreting the data, the amount of processing can be reduced by carefully matching selected pieces of data with discriminating or important features of a model (a frame or a script). A successful match tends to confirm the model as an explanatory hypothesis for the data. In a continuous-data interpretation task, the model, combined with periodic confirmatory matches, serves as the "cognitive fly-wheel" that maintains the ongoing "understanding." In driving a car, for example, our model of the road situation (prototypical highway characteristics, shapes of cars, their range of speed, their normal behavior, and so forth) saves us from continually having to process every bit of data within our visual range. We don't "notice" the color of the upholstery of the car in front of us even though that piece of information is often available because it is not relevant to the task of driving. The danger with this approach is that data can often match a wrong model for a long time, especially when the discriminating features are not carefully chosen.[7]

With this caveat, a model-driven approach is a very powerful device

[7] How often have you listened to a person and thought that person was talking about a particular topic before suddenly realizing it was a different topic all the time? (See Aiello (1983) for a simple experiment relevant to this topic.) The same pieces of knowledge from the PUFF Kunz et al., 1978 program were used in data-driven, goal-driven, and model-driven approaches. Although the model-driven approach ran the fastest, extra knowledge had to be added to keep it from making the wrong diagnoses.

in interpreting noisy data. In HASP a model-driven approach was used quite extensively and successfully. For example, it was used in determining which lines formed a harmonic set. In fact, the CBH served as a situation model from one time frame to the next. There was an implicit assumption that the current state of affairs was not significantly different from the state a few minutes earlier. To make this assumption work, HASP focused on finding counterevidence for a hypothesis as much as on finding supporting evidence.

Within an abstraction hierarchy, model-driven reasoning is usually a top-down process. For example, if a platform type is "known" with support from above (for example, intelligence reports) or with support from below (for example, data), the facts about the platform type can serve as a model. From this model, we can hypothesize the platform's range of speed, its sound-producing machinery, the machinery's acoustic signature, the platform's travel patterns, and so on. Pieces of data that can support the model-based hypothesis are sought in the signal data. As more supporting evidence is found, confidence in pursuing the model is increased.

Comparison Between HEARSAY-II and HASP

Problem solving by search and by recognition. The generate-and-test approach to problem solving produces combinatorial search. To reduce the amount of search, generation is carefully evaluated and controlled, often using domain-specific knowledge, within the context of a given state. HEARSAY-II used look-ahead, generator, and evaluator modules to implement the generate-and-test search. The first two modules were part of the knowledge source structure—the knowledge source precondition doing the look-ahead and local evaluation, the knowledge source body doing the generation; and the scheduler functioned as the overall-solution evaluator. The results of the look-aheads were carefully evaluated (by the scheduler) before an actual generation step was taken.

In recognition systems a knowledge module, often encoded as a set of if-then rules, knows what to do under what circumstances. That is, a piece of knowledge recognizes the situation under which it should be applied. The knowledge source in HASP consisted of a situation recognizer in the precondition and a body of action parts. The scheduler in HASP performed a simpler function than in HEARSAY; it merely decided what situation (state) to pay attention to, after which the knowledge sources that recognized the situation were executed.

The two different approaches to problem solving used by HEARSAY-II and HASP resulted in some basic differences in the design of the two systems:

A knowledge source was written as procedures in HEARSAY and as a set of rules in HASP.

In selecting a focus of attention, HEARSAY was concerned with selecting the next knowledge source to execute, which amounted to electing to generate more alternatives or process existing ones, whereas HASP was concerned with selecting the next solution island to pursue.

In HEARSAY a subset of knowledge sources was chosen for execution from a list of all applicable (invoked) knowledge sources. HASP executed all knowledge sources applicable to a focused event. However, not all the changes to the blackboard became focused events.

Temporal events. In HEARSAY-II, "time" meant the sequence in which words appeared in a spoken sentence. Based on the sequence of words, we could predict or verify the appearance of another set of words later or earlier in the sequence.

In HASP, time had different connotations. HASP's continuous input is somewhat equivalent to asking a speaker to repeat his utterance over and over again. After each utterance, the CBH would reflect the best that the system could do up to that point. There was information redundancy as well as new and different information (no two utterances sound exactly the same) as time went on. Redundancy meant that the system was not pressed to account for every piece of data at each time frame. It could wait to see if a clearer signal appeared later, for example.

In addition, time meant that the situation at any time frame was a "natural" consequence of earlier situations, and such information as trends and temporal patterns (both signal and symbolic) that occur over time could be used. One of the most powerful uses of time in this sense was the generation and use of expectations of future events.

Events. The concept of events is inherent in the HASP problem. For example, a certain type of frequency shift in the signal would be an event that implied the ship was changing its speed. An appearance or disappearance of a signal would be an event that implied a new ship was on the scene or a known ship was getting out of the range of the sensors, or it implied an expected behavior of certain types of ships. This inherent task characteristic made it natural for the HASP system to be an event-based system; that is, an occurrence of a particular event implied that new information was available for some a priori determined knowledge source to pursue. The goals of the task dictated what events were significant and what were not. This, in turn, meant that the programmer could a priori decide what changes in the blackboard, that is, events, were significant for solving the problem (as opposed to the system noticing every change). Furthermore, the only time a knowledge source needed to be activated was when some events occurred that it knew about. These task characteristics, together with the use of knowledge-based recognition approach, helped redefine and simplify the scheduler's task since each piece of knowledge was more or less self-selecting for any given change in the solution state.

Multiple input streams. Aside from the digitized data from many hydrophones, HASP had another kind of input—reports. Reports contained information gathered from intelligence or normal shipping sources. These reports tended to use descriptions similar to those used on the ship level on the blackboard (CBH). Whereas the ordinary data came in at the bottom level for both HEARSAY and HASP, HASP had another input "port" at the highest level. Given the input at this level, the system generated the kinds of acoustic sources and acoustic signatures it expected in the future based on information in its taxonomic knowledge base. This type of *model-based expectation* was one of the methods used to "fuse" report data with signal data.

Explanation. The purpose of explanation is to understand what is going on in the system from the perspective of the user and the programmer. Because the needs of the end users are different from those of the programmers, explanation can take many forms. Explanation for the user was especially important in HASP because there was no way to test the correctness of the answer. The only way to test the system's performance was to get human analysts to agree that the system's situation hypotheses and reasoning were plausible. CBH, with its network of evidential support, served to justify the hypothesis elements and their hypothetical properties. It served to "explain" the relationships between the signal data and its various levels of interpretation. The explanation of the reasoning, that is, "explaining" which pieces of knowledge had been applied under what circumstances, was made possible by "playing back" the executed rules.

In MYCIN and other similar rule-based programs, explanation consists of a playback of rule firings. In HASP the ordinary method of playback turned out to be useful only to programmers for debugging purposes. For the user, the rules were either too detailed or were applied in a sequence (breadth first) that was hard for the user to understand. In HASP the explanation of the line of reasoning was generated from an execution history with the help of "explanation templates" that selected the appropriate rule activities in some easy-to-understand order.

These differences between HEARSAY-II and HASP arose from different task characteristics and requirements mentioned earlier. Section E summarizes the architectural differences attributable to differences in search and recognition problem solving and to some task characteristics.

Additional Notes

The hierarchical control in HASP was an attempt to separate the domain-specific knowledge from knowledge about the application of that knowledge. It was the first attempt at such an organization and was rather simplistic.

In HASP the control-related information was made globally accessible. It was also decided to represent control functions in rule form. The grouping of control related rules into control knowledge sources was an obvious next step. However, by not integrating the control information into the blackboard structure, the control rules had to be expressed and processed differently from the domain knowledge sources. The basic architecture of HASP was generalized and implemented in the skeletal system AGE (Nii and Aiello, 1979, and Aiello et al., 1981), which then evolved into a commercial product ESHELL (Fujitsu Labs, 1987).

D3. TRICERO

THE TRICERO SYSTEM represents an extension of the blackboard system into the area of distributed computing.[8] There are many possible ways to design a blackboard system to use multiple, communicating computers. To design a multiprocessor blackboard system, either the blackboard model or the blackboard framework can be used as a design foundation. This choice will have a significant effect on the nature of the concurrency in the resulting system.

One way to use multiple processors is to partition the solution space on the blackboard into loosely coupled regions (for example, subregions of the ocean, parts of a sentence, pieces of the protein structure, and so on). For each of these partitions, create a copy of a blackboard system. For example, in HASP we might have a complete blackboard system for each sensor array. Because the arrays have overlapping coverage, the systems would have to coordinate their problem-solving activities. A system will notify an "adjacent" system if a platform is moving into that system's area, for example. In other words, the application problem can be partitioned into loosely coupled subproblems that need coordination. Research on this type of system is being conducted at the University of

---

[8] The TRICERO system was designed by Harold Brown of the Knowledge Systems Laboratory at Stanford University. It was built by programmers at Knowledge Systems Laboratory and Teknowledge. The TRICERO system was written using the AGE skeletal system (Nii and Aiello, 1979, and Aiello et al., 1981). The distributed-system aspects of TRICERO were simulated.

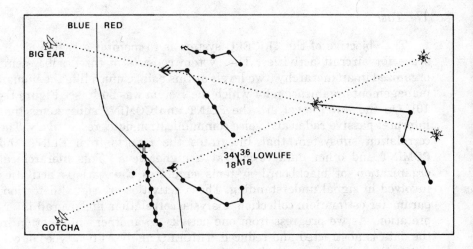

Figure D–9.   The TRICERO task.

Massachusetts under the direction of Victor Lesser (Lesser and Corkill, 1983; see also, Article XVIII in this Volume).

A second approach is to use the blackboard data in a shared memory and to distribute the knowledge sources on different processors (see Aiello (1986) and Ensor and Gabbe (1985) for examples). This distribution theoretically executes the knowledge sources in parallel. If the knowledge sources are represented as rules, their condition parts can be evaluated in parallel. The action parts can also be executed concurrently. The evaluation of the condition part and the action part can form a pipeline. The PSM project at Carnegie-Mellon University is targeted as a parallel rule execution system (Forgy et al., 1984).

Third, a more direct use of multiple processors can be accomplished by partitioning the problem into independent subproblems, where each subproblem is solved on a separate processor. For example, in the interpretation and fusion of multiple types of data, each type of data might be interpreted on different systems. Each system will have a different set of knowledge sources and a different blackboard organization. The results from the data analysis systems will be fused by another blackboard system. The TRICERO system is an example of this type of system.[9]

[9] The problems of designing and building blackboard systems capable of concurrent problem solving, distributed problem solving, and parallel computations are distinct from those of serial blackboard systems and are not discussed in this chapter. (See Nii et al., (1989) for discussions of some of the issues.) The TRICERO system is discussed here, because it does not fall into any of these categories. It is a variant of a distributed computing system that can be considered a direct extension of the serial systems. See Durfee et al., (this Volume) for distinctions between distributed-processing and distributed problem-solving systems.

The Task

The objective of the TRICERO system is to monitor a region of airspace for aircraft activities. The system consists of three subsystems organized in an hierarchy (two levels at this point), much like the human management organization for which the system was built (see Figure D–10). On the lower level are the ELINT and COMINT subsystems that interpret passive radar and voice communication data, respectively. The correlation subsystem that integrates the reports from ELINT and COMINT and other data resides at a higher level. This hierarchical organization of blackboard systems emulates the various activities involved in signal understanding. These activities are signal detection, parameter estimation, collection analysis, correlation, and overall interpretation. As we progress from one activity to another, information in the data is abstracted and reduced. TRICERO analyzes two types of collection data and correlates the analyzed data. Each data type is analyzed independently using different blackboard data organizations and different knowledge sources (see Figure D–11).

The Blackboard Structure

The ELINT blackboard consisted of three levels: observation, emitter, and cluster. The input data arrived at the observation level. These data

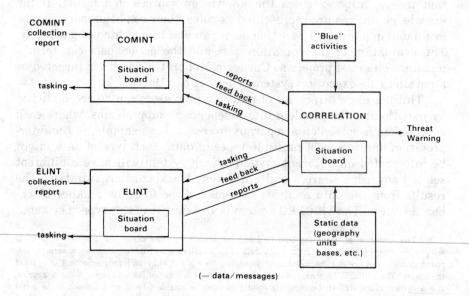

(— data/messages)

Figure D–10.   A distributed blackboard system. Control in TRICERO.

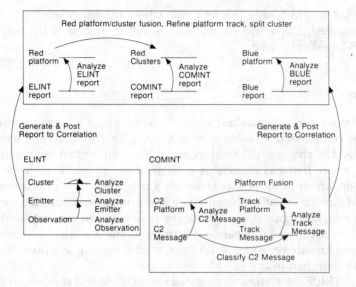

Figure D–11.   TRICERO blackboards and knowledge sources.

were tagged with the collection time and the site at which they were collected. Each node on the emitter level kept a history of detections from a site having the same identification tag. The history represented radar emissions believed to be emanating from one source. The identification tag could be in error; that is, different sources could have the same identification tag or one source could have multiple tags. The radar emissions detected at different sites were merged into an hypothetical platform (or a number of platforms "seen" as one platform) on the cluster level. Each level used descriptive vocabulary appropriate to that level: the platform types and speed history on the cluster level and the collection site and signal quality on the observation level, for example. The blackboard data structure in the COMINT and correlation subsystems were structured in similar fashions using abstraction levels appropriate to interpreting their data.

The Knowledge Source Structure

The knowledge sources were structured according to the requirements in the AGE (Nii and Aiello, 1979) skeletal system. Each knowledge source had a condition part and an action part. The condition part was a list of tokens, each representing a type of change that could be made on the blackboard. The action part consisted of a set of rules. The rules in each knowledge source could be processed as a multiple hit in which all rules whose condition sides were satisfied were executed, or as a single hit in which only the first rule whose condition side was satisfied was executed. There was no conflict-resolution process of the type found in OPS-based systems.

Control

Each of the independent subsystems in TRICERO used a subset of control components available in AGE. A globally accessible event list recorded the changes to the blackboard. At each control cycle, one event on an event list was chosen as a focus of attention. The choice of the event on which to focus was based on a predetermined priority of event types. Once an event (an event type and a node) was selected for focus, it was matched against the event-type tokens in the precondition, which served as a context-independent trigger of the knowledge source. The triggered knowledge sources were executed according to a predetermined priority assigned to the knowledge sources.

The TRICERO system augmented the AGE control component to handle the communication among the three subsystems. Each subsystem could send messages to designated subsystems. The receipt of a message by a subsystem was treated as an event, allowing the focus of attention to occur on a special node on the blackboard where the messages were stored. This construct allowed the subsystems to treat communication from other subsystems just like any other event.

The basic actions of the control component can be described in two parts:

1. Between subsystems
   a. The simulation of the distributed computation consisted of round-robin execution of the three subsystems—ELINT, COMINT, and correlation.
   b. Each subsystem sent report messages to designated subsystems. The receipt of a message was treated as an event with appropriate modification of the recipient's blackboard and event list.

2. Within a subsystem
   a. A control module selected a focus event using a list of event priorities. An event contained sufficient information to serve as a context for subsequent knowledge source execution, namely, the node on which the change was made, the knowledge source and the specific rule that made the change, and the actual change.
   b. Based on the focused event, knowledge sources whose precondition list contained the event (that is, knowledge sources triggered by the event) were chosen for execution.
   c. The rules in the activated knowledge sources were evaluated and executed according to the rule-processing method associated with

the knowledge source. Modifications to the blackboards and other associated information were put on the the appropriate event lists.

Knowledge-Application Strategy

Most of the knowledge sources engaged in bottom-up processing. They combined information on one level to generate a hypothesis on a higher level. The reports from ELINT and COMINT were treated as input to the higher level correlation subsystem. The reports from the correlation subsystem to ELINT and COMINT dealt primarily with information on the higher level (for example, platform identification) that improved or overrode the analysis done by the lower level subsystem. In such cases, the processing in these subsystems became top down and model driven.

Additional Notes

The partitioning of the overall task into subsystems in TRICERO was accomplished by assigning the analysis of abstract information to the correlation subsystem and the analysis of information closer to signal data to ELINT and COMINT. As mentioned in Section B, the knowledge sources that span the various levels of the blackboard hierarchy are logically independent. Thus the need for coordination among the subsystems is substantially reduced when the problem is partitioned into subsystems along carefully chosen levels of analysis.

As with the other systems described, the TRICERO data were noisy and the knowledge sources uncertain. The radar data, for example, contained "ghosts," detections of nonexisting objects. The ELINT subsystem handled the existence of this type of error by delaying the analysis until several contiguous detections had occurred. By doing so, it avoided the creation of hypothesis nodes that later needed to be deleted.

The issues relating to the deletions of nodes on the blackboard are quite complex. Suppose in TRICERO that a node on the cluster level (an object that represents a platform or a group of platforms) is to be deleted. What does it mean? Has the platform disappeared? Unless it somehow disintegrated, a platform cannot disappear into thin air. Was there an error in interpreting the radar data to begin with? Often, there are "ghost tracks," a characteristic of which is that the tracks disappear after a short duration. However, suppose the platform disappearance was not due to ghost tracks but to an error in reasoning. Unraveling the reasoning steps that led to the hypothesis and retrying often does not help. The system does not know any more than it did when the erroneous hypothesis was generated. Suppose the platform node is just deleted. What do we do about the network of evidence that supports the existence of the platform? Unfortunately there is no systematic way of handling node deletions. In HASP the nodes were never deleted. The nodes in error, the ones with negative confidence, were ignored and analysis continued ignoring the past errors. In TRICERO node creation was delayed until there was strong supporting evidence for the existence of an object represented by the node. When an error occurred, the hypothesis network was restructured using domain heuristics.

In TRICERO the confidence assigned to the hypothesis elements was expressed in a symbolic form. The vocabulary expressing the confidence consisted of "possible," "probable," "positive," and "was positive." The confidence level was changed according to heuristic criteria.

TRICERO was one of the first blackboard systems implemented on a computer system with a bit-map display (see Figure D–9 for an output display). The situation board, symbolically represented on the blackboard of the correlation subsystem, was displayed in terms of objects in an airspace and the objects' past behavior. The graphic-display routines were written as procedural knowledge sources and were executed when certain events occurred that warranted display updates. There might be some argument about the conceptual consistency of this approach because interfacing is usually not considered a part of problem solving. However, this engineering solution that integrated the display routines with the problem-solving components worked very well. An effective display interface requires knowledge about what is appropriate to display when. A knowledge-based control of displays and display updates is easily implemented using the knowledge source organization.

D4. PROTEAN

THE PROTEAN APPLICATION written in the BB1 skeletal system (Hayes-Roth, 1985) introduces an architecture that treats control as a task separate from the primary application task. Fundamental to this separation is the notion that control involves a dynamic creation of a plan consisting of sequences of domain actions. Put another way, as a solution to a problem evolves, problem-solving strategy and tactics can be revised dynamically. This notion can be traced back to the OPM system (Hayes-Roth et al., 1979; see also, Article XI.C, Vol. III). PROTEAN currently address the problem of determining the placement of groups of amino acids in three space formulated as a constraint satisfaction problem (Brinkley et al., 1987, and Hayes-Roth et al., 1987). Within this context, the control is intended to minimize the calls to an expensive constraint satisfaction routine written in C, focusing the control heuristics on the problem of resource allocation.

The Task

The task of PROTEAN is to determine the possible three-dimensional structures for a given protein molecule. In the CRYSALIS system the protein structure was inferred from the amino-acid sequence and a complete electron density map derived from crystallized protein (see Terry, 1983, or Volume II of the *Handbook*). PROTEAN must build the three-dimensional structure from nuclear magnetic resonance (NMR) data obtained from protein in solution. Because protein in solution has internal motion, the data are low in resolution and many not yield a unique solution, but a set of possible solutions. (In actuality, the program determines the regions within which a piece of protein may be located.) Three kinds of information are available to PROTEAN:

1. The primary structure, which is the amino acid sequence.

2. Secondary structures, which are pieces of the amino acid sequence that arrange themselves in recognizable structural patterns, such as alpha helices (see Figure D–12).

3. Proximity information for pairs of atoms obtained from high-resolution NMR.

Consider the following example of the input to PROTEAN (from Hayes-Roth et al., 1987).

Primary Structure: met1, lys2, pro3, val4, . . .
[The sequence is methionine, lysine, proline, valine, etc.]

Secondary Structures: (Coil met1 thr5) (Helix leu6 gly14) . . .
[A "random coil" formed by the first five amino acids, followed by a helix consisting of the 6th through the 14th amino acids, etc.]

Distance Constraints: (val4 3 try17 5) (val4 3 leu45 4) (val4 3 tyr47 5)
. . .
[The distance measure, called the nuclear Overhouser effects (NOEs), range from 2 to 5 angstroms. The constraints are read as: There is an NOE between the atom 3 of the valine in the 4th position and atom 5 of the tryptophan in the 17th position, etc.]

The overall problem is divided into two main subproblems, that of determining the shape and the volume of secondary structures from the constraints (local constraint satisfaction) and that of placing these "solids" in space. What is implemented in PROTEAN is the second problem with the human user determining the volume of the secondary structures. The remainder of the discussion is confined to the second problem.

The problem is formulated as a geometric constraint satisfaction

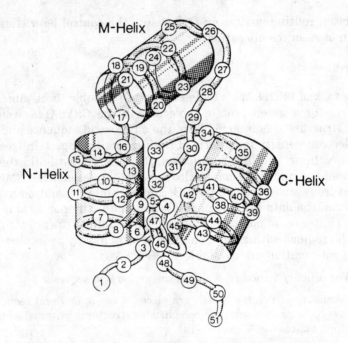

Figure D–12. Protein as a composite of secondary structures
(from Hayes-Roth, et al., 1987).

problem with the following iterative refinement. (Figure D–13 illustrates this process.)

1. Choose a solid (for example, a helix represented as a cylinder) as an *anchor* around which other solids will be placed.

2. Determine a region of space to be occupied by another solid, an *anchoree*, by applying all the constraints between the anchor and the anchoree. The resulting region in space around the anchoree is called an *accessible volume* of the secondary structure.

3. Reduce the accessible volumes by applying pair-wise constraints between the anchorees, a process called *yoking*.

4. Reduce and refine the accessible volume by iterative yoking with different sets of anchoree pairs.

The constraint satisfaction algorithms for a pair of secondary structures are written in C and run on an Iris workstation. A part of PROTEAN that determines *when* to call the constraint satisfaction algorithm with *which* pair of secondary structures is written in BB1, which runs on a LISP workstation. Once activated, the constraint satisfier can

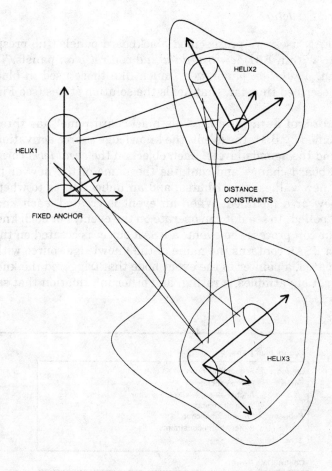

Figure D–13.   Anchoring and yoking.

run for hours for a pair of secondary objects. The choice of an object to serve as an anchor, the order in which the anchorees are chosen, and the order in which yokings are performed affect the cost of computing on the Iris workstation. The primary problem tackled in the blackboard portion of PROTEAN is that of dynamically creating a plan that minimizes the time spent in the constraint satisfaction algorithm. (The tradeoff is between a planned utilization of a resource, where the planning itself requires computational resource, and the unplanned use of the resource.) The dimensions of the tradeoff and some timing analysis can be found in Brinkley et al. (1987).

Blackboard Structure

PROTEAN uses two prespecified blackboard panels (the prespecification occurs within BB1), *control-data* and *control-plan* panels. There is, in addition, a *solution* panel, very much like those used in blackboard systems described thus far, that holds the solution states (see Figure D–14).

The control-data panel. This blackboard panel has three levels as prespecified by BB1: the event, the knowledge source activation record (KSAR), and the agenda levels. Each object on the *event level* corresponds to a blackboard change and contains the name of the new or modified node, the new values of attributes, and an indication as to whether the node is new or a modified. When an event is created, each knowledge source is "polled" to see if it can operate on the event. For each knowledge source that can process the event, a KSAR object is created on the *KSAR level*. Each KSAR contains the name of the knowledge source with which it is associated, a pointer to the event node that triggered the knowledge source, a set of variables, a rating, and other information that serves as

---

Control Plan Panel

Strategy:	Sequentially position all objects
Focus:	Pick an anchor
	Anchor all objects to the anchor
	Yoke all objects
Heuristic:	Prefer-long-anchor
	Prefer-strong-constraints
Schedule:	- - - - - - - -

Control Data Panel

Events:	- - - - - - - -
KSAR	- - - - - - - -
Agenda:	Executable:
	98 (orient PA1 about helix 1)
	94 (orient PA1 about helix 2)
	86 (orient PA1 about helix 3)

Solution Panel

Partial Arrangements   PA1

Secondary Structure   Helix 1   Helix 2   Helix 3
            length
            constraints
            weight- %
            location table

Figure D–14.   The PROTEAN blackboard panels.

a context for the knowledge source. We might view the combination of the knowledge source and a KSAR as a closure ("closure" is used loosely here) that represents an instance of the knowledge source. The *agenda level* has four nodes, each representing different states that an instantiated knowledge source can be in. These states are triggered, executable, obviated, and executed. What these states represent and how they are used are described in the following sections.

The control-plan panel. This blackboard panel contains four levels as specified in BB1: the strategy, focus, heuristic, and schedule levels. Information on the *strategy level* specifies the general strategy to be applied at any given point. The information structure can be arbitrarily complex, but in PROTEAN it usually contains one node. In Figure D–14, the strategy indicates that the secondary objects are to be positioned in the order described on the focus level. The *focus level* makes the strategy operational; that is, it contains a sequence of steps that, when executed, result in the realization of the strategy. Each focus step is generated dynamically by a knowledge source when the previous step is completed. (All the focus steps to be generated are shown in Figure D–14.) Continuing with the preceding example, a manifestation of the strategy is to first pick a secondary structure for an anchor, then place all other secondary structures to the anchor, and finally yoke all the anchorees. The strategy states that these three steps should be taken in the order specified.

When a focus step is selected, pieces of associated knowledge called heuristics are generated on the *heuristic level*. A heuristic is a procedure that evaluates an event based on some heuristic criteria. When executed, a heuristic returns an integer reflecting a rating of the event passed to it. In the example in Figure D–14, assume that "Pick an anchor" is the step to be taken. There are three possible candidates for an anchor, Helix1, Helix2, and Helix3. (The statement "Orient PA1 about Helix1" on the agenda level translates to "Orient Partial-Arrangement-1 around Helix1," which translates to "Pick Helix1 for an anchor for Partial-Arrangement-1.") A heuristic, for example, "Prefer-long-anchor," is applied to Helix1 to see if it would make a good anchor. If Helix1 is in fact a "long" secondary object, it will be rated high. The objects on the agenda level show the three helices with the ratings.

The solution panel. As of this writing, the solution panel contains two levels, the secondary structure and partial arrangements levels. The secondary structures are restricted to helices and "random coil." A partial arrangement is a clustering of the secondary structures, and theoretically, more than one possible arrangment can be created. The partial arrangements themselves could be configured further to form a complete protein structure.

The Knowledge Source Structure

As in HEARSAY-II and HASP, a knowledge source consists of a condition part and an action part. In PROTEAN, the condition part serves as a multistaged filter for applying the action part. The condition part is divided into three parts—the trigger, the precondition, and the obviate condition—representing different stages of knowledge source invocation. The condition parts are all LISP S-expressions. The action part of the knowledge source is a set of conditional rules as in HASP and TRICERO.

As mentioned earlier, when an event is posted, all the knowledge sources are polled for applicability. This is accomplished by evaluating all the knowledge source triggers. (In the actual implementation, some form of hashing is used to evaluate the knowledge source triggers. Note the similarity of this approach to the HEARSAY-II focus-of-control database.) If the trigger condition is satisfied, a knowledge source activation record, a KSAR, is created instantiating the knowledge source with the event as its context.

At this point two things happen:

1. The knowledge source is put in a "triggered" state, and the state is recorded on triggered-status-node on the agenda level (see the earlier description of the control data blackboard panel).

2. The remainder of the knowledge source (the precondition and the action part) becomes a schedulable activity.

When scheduled for execution, the precondition part of the knowledge source is checked, and if satisfied, the knowledge source is changed to "executable" state. All knowledge sources in the executable states are evaluated, and one is selected for execution. At any point, if the obviate condition is satisfied, the knowledge source is changed to the "obviate" state making it unavailable for execution. (See the Notes section for why the obviate condition is necessary.)

There is no difference between the domain and the control knowledge source structures. The distinction has only to do with whether a knowledge source operates on the control or the solution blackboard panels.

Control

In PROTEAN we can view the control panels and the knowledge sources that operate on them as parts of the control component or we can view them as a subsystem component whose task is dynamic planning. If we take the first view, the PROTEAN control component is very complex and indirect; that is, the execution of the constraint satisfier is preceded by a lot of control decision steps. If we take the second view, two tasks are being performed concurrently, neither of which is very complex. But the interleaving of the two tasks makes for complexity, especially since there is no clear way to know in advance how the task switching is to occur.

However we view the control component, it consists of three core modules and a core control loop. The core modules are the scheduler, the agenda maintainer, and the rating manager (see Figure D–15). These modules are used within the control loop as follows:

1. An action part of the knowledge source is executed, causing changes on the solution or control data panel. This causes the creation of one or more events on the event level.

2. Each of these events are checked against all knowledge source triggers by the *agenda maintainer*. For each knowledge source whose trigger is satisfied, a knowledge source activation record is created; that is, a knowledge source "closure" is formed with the event as its context. The knowledge source is recorded on the agenda as being in a triggered state.

3. The preconditions of the triggered knowledge source are then evaluated by the *agenda maintainer*. Each knowledge source whose precondition is satisfied is recorded as being in the executable state. At the same time, obviate conditions of all knowledge sources in exec-

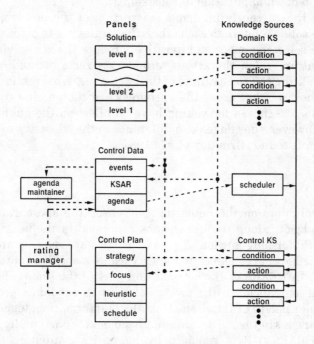

Figure D–15.   A schematic of PROTEAN control structure.

utable state are evaluated to determine if the knowledge state should be changed to the obviate state.

4. All the knowledge sources in the executable state are rated by appropriate "heuristic" procedures in the heuristic level. Note that there may be knowledge sources in the executable state from previous cycles. This process is managed by the *rating manager*.

5. The *scheduler* selects the highest rated executable knowledge source instance (as recorded on the agenda) for execution.

Knowledge-Application Strategy

From the perspective of knowledge-based systems, the PROTEAN problem is knowledge poor and the problem is underconstrained. Generally the method of choice for a knowledge-poor task is a generate-and-test search. The overall strategy in PROTEAN is to control the combinatorial explosion by searching at various abstraction levels of the protein structure, much in the way HEARSAY-II did in the speech domain. For example, by first satisfying the spatial constraints between secondary structures treated as an enclosed volume before placing the amino acids locally within the solid, the total search is reduced. This approach entails a top-down application of constraints.

Within the currently implemented portion of the problem, that of placing the solids relative to each other, the strategy is to place the solids around one selected anchor and iteratively reduce the accessible volume (a space within which the actual secondary structure could be placed without violating the constraints) of the anchorees. Which solid is chosen as the anchor, in what order the anchorees are chosen, and what pairs of anchorees are chosen for yoking have no affect on the quality of the solution. However, they do make a difference in the efficiency with which the solution is found (Brinkley et al., 1987).

Additional Notes

The evaluators on the heuristic level check the appropriateness of candidate objects along the dimensions expressed in the heuristics, for example, "Prefer-long-anchor." These heuristics are selected and posted by a knowledge source associated with various steps designated on the focus level. In HEARSAY-II, the condition part of the knowledge source served as a look-ahead in the process of solution candidate generation. The scheduler had to evaluate the look-ahead information, together with other pending activities, to decide what to do next. Functionally the look-ahead of HEARSAY-II is replaced by heuristics evaluators that rate objects on the solution panel. Since the evaluators return ratings, the task for the scheduler in PROTEAN is much simpler than in HEARSAY-II—it merely selects the highest rated knowledge source instance for execution. In essence, the many different functions performed within the scheduler of HEARSAY-II have been partitioned and made explicit in PROTEAN.

When the execution of the action part of a knowledge source does not immediately follow the condition part, as in HEARSAY-II and PROTEAN, a data (state) consistency problem arises. There is no guarantee, when an action part is finally selected for execution, that the condition part of the knowledge source still holds. To avoid the execution of now inappropriate, irrelevant, or undesirable action, the obviate condition is evaluated before the action part is executed.

When we look at the information used in the control panels and control knowledge sources, we wonder what is meant by "control." Close scrutiny of PROTEAN reveals that control knowledge consists of abstract representation of domain actions. Whether a knowledge source is called a domain knowledge or a control knowledge often seems arbitrary.

Since problem solving proceeds according to a plan, the notion of "opportunism" is defined as an action deemed appropriate that lies outside the plan in force. This definition is more intuitive and clearer than the loose use of the term in other systems. However, note that there is a need for knowledge sources, or rules within knowledge sources, that are looking for such opportunities.

There is no explicit mechanism for switching between the control task and the domain task to process next. Whether the focus of attention is to be on the domain task or the control task is controlled entirely by some rating function. This has the potential for rather arbitrary switching from one task to another.

Traditionally the blackboard held solution state data. In PROTEAN, some control nodes (for example, on the heuristic level) contain knowledge in the form of procedures. Although knowledge can be treated as data (as when looked at by metaknowledge), the particular organization in PROTEAN deviates from the simple, yet powerful, construct in which all active knowledge was represented by the knowledge sources.

D5. Summary

ALTHOUGH A PROBLEM-SOLVING MODEL can help in the general organization of domain knowledge and reasoning strategy, the blueprint of the architecture must account for the characteristics of the specific task at hand. Details of the task determine the specific choice of knowledge representation and reasoning methods. Therefore, there could be as many blackboard architectures as there are applications. Since HEARSAY-II and HASP, there have been many other programs whose system designs are rooted in the blackboard model. These programs include applications in the area of structure determination of proteins from electron density maps (Terry, 1983) and from NMR data (Brinkley et al., 1987), planning (Hayes-Roth et al., 1979), computer vision (Nagao and Matsuyama, 1980; and Raulefs and Thorndyke, 1987; and Draper et al., 1988), and signal understanding and situation assessment (Spain, 1983 and Williams, 1985).

Other applications are currently being built in the areas of process control, very large-scale integration (VLSI) design, crisis management, image understanding, and signal interpretation. Many applications in the Defense Advanced Research Project Agency's (DARPA) Strategic Computing Program in the areas of military battle management, a pilot's associate, and autonomous vehicles use the blackboard model. To date, there is no commonly agreed upon architecture or standards for blackboard systems. Rather, there are more or less strict interpretations of the model. Nonetheless there are many similarities in the design of blackboard systems. In Section E we attempt a rationalization of some of the differences in the designs and review the more common constructs used to date.

E. SUMMARY: ELEMENTS OF BLACKBOARD ARCHITECTURE

In section B we introduced the blackboard model of problem solving as a conceptual framework for organizing reasoning steps, solution and control state data, and domain knowledge useful for constructing solutions to problems. Various interpretations and implementations of the model for different application tasks were described in Section D. These applications are representative of architectural themes and variations to be found in current blackboard systems. Of the applications, HASP has the simplest architectural constructs and PROTEAN has the most complex. ("Architecture" here refers to design of structures. Within the context of our discussion, it means specific choices of constructs for the blackboard, knowledge sources, and control.) Yet, in terms of the complexity of tasks, as measured by the number of different objects to be manipulated, HASP is the most complex. The complexity of program behavior does not necessarily correlate with architectural complexity. Like the ant-on-the-beach metaphor used by Simon (Simon, 1969), simple mechanisms can give rise to complex behavior given a complex environment in which they must operate.

What then dictates the essential mechanisms needed to tackle different application tasks? What are the characteristics of tasks for which the blackboard approach has been applied? Within the blackboard framework what are the elements of the architectural space that system designers manipulate? There are no simple answers to these questions. Much depends on the specific requirements of the applications problems at hand. Some general things can be said about the nature of applications that have benefited from the use of a blackboard-system approach—we attempt such a description in Section E1. Aside from the task characteristics, the use of different problem-solving methods has a great influence on the design of blackboard systems. We discuss two problem-solving approaches that affect blackboard system architecture in Section E2. In Section E3 we summarize alternative designs for the major components gleaned from the different blackboard system applications discussed in Section D.

E1.　Blackboard Systems and Task Characteristics

THE APPLICATIONS for which the blackboard approach has been useful—
signal understanding, vision, situation assessment, and so on—share
common characteristics. First, they are all attempts at solving complex
and ill-structured problems. Second, the solutions involve the use of
many diverse sources of knowledge whose applicability is situation
dependent. We explore the nature of complexity and ill-structuredness
and show how the blackboard approach is an aid for dealing with this
type of problem.

Complex Problems

Simon (Simon, 1969) defines a complex system as "one made up of a
large number of parts that interact in a non-simple way. In such systems,
the whole is more than the sum of the parts, [in the sense that] given
the properties of parts and the laws of their interaction, it is not a trivial
matter to infer the properties of the whole." To understand complexity,
we describe complex systems in terms of less complex subsystems and
relationships among them. Often this description takes the form of a
hierarchy.

Software engineering techniques and methodologies tend to foster
hierarchical problem decomposition, and most complex programs are
organized according to some form of hierarchy. Usually the hierarchy is
organized along functional decompositions of the task to be performed,
forming a tree-like representation of the function-call relationships
among the modules. One advantage of this type of organization is that
it allows common modules to be shared. In blackboard systems, task
decomposition, often driven by the hierarchical decomposition of the
solution space, focuses on the functional independence of the modules in
order to limit the number of interactions among them. Loosely coupled
subsystems provide maximum flexibility in the software development
phase as well as during problem solving. In addition, due to the separation of task functions and the procedure for calling these functions,
these modules (knowledge sources) do not contain calling-sequence (control) information. Control is treated as a separate task, which may also
be decomposed as a hierarchy of subtasks, as in the case of PROTEAN.

The solution space represented as abstraction or part-of hierarchy on
the blackboard has pragmatic advantages. First, the hierarchical structure allows for the integration of diverse concepts and associated vocabularies. For example, in HASP the concept of a "platform" was defined
with properties such as type, speed, and location; whereas the concept of
"signal" was defined with properties such as frequency, intensity, and

bandwidth. Second, abstraction reduces the computational need in two ways:

1. Abstracted entities involve fewer components to manipulate than their detailed counterparts.

2. Abstractions can store information that would otherwise need to be recomputed from the detailed counterparts.

The hierarchical structure of the blackboard provides a favorable tradeoff between storage space and computational time. In HASP, for example, reasoning about platform movements is easier and faster at the platform level than reasoning at the level of its constituent propeller and engine parts, even though extra storage is needed to represent both levels of description.

Ill-Structured Problems

Ill-structured problems (Newell, 1969) are characterized by poorly defined goals and an absence of a predetermined decision path from the initial state to a goal. Often there is a lack of well-defined criteria for determining whether a solution is acceptable. (In many expert systems, the acceptability of a solution is determined by a panel of human experts who might disagree among themselves.) Often a problem is ill-structured because it is ill-defined or poorly understood, for example, assessing the merits of one's financial investments in light of proposed tax reforms. Although Newell's discussions about ill-structured problems occur within the context of weak problem-solving methods, he notes that a human's ability to solve an ill-structured problem may be due to the problem solver's ability to "recognize the essential connection or form of the solution" or due to the fact that "the problem solver always [has] available some distinctions that apply to every situation" (Newell, 1969). In short, many ill-structured problems might be solved by applying knowledge, especially knowledge in the form of empirical associations, or expertise. The condition part of a knowledge source serves as the recognizer of the situation under which the knowledge source can contribute to solving a problem.

Many non-blackboard expert systems deal quite well with ill-structured problems. What further aid can the blackboard approach provide? First, the blackboard approach requires no a priori determined reasoning path; the selection of what to do next is made while the problem is being solved. Second, from a knowledge engineering viewpoint, vague information and knowledge, which characterize ill-structured problems, must be made concrete in the process of building a solution to the problem. This can only be accomplished incrementally, by building a system and modifying the architecture and clarifying the knowledge, as the real nature of the problem reveals itself. The blackboard model is an excellent tool for *exploratory programming,* a conscious intertwining of system design and implementation, which is found to be effective for the development of the type of systems that are of concern here (Sheil, 1983).

Although useful for many problems, blackboard systems are generally expensive to run, primarily because the situation-specific control decisions are made dynamically, requiring space and time. It would be foolish to apply the blackboard approach when lower cost methods will suffice. For example, classification problems (Clancey, 1985) can in principle be solved using the blackboard method, but there are lower cost approaches to the problem. Determining the appropriate problem-solving methodology for an application problem is itself a difficult problem, and the reader is referred to Kline and Dolins (1985), Hayes-Roth et al. (1983), and Weiss and Kulikowski (1984) for some guidance. Generally, the occurrence of some combination of the following characteristics in a problem makes it an appropriate candidate for the blackboard approach:

- A large solution space.
- Noisy and unreliable data.
- A variety of input data and a need to integrate diverse information.
- The need for many independent or semi-independent pieces of knowledge to cooperate in forming a solution.
- The need to use multiple reasoning methods (for example, backward and forward reasoning).
- The need for an incremental and evolutionary construction of the solution.

E2.   "Problem Solving" Revisited: Search vs. Recognition

THE TERM "PROBLEM SOLVING" is used in two ways in the literature. First, it refers to a variety of cognitive activities that achieve well-defined goals, activities that we view as exhibiting "intelligent behavior." Second, it refers to a specific approach or a method designed to achieve intelligent behavior in programs. Our focus is on the latter use of the term. Carbonell (1983) categorizes the basic problem-solving approaches used to date: *search* (means-end analysis and heuristic search), *plan instantiation,* and *analogy.* The first two approaches have been used extensively, and the third approach, problem solving by analogy, is still a topic of current research.

Another way to differentiate problem-solving approaches is by the amount of task-specific knowledge needed or used to arrive at a solution.

From this perspective, knowledge-poor systems must rely on search techniques for problem solving, and virtually all systems using search techniques are knowledge poor. Knowledge-rich systems use recognition techniques for problem solving. *Recognition* is a term coined by McDermott and Newell (1983)—"the complete recognition system does not reason, it knows. Reasoning shows up in the occurrence of combinatorial search." At any particular computational state, instead of generating and evaluating the possible next states, a recognition system simply knows what the next state should be. Carbonell considers problem solving by recognition as a special case of the plan instantiation method. Plan instantiation suggests the existence of some structure, but in most recognition systems the plan is only implicit.

In the search paradigm, each problem-solving step requires an evaluator to select from a pre-enumerated or enumerable next state. Each problem-solving step consists of a generation of operators or state, followed by an evaluation, followed by a selection and an application of the state transforming operator. Often, evaluation precedes generation so that generation can occur selectively. The generator can be algorithmic or heuristic; it can be a legal-move generator or a plausible-move generator. The evaluator can be knowledge poor (general and weak), or it can be knowledge rich (task specific). To date most programs that use search use weak knowledge—the search paradigm is called a weak method.

Among the blackboard systems discussed, HEARSAY-II and PROTEAN use the search paradigm. In HEARSAY-II, all the possible states were enumerable by its knowledge sources. For example, given a grammar, a table of all legal adjacent words for each word could be generated; in PROTEAN, all the candidate secondary structures from which the anchor was selected were enumerable. In both HEARSAY-II and PROTEAN, the evaluator (the scheduler in HEARSAY-II and a combination of "heuristics" and rating function in PROTEAN) used weak criteria. In HEARSAY-II, criteria for selecting from a number of possible word sequences might be the number of words in the sequence. In PROTEAN, the criteria might be the number of satisfiable constraints. The knowledge is weak because it either does not rely heavily on task specific criteria or the task-specific criteria are very simple. Hypothetical, knowledge-rich criteria might be: "select a word sequence beginning with a preposition following a noun clause" or "select a secondary structure containing at least one tryptophan."

In the recognition paradigm, the knowledge base must be scanned for a piece of knowledge that can be applied to the current situation. This is called the *match* step. (Sometimes this is referred to as "search," in a general sense, but this causes confusion.) Each problem-solving step consists of a *match step* followed by the application of a state-transforming operator. If a piece of knowledge is encoded as conditional if-then rules, it not only contains what the next state would be, but also the situation under which the state transformation can occur. Most current expert systems are recognition systems.[10]

In HASP the search paradigm was tried and failed because there was no generator of the solution space (see Section C3). HASP was one of the first complete recognition systems. It consisted of fifty knowledge sources, each with an average of ten rules. The active knowledge sources consisted of domain- and situation-specific pieces of knowledge that "knew" what to infer or what action to take for each intermediate state. In addition, it had a plan for the application of the knowledge in the form of control knowledge sources.

We now elaborate on the basic differences in blackboard architectures attributable to the differences between the search and recognition methods of problem solving.

Search

As stated earlier, search requires at least a generator of the solution space and an evaluator. The evaluation can be of two types: a local look-ahead that evaluates possible future states and a global evaluator that selects the best operator based on the information provided by the look-aheads and the overall state of the solution. In the HEARSAY-II architecture, the action part of the knowledge source was used as a generator. (See Figure E–1.) Upon its execution, it placed new hypotheses on the blackboard. The condition part served as a look-ahead for the action part.

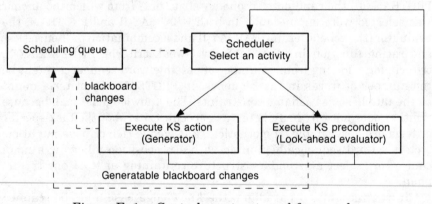

Figure E–1.   Control construct used for search.

[10] If-then rules are not necessary for a recognition system, and conversely the mere use of if-then rules does not imply a recognition system. The problem-solving approach is independent of the knowledge representation. (See Article XVIII in this Volume.)

When executed, it determined the state changes that *would be* produced if the action part were to be executed. The scheduler decided on the next activity (either to look ahead or to generate changes); that is, it determined the solution path by evaluating the current state of the solution and a set of possible future states.

In this scheme, the global evaluation criteria were hidden inside the scheduling module. The PROTEAN control structure is an attempt to make explicit the different activities involved in controlling search. These control activities are hierarchical in nature, consisting of the generation and evaluation of abstract strategies, tactics, and specific action within the context of a given solution state.

Within the search paradigm the quality of the solution may depend on the amount of search conducted, which is also a function of the quality of knowledge available for evaluation. The premise in HEARSAY-II and, especially in PROTEAN, is that a favorable tradeoff can be made between the amount of control knowledge and knowledge source activations— that is, spending time on evaluation pays off in reducing search and in improving the quality of the solution. Whether this tradeoff is generally true and whether the PROTEAN approach is the best way to achieve this still remain to be seen.

Recognition

The recognition problem-solving paradigm is conceptually simpler than the search paradigm (see Figure E–2). Here the knowledge base is scanned for a piece of knowledge that can be applied to a state. Of course, many pieces of knowledge may be applicable for a given state, and a

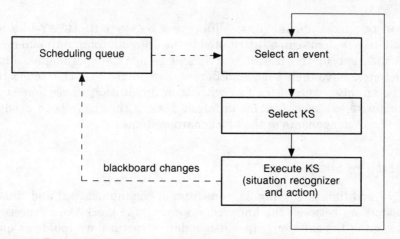

Figure E–2.   Control construct used for recognition.

decision must be made whether to apply all the pieces of knowledge or a subset of them. This control decision is also knowledge based. Thus there is a certain amount of uniformity between the way decisions are made about which knowledge to apply and about the manipulations of the solution-space objects. In recognition-oriented blackboard systems, the condition part of the knowledge source specifies the situations under which it can contribute to the solution state. The action part of the knowledge source changes the solution state. Since the applicable knowledge source for any given situation is predetermined, in the sense that knowledge sources are always associated with situations, the control module focuses on the selection of the best region of the solution space (the specific situation) to process next.

In this approach no distinction is made between control and domain-specific knowledge. However, since a domain knowledge source looks at blackboard data and a control knowledge source looks at a description of changes to the blackboard, in addition to the specifics of the changes, they are in fact different—we might say that the control knowledge source has a wider scope. Because control knowledge is different from other knowledge sources, systems can be designed to exploit the difference. Informal plans, can be either built into the control structure or dynamically generated. For example, in HASP, the control "plan" was the cyclic selection and execution of knowledge sources at different levels of control. In PROTEAN, control plans for the execution of the domain knowledge sources were dynamically created.

E3.   Component Design

SOME OF THE ARCHITECTURAL differences between HEARSAY-like and HASP-like systems can be attributed to the different computational methods inherent in the use of search and recognition paradigms. Many differences have their basis in different domain and task characteristics. Some of these were described with each application in Section D. To summarize, we now describe different designs that have been used for the major components of the blackboard systems.

Blackboard Structure

In addition to serving as a medium of communication, and thus of cooperation, between the knowledge sources, the blackboard represents a design of the solution. Since it is a data structure, we could not quite call it a problem-solving plan, yet in the process of problem formulation the structure of the blackboard serves as the backbone of the system design. It is where the design process begins. The blackboard partitions the solution space, and these partitions dictate what sources of knowledge will be needed to solve the problem. What constitutes a solution, what intermediate solutions are needed or available, and what relationships exist among hypotheses must all be expressed within the blackboard structure. Designing the blackboard is the first step in the divide-and-conquer process.

From the standpoint of structure, the blackboard has very little variability. It is organized into levels corresponding to the partitions of the solution space. These form either abstraction or compositional hierarchies. The objects on a given level share the same properties, or vocabulary.

Some of the components and considerations that go into the design of the blackboard data are listed here.

Levels. No limit is imposed on the number of levels in a hierarchy. In all the systems to date, the levels and templates for the nodes on the level (the attributes that the objects on the level will have) are created before run-time. This means that levels are not created dynamically. For discovery and learning tasks, the dynamic creation of levels as new concepts and constructs will be needed.

As a data structure, the level object holds information about the nodes on its level. For example, it must keep the names of the attributes of the nodes and maintain housekeeping information such as the number of nodes on the level at any given time. For these reasons, it is often convenient to view the level object as a class, and the nodes on the level as the instances of the class. This has the further advantage that nodes can inherit default property values at node creation time. Also, operators (methods) associated with creation and destruction of nodes can be stored with the level object.

Nodes. Nodes are objects on a level; for example, a particular word in a sentence is a node on the word level in HEARSAY-II. Nodes are created dynamically as they are needed. The vocabulary relevant to the level of analysis are represented as attributes and values; each node on the level share the same attributes (see Figure E–3). In an object-oriented programming language slots and slot-values can be used, and there is nothing to preclude the use of record structures available in other languages.

Attribute/value. The value of an attribute can have multiple fields; for example, credibility value and/or time stamps, as shown above. In HASP, both a weight and a time stamp were needed for some values (see Figure D–7). Often it is useful to maintain value history. This is especially true in continuous-input signal understanding programs in which temporal trends are important.

```
Aircraft-Node-2
Type:fighter
Position:((X 10) (Y 23) (Z 15000)(Weight .7) (Time 20:34))
Speed:((Knots 550) (Weight .8))
Heading:((Magnetic 120))
Supported-by: Emitter-Node-15
```

Figure E-3.   A node example.

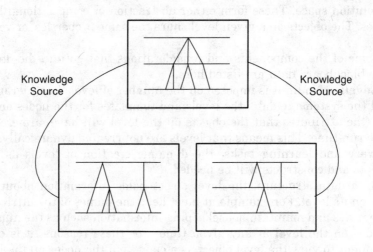

Figure E–4.   Blackboard panels.

Panels. There may be more than one hierarchy in the blackboard. Called blackboard panels, they are useful when more than one hierarchy is need to represent the solution-state data (see Figure E–4). They were first used in CRYSALIS (Terry, 1983; see also, Article VII.C3, Vol. II), which had an electron-density data hierarchy and a protein structure hierarchy. Multiple hierarchies were also used to represent plans and plan creation states in the OPM system (Hayes-Roth et al., 1979).

In PROTEAN, two of the three blackboard panels, the control plan and the solution panels, represented information needed by two closely coupled tasks, that of planning the application of constraints and that of applying constraints. The third panel held control data.

TRICERO had three self-contained blackboard systems. One note of interest in TRICERO is that messages were passed between each of the subsystems using nodes on the message level of each blackboard as mail boxes. This allowed for the uniform processing of externally and internally generated hypotheses.

Knowledge Source Structures

A knowledge source represents knowledge needed to solve a subproblem. All knowledge sources are event-triggered agents—the activation of knowledge sources are solution-state dependent, rather than being process dependent. This means that the most important thing about the design of knowledge source is that it must be able to evaluate the current state. In all blackboard systems, knowledge sources are designed with a condition part and an action part. When portions of the current state satisfy the condition part, that knowledge source becomes *triggered*. The condition part may be multistaged as in PROTEAN—a triggered knowledge source must pass other conditions before the action part can be executed. Upon its execution the action part produces a new state.

In HEARSAY-like search-oriented systems, the action and the condition parts are separately schedulable entities. The condition part serves as a look-ahead and the action part serves as a generator. In HASP-like recognition systems, the condition part serves as a situation filter for the action part and both parts are in one module.

Condition part. The condition part can make a context-independent or context-dependent evaluation of an event (a change to the blackboard). In HASP, possible changes to the blackboard are categorized into different event types. The name of the event type was used to record a blackboard change. It was also used as a triggering condition in the condition part of the knowledge sources. For example, if a blackboard modification was of a type "new-source-found," all the knowledge sources whose condition part contained the token "new-source-found" were executed. In this type of construct, the condition part is context independent because regardless of what the new-source might be, the knowledge sources would be executed. In PROTEAN, since both trigger and precondition parts are arbitrary predicates, the condition parts of the knowledge source could do a more elaborate state evaluation. For example, a knowledge source trigger part may stipulate that a new source be found, and the precondition part may stipulate that the new source be a diesel submarine whose speed is greater than 10 knots.

If the action part of the knowledge source is a collection of rules, the condition part of the knowledge source can be viewed as a high-level filter for the rule set. Rules have their own condition parts that serve as more detailed filters for the actions. Think of a condition part design as consisting of multistaged filters; for example, a context-independent filter followed by a number of context-dependent filters. (See Figure E–5).

Action part. The action part of a knowledge source modifies the current blackboard state. With the exception of HEARSAY-II, which used procedures, all the example systems used rule sets for the body of the knowledge sources. Each knowledge source can make one or more changes to the blackboard. In a rule-based knowledge source, multiple changes can come from multiple firing of rules or from multiple actions on the right-hand side of rules.

The changes to the blackboard are new hypotheses (and new data) or modifications to existing hypotheses. Changes can also be made to the control information, as in the case of PROTEAN. In addition to changes to intermediate solutions on the blackboard, state changes can occur from the posting of goals and subgoals to be achieved or posting of model-based expectations of changes to occur in the future, as in HASP.

Static knowledge. The discussion of knowledge in blackboard systems has been confined to knowledge sources, which are active knowledge. Active knowledge consists of algorithms and heuristic rules that directly transform one state of the world into another state, that is, change the blackboard. Other types of domain knowledge are awkward to represent in algorithms or rules, such as definitions and taxonomies. Such "static" knowledge is best represented as objects, frames, or tables. In HASP, the knowledge about ships was represented in an object hierarchy; in HEARSAY-II, the legal word sequences were represented in a network. The AGE [Nii and Aiello, 1979) and ESHELL (Fujitsu Labs, 1987) skeletal systems integrate object-oriented knowledge representation and rules by making objects accessible from rules.

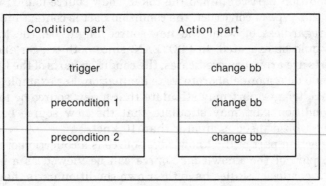

Figure E–5.   Knowledge source form.

Control

Control is the most complex component of blackboard systems and has the most variability in design. The basic function of the control component is to select and apply knowledge sources (or condition and action components of knowledge sources) within appropriate contexts. Major design differences occur in the following areas:

1. *Schedulable entities*—whether parts of the knowledge sources are separate schedulable entities or not.

2. *Scheduling*—whether the focus of attention is based on events or on knowledge sources.

3. *Noticing*—who notices the change in the blackboard.

4. *Control data*—where and in what form the control data are stored.

Schedulable entities.   In search-oriented systems, the condition part and the action part of the knowledge sources are scheduled separately. That is, the scheduler decides whether it wants to generate new hypotheses or do more look-aheads. In recognition systems, each knowledge source is scheduled as a single entity. If the condition part is satisfied, the action part is immediately executed. Scheduling structures arising from the two basic types are shown in Figure E–6.

As in HEARSAY-II, scheduling in PROTEAN was multistaged. When a knowledge source trigger was satisfied, the knowledge source was instantiated and the precondition part evaluated. If it was satisfied, the action part of the knowledge source became executable and was put on an agenda of pending activities. A knowledge source was selected for

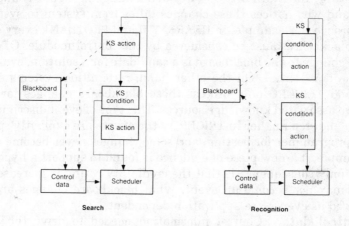

Figure E–6.   Basic scheduling approaches.

execution from those in executable states. HEARSAY-II can be viewed as a special case of a PROTEAN-like, multistaged scheduler design.

Note that if a state change is possible between the time a condition part and its action part is executed, the condition part must be reevaluated. Both HEARSAY-II and PROTEAN have this characteristic because both the condition and action parts are schedulable entities.

Scheduling.   There are two approaches to select the next thing to do:

1. A knowledge source, or knowledge sources, can be selected on the basis of the current state of the solution, or more specifically, on the latest changes to the solution state. Called event-oriented scheduling, the focus is on selecting the best solution island on which to base further computation. Most recognition systems (for example, HASP and TRICERO) take this approach. This is because in recognition systems, once a blackboard change is selected, the knowledge source that can process it is predetermined. (See Figure E–2.)

2. A knowledge source can be selected on the basis of what the knowledge source can contribute to the current state. This approach, called knowledge-oriented scheduling, is taken most often in search systems (for example, HEARSAY-II). The schedulable components of knowledge sources are the look-ahead evaluators and the generators of the solution space. The basic function of the scheduler in the control component is to evaluate the global situation and decide what to do next. (See Figure E–1.)

In reality, many problems can gain from a mixed strategy of search and recognition and BB1, for example, allows for both event-oriented and knowledge-oriented scheduling.

Posting and noticing blackboard changes.   What changes are posted and who notices these changes differ from system to system. In one approach (for example, in HEARSAY-II and PROTEAN), every change to the blackboard must be considered by the control module. Of course, if every change to the blackboard is a candidate for a solution, evaluating each one is essential. On the other hand, recognition systems such as HASP and TRICERO only process those blackboard changes for which there are associated knowledge sources. This type of event discrimination is taken one step further in TRICERO—the events are explicitly specified by the programmer for posting, and some changes never become events. For example, if a new piece of evidence is found to support a hypothesis, but the only consequence is that the credibility rating is increased, this change may not become an event. What blackboard changes are to be considered as events are application dependent.

Control data.   Control information needed to drive the system always resides outside the blackboard containing the solution state. In HASP and TRICERO, different types of changes to the blackboard (modification to nodes, goal posting, and so on) were stored in separate data structures. Each event was a recording of the type of change, the node that was modified, the new values, and the rule that made the modification. In HEARSAY-II, the control data was stored on a global list, the scheduling queue. The items on the queue were of two types—the stimulus-response frame generated by the condition part that pointed to its action part and all the places on the blackboard it could be applied to, and the names of the condition parts of knowledge sources. Because HASP-like systems focus on event scheduling, the control data are primarily about events; in HEARSAY-like systems, which focus on knowledge source scheduling, the control data are primarily about knowledge sources.

In PROTEAN, control was viewed as a problem separate from the primary task of satisfying constraints among pieces of protein. The control problem was to determine what domain knowledge source to apply and to what area of the blackboard. The control problem was formulated as a planning subproblem, and its solution state appeared on another blackboard, called the control panel. All data dealing with control were posted on the control-data panel and were shared by both the control-planning and the domain knowledge sources.

Domain-specific knowledge, meta-knowledge, and control knowledge. The distinction between domain-specific knowledge and meta-knowledge is not always clear cut. Meta-knowledge, knowledge about knowledge, is often thought to be weak, general, and domain independent. But, in both search and recognition systems, meta-knowledge is often treated as control knowledge about what to do next, and this type of knowledge is often very domain specific. For example, in PROTEAN the meta-knowledge "prefer long coils over short coils" is domain specific—it makes no sense outside the particular application. In general, making distinctions between domain-specific knowledge and meta-knowledge does not contribute much to the design of the system; rather, it tends to distract. Instead it is preferable to organize knowledge sources hierarchically according to some control hierarchy. In most systems, the control hierarchy partitions the knowledge sources into those that deal directly with the emerging solution states and those that deal with the process history or problem-solving states, called control states. The knowledge sources that operate on control states are called control knowledge sources. Some systems such as HASP, CRYSALIS, and OPM had more refined levels in the control hierarchy.

Summary

For a given application, a blackboard system can be designed by selecting from different constructs for the blackboard, knowledge sources, and control modules just described. An application could also be built on

one of the skeletal blackboard systems. We mentioned three in passing—
AGE, ESHELL, and BB1. AGE was used to build TRICERO and BB1 was
used to build PROTEAN. The description of several skeletal blackboard
systems, AGE, BB1, HEARSAY-III, GBB, MXA, and BLOBS, can be found
in Engelmore and Morgan (1988). A skeletal system is a programming
environment with predetermined architecture for blackboard systems.
The architecture is generally parameterized allowing the user some flexibility in the final details of the application system design.

   One of the key contributors to design differences in blackboard systems is the problem-solving paradigm. Whether the problem is formulated as a recognition or search problem, whether there is enough task
knowledge to solve a problem, and whether weak methods and knowledge
must be used affect the basic structure and the behavior of blackboard
systems. Search-oriented formulation of applications tends to favor
HEARSAY-II–like designs, whereas recognition-oriented formulation
tends toward HASP-like designs. Other design choices—whether a knowledge source is a set of rules or a procedure, whether there are multiple
data hierarchies in the blackboard, and whether attributes values
include certainty weights—depend on the requirements inherent in the
application problem.

Chapter XVII

Cooperative Distributed Problem Solving

Edmund H. Durfee—University of Michigan
Victor R. Lesser—University of Massachusetts
Daniel D. Corkill—University of Massachusetts

CHAPTER XVII: COOPERATIVE DISTRIBUTED PROBLEM SOLVING

A. OVERVIEW

COOPERATIVE DISTRIBUTED PROBLEM SOLVING (CDPS) studies how a loosely coupled network of problem solvers can work together to solve problems that are beyond their individual capabilities. Each problem-solving node in the network is capable of sophisticated problem solving and can work independently, but the problems faced by the nodes cannot be completed without cooperation. Cooperation is necessary because no single node has sufficient expertise, resources, and information to solve a problem. Different nodes might have expertise for solving different parts of an overall problem. For example, if the problem is to design a house, one node might have expertise on the strength of structural materials, another on the space requirements for different types of rooms, another on plumbing, another on electrical wiring, and so on. Different nodes might have different resources. For example, some might be very fast at computation, others might have connections that speed communication, and still others might have more memory. Finally, different nodes might have different information or viewpoints on a problem. For example, geographically separated nodes that are monitoring aircraft movements will have different perceptions because their sensors will pick up different signals. Only by combining information about their views will they be able to form an overall picture of aircraft movements.

CDPS nodes cooperatively solve a problem by using their local expertise, resources, and information to individually solve subproblems, and then integrating subproblem solutions into an overall solution. As they work together, the nodes face two very important constraints. First, because their subproblem solutions must eventually be integrated, nodes are constrained to form individual solutions that will fit into an overall solution. Even in situations where this overall solution is not represented at any one node, the distributed components of the solution must still be integrated by their mutual consistency. Thus the nodes must coordinate their asynchronous and parallel problem solving to build compatible solutions to their interdependent subproblems.

The second constraint is that nodes are limited in how much they can communicate. Limited internode communication stems from either inherent bandwidth limitations of the communication medium or because of the high computational costs of packaging and assimilating information to be sent and received among nodes. Limited communication between nodes that are working on interdependent subproblems

85

means that nodes must rely on sophisticated local reasoning to decide on appropriate actions and interactions. Each node must be capable of modifying its behavior as circumstances change and planning its own communication and cooperation strategies with other nodes.

Why CDPS?

From this description of CDPS, we might ask: If coordination among problem solvers is difficult, why not build a single, more powerful problem solver to perform the functions of a CDPS network? In short, why CDPS?

One answer to these questions has a technological basis. Advances in hardware technology for processor construction and interprocessor communication make it possible to connect large numbers of sophisticated, yet inexpensive, processing units that execute asynchronously. Interconnected processors can be a cost-effective way to provide the computational cycles required by AI applications. A range of connection structures is possible, from a very tight coupling of processors through shared or distributed memory, to a looser coupling of processors through a local area communication network, to a very loose coupling of geographically distributed processors through a communication network. Regardless of how tightly they are coupled, the processors must use their communication medium selectively; otherwise, they might overwhelm each other with more information than they can process. Whether because of limited communication bandwidth or limited processing power, the processors cannot share all of their information but must be able to work effectively together anyway.

A second answer is that many AI applications are inherently distributed. Some are spatially distributed; for example, interpreting and integrating data from spatially distributed sensors or controlling a set of robots that work together on a factory floor. Other applications are functionally distributed, for example, bringing together a number of specialized medical-diagnosis systems on a particularly difficult case or developing a sophisticated architectural expert system composed of individual experts in specialties such as structural engineering, electrical wiring, and room layout. Finally, some applications are temporally distributed (pipelined), as in a factory where production lines consist of several work areas, each having an expert system responsible for scheduling orders (Figure A–1).

A CDPS network that manages the distribution of data, expertise, processing power, and other resources has significant advantages over a single, monolithic, centralized problem solver. These advantages include: faster problem solving by exploiting parallelism; decreased communication by transmitting only high-level partial solutions to nearby nodes

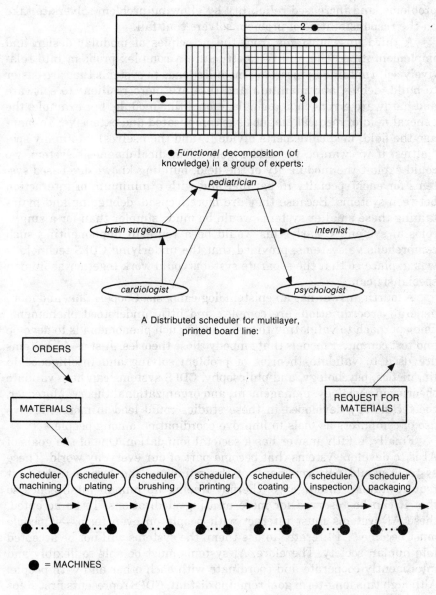

Figure A–1. Examples of spatial, functional, and temporal distribution.

rather than raw data to a central site; more flexibility by having problem solvers with different abilities dynamically team up to solve current problems; and increased reliability by allowing problem solvers to take on the responsibilities of problem solvers that fail.

A third answer stems from the principles of modular design and implementation. The ability to structure a complex problem into relatively self-contained processing modules leads to systems that are easier to build, debug, and maintain and that are more resilient to software and hardware errors than a single, monolithic module. For example, the general field of medical diagnosis is complicated and extensive. To manage the field, medical experts divide it (and themselves) into many specialties. If we wanted to build a general medical-diagnosis system, we could exploit the modularity of the field, building knowledge-based systems for each specialty in parallel and with a minimum of interaction between systems. Because they are more focused, debugging and maintaining these smaller systems would be much simpler than for a single, colossal system. Clearly this would be a route to implementing such comprehensive systems, provided that the underlying CDPS technology was in place so that the separate systems could work together as human specialists can.

A fourth answer has an epistemological basis. Cooperation, and more generally coordination, are complex and little understood phenomena. One approach to validating theories about such phenomena is to develop and test computer models that embody those theories. Just as AI systems are used to validate theories of problem solving and intelligence in linguistics, psychology, and philosophy, CDPS systems can help validate theories in sociology, management, and organizational theory. Moreover, the technology developed in these studies could lead to more effective use of computers as tools to improve coordination among people.

Finally, a fifth answer has a societal foundation. One of the goals of AI is to develop systems that become part of our everyday world. These systems would perform many of the mundane and boring tasks that require human intelligence, thereby freeing up human intelligence so that it can be reserved for more exciting meditations. To be accepted, these AI systems must interact with people on even terms—if people must become "AI literate" to use them, the systems will not be accepted into human society. Therefore, AI systems must be able to flexibly and intelligently cooperate and coordinate with each other and with people. Although this long-term goal remains distant, CDPS represents first steps toward it.

An Overview of CDPS Goals and Applications

CDPS, like other areas of AI, realizes theoretical advances in applications. In this section, we describe the general goals of CDPS, some tasks in which achieving these goals is important, and some specific technical problems that must be solved for CDPS to succeed. Four general goals for CDPS are presented in Figure A–2 (Durfee et al., 1987). Depending on the kind of application, some of these goals might be more important than others. The differences are highlighted by considering several of the application domains of CDPS research.

Distributed interpretation. Distributed interpretation applications require the integration and analysis of distributed data to generate a (potentially distributed) semantic model of the data. Application domains include distributed sensor networks (Lesser and Erman, 1980; Lesser and Corkill, 1983; Mason et al., 1988; and Wesson et al., 1981) and communication network fault diagnosis (Conry et al., 1988). In these applications, a central problem solver is inappropriate because it would be less reliable than a network, it would not exploit the potential parallelism in processing data from different regions, and it would require a substantial communication bandwidth to collect the large amounts of raw sensory data. A CDPS network is more reliable (performance degrades gracefully if individual nodes fail), would work on different parts of interpretations in parallel, and would communicate a relatively small number of high-level interpretations. However, to realize these benefits, the individual problem solvers in the network must each form partial solutions that are globally relevant. The nodes must selectively exchange enough information to allow each to decide what data to interpret in order to form such partial solutions. They also must coordinate the selective exchange of partial interpretations so that they can help each other resolve ambiguities and can integrate local results into complete interpretations.

Distributed planning and control. Distributed planning and control applications involve developing and coordinating the actions of distributed effector nodes to perform desired tasks. Application domains include distributed air-traffic control (Findler and Lo, 1986; and Thorndyke et al., 1981), cooperating robots, remotely piloted vehicles (Steeb, 1986), distributed process control in manufacturing (Smith and Hyny-

---

1. Increase the task completion rate through parallelism.
2. Increase the set or scope of achievable tasks by sharing resources (information, expertise, physical devices, and so on).
3. Increase the likelihood of completing tasks (reliability) by undertaking duplicate tasks, possibly using different methods to perform those tasks.
4. Decrease the interference between tasks by avoiding harmful interactions.

Figure A–2.   Generic goals of cooperation.

nen, 1987; Parunak et al., 1985; and Parunak, 1987), and resource allo-
cation/control in a long-haul communication network (Conry et al., 1985;
and Goyal and Worrest, 1988). Distributed planning and control applications often involve distributed interpretation to determine the appropriate node actions. As in the distributed interpretation domains, data
are inherently distributed among nodes, in this case because each has its
own local planning database, capabilities, and view of the world state.
Moreover, the combinatorics of planning potential activities for a large
number of nodes working in parallel can be overwhelming. Even if it
were possible, reliance on a central controller would generally lead to a
slow system (because of communication delays between controller and
controllees), and it would not be robust. A CDPS approach reduces these
problems, but once again, because no single node has an overall view of
the network, nodes must work together to coordinate their actions and
interactions.

Cooperating expert systems.   One means of scaling expert-system
technology to more complex and encompassing problem domains is to
develop cooperative interaction mechanisms that allow multiple experts
systems to work together to solve a common problem. Illustrative situations include controlling an autonomous vehicle that uses separate
expert systems for system status, mission planning, navigation, situation
assessment, and piloting (Arkin et al., 1987; and Smith and Broadwell,
1987); or negotiation among expert systems of two corporations to decide
price and/or delivery time on a major purchase. The heterogeneous char-
acter of cooperating experts means that individual agents might have
different goals, different approaches to problem solving, different evaluation criteria for solutions, and different internal representations of
problems and solutions. Getting them to cooperate is not simply a matter
of giving them a common communication language. For them to reconcile
different solutions to the same problem, they need detailed models of
each other—their capabilities, goals, plans, and preferences—to form a
compromise solution, or to reevaluate their solution criteria to cooperatively generate a completely new solution (Lander and Lesser, 1988).

Computer-supported human cooperation.   Computer technology
promises to provide people with more and better information for making
decisions. However, unless computers also assist people by filtering the
information and focusing attention on relevant information, the amount
of information can become overwhelming (Chang, 1987; Huhns, 1987;
and Malone, 1988). By building AI systems with coordination knowledge,
we can remove some of the burden from people. Domains where this is
important include intelligent command and control systems and multi-
user project coordination (Croft and Lefkowitz, 1988; Mazer, 1987; Nirenburg and Lesser, 1988; and Sathi et al., 1986). By building networks of
CDPS computer assistants for the people in an organization, we can

improve coordination by allowing these assistants to solve (initially routine) coordination problems such as scheduling meetings or routing messages to suitable people. The advantages of this CDPS approach, besides releasing humans from many coordination tasks, are that the assistants can work in parallel, can dynamically team up to coordinate the people they assist, and can work behind the scenes (in the background and at night) to share relevant information for making more coordinated decisions.

Cognitive models of cooperation.   Although the designers of CDPS approaches have consistently used insights about human cooperation to build similar capabilities into their systems, little research to date has worked in the opposite direction. However, AI methods have in the past served to implement and validate theoretical models of human intelligence, and CDPS provides a similar methodological framework for testing theories about human cooperation and coordination. For example, an important and common aspect of coordination among humans is negotiating through compromise (Sycara, 1988). Developing mechanisms that emulate human methods for coordinating their interactions can improve our understanding of humans, and in particular about how humans iteratively converge on decisions about how to share resources and avoid detrimental interactions.

These application areas provide the context for refining the general goals of cooperation (Figure A–2) into specific goals. We can list several specific goals (where the numbers in parentheses refer to the corresponding generic goals), and indicate one of possibly many application domains where they arise:

- Increase the solution creation rate by forming subsolutions in parallel (1). For example, distributed interpretation and distributed planning involve building partial interpretations or partial plans in parallel.

- Minimize the time that nodes must wait for results from each other by coordinating activity (1 and 4). For example, in distributed interpretation, the nodes should coordinate how, when, and where to exchange local interpretations to quickly construct an overall interpretation.

- Improve the overall problem solving by permitting nodes to exchange predictive information (2). For example, an expert system for room layout might quickly generate and share a rough view of a kitchen, so that the expert systems for wiring and plumbing can better predict where in the room they should concentrate.

- Increase the probability that a solution will be found despite node failures by assigning important tasks to multiple nodes (3). For example, in distributed planning, the nodes might be organized into small groups, each with a leader to coordinate the group. But the leader's information and expertise should also be available in one or more of the group members, just in case the leader becomes disabled.

- Improve the use of physical resources by allowing nodes to exchange tasks (2). For example, in computer-supported human cooperation, some assistants might be better suited for mail routing (have better network connections), whereas others might be better at scheduling meetings (have more computing capability for exploring possible schedules). Assistants should be able to exchange tasks to take advantage of each other's strengths.

- Improve the use of individual node expertise by allowing nodes to exchange goals, constraints, partial solutions, and knowledge (programs) (2). For example, cooperating expert systems should exchange information about constraints to focus how each applies its expertise to the current problem.

- Reduce the amount of unnecessary duplication of effort by letting nodes recognize and avoid useless redundant activities (4). For example, in distributed interpretation, nodes with overlapping sensors and identical expertise should not interpret data about the same phenomena if their interpretations are likely to be redundant.

- Increase the confidence of a (sub)solution by having nodes verify each other's results through rederivation using their individual expertise and information (2 and 3). For example, in distributed interpretation, nodes with overlapping sensors but different expertise might each interpret their shared data to make sure they get consistent results.

- Increase the variety of solutions by allowing nodes to form local solutions without being overly influenced by other nodes (1 and 4). For example, in distributed interpretation, each node should not necessarily ignore important local information just because it is incompatible with preferred network interpretations—the network might be wrong!

- Reduce the communication resource usage by being more selective about what messages are exchanged (4). For example, in modeling human negotiation through compromise, the nodes should not exchange all the details about how they came up with a proposal, but instead they should exchange just enough information to converge on an agreeable compromise.

These specific goals suggest that maximizing one specific dimension of effective cooperation, such as speed of solution, makes it impossible to achieve effective cooperation along other dimensions, such as limiting internode communication, or high reliability in case of hardware failure. Thus effective CDPS network control involves balancing the efficient use of communication and processing resources, high reliability, responsiveness to unanticipated situations, and solution quality based on application-specific criteria. The emphasis is shifted from optimizing the individual activities in the network to achieving an acceptable performance level of the network as a whole. This approach is similar to the concept of "satisficing" developed by March and Simon (1958) to describe human organizational problem solving.

Network coordination is difficult in CDPS networks because limited internode communication restricts each node's view of the network problem-solving activity. Network control must be able to tolerate the lack of up-to-date, incomplete, or incorrect control information due to delays in the receipt of information, the high cost of acquisition and processing of the information, and errors in communication and processing hardware. Furthermore, it is important that network coordination policies do not consume more processing and communication resources than are saved by the increased problem-solving coherence. Thus the cooperative problem solving necessary for effective network control may itself require a satisficing approach. Corkill and Lesser (1983) suggest that even in networks composed of a modest number of nodes, a complete analysis to determine the detailed activities at each node is impractical; the computation and communication costs of determining the optimal set and allocation of activities far outweigh the improvement in problem-solving performance. Instead, they suggest that coordination in CDPS networks must sacrifice some potential improvement for a less complex coordination problem. Problem solving and coordination must be balanced so that the combined cost of both is acceptable.

What CDPS Is Not

Networks of cooperating nodes, both conceptual and actual, are not new to AI. However, the relative autonomy and adaptability of the problem-solving nodes—a direct consequence of limited communication—sets CDPS networks apart from approaches such as the Actor framework (Hewett, 1977), HEARSAY-II (Erman et al., 1980), the ETHER language (Kornfeld, 1979), the BEINGS system (Lenat, 1975), CAOS (Schoen, 1986), Poligon (Rice, 1986), and Connectionism (McClelland et al., 1987). In all of these systems, knowledge is compartmentalized so that each actor or "expert" is a specialist in one particular aspect of the overall problem-solving task. The cooperative behavior exhibited by these systems stems from either a centralized scheduling mechanism or from predefined interactions between tightly coupled, simple processing elements. Each "expert" has little or no knowledge of the problem-solving task as a whole or of general strategies for communication and cooperation. As a result, an expert cannot function outside the context of the other experts in the system nor outside specific communication and cooperation protocols specified in advance by the system designer. Metaphorically speaking, an element in these networks is like a small piece of the brain: it is not intelligent alone, but intelligence emerges from a well-structured and tightly connected collection of such elements.

In contrast, each node in a CDPS network possesses sufficient overall problem-solving knowledge that its particular expertise (resulting from a unique perspective of the problem-solving situation) can be applied and communicated without assistance from other nodes in the network. This does not imply that a node functions as well alone as when cooperating with other nodes—internode cooperation is often the only way of developing an acceptable overall solution—but every node can at least formulate a partial solution using only its own knowledge. Each node also possesses significant expertise in communication and control strategies. This knowledge frees the network from the bounds of designed protocols and allows nodes the flexibility to develop their own communication and cooperation strategies dynamically. Appealing to a different metaphor, an element in a CDPS network is like a person who is part of a team. Each person can perform well with minimal intervention from teammates, but the team as a whole performs well only when the people coordinate their individual actions.

CDPS also differs significantly from distributed processing. A distributed processing network typically has multiple, disparate tasks executing concurrently in the network. Shared access to physical or other intelligent systems with *their* own goals? When deciding on an action to take, an intelligent system should use whatever knowledge it has to consider the potential actions of other intelligent systems and the effects of those actions. Reasoning about other systems is important whether the systems are cooperating, coexisting, or competing with each other. CDPS, as its name implies, concentrates only on forms of cooperation between AI systems. Note, however, that cooperation does not assume *benevolence* between nodes (Rosenschein and Genesereth, 1985), but instead that despite different viewpoints and goals, nodes must work together to meet the demands of their environment.

CDPS also differs significantly from distributed processing. A distributed processing network typically has multiple, disparate tasks executing concurrently in the network. Shared access to physical or informational resources is the main reason for interaction among tasks. The goal is to preserve the illusion that each task is executing alone on a dedicated system by having the network operating system hide the resource-sharing interactions and conflicts among tasks in the network. In contrast, the problem-solving procedures in CDPS networks work together to solve a single problem. These procedures are explicitly aware of the distribution of the network components and can make informed interaction decisions based on that information. Unlike CDPS networks, where cooperation among nodes is crucial to developing a solution, the nodes in traditional distributed processing applications rarely need the assistance of another node in carrying out their problem-solving function. However, more recent research into distributed scheduling for a network operating system has begun to take more of a CDPS perspective (Stankovic et al., 1985).

B. AN EXAMPLE OF CDPS

To HIGHLIGHT the general issues and challenges in organizing an AI computation for CDPS, we take a step back from examining specific application domains. Consider instead a more general AI problem where a knowledge-based system receives as input some data corresponding to some current situation and applies its knowledge to that data to form a response to the situation. This problem can be viewed as classification (using the data to classify the situation), interpretation (using the data to interpret the situation), diagnosis (diagnosing the situation based on the data), and planning (if the data includes both current state and desired goals, the system analyzes the data to respond with a plan for achieving the goals). In short, most AI systems take data of some form as input and apply knowledge to return some analysis of the data (e.g., an internal representation of the visual scene, medical situation, speech signals, actions to achieve a result, or concepts contained in a natural language dialog).

A Problem Solver

A single problem solver, $node_i$, receives a set of data $D_i = \{d_i^1, d_i^2, \ldots, d_i^m\}$. The data reside in the node's working memory. The node's knowledge base contains a set of operators for manipulating the data $O_i = \{O_i^1, O_i^2, \ldots, O_i^n\}$. Each operator contains knowledge about how pieces of data fit together to form some intermediate conclusion. The intermediate conclusion is essentially a new piece of data that can be used by other operators, and it is placed in the working memory. Thus data d_i^1 and d_i^2 can be used by operator o_i^1 to generate data d_i^{m+1}. Because the input to operators might be data given to the problem solver data generated by the problem solver, or (in a CDPS) data received from another problem solver, we will not distinguish between data based on their source. Finally, the node has an inference engine that decides, at any given time, which of the operators that could be applied to the current working memory should be invoked.

To give our problem solver flexibility, let us assume that the inference engine can work in either a data-driven or in a goal-directed manner. By data-driven, we mean that the node can choose to invoke an operator simply because the data that it uses is in working memory. By goal-directed, we mean that the node can identify a desired result and can give preference to operators that will eventually lead to that result. For example, all but one piece of data needed by operator o_i^j might be in working memory. The node can back-chain through the operators to determine whether any of the operators that could currently be applied to the working memory might create a new piece of data that might eventually lead to the desired data for operator o_i^j. If so, the node can use the goal of applying operator o_i^j to direct which operators it invokes, rather than just choosing among the currently applicable operators based on only their immediate results. Goal-directed reasoning is important in CDPS because a problem solver often receives a partial result from another node and must build a compatible partial result. After identifying a desirable partial result, it uses goal-directed reasoning to find a sequence of operators that will lead to that result.

The node searches through the possible consequences of the original data until it generates an "acceptable" solution d_i^s. In different applications, "acceptable" can mean different things, for example, achieving a particular confidence rating, being validated by some (often human) oracle, or covering the initial data most completely (Durfee, 1988). For our example, we will assume that a problem solver decides when a solution is acceptable based on how it covers the initial data, and we will not be concerned with the details.

A Network of Problem Solvers

This search process could be distributed among multiple nodes in many ways. The working memory could be distributed, meaning that the initial data might be divided among the nodes, and when the node applies an operator, the resulting data appears only in that node's working memory. The combined contents of each node's working memory is the *world state* (WS). Similarly each node maintains information about how it is controlling and focusing the search (application of operators to data). The combined information of the nodes concerning this focus of control is called the *focus-of-control-database* (FCD). In a CDPS situation, the WS and FCD would typically be distributed, sometimes with duplication of the same data at different nodes, or with inconsistent data at the nodes. In addition, the changes a node makes locally to the WS and/ or FCD may or may not be propagated to other nodes.

Similarly, the knowledge base—the set of operators—could be distributed. The distribution affects the control decisions a node makes such as whether it has the appropriate operators to locally process certain data, or whether it must request some other node that has the operators to process the data for it. Similarly the control decisions could be made by some centralized scheduler that controls all the nodes to ensure that they are pursuing compatible solutions, or different schedulers could control subsets of nodes, or each node could control its own decisionmaking. The potentially distributed operators and schedulers need access to the WS and FCD for their processing, and the problem solving in the CDPS depends on whether the operator/scheduler can access only local information or can access information from other nodes as well.

Table B–1, adapted from Lesser and Erman (1980), summarizes a taxonomy of information, processing, and control distributions. For simplicity, this taxonomy ignores many other CDPS concerns such as inconsistencies in the databases, protocols for transmission of information, strategies for distributed task allocation, organizational relationships among nodes, and techniques for terminating problem solving. The selection of options in this taxonomy depends on factors such as the speed of communication among nodes, the memory and the processing capabilities of individual nodes, the size and distribution of the WS and FCD, the needs of individual nodes for different parts of the solution state, the desired reliability of the network in the face of hardware errors, and so on.

The options listed in each area of the taxonomy were ordered from least to most difficult to deal with. That is, a CDPS network that could address the most difficult options could handle any other choice of options. However, difficult issues arise even with less difficult choices of options. Nor are the options in different areas independent. For example, if each node contains all the operators and data, each node could potentially solve the problem alone, and the nodes can thus solve the problem without ever sending each other requests for processing.

An Example CDPS Scenario

Consider a loosely coupled network of powerful processors such as a network of super-computers residing at mutually distant installations around the country. The nodes in the network work in parallel on parts of a large problem to solve the problem more quickly. The network solves problems for which the data are available in advance, such as characterizing last year's climatic conditions based on the copious amounts of daily weather data. Therefore, we have the opportunity to initialize the network so that each node has every operator (since each is a powerful processor) and each has all of the data. However, the decision (for now, imposed by a human) about what data each should process in parallel will affect which operators they apply.

As they progress in their problem solving, their initially identical world-state information will begin to diverge, as will their focus-of-control database information. Because of the distance between them, communication must be limited and slow, so mutually updating this information to keep consistent views of the WS and FCD is impractical.

Table B–1

A Taxonomy of CDPS

INFORMATION

Distribution of World State/Focus-of-Control Database (WS/FCD)
1. WS/FCD is distributed across the nodes with no duplication of information.
2. WS/FCD is distributed with possible duplication of information.
3. WS/FCD is distributed with possible duplications and inconsistencies.

Transmission of World State
1. Local changes to WS/FCD are not transmitted to other nodes.
2. Local changes to WS/FCD are transmitted to all nodes.
3. Local changes to WS/FCD are transmitted directly to fixed subset of other nodes.
4. Local changes to WS/FCD are transmitted to a dynamically determined set of relevant nodes.

CONTROL

Distribution of Operator Activity
1. Local data can be processed by operators within the node.
2. Local data can be processed by an operator within the node or by sending requests to all nodes in the network.
3. Local data can be processed by operator within the node or by sending requests to a fixed subset of nodes.
4. Local data can be processed by an operator within the node or by sending a request to a dynamically determined set of relevant nodes.

Distribution of Scheduling
1. A single, centralized scheduler is used to make scheduling decisions.
2. The nodes are statically partitioned into groups when there is one scheduler for each group.
3. The nodes are dynamically partitioned into groups where there is one scheduler for each group.
4. Each node does its own scheduling (possibly through interaction with schedules at other nodes).

PROCESSING

Distribution of Operators
1. Each node has only one operator.
2. Each node has all the operators.
3. Each node has a (not necessarily proper) subset of operators.

Access to World State/Focus-of-Control Database (WS/FCD)
1. An operator/scheduler can access the part of the WS/FCD that is contained in any node.
2. An operator/scheduler can access the part of the WS/FCD that is in a subset of nodes.
3. An operator/scheduler can access only the part of the WS/FCD that is in its local node.

Instead, nodes must work with incomplete views of each other. Because each node has all the data and operators, each could potentially solve the problem independently. However, to generate an overall solution faster, they should process different pieces of data in parallel and integrate the results of their local processing into a complete solution. Integration of results assumes that their local processing produced compatible partial results, so nodes must exchange locally generated partial results with nodes that could be working toward related results.

Given this network configuration and problem situation, we can characterize the CDPS situation using our taxonomy as:

- WS/FCD is distributed across the nodes with duplication of information.
- Local changes to WS/FCD are transmitted to a dynamically determined set of relevant nodes.
- Local data can be processed by an operator within the node (since each has all operators).
- Each node does its own scheduling (but might coordinate schedules with other nodes).
- Each node has all of the operators.
- An operator/scheduler can access only that part of the WS/FCD that is in its local node.

This scenario highlights several important CDPS issues, including: how to resolve interactions between subproblems, how to control activity to effectively exploit parallelism, and how to integrate partial local results into a complete global result. The first issue, how to resolve subproblem interactions, can be viewed as dealing with subgoal interactions. As it works toward its goal of solving a subproblem, a node must reason about how achieving that goal (solving the subproblem) will affect the achievement of other goals (solutions of other subproblems). Subgoal interaction is a common and important problem in classical planning research and is even more difficult in CDPS. Whereas a classical planner contains all the information about the problem, and so can detect any subgoal interactions, the relevant information is often distributed among nodes in a CDPS network, so they must explicitly exchange information to detect subgoal interactions.

For example, in our scenario, all nodes have identical initial data, so $node_1$ and $node_2$ both have data $d^1 - d^m$. Let us say that $node_1$ applies various operators to data $d^1 - d^j$, generating and applying operators to new data, and eventually produces a partial result d_1^{pr1}. Simultaneously $node_2$ applies its operators to data $d^{j+1} - d^m$ to eventually produce a partial result d_2^{pr1}. The nodes then send each other copies of their partial results. Unfortunately neither node has an operator that can generate an integrated result from the two partial results—they are incompatible.

We can illustrate this using the domain of characterizing climate based on weather data. $node_1$ might have characterized how moist the first half of the year was by computing the average relative humidity, whereas $node_2$ computed the average precipitation for the second half of the year. Each node has an operator to combine humidities and also an operator to combine precipitation, but they might not have an operator to combine humidity and precipitation.

Perhaps, when operators were developed for a centralized problem solver, its behavior might have been sufficiently predictable for the designer to determine that it would never need to combine humidity and precipitation data. For example, an operator for computing moisture in terms of humidity might include the precondition that the problem solver not have computed moisture in terms of precipitation. In our CDPS network, a problem solver will not know what has been computed by other nodes (unless it redundantly duplicates their computation, which would nullify parallelism), and this lack of knowledge might allow it to pursue a path that a centralized problem solver would have avoided. The partial results formed are incompatible because they cannot be combined. However, $node_1$'s operators *could* have computed a compatible partial result, as could $node_2$'s, if only it had (1) recognized that its partial result should be compatible with the results formed by some other node(s) and (2) communicated enough information with the other node(s) to decide what would constitute a compatible result.

CDPS research has developed techniques for helping nodes resolve subproblem interactions. One approach is to decompose the problem initially in such a way that each node knows how its partial result(s) should fit into complete solutions (for example, see Section C1). This approach cannot work when problems are inherently distributed so that no node has a view of the overall problem. In this case, a second approach is to insist that nodes must communicate everything about the problem solving to a coordinating node that builds the global view (such as in Section C4). Because this node might be a bottleneck and a reliability hazard, a third approach is for each node to exchange all its information with every other node; but in general nodes cannot afford the communication or the computation to share all their data (Section C2). A fourth approach is to allow nodes to selectively exchange a small subset of the data they form, where a node sends a piece of data if it believes that data is indicative of the node's eventual partial result. By exchanging relevant preliminary information, nodes can use goal-directed reasoning to redirect their efforts toward forming compatible results without incurring excessive communication overhead (for example, see Section C5). Finally, a fifth approach is to give a node the ability to predict or plan the sequence of operators it will apply in order to anticipate what results it might form and need. By abstracting and exchanging their plans, the nodes can coordinate their individual actions to more effectively form compatible results (Section C5).

The second CDPS issue highlighted by our scenario is how to control activity to exploit parallelism. This is essentially a distributed scheduling problem, where each node's scheduler has only a local view and communication between schedulers is limited. To work efficiently in parallel, the nodes must consider the potential for parallelism, the set of subproblems each node could currently pursue, and the interdependencies between subproblems. In our scenario, $node_1$ and $node_2$ have the same initial data. Let us assume that we can break the data into subsets $D_1 - D_3$, where each subset of data can be processed to generate a partial result. Now, suppose $node_1$ begins by processing data set D_1. The partial result generated by $node_1$ will strongly affect what operators the nodes should use on D_2. If $node_2$ begins processing D_2 while $node_1$ processes D_1, it is possible that $node_2$ will form incompatible results. Alternatively, $node_2$ might begin by processing D_3. If the nodes have only one way to process D_3, decisions about which operators to apply are unaffected by the partial results of D_1 or D_2. By initially focusing on D_3, $node_2$ uses knowledge about subproblem interactions to avoid potentially useless computation and to more efficiently use its resources in parallel with $node_1$. Another form of useless computation is redundantly processing the same data with the same operators. Unless required by performance criteria, the nodes' schedulers should avoid redundant computation such as both nodes processing data D_3.

CDPS research has made preliminary steps toward the scheduling problem. A simple approach is to have a centralized scheduler control all nodes. A more flexible but challenging approach is to provide each node with a scheduler and to have these schedulers coordinate their decisions (for example, see Sections C3 and C5). Assuming that nodes have techniques for recognizing subproblem interactions (discussed previously), the nodes can plan how they will pursue different subproblems so as to minimize the potential for unnecessary work while still promoting parallelism. In addition, having the potential for redundancy has several advantages, for example, reliability (if one node fails, another could solve the subproblem), flexibility of load balancing (nodes have more options about how to schedule their processing), and disjunctive parallelism (nodes could simultaneously solve the same subproblem using different operators).

Finally, the third CDPS issue that our scenario highlights is how to integrate partial results into a complete result. If the nodes have already identified the interacting subproblems they are pursuing, they at least know what partial results should be integrated. However, important problems remain about where and when to do the integration. In our example scenario, each node has every operator, so any node could potentially do the integration. However, reasons for preferring one node over another could still exist. For example, the network communication topology might make some nodes more suitable than others for collecting partial results, or scheduling decisions might have made some nodes shoulder more of a burden for processing the initial data, so others should take on the responsibility for integration. The question of where to integrate results is tied up with the question of when. When the network is trying to generate an overall solution as quickly as possible, intelligent decisions about where to integrate results require predictions about when and where different partial results will be formed, and about communication delays between nodes, and competing processing tasks at candidate nodes.

CDPS research has developed several approaches to integrating partial results. One relies on some node(s) to decompose the overall problem and distribute subproblems that explicitly indicate where the subproblem solutions should be sent (as in Section C1). A second approach allows nodes to transmit partial results to every potential integrator (see Sections C2 and C3). Although it could potentially lead to redundancy, this approach ensures that the network will generate an overall solution as rapidly as possible, typically at the cost of some unnecessary communication (of partial results) and computation (as several nodes compute the integrated result in parallel). A third approach is to once again give nodes the ability to plan their activities and exchange abstract views of these plans (Section C5). From these views, the nodes can recognize when and where relevant partial results will be formed and can plan how to integrate them appropriately.

A More Difficult CDPS Scenario

Consider what happens if we revise our CDPS scenario so that different nodes have different subsets of the operators, where each node does not necessarily know what operators another possesses. We also assume that each node receives data from a separate source, and we do not guarantee that the different data sources will necessarily generate consistent data. The result is a CDPS situation that corresponds to the most difficult options in our taxonomy:

- WS/FCD is distributed across the nodes with possible duplication and inconsistency.

- Local changes to WS/FCD are transmitted to a dynamically determined set of relevant nodes.

- Local data can be processed by an operator within the node or by sending a request to a dynamically determined set of relevant nodes.

- Each node does its own scheduling (but might coordinate schedules with other nodes).

- Each node has a subset of the operators.

- An operator/scheduler can access only that part of the WS/FCD that is in its local node.

Besides the issues that arise in the previous CDPS scenario, this new scenario highlights two additional issues: how to promote corroboration of results; and how to transfer subproblems and/or operators to improve network performance. The first problem, how to promote corroboration of results, is an aspect of the common AI problem of handling incorrect information. In most real-world situations, a knowledge-based system will at times acquire incorrect information that leads the system to develop solutions that cannot all be valid. When it recognizes that it has formed mutually exclusive views, it must reason about its information and knowledge to decide which information was incorrect.

In a CDPS network, the problem of identifying incorrect information is exacerbated because the information is distributed among the nodes. To identify incorrect data, nodes should redundantly attempt to solve the same subproblem using their different data and then compare their results to make sure they agree. When they do not, the nodes must exchange enough of their information to track down the source of the disagreement. Finally, they must decide (possibly by calling in additional nodes) on which information should be considered incorrect. CDPS research has so far done little to address the problem of corroborating results. One approach has been to allow inconsistencies in the data, and under the assumption that the correct data will lead to "better" solutions, the nodes will ignore poor data (Section C2). More sophisticated reasoning about inconsistencies—their causes, identification, and eradication—remains an open problem in CDPS.

The issue of transferring subproblems and/or operators has received considerably more attention. In general, it would be very restricting to expect that all nodes have the same operators and the same initial data. If the nodes' sets of operators could be different (but potentially intersecting), some nodes would be better suited to processing some data than others. The challenge, known as the *connection problem* (Davis and Smith, 1983), is to match tasks (subproblem data) with nodes that can perform those tasks (have operators and computing resources for processing the data). In our example scenario, $node_1$ might not have operators to process some of its data, and it must locate some other node(s) to do the processing. Meanwhile, $node_2$ might have no data at all and is sitting idle, and $node_3$ has a large amount of data that it could process locally. To work as an effective group, the nodes must reassign tasks (data) in order to process all the data as quickly as possible. A possible reassignment is for $node_1$ to send its problem data to one of the other nodes—preferably $node_2$ if it has suitable operators, but to $node_3$ otherwise. Depending on where the task was assigned and the amount of processing each node expects to do, $node_3$ should decompose its data into separate subtasks and transfer particular subtasks to other suitable nodes to better balance the processing load. In fact, $node_1$ and $node_3$ might swap tasks that each could do locally but could be done better by the other (because the other might have better operators for the particular tasks).

CDPS research has developed several approaches for allowing nodes to transfer tasks. A simple one is to have a central node that acts as a clearing-house for tasks. A second approach, which is distributed and much more flexible, is to have nodes locally decompose their tasks and announce subtasks to the network (Section C1). Other nodes will bid on tasks that they can perform, and the original node awards the task to the best bidder. This contracting approach has been used a great deal in applications where large tasks are originally localized in some node and must be decomposed and distributed for the network to perform acceptably. A third approach, which takes a planning perspective, is to view a proposed task transfer as a potential plan (Section C5). That is, a node with too many local tasks could develop a plan that specifies what tasks should be done by other nodes and how the results should be integrated. The other nodes would evaluate this plan, and they would accept, reject, or modify it until all nodes agree on the plan. At this point, they adopt the plan and transfer tasks based on the plan.

Conclusions

Our example has illustrated many of the issues that CDPS must address. In fact, the example corresponds in many ways to the task of having several geographically separated processors cooperatively track vehicles that move among them. This application domain is among the most completely studied in CDPS research and will be revisited later (Sections C1 and C3). The example illustrates how CDPS networks must address the cooperative goals shown in Figure A–2: Networks must transfer tasks and coordinate activity to exploit parallelism; they share resources and expertise so that each subproblem is adequately solved; they use redundant knowledge and information to corroborate results and ensure that all subproblems are solved even if some node fails; and they must detect and deal with interactions between subproblems to work as a more coordinated team.

The underlying problem encountered in CDPS networks is that nodes must make decisions about their actions (search, communication, problem solving, and so on) based on local views that might be incomplete, inconsistent, or out of date. They must use their communication and computation resources to not only perform in the application domain (domain problem solving), but also to control their actions and interactions. Solving this *control problem* entails dealing with interactions among subproblems (in the application domain), promoting parallelism, integrating local results into complete solutions, resolving inconsistencies, and transferring relevant information.

C. IMPORTANT CDPS APPROACHES AND EMPIRICAL INVESTIGATIONS

ALMOST EVERY CDPS approach developed to date has been motivated and evaluated in the context of an application domain, often by building a simulator for the domain. Here we discuss major CDPS approaches in the context of these applications. This makes the CDPS issues discussed in the previous section more concrete and provides empirical evidence (from simulations) to help us evaluate the capabilities and the costs of the approaches. In the following discussion, it is important to remember that the implementations are prototypes and simulations; to date, no CDPS networks have actually been used in real-world applications.

Important CDPS approaches can be categorized in terms of:

Negotiation: Using dialog among nodes to resolve inconsistent views and to reach agreement on how they should work together to cooperate effectively.

Functionally Accurate Cooperation: Overcoming inconsistency by exchanging tentative results to resolve errors and converge on problem solutions.

Organizational Structuring: Using common knowledge about general problem-solving roles and communication patterns to reduce nodes' uncertainty about how they should cooperate.

Multiagent Planning: Sharing information to build a plan for how agents should work together, and then distributing and following this plan throughout problem solving.

Sophisticated Local Control: Integrating reasoning about other agents' actions and beliefs with reasoning about local problem solving, so that coordination decisions are part of local decisions rather than a separate layer above local problem solving.

Theoretical Frameworks: Using mathematical and logical models of agents, their beliefs, and their reasoning to understand the theoretical capabilities of CDPS networks.

With a few exceptions, we will not discuss centralized approaches—where the network has a single coordinating node—because centralized control is contrary to CDPS. That is, CDPS focuses on networks and problem applications where centralization is not a viable option, for reasons such as limited computation (the problem of coordinating many nodes is computationally intractable for a single coordinator), limited communication (a single coordinator could be a communication bottleneck and could be overwhelmed with information from the network), and reliability (the network performance should not rely on one node).

C1. Negotiation

NEGOTIATION is a fundamental part of human cooperation, allowing people to resolve conflicts that could interfere with cooperative behavior. A perennial goal of CDPS researchers has been to capitalize on insights about human negotiation, to build mechanisms that enable AI systems to negotiate.

Unfortunately negotiation, like other terms that describe human behavior (e.g., "intelligence"), is difficult to define in mechanistic terms. For example, Sycara (1988) states that "the negotiation process involves identifying potential interactions either through communication or by reasoning about the current states and intentions of other agents in the system and modifying the intentions of these agents to avoid harmful interactions or create cooperative situations." We define negotiation as *the process of improving agreement (reducing inconsistency and uncertainty) on common viewpoints or plans through the structured exchange of relevant information.* Although these descriptions of negotiation capture many of our intuitions about human negotiation, they are too vague to provide blueprints for how to get AI systems to negotiate. The following subsections discuss more specific characterizations of negotiation.

The Contract-Net Protocol

One of the earliest and most influential research projects in CDPS is the Contract-Net framework developed by Smith and Davis (Smith, 1979, 1980; Smith and Davis, 1983, 1988; and Smith, 1978). The nodes use the Contract-Net protocol to form contracts concerning how they should allocate tasks in the network. *Contracting* involves an exchange of information between interested parties, an evaluation of the information by each member from its own perspective, and a final agreement by mutual selection. It differs from *voting* in that dissident members are free to exit the process rather than being bound by the decision of the majority.

In the Contract-Net protocol, nodes coordinate their activities through contracts to accomplish specific goals. Contracts are elaborated in a top-down manner. At each stage, a *manager* node decomposes its contracts into subcontracts to be accomplished by other *contractor* nodes. This process involves a bidding protocol based on a two-way transfer of information to establish the nature of the subcontracts and to determine which node will perform a particular subcontract. The elaboration procedure continues until a node can complete a contract without assistance. The result of the contract elaboration process is a network of control relationships, in the form of manager/contractor relationships, distributed throughout the network.

Nodes allocate tasks in the following stages:

1. A manager forms a task to be allocated.

2. The manager announces the existence of the task.

3. Available nodes evaluate task announcement.

4. Suitable nodes submit bids for task.

5. The manager evaluates bids.

6. The manager awards contracts to the most appropriate node(s).

7. The manager and contractor communicate privately during contract execution.

Before contracting can begin, a manager must recognize that it has a task to be allocated. Where this task comes from depends on the application and the manager's reasoning methods. Typically the manager receives a large task and decomposes it into smaller tasks in a predefined way. It announces a task to the network, and nodes that are currently idle receive and evaluate the announcement. Nodes with the appropriate resources, expertise, and information reply to the manager with bids that indicate their suitability to perform the task. After sufficient time has elapsed, the manager evaluates the bids it has received and awards the task to the most suitable node, or to several suitable nodes if redundancy is needed to ensure reliability. Finally, manager and contractor focus message exchanges between themselves. The manager supplies task information and the contractor reports progress and the eventual result of the task.

Smith and Davis investigated the performance of the Contract-Net protocol in several application domains. For example, they investigated a distributed interpretation application, where the network should track vehicles over a large geographical area. Their spatially distributed network was composed of two types of nodes: sensor nodes that can extract signal features from the data they sense, and manager nodes that can process the signal features from several sensor nodes to construct a map of vehicle movements. A manager node wants to form contracts with sensor nodes that are adequately distributed around an area and that have a complement of sensory capabilities. On the other hand, a sensor node wants to interact with a nearby manager to minimize communication. The Contract-Net protocol allows manager and sensor nodes to each have input into the contracts that are formed.

This application illustrates the use of message structures in the Contract-Net protocol, depicted in Figure C–1. Every message includes information about its source, destination, type, and contract identifier. A task announcement message includes abstract information about the task, expected capabilities of potential contractors, the information that

Task Announcement

$$N_{25} \to N_{42}$$

To: * indicates a broadcast message.
From: 25
Type: TASK ANNOUNCEMENT
Contract: 22-3-1
Task Abstraction:
  TASK TYPE SIGNAL
  POSITION LAT 47*N* LONG 17*E*
Eligibility Specification:
  MUST-HAVE SENSOR
  MUST-HAVE POSITION AREA *A*
Bid Specification:
  POSITION LAT LONG
  EVERY SENSOR NAME TYPE
Expiration Time: 28 1730Z FEB 1979
Signal task announcement

Bid

$$N_{25} \leftarrow N_{42}$$

To: 25
From: 42
Type: BID
Contract: 22-3-1
Node Abstraction:
  POSITION LAT 62*N* LONG 9*W*
  SENSOR NAME *S* 1 TYPE *S*
  SENSOR NAME *S* 2 TYPE *S*
  SENSOR NAME *T* 1 TYPE *T*
Signal task bid

Award

$$N_{25} \to N_{42}$$

To: 42
From: 25
Type: AWARD
Contract: 22-3-1
Task Specification:
  SENSOR NAME *S* 1
  SENSOR NAME *S* 2
Signal task award

Figure C–1.   Contract net messages. Examples of task announcement, bid, and award messages are shown for the distributed sensor net application.

a bid should contain, and a deadline for when bids should be received. In the vehicle monitoring application, the task abstraction specifies the task type and the manager's location; the expected capabilities indicate that a contractor must have certain sensory abilities and be in a particular area; and the information a bid should contain includes the sensor's location and sensory abilities. Furthermore, in the case of a task announcement, the message destination could indicate that the announcement should be broadcast to every node, or, if a manager node has information about which nodes are appropriate for the task, it can use *focused addressing* to send the message only to them.

Upon receipt of a task announcement, a node may send a task bid to the manager that announced the task. Besides the source, destination, type, and contract identifier, a task bid message includes the information requested in the task announcement's bid specification. In the vehicle monitoring application, the bid indicates the position and sensory capabilities of the sensor node.

Finally, following the expiration of the task announcement, the manager evaluates the bids and builds a task award message for each node that is awarded the task. In the vehicle monitoring application, the task award message indicates which of a sensor node's sensory capabilities are requested by the manager.

In addition to the basic message types, the Contract-Net protocol also allows nodes to announce their availability; this provides dynamic information to managers about loading in the network so that a manager can use focused addressing to reduce network communication. Other features of the protocol include special cases in which a contractor can avoid bidding and award a contract directly.

The Contract-Net protocol provides common message formats and a shared communication structure (i.e., nodes know about the order of message exchange to generate contracts). However, to use this protocol effectively, a manager must use some knowledge about the particular application to answer some key questions, including:

- What tasks should I contract out?
- How should I abstract the task to announce it?
- Who should receive the announcement?
- What information do I need to select the best candidate(s)?
- How many of the bidding nodes should receive the task?

In turn, the questions for the contractors include:

- What is the task about?
- Can I perform the task?
- Even if I *can* perform the task, is it desirable? Should I bid on it?

As a general framework for exchanging messages, the Contract-Net protocol does not include the application-dependent knowledge that nodes need to make these decisions. Hence it does not prescribe how nodes should cooperate. But it does provide a language for nodes to use when exchanging information that can lead to these decisions. In addressing the issue of how to structure communication to allow contracting, the Contract-Net protocol answered some questions but raised many others that CDPS researchers are still trying to answer, such as what knowledge nodes need to make cooperative decisions.

The Contract-Net framework concentrates on a subset of CDPS goals and issues. In terms of goals (Figure A–2), the Contract-Net concentrates on allocating tasks to increase parallelism and to make effective use of network resources. It assumes that the allocated tasks are independent, that is, that managers will decompose tasks to minimize subproblem interactions; and it assumes that the manager will implicitly know how to integrate the results of its contractors. In short, the Contract-Net framework is geared toward top-down decomposition of large tasks and allocation of the subtasks. It is thus best suited for CDPS applications with well-defined task hierarchies, with tasks that are initially presented to a few nodes in the network (in contrast to tasks that are distributed over all the nodes in a network) and that can be decomposed into essentially independent subtasks. Partial global planning (discussed in Section C5) subsumes contracting in an approach that allows nodes to suitably decompose and distribute tasks and to cooperatively solve inherently distributed problems by communicating in a more expressive framework.

Multistage Negotiation

Another use of a limited form of negotiation in task allocation has been developed by Conry and her colleagues (1988). They consider a class of task allocation problems called *distributed constraint satisfaction* problems, in which a coordinated set of actions is required to achieve the goals of the network, but each node has only limited resources available for completing all its assigned actions. The combination of local resource constraints and the need for coordination of actions among nodes gives rise to a complex set of global, interdependent constraints.

Conry and her colleagues have investigated task allocation in the long-haul, transmission "back-bones" of larger, more complex communications networks. These systems consist of networks of sites, each containing a variety of communications equipment, interconnected by links. Sites are partitioned into geographic subregions, with a single site in each subregion designated as a control facility. A control facility is responsible for monitoring and controlling its subregion. At any given time, the network may be supporting communication between several different sets of users. Each set of users is allocated a dedicated set of resources to create an end-to-end connection called a *circuit*. Normally the circuit lasts for the entire duration of the communication. However, equipment failures or outages can break a circuit. The control facilities of each subregion are monitored for interruptions, and when they occur, the control facilities interact as a CDPS network to assess the situation and to cooperatively develop alternative dedicated circuits to restore the end-to-end communication.

Conry and her colleagues have developed a multistage negotiation process for solving this class of task allocation problems. It extends the basic Contract-Net protocol to allow iterative negotiation during the bidding and awarding of tasks. Nodes tentatively choose local actions to allocate and link communication resources, and they iteratively exchange this information. At each iteration, each node assesses how its local choices and the current tentative choices of other nodes affect which circuits could be restored. Specifically each node detects whether a choice it has made violates the expectations of another node concerning the use of resources to restore a circuit. For example, $node_1$ might tentatively choose to allocate a communication channel to complete a circuit with $node_2$, and then $node_1$ receives a message from $node_3$ indicating that $node_3$ expects to complete a different circuit with the same resource. When conflicts are detected, a node can:

- Try to find different resources that will satisfy the other node's expectations (such as finding another communication channel to satisfy $node_3$'s needs).

- Retract its tentative choices and make new choices to satisfy the other node's expectations, hoping that alternatives to its retracted choices exist (such as choosing to allocate the channel for $node_3$'s request, and hoping that $node_2$ can route its circuit some other way).

- Recognize that the problem is overconstrained (the resources are not sufficient to restore every circuit) and transmit the observation to other nodes.

Nodes transmit information about their revised choices and repeat this process, iterating until they find a set of tentative choices that do not lead to violations, or until they recognize that the problem is overconstrained.

Multistage negotiation provides nodes with *sufficient* information about the impact of their local decisions on nonlocal state so that they may make local decisions that are globally acceptable. That is, nodes exchange only enough information to find a configuration that satisfies their constraints, rather than insisting that each node have a global view of all nodes' choices and their resource utilization requirements.

Negotiation in Air-Traffic Control

Negotiation is an important part of the cooperation strategies developed by Cammarata, McArthur, and Steeb (1983) for resolving conflicts among plans of a group of nodes. They have worked in the air-traffic control domain, where the goal is to develop CDPS techniques that will permit each node (aircraft) to construct a flight plan that will maintain an appropriate separation from other airplanes and will satisfy other constraints such as getting to the desired destination with minimum fuel consumption.

Their most well-developed approach to this problem is a policy they call *task centralization*. In this policy, airplanes involved in potential conflict situations (which occur when airplanes could become too close, based on their current headings) choose one of the agents involved in the conflict to resolve it. This airplane acts as a centralized planner to develop a multiagent plan that specifies the concurrent actions of all the airplanes (for more on multiagent planning, see Section C4). Although this technique is not itself distributed, the airplanes do use negotiation to decide which of them should do the planning. The chosen airplane is sent the detailed plans of the other agents involved in the potential conflict, and it attempts to modify only its own flight plan to resolve the conflict. The replanning airplane then transmits its revised flight plan to all agents that have received its earlier flight plan.

This replanning cycle iterates if one or more airplanes perceive a conflict based on the updated plan. This could occur if the replanning airplane could not completely resolve the conflict by modifying only its local plan or if the replanning airplane did not know that the new plan conflicts with the plans of airplanes not included in the original conflict set. The advantage of this centralized approach is that it avoids the possibility of agents generating inconsistent plans. In the decentralized case, agents can simultaneously change their plans (thus generating inconsistent views) so their plans might not avoid conflicts. The disadvantage of the centralized approach is that it may require many planning cycles to reach an acceptable solution. If too many iterations are needed, there may be insufficient time to carry out the plan. The centralized planning approach also requires that all the flight plans have to be communicated to a single replanning airplane, making that airplane a communication bottleneck and a reliability risk.

Three strategies for selecting the replanning airplane were explored: shared convention, least spatially constrained, and selection of the most knowledgeable, least-committed. The *shared convention* strategy avoids communication and serves as a baseline for evaluating the other two strategies. In it, agents use a preestablished protocol based on direct sensory information (current position, heading, and speed of other airplanes in the conflict set) to determine the replanning airplane. This approach assumes that each airplane has identical sensory information and uses identical decision procedures. If two airplanes are equally good candidates for selection, tiebreaking is based on arbitrary features such as an airplane's altitude or direction. In the air-traffic control domain, the shared convention strategy results in a poor selection because it does not consider the constraints on the chosen agent in modifying its plan, the knowledge it has of the plans of other airplanes, nor how modification of its plans will affect airplanes outside the conflict.

The other two strategies base negotiation on the exchange of information to improve the selection process. The *least spatially constrained* strategy selects the airplane with the most freedom in modifying its plan to resolve the conflict. Each aircraft in the conflict transmits a measure of its flexibility to the other airplanes in the conflict (Figure C–2). This measure is an aggregation of factors such as the number of other nearby aircraft, fuel reserves, and distance from destination. The airplane with the most freedom is selected to perform the replanning. This policy led to much better performance than the shared convention policy. It did particularly well in complex situations where a complete analysis of all possible intentions and actions of the airplanes is infeasible, so quickly finding a airplane with mobility is the best choice.

In the *most knowledgeable, least committed* strategy, each airplane in the conflict indicates its knowledge of the detailed flight plans of neighboring airplanes and how many airplanes are aware of its plans.

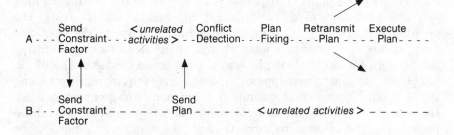

Figure C–2.   Task centralization: A typical sequence of communication, planning, and actions in the least spatially constrained strategy, where A is chosen as the planning node. Dashed lines are time lines for tasks executed by A and B, and solid lines indicate communications.

Specifically the plane that replans should preferably know about the plans of other planes, while its own plans should not be known to other planes. This way, it can make informed decisions based on its knowledge about the other planes and can freely change its own plans accordingly without the threat of violating other planes' expectations. This strategy worked better than the least spatially constrained strategy in situations involving few aircraft but where determining the best plan changes is difficult. However, in more complex situations involving many airplanes, this policy could lead to catastrophic results because the airplane chosen could not acquire and process information about other airplanes fast enough to avoid collisions.

Finally, although it was never evaluated in testbed experiments, a two-step negotiation called *task sharing* was also proposed. The task sharing strategy allowed the replanner to generate a modified plan for the least constrained airplane in the conflict set. The first step in this strategy requires choosing the least spatially constrained airplane's flight plan for modification. The second step chooses the most knowledgeable airplane to perform the replanning.

Cognitive Modeling of Negotiation

Although it has not been directly applied to CDPS, the work of Sycara, and of Sathi and his colleagues is relevant to CDPS applications. Sycara is developing a computational model for multistage negotiation leading to compromise between multiple agents dealing with multiple issues in both single and repeated encounters (Sycara, 1987, 1988; and Sycara-Cyranski, 1985). Her model is based on messages that contain:

- The proposed compromise
- Persuasive arguments
- Agreement or disagreement with the compromise or argument
- Requests for additional information
- Reasons for disagreement
- Agents' utility measures for the issues they disagree on

Sycara uses case-based reasoning techniques to drive the negotiation process, storing a history of past negotiations. When this approach fails, she relies on multiattribute preference analysis to decide on the most likely compromise that will be acceptable to the other agents. Thus, as they develop a compromise, the agents dynamically revise their goals. Her techniques for forming compromises, and for maintaining a history of previous negotiations and compromises, could be useful in CDPS networks.

In the negotiation framework developed by Sathi and his colleagues, agents iteratively relax their constraints until a compromise is reached (Sathi et al., 1986). Sathi defines a set of negotiation operators that an agent may use to propose a compromise:

- *Log-rolling*, where each agent slightly relaxes its interacting constraint
- *Reducing the cost* of a relaxation by agreeing to relax the solution criteria
- *Substitution* of a less preferred resource in place of the preferred resource
- *Bridging*, which involves the development of a completely new solution that satisfies only the most important constraints
- *Unlinking*, which involves overlooking weak interactions among constraints
- *Mediation and arbitration*, where third parties that possess additional knowledge and/or authority are drawn into the negotiation process

These operators would similarly be useful in a CDPS network for resolving conflicts and inconsistencies when problem solving nodes have different but related subproblems to solve.

Summary

Negotiation is a complex and variable phenomenon, and to date CDPS researchers have only been able to study some of its specific forms. It is important to CDPS research because it is a natural way for systems to coordinate decisions to achieve several cooperative goals, including assigning tasks to increase parallelism and to effectively use network resources (Figure A–2). Recalling the more specific goals of cooperation (Section A), negotiation allows nodes to improve the use of computing resources and expertise through exchanging tasks, to increase the solution creation rate through parallelism, and to increase the certainty of results or the likelihood of generating those results by assigning the same task to several nodes that may have different expertise.

C2.   Functionally Accurate Cooperation

A RECURRENT PROBLEM in CDPS research is how to get nodes with inconsistent views and information to cooperate effectively. Inconsistencies arise because nodes might have incomplete or out-of-date views of the states of other nodes, contradictory raw information about related subproblems (e.g., different but error-prone reports of the same events), conflicting long-term problem-solving knowledge, different views of the network's goals, and errors in hardware or software. Yet, despite these inconsistencies, the nodes should cooperate if at all possible.

One approach to dealing with inconsistency is to not allow it in the first place, or at least to not consider it. For example, the Contract-Net protocol (Section C1) decomposed and distributed tasks in such a way that there was always a manager node to coordinate its contractors, who would in turn always pursue the task as expected. A second approach is to resolve inconsistency through explicit negotiation. For example, mechanisms for negotiation (Section C1) allow nodes to recognize inconsistencies in the form of constraint violations, and to modify their plans accordingly.

A third approach is to build CDPS networks that continue to perform despite inconsistency. A purely practical argument for this approach is that, in many applications, it is too expensive to implement the necessary communication, synchronization, and hardware reliability to guarantee that each node has a complete, consistent, and up-to-date view of the information it needs to solve its subproblems in a way that does not lead to inconsistency. A second argument is more theoretical. As CDPS networks become very large and complex, operate in the real world, and evolve over time, it is impossible to guarantee that knowledge among the nodes will remain consistent. In fact, some have argued that some degree of inconsistency among nodes is beneficial to network problem solving (Corkill, 1983; and Reed and Lesser, 1980).

If the network permits inconsistencies, it must be able to resolve them. To do so, it should allow nodes to exchange inconsistent partial solutions, so that one or more of them has enough information to resolve the inconsistency. Exchanging partial solutions also helps prevent nodes from forming inconsistent partial solutions because a partial solution can represent *predictive information* that a recipient of this partial solution can use as context to predict the characteristics of partial solutions to build that will be consistent and compatible with it. The timely exchange of predictive partial solutions can thus reduce the search for compatible solutions and therefore make network problem solving faster (see also Section C5).

The Functionally Accurate, Cooperative Approach

Lesser, Corkill, and Erman were among the first researchers to explore the possibility of building CDPS networks that worked effectively despite inconsistencies (Lesser and Corkill, 1981; and Lesser and Erman, 1980). In their *functionally accurate, cooperative (FA/C) approach*, network problem solving is structured so that nodes cooperatively exchange and integrate partial, tentative, high-level results to construct a consistent and complete solution. A node's problem solving is structured so that its local knowledge bases need not be complete, consistent, and up to date in order to make progress in its problem-solving tasks. Nodes do the best they can with their current information, but their solutions to their local subproblems may be only partial, tentative, and incorrect.

Error resolution becomes an integral part of network problem solving as nodes try to combine (and assess the implications of) partial and tentative results received from other nodes. Thus the advantages of the FA/C approach are accrued at the cost of making local problem solving more complex. If we are willing to pay this cost, the FA/C approach can reduce the synchronization and communication among nodes that would be required to guarantee network consistency. Moreover, because FA/C networks can tolerate inconsistency, they can be more resilient and robust in face of processor, sensor, and communication failures.

Lesser and Erman (1980) developed a three-node FA/C network of modified HEARSAY-II speech understanding systems, in which each system sampled one time-continuous segment of the speech signal. The systems exchanged only high-level intermediate results consisting of phrase hypotheses, and yet they could still converge on complete interpretations despite the loss of some messages. For example, in Figure C–3 the phrases exchanged to build the complete interpretation "Have any new papers by Newell appeared" are shown. In (a), no messages are lost. Node 1 builds the phrase "Have any," which it sends to node 2, which combines the received phrase with "new papers by" and sends the result to node 3, which completes the phrase. In (b), 35% of the messages are lost, but the nodes converge on the solution anyway. Node 2 manages to send the phrase "new papers by" to node 1, which combines this with "Have any" and sends the result to node 3, which appends "Newell" and sends the result to node 1, which determines that the phrase beginning is complete and sends the result to node 3, which completes the end of the phrase.

Based on this work, Lesser and Corkill identified several characteristics of systems that tolerate inconsistent and incorrect information, and their implications for FA/C problem solving:

Asynchronous Nature of Information Gathering/Reduced Need for Synchronization: Problem solving is viewed as an incremental, opportunistic, and asynchronous process. A node does not have a predefined order for processing information and can exploit incomplete local information. Thus node processing and internode communication do not need to be synchronized.

Use of Abstract Information/Reduced Internode Communication Bandwidth Requirements: Nodes cooperate by exchanging abstract information in the form of high-level intermediate results. This reduces the amount of internode communication because nodes develop high-level views of network activity without exchanging low-level data.

Resolution of Uncertainty Through Incremental Aggregation/Automatic Error Resolution: Uncertainty is implicitly resolved when partial results

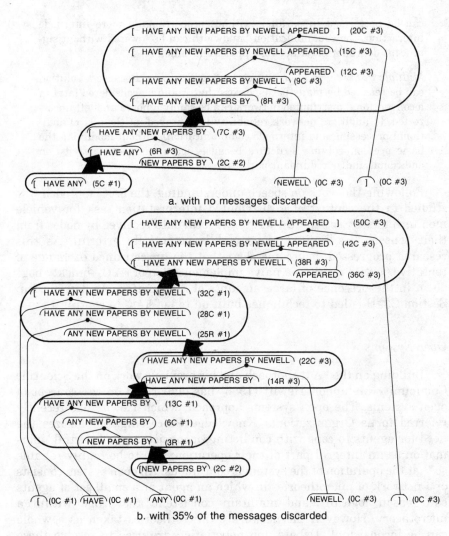

Figure C–3. Distributed HEARSAY-II message exchanges.

are aggregated and compared with alternative partial solutions. This incremental method of problem solving allows a distributed network to detect and reduce the impact of incorrect decisions caused by incomplete and inconsistent local information and by hardware malfunction.

Problem Solving as a Search Process/Internode Parallelism: Because many alternative partial solutions need to be examined, parallel search by different nodes is possible and desirable. Furthermore, the additional uncertainty caused by incomplete and inconsistent local information can be traded off against more search. To the degree that this extra search can be performed in parallel, without proportionally more internode interaction, the communication bandwidth can be lowered without significant degradation of network processing time.

Multiple Paths to Solution/Self-correcting Behavior: Because a solution can be reached by many paths, errors that would be considered fatal in a conventional distributed network can be safely ignored and left uncorrected. In addition, network reliability is improved (at the cost of additional processing and internode communication) without modifying the basic problem-solving structure because nodes can focus activity on additional and/or redundant paths to a solution.

Following the work on speech understanding, the FA/C approach was studied in the context of a distributed interpretation task for vehicle monitoring (see Section C3), where the local data received by nodes from their sensors has limited scope and is potentially errorful. As this research progressed, it became clear that the unrestrained exchange of tentative partial results—a naive implementation of FA/C—quickly bogs down in the presence of large amounts of information. As described in Section C3, this led to techniques built on top of FA/C to control it.

Open Systems

Building on the FA/C approach and his previous work on the Scientific Community Metaphor, Hewitt (1986) has elaborated on the concept of open systems. The open systems approach, which Hewitt has recently referred to as Organizational Knowledge Processing, emphasizes the need for agents to cope with conflicting, inconsistent, and partial information as an integral part of their operation; and to be highly reliable so that the operation of the system is continuous. An open system consists of a network of microtheories in which an agent or a small set of agents can reason logically and maintain consistent knowledge within a microtheory. However, the network of microtheories taken as a whole can be inconsistent. Debate and negotiation are used to resolve these inconsistencies. Hewitt further assumes that the "internal operation, organization and state of one computational agent may be unknown and unavailable to another agent. . ." (Hewitt, 1986). This assumption requires cooperative strategies that are similar to those needed to deal with heterogeneous expert systems, where individual systems may use different problem-solving strategies and knowledge representations and may have different criteria for judging acceptability of solutions.

Hewitt defines *due process* as the process of developing the appropriate cooperative framework for interactions among agents. Hewitt states that due process "is an inherently self-reflective process in that the process by which information is gathered, organized, compared, and presented is subject to evaluation, debate, and evolution within the organization." The open systems approach is currently a concept with no implementation, but it seems to represent an important conceptual framework for structuring large and complex CDPS networks made out of heterogeneous agents that can both passively tolerate and actively address inconsistencies.

Inconsistent Control Information

A node should also have the ability to tolerate inconsistency in its control information. In many applications, the information necessary to make informed local control decisions—decisions that are consistent with control decisions at other nodes—may not be located at the node making the decision. The costs to obtain consistent, complete, and up-to-date information might be prohibitively large in terms of delays due to synchronization and message transmission. Additionally, in a highly dynamic environment, the cost of recomputing network control for each minor change in the state of network may also be expensive (Durfee and Lesser, 1988). Thus it might be more cost effective to tolerate some level of inconsistency in control information than to try to resolve the inconsistency.

Inconsistencies in control information can be tolerated if the application domain allows a problem solver to recover from incorrect control decisions. In such domains, the most serious consequences of an incorrect control decision are that an incorrect partial result is generated and that the time and resources spent generating it are wasted. Because this partial result and any later partial results formed from it can be ignored, incorrect control decisions are easily tolerated—they delay but do not prohibit the successful formation of a correct overall solution. Durfee and Lesser have explored this issue in the context of a distributed vehicle monitoring task (see Section C5), where they have developed a mechanism to balance the benefits of reducing uncertainty about control information to improve coordination against the costs of acquiring and reasoning about this information.

Summary

Functionally accurate cooperation suggests that the exchange of tentative, partial results will allow nodes to eventually converge on correct and consistent larger results. More communication will generally reduce the inconsistency because nodes will have more common information. Less communication will result in more inconsistency, which will in turn force the nodes to perform extra computation because they generate a larger number of inconsistent results and must spend computing resources on resolving inconsistencies. Thus, functionally accurate cooperation highlights a basic tradeoff in CDPS networks between communication and computation. Nodes that are free to generate potentially incorrect and inconsistent tentative results can more completely explore the space of possible solutions. Functionally accurate cooperation can, therefore, increase the set or scope of achievable tasks by sharing information (Figure A–2), and in doing so it achieves the more specific cooperative goal of increasing the variety of solutions by allowing nodes to form local solutions without being overly influenced by other nodes (Section A2).

C3. Organizational Structuring

ONE IMPORTANT difference between negotiation (Section C1) and functionally accurate cooperation (Section C2) is that negotiation takes a top-down view of problem solving, whereas functionally accurate cooperation takes a bottom-up view. Functionally accurate cooperation allows nodes that are solving inherently distributed problems to work semi-autonomously, and through communication to build up overall solutions despite the fact that each is ignorant of how the others are contributing to overall solutions. The difficulty is that this ignorance can lead to excessive communication, duplication of effort among nodes, and generally ineffective use of network resources. In contrast, forms of negotiation such as contracting allow nodes to decompose and allocate their problem-solving responsibilities, to structure their actions and interactions to more effectively work as a team for a particular problem.

The trouble with this approach is that, in applications where problems are inherently distributed, the nodes might not initially know how their local subproblems fit together into the larger network problems. That is, they might not know what particular problem they are all trying to solve. In addition, their perception of the problem can change in the course of problem solving, dictating a need to dynamically alter the cooperative relationships between nodes.

Organizational structuring attempts to find a compromise between the strongly top-down view of contracting and the bottom-up view of functionally accurate cooperation. An *organizational structure* of a CDPS network is the pattern of information and control relationships that exist between the nodes and the distribution of problem-solving capabilities among the nodes. Whereas a contracting approach dynamically defines the relationships between nodes to solve a specific problem, an organizational structure gives more general, long-term information about the relationships between nodes. That is, contracts represent temporary alliances (as in a construction project, where the relationship ends when the structure is built), whereas an organization is more permanent (as in a corporation, where the roles of the president and vice president are stable for long periods of time). The organizational structure can augment a functionally accurate, cooperative system to give each node a high-level view of how the network solves problems and the role that the node plays within this structure. With this general, high-level view, the nodes can ensure that they meet conditions that are essential to successful problem solving, including (Corkill, 1983):

1. *Coverage*—Any necessary portion of the overall problem must be within the problem-solving capabilities of at least one node.

2. *Connectivity*—Nodes must interact in a manner that permits the covered activities to be developed and integrated into an overall solution.

3. *Capability*—Coverage and connectivity must be achievable within the communication and computation resource limitations and reliability specifications of the network.

The organizational structure must specify roles and relationships to meet these conditions. For example, to ensure coverage, the organizational structure could assign problem-solving roles to the nodes that make each node a specialist at a different type of subproblem. The organizational structure must then also indicate connectivity information to the nodes so that they can route subproblems to be solved to nodes that are able to solve them. On the other hand, the organizational structure might make the network more robust by assigning overlapping subsets of specialties to the nodes, so that no node is irreplaceable. The connectivity information should still allow nodes to redistribute subproblems, but it must also allow nodes with overlapping specialties to avoid redundantly solving the same subproblem. Because the network might be able to solve problems in several different ways, it must have nodes that have the authority to decide on and enforce a particular approach.

Table C–1 shows a range of control authority relationships among nodes, along the spectrum of self-directed (favoring problem-solving actions based on locally generated partial results) to externally directed (favoring actions based on partial results received from other nodes). An organizational structure can specify connectivity information about the flow of information and control between nodes in terms of topologies such as hierarchical, heterarchical, flat (lateral) structures, matrix organizations, groups or teams, and market or price systems (Figure C–4). Several possible organizations are shown in Figure C–4. For each the horizontal axis corresponds to locations and the vertical axis corresponds to infor-

Table C–1
Control Authority

A number of different authority relationships are shown, corresponding to different combinations along two dimensions. The horizontal dimension indicates whether a node generates goals from its own data and forms its own tasks to achieve them, whether it receives goals and forms its own tasks, or whether it receives tasks. The vertical dimension indicates whether a node gives preference to received information (externally directed), whether it gives preference to local information (self-directed), or whether it determines relative preferences dynamically through negotiation. The steps a node takes to choose the next task to perform is shown for each of the nine combinations.

	Data-directed	Goal-directed	Task-directed
Externally-directed	• receive evaluated data • generate goals from the data • prioritize the goals • determine tasks to achieve the goals • prioritize the tasks	• receive prioritized goals • determine tasks to achieve the goals • prioritize the tasks	• receive prioritized tasks
Negotiated	• receive data • negotiate an evaluation of the data • generate goals from the data • prioritize the goals • determine tasks to achieve the goals • prioritize the tasks	• receive goals • negotiate a priority for the goals • determine tasks to achieve the goals • prioritize the tasks	• receive tasks • negotiate a priority for the tasks
Self-directed	• receive data • evaluate the data • generate goals from the data • prioritize the goals • determine tasks to achieve the goals • prioritize the tasks	• receive the goals • prioritize the goals • determine tasks to achieve the goals • prioritize the tasks	• receive tasks • prioritize tasks

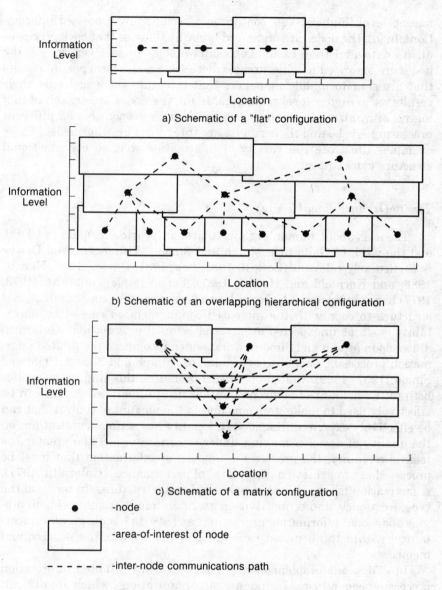

Figure C–4.   Control topologies.

mation level (higher levels contain more completely processed information). In (a), the nodes are organized laterally (flat), so that each processes all its data and they exchange results among themselves. In (b), the nodes are arranged in a hierarchy, where some nodes form partial results that are sent to middle managers that integrate them and pass their results on to higher level managers. In (c), the nodes are organized in a matrix orgranization, where separate nodes are responsible for different processing levels, and their results are integrated by other nodes. These examples illustrate the variety of information that an organizational structure can contain.

Ties to Organizational Theory

Theories about human organizations can provide insights to CDPS, and the work of Galbraith, March and Simon, Williamson, and Dewey is particularly relevant (Corkill, 1983; Fox, 1981; Gasser, 1986; Hewitt, 1986; and Kornfeld and Hewitt, 1981). For example, Galbraith (1973, 1977) has developed a set of paradigms for redesigning an organizational structure to cope with the increased communication caused by uncertainty (such as unexpected events and errorful information). Galbraith draws upon March and Simon's work, which recognized the limited information processing capabilities of humans (March and Simon, 1958; and Simon, 1957, 1969). Called *bounded rationality*, this limitation applies both to the amount of environmental (sensory) information that can be effectively used to make decisions and to the amount of control that can be effectively exercised. Bounded rationality has serious implications on the quality of decision making under uncertainty, for "the greater the task uncertainty, the greater the amount of information that must be processed . . . to achieve a given level of performance" (Galbraith, 1977). A motivation for variations in organizational structures (in terms of the type, frequency, and connectivity pattern on information flow) is to provide additional information processing capacity (to handle greater uncertainty) within the bounded rationality of the organization's individual members.

In CDPS, our problem-solving nodes also have limited information processing capabilities. Unlike human organizations, which are difficult if not impossible to fully characterize, CDPS systems are more easily characterized because each node in a system is (currently) much less complex than a human. Therefore, when applying organizational principles to a CDPS network, we are more likely to be able to measure those limitations of the nodes that will affect the choice of an appropriate organization (Lesser and Erman, 1980):

Control Bounds: What is the range of possible actions about which a node can make a decision? What is the amount of detail (level of abstraction) of this decision? What is its accuracy? Is the decision made explicitly or implicitly through the modification of other decisions?

Interpretation (Sensory) Bounds: What is the range of information that a node can access when making decisions? What is the detail of this environmental information? What is its accuracy? Is the information explicitly or implicitly available?

Bounds of the Nature of Decision Making: How much information about the history and future goals of the decision making process is available to a node? Is there only a single decision under consideration at a time or are alternatives considered simultaneously? What is the detail and accuracy of this information?

Fox concentrates on the effects of complexity and uncertainty on choosing suitable CDPS organizations (Fox, 1979, 1981). For example, he says, "Complexity and uncertainty are two opposing forces; complexity forcing a distribution of tasks ultimately resulting in heterarchical structure; uncertainty pushing in the opposite direction, vertically integrating tasks into a more hierarchical structure." Malone and Smith (1984) have also tried to develop theories about how distributed networks should be organized. They have used queuing theory models to analyze generic organizational classes to determine their performance strengths and weaknesses with respect to processing, communication, and reliability. Their analysis has shown that different organizational classes are appropriate given different problem situations and performance requirements, and that these characterizations change with the size of the organization. However, the implications of their work for CDPS are unclear because they assume that the individual tasks are independent and because they do not model uncertainty in terms of the accuracy of control and problem-solving decisions.

Gasser (1986) is pursuing a view of organization for CDPS that is less structural in perspective and more related to current organization theory. He views an organization as a "particular set of settled and unsettled problems about belief and action through which agents view other agents. Organizational change means opening and/or settling some different set of questions in a different way, giving individual agents new problems to solve and . . . a different base of assumptions about the beliefs and actions of other agents" (Gasser and Rouquette, 1988). The settling of questions about the belief and action of other agents comes from the need for agents "to conserve resources, to act under time constraints and to be predictable." From this perspective, Gasser believes, we can understand the underlying knowledge and problem solving that result in the external structure of an organization.

Gasser asserts that agents need to be able to recognize, diagnose, and repair violated expectations when other agents fail to meet default assumptions in previously settled questions. When expectations are violated, agents generate new questions that must be settled. Agents also require the ability to perform meta-level reasoning, change their goals and settle the associated set of questions that now need to be solved in order to effectively carry out their new goals. This latter capability leads to organizational change, whereas the former is more associated with local refinements of the organization.

Gasser is currently using the MACE testbed (Gasser et al., 1987) to simulate a game-like application domain where agents of one type attempt to surround and capture agents of another type (Benda et al., 1985). He is using this simulated application to empirically evaluate his coordination mechanisms (Gasser and Rouquette, 1988). His view of organization also has much in common with the recent work of Hewitt on open systems described in Section C2. For example, Hewitt's due process can be thought of as the meta-level reasoning that occurs when the organization's existing strategies for cooperation are no longer effective.

Coordination Using Organizational Structuring

Corkill and Lesser have applied organizational structures to CDPS to efficiently implement network coordination strategies. They use an organizational structure to limit the range of control decisions made by nodes (decreasing the demands on a node's information processing capabilities) and to ensure that information necessary for making informed decisions is routed to the appropriate nodes. The organizational structure provides a control framework that increases the likelihood that the nodes will work as a coherent team by providing a general and global strategy for network problem solving.

They have implemented and evaluated their ideas in one of the most flexible CDPS simulation testbeds developed to date: the Distributed Vehicle Monitoring Testbed (DVMT) (Corkill, 1983; and Lesser and Corkill, 1983). The DVMT simulates a network of nodes that perform distributed interpretation to track vehicles moving among them. The spatially distributed nodes detect the sounds of vehicles, and each applies knowledge of vehicle sounds and movements to track vehicles through its spatial area. Nodes then exchange information about vehicles they have tracked to build a map of vehicle movements through the entire area. This task requires functionally accurate cooperation because nodes work with potentially errorful data, leading them to generate potentially inconsistent and incorrect partial results. The nodes can converge on acceptable overall solutions if they exchange enough of their partial results. However, without an organizational structure to guide their processing and communication decisions, the nodes could quickly overwhelm each other with tentative partial results.

Corkill and Lesser recognized that, in designing a CDPS network to exploit organizational structures, they must have nodes with substantial sophistication. They suggest that it is unrealistic to expect to develop network-wide control policies that are sufficiently flexible and efficient and that require limited communication, while simultaneously making all the control decisions for each node in the network. Instead, each node needs to decide on its own activities based on its current local view of the problems being solved, but to use organizational knowledge about its problem-solving role in the network and the roles of other nodes to guide its decisions, so that it is a more effective participant in the network. This approach divides the problem of network coordination into two concurrent activities (Corkill and Lesser, 1983): the construction and maintenance of a network-wide organizational structure and the continuous local elaboration of this structure into precise activities using the local knowledge and control capabilities of each node. Thus, within the general bounds specified by the organizational structure, the nodes have substantial latitude as to what decisions they make.

In the DVMT, an organization is specified as a set of "interest areas" associated with each node that define what, when, and to whom information (partial results and goals to build partial results) should be transmitted, authority relationships indicating how much priority nodes should give to processing externally received goals versus internally generated goals, and goal priorities that indicate how to evaluate the importance of processing different types of goals. Interest areas allow the control relationships among nodes indicated in Table C–2.

Each node in the DVMT is a blackboard-based problem solver, with levels of abstraction and knowledge sources appropriate for vehicle monitoring. The DVMT problem-solving architecture is depicted in Figure C–5. It indicates how organizational roles are considered when goals are processed, affecting the ratings of KSIs (possible knowledge source executions). The planner decides which KSIs to invoke, triggering the knowledge source, which generates new hypotheses on the data blackboard. Finally, the goal processor builds goals to improve on these hypotheses and uses the organizational structure to influence the ratings of these goals.

A DVMT node's scheduler, which decides what knowledge source will be applied to the partial results on the blackboard, has been modified to use interest area specifications to prioritize the goals for generating different partial results. Goals (and their subgoals) to generate results in areas of high interest for the node have their priority raised. For example, to increase the range of tasks that a node could perform, the organization might allow it to interpret data from two different sensed areas, A and B. A neighboring node might also receive data for sensed area B. Thus, to avoid duplication of effort, the interest areas would

Table C–2
Possible Control Relationships

Several different types of organizations and their corresponding communication
and control relationships are shown. These can all be modeled in the DVMT.

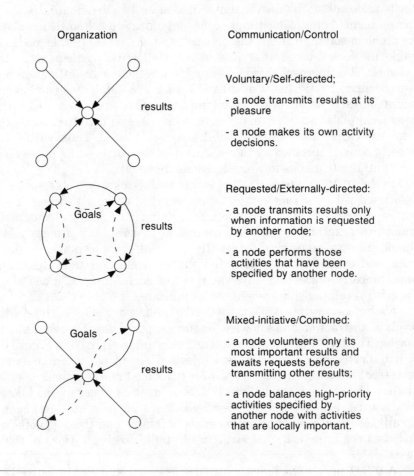

Organization	Communication/Control

Voluntary/Self-directed;

- a node transmits results at its
  pleasure

- a node makes its own activity
  decisions.

Requested/Externally-directed:

- a node transmits results only
  when information is requested
  by another node;

- a node performs those
  activities that have been
  specified by another node.

Mixed-initiative/Combined:

- a node volunteers only its
  most important results and
  awaits requests before
  transmitting other results;

- a node balances high-priority
  activities specified by
  another node with activities
  that are locally important.

specify that the node should prefer to achieve goals that generate partial
solutions in area A. But if it has no such goals, it can pursue goals in
area B to cooperate with its neighbor to process the data in parallel.
Similarly the ratings of goals to transmit and receive information are
influenced by the interest areas of both the sending and receiving nodes.

Without interest areas, a node would simply pursue its highest rated

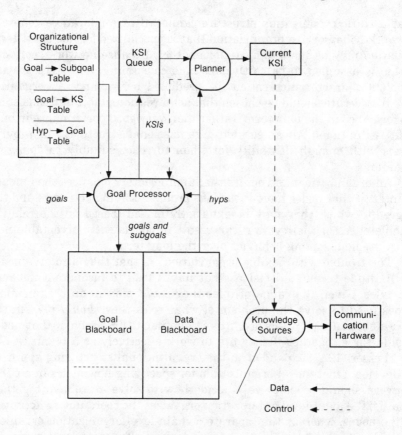

Figure C–5.   The DVMT problem solving architecture.

goal. This rating would be based on such factors as the confidence in the partial results that triggered the goal. The interest areas are themselves rated, and so when a node incorporates interest area information, it rerates a goal based on its initial rating combined with its interest area's rating. Thus the organizational structure only biases the node's decisions. Because goal ratings also involve other factors, a node could pursue a goal that is highly rated from a local perspective even if it falls in a poorly rated interest area. The organizational structure thus provides guidance without dictating local decisions and can be used to control the amount of overlap and problem-solving redundancy among agents, the problem-solving roles of the nodes (such as the "integrator," "specialist," and "middle manager"), the authority relations between nodes, and the potential problem-solving paths in the network.

Durfee, Lesser, and Corkill (1987) expanded these ideas and showed that a static organization structure cannot always guarantee coherent network behavior. An organization that is specialized for one short-term situation may be inappropriate for another. Because network reorganization is assumed to be costly and time consuming, and since specific problem characteristics cannot be predicted beforehand, an organizational structure should be chosen that achieves acceptable and consistent performance in the long term, rather than very good performance in only a few situations. An acceptable organizational structure will provide nodes with enough flexibility for them to react suitably to changing situations.

An organizational structure that appropriately balances the amount of interest that nodes have in various problem-solving activities and the degree to which they may be externally biased (based on the relative completeness of their views) can result in consistently acceptable network problem-solving behavior over the long term.

The trouble with flexible organizations is that they also give nodes the latitude to make decisions that might lead to incoherent network behavior. Given the range of roles they *could* play in an organization, nodes need to solve the problem of what roles they *should* play in the current situation. In essence, this is another CDPS problem that nodes should solve together if they are to work effectively as a team. Durfee and Lesser (1987) expanded on the organizational structuring approach to develop a meta-level organization for specifying how nodes in a CDPS network should cooperatively decide how to solve a problem together. That is, the meta-level organization organizes the coordination activities of the nodes, whereas the separate domain-level organization organizes their domain-level problem-solving activities. The meta-level organization specifies the type of control decision making that each node will perform, how its control decisions will be affected by decisions from other nodes, and what type of meta-information should be transmitted and to whom.

For example, a CDPS network in the DVMT might be composed of several nodes with equivalent problem-solving expertise, each of which might be connected to a different sensor. The domain-level organization might organize the nodes laterally. That is, nodes pass partial results to their neighbors until some node eventually forms a complete result. The meta-level organization for this network, however, could be centralized. One node is given the role of network coordinator, and the other nodes then know they should send information about their partial results to the coordinating node. That node, in turn, decides which partial results each node should form and where they should be exchanged to solve the problem as an effective team. Alternatively the meta-level organization could also be lateral, where nodes exchange information to their neighbors and each builds a view of how they should work together.

An unanswered question for this research is where organizational structure comes from in the first place. To date, they have all been developed by the human user and initialized with the network. A long-term goal of the research has been to automate the organizing process so that a network can reorganize when necessary. Reorganization is a costly process, both in communication and computation, and should only be undertaken infrequently, and only when problems arise with the current organization. Detecting problems with the current organization is difficult, because performance measures are distributed among the nodes. Perhaps no node has enough information to recognize when the organization is no longer effective. The work by Durfee and Lesser on meta-level organizations and on treating coordination as CDPS might provide tools for addressing the recognition problem. That is, if the coordination problem becomes overly difficult, it might indicate that the underlying domain-level organization is at fault. Once the nodes determine that they should reorganize, negotiation techniques could provide the basis for converging and agreeing on a new organization. Of course, the problem of detecting poor meta-level organizations remains.

Other CDPS Organizations

The contracting approach of Davis and Smith (Section C1) allows nodes to organize themselves to solve particular problems. When the network receives a large problem, the nodes recursively decompose the problem until nondecomposable tasks remain, assign subproblems to nodes through the Contract-Net protocol, solve the subproblems in parallel, and synthesize one or more answers from the subproblem solutions. Synthesizing the answer might require the nodes to locate and collect the best solution to each subproblem because several nodes might solve the same subproblem in different ways. Contracting allows the nodes to form simple organizations in terms of manager-contractor relationships. As the nodes solve one problem and move onto another, they reorganize themselves. Thus contracting provides an example of automated network organization, but the overhead of having to reorganize for each problem could be substantial. This is sufficient for many applications but would need to be extended to represent more complex organizations that combine hierarchical and lateral relationships between nodes.

From a different perspective, Kornfeld and Hewitt (1981) have proposed that CDPS can be organized in a manner analogous to the structure of scientific research. In their *scientific community metaphor* for CDPS, nodes posit either "questions" (goals) or "answers" (results) into a mutually accessible archive. The presence of this information allows a node to draw on work already performed by other nodes. They also propose using the economics of *funding* as the basis for controlling activity in the network. In essence, every goal in the network must have a *sponsor*, and every sponsor has limited resources. Thus goals that cannot command a sponsor are not pursued. Kornfeld and Hewitt implemented a parallel processing version of this system, called Ether, that embodies many of their ideas. However, although the metaphor is an interesting way of viewing CDPS networks, significant research on aspects of the implementation in a distributed environment remains to be done.

Summary

Imposing a general, high-level organization on a CDPS network gives nodes knowledge that improves how they coordinate, while still allowing them to pursue alternative solution paths that are not dictated by the network. The organization helps nodes focus their processing and communication resources on activities that are usually more likely to lead to effective network performance, although in any given problem-solving situation a more rigid, situation-specific organization could lead to even better performance. If the characteristics of the problem-solving situation are known beforehand, techniques such as contracting, which allow nodes to generate a situation-specific organization, are suitable. However, because CDPS networks often work in dynamic domains where the problem-solving situation can frequently change, organizational approaches have also focused on general-purpose organizations.

Organizational structures help nodes to cooperate and thus help to achieve the goals of cooperation (Figure A–2). Organizations allow nodes to work in parallel. Appropriate organizations assign network problem-solving roles to nodes with suitable resources so that network resources are used effectively. If specified in the organization, nodes can have overlapping roles to increase network reliability. Finally, the organization gives each node a global picture of the problem-solving roles of the other nodes so that each node can determine for itself whether or not any of its local activities might interact with those of another node. But note that some organizations such as those based on simple contracting relationships might not notice potential interactions between nodes because a manager only knows about its contractors, and not about all of their subcontractors.

C4. Multiagent Planning

IN A MULTIAGENT planning approach to cooperation, nodes (agents) form a multiagent plan that specifies all their future actions and interactions. Coordinating nodes through multiagent plans is different from other approaches in that one or more nodes possess a plan that indicates exactly what actions and interactions each node will take for the duration of the network activity. This differs from approaches such as contracting, in which nodes typically make pairwise agreements about how they will coordinate, and nowhere is any complete view of network coordination represented.

Contracting can lead to incoherent behavior that multiagent planning avoids. For example, in contracting, two different nodes might independently form and contract out the same subproblem to two other nodes so that these nodes are duplicating each other's effort because they are unaware of contracts in which they do not participate. In multiagent planning, one or more nodes would have information about each node's activities and could recognize and prevent the duplication of effort. Because it insists on detecting and avoiding inconsistencies before they can occur, multiagent planning is not like functionally accurate cooperation. Finally, unlike the general guidelines imposed by an organizational structure, a multiagent plan dictates exactly what actions each node should take and when.

A multiagent plan is built to avoid inconsistent or conflicting actions and is typically used in CDPS networks to identify and plan around resource conflicts. For example, in scheduling the use of airspace (Cammarata et al., 1983) or machining tools (Georgeff, 1983), an unexpected conflict for a resource can be costly in time, money, or human life. Rather than risking incoherent and inconsistent decisions that nodes might make using other approaches, multiagent planning insists that nodes plan out beforehand exactly how each will act and interact. Because multiagent planning requires that nodes share and process substantial amounts of information, it can also require more computation and communication resources than other approaches.

Centralized Multiagent Planning

Georgeff (1983) develops a multiagent planning approach where the plans of individual nodes are first formed, and then some central planning node collects them and analyzes them to identify potential interactions such as conflicts between the nodes over limited resources. The central node then performs a safety analysis to determine which potential interactions could lead to conflicts; for example, when a node modifies the world in such a way that another cannot continue with its plan. The central planning node next groups together sequences of unsafe situations to create critical regions. Finally, it inserts communication commands into the plans so that nodes synchronize appropriately. For example, if one node should wait until another has finished with a lathe before it begins operating the lathe, its plan contains an instruction to wait for a message from the other node before beginning to use the lathe. Georgeff and Lansky have pursued this centralized multiagent planning approach further, using alternative representations for events in multiagent domains (Georgeff, 1984, 1986; Lansky and Fogelsong, 1987).

Cammarata, Steeb, and McArthur (1983) have also developed a system for centralized multiagent planning. Their system, described more completely in Section C1, works in an air-traffic control application. Through a process of negotiation, the nodes (aircraft) choose a coordinator. Each node then sends this coordinator relevant information, and the coordinator builds a multiagent plan that specifies all the nodes' planned actions, including the actions that it, or some other node, should take to avoid collisions.

Distributed Multiagent Planning

When multiagent planning is done in a distributed manner, there may be no single node with a global view of network activities, so detecting and resolving interactions between nodes is much more difficult. The general approach is to provide each node with a model of other nodes' plans (Corkill, 1979; Georgeff, 1984; Konolige, 1983). For example, Corkill has developed a distributed hierarchical planner based on NOAH (Sacerdoti, 1977) where nodes represent each other using MODEL nodes (Corkill, 1979) and synchronize the plan execution with explicit synchronization actions. The nodes plan together level by level. They each build local plans at one level of detail and build suitable models of each other by communicating about shared resources needed for their goals. The nodes resolve resource conflicts using a protocol that Corkill has developed for a distributed version of NOAH's critics. When conflicts in their plans at this level have been resolved, the nodes then proceed to the next level of detail and repeat this process.

Using a logic-based approach, Rosenschein and Genesereth (1987) studied how agents with a common goal but different local information can exchange propositions to converge on identical plans. In their formulation, goals are propositions to prove, local information is represented in axioms, and plans are proofs of the goal propositions. They developed strategies for convergence based on assumptions about the correctness and completeness of agents' information, about what each agent knows about other agents' knowledge, about what each agent knows about itself, and about whether additional information can cause a previously acceptable plan to be unacceptable. In cases where agents might have incorrect information or incorrect views of the information of other nodes, Rosenschein and Genesereth show that convergence on a plan cannot be guaranteed, whatever strategy is used. Their results indicate that expecting sometimes unpredictable agents working in dynamic domains to always coordinate optimally is infeasible; perhaps the best we can hope for is that they will coordinate acceptably well and will tolerate any uncoordinated activity.

Durfee and Lesser (1987) have developed a CDPS approach called partial global planning (Section C5), in which nodes build local plans and share these plans to identify potential improvements to coordination. Unlike multiagent planning, which assumes that a plan is formed before nodes begin to act, partial global planning allows nodes to interleave planning and action. In partial global planning, nodes coordinate as best they can given their current view, rather than waiting for a complete view of the network. This ability is essential in dynamic domains where complete, up-to-date information might not be available to any node. Unlike conventional multiagent planning, partial global planning also gives nodes flexibility in deciding what node or nodes will build larger plans (represented in the meta-level organization discussed in Section C3).

Summary

Multiagent planning takes the view that interactions between the separate activities of the nodes must be identified, and any conflicts should be identified and fixed before the plans are executed. This view is critical in applications such as air-traffic control, where aircraft should wait until all their situations are taken into account in a plan before they begin executing the plan by changing course. Thus typical multi-agent planning approaches concentrate mostly on the particular cooperative goal of avoiding harmful interactions (Figure A–2). On the other hand, multiagent planning systems are poorly suited to dynamically changing domains, where nodes cannot wait for complete information about potential plan interactions before they begin acting. In most dynamic domains, nodes can make mistakes—take actions that are not well coordinated—without catastrophic results and can later take actions to rectify any problems resulting from earlier actions. For these domains, partial global planning can be a better approach (Section C5).

C5. Sophisticated Local Control

EXPERIENCE has taught us that a node in a CDPS network must be more sophisticated than a node that works alone because it must reason about its own problem solving, how this fits in with problem solving by other nodes in the network, and what it can do to improve network problem solving. It is a mistake to assume that effective coordination will result if we take nodes that are individually good problem solvers and then simply give these nodes a communication interface so that they can exchange messages. Coordination is not achieved just through exchanging information; nodes must reason about what that information represents and how exchanging information will affect their individual and group behavior.

Sophisticated local control allows a node to understand the implications of its planned problem-solving and communication actions on other nodes' goals, beliefs, and plans. This understanding forms the basis for deciding how to coordinate with others, for example, whether to contract out tasks, negotiate over how to achieve goals, exchange information to resolve inconsistent views, take on different organizational responsibilities, or plan specific actions and interactions to build complete solutions. Sophisticated local control concentrates on how to build nodes that can decide for themselves how and when to coordinate, rather than having a specific coordination approach imposed on them.

Communication Policies

Because nodes are influenced by the information they receive, they need policies to guide their decisions about what information to exchange, with whom, and when. Durfee, Lesser, and Corkill (1987) describe three major characteristics of the information communicated among nodes that affects global *coherence*—how well the nodes work as a team. These are relevance, timeliness, and completeness.

The *relevance* of a message measures the amount of information that is consistent with the solution derived by the network. Irrelevant messages may redirect the receiving node into wasting its processing resources on attempts to integrate inconsistent information, so higher relevance of communicated information can result in more global coherence because it stimulates work along the solution path.

The *timeliness* of a transmitted message measures how much it will influence the current activity of the receiving node. Since timeliness depends not only on the content of the message but also on the state of the nodes, a message's timeliness can vary as node activity progresses. If the transmitted information will have no effect on the node's current activity, there is no point in sending it. However, if the transmitted information will distract the receiving node to work in a more promising area, or if the node needs the information to continue developing a promising partial solution, then it is important that the information be sent promptly.

The *completeness* of a message measures the fraction of a complete solution that the message represents. Completeness affects coherence by reducing the number of partially or fully redundant messages communicated between nodes—messages that negatively distract nodes into performing redundant activity. Furthermore, as the completeness of received messages increases, the number of ways that the messages can be combined with local partial results decreases due to their larger context. Achieving completeness is important to minimize communication requirements in our loosely coupled distributed network.

These characteristics of communicated information are not independent. For example, higher completeness leads to higher relevance but, potentially, to a decrease in timeliness. Communication policies that guide decisions about what information should be sent, to what nodes, and when often involve tradeoffs among the three characteristics. With increased self-awareness, a node can be more informed about the relevance and completeness of its local hypotheses and can make more intelligent predictions both about how a hypothesis will affect its local decisions and about whether the timely transmission of the hypothesis is therefore likely to cause other nodes to alter their activities.

A node's communication decision is based on its communication policy. Durfee, Lesser, and Corkill (1987) have developed three communication policies for the DVMT (Section C3): the send-all, locally complete, and first-and-last policies. The *send-all* policy allows a node to transmit a partial solution to another node if the partial solution falls within the other node's interest areas, as specified in the organizational structure.

The second policy, called *locally complete*, allows a node to transmit a partial solution to another node if it falls within the other node's interest areas *and if the original node cannot itself improve on the partial solution*. This policy permits nodes to share only locally complete partial results and avoids the situation where a node sends a series of partial solutions where one is simply an extension of its predecessor. Sending all of the partial solutions can incur substantial communication overhead and computation overhead (the recipient must integrate each received partial solution into its local processing).

The third policy, called *first-and-last*, allows a node to transmit the first partial solution it forms in an area, and later the last (locally complete) one it forms. The purpose of transmitting the first is to provide the recipient with predictive information. That is, the first partial solution will indicate characteristics of the eventual locally complete solution, so the recipient can sooner predict what partial solution it should form that will be compatible with the locally complete partial solution it will eventually receive.

In evaluating these policies in the DVMT, Durfee, Lesser, and Corkill found that a policy's effectiveness depends on characteristics of the problem situation, for example, how much the nodes' subproblems overlap and how much data each node has. In all cases, the locally complete policy reduced network communication the most, and the send-all policy the least. In terms of the speed of network problem solving, the locally complete policy was generally superior because the other policies caused nodes to be *distracted* by the smaller partial solutions. The distraction often led to duplication of effort as the recipient node would extend the partial solution in the same way that the sending node was already extending it. Withholding incomplete partial solutions reduced distraction. However, first-and-last was superior to locally complete in situations where a recipient node had substantial uncertainty about which partial solution to pursue. The timely arrival of the incomplete, predictive partial solution would guide the recipient node into forming a suitable partial solution earlier. Overall, the experiments showed that making nodes aware of which of their partial solutions are locally complete and giving them knowledge about the potential impact of sharing their partial solutions allows the nodes to communicate less and still coordinate better.

Partial Global Planning

Durfee and Lesser have emphasized the need for sophisticated local control to make reasoning about coordination an integral part of a node's local decision making. Instead of having separate mechanisms for different forms of coordination, they have developed a unified, flexible framework in which nodes can form contracts, plan their actions and interactions, negotiate over their plans, use organizational information to guide their planning and problem-solving decisions, tolerate inconsistent views, and converge on acceptable network performance in dynamically changing situations despite incomplete, inconsistent, and out-of-date information. Their partial global planning approach (Durfee, 1988; Durfee and Lesser, 1987) thus addresses the different goals of cooperation (Figure A–2).

In the partial global planning approach, each node can represent and reason about the actions and interactions for groups of nodes and how they affect local activities. These representations are called *partial global plans* (PGPs) because they specify how different *parts* of the network *plan* to achieve more *global* goals. Each node maintains its own set of PGPs that it may use independently and asynchronously to coordinate its activities.

A PGP is a frame-like structure that nodes use as a common representation for exchanging information about their objectives and plans. The PGP's *objective* contains information about *why* the PGP exists, including its eventual goal (the larger solution being formed) and its importance (a priority rating or reasons for pursuing it). Its *plan-activity-map* represents *what* the nodes are doing, including the major plan steps being taken concurrently, their costs and expected results, and why they are being taken in a particular order. Its *solution-construction-graph* contains information about *how* the nodes should interact, including specifications about what partial results to exchange and when to exchange them. Finally, a PGP's *status* contains bookkeeping information, including pointers to relevant information received from other nodes and when it was received. A PGP is thus a general structure for representing coordinated activity in terms of goals, actions, interactions, and relationships.

Besides their common PGP representation, nodes also need at least some common knowledge about network problem-solving responsibilities and about how and when they should use PGPs to coordinate their activities. This common knowledge is represented in the domain-level and meta-level organizations (Section C3). Nodes use the domain-level organization to influence what goals they pursue and their plans to pursue them, and they use the meta-level organization to decide how, when, and where to form and exchange PGPs based on their local plans. Guided by the meta-level organization, nodes use transmitted PGPs to build models of each other. A node uses its models of itself and others to identify when nodes have PGPs whose objectives could be part of some larger network objective, called a *partial global goal*, and combines the related PGPs into a single, larger PGP to achieve it.

Given the more complete view of group activity represented in the larger PGP, the node can revise the PGP (and afterwards, its local plans) to represent a more coordinated set of group actions and interactions and a more efficient use of network resources. For example, a PGP could indicate that a certain partial solution to be formed by one node could provide useful predictive information to another node. This expectation, and the transmission of the partial solution, are explicitly represented in the PGP, and they indicate a plan to use information resources more effectively.

As a second example, nodes that are working on the same network goal might have different PGPs, reflecting their different local perspectives. These nodes could exchange PGP information so as to negotiate over a compromised, agreed upon PGP. As a third example, a node could survey its current view of network PGPs and identify nodes whose computing resources or expertise are being underutilized. At the same time, other nodes could be overwhelmed with subproblems. By modifying its PGPs, the node could propose how the nodes could transfer appropriate subproblems to work as a better team. It sends these PGPs to potential subproblem recipients, who in turn can accept or reject the PGP, or modify it and send it back as a counterproposal.

Thus, unlike a simple contracting protocol, partial global planning allows nodes to barter using proposals and counterproposals, where each proposal contains information about not only the subproblem to be transferred but also how that subproblem fits into network problem solving. This information helps a potential recipient make more informed decisions about how to respond to the proposal.

In complex CDPS networks, different subsets of nodes could need to coordinate in each of these ways at the same time. Partial global planning provides a unified framework that supports these different forms of coordination. This framework has been implemented and evaluated in the DVMT (Section C3) (Durfee, 1988). In this implementation, a node's local planner develops a plan at multiple levels of detail, including a representation of major plan steps. In the DVMT, a major plan step corresponds to extending a partial track into a new time frame (such as extending the track formed from d_i to d_j into d_{j+1}, where d_k is data sensed at time k). This step might take several processing actions to analyze the new data, filter out noise, and integrate the correct data into the track. For each major plan step, the local planner roughly estimates what partial results will be formed and when. By representing and coordinating their major plan steps, nodes cooperate effectively without reasoning about details that are frequently revised and quickly outdated.

Each node has a partial global planner (PGPlanner) as an integral part of its control activities. The PGPlanner builds a node-plan from each local plan, where a node-plan's objective indicates the possible track(s) being developed and its plan-activity-map is a sequence of plan-activities. Each *plan-activity* represents a major plan step and has an expected begin time, end time, and partial result, derived from the local planner's estimates. Guided by the meta-level organization, nodes exchange PGPs and node-plans so that one or more of them develops more encompassing PGPs. When combining PGPs into a single, larger PGP, a node merges the smaller PGP's plan-activity-maps to represent the concurrent activities of all participating nodes and can reorder the plan-activities to improve coordination. It also builds a solution-construction-graph to indicate which partial tracks formed by the plan-activities should be exchanged to share useful information and construct the complete solution. The PGPlanner then revises local plans based on the PGP and can propose transfers of subproblems to initiate negotiation that will lead to better use of network resources.

An important idea exemplified by the partial global planning approach is the distinction between "satisficing" network control and optimal network control. In environments that are highly dynamic and uncertain, and where an updated and consistent global view of the state of the network problem solving is very difficult to obtain, attempting optimal control at every moment is infeasible from both a computational and communicative perspective. Rather, partial global planning employs heuristic algorithms for reordering and revising PGP activities that achieve a reasonable balance between the interdependent requirements of global coherence, limited use of computational resources in controlling coordination, and responsiveness to dynamically changing conditions.

Two other ideas in the partial global planning framework contribute to our understanding of network coordination. The first is that increasing a node's understanding of its own activities is an important ingredient in designing effective coordination strategies. Durfee and Lesser show that providing a local node with the ability to develop high-level problem-solving goals and plans, to make reasonably accurate predictions of the time required to achieve its planned steps, and to make predictions about likely future goals all lead to more sophisticated network coordination. The second contribution is the concept of network coordination as a distributed problem-solving task in its own right, distinct from domain-level CDPS going on among nodes. Partial global planning introduces the concept of a meta-level organization to describe the organizational relationship among nodes required to solve the network coordination problem and permits the coordination tasks to go on asynchronously and in parallel with domain problem solving.

Summary

A node that by itself is a good problem solver will not necessarily be a valuable participant in a CDPS network. Coordination requires that a node have more sophisticated local control so that it can more fully reason about goals and plans, both its own and those of other nodes. This view allows a node to cooperate and communicate more effectively, allowing it to influence other nodes and be influenced by them so that they work as an effective team. Sophisticated local control thus opens nodes up to a wide range of capabilities, including being able to negotiate, form contracts, develop plans, conform (or rebel against) organizations, and share results. In essence, sophisticated local control is the foundation on which more complex forms of coordination activity must be built, and it allows the network to address all the goals of cooperation (Figure A–2), as exemplified in partial global planning.

C6. Formal Frameworks

ALTHOUGH an orientation toward techniques for particular application domains has dominated CDPS research, a number of researchers have instead concentrated on formal models of CDPS, using logic-based or game-theoretical nodes. Some of this work focuses on how nodes can form multiagent plans, including the work of Georgeff and of Rosenschein and Genesereth (see Section C4).

CDPS requires that the formalisms developed for logic-based agents that work alone must be extended in two ways. The first extension is that these systems must be able to model and reason about the concurrent activities of multiple agents, as discussed in Section C4. The second extension is that the agents must perform in situations where they have incomplete knowledge or limited computational resources. Both cases lead to the possibility of generating incorrect inferences, which in turn may result in agents having inconsistent beliefs about the world. As a result, agents might never converge on shared, coordinated plans (Rosenschein and Genesereth, 1987). Hewitt, in his studies of open systems (Section C2), addresses this problem and argues that formal logic is inadequate (Hewitt, 1986).

Researchers are following a number of different approaches to extending logical formalisms for CDPS applications. Konolige (1982, 1983) has developed the Deductive Belief model in which an agent's beliefs are described as a set of sentences in formal language together with a deductive process for deriving the consequences of those beliefs. This approach can account for the effect of resource limitations on the derivation of the consequences of beliefs. Appelt (1982) has used a possible world formalism to represent and reason about belief. Cohen and Levesque (1987) have developed a formal theory for reasoning about an agent's intentions as a combination of what it has chosen and how it is committed to its choice. Rosenschein (1983) has developed a more general theory of multiagent planning that allows for the existence of other agents and their mental states as part of the environment within which plans can be constructed. Halpern and Moses (1984) have investigated the issue of common knowledge between agents, discovering limitations in what agents can know about each other.

Research on dialog comprehension in natural language understanding is also relevant to CDPS research because both research areas must reason about multiple agents with distinct and possibly contradictory mental states (Allen, 1979; and Cohen, 1978). Mental states include not only facts or knowledge but also beliefs and goals. (See Chapter XIX in this Volume.) An agent must interpret messages from other agents, including what the messages imply about the agents' mental states, and must generate messages to alter the mental states of other agents, taking into account the potential actions of other agents that might affect how it can achieve its goals. Through an appropriate dialog, the agents can converge on shared plans for how they should coordinate their activities (Grosz and Sidner, 1985, 1988).

Another research approach toward developing a formal theory for understanding the nature of cooperation among multiple agents is that of Rosenschein and Genesereth (Rosenschein, 1982, 1983; and Rosenschein and Genesereth, 1985). They have based their model on game theory techniques and have shown the utility of communication to resolve conflicts among agents having disparate goals. Using a game-theoretic model, each agent attempts to choose an option to maximize its payoff, and since no combination of agents' options might lead to maximal payoffs for them all, they must somehow choose options that lead to acceptable payoffs given the circumstances. Rosenschein and Genesereth study how different assumptions about the rationality of the agents can lead to more or less effective choices. Certain assumptions about rationality allow agents to make reasonable choices without communication (since they each have complete information about the choices and payoffs for every agent), whereas the ability to communicate allows them to make deals about mutually beneficial activity in situations where complete information about the payoff matrix is not enough.

In summary, formal CDPS approaches attempt to use rigorous models of agent reasoning and interactions to develop insights into coordination that are independent of any domain. Many of these insights are useful to researchers attempting to build CDPS systems, illuminating crucial issues and limitations in what can be expected from CDPS networks. To remain tractable, however, the formal approaches often use simplified views of agents and their knowledge, such as assuming that all the choices and payoffs of agents are known in advance. Because of the complexity gap between the systems being modeled formally and the applications that are being studied, CDPS research has yet to adequately define rigorous approaches that work in real-world applications.

D. CONCLUSION

THE PROMISES and pitfalls of CDPS can be summed up by combining two proverbs: Many hands make light work, but too many cooks spoil the broth. CDPS networks where nodes work together effectively have many potential benefits in applications where information, resources, or expertise are naturally distributed, or where we can intentionally distribute them to improve the speed, modularity, or reliability of the system. We will not realize these benefits, however, if our CDPS networks are uncoordinated.

We have outlined many approaches for coordinating nodes in a CDPS network, including contracting, negotiation, organizational structuring, multiagent planning, and sophisticated local control. From these very different approaches, we can infer that effective coordination requires three things. First, it requires structure because without structure the CDPS nodes cannot interact in predictable ways. Structure is embodied in shared information such as organizations and communication protocols. Second, effective coordination requires flexibility because CDPS nodes typically exist in dynamically changing environments where each node might have incomplete, inaccurate, or obsolete information. Flexibility allows a contracting node to decide how to bid in its current situation, it allows a node in an organization to locally decide what partial solution to form given its current data, and it allows a node in a planning system to change its plan in response to changing circumstances.

The third requirement for effective coordination is the knowledge and reasoning capabilities to intelligently use the structure and flexibility. Nodes must form and reason about what they are doing—their goals, plans, and beliefs—and how this fits into what they know about others. They must rely on structure to guide this reasoning but must allow themselves the flexibility to adapt their activities to changing circumstances. In short, nodes need enough local sophistication to steer an appropriate course between regimentation and anarchy.

None of the approaches detailed earlier represents a general answer to the needs of intelligent coordination in CDPS networks, but our discussion has illustrated the richness of the ideas and approaches to date. Future CDPS research will build on this past work in many directions. One will be to improve our theories about organizing CDPS networks. These theories should provide guidelines for how domain and control problem-solving tasks should be distributed among agents based on the current network characteristics and problem-solving situation.

CDPS research will also extend its paradigms for how to get disparate agents to cooperate on a problem. These paradigms must address issues of how to resolve inconsistencies due to agents' different problem-solving approaches or knowledge; how to promote understanding between disparate agents of their beliefs, goals, and plans; and how to get agents to make intelligent communication decisions that influence each other to their advantage.

To incorporate CDPS into AI practice, we will need guidelines or frameworks for building AI systems that can become part of a CDPS network. If reasoning about coordination is an integral part of an agent, the agent must have knowledge representations, inference techniques, and control components that are adequate for this type of reasoning. Practical CDPS networks will also require advanced software infrastructures, languages and operating systems (Bisiani, 1986; and Hayes-Roth et al., 1988).

CDPS has opened a new door in the study of intelligence. CDPS research continues to reveal the complexity of coordination in all its forms, and the extensive though sometimes subtle connections between intelligent coordination and other aspects of intelligence. CDPS research brings to the fore issues in areas such as introspection, planning, language, and reasoning about belief. As Nilsson (1980) predicted in his early involvement in CDPS, research into CDPS forces us to address many of the basic problems of AI.

These insights have led some CDPS researchers to view reasoning about coordination—about how to interact with other intelligent agents—as a fundamental aspect of intelligent behavior. In fact, it could be argued that we judge the intelligence of an entity by how it interacts with us: whether we can understand its goals, plans, and beliefs as embodied in its actions, whether we can communicate with it, and whether it appears to be understanding us. CDPS research continues to study the knowledge and reasoning capabilities that must go into AI systems, if those systems are ever to meet these criteria for intelligence.

Further Reading

For further information on CDPS, the collection *Readings in Distributed Artificial Intelligence* edited by Bond and Gasser contains the seminal papers in the field (Bond and Gasser, 1988). In addition, the book *Distributed Artificial Intelligence*, edited by Huhns, provides papers on current research directions (Huhns, 1987). A second such book is due out late in 1989.

Acknowledgments

We would like to thank Clive Dym for helping us in our early drafts.

Chapter XVIII

Fundamentals of Expert Systems

Bruce G. Buchanan—University of Pittsburgh
Reid G. Smith—Schlumberger Laboratory for
Computer Science, Austin

CHAPTER XVIII: FUNDAMENTALS OF EXPERT SYSTEMS

A. OVERVIEW

EXPERT SYSTEMS are among the most exciting computer applications to emerge in the last decade. They allow a computer program to use expertise to assist in a variety of problems such as diagnosing failures in complex systems and designing new equipment. Using artificial intelligence (AI) work on problem solving, they have become a commercially successful demonstration of the power of AI techniques. Correspondingly, by testing current AI methods in applied contexts, expert systems provide important feedback about the strengths and limitations of those methods. In this review we present the fundamental considerations in designing and constructing expert systems, assess the state of the art, and indicate directions for future research. Our discussion focuses on the computer science issues, as opposed to issues of management or applications.

Characterization and Desiderata

Expert systems are distinguished from conventional programs in several important respects. Although none of the characteristics in the following list are missing entirely from other well-designed software, all of them together describe a distinct class of programs. Note that few expert systems exhibit all of the following five desiderata to the same degree. An expert system is a computer program that:

a. *Reasons with domain-specific knowledge that is symbolic* as well as numerical (this is what we mean by calling an expert system a knowledge-based system).

b. *Uses domain-specific methods that are heuristic* (plausible) as well as following procedures that are algorithmic (certain).

c. *Performs well* in its problem area.

d. *Explains* or makes understandable both what it knows and the reasons for its answers.

e. *Retains flexibility.*

One expert system that meets these conditions is the Dipmeter Advisor System (Smith and Young, 1984; and Smith, 1984). Its task is to help petroleum engineers determine the "map" of geological strata through

151

which an oil well is being drilled, e.g., the depth and the dip, or "tilt" of individual layers of sandstone, shale, and other rocks. It meets our desiderata in the following respects:

1. The knowledge used is partly mathematical (e.g., trigonometry) but largely nonnumeric geological knowledge (e.g., how sand is deposited around river beds).

2. Its reasoning is based on heuristics that well-logging experts use to interpret data from boreholes.

3. It aids specialists, providing interpretations better than those of novices.

4. It uses a variety of graphical and textual displays to make its knowledge understandable and to justify its interpretations.

5. It is flexible enough to be modified and extended frequently, without rewriting the programs that interpret the knowledge.

Figure A–1 shows an example of what the Dipmeter Advisor System's computer screen looks like, as an illustration of what the user of an expert system might see. This figure shows the input data and a partial explanation for a conclusion drawn by the system. The left-hand column shows natural gamma radiation against depth (which increases from the top of the screen to the bottom). To its right is shown dip against depth. Individual dip estimates (called "tadpoles") show the magnitude of the dip as horizontal position, depth as vertical position, and azimuth as a small direction line. Dip patterns, detected by the system, are explained in the text to the right.

Desiderata (a) and (b)—symbolic reasoning and heuristic methods—define expert systems as artificial intelligence programs. Desideratum (c) separates high-performance programs from others. By specifying human specialists as a standard of comparison, this condition also suggests using the knowledge of specialists to achieve high performance. Predefining the scope of problem solving to a narrow "slice" through a domain (still smaller than the slice mastered by most human specialists) has become a pragmatic principle of design. As covered in the following discussion, bounding the scope of the problem in advance avoids many of the challenges of building a generally intelligent robot that would behave appropriately in a wide range of situations.

Desiderata (d) and (e)—understandability and flexibility—are less frequently cited and less frequently achieved than (a) through (c). They may be seen as a means of achieving high performance, but they are included here to highlight their importance in designing and imple-

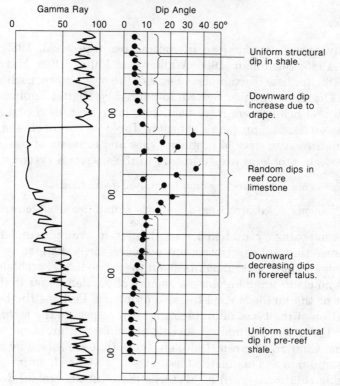

Figure A–1.   Screen from Dipmeter Advisor System.

menting any expert system. Understandability and flexibility are important both while expert systems are being designed and when they are used. During design and implementation, not all the requisite knowledge is in hand because not even specialists can say precisely what a program needs to know. As a result, expert systems are constructed incrementally. Important to understandability is the use of the same terminology that specialists and practitioners use. Understanding the static knowledge base allows us to decide what knowledge needs to be added to improve performance. Understanding the dynamics of the reasoning is also important in deciding what to change. Flexibility is thus needed to allow the changes to be made easily. Explanations help designers, as well as end users, understand the reasons for a program's conclusions. This capability is especially important when end users accept legal, moral, or financial responsibility for actions taken on a program's recommendations.

Examples

Many expert systems are in routine use (see AAAI, 1989; Rauch-Hindin, 1986; Buchanan, 1986; Walker and Miller, 1986; Harmon and King, 1985, for lists of examples). Some of the best known, such as XCON and the Dipmeter Advisor System (produced by Digital Equipment Corporation and Schlumberger, respectively) have been used commercially for many years. The programs shown in Table A–1 were chosen because they illustrate a variety of problem types and contexts of use. Roughly two classes of problems are addressed in these several systems:

1. Problems of interpreting data to analyze a situation.

2. Problems of constructing a solution within specified constraints.

Within each category are listed several different examples under general task names that are descriptive but not necessarily distinct.

We should note several points about these two lists of problems. First, there is no clear, unambiguous taxonomy of problem types that is independent of the methods used to solve problems. Perhaps the best characterization of the types of problems is with respect to the *methods* used to solve them. For example, heuristic classification problems (Clancey, 1985, and Chandrasekaran, 1986) are those that are solved by a method of the same name. This method assumes a predefined, enumerated list of possible solutions—such as MYCIN's list of antimicrobial drugs (Buchanan and Shortliffe, 1984)—and a set of heuristics for selecting among them efficiently—such as MYCIN's rules.

Second, for some problems we can specify a narrow enough scope so that the list of possible solutions is short enough for programs to deal with (dozens or hundreds, but not millions). For other problems we must

TABLE A–1

Several Examples of Expert Systems Working in Various Problem Areas.

CLASS I: PROBLEMS OF INTERPRETATION

Data Interpretation

Schlumberger (Dipmeter Advisor)—interpret down-hole data from oil well boreholes to assist in prospecting (Smith and Young, 1984).

St. Vincents Hospital (Sydney)—aid in interpreting diagnostic tests on thyroid function (Horn et al., 1985).

NL Baroid (MUDMAN)—determine causes of problems in drilling oil wells and recommend additives to the drilling fluid that will correct them (Kahn and McDermott, 1986).

Equipment Diagnosis

General Motors (VIBRATION)—determine causes of vibration noises and recommend repairs (Teknowledge, 1987).

Kodak (BLOW MOLDING INJECTION ADVISOR)—diagnose faults and suggest repairs for plastic injection molding machines (Teknowledge, 1987).

AT&T (ACE)—provide troubleshooting and diagnostic reports on telephone cable problems (Miller et al., 1985).

General Electric (CATS)—diagnose problems in diesel-electric locomotives (Sweet, 1985).

Troubleshooting Process

Hewlett-Packard—diagnose causes of problems in photolithography steps of wafer fabrication (Cline et al., 1985).

Elf Aquitaine Oil Company (DRILLING ADVISOR)—demonstrate reasoning used to find the cause of drill bit sticking in oil wells and to correct the problems (used for training) (Rauch-Hindin, 1986).

Monitoring

IBM (YES/MVS)—monitor and adjust operation of MVS operating system (Rauch-Hindin, 1986).

National Aeronautics and Space Administration (LOX)—monitor data during liquid oxygen tanking process (Kolcum, 1986).

Preventive Maintenance

NCR (ESPm)—monitor computers in the field, analyze error logs, and suggest preventive maintenance procedures before a computer fails (Teknowledge, 1987).

(*continued*

TABLE A–1 *Continued*

Screening

U.S. Environmental Protection Agency (EDDAS)—determine which requests for information fall under the exceptions to the Freedom of Information Act (Feinstein and Siems, 1985).

Credit Authorization

American Express (AA)—assist in authorizing charges from card members or in determining that a request is suspect or fraudulent (Klahr et al., 1987).

Financial Auditing

Arthur Young (ASQ)—assist auditors with planning and developing approaches to field audits (Hernandez, 1987).

Software Consulting

AT&T (REX)—advise persons on which subroutines in large statistical package to use for their problems and how to use them (Rauch-Hindin, 1986).

Equipment Tuning

Lawrence Livermore National Laboratory (TQMSTUNE)—specify parameter settings to bring a sensitive instrument into alignment (Rauch-Hindin, 1986).

Inventory Control

Federal Express (INVENTORY SETUP ADVISOR)—help decide whether or not to stock spares in inventory of 40,000 parts (Teknowledge, 1987).

CLASS II: PROBLEMS OF CONSTRUCTION

Configuration

Digital Equipment Corporation (XCON)—translate customers' orders for computer systems into shipping orders (Rauch-Hindin, 1986).

Design

Xerox (PRIDE)—design paper-handling systems inside copiers and duplicators (Mittal et al., 1985).

GM Delco Products (MOTOR EXPERT)—generate information necessary to make production drawings for low-voltage DC motor brushes by interacting with designers (Rauch-Hindin, 1986).

Loading

U.S. Army (AALPS)—design loading plan of cargo and equipment into aircraft of different types (AALPS, 1985).

(*continued*)

TABLE A–1 *Continued*

Planning

> Hazeltine (OPGEN)—plan and prepare "operations sheets" of assembly
> instructions for printed circuit boards (Rauch-Hindin, 1986).

> Hughes Aircraft (HI-CLASS)—set up sequence of hand-assembly steps for
> printed circuit boards (Hi-Class, 1985).

Scheduling

> Westinghouse (ISIS)—plan manufacturing steps in Turbine Component Plant
> to avoid bottlenecks and delays (Fox and Smith, 1984).

> Babcock & Wilcox—automate generation of weld schedule information (e.g.,
> weld procedure, pre-heat, post-heat, and nondestructive examination
> requirements) (Rauch-Hindin, 1986).

Therapy Management

> Stanford Medical Center (ONCOCIN)—assist in managing multistep
> chemotherapy for cancer patients (Hickam et al., 1985).

---

define a generator of alternatives, which can only be exercised with
strong guidance.

Third, some problems reason with a "snapshot" of a situation and
provide a static assessment; others require monitoring a data stream.

Fourth, some problems are solved routinely by people who have little
specialized training; others are problems that highly skilled persons
solve with considerable effort.

Fifth, the scope of competence of most of these programs is narrow
and well defined. To the extent that a problem is open-ended (or "open-
textured," i.e., requires reasoning about unbounded lists, such as the
intended meanings of a sentence), it is *not* a good candidate for an expert
system.

Sixth, criteria of the success of most of these programs are well
defined; e.g., either a suggested repair fixes a problem or it does not.

Historical Note

Expert systems emerged as an identifiable part of AI in the late
1960s and early 1970s with the realization that application of AI to
science, engineering, and medicine could both assist those disciplines
and challenge AI. The DENDRAL (Lindsay et al., 1980) and MACSYMA
(Moses, 1971) programs suggested that high performance in a subject
area such as organic chemistry or algebraic simplification was more

readily achieved by giving a program substantial subject-specific knowledge than by giving it the general axioms of the subject area plus a powerful, but general, deductive apparatus. The DENDRAL program represented many specific facts about organic chemistry in a variety of ways and used those facts in rather simple inferences (see Article VII.C2, Vol. II). For example, it represented the masses and valences of atoms as values of attributes; it represented classes of unstable chemical compounds as partial graph structures in a table; and it represented certain major patterns of molecular fragmentation in a mass spectrometer as predictive rules. From this work emerged the first principle of expert system building, as enunciated by Feigenbaum (Feigenbaum et al., 1971): "In the knowledge lies the power." The concept of a knowledge base has consequently become central in expert system.

In contrast, most other AI work of the day concerned reasoning by such general methods as theorem proving. Researchers sought to give programs power by means of general planning heuristics, exhibited, for example, in problem areas where knowledge about the objects of the domain was almost irrelevant. A favorite problem area was the so-called "Blocks World" of children's blocks on a table. General knowledge about stability and support, plus general knowledge about planning and constraint satisfaction, allowed programs to reason, say, about the sequence of operations needed to stack blocks in a specified order (see Section XV.A, Vol. III).

From the beginning (1950s–1960s), work in AI focused on two main themes: psychological modeling and search techniques (see Chapters II and XI). Expert systems build on much of that work, but they shift the focus to representing and using knowledge of specific task areas. Early work used game playing and reasoning about children's blocks as simple task domains in which to test methods of reasoning. Work on expert systems emphasizes problems of commercial or scientific importance, as defined by persons outside of AI. Newell calls MYCIN "the original expert system" (Foreword to Buchanan and Shortliffe, 1984) because it crystallized the design considerations and emphasized the application (see Article VIII.B1, Vol. II). In the 1970s, work on expert systems developed the use of production systems (see Article III.C4, Vol. I), based on the early work in psychological modeling. In the 1980s, fundamental work on knowledge representation evolved into useful object-oriented substrates (Stefik and Bobrow, 1986). Expert systems continue to build on—and contribute to—AI research by testing the strengths of existing methods and helping define their limitations (Buchanan, 1988).

Hardware developments in the last decade have made a significant difference in the commercialization of expert systems and in the rate of their development. Standalone workstations provide special hardware for AI programming languages, high-resolution interactive graphics, and large address spaces in small boxes at affordable prices (Wah, 1987). These have simplified development since it is no longer necessary to depend on large, time-shared central mainframes for development and debugging. They also provide an acceptable answer to questions of portability for field personnel. Development of expert systems—and the languages and environments (called "shells") for building them—in standard languages such as CommonLISP and C have essentially eliminated the last barriers to portability.

B. FUNDAMENTAL PRINCIPLES

ALL AI PROGRAMS, including expert systems, represent and use knowledge. The conceptual paradigm of problem solving that underlies all of AI is search (i.e., a program, or person, can solve a problem by searching among alternative solutions). Although immediately clear and simple, this formulation does not tell us how to search a solution space efficiently and accurately. The number of possible solutions may be astronomical, so exhaustive consideration of alternatives is out of the question. Therefore, most expert systems use heuristics to avoid exhaustive search, much as experts do. For example, the Dipmeter Advisor System is expected to delineate significant strata through which an oil well borehole penetrates. There are many hundreds of these in a one- or two-mile borehole. Then it is expected to classify the strata in any of several dozen geological categories. These interpretations are not totally independent: the endpoints of significant intervals are partly determined by the types of rock formations, and the identification of a type is partly determined by the identity of formations immediately above or below. Considerable knowledge of geology keeps the program from exhaustively searching this large, combinatorial space.

For problem areas in which experts are acknowledged to be more efficient and accurate than nonspecialists, it is reasonable to assume that what the experts know can be codified for use by a program. This is one of the fundamental assumptions of knowledge engineering, the art of building expert systems by eliciting knowledge from experts (Hayes-Roth, et al., 1983).

The term "expert system" suggests a computer program that performs at the pinnacle of human expertise, or one that models a human expert's thought processes. However, designers of expert systems subscribe to neither of these implications. Although high performance is a goal, a system need not equal the best performance of the best individuals to be useful: well-timed advice from a "good" system can help novices avoid trouble. On the other hand, programs can sometimes outperform the specialists by being more systematic in their reasoning. A commitment to achieving high performance, though, is not a commitment to achieving consistently unexcelled performance.

Similarly, designers of expert systems build into their programs much of the knowledge that human specialists have about problem solving. But they do not commit to building psychological models of how the expert thinks. The expert may describe how he or she would like others to solve problems of a type, as well as how he or she actually solves those problems. The expert system is a model of something, but it is more a model of the expert's model of the domain than of the expert.

One of the fundamental principles in the design of expert systems is the separation of knowledge about the domain (say, geology or medicine) from the programs that reason with that knowledge. This is sometimes briefly stated as separation of the knowledge base and the inference engine (Davis, 1982). The architecture of an expert system is a commitment to both the representation of knowledge and the form of reasoning.

In this section we attempt to elucidate principles that underlie architectural choices made to facilitate the design, implementation, fielding, and evolution of expert systems. We focus on the following important aspects: representation of knowledge, reasoning methods, knowledge base development, explanation (of both the contents of the knowledge base and of the reasoning process), tools used to facilitate system construction, and validation of performance. In the discussion, we relate each of the classes of choices to desiderata (a)–(e) for expert systems as enumerated in Section A. Finally, we conclude with a brief summary of factors that indicate when an expert systems approach is appropriate.

B1.   Representation of Knowledge

A HALLMARK OF an expert system is the use of specific knowledge of its domain of application (say, geology or medicine), applied by a relatively simple reasoning program. In this simple characterization, the term "knowledge base" is taken to mean the collection of knowledge of the domain, and the term "inference engine" refers to the programs that reason with that knowledge.

The phrase "knowledge programming" has been used to emphasize this aspect of building an expert system. The single most important representational principle is that of declarative knowledge enunciated by McCarthy in the formative years of AI (McCarthy, 1958). (See also Winograd's discussion of this principle in Winograd, 1975.) Simply put, this principle states that knowledge about facts and relations in the world must be encoded in an intelligent program explicitly, in a manner that allows other programs to reason about it, as opposed to relying on programs and subroutines to compute new facts. Arbitrary FORTRAN or LISP procedures, for example, cannot be explained or edited by other programs (although they can be compiled and executed), whereas stylized attribute-value pairs, record structures, or other, more complex data structures can be.

To a certain extent, a knowledge base is a database. The essential differences between knowledge bases and databases are flexibility and complexity of the relations. Current research on AI and databases, which are sometimes called expert database systems (Kerschberg, 1986) is reducing these differences. A knowledge base requires an organizational paradigm plus data structures for implementation. Together these two parts constitute the representation of knowledge in an AI program. Elements of a knowledge base may also be interpreted directly as pieces of the program, which is partly what we mean by the complexity of the relations expressed.

The contents of a knowledge base include domain-specific facts and relations. But many expert systems explicitly state generic facts and relations as well. For example, types and properties of various mathematical relations, or general knowledge of English grammar, may be included in a knowledge base. Also, many knowledge bases include declarative descriptions of the problem-solving strategy in meta-level statements (about how to use the domain-specific knowledge).

Elements of knowledge needed for problem solving may be organized globally around either the primary objects (or concepts) of a problem area or around the actions (including inferential relations) among those objects. For example, in medicine we may think primarily about the evidential links among manifestations and diseases, and the links among diseases and therapeutic actions, and secondarily about the concepts so linked. In this paradigm, we concentrate on the knowledge that allows inferences to be drawn and actions to be taken—the "how to" knowledge. Alternatively, we might organize medical knowledge primarily around the taxonomy of diseases and the taxonomy of their manifestations and secondarily around the inference rules that relate manifestations to diseases and problems to treatments. In this second paradigm, we concentrate on what might be called the "what is" knowledge. These two conceptual views are known as *action-centered* or *object-centered* paradigms for representing knowledge. They have counterparts at the implementation level in program organization.

For each type of representation, we may identify the primitive unit and the primitive action. The primitive unit, in the case of action-centered representations, is the fact (e.g., the freezing temperature of water is 0 degrees C). Primitive facts are linked in conditional sentences by rules ("If . . . then . . . " statements). Note that these links may reflect causal associations based on theory, or empirical associations based on experience. An example from the Dipmeter Advisor System, which is an abbreviated causal description as found in geology texts, is shown in Figure B–1. It is one of a set used to perform sedimentary environment analysis. This rule is attempted only after the system has determined that the overall sedimentary environment is a deltaic plain.

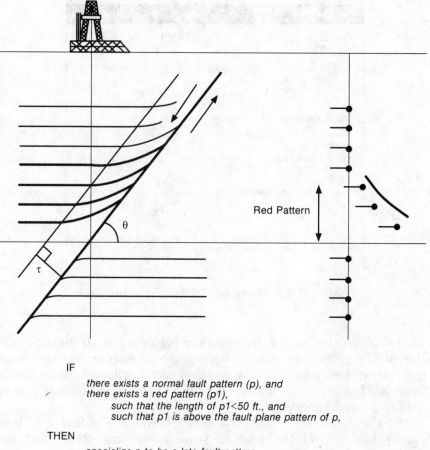

IF

there exists a normal fault pattern (p), and
there exists a red pattern (p1),
    such that the length of p1<50 ft., and
    such that p1 is above the fault plane pattern of p,

THEN

specialize p to be a late fault pattern

Figure B–1.   Dipmeter Advisor System rule.

Conversely, the primitive unit of an object-centered representation is the object with a number of attributes (called *slots*) and values (e.g., a spur gear with number-of-teeth = 24, material = cast-steel, and diameter = 5 cm). Objects typically also encapsulate procedures (called *methods*). In addition, they may contain defaults, uncertainty, relations to other objects (e.g., generalizations and parts), and a variety of other information. An object can be viewed as a structured collection of facts. Minsky (Minsky, 1975) popularized the use of objects (then called *frames*) for AI (see Article III.C7, Vol. I). An example of an object definition from the Dipmeter Advisor System is shown in Figure B–2. This model encapsulates information about normal or tensional geological faults. Individ-

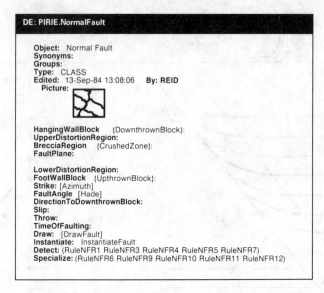

Figure B–2.   Dipmeter Advisor System object.

ual attribute (slot) names are shown in boldface (e.g., **Hanging-Wall-Block**). Where used, synonyms for attribute names are enclosed in braces (e.g., {Downthrown-Block}). The "type" of each attribute value is shown in square brackets (e.g., the value of the **Strike** slot is expected to be a datum of type [Azimuth]).

Smalltalk (Goldberg and Robson, 1983) was one of the early languages that showed both the power of objects as programming constructs and the power of an integrated graphical programming environment. Many commercial expert-system shells now contain an object-oriented component (Stefik and Bobrow, 1986).

The primitive action in action-centered representations is often referred to as *firing a rule*: If the premise conditions of a conditional rule are true in a situation, take the actions specified in the consequent part of the rule. For example, in a medical system, conclude that an organism may be streptococcus if its gram stain is positive. This style of programming began as production systems, made popular by Newell's work in the 1960s (see Chapter 2 of Buchanan and Shortliffe, 1984).

Given that rule-oriented programming often involves making deductions, it has been argued that various forms of logic are well suited for use in expert systems. Simple systems have used propositional logic; more complex systems have used first-order predicate logic; and there is ongoing research in the use of higher order logics to express relations among beliefs, temporal relations, necessity, and uncertain information (both the uncertainty with which data must be regarded in many real systems and the uncertainty about the strength of heuristic rules, which reflects a lack of detailed understanding of a domain) (Allen, 1984; Allen and Koomen, 1983; Szolovitz and Pauker, 1978; Pearl, 1986; Pearl, 1989; Shafer et al., 1989).

In object-centered representations, the primitive action is called *sending a message*: If an action needs to be taken (e.g., a value of an attribute is needed), send a request to the object that can take the action (e.g., compute, or conclude, the value). For example, in a geology system, send the *Analyze-Sedimentary-Environment* message to an instance of the Borehole-Interval object. The effect is to perform an arbitrary action, which could include drawing inferences. In our example, the action performed is to draw conclusions about the geological "story" of sedimentation at a specific depth interval penetrated by the oil rig's drill. This style of object-oriented programming was defined by Hewitt (1977).

In terms of data structures, objects are much like record structures. Each object has a number of fixed fields. Unlike record structures, however, new fields can be added to objects during a computation. Objects are typically divided into two types: instances and classes. Instances represent individuals in a domain (e.g., a specific depth interval from 1200 to 1225 feet in a specific borehole). Classes represent sets of individuals (e.g., any depth interval). They define the common characteristics of the individuals that are their instances. Classes are usually organized into hierarchies according to different relations. The most common relations are the specialization, subclass, or "is-a" relation (e.g., a reverse geological fault is a kind of geological fault) and the "part-of" relations (e.g., a fault plane is part of a geological fault). Object-oriented systems allow arbitrary relations to be encoded, but they often provide efficient support for one or two specific relations.

To support the characteristics of expert systems listed in Section A, representation mechanisms must have sufficient expressive power to state, clearly and succinctly, both "what is" knowledge and "how to" knowledge. (This distinction and an important early discussion of representing facts about the world—the "what is" knowledge—are in McCarthy and Hayes (1969). Expressive power has both design-time and run-time implications. One of the key problems for designers of expert systems is the management of complexity. Impoverished representation mechanisms force designers to encode information in obscure ways, which eventually leads to difficulty in extending and explaining the behavior of expert systems. Representation mechanisms that permit efficient compilation and structuring of knowledge reduce run-time requirements of both time and memory.

As an example, an object-oriented language allows some information to be stated once, in an abstract class, and accessed (by inheritance) in a large number of subclasses. A representational mechanism that does not allow this forces designers to confront the complexity of stating essentially the same information many times. This may lead to inconsistency and difficulty in updating the information. It also has an obvious memory cost. At run time, each of the separate encodings of the information may have to be considered individually, resulting in an obvious performance penalty. An example of a taxonomic hierarchy is shown in Figure B–3.

To facilitate the incremental development of expert systems, representation schemes must also be extensible. Since there is rarely a complete specification of either the problem or the knowledge required to solve it, incremental development is required. When new concepts, attributes, and relations are added incrementally, a designer must not be forced to recode substantial portions of the knowledge already encoded.

Experience has shown that declarative, modular representations are useful for expert systems. Some information is more difficult to encode

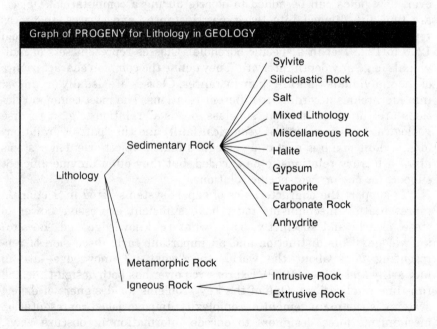

Figure B–3.   Dipmeter Advisor System tectonic feature
              hierarchy.

in the action-centered paradigm, whereas other information is more difficult in the object-centered paradigm. For example, sequencing of actions is difficult to encode in an action-centered paradigm. The same is true of information that is essentially static such as causal or structural descriptions. On the other hand, object-centered representations have no built-in inference mechanism beyond inheritance (although they support them, and many commercial shells have an integrated rule-oriented component). In addition, in some domains, subclasses are "soft," and it may be inappropriate to wire in hard distinctions between classes. For example, in geology, classification of rocks according to lithology (sandstone, shale, and carbonate) is not firm because the end members are mixed to varying degrees. Consequently, there is no single answer to the question, "Which representation method is best?" Action-centered and object-centered paradigms are in fact two ends of a spectrum of representational possibilities. The two emphasize different aspects of modeling. Contemporary expert systems often use heterogeneous representational paradigms, but they attempt to integrate them into a uniform framework. As systems become more complex, it will be more and more difficult to maintain a uniform view.

The problem of representation spans from deciding globally what to represent through deciding locally how to use the data structures of a specific programming language. At the global level, designers (sometimes called *knowledge engineers*) must determine an overall organizational paradigm within which an expert system can reason effectively. Since the knowledge engineer and the expert are discussing at this point the objects and relations that are important enough to name, this phase is sometimes called determining the ontology. As an organizing principle, it is important that the ontology of the expert system closely reflect the ontology of the experts. Otherwise, the experts will not be able to understand and debug the system's reasoning.

B2.   Reasoning Methods

INFERENCE METHODS are required to make appropriate and efficient use of the items in a knowledge base to achieve some purpose such as diagnosing a disease. Logically speaking, the two rules of inference most used in problem solving are *modus ponens* ("If A implies B and you know A, then infer B") and *modus tollens* ("If A implies B and you know not-B, then infer not-A") (see Section XII.B, Vol. III). Linking several applications of modus ponens together is sometimes called the "chain rule" because inferences are chained together in a sequence:

$$
\begin{array}{l}
A \\
A \;\rightarrow\; B \\
B \;\rightarrow\; C \\
\underline{C \;\rightarrow\; D} \\
\text{Therefore,} \quad D
\end{array}
$$

In addition to these two simple rules, rules of quantification are sometimes used. For example, "If all As are Bs and x is an A, then x is a B." With a few simple rules of inference such as these driving the problem solving, a knowledge base full of many special facts and relations about the problem area can provide the expertise on which high performance is based.

Some expert systems (e.g., those written in PROLOG) use a theorem prover to determine the truth or falsity of propositions and to bind variables so as to make propositions true. Others use their own interpreters in order to incorporate more than a theorem prover provides—most importantly, capabilities for controlling the order of inferences, strategic reasoning, and reasoning under uncertainty. Most fielded rule-based expert systems have used specialized rule interpreters that are not based directly on logic. To some extent this reflects timing—efficient PROLOG interpreters and compilers that can be integrated with other systems have only recently become available. However, it also reflects a need for more flexible styles of inference (in addition to a theorem prover's depth-first backtracking) and control over the strategies guiding the order of inferences.

Controlling the Order of Inferences and Questions

From a logical point of view, the order in which new facts are derived is irrelevant, if all logical consequences of the initial facts are to be considered. However, for pragmatic reasons, expert systems often need to be selective about which facts to consider and which consequences to pursue. Space and time are often limited, for example, and it may also be important to develop a line of reasoning, and an order in the inferences, that a user can follow.

Matching the premise clauses of all rules—or the templates of all objects—in a knowledge base against each new situation can be prohibitively expensive where there are many rules or objects, and many new situations created in the course of problem solving. Rules and object definitions often contain variables that can be bound in many different ways, thus creating additional ways that they can match a situation. Rule interpreters commonly provide mechanisms for compilation of rules and rule-matching procedures (Brownston et al., 1985). In addition, all but the simplest rule-based systems organize and index rules in groups in order to control the expense of matching and invocation. Rule groups (called *rule sets, tasks,* or *control blocks*) are also used to control the expert system's focus of attention in order to make interactions with users more comprehensible.

Rule-based expert systems are often organized around one (or a combination) of three different reasoning paradigms: forward, backward, and opportunistic reasoning.

Forward reasoning from data to conclusions is used when the cost or inconvenience of gathering and filtering low-level processing data is low and there are relatively few hypotheses to explore. A forward-chaining system starts with a collection of facts and draws allowable conclusions, adding those to the collection and cycling through the rules. The stopping conditions vary from stopping with the first plausible hypothesis to stopping only when no more new conclusions can be drawn. The XCON computer configuration system is a classic example of a forward-chaining system.

Backward reasoning is goal-directed and does not require all relevant data to be available at the time the inferences are begun. It is also more appropriate when a user supplies many of the data, and when the user cares about the order in which data are requested. MYCIN is a classic example (see Article VIII.B1, Vol. II). A backward-chaining system starts with a hypothesis (goal) to establish and asks, in effect, "What facts (premise clauses of rules) would need to be true in order to know that the hypothesis is true?" Some of these facts may be known because they were given as initial data, others may be known after asking the user about them, and still others may be known only after starting with them as new subgoals and then chaining backward. The stopping conditions vary from stopping with the first hypothesis found true (or "true enough") to stopping only after all possibly relevant hypotheses have been explored.

Opportunistic reasoning combines some elements of both data-directed (forward) and goal-directed (backward) reasoning. It is useful when the number of possible inferences is very large, no single line of reasoning is likely to succeed, and the reasoning system must be responsive to new data becoming known. As new data are observed, or become known, new inferences can be drawn; and as new conclusions are drawn, new questions about specific data become relevant. An opportunistic reasoning system can thus set up expectations that help discriminate a few data elements from among an otherwise confusing mass.

The key element of such a system is an agenda of actions with an associated scheduler that enables explicit decisions to be made about which actions are to be taken (e.g., which rules to apply, whether to apply them in a forward- or backward-chaining manner, and which object is to be the focus of attention). Such decisions, by contrast, are hardwired into forward- and backward-chaining systems. Two successful prototypes based on this paradigm are the HEARSAY-II and HASP systems. In both cases, acoustic data are received and need to be interpreted (as a spoken English sentence in HEARSAY-II or as a description of types and locations of ships in the ocean in HASP). Opportunistic processing, blackboard architecture, and specific systems, including HEARSAY-II and HASP, are described in Chapter XVI of this volume. As data are received over time, hypotheses are revised. With each revision, new ambiguities arise, which can be resolved by reprocessing old data or looking for new signals.

Object-centered expert systems generally make inferences with rules, and thus include one or more of the rule-based reasoning paradigms. They also include built-in mechanisms for inheritance of features of one object from another. For example, individual persons will inherit defining characteristics of the classes they belong to so that the default characteristic diet of Joe Jones is inferred to be omnivorous, provided that the object representing Joe has been defined to be an instance of the class object of omnivores.

Using Explicit Strategies

Any simple reasoning paradigm may need refinement and coordination in order to reflect a complex decision strategy such as medical diagnosis. There are many high-level strategies for solving problems that have been discussed in the AI literature such as means-ends analysis, stepwise refinement, or plan-generate-and-test.

Many environments—or *shells*—for building expert systems provide a built-in problem-solving paradigm at a conceptual level. EMYCIN and its commercial derivatives, for example, work under the strategy of evidence gathering, in which data are collected for and against hypotheses (individually or in classes). Then the data, and the facts inferred from them, are weighed (using a built-in weighting function) in order to decide which hypothesis is best supported by the data. This is a description at the conceptual level; at the implementation level this is all accomplished using backward and forward chaining. (This paradigm is sometimes called *heuristic classification* (Clancey, 1985) because data and heuristics are used to classify a situation into one of a fixed number of categories.)

Representing strategic knowledge explicitly is an important trend in expert systems. It is especially important whenever there is no clear choice as to the best strategy and some experimentation with prototype systems may be required—under different strategies—to determine good and bad choices. It is also important because users may be puzzled about the line of reasoning of an expert system when the expert's strategy for attacking a problem (and thus the expert system's approach) differs from that of the user. With an explicit representation of the strategic rules or procedures, an expert system can explain those just as it explains its domain-level knowledge.

MYCIN's metarules, a solution to this problem in the late 1970s, represent knowledge of reasoning strategy as rules (Buchanan and Shortliffe, 1984). They differ from the other "domain knowledge" rules in the system in that they refer to those rules in some of their premise or conclusion clauses:

IF <medical context> AND there are rules that mention fact A and rules that mention fact B,

THEN reason with the rules mentioning A before the others.

Strategies can also be represented as an organization of steps to perform, in a stylized definition of a procedure (Clancey, 1986; Hickam et al., 1985; Laird et al., 1987; Newell and Simon, 1976; Gruber, 1987; Marcus, 1987; Hayes-Roth, 1985).

Reasoning Under Uncertainty

Reasoning under uncertainty is essential in problem areas outside of logic and mathematics, in which information is incomplete or erroneous. In every empirical discipline from physics to biology and engineering to medicine there is rarely complete certainty about having *all* the data or about the accuracy of the data. Data are never complete enough; tests that would confirm or disconfirm a hypothesis are often too expensive or too risky to perform. Measurement errors are known to occur. Thus expert systems must address these problems if they are to be useful in the real world.

Several methods are used in expert systems to deal with uncertainty arising from either uncertain and incomplete data, or uncertain associations between data and conclusions. The major methods for addressing these issues are listed below.

1. Abstraction—Assume that the uncertainty is small and can safely be ignored, thus treating all knowledge as categorically true (Szolovits and Pauker, 1978). The method is extremely simple and efficient to use. It often works. However, many problems require more precision in estimating uncertainty.

2. Bayes's Theorem—Use prior and posterior probabilities to represent less than certain data and associations; then compute new probabil-

ities with some variation of Bayes's Theorem (Gorry, 1970). This method is based on a solid formalism, but it requires either frequency data or subjective estimates for many combinations of events.

3. Fuzzy Logic—Represent the uncertainty of propositions such as "John is tall" with a distribution of values; then reason about combinations of distributions (Zadeh, 1979). This is intuitively appealing because it is based on ordinary linguistic concepts. It is computationally more complex than other mechanisms, however, because it propagates uncertainty through distributions of values.

4. Criterion Tables—Assign categories or weights to clauses in rules based on their relative importance in drawing conclusions (e.g., major and minor findings associated with a disease); then allow a conclusion to be drawn if sufficient numbers of clauses in each category are true (Kulikowski and Weiss, 1982). This simple mechanism is computationally very fast. It fails to capture gradations between categories, however, and thus lacks the expressive power to reason in some complex problem areas.

5. Certainty Factors (CFs)—Assign single numbers to propositions, and to associations among propositions, representing increases in belief—either probabilities or a combination of probabilities and utilities; then use MYCIN's formulas to determine the CFs for inferred beliefs (Buchanan and Shortliffe, 1984). This calculus has been frequently used and has been shown to have a formal interpretation in probability theory (Heckerman, 1986).

A general problem with methods 2 through 5 is arriving at a coherent set of numbers. Typically these are obtained from experts over several iterations, with empirical testing, because valid, objective numbers are not available. Another problem is that one person's subjective estimates are not always applicable in novel situations, nor are they always easy for others to change.

Summary

There is no single answer to the question, "Which inference method is best?" Each expert system, or system-building shell, provides a nearly unique set of choices for controlling inferences, using strategies, and reasoning under uncertainty. Some also contain methods for backtracking (recovering from local failures), critiquing (making no recommendations unless the user needs them), reasoning about shapes or positions, and reasoning about temporal dependencies. Most present-day systems allow no modification of the inference methods they use. This is a shortcoming that has not received widespread attention, but that sometimes causes system builders to make inappropriate or unhappy choices because they must work with an inference procedure within a shell in which someone else made those choices.

B3. Knowledge Base Development

FOR THE LAST decade, everyone involved has referred to the process of putting knowledge into a knowledge base as a "bottleneck" in building expert systems (Hayes-Roth et al., 1983). Usually this process involves two persons (or teams): an expert whose knowledge is to be partially mirrored in the knowledge base, and a knowledge engineer who interviews the expert to map his or her knowledge into the program's data structures holding the knowledge base. The process is time consuming and difficult, yet the performance of the resulting expert system depends on its being done well. This is exacerbated by the fact that knowledge base design often involves integrating the knowledge of several experts because relying on a single expert may cause implicit assumptions to be overlooked. A survey conducted by SRI International indicates that the average cost of developing an application (knowledge engineering plus end-user interface alone) is about $260,000. For small systems, these costs are about $5,000; for large systems, more than $1.5 million (Fried, 1987). Note that these estimates do not include the cost of constructing an expert system shell.

Much of the process of knowledge engineering is engineering. Yet there are several difficult issues of a fundamental nature wrapped up in the steps of the process.

1. During the first step, problem assessment, the knowledge engineer must match the characteristics of the proposed problem against the characteristics of known solution methods. Unfortunately there are no expert systems that match a description of a problem to a best method for solving it.

2. The second major step is exploratory programming, in which a few experimental prototypes are constructed quickly—first as a proof-of-concept, and then with successively larger fractions of an expert's knowledge—showing that a part of the problem can be (partially) solved with that knowledge encoded in a specific environment. Two substantial issues here are
   a. Formulating an accurate conceptual framework, including terminology, to allow knowledge to be added incrementally.
   b. Iteracting with—not just passively listening to—the expert efficiently to elicit what he or she knows about the problem that is relevant for the expert system.

3. Developing the knowledge base to increase both the breadth and depth of the system's competence is the third major step. This step takes the most time (several person-years), but it is relatively straightforward if steps 1 and 2 have been done well. One difficult issue here is anticipating characteristics of end users and their context of use. Another is deciding which new facts and relations are and which are not relevant for the system's performance and understandability in context. The competing paradigms for making this decision—and for knowledge engineering generally—may be called *model-directed* and *case-directed* knowledge base development. In the former, the knowledge base is largely developed along the lines of a model, or theory, of the problem area. In the latter, it is largely developed in response to errors exhibited in solving test cases. Neither is entirely adequate by itself; knowledge engineers must use both. Whatever combination of development paradigms is used, there is no clear stopping criterion for development. This presents problems in providing for continual additions and modifications to a knowledge base—the extensibility mentioned earlier.

4. The last step of the process is software engineering, that is, ensuring that the system fits into the end users' environment, is responsive to their needs, and so on. The difficult issues at this step are not unique to expert systems. It is included as a reminder that a successful application requires more than developing a knowledge base.

B4.   Explanation

ONE OF THE defining criteria of expert systems is their ability to "explain" their operation. Early forms of explanation focused on showing the line of reasoning, typically a sequence of rule firings, that led to a particular conclusion. This was normally done in stylized natural language (Part Six of Buchanan and Shortliffe, 1984). The user could ask the system questions of the form, "How did you conclude . . . ?" In a sense it is an extension to the kind of dialog that was originally shown in the SHRDLU system (Winograd, 1972; Article IV.F1, Vol. I). That system answered questions by actually looking in its environment and on its own goal stack (i.e., agenda of goals and subgoals).

Although natural language interfaces were used almost exclusively in early expert systems, powerful, low-cost graphics workstations have fueled a trend toward graphic interfaces, for example, the STEAMER system, used to train naval personnel to operate steam power plants onboard ships (Hollan et al., 1984). Contemporary systems often provide mixed natural language and graphical interfaces, for example, the Drilling Advisor (Rauch-Hindin, 1986).

Lines of reasoning, for example, the Guidon-Watch System (Richer et al., 1985) may be shown as graphs that permit user interaction to explore alternative possible lines of reasoning. Perhaps this makes clear the fact that current explanation facilities are much like sophisticated program debugging facilities and are often used as such. Like all good debugging systems, they permit the programmer/user to examine system operation in high-level terms, rather than in terms of the low-level machine instructions actually executed. There is a trend today toward recording justifications that underlie the items in the knowledge base (Smith et al., 1985). These can be used to augment explanations. Research is ongoing to enable expert systems themselves to use this information.

The term "explanation" can also be used to cover examination of the static knowledge base. Object-oriented representations and sophisticated graphics facilities enhance the ability of a domain specialist to understand what has been encoded (Smith et al., 1987). As found in the GUIDON system (Clancey, 1986) (see Article IX.C6, Vol. II), however, such facilities do not in and of themselves constitute a tutoring system.

We could argue that the user of a conventional FORTRAN program can also examine the "knowledge base" of the program. Depending on how the program is written, this is true to a certain extent. It would typically be done with a text editor. One thing that sets expert systems apart, however, is their ability to be queried in the run-time context. Whereas a conventional program can be examined only statically, an expert system can be examined dynamically. It is true that a programmer can examine the stack of a conventional program with a debugger, but such programs do not maintain an explicit goal stack or line of reasoning. This is not a statement about implementation language but rather about system design style.

B5.   System-Building Tools/Shells

WHEN THE FIRST commercial expert systems were being developed, the developers faced two major problems:

1. Eliciting and encoding the domain knowledge to solve the problem at hand.

2. Building programming systems with which to encode/apply the knowledge.

There were almost no generally applicable rule interpreters or object-oriented programming languages. Most of the early "shells" had been constructed in universities as parts of specific applications. They typically made too many assumptions about either the domain of application or the problem-solving methods to be used. Furthermore, they typically could only be used by highly trained specialists. Finally, their run-time, space, and implementation language requirements precluded their use in a wide variety of environments. Nevertheless, these shells represented generalizations, in code, of principles learned from experience with prior expert systems.

One of the most practical effects of the recent commercial application of expert systems has been the development of many dozens of robust shells and tool sets (Bundy, 1986; Gevarter, 1987; Harmon, 1987; and Richer, 1986). These shells range in capability from those that can support little more than experimentation with rule-based techniques to those that can support efficient development and operation of substantial systems. A few of the more powerful shells are used to support current research in expert systems. The shells are implemented in a number of programming languages (e.g., LISP, C, and PROLOG) and run on a variety of hardware, including inexpensive PCs, workstations, and mainframe computers.

Today, users can expect a high-end shell to offer support for a number of programming paradigms. The two most common are rule-oriented programming and object-oriented programming. Both forward and backward chaining are standard, as is support for structuring rules into collections (or rule sets) according to task. Typically rules are efficiently compiled into code in the underlying implementation language. Not all rule languages are extensible. The OPS5 rule language, for example, allows new action functions to be defined but does not allow new matching predicates (Brownston et al., 1985).

When support for object-oriented programming is provided, it includes multiple inheritance, message-passing, and active values. A common way to combine rules and objects is to construct a method that responds to a message by applying a set of rules, with either forward or backward chaining. Such a method may also be invoked in response to a change in an active value. The REACTORS system, for example, uses active values to respond to changes in the operating conditions of a nuclear power plant to invoke rules that suggest new responses (Rauch-Hindin, 1986).

Some shells provide support for uncertainty in rules and in facts. The certainty factor calculus originally developed for the MYCIN system is widely used. Complete integration of inexact reasoning and objects has not yet been achieved. It is currently limited to support of uncertainty for slot values. Support for uncertainty in interobject relations is less common.

In the early years of commercial systems, expert systems were designed as standalone tools. As a result, they were not well integrated with database management systems, large numerical packages, or other existing software and systems. Today's commercial systems are considerably better integrated with other uses of computers. It is now common to see support for mixed language environments (e.g., with some code in LISP and some in C).

Over the past few years increasing attention has been focused on tools to support interaction between humans and expert systems. There are two major reasons for this:

1. In many fielded systems, the end-user interface accounts for a substantial portion of the overall system and success depends heavily on the quality of user interaction (Smith, 1984).

2. The knowledge acquisition process is simplified and enhanced when the expert can readily examine the evolving knowledge base and directly interact with the system to refine its understanding of the domain (Davis and Lenat, 1982).

It has also been found that the tools used to represent domain knowledge and strategy knowledge (e.g., objects and rules) can be applied to structuring user interfaces. Extensible systems and tools have been developed to support interaction requirements for knowledge engineers, experts, and end users (Smith et al., 1987).

B6. Validation

THERE ARE many dimensions along with which we might wish to judge an expert system. The three most important of these are computational, psychological "look and feel," and performance. Computational issues include speed, memory required, extensibility, portability, and ease of integration with other systems. Psychological issues include ease of use, understandability and "naturalness," and online help and explanation. Performance issues—the sine qua non—include the scope of competence, percentage of false positive and negative solutions (false alarms and misses), and time or money saved. Some involve evaluations of the static knowledge base (e.g., its scope), whereas others involve looking at the program in use (e.g., its ease of use or statistics on correctness). (See Cohen and Howe, 1989 and 1988 for specific recommendations.)

Formal validations of expert systems are rarely published, if done at all. The formal validation of MYCIN's performance (Part 10 of Buchanan and Shortliffe, 1984) stands out as an exception. In that study, outside evaluators reviewed the therapy recommendations for several randomly selected patients as made by MYCIN and nine persons whose expertise ranged from acknowledged specialist to medical student. The evaluators (in a blinded study) judged MYCIN's recommendations to be indistinguishable from those of the specialists. In practice, expert systems are validated in the same way as conventional software. Developers mostly demonstrate that a new system solves a variety of difficult problems before it is turned over to end users (O'Keefe et al., 1987). A few of the end users then try the new system in context on a large number of cases, often in parallel with the old method for solving these problems. Any errors that are detected are fixed. When the end users and their managers are convinced of the program's effectiveness, the program is put into routine use, often at a single site first.

With small conventional programs, we often test each branch of each subroutine with boundary values of variables to assure ourselves that the program's parts behave as specified. With large systems, complete testing is not possible, and software engineering practices prescribe testing boundary conditions, exercising new code under as many variations as possible, and empirical testing with a variety of cases—with no guarantees of complete testing. As a consequence, programmers (as well as managers) hesitate to make any changes at all in code that has worked in the past for fear that unforeseen errors will be introduced.

In an expert system, each element of the knowledge base can be examined in the same fashion as a single, small subroutine. As with subroutines, the places where unforeseen errors occur are in the interactions among the elements. These have to be uncovered by empirical tests—running the program on a large random sample of problems (within the specified scope) and determining which cases are solved correctly and which are not. In the absence of a complete logical analysis that proves the correctness of both the knowledge base and the inference engine, we must analyze performance empirically. The criteria for "acceptable" levels of errors of any type, however, must be determined by weighing costs of errors of each type against the benefits of correct solutions.

B7.   Reasons for Using the Methods of Expert Systems

IN GENERAL, the main issues in building expert systems can be classed as issues of complexity, interpretability, and explicit, modular forms of knowledge. In this section we summarize some of the factors that suggest using expert systems instead of conventional software. Note that many of the points are true of the programming technology that underlies AI programs in general—not simply expert systems.

Complexity: Problems, Project Management, Systems

Often when we begin designing an expert system, neither the problem nor the knowledge required to solve it is precisely specified. Initial descriptions of the problem are oversimplified, so the complexity becomes known only as early versions of the system solve simple versions of the problem. Expert systems are said to approach competence incrementally. A declarative, modular representation of knowledge, applied in a uniform manner, is the key to managing this kind of complexity. Time after time, commercial developers of expert systems report that one major benefit of building a system has been that they, and others in the organization, better understand the problem and the information requirements for a solution.

The traditional life-cycle model of software construction and maintenance presumes that problems are well specified. An alternative model, used in constructing expert systems, is exploratory programming, in which problem definition and problem solution are mutually reinforcing. A key element in exploratory programming is a powerful, integrated development environment (Sheil, 1984).

Conventional software can in principle be written by good programmers to solve any problem that an expert system solves. Frequently a system that is initially constructed in a shell system is rewritten in FORTRAN, PL/I, C, or some other well-known language. Constructing the system in the first place, however, requires considerably more ability than most, or unless the shell system (itself in C or some other language) provides an interpreter for elements in its knowledge base.

Interpretation

One of the facilities commonly used to advantage in expert systems is evaluation—*EVAL* to the LISP programmer. This facility allows the user (or the system itself) to specify a query or arbitrary computation to the running system and evaluate it in the run-time context. It lays open to examination the entire state of the system and its environment, including the knowledge base, the line of reasoning, agenda, and so on. This is the sense in which programs written in interpretive languages like LISP are said to themselves constitute data. It is one of the most important facilities on which an expert system depends. It allows a system to reason not only about incoming data but also about past inferences and even about how it makes inferences. To a certain extent, operating systems also perform this kind of introspection. However, these systems can usually only be tuned in a number of predefined ways, according to a fixed set of parameters; operating systems typically cannot look at their own procedures. By contrast, expert systems in principle can do this kind of detailed introspection, examining their procedures as well as their data.

In order for this capability to be used effectively, it is important that the knowledge be represented explicitly (declaratively) and uniformly, and that it be applied in a relatively uniform manner. Although it may be possible in principle to reason about pure LISP code, in practice it is extremely difficult—for humans as well as programs. Thus a simpler syntax, like objects or rules, is usually defined as the fundamental representation, and an interpreter is written for that syntax.

Knowledge

Specialized knowledge of a problem area is the key to high performance. And the key insight from AI has been that representing a program's knowledge declaratively provides considerable advantages over hard-wiring what a program knows in coded subroutines. There is a continuum, of course, from parameterized procedures to completely stylized, understandable, high-level procedure descriptions. For different purposes, designers of expert systems use different ways of representing knowledge explicitly, but they all focus on the knowledge—representing it, reasoning with it, acquiring it, and explaining it. Today's expert systems demonstrate the adequacy of current AI methods in these four areas, for some well-chosen problems. Shells, or system-building environments, codify many of the present methods.

C. STATE OF THE ART

SEVERAL recent books and publications provide extensive overviews and details about the state of the art. See, for example, Feigenbaum et al. (1989), Waterman (1986), Rauch-Hindin (1986), Mishkoff (1985), and Scown (1985), plus numerous current journals and newsletters such as *Expert Systems*, *IEEE Expert*, *AI Magazine*, *Expert System Strategies*, and *The Applied Artificial Intelligence Reporter*. In this section we encapsulate our own understanding of what can be done easily with standard tools, and distinguish that from work that requires ingenuity or new research because present methods are inadequate.

C1. Size of System

THE NUMBERS of expert systems and persons working on them have grown to the point where building expert systems has become routine. This is especially true for small, rule-based systems, and many companies are choosing to develop many small systems instead of concentrating on one or two "big wins" (Feigenbaum et al., 1989). A few expert system shells have small upper limits on the size of the knowledge bases that can be accommodated, mostly for reasons of memory size of the underlying personal computer. Even systems that today are counted as modestly large or complex mention only a few thousand objects (or classes of objects) or a few thousand rules. These limits may be due more to experts' and knowledge engineers' limitations in keeping track of larger numbers of items (and their interactions)—and to managers' unwillingness to spend more than 12–24 months in developing a system—than to hardware or software limits. New technology will be required for managing knowledge efficiently, however, when we try to build knowledge bases that contain millions of items. (See Lenat et al., 1986, for work in progress on methods for defining and managing truly encyclopedic knowledge bases.)

Although it is difficult to characterize the size of a system, either numerically or symbolically, there are some rather crude ways of describing how large present systems are. For example, MYCIN contained about 1,000 rules and 20 class names, and XCON contains about 6,000 rules and 100 class names. The INTERNIST system (see Article VIII.B3, Vol.

II) contains about 2,600 rules, with another 50,000 links among roughly 600 diseases (objects), and 80 manifestations (slots) per disease (chosen from approximately 4,500 manifestations in all). Numbers like these are difficult to compare for many reasons: there may be substantial differences in the level of conceptual detail covered in a rule in different shells (e.g., EMYCIN vs OPS5); there is more in a knowledge base than rules and object names; complex procedures contain considerable knowledge, even though not represented declaratively; and a single concept, or a single clause in a rule, may stand for something very complex (e.g., "state of the patient") or for something quite straightforward (e.g., "patient's age").

An approximate characterization of the complexity of present-day knowledge bases is shown in Table C–1. Assuming that the facts are represented as object-attribute-value triples (e.g., "the identity of Organism-2 is *E. coli*"), it makes some sense to ask how many there are. The numbers in Table C–1 represent empirical, not theoretical, upper bounds on several key parameters. With problems much smaller than those in Table C–1, along these dimensions, the flexibility of expert systems may not be required. With much larger problems, resource limitations (especially time for construction) may be exceeded. There are complications,

TABLE C–1.

Approximate Measures of Complexity of Expert Systems Built Routinely in the Late 1980's.

Vocabulary	
# Objects	1,000s of objects or classes of objects
# Attributes	10–250 named attributes per object
# Legal values	3–100 discrete values per attribute, or arbitrarily many discrete ranges of values of continuous attributes
Inferential Relations	
# Rules or Taxonomic Links	100s to 1,000s
Depth of Longest Reasoning Chains	2–10 steps from primary data to final conclusion
Breadth of Reasoning	2–10 ways of inferring values of any single attribute
Degrees of Uncertainty	Facts and relations may be expressed with degrees of uncertainty beyond "true or false" (or "true, false, or unknown")

however, because classes may be defined for arbitrarily many instances; and attributes may take on continuous values (e.g., any real number). So, instead of showing only the number of rules, Table C–1 indicates the depth and breadth of the chains of inferences. It also suggests that knowledge bases are more complex when they must deal with uncertain facts and relations.

As developers attempt to encode more information in objects (attempting to make fewer assumptions about how the knowledge will be used), the number of rules tends to be reduced. This occurs because the rules are written to be applied to members of hierarchically organized classes of objects and not just to single individuals. An important strategy in scaling up from a small system to a large one is to find nearly independent subproblems and build subsystems that address them, with other subsystems addressing the (few) interactions. When followed, this simple idea keeps the complexity of the composite system from growing exponentially with the number of objects or facts being related.

The amount of detail required in a knowledge base is determined by the degree of precision required in the solution to a problem. If a diagnostic system, for example, is useful in locating errors within large, replaceable components (such as an aircraft's radar system), it need not reason about all the individual parts within the component. This would be reflected especially in the size of the vocabulary and the depth of the reasoning. Often this consideration is called the *grain size* or *granularity* of the description.

The time it takes to build a system varies greatly depending on the scope of the problem and the expectations about the end product. A prototype that is expected to demonstrate feasibility on a small troubleshooting problem, for example, may be built by a single person in one to ten weeks. A fully developed system ready for field use on a complex problem, on the other hand, may take a team of several persons one to three years or more. One measure of our increased understanding of knowledge programming is that students are now routinely assigned one-term class projects that would have been two-year doctoral research projects a decade ago.

C2. Type of System

SEVERAL TYPES of problems for which systems can be built were listed earlier in the categories: interpretation and construction. We lack a robust taxonomy of problem types (among the most complete so far is the one proposed in Chandrasekaran, 1986), so the individual examples still provide a better characterization of the types of problem than general descriptions. Most expert systems described in the open literature address problems of data interpretation, mostly for purposes of troubleshooting or equipment diagnosis. They are mainly organized around the method of evidence gathering, in which evidence is gathered for and against a fixed set of hypotheses (or solutions), and the answer(s) with the best evidence is selected (Buchanan and Shortliffe, 1984). This is also known as *catalog selection* or *heuristic classification* (Clancey, 1985). Most commercial shells address problems of this type. However, more and more systems are being built for problems of the second category, construction, and shell systems are emerging to handle the myriad constraints that shape a design, assembly, configuration, schedule, or plan.

C3. Some Observed Limitations

EXPERT SYSTEMS are designed to solve specific problems in well-circumscribed task domains in which specialists can articulate the knowledge needed for high performance. Current methods for designing and building them have limitations, naturally, so that attempts to implement and use an expert system may not always be successful. Working within known limitations is more likely to lead to success, however, than working without regard for them.

The observations about the limitations of today's tools highlight opportunities for further research. Taken together with current research, the limitations also point to extensions of our methods that can be expected in the future. In the following subsections we mention several pieces of current research on some of these topics, and additional ones that are likely to advance the state of the art over the next several years. This is not a complete list by any means, but it points to several areas of active work in which improvements are likely. It is also not a list that does justice to any of the topics or any piece of work mentioned.

Traditionally, research in artificial intelligence generally has focused on problems of *knowledge representation* and knowledge use, or *reasoning*. Advances in these fundamental areas will certainly advance the state of the art of expert systems. There are additional demands that expert systems make on programmers, however, because of the desired high performance, flexibility, and understandability. The corresponding areas of research in expert systems work are known as problems of *robustness* and *validation*, *knowledge acquisition* and *maintenance* of knowledge bases, and *explanation*.

In addition, several problems crop up repeatedly in work on expert systems that are broader issues of software engineering or computer science generally. Pragmatic problems of putting expert systems into actual routine use involve research on the *integration* of expert systems with existing applications software, the *security* of knowledge and data in expert systems, design *specification* and *testing*, and the costs and logistics of *hardware* for AI applications. There is also considerable work on *interfaces* and *human factors* whose advances will make a difference in future expert systems.

Expertise. Expert systems work within narrow areas of expertise (Davis, 1982 and 1989). Technical domains, in which terms are well defined and in which subproblems can be solved separately, are more amenable to the introduction of expert systems than more open-ended domains. Engineering and business are thus better problem domains than political science and sociology. When the limitations are well understood, there is little problem in using an expert system reliably for substantial gains in productivity, and many of the notable successes are of just this sort (Feigenbaum, 1989).

Difficulties arise, however, when a user of a system expects that the system can solve a problem for which the knowledge or reasoning principles are totally inadequate. Often, regrettably, this is the fault of overselling on the part of the designers; sometimes it is the result of misunderstanding on the part of the user; and sometimes the result of blind spots or errors in the program.

Applications over the last several years have become larger and more complex. In the past we had to choose between building a 3,000-rule (or 5,000-object) system that is either narrow and deep, or shallow and broad. Mostly it has been easier to demonstrate proficiency and utility with the former. With advances in our methods for dealing with very large problems, we will be able to have both breadth and depth. Several of the techniques from AI that help us manage large, combinatorial problems will also apply to large expert systems. These include problem decomposition, omitting (nearly) irrelevant details, reasoning at successively finer levels of detail, and reasoning at a strategic level before (and during) problem solving.

First Principles. The domain models used by expert systems are not generally the theoretical first principles of textbooks, but are a looser collection of facts and associations (Davis, 1987). Expert systems rely more on special-case formulations of relations than on "first principles." Although a set of general principles such as Maxwell's equations governs the behavior of a large class of devices, designers of expert systems prefer to codify special cases, exceptions, and empirical associations, as well as some causal associations, in order to put the general principles in forms that can be applied more quickly and more precisely. As a result, they are unable to fall back on a better theory in some situations. There is substantial research in AI on using first principles in reasoning, much of it in the area of electronics troubleshooting (Davis, 1987). As this matures, it will allow us to build expert systems that blend the theoretical soundness of the first principles with the precision of special-case exception clauses that map the theory into the world of practical applications.

Limits of Knowledge. Expert systems tend to perform well on the classes of cases that have been explicitly considered but may fail precipitously on new cases at the boundaries of their competence (Davis, 1987; Lenat, 1986). In part this is due to lack of knowledge of first principles. The performance of humans is more robust. As we reach the extent of what we know about a problem area, we often can give appropriate answers that are approximately correct, although not very precise—and we know that we have reached the limits of our knowledge. For expert systems, the standard solution today is to codify rules that screen out cases that are outside the intended scope in order to further ensure that the system is being used in an appropriate way. Current research on reasoning from a sound theoretical basis mentioned earlier will help overcome this problem. The general approach is to back up (or perhaps replace) the specialized rules that are now encoded by expressions of a sound theory. Thus, when a system finds few or no specialized items in its knowledge base covering a situation, it can resort to reasoning from first principles. It can also use the theory to check the plausibility of conclusions reached by using the specialized knowledge.

Self-knowledge. Expert systems have little or no self-knowledge, and thus do not have a sense of what they do not know (Lenat et al., 1983). Although expert systems can often give explanations of what they know, they do not have a general "awareness" of what the scope and limitations of their own knowledge are. Meta-level knowledge, such as rules of strategy, can offset this shortcoming in special situations but does not constitute a general capability.

Commonsense Knowledge. Expert systems can only represent commonsense knowledge explicitly and do not use commonsense modes of reasoning such as analogical reasoning or reasoning from the most similar recent case (McCarthy, 1983). Designers of current expert systems resolve this by assuming that users can exercise some common sense, and by specifying common facts explicitly when needed. The INTERNIST system, for example, contains about 100,000 commonsense medical facts such as "males do not get pregnant" and "aspirin obscures the results of thyroid tests" (personal communication from R. Miller). The challenge is to construct a "commonsense reasoning component" that is general enough to avoid errors that "any fool" would avoid and specific enough to reason reliably and efficiently. Current research on case-based reasoning attends to some of these difficulties (See, for example, the 1989 Proceedings of the Case-based Reasoning Workshop, published by Morgan-Kaufman, San Mateo, CA).

Explicit Knowledge. The knowledge of expert systems must be made explicit; they have no intuition (Dreyfus and Dreyfus, 1986). So far, the problems that have been most successfully solved with expert systems have been those in which inferential knowledge is easily formulated as rules and the organization of objects and concepts is easily formulated as taxonomic (class-subclass-instance) hierarchies and part-whole hierarchies. Reasoning by analogy or by intuition is still too unpredictable (and ill-understood) to use in high-performance systems. Because expert systems depend on knowledge formulated explicitly, it is important to develop better methods for facilitating the process through which experts articulate what they know. Any task for which knowledge cannot be articulated for any reason is not a good candidate for an expert system.

Reusable Knowledge. Knowledge bases are not reusable (Lenat, 1986). Since the cost of building a knowledge base is substantial, it is desirable to amortize it over several related expert systems, with unique extensions to cover unique circumstances. For example, many medical systems use facts about anatomy and physiology, yet often each encodes those facts specifically for use in a unique way. The challenge is to develop knowledge representations that can be used efficiently, independent of the specific context of use. By contrast, considerable progress has been made in building lower level components of expert systems that are reusable—this has led to the widespread use of expert system shells. Representing knowledge in structured objects improves the chances of reusability, and substantial current research is exploring this and other means of improving reusability of knowledge bases (see, for example, Lenat, 1986).

Learning. Expert systems do not learn from experience (Schank, 1983). Research on machine learning is maturing to the point where expert systems will be able to learn from their mistakes and successes. Learning by induction from a large library of solved cases is already well enough understood to allow induction systems to learn classification rules that an expert system then uses (Michie et al., 1984; Michalski et al., 1986). Prototype systems have been built that emphasize learning in context, sometimes called explanation-based learning or apprentice learning, which appears to hold promise for expert systems (Mitchell et al., 1986). The challenge is to design learning mechanisms that are as accurate as knowledge engineering but are more cost effective.

Reasoning Methods. It is generally not possible to prove theorems about the scope and limits of an expert system because the reasoning is not formal (Nilsson, 1982). Although some systems are implemented in a logic programming language such as PROLOG, or otherwise use predicate calculus as a representation language, many systems are more "ad hoc." In this regard, though, expert systems are not in a much different state than other software in which complex reasoning with heuristics defies proofs of correctness. There is considerable research on formalizing the reasoning methods of AI programs and combining those with a predicate calculus representation of knowledge.

Knowledge Context.   Expert systems may fail if the user's conceptual framework is not the same as that of the expert and others on the design team (Winograd and Flores, 1986). Knowledge engineers work under the assumption that the experts they work with know the context of intended use and the intended users' terminology and point of view. This may result in misuse of a system when a user attaches different meaning to terms than did the expert who designed the knowledge base. There are no safeguards built into today's systems to test this assumption. Thus the challenge is to provide enough ways of explaining what is in a knowledge base to make its contents clear to all users. But a simple, more pragmatic remedy is to include members of the intended user community on the design team.

A related problem is that the conceptual view of the design team— even if only a single expert—may change over time, and thus maintaining a knowledge base over time becomes difficult.

D. DESIGN PRINCIPLES AND SUMMARY

D1. Design Principles

OUT OF THE experimental work with expert systems over the last five to ten years, several "architectural principles" of expert systems have emerged. In 1982, Davis (1982) articulated an early set of principles based on experience with a few rule-based systems. (See also McDermott, 1983, for another set of generalizations and Chapter 5 of Hayes-Roth et al., 1983, and practical advice for knowledge engineers.) Given additional experience, we can augment and refine these principles. Note that many of these "principles" in fact represent design tradeoffs. Where appropriate, we identify the relative advantages of each side of tradeoffs.

Modular, Declarative Expressions of Knowledge Are Necessary

1. *Represent all knowledge explicitly.* This simplifies the explanation of system behavior as well as refinement, both by human designers and by the system itself. The main feature of an expert system is the suite of specific knowledge it has about its domain of application. For reasons of extensibility and flexibility, it is important to separate the abstract concepts and relations of the target domain from inferences that can be made in the domain, i.e., "what is known" from "how to use it."

2. *Keep elements of the knowledge base as independent and modular as possible.* When updating rules or links among objects, the fewer the interactions with other parts of the knowledge base the easier the isolation and repair of problems. Although complete independence of rules or objects is impossible (without complex, lengthy descriptions of the context of relevance), partitioning the knowledge base into small, nearly independent modules facilitates maintenance. Common partitionings include:
   a. Domain-specific knowledge (e.g., a model of structural geology, which could be used in a variety of applications).
   b. Task-specific knowledge (e.g., the knowledge of how to use the model of structural geology, together with a model of the data sensed by a dipmeter tool, to interpret the data in terms of geological structures).
   c. Knowledgeable interaction with developers and users.

    d. Problem-solving knowledge (e.g., strategies like top-down refinement and least-commitment constraint propagation).

    e. Other domain-independent knowledge (e.g., commonsense facts and mathematics).

3. *Separate the knowledge base from the programs that interpret it.* Historically this has been phrased as "separate the knowledge base and the inference engine" (Davis, 1982).

4. *Consider interaction with users as an integrated component.* It is important to avoid dealing with user interaction issues in an "add on" manner, after the expert system has been designed. High-quality user interaction frameworks are often essential to end-user utility. They are also important to widen the knowledge acquisition bottleneck.

5. *Avoid assumptions about context of use.* Extending a knowledge base is made difficult when assumptions about how the individual packets of knowledge will be used are implicitly encoded. For example, important premise conditions of a rule may be omitted because the system developer knows the context in which that rule will be applied (as noted earlier with the sample rule from the Dipmeter Advisor system). This is also important if domain-specific knowledge bases are to be reused for a variety of applications.

Uniformity, Simplicity, Efficiency, and Expressive Power Are Interdependent

1. *Use as uniform a representation as possible,* although specialized representations are often worth the cost of translating among representations because they may improve run-time performance and simplify knowledge acquisition.

2. *Keep the inference engine simple.* A program's ability to reason about its actions depends on its ability to reason about the way it makes inferences, and complex inference procedures make this task more difficult. However, this must be balanced against problems that simplicity may cause in expressing knowledge in "appropriate" ways and in run-time efficiency.

3. *An object-centered paradigm offers the most flexibility,* and thus the most expressive power, even though there is a logical equivalence among representational choices.

4. *Be sure the reasoning is based on sound, conceptually simple strategic knowledge.* A knowledge base is more than a bag of facts and relations; it is used for a purpose, with a reasoning strategy in mind. The clearer that strategy is, the more coherent the knowledge base

will be. Again, however, this must be balanced against possible deterioration in run-time performance.

Redundancy Is Desirable

Exploit redundancy. One advantage of a modular representation of the domain knowledge is that it allows the system to explore multiple lines of reasoning. By contrast, a conventional program typically has a single procedure with a fixed sequence of steps for achieving a goal. Reasoning with uncertain or missing data, or with knowledge that is uncertain or incomplete, requires building redundancy into the reasoning to allow correct conclusions to be drawn in spite of these deficiencies.

D2. Summary

EXPERT SYSTEMS use AI methods for representing and using experts' knowledge about specific problem areas. They have been successfully used in many decision-making contexts in which:

1. Experts can articulate much of what they know (e.g., in training manuals).

2. Experts reason qualitatively (e.g., based on what they have learned from experience) to augment the formulas in textbooks.

3. The amount of knowledge required to solve problems is circumscribed and relatively small.

Although many interesting and important research problems remain open, expert systems—and the shell systems that make them easy to build—encapsulate solutions to many problems associated with the representation, use, acquisition, and explanation of knowledge. The engineering solutions used in today's expert systems are not without limits, but they are well enough understood and robust enough to support commercial applications of importance. Many applications are in routine use, with annual savings of millions of dollars each (AAAI, 1989; Feigenbaum et al., 1989), and all of them were built with the tools and methods developed in the last decade or so. Future research will extend the scope of the commercial successes, but there is no limit to the number of systems that can succeed using tools available today.

Acknowledgments

Eric Schoen and David Hammock assisted in generating the Dipmeter Advisor System figures. The ideas in this chapter synthesize articles by and discussed with many friends and colleagues, no one of whom will agree with every statement (including this one). We are grateful to them all. An earlier version of this paper appeared in the *Annual Review of Computer Science* 1988, Vol. 3: 23–58.

Chapter XIX

Natural Language Understanding

James Allen—University of Rochester

CHAPTER XIX: NATURAL LANGUAGE UNDERSTANDING

A. OVERVIEW

RESEARCH in natural language understanding is entering a new phase of development where significant progress will be made toward building comprehensive conversational systems. There are two major reasons for this, one relating to methodology and system organization and the other relating to the steady growth in our knowledge of how extended discourse is organized. This chapter addresses both of these areas in some detail and describes some directions for future research.[1]

The methodological change results from a growing trend to separate the description of linguistic structure from the methods for actually processing language. As a result, computational models have moved closer to formal linguistic theories, and a rich interaction has arisen between the two disciplines. On the computational side, this separation allows particular aspects of language to be formulated in detail without regard to how and when the information will be used in the actual system. To better grasp this point, consider the traditional division made between a grammar and a parser (see Article IV.C and D, Vol. I). The grammar defines the structure and, in simple formulations such as an unextended context-free grammar, many different parsing strategies can be explored. More importantly, different strategies for combining syntactic processing with other aspects of the system can be explored as well. The surprise is that, until recently, a large number of computational grammar formalisms did not have this property. In particular, most parsing systems have been based on network grammars or context-free grammars (CFG) that are then augmented with operations that are performed whenever that particular part of the grammar is used in the parse.

Although the augmentation produces the extra power needed for natural language analysis, the augmentations usually depend on the parsing strategy. If the parsing strategy is changed, the augmentations may also need modification. In recent years, augmented formalisms based on unification have been developed that allow the augmented grammar to be completely independent of the parsing strategy. In other words, the result of using a set of rules to analyze a sentence is the same regardless of the order in which the rules are applied. Besides effecting

---

[1] All of the terminology and early research referred to in this chapter was introduced in Chapter IV, Volume I Handbook of AI.

the obvious simplifications, this separation also opens the door to more flexible parsing strategies involving other parts of the system such as semantic and pragmatic interpretation.

If the division between grammars and parsers was not quite complete, the division between semantic interpretation rules and the semantic interpreter has for the most part been nonexistent. In systems such as LUNAR (Woods, 1978; see also, Article IV.F3, Vol. I) and DIAGRAM (Robinson, 1982), the semantic interpreter is little more than LISP code that produced the semantic representation from the syntactic analysis. Recent work, however, shows the possibility of interpretation rules independent of the interpretation algorithm. One great advantage of this is that the resulting system is much more easily comprehended. In addition, the wide range of techniques for combining syntactic and semantic interpretation found in the literature can all be examined within essentially the same framework.

The second reason to believe natural language understanding is entering a new phase is the development of a wide range of theories describing particular aspects of multi-sentence discourse. This includes models that apply general world knowledge about actions and communication to integrate multiple sentences into a coherent structure as well as work that examines the more structural aspects of discourse itself. Substantial progress has been made in particular problem areas, and I believe it is now time that these individual solutions can be integrated into a comprehensive system.

Virtually all language understanding systems divide their work into subcomponents, at least between the parsing processes and the contextual interpretation processes. Many also separate syntactic and semantic processing. I will pursue a similar strategy here, though it has a significant difference: the division is based on the different types of linguistic structural knowledge, not on the processes. Whereas a process-based division typically creates a less integrated model of processing, the descriptive-based division does not, because the processor might apply all descriptive rules in a parallel fashion. Each module (in the descriptive-based model) specifies a mapping from one or more input representations to an output representation. Ultimately there will be many different such modules (as contextual processing becomes better understood), but this chapter keeps to a fairly traditional division as shown in Figure A–1. The mapping from a sentence to a syntactic form is specified by the syntax component, the mapping from the syntactic form to a logical form by the semantic interpretation component, and the mapping from both the syntactic and logical forms to a final representation by a contextual/world knowledge component.

First, this chapter examines the emergence of unification-based grammars that give exactly the separation between description and pro-

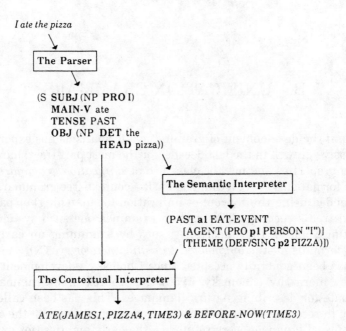

I ate the pizza

The Parser

(S SUBJ (NP PRO I)
   MAIN-V ate
   TENSE PAST
   OBJ (NP DET the
            HEAD pizza))

The Semantic Interpreter

(PAST a1 EAT-EVENT
   [AGENT (PRO p1 PERSON "I")]
   [THEME (DEF/SING p2 PIZZA)])

The Contextual Interpreter

ATE(JAMES1, PIZZA4, TIME3) & BEFORE-NOW(TIME3)

Figure A–1.   The flow of information.

cessing needed for syntax. Next, it considers work suggesting a similar formalism for semantic interpretation. The flexibility of these representations is then demonstrated by showing how a wide range of different processing strategies found in existing systems can be specified without changing the syntactic or semantic specifications. Finally, the last two sections consider the application of contextual knowledge in interpreting sentences and the exploitation of constraints based on the structure of extended discourse.

B. UNIFICATION GRAMMARS

ALTHOUGH the development of grammatical formalisms has experienced an explosive growth in the last decade, for the most part they share some common properties and may be classified as *unification grammars*. Most of these formalisms share a common basis—context-free grammars—and are extended using the concept of unification (or matching) or partially specified tree structures. This section examines one such system after motivating some of the important issues by examining an early augmented formalism—the *augmented transition network* (ATN).

It has been generally accepted since Chomsky's development of the Chomsky hierarchy (Chomsky, 1956) that context-free grammars are inadequate for describing natural languages. This has been called into question in recent years, and all the early arguments against the context free nature of language were refuted in the early eighties (for example, see Gazdar, 1982). The debate is now more active than it has been in years. Whatever the outcome, however, it is clear that the pure context-free grammar notation is at best unwieldy for capturing the syntax of natural language. (Context-free grammars are described in Article IV.C1, Vol. I.)

In computational systems, the standard way to extend the notation has been to allow augmented grammars. Most prominent among these have been the augmented transition network (ATN), which has been the basis of many practical systems such as Woods (1970), Kaplan, (1973), and Bates (1978). (See Article IV.D2, Vol. I.) In addition, many augmented context-free grammar formalisms have been developed such as Robinson (1982) and Sager (1981). In essence, an augmentation specified a set of procedures to execute whenever the grammatical rule (or network link) was used in a parse. These procedures could save state in a set of variables, called registers, as well as test state to determine whether the rule should be applied. Figure B–1 shows an example of a very simple ATN that checks for subject-verb agreement and for a simple form of passive.

The ATN in Figure B–1 contains four nodes and three transition arcs. The first arc (labeled 1) can only be followed if a noun phrase (NP) can be found in the input. (The noun phrase structure would be defined by another network using this same notation.) The second arc can only be followed if a word in the AUX category (an auxiliary verb) is found in the input, while the third can only be followed if a verb is next in the

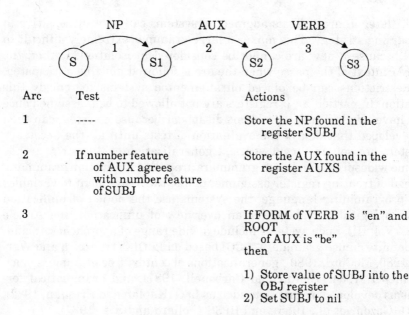

Figure B–1.   A simple ATN.

input. The annotations are listed below the network for each arc. For example, arc 2 can only be followed if the number feature of the auxiliary (the AUX) agrees with the number feature of the subject NP (in the register SUBJ, set in the action on arc 1). The action on arc 2 indicates that the auxiliary verb found should be stored in a register called AUXS. Arc 3 is annotated with a conditional action that checks the verb form and auxiliary to detect the passive, and if found, moves the noun phrase in the SUBJ register to the OBJ register. This specification works fine as long as the parsing algorithm is determined in advance. In particular, ATNs typically use a top-down search through the network. Thus the actions on arc 1 in Figure B–1 are performed before those on arc 2 and so on.

In some applications, however, a different parsing strategy might be desirable. For instance, in speech understanding, one parsing strategy starts with the most reliable word information and works outwards, to the right and to the left. This immediately causes difficulties. For example, say the input is "Jack was seen" and the word "was" is reliably recognized. Unfortunately the test on arc 2 cannot be performed since the SUBJ register is not set yet. Similarly, if arc 3 were executed before arc 1, the NP "Jack" would still end up in the SUBJ register since setting SUBJ to nil in arc 3 will have no effect on setting the SUBJ register to

"Jack" later in arc 1. Thus augmented systems can be very sensitive to the parsing strategy. This makes a large grammar extremely difficult to build because a new arc cannot be considered in isolation. Rather, the entire context of the parse when the arc is followed must be anticipated.

Restrictions can be placed on augmented systems to remedy this situation. In particular, if registers are not allowed to be reassigned once they have a value, many problems disappear because a system can then be developed that delays the evaluation of tests until all the necessary registers are set. In recent years, a generalization of this strategy has become widespread, and such grammars are called unification grammars. Instead of treating register assignments like the assignment to variables in a programming language, the systems use the notion of unification between logical variables (for an overview of unification, see Article XII.B, Vol. III). Such systems include a wide range of approaches, including definite clause grammars (DCG) based on PROLOG (Pereira and Warren, 1980; McCord, 1980), generalizations of context free grammars (such as Shieber, 1984; Tomita and Carbonell, 1987), and grammatical formalisms developed by linguists such as LFG (Kaplan and Bresnan, 1982), GPSG (Gazdar et al., 1985), and HPSG (Pollard and Sag, 1987).

This approach has gained popularity due to its flexibility and generality, and its clean theoretical foundations. The most notable advantages stem from the independence of the grammar from a particular parsing algorithm, so each rule in the grammar can be better isolated as a unit of study, and from the unification-based representation of uncertainty. In particular, a variable can be assigned a structure that contains other variables representing information that will be filled in later.

The remainder of this section introduces a simple unification-based formalism that captures the essential ideas. Consider a notation common to many augmented systems: a constituent is represented by a list starting with the type of constituent (i.e., S, NP, PP) and followed by a number of slot-filler pairs (or register values). Thus

(S **MAIN-V** (VERB **ROOT** LOVE))

is an S constituent with a slot **MAIN-V** filled with a VERB constituent consisting of the **ROOT** slot filled with the word *love*. Uncertainty can be represented by a disjunction of values enclosed in curly braces. Thus

(NP **NUM** {3s 3p})

is an NP with the **NUM** slot filled either with the value 3s (i.e., third person singular) or 3p (i.e., third person plural). Such a disjunction would capture the ambiguity inherent in the word *fish*, which can be singular or plural.

This system is defined as an extension of a standard context-free formalism where each rule is annotated by a set of unification equations. Specifically, two register-value structures unify if each of the specified register values is consistent with that same register's value in the other structure. Any register specified in one but not the other is simply copied to the resulting structure. For example, the structures

```
(S MAIN-V (VERB ROOT LOVE))
```

and

```
(S MAIN-V (VERB FORM en)
   NUM {3s})
```

unify to produce a new structure

```
(S MAIN-V (VERB ROOT LOVE
                FORM en)
   NUM {3s})
```

Registers that take a set of disjunctive features (indicated with curly brackets) are unified in the obvious way by intersecting their sets. If the intersection is empty, the unification of the structures fails. This is the way that agreement restrictions can be enforced. For example, the word *sing* agrees with any person and number subject except third person singular. Its **NUM** register is {1s 2s 1p 2p 3p} (allowing first person singular, second person singular, first person plural, second person plural, or third person plural). The noun phrase *the fish,* on the other hand, can be singular or plural and thus has the number feature {3s 3p}. When these two features are unified in the sentence *The fish sing,* the intersection of the **NUM** registers is unambiguously third person plural, {3p}, as desired.

All unification equations are of the form *structure = structure,* as in

```
(NP NUM {1s 3p}) = (NP NUM {1s 2s})
```

which has the result (NP **NUM** {1s}). To be useful as a rule annotation, equations may specify registers in the current constituent being built and in the subconstituents (i.e., the right-hand side of the rule). Thus the following are possible unification equations with the rule NP ← ART ADJS NOUN:

```
DET = ART
```

This equation unifies the **DET** register (in the NP being built) with the structure built as the ART. Note that if the **DET** register is empty prior to this unification, this situation is similar to the register assignment in a traditional augmented formalism. If the **DET** register is set to some value before the unification, the two values are unified, and both the

DET register and the ART constituent are changed to the resulting structure.

$$\textbf{NUM} = \textbf{NUM}_{ART} = \textbf{NUM}_{NOUN}$$

The values of the **NUM** register in the constituents ART and NOUN are unified, and the result is unified with the **NUM** register in the new NP. If the result of the unification is empty, the entire rule is rejected. This equation is equivalent to both testing for number agreement and the register assignment action to the **NUM** register.

This formalism can be defined precisely by defining each slot name as a function from its containing constituent to its value. You can see this by using a representation based on directed, acyclic graphs. In particular, each constituent and value is represented as a node, and the slots are represented as labeled arcs. Thus the constituents

```
(ART₁  ROOT THE        (NOUN₁  ROOT FISH
       NUM {3s 3p})            NUM {3s 3p})
```

would be represented by the graphs in Figure B–2.

The unification equations on a rule state how to construct a new constituent out of the subconstituent graphs. Most importantly, nodes may be collapsed together as the result of a unification (assuming the intersection of their values is nonempty, of course). For example, if ART₁ and NOUN₁ represent the entries for a noun phrase *the fish,* the equations associated with the rule

```
NP ← ART NOUN    DET = ART
                 HEAD = NOUN
                 NUM = NUMₐᵣₜ = NUMₙₒᵤₙ
```

specify how to construct the graph defining the new NP constituent, as shown in Figure B–3. Assume that the verb phrase *is sick* has been analyzed in a similar fashion and is represented as in Figure B–4. Given these initial analyses, the analysis of the sentence *The fish is sick* constructed by the following rule is shown in Figure B–5.

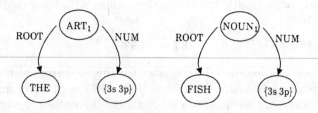

Figure B–2.   Lexical entries for *the* and *fish.*

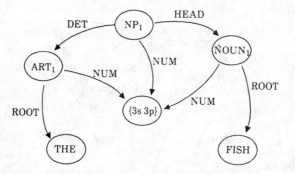

Figure B–3.   The graph for the NP *the fish*.

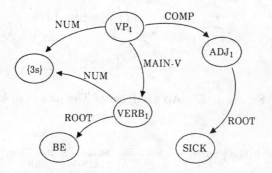

Figure B–4.   The analysis of the VP *is sick*.

$$S \leftarrow NP\ VP$$

SUBJ = NP
MAIN–V = **MAIN–V**$_{VP}$
COMP = **COMP**$_{VP}$
NUM = **NUM**$_{NP}$ = **NUM**$_{VP}$

Note that the value of the **NUM** slot is now the same node for S$_1$, NP$_1$, ART$_1$, NOUN$_1$, VP$_1$, and VERB$_1$! Thus the value of the **NUM** slot of ART$_1$, for instance, changes as the **NUM** slots of NP$_1$ and VP$_1$ are unified. In Figure B–5, all these slots now have the value {3s}, disambiguating the noun phrase *the fish*.

The ability to maintain partial information allows you to represent constraints between constituents easily. For example, to handle infinitive constructs as in *I hope to eat a fish* in a traditional ATN system, a new mechanism is introduced to preset registers. This is used to set the **SUBJ** of the embedded clause to the value of the **SUBJ** of the outer clause, so the final representation corresponds closely to the sentence *I hope that I*

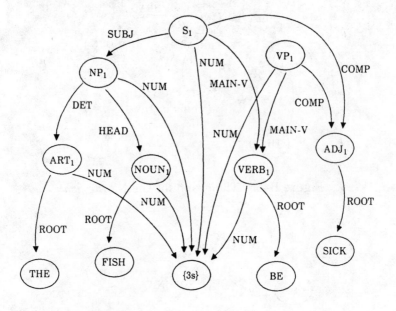

Figure B–5.   An analysis of *The fish is sick*.

1.   S ← NP VERB S-INF

   SUBJ = **SUBJ**$_{\text{S-INF}}$ = NP
   MAIN-V = VERB
   SUBCAT$_{\text{VERB}}$ = {TO-INF}
   COMP = S-INF

2.   S ← NP$_1$ VERB NP$_2$ S-INF

   SUBJ = NP$_1$
   MAIN-V = VERB
   SUBCAT$_{\text{VERB}}$ = {OBJ + TO-INF}
   OBJ = **SUBJ**$_{\text{S-INF}}$ = NP$_2$
   COMP = S-INF

3.   S-INF ← AUX VERB NP

   AUXS = (AUX ROOT TO) = AUX
   MAIN-V = VERB
   OBJ = NP

Figure B–6.   A simple unification-based grammar for infinitive
            complements.

eat a fish. No such extension is necessary in the unification grammar
because the notation already allows the necessary manipulations. For
example, a unification-based context-free grammar dealing with simple
infinitive complements is shown in Figure B–6. Consider the first unification equation on rule 1, that is, **SUBJ** = **SUBJ**$_{\text{S-INF}}$ = NP. This equation unifies the **SUBJ** register in the new S being built, the **SUBJ** register

in the infinitive complement (S-INF), and the NP constituent. In particular, if both **SUBJ** registers are initially unset, both will be assigned the NP constituent as desired. As another example, the equation **SUBCAT**$_{\text{VERB}}$ = {TO-INF} simply checks that the verb in the sentence allows this form of complement.

Because the **SUBJ** register of S-INF is always set from outside rule 3, there is no mention of the **SUBJ** register in rule 3. The structure built when this rule is successfully applied, however, will always have its **SUBJ** register set as appropriate.

An important property of graph unification, which is shared with the traditional unification, is that you get the same result from unifying a set of structures regardless of the order in which they are combined. A direct consequence of this property is that any parsing strategy could be used, and given that the same rules were eventually used in the analysis, the resulting structures would be the same. Not only does this allow different parsing strategies to be explored easily, it also opens the door for the parsing strategy to be modified by other parts of the system, such as semantic interpretation.

C. SEMANTIC INTERPRETATION

DERIVING the syntactic structure of a sentence is just one step toward the goal of building a model of the language understanding process. It is important to also identify the sentence's meaning. Although it is difficult to define precisely, sentence meaning allows you to conclude that the following two sentences are saying much the same thing:

I gave a contribution to the Boy Scouts.
The Boy Scouts received a donation from me.

Sentence meaning, coupled with general world knowledge, is also used in question answering. Thus, if it is asserted that *John drove to the store,* the answer to the question *Did John get into a car?* is *yes.* To answer such a question, you need to know that the action described by the verb *driving* is an activity that must be done in a car (see Article IV.F5-6, Vol. I).

These two examples of semantics involve quite different mechanisms, however. The two sentences about contributing to the Boy Scouts can be identified as saying the same thing based on the knowledge of the structure of the sentences and the words used. Answering the question about driving, however, involves general world knowledge about what is usually involved in the driving action. The answer is derived not directly from the structure of the sentence and the words used, but by applying other knowledge about the world as well. The approach taken here makes a clear distinction between structural meaning and interpretation in context, and it divides the problems of semantic interpretation into two stages. In the first stage the appropriate meaning of each word is determined, and these meanings are combined to form a *logical form* (LF). The logical form is then interpreted with respect to contextual knowledge, resulting in a set of conclusions that can be made from the sentence.

An intermediate semantic representation is desirable because it provides a natural division between two separate, but not totally independent, problems. The first problem concerns the ambiguity inherent in word senses and in the structure of sentences. Just as many words fall into multiple syntactic categories, each word within each syntactic class may have several different meanings, or "senses." The verb *go,* for instance, has over fifty distinct meanings. Even though most words in a sentence have multiple senses, a combination of words in a phrase often has only a single sense since the words mutually constrain each others' possible interpretations. Encoding and enforcing these constraints, which is a complex process worth study in its own right, is essentially the process of deriving the logical form.

The second problem involves using knowledge of the world and the present context to identify the particular consequences of a certain sentence. For instance, if you hear the sentence *The president has resigned,* you must use knowledge of the situation to identify who the president is (and what organization he or she heads) and to conclude that that person no longer holds that office. Depending on the circumstances, you might also infer other consequences, such as the need for a replacement president. In fact, the consequences of a given sentence could have far-reaching effects. Most attempts to formalize this process involve encoding final sentence meaning in some representation (often based on logic) and modeling the derivation of consequences as a specialized form of logical deduction.

The logical form is the intermediate representation between the syntactic form of the sentence and a logical representation of the sentence. It resembles a logic in many ways but has a syntax closer to that of syntactic structure. Any decisions that require contextual knowledge will not be made in deriving the logical form. Rather the information from the sentence structure is recorded in the logical form for use later by the contextual analyzer.

Before you can specify the meanings of words and sentences, you need some methods of expressing knowledge about the structure of the world. The most important aspect of this knowledge is the way that objects in the world are classified into groups by their properties. One of the most fundamental properties of any object is its type, which identifies what kind of object it is. For example, some objects can be classified as dogs and others as cats. More generally, these same objects can be classified as examples of animals or living creatures.

You can construct type hierarchies describing the physical world, as shown in the simple example in Figure C–1. Note a few things about this hierarchy. Some decompositions are exhaustive; for example, every physical object (PHYSOBJ) must be either living or nonliving. Similarly, every LIVING thing is either ANIMATE or VEGETATIVE. Others are not exhaustive; there are more classes of ANIMATE objects than HUMAN, CAT, and DOG. The presence of such hierarchies will allow the specification of general constraints between words. For instance, the adjective *healthy* constrains the word it modifies to be some living object (e.g., dogs or trees). This constraint can be expressed as saying that *healthy* can only modify words with senses under the general sense of LIVING on the hierarchy. This one general statement allows *healthy* to modify any animal or plant, but no rocks, cars, or other kinds of objects not classified under LIVING.

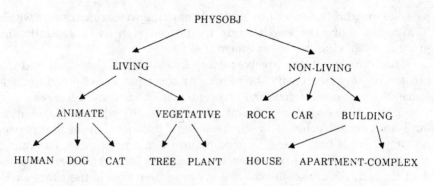

Figure C–1. A type hierarchy of physical objects.

These modification constraints are often called *selectional restrictions,* and one of the most fruitful examples of such restrictions involves how noun phrases are semantically related to the main verb in a sentence. The most influential work for computational approaches has been *case grammar* (Fillmore, 1968; Article IV.C4, Vol. I) and its successors and modifications. For present purposes, case grammar outlines the range of semantic roles, called *cases,* that a noun phrase may play with a verb. One of the most interesting claims of case grammar is that the number of possible semantic relationships is quite small, although there has been little agreement on what this small set consists of. The approach discussed here assumes that the set of possible semantic cases forms a well-defined hierarchy (distinct from the word sense hierarchy) and that the number of immediate subcases for any case is limited to a small quantity. Given this framework, different researchers may have proposed different sets of cases because they based their semantic analysis at differing levels in the case role hierarchy.

Since the ultimate goal of this analysis is to extract the meaning of a sentence, the analysis of sentences with different meanings should lead to different results. Similarly, sentences with different syntactic structures but the same meaning should get mapped to similar structures. For example, consider the group of sentences:

John broke the window with a hammer.
The hammer broke the window.
The window broke.

John, the hammer, and *the window* play the same semantic roles in each of these sentences. *John* is the actor, the *window* is the object, and the *hammer* is an instrument used in the act "breaking of the window." The logical form, a representation based on case roles, captures these intuitions directly.

The Logical Form

The logical form (LF) introduced here can be viewed as a linear form of a semantic network or frame-like representation used in many representation systems. (See Chapter III in Vol. I.) The basic structure identifies an instance of a particular type in the type hierarchy, followed by a list of additional facts about the instance. For example, the sentence *Jack kissed Jill* would be represented by a form that can be paraphrased as follows: An instance s1 of a kiss event in the past has as its AGENT case a person named Jack and as its THEME case a person named Jill. In LF notation this is:

```
(PAST s1 KISS-ACTION [AGENT (NAME j1 PERSON
                             "Jack")]
                     [THEME (NAME j2 PERSON
                             "Jill")])
```

Each LF statement is made up of the following components:

- **Operator** indicating the type of structure (in this case, PAST means that this represents some event occurring in the past).
- **Name** for the object being described (in this case, the instance of KISS-ACTION called s1).
- **Type** of the object (in this case, KISS-ACTION).
- **Modifiers** of the object, which may be a list of LF structures (in this case, the modifiers defining two cases, AGENT and THEME).

Other simple operators for sentence structures will include PRES (simple present tense), FUT (simple future), and INF (infinitive clauses).

The Logical Form of NPs

Noun phrases can be represented in the same language. The operator for simple noun phrases is used to indicate the determiner information for later use in processing. Some of the possible operators for NPs are:

Operator	Description	Example
DEF/SING	Definite singular reference	*the boy*
DEF/PL	Definite plural reference	*the boys*
INDEF/SING	Indefinite singular reference	*a boy*
INDEF/PL	Indefinite plural reference	*boys*

The name and type for simple NPs are as expected, and the modifiers consist of any qualifications produced by adjectives or other modifying phrases. Thus the LF for the NP *the large boy* would be:

```
(DEF/SING b1 BOY (LARGE b1))
```

The quantified NPs map to similar structures using different operators as appropriate. Thus the sentence *Every boy loves a dog* would be
represented as

```
(PAST a1 LOVE-EVENT
  [AGENT (EVERY b2 BOY)]
  [THEME (INDEF/SING p1 DOG )])
```

Note that the logical form does not force any quantifier scoping. The
two quantified noun phrases *every boy* and *a dog* are not scoped, so the
logical form retains the ambiguity between the situation where there is
one dog that every boy loves and the situation where every boy loves
some dog (though they do not all love the same dog). The ambiguity is
retained in the logical form because quantifier scoping usually can only
be determined using contextual information.

The logical form for NPs that describe events is virtually identical
to the representation of event sentences, except that the marker indicates
a determiner rather than a tense marker. For example, the NP *The
arrival of George at the station* would be represented as:

```
(DEF/SING a1 ARRIVE-EVENT
  (AGENT a1 (NAME g1 PERSON "George"))
  (TO-LOC a1 (DEF s4 STATION)))
```

whereas the sentence *George arrived at the station* would be represented
by the logical form:

```
(PAST a2 ARRIVE-EVENT
  [AGENT (NAME g1 PERSON "George")]
  [TO-LOC (DEF s6 STATION)])
```

With the logical form and the syntactic structure of sentences well
defined, semantic interpretation rules can now be formulated to map
from one to the other. These are specified as a set of mapping rules that
relate fragments of syntactic structure to fragments of logical form. The
final LF is generated by unifying the partial logical forms. Allen (1987)
provides a detailed description of this; here only a brief introduction and
a few examples are given.

Patterns are specified in the same notation as the syntactic structure,
except that there may be additional semantic tests on the LF of subconstituents. Thus a pattern that matches any sentence with a verb that
can denote an action and an animate subject would be:

```
(S SUBJ    + animate
   MAIN-V  + action-verb)
```

The partial logical form is specified by allowing special symbols:

- ? for no information
- * for a new instance to be generated by the interpreter to stand for the object denoted by the constituent

and special functions:

- **T** (slotname) that returns the semantic type of the LF of a constituent in the indicated slot
- **V** (slotname) that returns the LF of the constituent in the slot

Thus a mapping rule that sets the semantic type and the AGENT case for an action verb would be:

```
(RULE 1)
(S SUBJ    + animate
   MAIN-V  + action-verb) → (? * T(MAIN-V)
                             [AGENT V(SUBJ)]
```

The right-hand side is a specification of a partial description consisting of

- No information on the tense (the ?)
- A new instance (the *)
- The type of the verb denoting an action (i.e., the sense of the verb in **MAIN-V**)
- The restriction that the AGENT case (of the new instance) is the semantic interpretation of the **SUBJ** slot

Applying this rule to the syntactic structure:

```
(S MAIN-V   ran
   SUBJ    (NP DET the
               HEAD man)
   TENSE past)
```

produces the partial description (assuming other rules interpret the embedded NP):

```
(? r1 RUN1 [AGENT (DEF/SING m1 MAN)])
```

The tense information could be analyzed by another rule such as

```
(S TENSE past) → (PAST ? ?).
```

Unifying the results of these two rules gives the final LF, namely,

```
(PAST r1 RUN1 [AGENT(DEF/SING m1 MAN)]).
```

A set of semantic interpretation rules in this notation is given in Allen (1987). An important point here is that the rules have been specified independent of an interpretation strategy to apply them. As demonstrated in the next section, a wide range of interpretation strategies are now possible.

D. SEMANTIC INTERPRETATION STRATEGIES

SEMANTIC INTERPRETATION STRATEGIES differ in the way they interact with syntactic processing. One method is a strict separation of the processing. The syntactic module produces complete interpretations that the semantic module then maps to a logical form. There are many ways to make the processing more integrated. Some methods such as the *semantic grammar* approach (Brown and Burton, 1978; Hendrix et al., 1978; Article IV.F7, Vol. I; Article IX.C3, Vol. II) encode semantic information directly into the grammar, whereas others interleave semantic interpretation with syntactic processing. Constituent-based interleaving involves the semantic interpretation of each major constituent (e.g., S, NP, and PP) as it is completed, whereas rule-by-rule systems perform the semantic interpretation incrementally as each syntactic rule is used. Finally, there are semantically driven parsers that use minimal syntactic information during the parsing (Birnbaum and Selfridge, 1981). Although these systems do surprisingly well, a rich syntactic model needs to be reintroduced to capture sentences with more complex structure (see Lytinen, 1986).

There are advantages to each of these approaches. Semantic grammars tend to be easily built for small domains and can be very efficient. They are not easily transportable to new domains, however. The interleaved strategies are generally more domain-independent because of the syntactic grammar. Most of the work in moving to a new domain involves changes or extensions to the semantic interpreter. The rule-by-rule analysis offers the strongest form of interaction and can be used to eliminate syntactically valid but semantically anomalous interpretations as early as possible. These methods, however, do incur a hidden cost over the completely separate syntactic and semantic processing. In particular, syntactic analysis may cost considerably less than semantic interpretation. Because of this, much time could be wasted building semantic interpretations of fragments that turn out later not to be syntactically possible. If the syntactic processing were to complete before semantic interpretation was tried, the cost of interpreting such structurally impossible fragments could be saved.

In the remainder of this section, a few of these strategies will be explored in enough detail to give a flavor of the techniques. A more detailed survey can be found in Allen (1987).

Semantic Grammars

The first technique for combining syntactic and semantic processing involves collapsing them into a single uniform framework—either a context-free grammar or an ATN. This result, called a *semantic grammar*, looks like a standard syntactic grammar, except that it uses semantic categories for terminal symbols. For example, rather than having a rule such as

```
           VP ← SIMPLE-VP PPS
```

a semantic grammar would have a separate rule for each semantic verb class. Thus, in a simple airline query domain, you might replace this rule with the following rules:

```
(sem.1)  RES-VP ← RESERVING RES-MOD
(sem.2)  RES-VP ← RESERVING
(sem.3)  DEP-VP ← DEPARTING DEP-MODS
```

Rule (sem.1), which might be realized by the phrase *book a flight for me*, involves verbs of reserving, such as *book,* plus their allowable complements. Rule (sem.3), on the other hand, is for verbs of departure and might be realized by the phrase *leaves for Chicago.*

Similarly the rules for SIMPLE-VP and PPS are replaced by their semantic grammar equivalents. For the RESERVING verbs, you need the rules:

```
(sem.4)  RESERVING ← RESERVE-VERB FLIGHT
(sem.5)  RES-MOD   ← for PERSON
```

Notice that only those PP modifiers that are semantically interpretable are now allowed by this grammar fragment. In particular, for any RESERVE-VERB, a modifying PP such as *for me* is acceptable, as in *book it for me,* but the PP *to Boston* is not acceptable (since no RES-MOD rule allows a *to*). Neither is the PP *for Boston* an acceptable modifier as Boston is not in the class PERSON, and thus the PP cannot be RES-MOD.

For the DEPARTING verbs, you need the rules:

```
(sem.6)   DEPARTING ← DEPART-VERB
(sem.7)   DEPARTING ← DEPART-VERB SOURCE-LOCATION
(sem.8)   DEP-MODS  ← DEP-MOD DEP-MODS
(sem.9)   DEP-MODS  ← DEP-MOD
(sem.10)  DEP-MOD   ← to DEST-LOCATION
(sem.11)  DEP-MOD   ← from SOURCE-LOCATION
```

Again, only the PPs that are semantically acceptable with verbs of departing are now accepted by this grammar.

So far, a few syntactic rules have been replaced with eleven semantic grammar rules to cover two verb categories. Adding more verb categories in this domain could continue to expand this semantic grammar at approximately this same rate of about six new rules per verb category. Thus semantic grammars tend to be much larger than their corresponding syntactic grammars. In compensation, the number of words in each terminal category is considerably smaller, so only a small fraction of the grammar is applicable with any given sentence. The main disadvantage of semantic grammars is thus not efficiency, but the difficulty of constructing the large grammar itself. This problem can be avoided by specifying the syntactic and semantic rules separately and then compiling them together to form a semantic grammar (e.g., Tomita and Carbonell, 1987). For example the syntactic rule:

$$S \leftarrow NP\ VERB$$

with an annotation assigning the registers SUBJ and MAIN-V appropriately might be combined with the semantic interpretation rule:

```
(S SUBJ    + animate
   MAIN-V  + action-verb) → (? T(MAIN-V)
                               [AGENT V(SUBJ)])
```

to produce the semantic grammar rule:

$$S \leftarrow ANIMATE\text{-}NP\ ACTION\text{-}VERB$$

Semantic Filtering

Perhaps the simplest way to combine syntactic and semantic processing is to invoke the semantic interpreter each time the parser builds a major syntactic constituent. If the constituent cannot be interpreted, the parser rejects it and continues the parse as though it were never constructed. Thus the semantic interpreter acts as a filter on constituents proposed by the parser.

Consider an abstract example that demonstrates the point. A sentence consisting of the structure $NP_1\ V_1\ NP_2\ PP_1\ PP_2$ is structurally ambiguous in five ways, depending on whether the PP_1 modifies V_1 or NP_2, and whether PP_2 modifies V_1, NP_2, or the noun phrase in PP_1. The different structural interpretations are shown schematically in Figure D–1, where parentheses indicate subconstituent grouping.

Without semantic filtering, a syntactic parser must generate all five interpretations and then pass them on to the semantic interpretation module. If we assume that it is semantically anomalous for PP_1 to modify NP_1, the semantic interpreters would reject interpretations (3), (4), and (5). If it is then anomalous that PP_2 could modify V_1, interpretation (1)

(1)   NP, V_1 NP_2 PP_1 PP_2

(2) NP_1 V_1 NP_2 (PP_1 PP_2)

(3) NP_1 V_1 (NP_2 PP_1 PP_2)

(4) NP_1 V_1 (NP_2 (PP_1 PP_2))

(5) NP_1 V_1 (NP_2 PP_1) PP_2

Figure D–1. Five structural interpretations.

is eliminated and interpretation (2) remains as the analysis of the sentence.

Consider the same example if the semantic interpreter were called each time a noun phrase constituent was suggested. In this case, the first time the structure (NP_1 PP_1) (i.e., PP_1 modifies NP_1) is suggested, the semantic interpreter rejects it as impossible. The parser then acts as though the structure (NP_1 PP_1) never existed and consequently never goes further to build interpretations (3), (4), and (5). The decision is made once, and the effect is a large pruning of the search space generated by the grammar. In fact, these interpretations can be eliminated even before the phrase PP_2 is processed at all. The end result is the same, but the work the parser does constructing interpretations that will later be eliminated is dramatically reduced.

There are problems with this method, however. In particular, an NP may appear anomalous in isolation, but it can participate in a legal sentence. For instance, the NP *the moon in our car* makes no sense in isolation, yet it could be used in a sentence such as *It's impossible for you to have seen the moon in our car, because it wouldn't fit*. On the other hand, if you relax the semantic filtering so that this NP is acceptable, the semantic filter will be of no use in disambiguating a sentence such as *We saw the moon in our car,* which has a good interpretation corresponding to *We saw the moon while we were in our car.* Since the bad interpretation involving the NP *the moon in our car* would be acceptable in order to handle the first sentence, this second sentence would remain ambiguous. The problem, of course, is that the semantic filter is an all-or-nothing filter. It can only accept or reject, and as you find various strange sentences, the boundary of acceptance must keep moving closer and closer to accepting everything. What is needed is a way of rating semantic interpretations so that some are preferred over others. The job of the parser then would be to find the best interpretation. Some techniques for designing such a system are discussed in the next section.

Semantic Interpretation Based on Preferences

The strategy of having the semantic interpreter simply accept or reject a proposed syntactic constituent can be shown to be too rigid for many situations. In particular, it either eliminates many sentences that should be interpretable or weakens the mechanism of case-value restrictions on verbs to the point that they do not reduce ambiguity at all. This section considers a generalization of the interleaved parser in which the semantic interpreter assigns a *well-formedness rating* to each constituent and thereby avoids this dilemma.

For example, assume that the verb *give* is defined by using the case-value restrictions that the THEME case is nonhuman and the TO-POSS case is a human or an organization. This information allows sentences such as:

We gave the man the money.
We gave the money to the man.

With the former, the NP immediately following the verb is of type HUMAN and is classified as the TO-POSS. With the latter, the NP immediately following the verb is nonhuman and so is classified as the THEME.

Although these restrictions seem reasonable, they can easily be violated, as in the sentence *We gave the man to the police*. To handle this sentence in the present framework, the case restriction on the THEME case would have to be revised to simply be a PHYSOBJ. But even this is too restrictive because there are contexts where nonphysical objects might fill the THEME case, as in *The water gave the plant a new lease on life*. Similar examples could be formed to nullify virtually all the case-value restrictions. If there were no case-value restrictions, however, the number of spurious readings of sentences would grow dramatically.

The solution to this dilemma is to allow the semantic interpreter to return some *rating* of semantic well-formedness rather than a simple accept or reject. The parser can then be modified to find the best rated interpretations. Thus in the usual situations the case-value restrictions eliminate many spurious readings (that are not as semantically well rated), but in the exceptional cases an interpretation can still be found. The idea is that if a case-value restriction is violated, the interpreter still returns a semantic interpretation but reflects the violation in a measure of well-formedness. One simple measure might be just to count the number of violations that occurred in an interpretation. A perfectly acceptable sentence would have a reading of 0 (no violations), whereas a sentence with a single violation would have a rating of 1, and so on. Wilks (1975) was the first to suggest this type of strategy and built one entire system with preference criteria as the organizing principle (see Article IV.F2, Vol. I). Techniques closer to those just described can be found in work dealing with "ill-formed input" such as Weischedel and Sondheimer (1983) and Fass and Wilks (1983).

Rule-by-Rule Semantic Interpretation

One of the unsatisfying characteristics of the interleaved parser involves the size of the constituents that are built before the semantic filter is called. In particular, whole NP and S structures were constructed without any semantic guidance and were verified only after the fact. This section pushes the interleaved approach to its logical conclusion and examines methods of calling the semantic interpreter each time a syntactic rule is applied. This technique is called the rule-by-rule approach because there is a pairing of syntactic and semantic rules.

To employ this approach, you have to have a valid logical form corresponding to each syntactic category. For example, many grammars have rules such as:

1. S ← NP VP

2. VP ← VERB NP

If you perform semantic interpretation whenever a rule is used, you must have for rule 2 an interpretation of the VP (built from the interpretation of the VERB and the NP), which can later be combined with an NP interpretation to produce an S interpretation. Presumably the VP analysis would look like the S analysis, except that the subject NP would be missing. A formal way to allow such forms is to use a version of the *lambda calculus*. The lambda (λ-) calculus provides a general mechanism for specifying functional expressions. For instance, if the final logical form for the sentence *The man kissed the dog* is:

```
(PAST k1 KISS [AGENT (DEF/SING m1 MAN)]
              [THEME (DEF/SING d1 DOG)])
```

then the semantic interpretation of the VP *kissed the dog* would be the function:

```
λ (x) (PAST k1 KISS [AGENT x]
                    [THEME (DEF/SING d1 DOG)])
```

In general the form of these expressions is:

```
λ (x) Px
```

which denotes a function of one variable (x), which takes an argument and produces an expression that is the result of substituting the argument for x in the expression Px. An operator Apply is defined to compute the value of the function. Thus:

```
Apply (λ (x) (PAST k1 KISS [AGENT x]),
       (DEF/SING m1 MALE-HUMAN))
```

would produce:

```
(PAST k1 KISS [AGENT (DEF/SING m1 MALE-HUMAN)]).
```

How would the VP interpretation be constructed from the VERB and NP interpretations when rule 2 is used? One way is for the lexicon entry for each transitive verb to specify a function that maps an NP interpretation into a VP interpretation. In our example, the meaning for *kissed* would be:

```
λ (o) (λ (x) (PAST k1 KISS [AGENT x] [THEME o]))
```

Consider a parser operating on this example. The grammar is as shown in Figure D–2. Each rule has a semantic interpretation formula attached that indicates how the analysis of the subconstituents are combined to form a semantic analysis of the whole. Any framework that always produces the interpretation of the constituent as a function of the interpretation of its subconstituents is called a *compositional* system. The lexicon, besides defining the syntactic properties of each word, specifies a semantic value as well. Figure D–3 shows a simple lexicon.

Consider a parse of the sentence the *man kissed the dog*. As each grammar rule in the parse is completed, its semantic value is computed using the formula. Most left-to-right parsing strategies would produce

	Syntactic Rule	Interpretation Function
(1)	S ← NP VP	Apply (VP, NP)
(2)	VP ← VERB NP	Apply (VERB, NP)
(3)	NP ← ART NOUN	Apply (λ (x) (DEF/SING * x), NOUN)

Figure D–2.   A simple grammar.

Word	Semantic Interpretation
kissed	λ (o) λ (x) (PAST * KISS [AGENT x] [THEME o])
man	MALE-HUMAN
dog	DOG

Figure D–3.   A simple lexicon.

constituents in the following order: Using rule (3), the parser would construct the constituent:

```
(NP ART the
    NOUN man)
```

The interpretation function for rule (3), namely, `Apply (λ (x) (DEF/SING) * x), NOUN)`, with the semantic value of the NOUN slot being MALE-HUMAN would produce the semantic value:

```
(DEF/SING m1 MALE-HUMAN).
```

Next is the constituent:

```
(NP ART the
    NOUN dog)
```

This is interpreted in the same way to produce the value (DEF/SING d1 DOG)). Next rule (2) applies to build a verb phrase:

```
(VP VERB kissed
    NP (DEF/SING d1 DOG)).
```

Applying the interpretation of *kissed* to the NP produces the semantic value

```
λ (x) (PAST k1 KISS [AGENT x]
                    [THEME (DEF/SING d1 DOG)])
```

The final constituent produced is:

```
(S NP (DEF/SING m1 MALE-HUMAN)
   VP λ (x) PAST k1 KISS [AGENT x]
                        [THEME (DEF/SING d1
                                DOG)])).
```

Applying the interpretation of the VP to the NP produces the final logical form:

```
(PAST k1 KISS [AGENT (DEF/SING m1 MALE-HUMAN)]
             [THEME (DEF/SING d1 DOG)]).
```

Work in this area usually draws from the work of Montague (see Dowty, et al., 1981). Computational systems include Rosenschien and Shieber (1982), Schubert and Pelletier (1982).

Many computational systems use a different technique and directly represent partial structures and use pattern matching to produce a rule-by-rule system. Hirst (1987), for example, uses a frame-based system similar in many ways to the logical form represented here. His system is compositional in the strongest sense, and besides interpreting S and NP constituents, it interprets every smaller constituent down to the word level. For example, prepositions map to slot names, and prepositional phrases are handled by a single rule: the interpretation of a PP is a slot-value pair in which the slot is the interpretation of the preposition and the value is the interpretation of the NP.

In systems based on unification grammars, the semantic interpretation can be accomplished using variables to represent the partial logical forms. For example, allowing a register **SEM** for the semantic interpretation, some rules for simple intransitive sentences in the notation introduced in Section 1 might be as follows:

```
S  ← NP V    SEM  = (TENSEᵥ ?e SEMᵥ [THEME SEMₙₚ])
             SUBJ = NP
             VERB = V
NP ← ART N   SEM  = (SEMₐᵣₜ ?o TYPEₙ)
             DET  = ART
             HEAD = N
```

If the **SEM** of *the* is DEF, the **SEM** of *cat* is FELINE, and the **SEM** of *slept* is SLEEP and **TENSE** of *slept* is PAST, then the sentence *the cat slept* would be parsed by this grammar as an S with its **SEM** set to

```
(PAST ?e SLEEP [THEME (DEF ?o CAT)])
```

by the unifications outlined earlier. Thus the semantic interpretation is built using the same mechanism that builds the syntactic structure. Systems using techniques like these include Pereira and Warren (1980), McCord (1985), and Kaplan and Bresnan (1982).

Semantically Directed Parsing Techniques

Since at the syntactic level of analysis there may be considerable ambiguity that can be resolved by semantic interpretation, researchers have done a fair amount of work to design parsers that primarily perform semantic interpretation directly on the input and use syntactic information only when necessary. Typically these systems do not construct a syntactic representation of the sentence, and thus only local syntactic information about the sentence is available to the parser.

Although the actual representation details vary, these systems all perform a case analysis of sentences directly from the input words. The grammatical and semantic information is stored in the lexicon entries for the words. In particular the lexicon contains essential information such as the different senses possible for the word, including case-frame information for verbs and adjectives, and a specification of a procedure for disambiguating the word and integrating it into larger semantic structures by combining it with other words. A good example of such a system is by Birnbaum and Selfridge (1981).

Although parsers can be built quickly in such a framework to handle some specific sets of sentences, problems arise in viewing these systems as a general model of parsing. In particular, since all the rules are indexed by individual words, there is no opportunity to capture linguistic generalizations conveniently. More importantly, these systems can use only local syntactic information since the only state they maintain consists of the current case-frame structure being specified and the current input. Thus, to disambiguate a word, you can at best inspect one word or so before it and a few words after. In practice, as these rules become more complex, they apply to fewer and fewer situations, and more equally complex rules need to be added to handle simple syntactic variants.

Recent work such as by Lytinen (1986) has aimed at remedying these deficiencies by reinstating a syntactic component that can be used to aid the interpretation in complex sentences. You can maintain syntactic context by running a syntactic parser in tandem with this interpreter. The actions of the parser, however, will be suggested by the semantic analyzer. The syntactic parser can simply return whether the syntactic operation identified by the semantic analyzer is a possible next move or not. If it isn't, the semantic interpreter attempts to find a different analysis. It is not clear, however, whether the semantic analyzer can handle complex sentences involving movement in a clean way. When the syntactic analyzer is controlling the processing, the syntactic component can be used to eliminate these complexities before the semantic analyzer is invoked. With the control scheme suggested here, the semantic analyzer itself would have to be able to handle the complexities, and only then would it have the syntactic component verify the analysis.

Discussion

Although the representations and parsing techniques differ dramatically among the preceding systems, all can be described within a reasonably uniform framework of combining the same syntactic and semantic interpretation rules in different ways. We saw systems that produced full syntactic analyses first and then interpreted them semantically, systems that interpreted each major constituent as it was built during the syntactic analysis, and systems that performed semantic analysis directly in parallel to the syntactic analysis using the rule-by-rule approach. If the semantic interpretation rules themselves are specified using mechanisms such as unification and do not contain the equivalent of variable assignment, we can be confident that the same rules should work for any one of these strategies since the order in which the rules are applied has no effect on the final result. This property will become even more important as systems using true parallelism are developed and as systems start to integrate more contextual processing.

E. MODELING CONTEXT

EXAMINATION of even simple dialog illustrates the necessity of extra-linguistic knowledge such as plans and goals for understanding language. For example, imagine the demands that would be placed on a computer system capable of taking the role of the clerk in the following dialog:

1. Passenger: The eight fifty to Milan?
2.   Clerk: Eight fifty to Milan. Gate 7.
3. Passenger: Could you tell me where that is?
4.   Clerk: Down there to the left. Second one on the left. No need to hurry though. The train is running late.

To process fragmentary or incomplete utterances such as (1), the system needs knowledge regarding the context of the utterance. For example, if the train clerk knows that persons seeking information typically are boarding a train, meeting a train, or looking for a room in the station, utterance (1) can be understood by recognizing that the speaker wants to board a train and that to do this the speaker needs to know what gate to go to. Plan analysis is also useful for understanding full utterances as well. Since the system not only knows what was said but also why, recognition of how an utterance connects with a speaker's underlying goals provides a deeper level of understanding.

Knowledge of a speaker's domain plans and goals is also useful for understanding indirect speech and providing more information than requested. Consider indirect speech. Although utterance (3) is literally a yes-no question, the clerk responded as if the passenger had asked the clerk the location of gate 7. The clerk inferred that this was the intent behind the passenger's utterance since the literal interpretation corresponded to achieving what was likely an already satisfied passenger goal (i.e., knowing if the clerk knew the location of gate 7). Furthermore, note that the clerk's reply included information irrelevant to the location of the gate, but important from the perspective of the passenger's plan.

The next section presents a simplified representation of actions and plans (for example, Fikes and Nilsson, 1971; Sacerdoti, 1977) that supports a model of reasoning typical of general-purpose problem solvers. (See Chapter XV, Vol. III and Article IV.F6, Vol. I.) The following sections then show how this framework can provide a model of the topic of simple stories and task-oriented dialog. Finally, the last section shows how to introduce speech acts into the framework and use them to model the communication process.

Plans and Goals

To be concrete, consider a simple representation for actions, plans, and goals. Assume that the world at any particular time is described by a set of propositions in the first-order predicate calculus. (See Article III.C2, Vol. I and Article XII.A-B, Vol. III.) In addition, there is a set of action-types defined by conditions that fall into the following three classes:

- *Preconditions*: A set of logical formulas that must be true before the action can successfully be executed.
- *Effects*: A set of formulas that will be true after the action has been successfully executed.
- *Body*: A set of actions that describe the decomposition of the action into subactions. Each subaction can itself either be executed or decomposed into subactions.

Intuitively, if the body of (an instantiation of) an action-type is executed in a situation where the preconditions hold, the action is said to have been executed and the effects will hold. A plan is represented as a tree of nodes representing action instances, annotated with the relevant preconditions and effects as shown in Figure E–1. The tree represents both a hierarchy of actions (i.e., subactions are below their parent action) as well as a temporal ordering indicated by reading from left to right across one level of the tree.

In particular, the TAKE-TRIP action consists of three substeps: a BUY action, a GOTO action, and a GET-ON action. The BUY action is further decomposed into substeps, specifically, GOTO and GIVE, both of which are considered basic (i.e., it is not decomposed further).

Consider a set of propositions, functions, and actions that could be used in modeling a train station. We must have predicates such as:

HAS(actor, object)—The actor possesses the object.

ON-BOARD(actor, train)—The actor is on the train.

AT(actor, object)—The actor is located next to the object.

IN(actor, city)—The actor is located in the specified city.

and functions such as:

Price(ticket)—The price of a ticket

Loc(object)—The location of an object

TAKE-TRIP(Actor, Train, Dest)
Preconditions: DESTINATION(Train, Dest)
Effect: IN(Actor, Dest)

PURCHASE(Actor, Clerk, Ticket-for(Train)))   GET-ON(Actor, TR1)
Preconditions:HAS(Actor, Price(Ticket-for (Train))) Preconditions: AT(Actor, Train)
Effects: HAS(Actor, Ticket-for(Train))   HAS(Actor, Ticket-for(Train))
                                              Effects: ON-BOARD(Actor, Train

GOTO(Actor, Train)
Effects: AT(Actor, Train)

GOTO(Actor, Clerk)   GIVE(Clerk, Actor, Ticket-for(Train))
Effects: AT(Actor, Clerk)   Preconditions: HAS(Clerk, Ticket-for(Train))
                                 Effects: HAS(Actor, Ticket-for(Train))

GIVE(A, Clerk, Price(Ticket-for(Train)))
Preconditions: HAS(Actor, Price(Ticket-for(Train)))
Effects: HAS(Clerk, Price(Ticket-for(Train)))

Figure E–1.   A plan to take a trip to Milan.

Ticket-for(train)—The ticket for a train (making the simplification that there is only one ticket for each train)

The Use of Plans to Model Topic Structure

If an agent constructs and executes plans, a crucial part of understanding another agent's actions should be to recognize the plans that motivate the actions. Plan recognition then can be viewed roughly as the inverse of the process of plan generation. Rather than start with a goal and plan a sequence of actions to achieve the goal, the system observes an executed action and uses its knowledge of other actions to construct a motivating plan and goal. That plan can be used to model the topic structure of simple stories involving activities as well as the topic structure in dialog discussing activities. The former application originates from the use of scripts and plans (Schank and Abelson, 1977;

Wilensky, 1983) in story understanding. In particular, such knowledge can be used to characterize our intuition as to why language can be coherent or incoherent as well as to help analyze difficult problems such as reference.

The reference problem concerns identifying the object to which a particular noun phrase (or other phrase) refers. The simplest form of reference is the use of proper names, in which all systems simply use a predefined table lookup to associate the name with the object in knowledge representation. Definite noun phrases (such as *the ticket*) are considerably more complicated since their interpretation depends on the context. The plan-based model provides an elegant solution to one class of such noun phrases.

As a simple example, assume the context is such that an agent JACK1 is going to take a train trip somewhere. Consider the simple story fragment:

1. Jack bought a ticket to Milan.

2. He rushed for the train.

The logical form of sentence 1 might be:

```
(PAST b1 BUY [AGENT (NAME p1 PERSON "Jack")]
            [THEME (INDEF/SING t1 TICKET
             (DESTINATION t1
                (NAME c1 CITY "Milan"))])
```

Assuming that the name table maps "Jack" to JACK1, that the indefinite noun phrase introduces a new object tic1 of type ticket, and that the word sense BUY maps to the action PURCHASE in the plan representation, the final representation of the sentence might be:

```
PURCHASE(JACK1, Clerk1, tic1)
DESTINATION(tic1, MILAN)
```

Matching this into the TAKE-TRIP plan (Fig. E–1) would find the obvious PURCHASE step, and bind the plan parameters Actor to JACK1 and Ticket-For(Train) to tic1, and derive DESTINATION(Train, MILAN). Thus the system could conclude that Jack is taking a train to Milan and expects further sentences to be relevant to this plan.

Now consider processing sentence 2. Assume its logical form is as follows:

```
(PAST r1 RUSH [AGENT (PRO p1 PERSON "he")]
              [TO-LOC (DEF/SING t1 TRAIN)]).
```

The pronoun *he* could easily be resolved to JACK1 by simple techniques based on the pronoun gender and number information. The definite NP *the train*, however, cannot be analyzed out of context—the system could not identify the referent unless only one train existed in the entire world. This is where the plan representation helps significantly. Assuming a dummy referent train2 for the moment, the final meaning of sentence 2 in the plan representation might be the action:

$$GOTO(JACK1, \ train2).$$

This can be interpreted as a continuation of the plan recognized above. There is a strong convention in simple narratives that the temporal ordering of the actions is the same as the order in which they are described. Thus the system should check for GOTO actions in the plan following the PURCHASE act. The second step of the TAKE-TRIP plan is recognized and the referent of *the train* is found to be the Train parameter in the plan (Fig. E–1). Thus, although a particular train is not identified, the sentence is fully integrated into the context and much is known about what train is being referred to (i.e., it is going to MILAN and JACK1 will be on it). Subsequent sentences in the story could be interpreted and integrated with the previous sentences in the same way.

The plan-based model becomes even more useful as we consider natural language dialog systems. Assume we want to model conversations between two actors who want to cooperate with each other. Then a dialog such as:

A: I want to buy a ticket to Milan. Here's the money.
B: OK. (Hands A the ticket)
A: Where do I go?
B: Gate 7. Better hurry though—the train is about to leave.

can be explained in much the same way as the preceding stories. For example, A's first utterance both identifies a goal to perform a PURCHASE action and indicates the execution of the second subaction of PURCHASE (recall Figure E–1). B can then use knowledge of the decomposition of A's PURCHASE action to perform the next and final subaction. Furthermore, just as in the previous example, B can use the library of actions to hypothesize that A is performing a PURCHASE action as part of the action TAKE-TRIP(A, train1, MILAN). Knowledge of the decomposition of TAKE-TRIP can then be used to capture the coherence of A's question "Where do I go?" This is because in task-oriented dialog such as the preceding one, the topic structure naturally follows the execution of the actions in the plan (Grosz, 1977). Thus B assumes that A's question is related to the next action in TAKE-TRIP, i.e., GOTO(A, train1). Finally, B can use knowledge of TAKE-TRIP to include in the reply not only the information explicitly requested, but also useful information with respect to A's overall goals. Some systems built using this type of model include Allen, (1980); Carberry, (1983); and Sidner, (1985).

Plans about Language

The preceding discussion showed how using plans to represent the topic of conversation was essential to complete understanding. Similarly, plans can be used to model the conversational goals of the participants of a dialog with further added benefits. This requires the introduction of explicit linguistic acts called *speech acts*. To see this, consider for a moment a problem in generating language. Once speech acts are introduced, they can then be reused for language understanding. Consider taking the role of agent A as A tries to buy a ticket to MILAN. Recall that the decomposition of the PURCHASE action involved three steps:

```
1. GOTO(A, CLERK);
2. GIVE(A, CLERK, Price(Ticket-for(TR1)))
   where TR1 goes to, MILAN;
3. GIVE(CLERK, A, Ticket-for(TR1)).
```

Two major problems arise when A attempts to execute this plan. The first is that A may not know what the price of a ticket to Milan is and so cannot execute step 2. The second is that since this is A's plan, there is no reason to suppose that the clerk knows about the plan; the clerk will thus probably not know to execute step 3. Both problems can only be solved by using some means of communication. Intuitively the first problem may be solved by asking the clerk how much the ticket is, and the second by asking the clerk to give A the ticket. To formalize this, some actions must be defined that correspond to linguistic actions such as "inform" and "ask." Such actions are usually called speech acts, adopting the terminology used by philosophers (for example, Searle, 1969).

Consider defining an act of asking called REQUEST. REQUEST must be defined so that it affects the goals and plans of another agent. To represent this, a new predicate WANT(agent, action) is introduced, which is true when an agent intends to perform an action. For the purposes of this chapter, we can assume this means that the agent has a plan that contains the action. To incorporate this type of knowledge into plans, a new precondition is added to every action, namely, that the actor intends to perform the action. This condition should be trivially true for one's own actions in one's own plans because having the action in the plan is equivalent to intending to perform the action. For other agents, however, this precondition may have to be explicitly achieved. Given these additions, a simple formulation of the act REQUEST is:

```
REQUEST(a, b, action)
Preconditions: none
Effects: WANT(b, action)
```

In a richer framework, the effect of REQUEST might need to be modified. In particular it might be that the hearer knows that the speaker wants the hearer to want to perform the act. This second formulation allows for the case where a request can be refused, i.e., it is up to the hearer to "decide" whether to adopt the action since the effect only changes the hearer's beliefs and not the hearer's goals. For a detailed analysis of these issues see Cohen and Perrault (1979).

The other speech act needed for our examples is the inform act, which consists of the speaker telling the hearer the value of one of the functions (e.g., Price(ticket)). To model the effect of this act, a new predicate (or modal operator) KNOW-REF(agent, function) is needed, which means that the agent knows the value of the function. Various semantics have been suggested for such an operator, but there is no space to discuss them here (see Moore, 1981; McCarthy, 1980; Haas, 1986; Konolige, 1985). Here, we will refer to KNOW-REF informally as a predicate. We again need to add additional implicit preconditions on every act, namely, that in order to execute any action with functional parameters $P_1, P_2 \ldots, P_n$, the actor must know the value of each of the parameters (e.g., KNOW-REF(A, P1), and so on). Given these additions, the action of a sincere informing can be defined as follows:

```
INFORM-REF(speaker, hearer, function)
Effects: KNOW-REF(hearer, function)
Preconditions: KNOW-REF(speaker, function)
```

As with the definition of REQUEST, more complicated definitions are needed if we need to reason about situations where the hearer doesn't automatically believe what was said. To handle these cases, the effect would have to be that the hearer believes the speaker wants the hearer to know what the value of the function is.

Consider agent A again trying to buy a ticket to MILAN. To execute step 2, A needs to achieve the implicit precondition:

```
KNOW-REF(A, Price(Ticket-for(TR1)))
```

Looking for an action that can achieve this goal, we see that an INFORM-REF act would do the trick, so A plans for the action:

```
INFORM-REF(actor, A, Price(Ticket-for(TR1)))
```

Checking the preconditions of this action, A sees that whoever fills the actor parameter should already know what the price of the ticket is. If it is known in the train domain that the clerk knows such prices, i.e.,

```
KNOW-REF(CLERK, Price(Ticket-for(TR1)))
```

then by making actor = CLERK, the precondition is satisfied. Now A only needs to satisfy the "want" precondition of the just-introduced INFORM-REF, i.e.,

```
WANT(CLERK (INFORM-REF(CLERK, A, Price(Ticket-
           for(TR1))))
```

This can be accomplished by having A request CLERK to perform the act. Thus A can accomplish step 2 by executing the new subplan:

```
2.1) REQUEST(A,CLERK,INFORM-REF (CLERK, A,
     Price(Ticket-for(TR1))))
        achieving
     WANT(CLERK, INFORM-REF(CLERK, A,
     Price(Ticket-for(TR1))))
2.2) INFORM-REF(CLERK, A, Price(Ticket-for(TR1)))
        achieving
     KNOW-REF(A, Price(Ticket-for(TR1)))
2.3) GIVE(A, CLERK, Price(Ticket-for(TR1)))
```

Similarly, A can ensure that step 3 is executed by planning another request action,

```
REQUEST(A, CLERK, GIVE(CLERK, A, Ticket-for(TR1)))
```

An example dialog reflecting these speech acts is as follows:

        A: How much is a ticket to Milan? (request (2.1))
    Clerk: Thirteen Fifty (inform (2.2))
        A: Could I have a ticket please (request for (3))

Note that the discussion to this point has said nothing about the mapping of sentences to their speech act forms. In particular, there are many cases when the system will not be able to compute speech act descriptions directly from the input. Consider the widespread use of indirect speech acts (Searle, 1975), utterances where the speaker, if taken literally, says one thing yet actually means another. For example, "Do you know the time?" is literally a yes-no question, but it is usually used as a request for the time (i.e., REQUEST to INFORM-REF the time). In some settings, where the speaker knows the time and the hearer doesn't, it can even be meant as an offer to tell the hearer the time! Thus, instead of computing a speech act from the actual sentence, we assume that the system will compute a surface speech act form encoding the literal meaning of the sentence out of context. There is not the space to go into this in detail. The interested reader should see (Perrault and Allen, 1980).

Speech Acts and Understanding

Recognizing the plan underlying an agent's speech acts will be useful for generating an appropriate response in conversations. For an example demonstrating this, consider the issue of generating helpful responses. For instance, if the CLERK observed the speech act:

    REQUEST(A, CLERK, GIVE(CLERK, A, Ticket-for(TR1)))

with

                DESTINATION(TR1, MILAN),

then he could infer from the effect of the REQUEST (i.e., that A wants the clerk to give A a ticket) that A's plan is:

                TAKE-TRIP(A, TR1, MILAN)

This would be inferred in the same way that we constructed a plan earlier. To be helpful, the clerk inspects the plan to see if he can assist A in other ways besides those that were explicitly asked. For instance, since the clerk believes that A will next perform the act GOTO(A, TR1), he believes A will need to know where TR1 is since:

                KNOW-REF(A, Location(TR1))

is an implicit precondition of GOTO(A, TR1). Thus the clerk might plan to perform the action:

                GIVE(CLERK, A, Ticket-for(TR1))

as requested, but in addition might perform:

                INFORM-REF(CLERK, A, Location(TR1))

to satisfy the precondition on the GOTO act. Of course, if the clerk had believed that A already knew where TR1 left from, the precondition would have already been satisfied and we would not have generated the additional action. Such a situation would occur in a small country rail station where all trains left from the same single track. This model thus provides some account of helpful behavior in dialogs, where the participants do not simply respond to every request with the minimum effort required.

The preceding approach shows how both linguistic and nonlinguistic actions can be incorporated into the same formalism to provide a rich theory of the events that occur during a dialog. It also shows that an appropriate response can be generated from sentence fragments where the initial speech act is not known. In the first case, the clerk responded as though A's utterance were a question about the price of a ticket to

MILAN (i.e., a REQUEST to INFORM-REF), whereas in the second case, when A also gave the clerk some money, the clerk responded as though the utterance was a request to give A a ticket.

There is a built-in assumption, however, that the clerk and passenger agree on what the actions are and what makes up a reasonable plan. Pollack (1986) has investigated ways of generalizing this model to handle conversations in which one agent's plan is faulty and/or unexecutable.

F. DISCOURSE STRUCTURE

THIS SECTION examines a model of discourse structure that allows the previously described techniques to be generalized and integrated with other processing techniques based on the structural properties of discourse. The key idea is that discourses can be broken down into *discourse segments*, each one a coherent piece of text, that can be analyzed using techniques similar to those presented already.

Until the last ten years, computational models of language dealt with multiple sentences as though the discourse had a linear structure. The plan-based understanding in the last section was a good example of this. Each new sentence was integrated into the plan at some time after the point of the previous sentence. There was no opportunity for topic change, interruption, or resumption. As another example, techniques for finding the referents of pronouns have typically been based on recency. A list was kept of all the objects mentioned so far, and the antecedent of the pronoun was taken to be the most recently mentioned object that satisfied the pronouns restrictions. For example, the pronoun *he* would check for a male individual, whereas *they* would check for a set of individuals. This technique can be extended by considering the plan inference techniques as discussed in the previous section, but it still uses a new form of linear ordering of candidates. In particular, the antecedent would be searched for in the next part of the plan following the event described in the last sentence.

In dialogs where the topic may shift and change, however, you can easily see that these techniques are inadequate. For instance, consider the following constructed dialog fragment (say, over the telephone) between some expert E and an apprentice A while E helps A fix a lawn mower:

1. E: Now attach the pull rope to the top of the engine.
2.   By the way, did you buy gasoline today?
3. A: Yes. I got some when I bought the new lawn mower wheel.
4.   I forgot to take the gas can with me, so I bought a new one.
5. E: Did it cost much?
6. A: No, and we could use another anyway to keep with the tractor.
7. E: OK, how far have you got?
8.   Did you get it attached?

The referent of *it* in sentence 8 was last mentioned seven sentences earlier. In addition, several of the objects mentioned since then would satisfy any of the selectional restrictions that would be derived for *it* from its thematic role with *attach* (for example, the wheel is something that can be attached to the lawn mower). Thus the history list mechanism would fail to find the correct referent in this situation, and no simple generalization of that mechanism that retained its linear ordering of referents can provide a satisfactory solution. Intuitively you know what is going on. Sentences 2 through 6 are a subdialog incidental to the other interaction involving attaching the pull rope. In sentence 7, E makes it clear that the original topic is being returned to. Thus in the interpretation of sentence 8, the relevant previous context consists only of the analysis of sentence 1. An account of this structure needs a notion of *discourse segments*, stretches of discourse in which the sentences are addressing the same topic, and requires a generalization of the history list structure that takes the segments into account.

A generalization of the plan inference models derived in the last section might be useful for identifying the segments. Using such techniques, the system could recognize that sentence 2 is not the expected continuation of the plan to attach the pull rope and thus represents a digression. But this could be quite expensive, and it may not be possible in some cases because there could be an obscure interpretation that would allow a sentence such as 2 to be viewed as a continuation of the action described in sentence 1 (for instance, the gasoline might be used to clean the engine before attaching the rope).

Intuitively, however, you no doubt recognize that E explicitly told A that the topic had changed in sentence 2 by using the phrase *By the way*. Such phrases, called *cue phrases* by Grosz and Sidner (1986) and *clue words* by Reichman (1985), play an important role in signaling topic changes in discourse. There must be some other form of discourse structure beyond the plan or topic reasoner to allow a clean analysis of cue phrases.

Segmentation

Although the need for segmentation is almost universally agreed upon, there is little consensus on what the segments of a particular discourse should be or how segmentation could be accomplished. One reason for this is that there is no precise definition of a segment beyond the intuition that certain sentences naturally group together. A good model of segmentation is essential to simplify the problem of understanding discourse. In particular, it should divide the problem into two major subproblems: what techniques are needed to analyze the sentences within a segment and how segments can be related to each other.

A segment of discourse can be defined as a sequence of sentences that display local coherence. In particular, a segment should have:

- A recency technique (for example, a history list) for reference analysis and handling ellipsis.
- A simple time and location progression.
- A fixed set of relevant background assumptions.

Note that this definition allows segments that include sentences not adjacent to one another in the text. For example, the dialog given earlier has a segment consisting of sentences 1, 7, and 8 that satisfies the definition. The simple history list generated from this sequence will correctly predict the referent for *it* in sentence 8, and sentences 1 and 8 are describing the same activity.

Consider some examples that show that identifying the structural properties of discourse can be very useful for determining reference and for constructing causal analyses of a text. In stories where the simple past is used to indicate a normal temporal progression for the events in the story, a shift to the past perfect signals a new segment and indicates that the new segment describes a situation prior to what was described in the last segment (Webber, 1988). Now the story could continue discussing more detail at the time in the past (thus continuing the new segment), or it could resume discussing the story where it left off before the tense shift (thus resuming the first segment). By maintaining a *now point* relative to each segment, the same plan reasoning mechanism can be used for both of these cases. For example, consider the following simple constructed story:

```
2.1  Jack and Sue went to a hardware store to
     buy a new lawn mower
2.2  since their old one had been stolen.
2.3  Sue had seen the men who took it
2.4  and had chased them down the street,
2.5  but they'd driven away in a truck.
2.6  After looking in the store, they realized
     that they couldn't afford a new one.
```

Here, clause 2.1 starts a segment that is then interrupted by a second segment (in the past perfect) that describes what happened to the old lawn mower (clauses 2.2 to 2.5). The initial segment is resumed in sentence 2.6 by resuming the simple past. Identifying this structure is crucial for determining the referent of the pronoun *they* in sentence 2.6, since the most recent candidate using a linear history list would be *the men*. Thus the segmentation is needed to provide the information necessary to eliminate the most recent (but wrong) candidate.

Another major source of information about discourse segments is the use of cue phrases to signal segment boundaries. For example, the preceding story might continue as follows:

```
2.7   By the way, Jack lost his job last month
2.8   so he's been short on cash recently.
2.9   He has been looking for a new one,
2.10  but so far hasn't had any luck.
2.11  Anyway, they finally found one that met
      their needs at a garage sale.
```

The phrase *By the way* explicitly signals that a new segment (which will be some sort of digression) is starting. Thus a new segment is signaled even though the tense remains in the simple past. The digression continues on until sentence 2.11, where another cue phrase is used. The word *Anyway* signals that the current segment is completed and the speaker will be returning to a previous segment. Without the cue phrase in clause 2.7, some direct connection would be searched for between clauses 2.7 and 2.6. If the information in the cue phrase were used, however, such a search could be avoided because a digression is explicitly signaled.

The structural organization of segments in a discourse can be revealed by considering the three main types of functions that cue phrases can signal:

- Those that signal that the clause ends a segment (OK, fine, that's all)
- Those that signal that the clause resumes a previous segment (anyway, in any event, so)
- Those that signal that the clause begins a new segment, not completing the previous segment (now, by the way, next)

Given these functions, a stack-based organization of segments, where the top segment is always the one being extended by the next sentence, is a reasonable starting model. Newly created segments are pushed onto the stack, completed segments are popped off the stack, and a segment is resumed by popping off the segments above it on the stack. Most notations for segmentation reflect this stack-based organization. For instance, the structure of a dialog can be represented as a tree, a boxing of text, or a sequence of states of the stack, but all of these (see Figure F–1) are essentially equivalent. Since computational models emphasize the process of integrating the next sentence of a discourse at a particular time, the stack-like representation is the most convenient.

The diverse area of discourse analysis has mainly consisted of work that addresses only one particular aspect such as focus of attention, plan tracking, and so on. Only recently have attempts been made to specify an overall framework into which all these pieces fit. In particular, Grosz and Sidner (1986) and Allen (1987) have the most concrete proposals, but no comprehensive discourse system has yet been built.

The Structure Represented by Boxing:

```
┌──────────────────────────────────────────────────────────────────┐
│ SEG1                                                               │
│ 2.1    Jack and Sue went to buy a new lawnmower.                   │
│        ┌──────────────────────────────────────────────────┐       │
│        │ SEG2                                             │       │
│        │ 2.2    since their old one had been stolen.       │       │
│        │ 2.3    Sue had seen the men who took it and       │       │
│        │ 2.4       had chased them down the street,         │       │
│        │ 2.5       but they'd driven away in a truck.       │       │
│        └──────────────────────────────────────────────────┘       │
│                                                                    │
│ 2.6    After looking in the store, they realized they couldn't afford a new one. │
│        ┌──────────────────────────────────────────────────┐       │
│        │ SEG3                                             │       │
│        │ 2.7    By the way, Jack lost his job last month   │       │
│        │ 2.8       so he's been short on cash recently.     │       │
│        │ 2.9    He has been looking for a new one,          │       │
│        │ 2.10      but so far hasn't had any luck.          │       │
│        └──────────────────────────────────────────────────┘       │
│                                                                    │
│ 2.11   Anyway, they finally found one at a garage sale.            │
└──────────────────────────────────────────────────────────────────┘
```

The Structure Represented as a Tree:

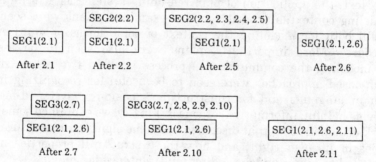

The Structure Represented as a Sequence of Stacks:

Figure F–1.   Three equivalent representations of segment structure.

G. CONCLUSION

WE CAN EXPECT great progress in the next decade toward practical conversational natural language systems. The area of syntactic processing is at an advanced stage of development, and the methods of integrating syntax and semantics are well understood. Considerable work remains to be done in defining a sufficiently general logical form notation and in dealing with extensive word sense ambiguity. In particular application areas, however, many of these problematic areas can be avoided.

This chapter first examined the recent development in syntactic theory based on the technique of graph unification. It was shown that systems built with these techniques are both theoretically better motivated, being close to recent work in formal linguistics, and also are more adaptable to experimentation with different parsing strategies. Next the chapter explored a similar approach to define the semantic structure of sentences and examine the range of possible system organizations based on different ways of combining syntactic and semantic processing.

Next, the application of plan reasoning systems as a technique for modeling contextual knowledge was examined. Plans were seen to be useful both for modeling the context of some forms of multisentence discourse. More importantly, plans were also seen to be essential for modeling the communicative process itself in two person dialogs. Plan-based approaches were seen to be useful for recognizing indirection in language and for constructing a computer system that could provide helpful, informative responses. Finally, we examined some recent work demonstrating that discourse has some significant structural properties in its own right, and how these structural properties may be exploited to aid in understanding multisentence language.

Although no comprehensive multisentence discourse system has been built to date, the groundwork has been laid for such projects in the near future. Crucial to the success of these projects will be the ability to define each part of the language understanding process in a way that separates the description of the structure from the processing to build the structures. This separation has been achieved for syntactic processing, is close for some stages of semantic interpretation, and remains to be done for contextual processing. It is this separation that will allow focused research on a particular topic area to be used in a highly integrated system where the control structure will necessarily need to be highly dynamic, using and exploiting information from syntax, semantics, and context, wherever it is best defined at a given moment, to lead the system to the appropriate interpretation.

Chapter XX

Knowledge-based Software Engineering

Michael Lowry—Kestrel Institute
Raul Duran—Stanford University

CHAPTER XX: KNOWLEDGE-BASED SOFTWARE ENGINEERING

A. OVERVIEW

SOFTWARE ENGINEERING IS the discipline of defining, designing, developing, and maintaining software systems. The current generation of *computer-aided software engineering (CASE)* tools helps to reduce the clerical overhead involved in software engineering. Since software engineering is a knowledge-intensive activity, even greater productivity gains will be achieved with intelligent computer-based tools. Artificial Intelligence (AI) is just beginning to achieve a commercial impact on software engineering through intelligent computer-based tools. The application of AI technology to software engineering is called *knowledge-based software engineering (KBSE)*. As AI research matures and knowledge-based tools are developed, the future impact will likely be significant.

Motivation for KBSE

The potential economic impact of increasing software design quality and productivity is enormous (Boehm, 1981). Software now accounts for 80% of the average total cost of a computer system. In the next decade, software engineering is projected to be a one hundred billion dollar per year industry in the United States alone. In the United States, software engineering professionals now number over one million people. Despite this large existing market, software engineering is still in its infancy and is not satisfying current needs, much less projected future needs. The potential of new computer hardware to run sophisticated software applications is not being met by current software engineering technology. Large software projects typically cost twice as much as budgeted, are delivered late or never at all, and have so many errors that the cost of eliminating the defects can exceed the cost of the design and coding combined. Furthermore, modification is so difficult that maintenance soaks up more than half of the total resources. This state of affairs is often called the "software crisis."

The origins of the software crisis lie in the difference between software technology and hardware technology. Hardware has always been limited by material and manufacturing technologies. Advances in these technologies have led to over a thousandfold price/performance gain in hardware in the last three decades, primarily by vastly increasing the number of components that can be placed on one chip. This is illustrated by the improvement from the magnetic core memories of the 1960s to

243

the 1-megabit memory chip in 1987. In contrast to hardware, software is a design problem and not a manufacturing problem. The tenfold gain in software design productivity is due to the development of higher level languages, structured methods for developing software and managing project complexity, and better educated software engineers.

The emerging technology of computer-aided software engineering (CASE) provides computer support for structured software development and project management. CASE is expected to mature in the mid 1990s. However, CASE technology does not address the basic characteristic of software engineering: Software design is a knowledge-intensive activity that begins with an informal, vague requirement of what needs to be done and results in a highly detailed formal object, namely, a software system. Currently this process is labor intensive and error prone. Moreover, the end result is devoid of the design knowledge that led to the software system. It is precisely this design knowledge that is needed to maintain and update a software system, and that can profitably be reused in developing new software systems.

What is KBSE?

The technology of software engineering has evolved significantly since the introduction of the digital computer. At first, programmers encoded knowledge into computers as strings of 0s and 1s—machine-level programming. This level of programming is far removed from the level at which humans conceive of problems and their solutions. Then the computer itself was turned to the task of raising the conceptual level of programming. Compilers were one of the first automatic programming tools developed, enabling knowledge to be encoded at the level of algebraic formulas and high-level control structures.

In the 1980s, three groups of software development tools collectively known as CASE (computer-aided software engineering) were introduced into the commercial market: code generators, analysis and design aids, and project management tools. Code generators take over routine programming tasks such as generating programs that produce reports, video display screens, and transaction processing. Code generators usually consist of program templates that are filled in interactively through a graphical user interface. Design aids provide computer support for structured and hierarchical software design. A user designs a software system as a hierarchy of modules interlinked by control and data flow. The design tool provides a convenient graphic interface and a dictionary of data structure definitions and checks overall consistency of the hierarchy of modules. Project management tools help a manager produce a plan for a software project, lay out the interdependencies between tasks, allocate resources, and then track the project under development.

Knowledge-based software engineering will probably succeed computer-aided software engineering by supplanting data-based tools with knowledge-based tools. A knowledge base is a database augmented with rules for reasoning about the data and an inference engine that applies the rules. Because of this added reasoning capability, knowledge-based tools are more powerful than data-based tools; intuitively the difference is between reasoning about the semantics of a software system versus merely reasoning about the structure of a software system. Program synthesis tools that greatly expand the capabilities of current code generators have been developed in research laboratories, and some are available commercially. Design tools are being developed that reason about the semantics of a domain and help the user develop a correct design. Current CASE design tools only help to ensure the internal consistency of the hierarchy of modules. Finally, project management tools that effectively coordinate large groups of people and understand the integration of their separate tasks will supplant current tools that only help to track the statistics and costs of a project.

Goals of KBSE

Knowledge-based software engineering introduces a fundamental change in the software lifecycle—maintenance and evolution occur by modifying the specifications and then rederiving the implementation, rather than by directly modifying the implementation. This fundamental change is reflected in the organization of this chapter into separate sections on specification acquisition and program synthesis. KBSE uses knowledge-based and other AI techniques to go beyond the capabilities of current CASE tools. The overall objective is to provide intelligent computer-based assistance for all parts of the software lifecycle. More specifically, KBSE has five goals (Green et al., 1983):

1. To formalize the artifacts of software development and the software engineering activities that produce these artifacts (Scherlis and Scott, 1983). For example, formal specification languages enable specifications to be stated precisely and unambiguously (Spivey, 1989).

2. To use knowledge representation technology to record, organize, and retrieve the knowledge behind the design decisions that result in a software system. This knowledge base would form a computer-based "corporate memory" that coordinates the efforts of the software development team and facilitates evolution and maintenance. An explicit record of design decisions and their rationale would be a considerable improvement over current debugging and maintenance methods, which essentially require reconstructing design decisions from the source code and written documentation.

3. To produce knowledge-based assistants to synthesize and validate source code from formal specifications. This will enable maintenance to be performed by altering the specification and then replaying the steps for synthesizing source code, with appropriate modifications. There is also a need for knowledge-based assistance to recover high-level specifications from source code. Many institutions are locked into existing software systems that are largely undocumented and so brittle that maintenance is extremely difficult. Computer assistance for program understanding complements the synthesis of source code from specifications.

4. To produce knowledge-based assistants to develop and validate specifications. Knowledge-based assistance for specification development will help a user resolve conflicting requirements, refine incomplete and informal requirements into precise specifications, and use domain knowledge in developing system designs. Validation methods may use the specification itself as an executable prototype or perform various types of analysis on specifications.

5. To produce knowledge-based assistants to manage large software projects. The knowledge bases will form semantic models of an entire project, including history, procedures, and policies. In the near term, existing expert system technology can be used to integrate the information of a large software project (Garg and Scacchi, 1989) and to automate non-creative aspects of project managment (Kaiser et al., 1988; Perry, 1987).

Software Development: Present and Future

Software development logically proceeds along an extended what-to-how spectrum. This ordering is the basis of the "waterfall model" (Royce, 1970) of software development, shown in Figure A–1. The waterfall metaphor suggests the development of software through separate successive phases. The U.S. Department of Defense currently requires contractors to adhere to this model of software development (designated DOD Standard 2167A). DOD spent $11 billion on new software in 1986; so several CASE tools support aspects of this model. The waterfall model works well for developing familiar types of software; however, recent studies have shown that for new types of software the waterfall model is flawed and that prototyping is needed early in software development (Boehm, 1986). Prototyping will be discussed at the end of this section; AI technology provides good tools for rapid prototyping. The waterfall model also does not effectively reuse the design knowledge gained from previous software projects for familiar types of software (Biggerstaff and Perlis, 1989). AI technology provides a foundation for recording and reusing design knowledge.

As an example of the software lifecycle we will consider the U.S.

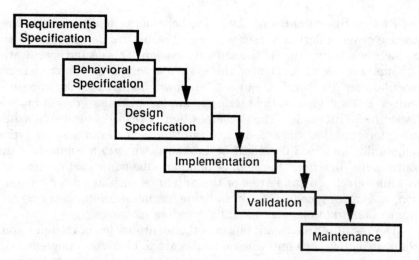

Figure A–1.   The waterfall model of software development.

space station scheduled to be built in the 1990s. Although project Mercury required 1 million lines of machine instructions and the space shuttle required 40 million lines, the space station is estimated to require 1,000 million lines of machine instructions. The reliability of the software will be crucial to the lives of the space station's inhabitants. The efficacy of tools for software design and for coordinating 4,000 personnel in 30 major companies will be a major factor in bringing the space station on line, on budget, and on time. It is unlikely that this software could be successfully developed without advances in software engineering.

Requirements and Behavioral Specifications.   The first step in the software lifecycle is to consider what needs the software will fulfill. The space station will require life support, orbital maintenance, communication, and support for activities such as scientific experiments. These needs are elaborated into an analysis of the requirements for the software. The result is a requirements specification. The second step is the behavioral specification, sometimes simply called specification, which describes the system's external behavior as well as constraints on the system's performance. This specification treats the system as a "black box," describing required characteristics of its external behavior ("what"), but not the internal structure that will generate that behavior ("how"). At present, the product of requirements and behavioral analysis is usually a written document. In the research stage are knowledge representation tools that will aid the development of conceptual models of a domain and the requirement and behavioral specifications.

Design Specification. After the behavioral analysis phase, there are one or more design phases whose end result is a design specification of the internal structure of the software system. This design specification is usually a decomposition of the system into a set of interconnected modules (module specifications)—a top-down, hierarchical decomposition with modules higher in the hierarchy implemented in terms of modules lower in the hierarchy. The decomposition is such that the submodules are interconnected via well-defined interfaces. For example, the overall communications module might be broken down into a submodule that controls the direction of antennas, another submodule that controls and monitors electrical properties of the antennas such as power consumption, and various modules for initializing communication, observing communication protocols, and encoding/decoding messages.

The result of the design phase is the identification of modules and a graph structure showing which modules are to be used in implementing other modules. Later design phases are often used to elaborate the structure of modules that were considered as black boxes in earlier design phases, in a recursive fashion. This work is usually done by a systems analyst, who again typically produces a written document. In a large project like the software for the space station, the systems analyst is likely to be a different person than the one developing the requirements specification. Consequently misunderstandings are likely to arise, perhaps due to the ambiguity of natural language. An important aspect of project management is to ensure that misunderstandings are resolved early in the software lifecycle, before they become costly to correct.

Implementation. The implementation phase turns the design into code executable in the run-time environment. This entails defining the internal mechanisms by which each module will meet its module specification, and then mapping module mechanisms and interface properties into the implementation language. Program synthesis research in AI attempts to automatically or semi-automatically generate implementation language code from module specifications. Algorithm synthesis defines the high-level control and data flow for the internal module mechanisms. The output of algorithm synthesis is typically a high-level specification of the internal mechanism, independent of the details of programming language. Transforming a high-level algorithm into target language code has been the focus of much automatic programming research.

Validation. Validation checks whether the software system satisfies the needs for which it was developed. Validation failure can result from problems due to errors in the requirements, behavioral, or design specification, miscommunications, or a poor understanding of the initial needs. Techniques for incremental validation facilitate testing software systems that have not been completely implemented, thereby detecting problems early in the lifecycle. One technique is rapid prototyping, where an inexpensive prototype is developed that is sufficient to refine ideas about the desired functionality. Rapid prototyping is particularly useful when the initial needs are not well understood. AI languages, environments, and expert system shells are useful tools for rapid prototyping. For example, communication protocols can now be rapidly prototyped using the ProSpec system developed within the REFINE software development environment (Section E6). In the future knowledge-based technology will enable aspects of validation to be done prior to prototyping. For example, the Watson system (section D7) interacts with telephone design engineers to derive specifications for new telephone features, like call-forwarding. Watson uses knowledge of the telephone domain to interactively resolve ambiguities and inconsistencies in natural language scenarios of new features.

Critical software is sometimes *verified* (mathematically proven) to be correct with respect to a formal specification. Program synthesis tools based on formal mathematics produce verifiably correct code. The orbital maintenance software would be a good candidate for formal verification since it is critical and its functionality is easy to specify mathematically.

Maintenance.   As the needs for which a software system was developed evolve, the software system is updated and maintained. Over half of current software costs are due to maintenance, including fixing bugs. Maintenance is the transformation of an existing system satisfying previous needs to a new system satisfying present needs. Maintenance is in part an incremental reiteration of the entire software lifecycle. Much of a programmer's time for maintenance is spent simply trying to understand the existing program, by reconstructing the rationale for implementation decisions. Good documentation and structured programming techniques of the last decade facilitate program understanding. In the near future, knowledge-based techniques could be used to explicitly record, index, and explain the program implementation; thereby providing interactive assistance in program understanding. Further along, success in program synthesis could enable maintenance to be done at the specification level instead of at the code level.

A difficult challenge for maintenance is older systems, written ten to twenty years ago, before the widespread acceptance of structured programming techniques. The older systems that have experienced significant enhancements resemble inner tubes that have been patched so many times that additional patches cause the system to break in new places. AI research has directly addressed automated program understanding of undocumented code (see Section B6).

Alternative Models of Software Development.   The waterfall model is appropriate where errors in the early stages of requirements analysis and design specification are unlikely, for example, in well-understood domains. The resulting implementation will probably be conceptually clear and well modularized. However, this is a risky approach since it costs 10 to 1,000 times as much to fix an error in a requirement during the implementation phase than in the requirements analysis phase. Thus early validation of requirements and specifications is crucial for controlling costs.

Another model for software development is the evolutionary approach, which is often used in AI research systems. Software development starts with a prototype and proceeds by incremental modification and maintenance of the prototype. The development of the system changes the understanding of the problem; in interactive environments, the existence of the system might even change the environment, resulting in an evolutionary process. The evolutionary approach is appropriate for poorly understood domains or problems and in highly interactive systems. The risk is that the resulting implementation will be highly convoluted and become progressively more difficult to modify. This risk is ameliorated if modification is done at the specification level rather than at the low-level language level. Very high-level languages, which are compiled using program synthesis techniques, support modification near the specification level.

The spiral model of software development, illustrated in Figure A–2 and developed by Barry Boehm (1986), encompasses both the waterfall and evolutionary models. It incorporates early validation through prototyping and also a top-down approach to software development. The idea is to start with a small set of the core requirements, and then to develop

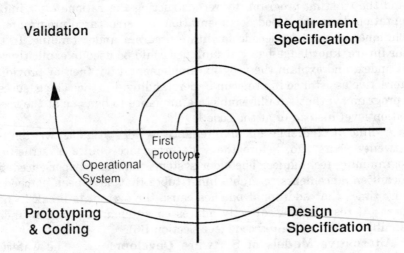

Figure A–2. The spiral model of software development.

a prototype of the key components of the system, which can be used to validate and refine the basic functionality. This is the first complete turn of the spiral. The second pass expands the set of requirements and the functionality of the system. Since relatively little effort was deployed in the first pass prototype, it can be discarded if modification would become too convoluted. Successive turns of the spiral expand the requirements and the system's functionality, until the final turns become maintenance phases. The spiral model minimizes both risk and costs by combining both the well structured management techniques of the waterfall model and the early validation techniques of the evolutionary model.

Current Status of KBSE

Since 1982 and the publication of Volume II of the *Handbook of Artificial Intelligence* (which included a chapter on automatic programming), two major trends have emerged in automatic programming research. The first is the maturation of work on program synthesis, where a high-level specification is transformed into a working program. It is now possible to buy commercial systems such as REFINE (see Section E6), in which programs are specified declaratively at the level of sets and logic. Knowledge-based compilers transform these high-level constructs to procedural control and data flow constructs. Interactive design assistants such as KIDS (see Section E3) are approaching the break-even point where even high-level algorithm development is faster when machine assisted than manual development. The use of program synthesis tools will leverage other KBSE tools.

The second trend is the broadening of automatic programming to include the entire software lifecycle: knowledge-based software engineering. In particular, specification acquisition research has progressed from program specification to system specification. Knowledge-based assistants for acquiring, validating, and maintaining specifications have been developed in research laboratories. This work is still in the basic research phase. However, the development of knowledge-based techniques is likely to radically transform the software lifecycle.

AI technology is currently being introduced to the commercial software engineering market through three channels. First, CASE vendors are enhancing the performance of their products by incorporating AI technology. For example, some CASE vendors offer expert systems to tutor and assist users of particular CASE tools. Second, expert system companies are integrating their expert system shells into conventional software engineering environments and languages. These shells are then used for rapid prototyping and also for developing "moving-target" subsystems that are subject to frequent revision. Third, several large corporations are developing in-house software engineering environments that incorporate KBSE technology.

Guide to This Chapter

This chapter is a survey of knowledge-based software engineering. Section B reviews techniques and tools for specification acquisition, the process of developing models that describe a problem, and the software system that provides its solution. In particular, specification acquisition entails both domain modeling and requirements. Domain modeling is the construction of a conceptual model of the domain in which the desired software system will be operating. Domain modeling and system specification draw heavily on AI techniques for knowledge representation. Section C reviews program synthesis, which is the technology for automating traditional programming tasks such as algorithm design and data structure selection. The objective of automatic program synthesis is to enable humans to specify what they want done to solve particular problems, without the details of how it should be done. Section D surveys current research in knowledge-based specification acquisition. Section E surveys research in knowledge-based program synthesis. Section F is a guide to further readings in knowledge-based software engineering.

B. SPECIFICATION ACQUISITION

B1. Knowledge-based Specification Acquisition

PRIOR TO the development of computer-aided software engineering (CASE) tools, a specification was just a written document. A *requirements* document describes what the customer wants; a *specification* document describes the external behavior of a software system including the user interface; and a *design* document describes the internal structure of the software system, particularly, the hierarchical decomposition of the system into modules and the external data formats used by the modules. Specification acquisition is the process of producing these three types of specifications.

Current CASE tools are relatively unsophisticated and perform without benefit of semantic models of problem domains. They include design and analysis tools that provide computer support for creating and maintaining a design specification. Using an interactive graphics editor, a system designer specifies the hierarchical decomposition of a system into modules and the control and data flow linking modules. CASE design tools perform limited syntactic consistency checks such as determining whether or not there are any dead ends in the flow of control between modules.

The goal of AI research in specification acquisition is to develop knowledge-based tools that rely on semantic models of problem domains to help users produce complete, consistent, and correct specifications. A problem domain model enables a knowledge-based tool to communicate with a user in domain-oriented terms, to perform semantic consistency checks, and to guide the user according to the constraints of the problem domain. Because software development is knowledge intensive, knowledge-based tools should ultimately be more effective and cover more of the software lifecycle than current CASE tools. The key idea is to use knowledge acquisition techniques to formulate a semantic model of a problem domain. Once a computer-based model exists for a problem domain, intelligent assistants can help users develop requirements, specifications, and designs. (Section D reviews several projects developing such intelligent assistants.) Next we discuss the major components of knowledge-based specification acquisition.

253

Domain Models

Knowledge representation formalisms provide a means of specifying a computer-based model of a real-world problem domain. Knowledge acquisition techniques provide a means of developing problem domain models. Domain models serve as knowledge bases for expert systems that assist users in specification acquisition. Furthermore, a domain model specifies some of the information needed for program synthesis. A computer-based domain model should represent the following aspects of a problem domain (Brodie et al., 1984):

1. *Static properties*, which include the objects of a domain, attributes of objects, and relationships between objects.

2. *Dynamic properties*, which include operations on objects, their properties, and the relationships between operations. The applicability of operations is constrained by the attributes of objects.

3. Integrity constraints that express the regularities of a domain.

Application domain knowledge is necessary to write good programs within a domain (Adelson, 1985) and is required for program generators (Barstow, 1984). However, this knowledge is usually poorly defined within a field and frequently takes years to gather (Curtis, 1988). Developing a computer-based domain model is a knowledge acquisition problem. It is a difficult process, currently requiring a sustained collaborative effort between domain experts and knowledge engineers. Domain modeling is known to be a bottleneck in developing intelligent assistants for specification acquisition and program synthesis (Iscoe et al., 1989). Preliminary research has already begun on developing intelligent assistants to help domain experts develop domain models for software engineering (see Ozym in Section D6).

Requirements and Specifications

A domain model provides the knowledge needed by intelligent assistants to help users develop requirements and specifications. Several approaches are being studied in research laboratories; all of them use the domain model as a communication medium between the automated assistant and the user.

1. Requirements and specification decisions can be recorded in domain terms and partially justified by reference to the domain model. This explicit record facilitates maintainance, as explained in Section B6.

2. Portions of previous requirements and specifications can be reused; the domain model provides the domain definitions that enable previous requirements to be retrieved and suitably modified.

3. Knowledge-based assistants such as KATE (see Section D5) serve as

analysts that use the domain model to find potential problems with developing requirements.

4. Knowledge-based assistants such as the Requirements Apprentice (see Section D4) can help the user generate formal and consistent specifications from initial vague, informal requirements.

In all these approaches, intelligent assistants use the domain model to provide semantic support for specification acquisition.

Design Specifications

Expert system technology can be applied to the existing CASE framework to make CASE design tools more powerful, flexible, and interactive. Whereas previous CASE tools only provided batch design checking, expert system technology facilitates the development of interactive and user-friendly assistants. Essentially these are experts in the structured design methods developed for software engineering in the 1970s. They guide a user in developing a data dictionary and a decomposition of a design into a hierarchy of modules. An example is the Exsys system, which originated at the University of Wellington. Exsys is a design tool that uses expert system techniques to guide a user in developing a system specificiation by prompting the user with a series of analytical questions. Exsys steers developers in the right direction and provides interactive checking of completeness and consistency of a design.

Knowledge-based tools use a domain model to provide support in developing a system design. Although not yet commercial products, research prototypes such as DRACO (Section D3), IDeA (Section D1), and the Explainable Expert Systems project (Section D2) support reusing existing design knowledge in the context of a new requirement. In order to reuse previous system designs a domain model must enable intelligent retrieval from a knowledge base and context-sensitive modification. This is one substantial advantage knowledge-based design tools will have over existing CASE design tools. Another advantage is their ability to explain an evolving design in domain terms. This requires both a domain model and an explicit record of the rationale for a design.

B2.   Specification Languages

SPECIFICATION LANGUAGES provide the means for describing problem domains, the required behavior of a software system, and also the overall design of a software system. The tradeoff in specification languages is between their expressive power and the degree to which they can be supported with tools such as compilers, interpreters, and theorem provers. The more expressive the language, the more difficult it is to support with automated tools; progress is measured by the expressiveness of languages that can be computer supported. For example, FORTRAN (FORmula TRANslator) was developed in the 1950s to enable users to specify programs at the level of algebraic formulas; these are then automatically translated to machine language by a compiler. When it was developed, the FORTRAN compiler was considered an automatic programming tool.

Today the frontier has progressed to logic programming languages such as PROLOG and *executable specification languages* such as REFINE (Section E6). The languages at this frontier are expressive enough to facilitate rapid specification yet limited enough so that specifications can be executed on test cases. These languages are suitable in many cases for rapid prototyping and exploratory development. However, even if a specification can be compiled, the resulting code might be so inefficient that it takes days to run even small test cases. Research on automatic algorithm synthesis, reviewed in Sections C and E, addresses the issue of transforming a high-level specification into high-level algorithms that compile into efficient code.

Specification languages differ in what can be stated concisely, what must be stated redundantly, and what is stated by default. For example, languages that directly support constraints and class hierarchies facilitate specification development because constraints economically express relationships that would otherwise need to be repeated in multiple locations. Consider the constraint that two things glued together are always in the same location. In a specification language with constraints, this can be stated once; without constraints, statements must be inserted in the specification of each operation that moves things to also update the location of any attached item.

Similarly, class hierarchies group together objects that share similar structure and similar operations. Languages with class hierarchies enable this similarity to be stated explicitly and concisely. A subclass consists of objects with additional structure; the subclass relationship defines a hierarchy. By default a subclass inherits the properties and operations of its superclass. This achieves both an economy of expression and ensures consistency since any changes to the superclass are automatically inherited by its subclasses.

AI languages are useful as specification languages because they support different ways of conceptualizing a problem and its domain. Furthermore, they are relatively close to the conceptual level at which humans conceive of problems. Next we discuss various types of AI languages and how they are used as specification languages; consult Chapter VI, in Vol. II, for more information on programming languages for AI research.

Logic Programming Languages

The key idea underlying logic programming is specification through the development of a logical description of a problem domain. When combined with an inference engine, this problem domain description can be used to directly solve problem instances. The specification is maintained in a database, and the logic programming system provides pattern matching facilities and an application-independent inference procedure. (Logic programming was discussed in Article XII.F, in Vol. III.)

A logic programming system can be viewed as a type of rule-based system or production system. All encode transformations in terms of a left- and right-hand pair of patterns. The transformations are applied by matching a left-hand pattern to a particular instance and then transforming it to the corresponding instantiation of the right-hand pattern. Though similar, these approaches have different cultural legacies: Logic programming grew out of automatic theorem proving, production systems grew out of cognitive modeling, whereas rule-based systems grew out of research on expert systems. A more substantial difference is that of formality: Logic programming languages have a formal declarative semantics that is defined independently of the operation of the inference procedure. In contrast, rule-based systems and production systems are defined only by reference to the operation of their inference procedures. It is important for a specification language to have a formal declarative semantics in order to verify the correctness of programs derived from a specification.

Object-oriented Languages

Object-oriented languages were developed because real-world entities were not adequately represented in conventional programming languages. The first object-oriented language, SIMULA, was an extension of ALGOL 60 (Dahl, 1966). This SIMUlation LAnguage was designed to provide a set of basic building blocks for programming discrete event simulation problems. SIMULA was extended by adding structuring primitives called *classes*. Objects and their classes provide a convenient way to encapsulate data and the procedures that access or change the data.

Object-oriented languages can be used as executable specification languages in which domain objects are classified in a hierarchy and in which the properties, relationships, and attributes of an object are directly associated with an object. Procedural attributes are called methods; objects inherit methods by default from classes higher in the hierarchy. This inheritance reduces the need to specify redundant information and simplifies modification since information can be entered and changed in one place. A specification formulated in an object-oriented language can be used to simulate a domain model, thereby facilitating rapid prototyping and specification validation.

System Specification Languages

System specification languages include constraints for specifying the relation between system components, and a means of specifying states and state transitions. For example, in the GIST specification language (Balzer, 1985) a system is specified in terms of its components, the attributes of components, and the relations between components. A state is described as a snapshot of the attribute values of the components of the system. A history is a sequence of states. The specification of a system in GIST denotes a set of alternative possible histories, also called *behaviors*.

GIST supports the refinement of system specifications: starting with an underconstrained, nondeterministic system specification, the user adds constraints to prune the set of behaviors. Constraints are used for several purposes, the most important is to denote the set of admissible behaviors. Constraints restrict both the admissible state transitions and the legal states. GIST has historical reference so that a description of a state can make reference to the attribute values in previous states.

The REFINE language (Section E6) also supports system specifications. In addition to GIST's capabilities, REFINE can compile a system specification to LISP. To enable compilation, REFINE's constructs for specifying nondeterministic system constraints are more limited. REFINE incorporates the styles of logic-programming, constraint-based programming, transformational technology, and object-oriented programming— all within a unified framework. The object-oriented style can be used to describe the system components and their attributes. Constraints can then be used to describe relationships among components in a legal state.

In summary, a system specification language needs constructs for denoting states, attributes of states, and transitions between states. Constraints facilitate the refinement of system specifications. For system prototyping and validation, the specification should be executable.

B3.   Specification Acquisition Methodologies

A SPECIFICATION acquisition methodology is a set of methods and guiding principles for prescribing what is to be modeled by a specification and how the specification should be developed. A methodology focuses the activities of the specification acquisition process. Here we describe several specification acquisition methods and evaluate when they are appropriate.

Conventional Approach

The conventional approach, which is epitomized by the waterfall model in Figure A–1, reduces the complexity involved in transforming the initial requirements into a software system by first concentrating on what the system should do and only then addressing how the system should accomplish its objectives. The conventional approach is suitable in well-understood domains where the problems are familiar, and realistic requirements can be specified without first testing out a prototype.

The conventional approach was developed in response to software implementation disasters of the 1960s that resulted from the lack of a clear set of fixed requirements and overall design. It leads to a rational, well-structured development of software systems in which a fixed set of requirements forms a stable base for an implementation. Its advantage is at once its disadvantage. By fixing requirements early and only allowing each phase to feedback to the preceding phase, errors in the requirements or design might not manifest themselves until the system is implemented and repair is costly or impossible. In poorly understood domains, design errors are inevitable.

Reuse

In familiar problem domains, much software has already been designed, and the designers have a good deal of experience and knowledge. One deficiency of the waterfall model is that it provides for only limited reuse of previous design efforts, mainly at the level of subroutine libraries and text editing of existing programs. For example, a growing trend in commercial data processing is to buy a generic software package (e.g., an accounting package) and then customize the programs for a particular application (e.g., customer's accounts).

For reuse to become a full-fledged methodology, it will require support from more powerful tools than simple text editors. In addition to reusing programs (Dershowitz, 1983), we would like to reuse requirements specifications, design specifications, and program derivations (Tracz, 1988). In particular, we need three kinds of knowledge-based support tools:

1. Tools for retrieving relevant previous designs.

2. Tools for determining which portions of a previous design can be directly reused and which need to be redesigned.

3. High-level editing tools for modifying a previous design based on
   semantic changes. One high-level edit command can result in many
   text level changes.

All of the systems reviewed in Section D reuse knowledge for developing requirements specifications or design specifications. However, since these are research prototypes, the knowledge bases were hand-crafted. From these prototypes we have a better understanding of the type of knowledge that needs to be recorded in order to achieve reuse. The next step is to tackle the knowledge acquisition issue: developing methods for extracting reusable design knowledge during the course of developing real systems with real users.

Experimentation and Evolution

The rapid prototyping capabilities of AI languages support an entirely new methodology for software development: exploratory programming. In unfamiliar problem domains, a client has no experience upon which to base a requirements specification. By empirically exploring the properties of some putative solutions, a client can determine what is really needed. Unfamiliar problems require programming systems that allow the requirements and design to emerge from experimentation with a program; the program is an experimental tool. A good example is AI research systems. Since intelligent activity is always poorly understood, the AI system designer invariably has to restructure and modify the system many times before it becomes proficient. Exploratory programming environments first emerged in the AI research community.

Several options follow the initial experimentation phase. The first is to branch off into the conventional approach, viewing the experimental program as a throw-away prototype (Brooks, 1982). This option is used in commercial data processing, where a limited prototype is often developed to experiment with the user interface. Consider, for example, the user interface of an airline reservation system, which displays information on video screens to ticketing agents. It is difficult to predict without experimentation exactly what information should be presented and how it should be displayed. Special commercially available screen prototyping tools simulate the "look and feel" of screen-oriented transaction systems; these tools have been quite successful.

A more radical option, suitable for domains with continuously evolving requirements, is to view the entire software development lifecycle as one of evolution and adaptive maintenance. For example, in the mid- to late-1980s, federal and state tax codes underwent major revisions every year. Thus, every year, tax preparation programs also underwent major revisions. Instead of viewing revision and evolution as necessary evils of maintaining a software system, exploratory programming methodologies make them a central feature. Since maintenance is the dominant cost of software engineering, it is likely that as exploratory programming methodologies are developed and become proficient they will supplant the conventional approach. The spiral model of software development (see Figure A–2) incorporates features of the conventional approach and the exploratory approach.

One goal of current KBSE research (Green et al., 1983) is to develop tools to support evolution at all levels of software design. Specifications can be very complex, and they often describe some part of the environment in which the system will be embedded. Often the only way to understand or develop the specification is to evolve it. The first step toward tools for specification evolution is to categorize the types of changes that are commonly made to specifications. The next step is to develop a high- level editor that can make these changes to a specification when guided by a user. This step is the current state of KBSE research (see Davis, 1984; Johnson, 1988; Balzer et al., 1983).

Specification evolution is a restricted type of reuse; the modifications are incremental. The technology developed to support specification evolution will likely support aspects of reuse. These methodologies require that validation and maintenance can be done at the specification level, which are the subjects of the next two subsections.

B4.   Specification Validation

A VALID specification describes a software system that satisfies the needs of the client. Validating a specification is necessarily an interactive process. In contrast, verifying the correctness of a program can in principle be done automatically. A program is verified by proving that it is a mathematically correct implementation of a formal specification.

In many contracted software projects, the requirements are negotiated with a client, and then the specification document is developed and presented to the client for validation. However, the real validation occurs only after the system is implemented and delivered to the client. This is an inherently risky approach since major revisions are much more expensive after the system is implemented than during the earlier phases of the software lifecycle. A client often has only a vague idea of the behavior he or she wants in a system; furthermore the ambiguity inherent in natural language can lead to misunderstandings between the requirements analyst and a client. How many analysts, designers, and programmers have not heard the dreaded words, "But this isn't what I asked for!" at the end of some software development project?

Prototyping is widely used in engineering disciplines to test a design before manufacturing. Since software is a design problem, not a manufacturing problem, software prototyping has a different purpose than hardware prototyping. The objective of software prototyping is to validate a proposed design by constructing a low-cost system that has enough functionality to test out major design decisions on examples. As we discussed in the previous section, many AI languages and environments are good for rapid prototyping because they have very high-level constructs and provide good interactive facilities.

As part of the knowledge-based specification assistant project at ISI (Johnson, 1988), research prototypes of the next generation of specification validation tools have been developed. These tools provide richer feedback than just running a prototype on test cases. The following tools perform various types of analysis on specifications written in GIST, thereby clarifying for a user the actual meaning of the specification:

1. *The symbolic evaluator*—takes a system specification and deduces properties of a generic initial state. The user is then prompted with a list of possible actions that could take place. When an action is chosen by the user, the symbolic evaluator deduces properties of the new state by propagating the description of the initial state through the specification of the operators. The symbolic evaluator has facilities for going back and forth in a history, and even for adding new assumptions to a previous state. The difference between the evaluation of test cases and symbolic evaluation is that the latter uses generic or symbolic test cases. The system's behavior at the boundary of its legal inputs is often made explicit as a result of symbolic evaluation.

2. *The paraphraser*—creates a natural language paraphrase of a GIST specification. Paraphrasing can make implicit consequences of a specification explicit. This feedback helps users see their specification from a different viewpoint and also alerts them to unintended consequences of their specification. Paraphrasing also provides automatic documentation.

3. *The static analyzer*—checks that the specification is consistent, which means that there is at least one realizable system that implements the specification. A consistent specification is free of contradictions. Users can also annotate specifications in GIST. An extension of the static analyzer, called the ontological analyzer, checks for semantic consistency between a GIST specification and user annotations.

B5. Specification Maintenance

THE MOST expensive phase of software engineering is maintaining a system after it has been placed into service. Currently maintenance accounts for over half of software engineering resources; at present maintenance is done by directly patching code. The major effort in maintenance is program understanding, which entails reconstructing the design information lost during implementation and furthermore determining that making a change to a program will not have any unintended effects. It is not unusual for a maintenance programmer to spend all day studying a program and then change only one line of code. The goal of AI research on program understanding is to recover a high-level specification from source level code (see Section B6). Maintenance includes the following activities:

1. Corrective maintenance to fix bugs and other defects.

2. Perfective maintenance to improve the quality, efficiency, and reliability of a software system.

3. Adaptive maintenance to update a system to meet changing needs.

The first two activities are partially addressed by research on program synthesis whose principle objective is technology for deriving correct and efficient code from formal specifications. If this research is successful, maintenance will be raised to the specification level since correct and efficient code can be rederived from an updated specification. Rederiving efficient code might be done by replaying the program derivation for the previous version of the specification, as discussed in Section C6. To replay a program derivation, a design record must be kept linking the steps of the derivation to their justification in the formal specification. Thus only those steps whose justification is no longer true in the updated specification need to be changed.

Adaptive maintenance is greatly facilitated if updates are made at the specification level rather than at the code level. Ultimately, with appropriate tools and with specifications sufficiently close to a conceptual understanding of a problem, the end users themselves will be able to perform adaptive maintenance. Small changes in the desired functionality of a system are reflected in small changes to the specification. However, small changes to a specification can result in large changes to the code. For example, adding an argument to an operation is a small change at the specification level, but it can require completely changing the procedure that implements the operation and furthermore all the calls to the procedure. For this reason, enabling maintenance to be done directly on specifications will result in large gains of software development productivity by decreasing the effort required for adaptive maintenance.

Specifications are designed artifacts just like programs. Successfully reiterating the design during adaptive maintenance requires understanding the previous design rationale and the ramifications of any proposed changes. For example, consider the design specification of a computer system that monitors a small switching network for a regional telephone company. A requirement for high performance would justify the design decision to assign one processor to each node in the network. A small number of processors is then justified if the network is expected to remain small. If in the future the telephone company decided to go national, the design rationale either requires purchasing additional processors or sacrificing performance by assigning one processor to multiple nodes.

A specification maintenance assistant keeps a record of specification design decisions and the justification links for design decisions. This is similar to recording the derivation history of a program. The justification links can span multiple levels; for example, a fact in a domain model might justify a requirement that in turn justifies a design decision. Then a change in the domain model—for example, a state law being repealed—would propagate down to multiple design decisions. Conversely, if a user did not like some aspect of a system's behavior, the system could be debugged by tracing up through justification links. The explainable expert systems project (Section D2) is based on this architecture. Likewise future versions of IDeA (Section D1) will be based on an explicit record of design decisions and a dependency maintenance system.

Dependency maintenance systems (DMS) (Doyle, 1979; deKleer, 1985) were first developed in the mid-1970s to facilitate automated reasoning about qualitative physics. When applied to specification maintenance, a DMS is used first to record justification links between design decisions, requirements, and domain models. The "state changes" are in response to a user updating a specification. The DMS performs the following functions in response to a state change:

- Maintains the dependencies in the face of change.
- Indicates when a dependency cannot be maintained.
- Reports when changes occur that affect dependencies.

Thus a DMS performs the dependency record keeping that enables a specification maintenance assistant to explain the rationale for a specification and the ramifications of any proposed updates.

B6. Recovering Specifications from Code

THE PREVIOUS PARTS of Section B have reviewed how specifications will
be developed, validated, and maintained in the KBSE paradigm. However, more than half of present software engineering resources are
devoted to maintaining the current stock of software, which is often
poorly documented and difficult to understand. Moreover, institutions
are frequently locked into using outdated systems that are difficult to
update. In order to make KBSE relevant to existing software, it is necessary to recover specifications from existing code. To a first approximation program synthesis rules, reviewed in Section C, are applied in
reverse to recover specifications from code.

There is a spectrum of specification recovery tasks. At one extreme,
reverse engineering seeks to recover low level specifications from code.
These specifications are usually at the level of abstract syntax or data
flow and control flow. These low level specifications can be used to
restructure programs and to translate programs into different dialects
and different languages. At the center of the spectrum, program understanding systems seek to recover information about the design of a
system from source code and other information in order to assist human
maintenance. At the other extreme, programming tutors seek to understand the intentions behind a student's bug-ridden code in order to assist
teaching software design.

Adapting existing code to new environments consumes a large fraction of current maintenance budgets. Current reverse engineering tools
apply compiler technology in reverse to derive intermediate level representations from which restructured code is derived. KBSE technology
can improve upon compiler technology for developing reverse engineering tools. First, knowledge-based technology enables the rapid construction of program transformation systems, including reverse engineering
tools (see Section E6). Second, KBSE technology enables a semantically
deeper analysis of existing code than the syntactic methods of current
compiler technology. This is illustrated by the UNPROG program understander (Hartman, 1989), which recognizes plans such as "bounded linear
search" in large, unstructured, imperative programs. The plans are
stored in a library of programming concepts. A restructuring system,
which uses UNPROG's semantic recognition capabilities, performs COBOL
restructuring with much higher quality than existing syntactic methods.

Program understanding systems recognize abstract concepts, called
plans or clichés, in the text of existing programs. Program understanding
is arbitrarily difficult, depending on the depth of the semantic analysis.
While reverse engineering systems apply a shallow but complete analysis

in order to automatically restructure code, program understanding systems apply a deeper but possibly partial analysis, usually in order to assist human maintenance of code. Program understanding systems differ in the representation they use for programs and the sources of information they use in recovering a specification. The CPU system (Letovsky, 1988) represents programs in the lambda calculus, which is a mathematical formalism for LISP. CPU applies transformational implementation rules (see Section C2) in reverse, thereby transforming parts of concrete programs into instances of clichés. CPU's output is a hierarchical description of a program from abstract clichés to the concrete program.

KBEmacs (Section E4) represents programs in the plan calculus, which is a graph grammar for describing data flow and control flow. The recognizer component of KBEmacs (Wills, 1986) applies graph matching algorithms to the graph representation of a program in order to identify instances of clichés, which are stored in a library. The recognizer uses implementation relationships between clichés to construct a hierarchical description of a program's design. Because the plan calculus is a general graph representation instead of the tree structured representation of the lambda calculus, the matching process is more expensive. However certain operations, such as recognizing clichés in source code with variable references, can be done in one step.

Both CPU and KBEmac's recognizer use only the source code for program understanding. In system maintenance, human programmers use many clues to recover the design specification, including comments, identifier names, and knowledge of the application domain. The interactive DESIRE design recovery system (Biggerstaff, 1989) uses these informal clues to assist program understanding. DESIRE's domain knowledge is stored in a distributed representation similar to a semantic network. DESIRE's first step in program understanding is to use string matching to locate instances of "linguistic idioms", like the words 'queue', 'head', or 'tail' that provide informal evidence for the use of plans. The second step is a neural network algorithm that computes the likelihood that a program plan such as QUEUE is present in the text under examination. Program understanding based on informal clues complements program understanding based on the formal analysis of source code.

Automated programming tutors such as Proust (Johnson, 1986) and Talus (Murray, 1988) try to find the clichés that best fit a possibly "buggy" student program. In order to effectively diagnose novice programming errors they need to correlate the problem specification to the student's written code. To diagnose buggy code, this process must be robust. Conceptually, Proust uses a two step process. First the problem specification is decomposed into subgoals. These subgoals are correlated with clichés in a library. The second step is to map the clichés to the actual code written by the student. Because of the size of the search space, Proust actually performs the specification decomposition and the mapping of clichés to source code in tandem. The tandem processing enables these steps to be mutually constraining and robust. In addition to knowledge of correct decompositions and mapping of clichés, Proust also has knowledge of buggy decompositions and buggy cliché realizations. Proust was tested on 206 different student programs for the same problem specification. Each program was the first syntactically correct program the student wrote for the programming exercise, so there were still many semantic bugs. Proust was able to completely analyze 79% of the student programs, and of these it's analysis was correct 95% of the time.

C. PROGRAM SYNTHESIS

THE GOAL of program synthesis research is to develop tools that synthesize efficient programs from program specifications. A program specification is a description of the preconditions that hold before a program is entered and the postconditions that hold after a program terminates. Most work on program synthesis has focused on deriving applicative programs, which produce an output given an input and have no side effects. A program specification for an applicative program consists of an input predicate that defines the legal inputs and an input-output relation that defines the legal outputs for each legal input. The input predicate is the precondition and the input-output relation is the postcondition. Program synthesis techniques for imperative programs, which are applied for their side effects, are less well developed than those for applicative programs. Research has just begun on techniques for specifying and synthesizing programs that do not terminate, such as operating systems, and also programs that execute on parallel-processing hardware. This section only overviews techniques for synthesizing applicative programs.

The central idea behind many approaches to program synthesis is to incrementally refine a high-level specification until an implementation as a procedural program is derived. The two major approaches to this incremental refinement are the transformational approach and the constructive theorem-proving approach. In both, a program is usually derived by repeatedly applying rules, transformation rules in the first case and logical inference rules in the second case. At each step of a derivation, many rules could apply. If at each step just two could be applied, there are eight three-step possibilities, one thousand ten-step possibilities, and 2^{100} hundred-step possibilities. As the number of steps increases the total possibilities grow exponentially; computer scientists call this growth *combinatorial explosion*. It is beyond the capabilities of any present day computer to search through 2^{100} possibilities in even a thousand years. Faster computers are not the answer to combinatorial explosion. Because of combinatorial explosion, the major issue in both approaches to program synthesis is guiding the search through the large number of possibilities.

The first approach to program synthesis is to apply transformations that incrementally modify a high-level specification until a procedural program is derived. This approach is often used with wide-spectrum languages that encompass within one language the spectrum from high-level specification constructs to lower level procedural constructs. In a wide-spectrum language, a transformation can be written as a rule consisting of two patterns. The first pattern matches against parts of a specification; the second pattern shows how these parts are then replaced and modified.

The second approach to program synthesis is to apply rules of logical inference to prove from a high-level specification and domain axioms that for any legal input there exists a legal output. A constructive proof not only shows existence of a legal output but moreover produces a term that shows how to compute a legal output from a legal input. This term consists of nested functions applied to the input. If each function is a primitive in the target programming language, then this term is an applicative program.

This section first gives a historical overview, starting with the roots of program synthesis in automatic theorem proving and concluding with an outlook on how program synthesis technology may be used in future software engineering environments. The next two subsections present an overview of the transformational approach and then the theorem proving approach. The last five subsections discuss the issue of guiding the search through the large number of possible implementations. The first topic is basic sets of rules adequate just to generate the possible implementations. However, program derivations using basic rule sets are far too long and tedious to be suitable even for manual guidance through the search space, much less feasible for automatic guidance. Therefore, the second topic is large-grained rules that are more suitable to program synthesis since derivations require only a fraction of the steps required for derivations with minimal rules. The third topic discusses how program derivations can be recorded and partially reused through analogy to derive new programs. The fourth topic is how traditional AI search techniques like best-first search can be used to automate or partially automate program derivations. The last subsection shows how knowledge about program derivations can itself be encoded as tactics to automate program derivations.

C1.   Historical Perspective

ROBERT FLOYD began the study of program synthesis by showing how a verifiably correct program could be constructively derived from a formal specification (Floyd, 1967). Since then, the study of algorithm derivations has provided fresh avenues of research to the more established fields of verification theory and complexity analysis. Soon after Floyd's paper, the AI community began research on automatically deriving programs from specifications. If successful, a human could specify what should be done; an automatic programming system would then determine how to do it and derive a correct program.

An early effort was Cordell Green's application of resolution theorem proving first to problems in planning (straight line programs) and then to conditional programs and recursive programs (Green, 1969). Resolution theorem proving fell out of favor in the early 1970s because of seemingly intractable problems with the combinatorial explosion of the search space. Then, in 1975, a group at the University of Marseille in France developed a restricted and efficient application of resolution called PROLOG (Roussel, 1975). PROLOG and other types of logic programming have had a significant impact on both AI and software engineering research. One use of logic programming is to rapidly prototype a software design before committing resources to a full-scale system. A related use is as an executable specification language, which enables a user to interactively develop a precise specification of a system before developing production code.

The theorem proving and transformational approaches to program synthesis have continued to develop, as discussed in subsequent subsections. In its purest form, the transformational approach is inference using the rules of equational logic. Thus the approaches are closely related; both use rules of logical inference to derive programs from formal specifications. In fact, Manna and Waldinger's deductive tableau, described in Section C4, uses many of the same inference rules developed in their earlier transformational system called Dedalus (see Article X.D5 in Vol.II)

Transformational development encompasses a wide range of approaches from equational logic to expert system approaches. Early work in transformational development includes work at Edinburgh (Burstall and Darlington, 1977), the CIP group in Munich (Section E1), and Cordell Green's group at Stanford University and later Kestrel (see Article X.D1 in Vol. II). In the *transformational implementation* approach, an abstract construct is substituted with a more concrete but equivalent construct. Transformational implementation is easier to control than undirected theorem proving since the search space is directional from abstract to concrete. The inverse of transformational implementation is *transformational analysis* (Letovksy, 1987; 1988). Transformational analysis starts with the concrete source code and incrementally applies transformation rules in reverse to derive an abstract specification of the original source code. Transformational analysis is facilitated by wide-spectrum languages that can represent a program at many levels of abstraction.

To date, the field of program synthesis has had only a minor impact on commercial software development. Although it is now possible to buy commercial products that transform high-level specifications into programs, they typically limit the search space by considering only one predefined alternative, so the resulting code is not efficient enough for commercial systems. These products are currently used commercially for rapid prototyping and for generating efficient code in restricted domains. To date, AI has contributed to software engineering through its programming languages and environments. Examples include logic programming languages such as PROLOG, object-oriented languages such as Smalltalk, and development environments such as the Symbolics Lisp machine environment. Expert system shells are also used as development environments and rapid prototyping systems.

In the future, program synthesis may have significant impact. For example, program synthesis technology can be applied to MIS (management information systems) in two ways. It can help to generate nonstereotyped code, which will become the next bottleneck after the widespread adoption of current fourth-generation languages (these can generate 70% to 90% of the highly stereotyped code). Second, code generators based on AI technology such as transformation rules are much more flexible and modular than current code generators, permitting customization for particular applications.

Whereas the algorithms used in MIS applications are highly stereotyped, those used in engineering applications are much more varied and difficult. This second major class of commercial software encompasses applications from controlling a microwave oven to controlling the future U.S. space station. Technically the software is embedded in mechanical and electrical systems and driven by real-time inputs requiring real-time outputs. Because of the complexity and variety of these algorithms, general-purpose automatic code generators do not yet exist for engineering applications.

Program synthesis research can be applied to these applications in two ways. First, we can construct special-purpose code generators for restricted domains and restricted classes of algorithms because in restricted domains it is feasible to build in the knowledge of domain concepts and domain problem solving techniques. Unfortunately there are too many domains and too few experts to rely on special-purpose code generators; and, at the boundaries of their knowledge, special-purpose code generators are limited and brittle (which is also true of conventional expert systems). Second, program synthesis techniques can be used to provide general purpose interactive program development environments, such as KIDS (Section E3).

C2.   Transformational Approach

TRANSFORMATIONAL PROGRAMMING is a method of incremental program construction by successive modifications by transformation rules. Usually the input to a transformation system is a high-level formal specification, though transformational programming can also be applied to the task of refining an incomplete, informal set of requirements into a complete, formal specification. In transformational implementation, transformations refine a high-level algorithm into a target language program by incrementally transforming high-level control and data structures into low-level target language constructs. Optimization transformations may also be applied. The transformational approach can be applied to many phases of software development, including the refinement of an incomplete specification, the development of a high-level algorithm, the implementation in target language constructs, and program optimization.

The basic unit of knowledge in the transformational approach is a transformation rule, which is a partial mapping from programs to programs. Transformation rules are either procedures or production rules that transform a pattern matching part of a program into another pattern. Global transformations such as transformations based on data flow analysis and consistency checks are usually encoded as procedures. Global transformations transform the whole program into another program; in contrast, local transformations only transform part of a program. Local transformations are usually encoded as conditional production rules whose left-hand sides match part of a program and whose right-hand sides give a schematic pattern for the result. These production rules can express domain knowledge, algebraic properties, and knowledge of how to implement higher level program constructs in terms of lower level constructs. The application of a transformation rule can be conditional, thereby requiring some deductive capability to determine when a rule can be used:

> If Condition
> then Left-Hand-Pattern → Right-Hand-Pattern

The most important semantic property of a transformation rule is whether or not it preserves correctness. The application of correctness preserving transformations to a formal specification ensures the correctness of the resulting program. The strongest correctness property is strict equivalence, which means that the transformed program behaves exactly the same as the original specification on all inputs. A weaker condition is descendence, which ensures correctness only for inputs satisfying the input predicate.

Sets of transformation rules can be broadly classified as either *minimal generating sets* or *catalogs of rules*. A minimal generating set that is language independent will be described in Section C4, and the catalog approach will be discussed in Section C5. Catalogs of rules, often called the *knowledge-based approach* or *expert systems approach*, can in principle be constructed by composing basic transformation rules. In practice, catalogs of transformation rules are usually constructed with the same development process as applied to expert systems.

The application of transformation rules can be manually guided, semi-automatic, or fully automatic. The full manual guidance of a set of basic transformation rules is far too tedious and detailed to be a viable method of program development. It is almost always easier to develop the program by hand. An exception is when the correctness of the resulting program is of utmost importance, in which case manual guidance of minimal but verifiably correct transformation rules is an alternative to developing a program by hand and then verifying it interactively with a program verification system.

Semi-automatic control of transformation rules provides substantial assistance to human guidance, suppressing detail but leaving difficult choices to human control. Using large-grained transformation rules is one method of suppressing detail. Another approach is to have the programmer provide high-level strategic advice, perhaps in the form of schematized intermediate steps in the derivation, while letting the system fill in the details of the derivation. Another approach toward semi-automatic control is the use of directives in transformational implementation. For example, the human provides both a high-level algorithm using set-theoretic constructs and indicates how the sets should be implemented—as hash tables, lists, bitmaps, and so on. The system fills in the implementation details.

Full automatic guidance in a commercial strength system is currently feasible when the choices are relatively few and can be determined with little search. Examples include the REFINE and SETL compilers, both of which use predefined implementations of high-level data structures such as sets. In the research stage are systems that automate the application of transformation rules when significant choices are made. One approach is the use of strategies and tactics described in Section C7. Full automation of search control will be approached asymptotically; robust commercial systems will either be semi-automatic or will limit the scope of possibilities. However, if a record is kept of the choices made in deriving a program from a specification, it should be possible to "replay" the derivation for a similar specification. This would be particularly useful when maintaining a slowly evolving system, enabling the changes to be made at the level of specifications while reusing the work done on the derivations.

C3.   Deductive Approach

ANOTHER TECHNIQUE for program synthesis is automatic theorem proving. First, the specification is transformed into a theorem to be proved. Then, a constructive proof that the theorem is true is generated. The basic idea is that each step of a constructive proof corresponds to a step in a computation (Constable, 1971). For example, case analysis in a constructive proof corresponds to a conditional statement in a program. Finally, a program is extracted from the constructive proof.

Suppose that a desired program is specified as taking an input x and producing an output y. Furthermore, suppose the specification states that the input x satisfies a precondition $P(x)$ when the program is entered and that when the program terminates the output y satisfies the postcondition $R(x,y)$, relating the input to the output. For example the specification for a sorting program has the precondition that the input is a list of elements and the output is a sorted list with the same elements as the input but in ascending order. The specification of the precondition and postcondition of the desired program can be turned into a theorem of the following form:

$$\forall x \, \exists y \, [P(x) => R(x,y)]$$

This theorem states that for every input satisfying the precondition there is a suitable output satisfying the postcondition. This theorem and the domain axioms are then given to a constructive theorem prover. The theorem prover either proves that the theorem is false, in which case there is no feasible program, or it proves that the theorem is true by constructing the definition of a function f that makes the following theorem true:

$$\forall x \, [P(x) => R(x,f(x))]$$

The definition of the function f is a program satisfying the specification.

By reformulating program synthesis as an application of theorem proving, automatic programming can be cast in a formal, precise framework. Automatic theorem proving dates back to 1963 when Robinson (Robinson, 1965) showed that a single easily programmed rule of inference, resolution, is a complete inference method for proofs by contradiction. In the late sixties, Cordell Green (Green, 1969) and Richard Waldinger (Waldinger, 1969) showed how programs could be synthesized as a side effect of doing resolution proofs.

Theoretically, given enough computational power, the reformulation of program synthesis as automatic theorem proving solves the automatic programming problem. However, there are two practical problems with this approach. First, the brute force application of the resolution rule leads to a combinatorial explosion in the computational resources required to synthesize moderately long programs. Roughly, each additional instruction in a synthesized program doubles the amount of computational resources required for the formal derivation. This means that a computer the size of the universe, based on the fastest and smallest conceivable quantum devices, would still require more than a billion years to synthesize a medium-sized program such as a word processor. Clearly, practical success requires applying automatic theorem proving in an intelligent manner to avoid this combinatorial explosion.

The second practical problem is inherent to any formal approach to program synthesis: The creation of a formal domain theory and a formal specification is a difficult task for humans. Practical success necessitates reusing domain models so that the cost of creating them can be amortized over many different programs. Furthermore, mechanical assistance in developing formal specifications is needed. Sections B and D discuss research work that address these issues.

C4. Basic Rules

THE OBJECTIVE of defining a minimal set of basic rules is to obtain a small set that is logically sufficient for deriving programs. If more complex rules can always be generated as combinations of the basic rules, the set is complete. This provides a way for proving that a set of rules is correct. First, find a minimal set and prove that each rule is correct. The other rules are then correct if they can be defined as combinations of the correct minimal rules. This subsection defines a basic set of transformation rules and a basic set of inference rules.

Transformation Rules: Substitution of Equals for Equals

The mathematical basis for transformation rules is the substitution of equals for equals. By iteratively replacing parts of a specification with equivalent forms, an efficient program can be derived that is functionally equivalent to the original specification. The cleanest example of a minimal set of transformation rules founded on the substitution principle are the fold/unfold transformations developed by Burstall and Darlington (1977). These transformations have been incorporated into a program development environment at Imperial College in London under the Flagship project (Darlington et al., 1989). Flagship is sponsored by Alvey, which is a British funding program charged with developing next generation computers and computing environments.

A prototype transformation system was developed earlier that transformed program specifications written in NPL into efficient programs (Darlington, 1981). The NPL language itself is based on the principle of substitution of equals for equals, also known as *equational logic*. As an example, consider the NPL specification of the factorial function:

```
fact(0) => 1
fact(N+1) => N+1 * fact(N)
```

Instead of using just ordinary equalities (=) the NPL language uses oriented equalities (=>) called *rewrite rules,* which are applied left to right. This means that NPL is a logic programming language (see Section B3) since the rewrite rules are applied like production rules. A specification in the NPL language consists of a set of rewrite rules that define the value of a function on various inputs. For example, the first equation defines the value of factorial on the input 0, whereas the second equation defines the value of factorial on all the positive integers. This specification of the factorial function is executable, which means that by repeatedly applying the rewrite rules an expression such as fact(0+1+1) is reduced to its value. An expression is reduced by repeatedly matching parts of the expression against the left-hand side of rewrite rules and then substituting the corresponding right-hand side. For fact(0+1+1) the reduction proceeds as follows:

```
fact(0+1+1) ->
(0+1+1)*fact(0+1) ->
(0+1+1)*(0+1)*fact(0) ->
(0+1+1)*(0+1)*1 ->
(1+1)*(0+1)*1 ->
(1+1)*1*1 ->
(1+1)*1 ->
(1+1)
```

The reduction illustrates rewrite rules defining fact, as well as simple algebraic laws. One of the strengths of equational logic is that it provides a uniform framework for specifying both algebraic laws defining the regularities of a domain and also recursive definitions of functions for which efficient programs are desired.

The unfold transformation is similar to reduction except that, instead of rewriting an expression, unfold rewrites rewrite rules! The unfold transformation takes a rewrite rule and unfolds the right-hand side by applying other rewrite rules, thereby deriving a new rewrite rule. Consider the following example of developing an efficient program for the double append function. The first equation defines the append function when its first argument is the empty list nil, and the second equation defines the append function when its first argument is a nonempty list, that is, a list formed by prefixing an element X1 onto the front of a list X (the cons function).

```
append(nil,X) => X
append(cons(X1,X),Y) => cons(X1,append(X,Y))
dblappend(X,Y,Z) => append(append(X,Y),Z)
```

The third equation defines the double append function as two applications of the append function. However, as specified the double append function is inefficient since the list append(X,Y) is computed as an unnecessary intermediate result. Applying fold/unfold transforms the inefficient double append specification into a version optimized for execution. First, the definition of double append is instantiated to the two different cases for the first argument, nil and cons. Second, these instantiations are unfolded by applying rewrite rules. The result of an unfold transformation is a new rewrite rule:

```
dblappend(nil,Y,Z) ->
  append(append(nil,Y),Z) -> append(Y,Z)
New rule:dblappend(nil,Y,Z) => append(Y,Z)
dblappend(cons(X1,X),Y,Z) ->
  append(append(cons(X1,X),Y),Z) ->
  append(cons(X1,append(X,Y)),Z) ->
  cons(X1,append(append(X,Y),Z))
New rule:dblappend(cons(X1,X),Y,Z) =>
        cons(X1,append(append(X,Y),Z))
```

Third, the fold transformation takes the right-hand side of the second derived rewrite rule and folds it back into an instance of double append. The result is an optimized version of the double append rewrite rule that does not compute the unnecessary intermediate list append(X,Y):

```
cons(X1,append(append(X,Y),Z)) ->
cons(X1,dblappend(X,Y,Z))
New rule:dblappend(cons(X1,X),Y,Z) =>
        cons(X1,dblappend(X,Y,Z))
```

The fold transformation folds a definition back into itself. It is the inverse of the unfold transformation since it applies the rewrite rules in the opposite direction. Both fold and unfold transformations are based on the principle of substitution of equals for equals, which is the basis for equational logic. Fold/unfold together with instantiation are a complete set of transformations, which means that from a set of oriented equations any valid rewrite rule can be derived from this minimal set of transformations. The reason they are complete is because equational logic is complete; fold/unfold account for the two directions in which oriented equations can be applied.

Fold/unfold transformations use rewrite rules to transform rewrite rules. These transformations can also be applied to transform languages that are not based on equational logic or rewrite rules. In this case, there is a distinction between the language constructs and the rewrite rules used to transform language constructs. By convention, these rewrite rules are themselves called *transformation rules* and are applied left to right.

As implemented in the Flagship programming environment, the fold/ unfold transformations are applied by meta-programs called scripts (Darlington and Pull, 1987). The use of meta-programs and tactics for applying rules will be discussed in later subsections.

The Nonclausal Resolution Rule

The clausal resolution rule developed by Robinson (1965) is a complete inference rule for proofs by contradiction. If a theorem logically follows from a set of axioms, there is a proof using resolution that the negation of the theorem is inconsistent with the set of axioms. The clausal resolution rule and its use in AI is explained in many introductory text books, including (Genesereth and Nilsson, 1987). Early approaches to automatic program synthesis such as (Green, 1969) and (Waldinger, 1969) used clausal resolution. However, the clausal resolution rule has several disadvantages for program synthesis. One disadvantage is that it leads to long proofs for even simple programming constructs such as conditional statements. A second disadvantage is that to apply clausal resolution both domain axioms and specifications need to be converted into a special syntactic form called *conjunctive normal form*. This conversion can greatly increase the number of axioms and also obscure the meaning of axioms. For example, the sentence "All humans are mortal" is converted into the sentence "Not human or mortal". A third disadvantage is the difficulty of representing mathematical induction with clausal resolution, which impedes the synthesis of iterative and recursive programs. Because of these and other disadvantages, clausal resolution was abandoned as a viable method for automatic program synthesis in the 1970s.

To make resolution theorem proving suitable for program synthesis, Manna and Waldinger (1980) developed the nonclausal resolution rule. Like clausal resolution, this too is a complete inference rule for proofs by contradiction. Hence it is also a minimal rule that can generate all possible programs. However, nonclausal resolution applies directly to axioms and specifications without conversion to a special normal form, thereby making proofs shorter and easier to follow. Manna and Waldinger also developed a formalism called the *deductive tableau* that incorporates nonclausal resolution, transformation rules, and structural induction. Nonclausal resolution directly synthesizes conditional statements in a developing program, as will be shown here. Structural induction is used to synthesize recursive programs. The deductive tableau formalism has the power of Manna and Waldinger's earlier transformation-based system called Dedalus (see Article X.D5, in Vol. II) in a simple, uniform structure. This formalism also addresses many of the shortcomings of clausal resolution when applied to program synthesis. However, the deductive tableau formalism by itself does not solve the combinatorial explosion inherent in automatic theorem proving.

A deductive tableau consists of rows with separate columns for assertions, goals, and outputs. The specification for an applicative program with input variable x, output variable y, precondition $P(x)$ and postcondition $R(x,y)$ would be represented as follows:

Assertions	Goals	Outputs
$P(x)$	$R(x,y)$	y

A derivation proceeds by adding new rows through rules of logical inference. As part of these rules, variables such as y are unified with terms such as $f(x)$. Unification is a bidirectional matching procedure that given two terms with variables finds substitutions for the variables that makes the two terms equal. Through unification the output column is transformed from an output variable in the specification row into terms denoting program fragments in new added rows. A derivation succeeds if a row with the goal true is derived and whose output column is a term consisting entirely of primitives from the target programming language; this term is the desired program.

Consider the following derivation of a min2 program that takes two inputs u and v, returning as output y the lesser of the two inputs. The first row is the specification, the second and third rows are intermediate rows, and the fourth row is derived through nonclausal resolution from the second and third rows. The final row is the result of applying a simplification transformation to the goal of the fourth row. This simplified goal is true so the output column of the final row is the desired min2 program:

Assertions	Goals	Outputs
1.	`min2(<u,v>,y)`	`y`
2.	`u<v`	`u`
3.	`not(u<v)`	`v`
4.	`TRUE And not(FALSE)`	`if u<v then u else v`
5.	`TRUE`	`if u<v then u else v`

Nonclausal resolution takes two rows (2 and 3) that have a common subexpression (the expression `u<v`) and then generates a new row (4) that joins the two rows together and substitutes `TRUE` for the common subexpression in one row and `FALSE` for the common subexpression in the other row. Two goals are joined together `And`. Thus to derive row 4 from rows 2 and 3, nonclausal resolution takes the following steps:

1. It finds a common subexpression, which is `u<v`.

2. It substitutes `TRUE` for `u<v` in row 2, yielding `TRUE`.

3. It substitutes `FALSE` for `u<v` in row 3, yielding `not(FALSE)`.

4. It joins the two together with `And`, yielding `TRUE And not (FALSE)`.

5. It joins the output columns of row 2 and 3 together with a conditional expression, yielding `if u<v then u else v`. This is the final conditional program for `min2`.

Consider the following general schema for joining two goals. The common subexpression, denoted `P`, must have a boolean type. This means that the common subexpression can have one of two possible values: `True` or `False`. The conditional expression has `P` as the test and the two outputs as the separate branches of the conditional expression.

Assertions	Goals	Outputs
1.	`F[P]`	`t1`
2.	`G[P]`	`t2`
3.	`F[True] And G[False]`	`if P then t1 else t2`

The justification for the nonclausal resolution rule can be found in Manna and Waldinger (1980), as well as an extension of this rule to the general case when the common subexpressions are not identical, but they can be matched together through unification.

In summary, this subsection has described a minimal set of transformation rules and a minimal inference rule, both of which are logically adequate for synthesizing programs. In principle, these rules enable a sufficiently powerful computer to mechanically synthesize programs from formal specifications. However, in practice, the brute force application of these rules results in a combinatorial explosion of possibilities. The key is to apply these rules intelligently, through some combination of manual guidance and/or automatic guidance. Although automatic guidance is not yet feasible, research in combined manual/automatic guidance is approaching the break-even point, where use of computer-assisted program synthesis is more efficient than complete manual derivation of programs. The next subsections overview some of this research.

C5.   Large-grained Rules

IN THE LAST subsection we discussed how a small set of basic rules could be used to derive programs from specifications. However, because these rules take very small steps, the derivations are very long, detailed, and unnatural. This is a severe disadvantage for manually guided or semi-automatic program synthesis systems because a human will become mired in the level of detail. Large-grained rules result in derivations that are shorter, more natural, and are easier to understand. It is also easier to develop automatic program synthesis systems that guide the application of large-grained rules rather than small-grained rules.

There are several approaches to developing large-grained rules. The first is to write meta-programs or scripts in a language whose primitives are minimal rules and whose programs are larger grained rules. Most interactive tools like text editors or spreadsheet programs have a scripting language whose constructions denote various ways of composing primitives together. For example, one meta-program is to iteratively apply unfold transformations until a fold transformation can be applied; this meta-program would transform the double append function described in Section C4. The larger grained rules defined by meta-programs are suitable for manual interactive application. This is the approach being taken by the Flagship project.

A second approach to developing a catalog is to represent the knowledge of human programmers as large-grained rules (Barstow, 1979). This knowledge engineering approach uses the knowledge acquisition methods of expert system development to construct rules corresponding to human expertise. Barstow's PECOS program (see Article X.D4, in Vol. II) used a catalog of these rules for transformational implementation, which transforms abstract algorithms into implementations as concrete programs. An example is the following English paraphrase of a PECOS transformation rule: "The intersection of two sets may be implemented by enumerating the objects in one and collecting those that are members of the other."

A third approach is to develop procedures that directly transform parts of a specification or do some portion of a proof. An example is Manna and Waldinger's use of theory resolution to define new inference rules. Theory resolution is a general method for interfacing inference procedures to the deductive tableau formalism (Stickel, 1983). Suppose we have a procedure for solving sets of linear inequalities; theory resolution then allows us to add this procedure as a new inference rule to the deductive tableau formalism. Let `H[P,Q]` be a valid consequence of a theory that is computed by our new inference procedure. Then given the following rows in a deductive tableau:

Assertions	Goals	Outputs
1.	`F[P]`	`t1`
2.	`G[Q]`	`t2`

we add the following row through theory resolution:

3.	`F[true] And G[true]`	`if P then t1 else t2`
	`And ¬H[false,false]`	

Normal resolution is a special case of theory resolution, so we can view the deductive tableau formalism as providing a common interface and data structure for a catalog of inference procedures.

We have discussed three approaches to developing a catalog of large-grained rules. The unguided application of a catalog of rules results in combinatorial explosion. Although the larger grained rules result in shorter derivations than minimal rules, there are many more large-grained rules, so the possibilities multiply faster. However, the large-grained rules are suitable for manual guidance since they abstract from tedious detail, and if well chosen, they appear natural to a human. The next three subsections discuss complementary approaches to automatically guide the application of a catalog of rules.

C6.   Reusing Derivations

BARRY BOEHM, a noted expert on the economics of software engineering, exhorts us to write less code; instead, we should reuse code developed in previous efforts. However, with the exception of subroutine libraries of well-defined mathematical functions there is relatively little code that can be reused without considerable reworking. The problem is that programs written in concrete programming languages are the result of transforming abstract specifications into efficient code. As a result of this transformation, constructs that are conceptually independent at the specification level become distributed throughout a concrete implementation and intertwined (Chetam, 1984). This makes reuse difficult at the code level because small changes in the desired functionality of a program or run-time environment require many changes to the concrete program.

Object-oriented languages and ADA were developed with the intention of localizing small conceptual changes to limited areas of a program. Although they do succeed in localizing some changes, transformational programming offers the potential for a more general solution. In transformational programming, the user first develops a high-level specification and then manually or semi-automatically applies a sequence of transformation rules to derive a concrete program. When the user later makes a small change to the specification, the sequence of transformations is replayed, only being modified for those parts of the specification that were modified. Reuse at the level of specifications and transformational derivations is more flexible than reuse at the level of concrete programs because the relationship between the specification and the program is made explicit in the derivation history.

There are several contexts in which reusing derivations is feasible and profitable. The first is adaptive maintenance (see Section B5), where the specification changes but most of the derivation decisions still apply. The second is experimentation and evolution (see Section B3), which is a software development methodology that views the entire software lifecycle as one of adaptive maintenance. In both of these contexts, the original derivation sequence is replayed with modifications. A third context is in developing an implementation for a new specification. Often the derivation is similar to some previous derivation, but finding the appropriate previous derivation can be difficult. Derivational analogy (Carbonell, 1986) is a method for retrieving a previous derivation from a library and determining the correspondence that maps the previous derivation steps onto a derivation for the new specification.

To reuse a derivation, it must first be recorded and its hierarchical structure made explicit. Although a derivation is realized as a sequence of transformation steps, the internal structure of a derivation is a goal/subgoal tree whose leaves are transformation steps. Languages such as PADDLE (Wile, 1983) have constructs such as goals, subgoals, and dependencies that make this structure explicit. A derivation step depends on another derivation step if the first needs to be applied either to make the application of the second legal or to enable the second to achieve its goal.

A derivation is reused during adaptive maintenance by traversing down the hierarchical goal structure and replaying the derivation steps until one does not apply because the relevant part of the specification was changed. At this point, the replay mechanism either invokes an automatic derivation system or notifies the user to achieve the subgoal that was the purpose of the now inapplicable derivation step. After the subgoal is achieved, the replay mechanism resumes applying the original derivation steps, suitably modifying those steps that depended on the now inapplicable step. Preliminary work on reusing derivations is reported in Mostow and Barley (1987), and Steinberg and Mitchell (1985).

Reusing a derivation on a new specification is much more difficult than reusing a derivation for adaptive maintenance. The key issue is to develop an analogy between the previous specification and the new specification that extends to an analogy between the derivations. Preliminary research on derivational analogy is reported in Dietzen and Scherlis (1986), Mostow (1987), and Huhns and Acosta (1987).

C7. Basic Search Techniques

A WELL-DEVELOPED area of AI is the theory of search. A search strategy takes a set of generation rules, such as the basic rules described in Section C4 or large-grained rules described in Section C5, and guides the application of these rules. In this subsection we describe how two basic AI search techniques—problem decomposition and best first heuristic search—have been applied in program synthesis systems.

Using Decomposition in a Transformation System

Even synthesizing a moderately sized software system can require more than 10,000 transformations, the exact number depending on the grain size of the transformation rules and the conceptual distance between the specification and the implementation. The REFINE compiler manages this complexity by partitioning the rules into packages that are exhaustively applied in separate passes. This partitioning of transformation rules decomposes the search space into subspaces. Since the rules are exhaustively applied and there is currently only one default implementation, little search control is necessary. See Nilsson (1980) for an introduction to decomposable transformation systems. Programs produced by REFINE are suitable for rapid prototyping, but are usually not efficient enough for production code (see the KIDS system, Section E3, for further elaboration of this point). As commercial systems move toward producing efficient code requiring significant choices in program derivations, search control will become a dominant concern. Research in transformational programming has already addressed some of the search control issues.

Although REFINE statically decomposes the set of transformation rules, systems that make significant design decisions usually decompose a specification into quasi-independent subspecifications. The programs for the subspecifications are then joined together into a program for the whole specification. Given a large specification AB that can be decomposed into two independent specifications A and B, the combined search space is roughly proportional to the sum of the search spaces for A and B. In contrast, if A and B are dependent on each other, every choice for

A must be considered with respect to every choice for B. In this case, the combined search space is roughly proportional to multiplying the search spaces for A and B. Applied hierarchically, multiplicatively dependent search spaces result in a combinatorial explosion. In contrast, independent search spaces applied hierarchically still result in combined search spaces proportional to the sum. This is the reason that a design specification decomposes a software system into a hierarchy of quasi-independent modules. Similarly, to effectively apply a transformation system to a specification, some of the transformations must decompose the specification into quasi-independent subspecifications. The KIDS, MEDUSA, and STRATA systems reviewed in Section E all use decomposition to factor a specification into subspecifications. An analysis of quasi-independence in factoring the search space can be found in McCartney (1988).

Search control can also be formulated as an explicit goal/subgoal relationship between derivation steps. An expert system can then guide a program derivation by decomposing the overall goal of deriving a program into a hierarchy of subgoals; a primitive subgoal is achieved directly by a single transformation. For example, "jittering" transformations are applied to massage a developing program so that a major program transformation can be applied. Performing the jittering transformation is a subgoal of the goal of achieving the major transformation. This idea was used in the PADDLE system (Wile, 1983), which began as an editor for derivation histories. A grammar was created for parsing derivation histories, which was then used as a generative grammar to create derivations.

Applying Best First Search to Guide a Theorem Prover

Best first heuristic search is a search strategy that at each step uses a heuristic evaluation function to score the possible next moves. The best scoring move is then taken, and the cycle repeats until the final state is achieved. A heuristic is a rule of thumb that is not formally justified yet empirically yields good results. The PSEUDS system, developed by Stuart Russell (1985), guides the derivation of a deductive tableau proof using a best first heuristic search. Consider how we can view the derivation of a deductive tableau proof as a search space:

- Each node in the search is a deductive tableau consisting of a number of rows. The rows are either assertions or goals whose output column is a term corresponding to a program fragment.
- The moves are inference rules that add new rows to the tableau.
- The final state is a deductive tableau with a row that has "true" in the goal column and a term consisting of programming language primitives in the output column.

A nice feature of this search space is that it is additive: adding a new row does not preclude adding any of the other rows that are possible next moves. This means that the search space is commutative-the choices can be taken in any order. Hence no backtracking is necessary.

In a deductive tableau proof, the main difficulty is to establish a structural induction step that corresponds to recursion in the synthesized program. Accordingly the PSEUDS system uses a set of heuristic rules to evaluate which next move is most likely to lead to developing the inductive part of a proof. Each heuristic rule returns an integer value; the evaluation function simply sums all the integer values.

C8.   Knowledge-intensive Search Techniques

THE UNGUIDED use of theorem proving or transformation rules quickly leads to combinatorial explosion. The tree of possibilities grows exponentially with the depth of the moves. In contrast to the basic search techniques discussed in Section C7, knowledge-intensive search techniques provide a global plan for guidance throughout a derivation. Strategic knowledge should be general enough to cover an interesting class of derivations, but not so broad that it does not provide sufficient guidance for limiting possible moves. Strategic knowledge can be applied to both the theorem proving approach (Bundy and vanHarmelen, 1988) and the transformational approach.

Strategic search control continues to be a fundamental research issue in artificial intelligence. Strategic knowledge in program synthesis is knowledge about program derivations. One source of strategic knowledge comes from design analysis, in which a class of algorithms such as divide and conquer algorithms is analyzed to understand their common logical structure, computational structure, and derivational structure. This analysis is formalized in terms of a theory, a program schema, and a design tactic. These three components can then be automated in order to derive algorithms of this class from specifications.

Strategic knowledge will be illustrated by showing how a design tactic for divide and conquer can be applied to the specification of sorting to derive insertion sort. The design analysis of divide and conquer algorithms was formalized in Smith (1985). There are three parts to the formal structure of an algorithm class (Smith and Lowry, 1989).

1. A theory that specifies the logical components of an algorithm and the constraints between the components. These constraints can be arranged in a hierarchy (Lowry, 1987a).

2. One or more program schemas that are parameterized program tem-

plates. After the theory is instantiated with the theory for a particular algorithm, a program schema is then directly instantiated to
obtain a program.

3. A design tactic that encapsulates strategic knowledge for instantiating the theory and hence deriving an algorithm.

For the class of divide and conquer algorithms both the theory and
the program schema are illustrated by Figure C–1:

The divide and conquer program schema for computing a function F
consists of two cases. The first case is when the input to F is primitive,
then the function F is computed directly without recursion. The second
case is when the input to F is complex and decomposable (not primitive),
then the input is decomposed, the function F is recursively applied, and
the outputs are composed together to obtain the output for the original
input to F. There are really two varieties of decomposition, one in which
an input is decomposed into two or more inputs of the same type, and
the second in which an input is decomposed into an auxiliary type and
another input of the same type. For example, a sequence of cards can be
decomposed into the first card (of type card) and the rest of the sequence
(of type sequence). In this second variety of decomposition (see Figure
C–1) the function G is applied to the auxiliary type after the decomposition step. To ensure termination, the output of the decomposition step
must be less than the input in some well-founded ordering, which is an
ordering that always bottoms out. For example, the sequence [2 3 4] is
a suffix of the sequence [1 2 3 4] since it consists of all elements but the

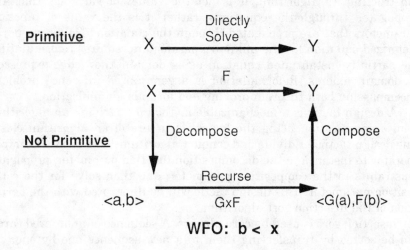

Figure C–1. Schema for divide and conquer algorithms.

first. The suffix relation defines a well-founded ordering, since it eventually bottoms out in the empty sequence.

The key to the theory of divide and conquer algorithms is the *Strong Problem Reduction Principle* (SPRP) constraint, which is illustrated by Figure C–1. This constraint relates the function F, the decomposition function, and the composition function. The arrows in figure C–1 define two paths from the input of F to the output of F; these two equivalent paths are the two sides of the conditional equation which formalizes the SPRP constraint:

$$\text{not(primitive}(x)) => F(x) = \text{compose}(\text{GxF}(\text{decompose}(x))$$

The other axioms of the divide and conquer theory are concerned with the nonprimitive case and the well-founded ordering:

$$\text{primitive}(x) => F(x) = \text{directly-solve}(x)$$
$$\text{WFO}(x,\text{Second}(\text{decompose}(x)))$$

The axioms of divide and conquer theory not only define the class of divide and conquer algorithms, but they can also be used to derive a divide and conquer algorithm from a formal specification with a design tactic. The axioms are constraints; given instantiations for some of the components of a divide and conquer algorithm the constraints can be used to "solve" for the remaining components. An analogy can be made to spreadsheets in which the instantiated value for a cell is propagated through equations to instantiate the value of dependent cells. The SPRP constraint is also an equation: Given a value for some of the parameters, the equation can be solved for the unknown parameters. However, in constructing an algorithm, it is not the values of variables that are propagated through the equations, rather it is the value of function parameters that are propagated through the equations. Solving a parameterized equation for the unknown parameters requires reformulating the partially instantiated equation using domain knowledge expressed as domain axioms. Reformulation is a generalized inference problem encompassing both theorem proving and formula simplification.

A design tactic is a mechanizable method for deriving an algorithm from a specification using the logical structure of an algorithm class. One design tactic for divide and conquer algorithms is to choose a simple operator to instantiate the decomposition function parameter, propagate constraints to the composition parameter, and then solve for the composition parameter. This design tactic will be illustrated with the derivation of the insertion sort algorithm.

Insertion sort is used by card players. A sequence of unordered cards can be sorted by transferring them to a new sequence one by one. As each card is transferred, it is inserted into its proper order in the new sequence. First, the last card is transferred, then the second to last card is transferred and inserted either before or after the last card, then the third to last card is transferred and inserted into its proper order, and so on until all the cards are transferred and put into their proper order. Insertion sort can be formulated as a recursive program that calls itself on the tail of a sequence of cards, sorts the tail, and then inserts the head of the sequence into the sorted tail. The head is the first card in a sequence, whereas the tail is the rest of the sequence. Note that since the tail is a suffix of the whole sequence, this means that head-tail decomposition satisfies the constraints of a well-founded ordering.

The divide and conquer design tactic starts the derivation of an algorithm for sorting by choosing a simple decomposition operator for sequences. There are two possibilities in the library: head-tail decomposition and splitting the sequence into two equal-sized subsequences. Insertion sort is derived by choosing the first possibility, whereas merge sort is derived by choosing the second possibility. Let us assume that head-tail decomposition is chosen, so the next step is to propagate this constraint to the other parameters through the SPRP constraint. We will assume that the nonprimitive parameter is instantiated with x ≠ EMPTY since this is a precondition for being able to apply head-tail decomposition. Furthermore, we will assume that the auxiliary function parameter G is instantiated to the identity function. The result of these instantiations, which include the instantiation of F to sorting, can be viewed in terms of Figure C–2.

With these instantiations, SPRP constrains the unknown parameter

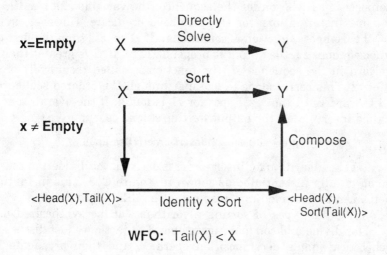

WFO: Tail(X) < X

Figure C–2.   Partial instantiation of schema for insertion sort.

Compose from both the input side and the output side. This constraint is expressed by the following conditional equation:

$$x \neq empty \Rightarrow sort(x) = compose(head(x), sort(tail(x)))$$

This equation can be "solved" to obtain a specification for the unknown Compose parameter using the definition of sort and a form of deductive reasoning called *directed inference*. Directed inference reformulates this constraint into constraints on the input $(z1, z2)$ and output (y) variables of the unknown Compose function. Directed inference uses the domain axioms that describe the sorting domain in order to reformulate the constraint to the following specification:

Compose$(z1, z2)$ <= y such that permutation(prepend$(z1, z2), y$)
AND Ordered$(Z2)$ => Ordered(y)

A permutation of a sequence of cards is a reshuffling of the cards, and prepending a card to a sequence of cards means to insert it at the beginning of the sequence. Thus the reformulated constraint states that the output of the unknown compose function is some reshuffling of inserting the card $z1$ at the beginning of the sequence $z2$, and furthermore that if the sequence $z2$ is ordered, the output will also be ordered. What directed inference has done is to take the constraint that the inputs to the Compose function are the head of a sequence of cards and the sorted tail of a sequence of cards and reformulated the constraint in terms of an input-output specification.

The divide and conquer design tactic can be applied again to derive an algorithm for this specification of Compose. Once again, a head-tail decomposition is chosen for the sequence (the variable $z2$), resulting in the same instantiations for the primitive predicate. However, in this case, the Compose function is conditional. If $z1$ is less than the first card in the sequence $z2$, the output is prepend$(z1, z2)$. If $z1$ is greater than the first card in the sequence $z2$, the function is called recursively on the tail of $z2$. This corresponds to looking through the ordered sequence $z2$ card by card until the right spot for $z1$ is found. If the overall function is called insert-order, the output for this second case is:

prepend(head(z2), insert-order(z1, tail(z2)))

After the algorithm for insert-order is derived, the divide and conquer schema is fully instantiated as shown in Figure C–3. This instantiated schema can be compiled into Lisp using the REFINE compiler.

Many other types of sorting algorithms can be synthesized using tactics for divide and conquer algorithms. The tactic we just discussed is to choose a simple decomposition operator, and then propagate constraints to the composition operator. A different tactic is to choose a simple composition operator and then propagate constraints to the

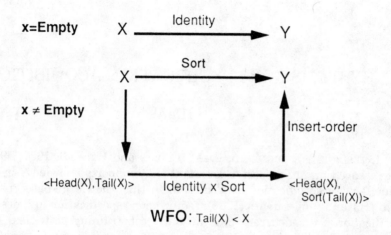

Figure C–3.   Instantiated schema for insertion sort.

decomposition operator. Both tactics use the SPRP constraint to propagate constraints. For each of these two tactics, there is a choice of whether the simple operator works on two subsequences or a single card and a sequence of cards. For example, a simple operator that takes two sequences and joins them together is append, whereas a simple operator that takes a card and a sequence and joins them together is prepend.

Depending on which tactic is chosen and which simple operator is used different sorting algorithms are derived, each derivation uses the SPRP constraint.

	Singleton	Equal-Sized
Simple Composition Operator	Selection Sort	Quick Sort
Simple Decomposition Operator	Insertion Sort	Merge Sort

D. SYSTEMS FOR SPECIFICATION ACQUISITION

D1. IDeA

THE INTELLIGENT DESIGN AID (IDeA) (Lubars and Harandi, 1987; 1988) is a research prototype design assistant that supports knowledge-based refinement of specifications and design. In this knowledge-based paradigm (Harandi and Lubars, 1986), requirement specification and design specification are concurrent and mutually constraining activities. The objective is for the designer, IDeA, to provide the requirements analyst with incremental feedback on the completeness and consistency of a developing requirements specification. This paradigm contrasts with the waterfall model of software development where the requirements analysis phase completely precedes the design phase, without any intermediate feedback.

IDeA represents designs as dataflow diagrams with inputs and outputs described in terms of domain-oriented data types and properties. This allows the human analyst to use these domain concepts to communicate with IDeA. The initial unrefined requirement specification is given to IDeA in terms of domain-oriented system inputs, outputs, and general system function. IDeA generates an initial top-level design specification by selecting an abstract design schema from its knowledge base of design abstractions, using partial matches on dataflow and system function. IDeA then applies refinement rules to add new levels in the hierarchical dataflow design. Each refinement rule specializes a component of the schema or decomposes a component into subcomponents. The human analyst supplies requirements constraints that guide IDeA in the selection of refinement rules and the specialization of data types. IDeA also propagates constraints through the dataflow diagram in order to refine data types and other related components. IDeA provides feedback to the human analyst through a graphical interface that presents the current system design as a dataflow diagram and definitions of data types. The overall paradigm is illustrated in Figure D–1.

As an example, consider how IDeA could be used in specifying and designing a library system. Assume that IDeA's knowledge base contains an abstract design schema for inventory control systems, with library systems being a type of inventory control system. The analyst specifies a library system that checks books in and out of the library. IDeA then matches this specification against the abstract design schema for inven-

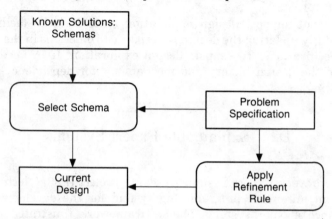

Figure D–1.   Architecture of IDeA.

tory control systems to generate an initial design for the library system. As a result of the partial match, constraints that are particular to the library specification are propagated so that they can direct the refinement of other components and data types. For example, the constraint that books are returned causes IDeA to refine the return inventory suboperation of inventory control systems to the correct design for book checkin.

An agenda of goals tracks components that need to be further refined and to resolve mismatches between the analyst's specification and the abstract design schema. For example, the abstract design schema for inventory control systems contains a component for generating inventory reports, but there is no corresponding component in the analyst's specification for the library system. Resolving this mismatch would be put on the goal agenda. Later, when this goal is selected, the analyst could decide to add a component for generating an inventory report. Constraint propagation would cause this component to be specialized to generating reports about books available for loan.

IDeA facilitates the incremental and parallel development of requirements specifications and design specifications. The requirements specifications are validated by developing a complete and consistent design. IDeA's knowledge base of domain-dependent abstract design schemas and refinement rules enables the analyst to express requirements specifications and to understand IDeA's design specifications using application-specific terms. Moreover, IDeA supports the reuse of existing design knowledge that is encoded as abstract design schemas and refinement rules.

Future work will support design exploration and the construction of knowledge bases for new application domains. The current prototype of

IDeA does not support design exploration since it lacks facilities for incrementally updating the design in response to deletions in the requirements specifications. To support design exploration, IDeA needs better records of the design history and mechanisms for dependency-directed backtracking.

D2.   Explainable Expert Systems

THE EXPLAINABLE Expert Systems research project (ESS) (Neches et al., 1985) is an automatic programming system for the development and maintenance of expert systems. The ESS framework, illustrated in Figure D–2, is based on the principle that by formally recording the knowledge used in designing an expert system, the resulting system will be able to explain its own behavior, enabling domain experts to debug and maintain the expert system.

In the Explainable Expert Systems approach, knowledge engineers and domain experts collaborate to produce a model of the declarative and procedural knowledge of a problem domain. The resulting knowledge base is the foundation of the EES framework; it contains knowledge such as causal links, domain problem solving strategies (called *domain principles*), and optimization knowledge. The knowledge base is used to guide an automatic program writer in designing an expert system. The program writer maintains a record of its choice points and decisions, which constitutes the design history. The design history is organized as a tree structure whose leaf nodes represent system implementation code and

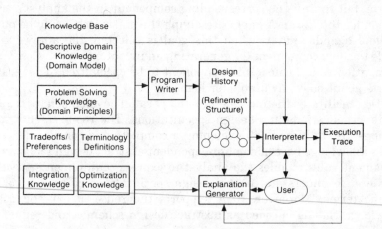

Figure D–2.   Architecture of Explainable Expert System
              generator.

whose interior nodes represent goals and decisions made on the way to generating the implementation. The resulting code is executed by an interpreter, which maintains a record of the execution history.

All together the knowledge base, design history, code, and the execution history provide domain experts with the means to critique the system, to understand the abilities and limitations of the system, and to find the parts of the domain model or implementation responsible for an error. When an error occurs the domain expert searches the execution trace to determine which component of the expert system was responsible. The design history is then analyzed to determine which design decisions were responsible for the faulty component. These decisions are analyzed to determine the parts of the domain model on which they are based. Finally, the domain model is modified to resolve the error. The expert system is then regenerated.

The program writer creates an expert system in a top-down fashion, by refining a high-level goal into subgoals. The writer iteratively implements goals using goal/subgoal refinement until the level of system primitives is reached. Goals are decomposed through the domain principles, which have three components: a goal, a method, and a domain rationale. The goal states what the method can accomplish, whereas the method itself refines the higher-level description of the goal into one expressed in lower level terms. When the program writer tries to refine a goal, it examines the domain problem solving strategies to find one whose goal most closely matches the goal to be refined. The purpose of the domain rationale is to integrate knowledge from the descriptive domain model into the refinement process by defining terms at one level of refinement using terms at the next level down.

The EES framework is a first step toward self-aware, self-healing software. The recorded design history enables the expert system to explain its own behavior so that a human can determine how to modify the domain model used to generate the expert system. In the future, we would like our software systems to understand and modify themselves.

D3. DRACO

DURING THE traditional requirements analysis phase of software construction, an end user interacts with an analyst who specifies what the system should do. This specification is then given to a systems designer who produces a system design. The DRACO research project (Neighbors, 1984) defines two new human expert roles: the *domain analyst* and the *domain designer*. The objective is to encode the expert knowledge of the domain analyst and domain designer as a domain model within the

DRACO knowledge base so that the knowledge can be reused. A domain analyst is a person who examines the needs and requirements of a collection of systems in a specific domain. The goal of the domain analyst is to define the objects and operations of the domain; the result is a domain language that can be used as a specification language for the domain. A domain designer then determines different implementations for these objects and operations in terms of other domains already known to DRACO.

A systems analyst can then develop the specification for a new system in terms of a domain language, developed previously by a domain analyst. This makes the job of the systems analyst much easier since his or her specification is now at the level of domain concepts; in fact, an end user with little formal training might now be able to do this job for simple systems. After a system has been specified, a systems designer interacts with DRACO to refine the specification to executable code. In this interaction, the systems designer can decide between different implementations as specified by the domain designers.

The domain designers can reuse the knowledge encoded into DRACO for previously analyzed domains. For example, suppose that DRACO already has the inventory control system domain, and the library domain is given to a domain analyst. The domain analyst specifies the pertinent objects and operations of the library domain, for example, borrower, book, lend, and return. The domain designer can then implement the library objects and operations in terms of the objects and operations in the domain of inventory control systems. For example, books in a library correspond to inventory in stock, and borrowers to customers. By setting up this correspondence, implementations for the inventory domain can be used for the library domain.

The DRACO approach enables reusing knowledge about domain analysis and system designs by reusing designs from other domains, as shown in Figure D–3. DRACO provides language creation facilities (e.g., parser generators) and a transformation system that allows the user to relate the constructs of the newly defined language to those of the languages already known to DRACO. Furthermore, the constructs are at the conceptual level of several domains, and the users are free to express their needs and requirements using the terms and operations that are most natural to them.

D4.   The Requirements Apprentice

THE GOAL of the Programmer's Apprentice (PA) research project at MIT is to provide intelligent assistance in various phases of software devel-

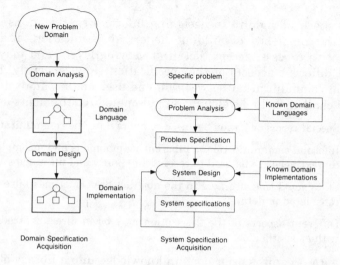

Figure D–3.   The DRACO approach. Reuse of domain analysis
and domain implementations.

opment (Rich and Waters, 1988). Viewed at the highest level, software
development is a process that begins with the desires of an end user and
ends with a program that can be executed on a machine. The first step
of this process is traditionally called *requirements acquisition*, and the
last step is called *implementation*. To date, two demonstration systems
have been developed as part of the PA project: the Knowledge-Based
Editor in Emacs (KBEmacs) and the Requirements Apprentice (RA).
Emacs is a standard text editor which can serve as an interface for other
programs. KBEmacs supports program implementation; it is reviewed in
Section E5. The RA supports requirements acquisition.

The Requirements Apprentice (RA) (Reubenstein and Waters, 1989)
helps a human requirements analyst create and modify software requirements. Unlike current requirements analysis tools, which assume a formal description language, the focus of the RA is on the boundary between
informal and formal specifications. The RA is intended to support the
earliest phases of creating a requirement, in which incompleteness, contradiction, and ambiguity are common features.

From an AI perspective, the central problem the RA faces is one of
knowledge acquisition—it has to develop a coherent internal representation from an initial set of disorganized statements. Research on the
RA addresses two fundamental issues: informality and the process by
which informal descriptions evolve into formal specifications, and the
role of prior domain knowledge in developing a formal specification.

Informality is an inevitable and desirable feature of the specification process. Lack of rigidity in designing informal specifications serves to reduce the complexity of building the formal specification—it allows for an iterative process, accepts detail at varying levels, and may develop several different aspects of the specification simultaneously. However, informal communication between an end user and an analyst presents several challenges to developing an automated requirements assistant:

1. Special terms or jargon are used to abbreviate the communication.

2. Informal communication is inherently ambiguous and incomplete so context needs to be used to resolve ambiguity and fill in gaps.

3. Statements that are true in the abstract are sometimes false when considered in detail.

4. Different aspects of the description may be in direct contradiction with each other.

The RA organizes prior domain knowledge into a library of requirements clichés, which capture the common structures of the domain. An example of a cliché is the term "repository". This cliché has a number of roles including: the items that are stored in the repository, the place where the items are stored, and the users that utilize the repository. The term "cliché" refers to commonly occurring structures. Formally, a cliché consists of a set of roles embedded in a body. The roles of a cliché are the parts that vary from one use of the cliché to next. The body contains both constraints and fixed elements of structure, which are parts that are present in every occurrence of the cliché. Constraints are used to check that the parts that fill the roles of a particular occurrence are consistent and to compute parts to fill empty roles in a partially specified occurrence.

The implementation of the RA is based on a hybrid, knowledge-representation and reasoning system called Cake (Rich, 1985), which has been developed within the Programmer's Apprentice project. Among other things, Cake supports dependency-directed reasoning with full retraction and a frame-based knowledge representation. In the RA, clichés are represented as frames with associated logical constraints, and the reasoning capabilities of Cake are used to support disambiguation and contradiction detection.

D5.　KATE

KATE (Fickas, 1987) is a proposed interactive analyst used for developing a requirements specification. The key idea is that developing a requirements specification is an interactive problem-solving process between an end user (client) and an analyst. In contrast to the traditional viewpoint that sees analysis as a process of translating user intent to a formal document, KATE assumes that an end user might only have a vague idea of what he or she wants. This means that the analyst must be both a domain expert and an expert in the software development process.

KATE is based on observations and protocol experiments with clients and human analysts at the University of Oregon. First, client complaints with software systems were traced back to bugs in analysis. From these observations a classification of analysis bugs was developed, as well as insights into which analysis techniques avoided bugs and which analysis techniques created bugs. Second, protocols of human analysts interacting with clients were used to understand the knowledge and techniques used by expert analysts. Experienced analysts use their domain knowledge to zero in on key questions. Experienced analysts also use hypothetical examples both for interviewing clients and for explaining issues to a client. Finally, experienced analysts use summarization and paraphrasing to validate a requirements specification and to ensure that there is a complete understanding between analyst and client.

The proposed KATE system is built around four components:

1. A knowledge base that models the problem domain.

2. A problem acquisition component that controls the interaction between client and system.

3. A critic that attempts to poke holes in the current problem description.

4. A specification generator that can map a requirements model into an existing specification language.

The objective of KATE is to find bugs with a requirement specification before design and implementation. The method uses domain knowledge to find bugs with a problem description that could not be found using solely syntactic criteria. A prototype research system called SKATE has been developed and has shown the usefulness of an automated critic that uses a domain model. Future work will concentrate on an interactive problem acquisition component.

D6.   Ozym

THE LONG TERM goal of the Ozym research project (Iscoe et al., 1989) is to provide the means for application program designers, who are neither domain experts nor computer programmers, to directly specify and implement application programs. The focus of the research is to create a domain modeling system that enables a domain expert to create a domain-specific application program generator. The application program designer then uses the application program generator to generate application programs. Thus the domain modeling system is a meta-generation system. Figure D–4 illustrates the paradigm.

Modeling domain knowledge (the top right portion of Figure D–4) is the focus of this research. An object-oriented model has been developed that provides a conceptual structure for the types of domain knowledge required to specify application programs. Libraries of domain-independent and domain-specific classes are populated by a domain expert who uses attribute characteristics to structure class taxonomies and to constrain the definitions and runtime behavior of class methods and object states. The attribute characteristics that are common across domains are identified and classes are specified in terms of parameterized properties such as scales, units, defaults, and population parameters. The lower right portion of Figure D–4 represents a domain-specific transformational program generation system. The figure is meant to imply that application designers, who range in sophistication from domain experts to endusers,

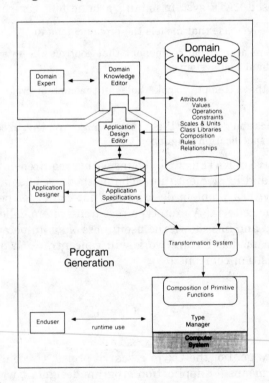

Figure D–4.   Domain modeling for application program generation.

interact with a design editor to create a set of application specifications. These specifications are then transformed into a composition of primitive functions that can be executed by a type manager. Program synthesis is described elsewhere in this chapter, and is not the focus of this research. Instead, Ozym should be viewed as a project to create a system for the generation of program generators in a manner analogous to the way EMYCIN was created to provide a system for the creation of expert systems.

D7.   Watson

WATSON (Kelly and Nonnenmann, 1987), is a specification acquisition research system developed at AT&T Bell Laboratories. Watson uses domain knowledge of telephone switching software to allow designers to specify new features, such as call waiting, through English-language scenarios. Watson inductively generates a finite state machine (FSM) specification from a scenario. The telephone domain knowledge is crucial in both constraining the induction of FSMs from scenarios and in being able to communicate with users in the English sub-language of telephone engineers. Watson needs a variety of background knowledge about telephone hardware, telephone network protocols, expected end-user etiquette, and principles of finite-state machine design.

Watson interacts with two types of users: domain experts and telephone design engineers. Watson's knowledge base is maintained by domain experts who must be comfortable with the mathematics of temporal logic. Watson provides knowledge base audit tools which assist domain experts in testing new knowledge bases against "benchmark" scenarios. In contrast, interaction with telephone feature designers hides the mathematical rigor of temporal logic. After a feature designer presents an English-language scenario, Watson proposes expanded scenarios to the designer in order to resolve incompleteness and inconsistencies with its background knowledge.

Figure D–5 shows the relationship between Watson's three knowledge representations for background knowledge and new features: goal-directed plans, temporal logic formulas, and relational approximations to FSMs.

Scenarios and plans are the medium for interaction with telephone feature designers. These are converted to temporal logic constraints on state transitions through justified generalization. The relational model is an approximation to a finite state machine which realizes a feature being designed. During a session with Watson, this relational model converges upon a minimal FSM which is compatible with the scenarios

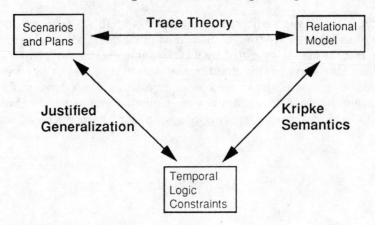

Figure D–5.   Watson's three knowledge representations.

and obeys all the temporal logic constraints in the knowledge base. The scenarios must be realizeable as traces of paths through the FSM. The relational model is constructed from the temporal logic constraints in accordance with the mathematics of Kripke semantics. After the model is constructed, Watson reasons directly with the model whenever possible rather than its temporal logic theorem prover.

In summary, Watson uses extensive domain knowledge to derive specifications from examples. Heterogenous knowledge representation enables Watson to hide the details of its formal, mathematical specifications from users and to communicate in a restricted subset of English.

E. PROGRAM SYNTHESIS SYSTEMS

E1. CIP

THE CIP (Computer-Aided Intuition-Guided Programming) project (Broy and Pepper, 1981) has been an ongoing effort at the Technical University of Munich since 1974. This project was a pioneering effort in the transformational approach to program synthesis. The CIP project produced a wide-spectrum language, CIP-L, and an associated manually guided transformation system, CIP-S. The emphasis of the CIP project has been on mathematically clear semantics and correctness preserving transformations. The semantics are built upon a functional kernel language with well-defined semantics. New language constructs are defined as extensions of the functional kernel; the definitions also serve as transformations from the new language constructs to the functional kernel. The CIP system has been specified in CIP-L itself.

At the beginning of the project, CIP-L was designed to consist of several discrete language layers, with transformations between layers. This approach was found to be unworkable. The problem was that in the course of transforming a high-level specification into a program at the level of the functional kernel, different parts of the program would be distributed in different language layers. The machinery that was needed to keep track of interrelated program fragments at different language layers was found to be significantly more complex than having one wide-spectrum language. The current wide-spectrum language encompasses constructs at all different levels.

A user of the CIP system repeatedly specifies transformations to apply to a high-level specification. CIP applies these transformations and records them in a history. CIP also collects the preconditions of the transformations into a theorem. If the theorem can be proved, the concrete program is a verifiably correct version of the abstract specification. Members of the CIP project expressed the view that a manually controlled transformation system was a cost-effective way of deriving programs only when extreme reliability is required. In the absence of extreme software reliability requirements, it was usually faster for a human to write a concrete program by hand than to write an abstract specification, and then manually guide the detailed transformations to a concrete program. More recent work has focused on automating the selection of

303

transformations. This work has been influenced by the ML language at the University of Edinburgh.

E2. Designer

THE DESIGNER research project investigated knowledge-based automatic algorithm design, focusing on understanding the methods used by human algorithm designers (Kant, 1985; Kant and Newell, 1984; Steier, 1989). Based upon a protocol analysis of colleagues at Carnegie Mellon University deriving algorithms in computational geometry, four systems were developed: Designer, Designer-Meets-Soar, Cypress-Soar, and Designer-Soar. The original Designer system was implemented in OPS5 (Forgy, 1981), which is a general purpose production system, while the last three systems were implemented in Soar (Laird et al., 1987), which is described here.

The protocol analysis identified the following cognitive aspects of human algorithm design:

1. Designers used an abstract representation of algorithms based upon dataflow and a small set of general primitive steps such as generate, test, and store.

2. Designers typically chose a basic scheme like divide and conquer for the algorithm relatively quickly, and then spent considerable time refining the initial scheme.

3. Designers refined an algorithm through means-ends-analysis (MEA) of symbolic and test-case execution of partial algorithms. MEA finds differences between the desired properties of the algorithm and the properties present in the partial design. These differences triggered a locally-driven process of refinement.

4. Designers used a strategy of repeatedly executing the partially refined algorithm, progressively extending the execution on each repetition. This progressive deepening strategy is similar to that encountered by Newell and Simon in protocol analyses of chess players (Laird et al., 1987).

These protocol findings formed the foundation of a model of algorithm design that was partially implemented in the Designer system. Designer represented algorithms using dataflow graphs of process components, and each component of the graph could be recursively refined into its own dataflow graph. The refinement process was driven by MEA based on the results of symbolic and test-case execution. Execution consisted of manipulating assertions on data items arriving on an input port of a component to produce appropriate assertions on the output port. These output assertions were compared against expected values in order to flag opportunities and difficulties. These in turn triggered design rules which modified the configurations. An example of a design rule is that if an item on the input port of a component does not satisfy a precondition, and it is known that some other component can produce an object satisfying the precondition, then this other component is spliced into the configuration. The rules controlling design and execution in Designer were implemented in OPS5.

In 1985 the Designer project moved from OPS5 to Soar, which is a general architecture for problem-solving and learning. Soar formulates all problem-solving in terms of problem spaces. A problem space consists of a set of states and operators which map from state to state until a goal state is reached. Knowledge is represented as productions which operate on data stored in working memory. The basic problem-solving cycle in Soar follows these steps:

1. Fire productions that add information about which operator should be applied next.

2. Select an operator.

3. Apply the operator, resulting in a new state.

Whenever there is insufficient information to proceed in this cycle, Soar automatically generates a subgoal. In response to a subgoal, Soar selects a problem space to acquire the necessary information. When this subgoal is achieved, Soar pops up and continues in the original problem space. Subgoaling can be applied recursively.

Another key aspect of Soar is a learning mechanism called *chunking*, which encapsulates the result of subgoaling as a new production rule in the original problem space. This new production has as left-hand side a generalized version of the state prior to subgoaling and as right-hand side a generalization of the information derived through subgoaling. Thus when Soar encounters a similar situation, instead of subgoaling it immediately applies the new production rule to select the next operator. Systems implemented in Soar have solved problems and learned in domains ranging from the traditional AI toy problems to more complex knowledge-intensive tasks, such as configuring VAX computer systems. The latter is a re-implementation in Soar of part of the R1/XCON expert system.

Designer-Meets-Soar (DMS) was a direct re-implementation of Designer in Soar's architecture. The data flow networks representing partial algorithms were kept in Soar's working memory. While DMS was successful in designing five simple algorithms, its performance on larger algorithms was too slow for practical use, due to the overhead of keeping data flow networks in working memory.

Cypress-Soar (Steier, 1987) is a partial re-implementation in Soar of the divide and conquer design strategy described in Section C8. Cypress-Soar represented the abstract divide and conquer scheme as a set of instantiation operators in a problem space. Cypress-Soar showed that an algorithm design system could learn and improve its performance through chunking. However, Cypress-Soar's propositional representation for algorithms led to slow performance in Soar. Cypress-Soar also had no clear role for the use of examples, which is an important source of knowledge used by human designers.

Designer-Soar (Steier and Newell, 1988) combines elements of both DMS and Cypress-Soar in a new formulation of the algorithm design task. Designer-Soar represents algorithm designs directly as problem spaces for a computational domain. Each state in these problem spaces represents a computational state. Execution sequences are paths through the problem space. In Designer-Soar, designing an algorithm is equivalent to learning to execute it. Designer-Soar learns the generalized execution path representing an algorithm from repeated executions.

Chunking and production-rule matching are used to store and retrieve this generalized execution path as operator selection and implementation knowledge in the computational domain problem spaces. Designer-Soar also uses another set of problem spaces that model the objects and operators of the application domain. Designer-Soar essentially designs algorithms by mapping methods defined in terms of application domain operators to the computational domain. In contrast to Cypress-Soar and DMS, Designer-Soar's formulation of the algorithm design task is far less expensive and cognitively more plausible than storing all parts of previous and current designs as explicit data structures in Soar's working memory.

Designer-Soar can design several simple generate and test, and divide and conquer algorithms in a few application domains. It uses multiple levels of abstraction in problem solving in the computational spaces, and generalizes from examples in the application domain spaces. Furthermore, it learns from experience, transferring knowledge acquired during the design of one algorithm to aid in the design of others. For example, Designer-Soar took 860 decision cycles to design merge sort. However, if insertion sort was designed first, Designer-Soar took only 551 decision cycles to design merge sort. Designer-Soar was able to reuse knowledge gained in designing insertion sort while designing merge sort. Designer-Soar is consistent with what is known from cognitive psychology about human designers, and is shaped by the necessity to cope with both diversity in knowledge and limitations on problem-solving resources.

E3. KIDS

THE KESTREL interactive development research system (KIDS) is an interactive program synthesis system that integrates a number of sources of programming knowledge (Smith, 1988). The KIDS' user interface is an interactive display whose left side is a textual representation of a program under development and whose right side is an abstract representation for the program specification and various assertions used in program synthesis. The user develops a program by choosing program development operations from a menu and then selecting the expression to operate on with the mouse. Figure E–1 shows a user specifying an unfold operation on part of a program under development to solve the K-queens problem. The K-queens problem is to place K queens on a K × K chessboard such that no queen attacks another queen.

KIDS is built on top of REFINE and uses REFINE's object-oriented knowledge base and compiler. Both specifications and programs can be represented in REFINE's wide-spectrum language. KIDS translates from a textual representation of a developing program to an abstract representation using REFINE's grammar-based parsers and unparsers. KIDS also uses an inference system (RAINBOW II) in which inference rules are implemented as transformation rules in REFINE.

A user develops a program with KIDS by first developing a mathematically oriented domain model through definitions of appropriate domain concepts and laws for reasoning about them. RAINBOW II supports a generalized form of algebraic law to reason about specifications at the level of domain concepts and mathematical properties rather than at the level of detailed definitions. This vastly simplifies the inference search space. The user then defines a high-level specification in REFINE of the program he or she wants to develop.

KIDS then enters into an interactive loop with the user. The first step is to choose an algorithm design tactic to apply to the specification; current choices are divide and conquer, local search, and global search. After semi-automatic development of a high-level algorithm (Section C8), the user chooses further program development operations from the menu such as simplifying an expression. Finally, based on the operations performed on data types, KIDS chooses efficient implementations; for example, sets taken from a fixed universe are implemented with bit-vectors. An experimental knowledge-based compiler then produces efficient imperative code from the REFINE program and data structure implementations.

The initial algorithm KIDS designed for the K-queens specification takes 60 minutes to find all 92 solutions for an 8 × 8 chessboard; the final optimized version designed with KIDS takes 2 seconds to find all

Kestrel Interactive Development System

Canonicalize Compile Expose FD-Condition FD0 Initialize Pop Context Refine Interface Rename Simplify Tactics Unfold

```
function QUEENS-AUX-2-1 (K: integer, V: seq(integer), POOL)
: set(seq(integer))
= (V | () empty(POOL))
  ∪ reduce
    ('UNION,
     {QUEENS-AUX-2-1(K, append(V, I), POOL less I)
      | (I)
      I ∈ POOL ∧ UDD-OVER-SEQS(V, [I])
        ∧ UDD-OVER-SEQS(V, [I]) })

function QUEENS-2 (K: integer): set(seq(integer))
= QUEENS-AUX-2-1(K, [], SET-WITH-RANGE(1, K))
```

```
(OPERATOR-SPECIFICATION QUEENS-AUX-2
 input-types integer, seq(integer), any-type
 output-types set(seq(integer)) input-vars K, V, POOL
 output-vars SO
 input-condition
   1 ≤ K ∧ range(V) ⊆ SET-WITH-RANGE(1, K)
   ∧ INJECTIVE(V, SET-WITH-RANGE(1, K))
   ∧ UNIQUE-UP-DIAGONALS(V)
   ∧ UNIQUE-DOWN-DIAGONALS(V)
   ∧ POOL = setdiff(SET-WITH-RANGE(1, K), range(V))
 output-condition
   EXTENDS(SQ, V)
   ∧ UNIQUE-DOWN-DIAGONALS(SQ)
   ∧ UNIQUE-UP-DIAGONALS(SQ)
   ∧ BIJECTIVE(SQ, SET-WITH-RANGE(1, K)))

(OPERATOR-SPECIFICATION QUEENS-2 input-types integer
 output-types set(seq(integer)) input-vars K output-vars SO
 input-condition 1 ≤ K
 output-condition
   BIJECTIVE(SQ, SET-WITH-RANGE(1, K))
   ∧ UNIQUE-UP-DIAGONALS(SQ)
   ∧ UNIQUE-DOWN-DIAGONALS(SQ))
```

```
Goal: BIJECTIVE(V, SET-WITH-RANGE(1, K))
Search goal: BIJECTIVE(V, SET-WITH-RANGE(1, K))
Search goal: SURJECTIVE(V, SET-WITH-RANGE(1, K))
Search goal: SETEQUAL(range(V), SET-WITH-RANGE(1, K))
Search goal: SET-WITH-RANGE(1, K) ⊆ range(V)
Search goal: empty(setdiff(SET-WITH-RANGE(1, K), range(V)))
Search goal: empty(POOL)
RAINBOW result: empty(POOL)
Ids command:
Ids Unfold:    [Abort]
Ids command:
Ids Unfold: (Select a program expression.) ■
```

Figure E-1. The KIDS' user interface.

solutions. Equally important, each version of the program from initial algorithm to final version is a mathematically correct implementation of the initial specification.

Figure E–2 shows timing results for a job scheduling program at various stages of development with KIDS. The initial specification is to schedule a set of jobs subject to partial constraints on their order; mathematically this is known as topological sort. The combinatorics of job scheduling is similar to that of K-queens and many other problems.

At the very left is the curve showing the performance from just compiling the initial REFINE specification. The performance is worse than exponential, increasing in proportion to the factorial of the number of jobs. Although scheduling five jobs takes 4 seconds, scheduling seven jobs takes 75 hours. This is unacceptable even for validating a specification by execution of test cases. The second curve shows the performance after developing a high-level algorithm (see Section C8) and then compiling. This performance is adequate for specification validation, but it is inadequate for production code that must work on very large numbers of jobs. The third curve shows the performance after applying a finite differencing transformation to the initial algorithm. Note that the performance is actually slightly worse than the initial algorithm on small number of jobs, but as the number of jobs increases performance improves.

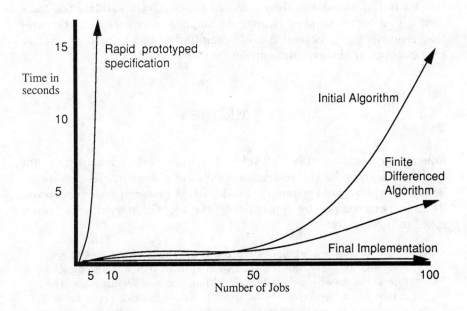

Figure E–2. Program development with KIDS.

Finite differencing is a transformation that improves performance by reusing partial results. For example, if the size of a set is used in a program, instead of counting the elements each time the size is needed, an alternative is to update the size each time an element is added or deleted from the set. For small sets this can lead to worse performance, as shown in Figure E–2, but for large sets the performance can be enhanced considerably. The application of finite differencing is very similar to the unfold/fold transformation of double append described in Section C4.

The final curve shows the performance after transforming the program to use efficient data structures. This version of the program was slightly faster than one developed by an experienced programmer; it takes only 15 milliseconds to schedule 100 jobs.

Several lessons are to be learned from this example. First, it demonstrates that it is possible to use current program synthesis technology to traverse the whole distance from high-level specification to efficient program. Second, it lends credibility to the aspiration of greatly improving software design productivity through automation. Once the domain axioms were developed, the human effort to synthesize the job scheduling program was comparable to manual development. Since the domain axioms are highly reusable, this indicates that the technology is already within an order of magnitude of the break-even point. Third, this example demonstrates the need for transforming a high-level specification into an initial high-level algorithm just to effectively validate the specification on test examples. Fourth, developing an efficient implementation requires going beyond default compilation techniques in order to reason about alternative data structure implementations.

E4. MEDUSA

ROBERT MCCARTNEY (1987) developed a high performance algorithm synthesis system for the restricted domain of planar intersection problems in computational geometry. The MEDUSA research system achieved its high performance by constraining the algorithm synthesis search space in three ways:

1. MEDUSA synthesized algorithms top down; the top-level task of synthesizing an algorithm from a formal specification was decomposed into subtasks of synthesizing algorithms for subspecifications. The result was a tree structure with the leaves of the tree being known algorithms. Algorithm synthesis can be viewed as generation within a grammar where the terminals are known algorithms. The decom-

position of specifications into subspecifications helped to make the search space tractable (see Section C7).

2. Part of the input to MEDUSA was a cost constraint for the final algorithm. MEDUSA used the cost constraint to prune subtasks that it estimated would violate the cost constraint, and to order the remaining subtasks by simplicity. Cost constraints are propagated from tasks to subtasks. MEDUSA used asymptotic time complexity as a cost constraint, which considerably simplified estimating costs as compared with Libra's cost estimates (see Article X.D8, in Vol. II, for a description of Libra).

3. Subtasks were generated in only a small number of ways. First, a task could be decomposed into a functionally equivalent skeletal algorithm; the total cost was defined in terms of the costs of the subcomponents. Second, a task could be transformed into an equivalent task using domain knowledge. Third, a task could be decomposed into disjoint subcases through case decomposition. Fourth, a task could be transformed into dual task, for example, to determine if three points are colinear transform the points to lines and determine if the lines intersect. Dual transforms are a type of problem reformulation.

The basic synthesis loop of MEDUSA was to take a task and generate a functionally equivalent sequence of subtasks while propagating the cost constraints from the task to the subtasks. Then MEDUSA recursively calls itself on each subtask. The recursion stops when the current task can be solved by a known algorithm.

E5.   KBEmacs

ONE OF the central developments of the Programmer's Apprentice research project (see Section D4. and also Article X.D3, in Vol II) has been the Knowledge-based Editor in Emacs (KBEmacs) (Waters, 1985). KBEmacs allows a programmer to build up a program rapidly and reliably by combining prototypical program fragments called clichés. KBEmacs also enables a programmer to modify a program in terms of its component clichés.

The key basis for KBEmacs is a representation for programs and programming knowledge called the Plan Calculus (Rich, 1981). The key virtue of Plans is that they facilitate the manipulation of programs by representing data flow and control flow explicitly and by representing the algorithmic structure of a program in terms of the clichés out of which it is built. In both development and modification, KBEmacs gains most of its power from the fact that its actions are performed on an abstract plan for the program rather than on the program text.

The architecture of KBEmacs is shown in Figure E–3 (Waters, 1985). At each moment, KBEmacs maintains two representations (program text and a plan) for the program being developed or modified. Given the text for a program, the analyzer module can construct the corresponding plan. The coder module performs the reverse transformation, creating program text from a plan. The text editor can be used to modify the program text. The plan editor can be used to modify the plan. The library contains common program fragments (clichés) represented as plans.

The leverage provided by KBEmacs comes primarily from two sources. First, the programmer can rapidly and accurately build up a program by referring to the fragments in the plan library. Second, the editor provides a variety of commands specifically designed to facilitate the modification of programs to suit different needs. In particular, KBEmacs enables a programmer to develop and modify systems via knowledge-based editing—the direct manipulation of a program in terms of its component clichés.

KBEmacs adds to Emacs, rather than replacing it. The programmer is able to modify a program by editing the program text as well as by using the special knowledge-based commands that deal with clichés. This requires that the analyzer module be able to recognize clichés in the textually edited code, so that KBEmacs can maintain an accurate model of the program's structure.

A prototype program recognition system has been developed which

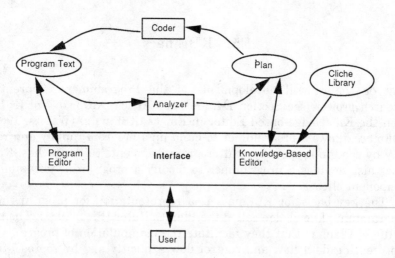

Figure E–3.　Architecture of KBEmacs.

identifies instances of clichés in a program (Wills, 1986). Based on the implementation relationships between the clichés, the system constructs a hierarchical description of the program's design. The recognition system represents the program as a Plan, encoded as a graph. Recognition is achieved by parsing this graph in accordance with a graph grammar, which encodes the cliché library. This yields a hierarchical description of the program in the form of a derivation tree.

E6. REFINE

REFINE is a commercially available interactive software development environment from Reasoning Systems, a company based in Palo Alto, California. REFINE provides an executable specification language, object-oriented knowledge base, and facilities for constructing knowledge-based compilers built with transformation rules. The knowledge base can represent all aspects of a software system, including specification, code, and documentation.

The specification language is a very high-level, wide-spectrum language that supports a variety of specification techniques including set theory, logic, transformation rules, procedures, and object-oriented programming. The REFINE compiler is implemented in REFINE itself as a program transformation system; the current version produces Common Lisp and a code generator for C is currently under development.

Particularly noteworthy are facilities for creating new languages and re-engineering existing languages with knowledge-based compilers. Typically, a user defines a textual representation for a language and the corresponding abstract syntax with REFINE's grammar definition facilities. Then REFINE compiles a lexical analyzer, parser, and pretty-printer from the grammar. The user can then develop a knowledge-based compiler using transformation rules defined on the abstract syntax.

Commercial users of REFINE typically develop software systems three times faster than with high-level languages such as ADA and Lisp. For example, a communication system that took 9 person-months to develop in ADA only took 3 person-months to develop in REFINE. Programming-language oriented applications such as compilers, program translators, and re-engineering tools show even larger productivity gains, usually exceeding an order of magnitude. For example, a system to translate logic expressions to SQL database queries took 3 person-months to develop in Lisp but only 5 person-days in REFINE. Productivity gains over older languages are even more substantial. For example, a computer equipment configuration system took 36 person-months to develop in COBOL but only 1 person-month in REFINE.

One application of REFINE is the rapid construction of re-engineering tools that port programs between different environments and dialects. This application uses REFINE's language definition facilities and the capabilities for directly specifying transformation rules. In theory, high-level languages make it easy to port a program from one machine and operating environment to another. In practice, popular languages such as FORTRAN and COBOL have a maddening variety of incompatible dialects. Thus a substantial portion of human resources in commercial data processing is devoted to converting programs. An example is converting programs written in NATURAL 1.2 to NATURAL 2.0. NATURAL is a COBOL-like language used primarily for business applications. The most recent version is NATURAL 2.0, which runs almost identically on IBM mainframes and DEC equipment. The older and most widely used version for IBM mainframes is NATURAL 1.2, which is largely incompatible with NATURAL 2.0. Thus customers must convert NATURAL 1.2 applications to NATURAL 2.0 and then recompile them in order to run them on DEC equipment.

A fully automated NATURAL 1.2 −> 2.0 converter is currently under development using REFINE. Before choosing REFINE, the customer investigated several strategies for conversion tools, including text-based approaches and approaches using YACC and C. The customer and Reasoning Systems jointly developed a prototype converter using REFINE in two weeks. The prototype included parser/printers for subsets of both NATURAL 1.2 and NATURAL 2.0, and transformation rules that handled several key incompatibilities between the two language versions. The prototype was able to completely convert several small examples.

Consider the following sample conversion rule used in the NATURAL 1.2 −> 2.0 prototype converter. This rule makes a conversion that is necessary because NATURAL 1.2 allows variables to be defined anywhere within a program, whereas NATURAL 2.0 requires that all variable definitions occur within a single "data definition" clause at the beginning of the program.

```
rule hoist-variable-definition (node)
  variable(node)
  var-fmt = variable-format(node) &
  *data-def-clause* =
  'DEFINE DATA LOCAL $old-defs END-DEFINE'
->
      variable-format(node) = undefined &
      new-var = make-variable(var-name, var-fmt) &
      *data-def-clause* =
      'DEFINE DATA LOCAL $old-defs,
      @new-var END-DEFINE'
```

The terms in this rule are part of the abstract syntax defined for the NATURAL 1.2 and 2.0 languages. In this rule, the input node is first tested to see if it is an inline variable declaration. If so, `var-fmt` is set to the format of the inline declaration. On the right-hand side of the rule, a new variable declaration `new-var` is created and added to the "data definition" clause `*data-def-clause*`. Also, the variable format of node is erased, effectively deleting the inline variable declaration from the program.

In summary, the commercially available REFINE system is based on technology developed through program synthesis research over the last two decades. Substantial software development productivity gains have been achieved by customers, exceeding an order of magnitude in the area of programming language applications.

E7. SETL

SETL (Dewar et al., 1979) is a very high-level language that provides set theoretic data types with the conventional control structures found in block structured languages like Pascal. It also has language constructs for backtracking, universal quantification, and existential quantification. The SETL project was started in the early 1970s and is an ongoing effort at New York University. Many regard SETL as the first executable specification language. SETL was used to construct the first verified correct ADA compiler in 1982. Despite being a rapid prototype, this ADA compiler actually ran faster than the hand-coded ADA compilers built at that time.

The key issue addressed by SETL is the compilation of set data types into efficient concrete data structures. SETL compiles sets into dynamic linked hash tables, which provide asymptotically optimal performance for set operations such as enumeration, membership tests, insertion, and deletion. However, even though asymptotically optimal, there can be a large constant time overhead for set operations implemented with these hash tables.

SETL augments dynamic linked hash tables with BASES—auxiliary data structures that do not have the large constant time overhead of dynamic linked hash tables. For example, if A is a subset of B, then BASING would represent A by a bit on each object in B. A heuristic algorithm for choosing bases was developed and implemented for the SETL compiler (Schonberg et al., 1981). BASING significantly reduces the constant time overhead of dynamic linked hash tables, thus making set operations efficient in practice.

Another key efficiency issue for the SETL compiler is to determine when data structures can be shared—that is, when it is possible to pass pointers instead of copying data structures. The SETL language has value semantics like APL, rather than pointer semantics like LISP. Value semantics are a higher level of abstraction than pointer semantics, but they can lead to repeated copying of data structures especially in recursive programs. The SETL compiler automatically determines when pointers can be passed instead of copying data structures.

E8. STRATA

THE STRATA research system (Lowry, 1987b) synthesizes algorithms through problem reformulation. The basic idea is illustrated in Figure E–4.

An algorithm that solves a problem through reformulation consists of an encode step, an algorithm to solve the reformulated problem in the new domain, and a decode step. For example, to compute decimal arithmetic operations, a computer first encodes the decimal numbers into binary numbers, computes the answer in binary arithmetic, and then decodes the result back to decimal arithmetic. A fundamental theorem of problem reformulation (Lowry, 1989) states that whenever there is an

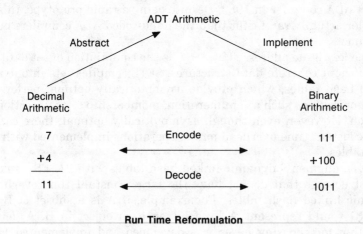

Figure E–4.   Problem reformulation through abstraction, then implementation.

encode/decode reformulation, the original problem and the reformulated problem are both implementations of the same abstract problem specification. In Figure E–4 this abstract specification is the abstract data type (ADT) for arithmetic. All concrete representations of arithmetic are implementations of this ADT.

This theorem suggests that to synthesize an algorithm the problem and its domain theory should first be abstracted to generate an abstract problem specification and abstract domain theory. Then, the program synthesis methods described in Section C can be applied to this abstract specification. First, an abstract algorithm is designed, and then this abstract algorithm is implemented with efficient concrete data structures and concrete operations. If different data structures are derived than those in the original problem specification, encode/decode functions also need to be synthesized to reformulate problem instances at run-time. The encode/decode run-time reformulation is a side effect of abstracting the problem specification and then implementing the abstract algorithm in a different representation. STRATA synthesizes algorithms in three steps, as shown in Figure E–5.

The main contributions of STRATA are methods for abstracting problem specifications. These methods are based on a semantic theory of problem reformulation (Lowry, 1989), developed by extending the mathematical theory of abstract data types (Goguen et al., 1978; Goguen and Burstall, 1985). These methods can generate new abstract data types because they are based on first principles. In contrast, the program understanding systems discussed in Section B6 use predefined libraries of abstractions. One of STRATA's abstraction methods is to discover behavioral equivalences and then incorporate them into the domain

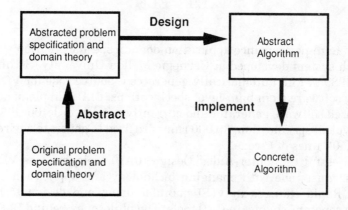

Figure E–5.   STRATA's algorithm synthesis method.

theory. A behavioral equivalence is a relation among domain objects which behave equivalently with respect to a problem. Behaviorally equivalent objects can be grouped together into the same abstract object. STRATA transforms the domain theory into a new domain theory denoting these abstract objects.

STRATA is interfaced to KIDS (Section E3), which provides a shell for the algorithm design and implementation steps. STRATA includes a design tactic for local search algorithms (Lowry, 1988b), also known as hill-climbing algorithms. This design tactic is similar in structure to the divide and conquer design tactic described in Section C8. A hill-climbing algorithm starts with a feasible solution and searches its neighborhood to find a better solution. If a better solution is found, then this solution becomes the current solution, and the algorithm iterates. If the current solution is the best in its neighborhood, the algorithm returns this locally optimal solution and then terminates.

The major issue in designing a hill-climbing algorithm is to define a neighborhood structure over the space of feasible solutions. STRATA does this with mathematical techniques related to abstraction through symmetry (Lowry, 1988). A symmetry is defined by a group of transformations. STRATA's hill-climbing design tactic first defines a group of transformations that map feasible solutions to feasible solutions. A subset of these transformations then defines the map from a feasible solution to neighboring feasible solutions. The effectiveness of this design tactic was demonstrated by synthesizing a variant of the simplex algorithm from the abstract specification of linear optimization problems.

E9. ELF

ELF is a high-performance application-domain specific program synthesis research system developed at Carnegie Mellon University (Setliff, 1988; 1989; 1989a). ELF automatically generates C source code for VLSI wire-routing software from high-level specifications. ELF is implemented as a rule-based software generator and currently consists of 1,400 OPS5 rules. For a typical specification, 30,000 rules are fired to generate a wire router with 2,500 lines of C code.

Successful Computer-Aided Design (CAD) tools, such as VLSI wire routers, must cope with changing technology and application environments. Rapid changes in VLSI manufacturing and design technology require constant change in CAD tools. The philosophy behind ELF is that the appropriate place for technology-dependent information is not as run-time parameters for CAD tools, but in a high-level specification given to a generator for CAD tools. To generate wire-routing software, ELF integrates application-domain knowledge with algorithm and programming knowledge.

ELF has three key features. First, algorithms and data structures are represented and developed at a very abstract level. A custom-designed language called ADL (Algorithm Development Language), which is essentially a simplified version of SETL (see Section E7), is used to describe algorithm design schemata. ADL is based on sets and lacks data structure implementation specifications. Instead, data structures are specified separately by hierarchically composing simple templates for elementary structures such as arrays and lists.

Second, wire-router design knowledge and generic program synthesis knowledge are used to guide search, to select among candidate algorithm design schemata for all necessary component algorithms, and to deduce compatible data structure implementations for these components. Candidate representations are analyzed and modified to reflect selection decisions. An important aspect of ELF's architecture is its logical separation of algorithm selection and data structure selection. ELF alternates algorithm selection decisions with data structure selection decisions to ensure that dependencies between algorithms and data structures are taken into account.

Third, code generation is used to transform the resulting abstract descriptions of selected algorithms and data structures into C source code. Code generation is an incremental, stepwise refinement process that uses wire-router design knowledge, generic program synthesis knowledge, and knowledge of how these two interact.

ELF has synthesized wire routers for a variety of VLSI technologies, illustrating how its architecture copes with shifting technology. These wire routers compared well against hand-crafted production-quality wire routers, and were verified on both synthetic and industrial wire-routing benchmarks. ELF has proven its ability to generate high-quality wire-routing code.

In summary, ELF is a software generator based on AI technology. ELF efficiently generates high-quality CAD software using application-specific and generic program synthesis knowledge. Like current CASE code generators, ELF selects and composes templates. However there are substantial differences. The templates ELF composes are very high-level algorithm schemata and data structure templates, as opposed to source level templates. ELF also uses a sophisticated rule-based architecture for selecting and composing templates. Finally, ELF uses stepwise refinement to convert abstract algorithm and data structure specifications into source code.

E.10. PhiNix

PHINIX is a transformational implementation research system that generates programs that interact with physical devices through temporal streams of data and control (Barstow, 1988). Abstract specifications are stated in terms of constraints on the values of input and output streams. The target language is the Stream Machine (Barth et al., 1985), which includes concurrently executing processes communicating and synchronizing through streams. PhiNix 's specific domain of expertise is device drivers for controlling oil well logging tools (Barstow, 1985). These tools are inserted into an exploratory oil well to gather geological data relevant to oil exploration.

PhiNix is distinguished in two ways from other transformation systems based on wide-spectrum languages. First, its target domain is embedded software which reacts to its environment, unlike the target domain of most program synthesis systems which produce applicative programs that take an input, produce an output, and then terminate. Second, this target domain requires that PhiNix's wide-spectrum language, PhiLang, includes both applicative constructs for specification and imperative constructs for the target language. PhiNix first transforms an abstract specification into an applicative expression, and then into imperative expressions denoting processes that consume and produce streams. An applicative operator takes input values and produces output values, while an imperative operator takes values from a computational context (e.g. global memory) and produces side effects on that context.

PhiLang varies along two dimensions. The first dimension varies from abstract data types such as sets to concrete data types such as sequences. A stream is a sequence that is temporally ordered. The second dimension varies from applicative to imperative. During transformational implementation a program will contain a mixture of applicative and imperative constructs. PhiLang supports this mixture through environments. An imperative environment is an applicative operator defined in terms of imperative constructs, whereas an applicative environment is an imperative operator defined in terms of applicative constructs.

Currently (Barstow, 1988), the language PhiLang has been defined and implemented with enough transformations to generate a small error correction data routine. PhiNix transformations are guided either manually or through a script. In the future, a tactic and strategy language will be developed for controlling the transformational search space. Another future extension is to incorporate language constructs for specifying real-time performance constraints, which is an important aspect of embedded software. These performance constraints will help to guide the search in program synthesis.

In summary, the major significance of the PhiNix project is the extension of the transformational implementation paradigm to the synthesis of embedded, reactive software. This type of software is an important component of many engineering applications.

F.   FURTHER READINGS IN KNOWLEDGE-BASED SOFTWARE ENGINEERING

Survey Articles

"Artificial Intelligence and Software Engineering," David Barstow, 9th International Conference on Software Engineering, Monterey, CA., pp. 200–211, March 1987.

"Automatic Programming: Myths and Prospects", C. Rich and R.C. Waters, IEEE Computer, Vol 21(8) pp. 40–51, August 1988.

"Knowledge-Based Programming: A Survey of Program Design and Construction Techniques," Allen T. Goldberg, IEEE Transactions on Software Engineering, Vol. SE-12 (7) pp. 752–768, July 1986

"Program Transformation Systems," Helmut Partsch and R. Steinbruggen, ACM Computing Surveys, Vol 15(3) pp. 199–236, September 1983

Special Issues

IEEE Expert, Special issue on "Building Intelligence into Software Engineering," Vol. 1(4), 1986

IEEE Transactions on Software Engineering, Special issue on "Artificial Intelligence and Software Engineering," November 1985, Volume SE-11, Number 11, Jack Mostow (Ed.)

Books

Algorithm Synthesis: A comparative study, David Steier and Penny Anderson, Springer-Verlag, New York, 1989

Artificial Intelligence and Software Engineering, Derek Partridge (Ed.), Ablex Publishers, New York, 1989

Automatic Program Construction Techniques, Alan Biermann, Gerard Guiho, and Yves Kodratoff (Eds.), Macmillan Publishing Company, 1984

Automating Software Design, Proceedings of Workshops held at AAAI-88 and IJCAI-89, Michael Lowry and Robert McCartney (Eds.), AAAI Press, 1990

IEEE Tutorial on New Paradigms for Software Development, W. W. Agresti (Ed.), IEEE Computer Society Press, 1986

Readings in Artificial Intelligence and Software Engineering, Charles Rich and Richard Waters (Eds.), Morgan Kaufmann Publishers, 1986

Chapter XXI

Qualitative Physics

Yumi Iwasaki—Stanford University

CHAPTER XXI: QUALITATIVE PHYSICS

A. OVERVIEW

QUALITATIVE PHYSICS is an area of artificial intelligence concerned with reasoning qualitatively about the behavior of physical systems. Physical systems include any systems, natural or man-made, operating under the laws of physics. Although numerical simulation using computers has been a tool for predicting behaviors of systems in many disciplines of natural and social sciences for a long time, interests in the topic of qualitative physics has grown very rapidly in the recent years. Qualitative physics is different from numerical simulation of physical system behavior in that reasoning about behavior is carried out not at the level of a collection of numerical values of variables at different time points, but at a more abstract level of qualitative characteristics of its behavior. Many of the qualitative physics systems described in this chapter perform qualitative simulation or prediction, but the goals of qualitative physics go beyond being able to simulate behavior. The goals are to understand the types of knowledge required for carrying out qualitative reasoning about behavior, to develop a general representation scheme for such knowledge, and to develop procedures for making useful inferences about the behavior of physical systems.

This chapter gives an overview of qualitative physics, discussing basic issues and techniques and describing some people's work in the field. The discussion in this chapter focuses on what can be called *qualitative dynamics*—qualitative representation of time-varying quantities and its use in reasoning about behavior.

One important type of physical reasoning that this chapter does not attempt to cover is reasoning about shapes and motion. Much work has been done on spatial reasoning in the field of robotics, and also some researchers in qualitative physics have been studying the problem of qualitative spatial reasoning. We do not attempt to cover this area in this chapter because issues involved in spatial reasoning are considerably different from and in some ways much more difficult than issues in qualitative dynamics. For the readers interested in the problem of qualitative spatial reasoning, references are included at the end of this section.

Motivations for Qualitative Physics

In his work on naive physics (Hayes, 1978 and 1979) Hayes attempted to construct a formalization of ordinary, everyday knowledge about the physical world. This work provided much inspiration to the research in qualitative physics. Today, modeling commonsense physical reasoning is still an important goal for some researchers in qualitative physics, but there are many more motivations for studying qualitative physics that go beyond the scope of commonsense reasoning.

Commonsense Reasoning About the Physical World.   People perform commonsense reasoning all the time about everyday physical situations in daily life, and they seem to do so without much effort. For example, if we put a kettle filled with water on a stove, we can predict that the water will eventually start boiling, the amount of water in the kettle will decrease and eventually the kettle will be empty. If we throw a ball up into the air, we can easily predict that at first the ball will keep rising for a while with the upward speed steadily decreasing. Eventually the upward speed will reach 0 and the ball will start falling. The ball will continue to fall with an increasing downward speed until it eventually hits the ground. Though we could certainly set up mathematical equations and solve them to compute the trajectory of the ball, people make such a prediction even without knowing mathematics nor the precise physical laws. People's intuitive physical reasoning in these cases seems very different from that taught in formal physics classes. One of the motivations for qualitative physics research is the desire to identify the types of knowledge required to perform commonsense physical reasoning and also to learn how people use such knowledge.

Qualitative Reasoning.   People often reason qualitatively not only about everyday situations, but also about situations that are beyond the scope of commonsense reasoning and that require much specialized knowledge of the domain. There are many advantages to being able to reason qualitatively about a complex situation.

In many areas of natural and social sciences, we have only qualitative knowledge about behavior. Precise information may be unavailable both about variable values or about relations among variables. For example, in ecology, a person studying the population balance between foxes and rabbits may know that an increase in the population of foxes tends to cause the population of rabbits to decrease because foxes prey on rabbits. He may also know that a decrease in rabbit population has a negative effect on the fox population because there will be less food for foxes. However, it may be impossible to know the precise form of the mathematical relations between the two populations implied by these statements. Even then, we may need to make some qualitative predictions, and people in fact do so in the absence of quantitative information.

Some problems are simply too difficult to completely solve analytically. Numerical simulation, a tool widely used for prediction of behavior when an analytic solution is unavailable, may require more computational efforts than it is worth. In such circumstances, it may still be possible to make some statements about the future course of events through a qualitative analysis of the problem. Even when an analytic or numerical solution is possible, a detailed quantitative prediction may be unnecessary. If all that is desired is a qualitative description of behavior, it may be more efficient to figure out roughly what will happen using qualitative information, and then to resort to more detailed quantitative reasoning only when it is necessary to do so to resolve ambiguities in the prediction.

Model-based Reasoning from First Principles. The last decade has seen a great success of expert systems research (see Chapters VII, VIII, and IX), and many programs have been built that achieve human expert level performance in their area of application. The high level of performance of these expert systems is made possible by their rich body of heuristic knowledge that enables them to search a very large search space efficiently. Reliance on heuristic knowledge acquired from experts makes it possible to build a system relatively easily that achieves expert level performance. However, their lack of explicit representation of more fundamental knowledge about the domain that underlies heuristic knowledge causes some serious problems for these systems. One of the main goals for research described in this chapter is to study reasoning from fundamental knowledge of the domain to overcome these problems.

One problem with conventional heuristic reasoning systems is that their performance degrades sharply outside their narrow domain of expertise. When a human expert encounters a novel problem for which he does not have hard-and-fast rules, he can still try to solve the problem using more basic knowledge of the domain. However, if a given problem falls slightly outside its area of expertise, a system that lacks fundamental knowledge of the domain can only give up or, worse yet, it may draw an erroneous conclusion by failing to recognize the limitation of its own knowledge.

Another problem is the inability to transfer knowledge to other tasks. Since their knowledge is encoded as heuristic associations that are specific to the particular type of tasks they are designed to solve, it is not easily reusable for other tasks even in the same domain. For example, the rule that says, "If the gas mileage is below normal and the color of the exhaust gas is blue, clean the carburetor" may be useful for diagnosing automobile malfunctions, but it cannot be used for designing better cars even though the underlying mechanisms and physical principles are the same for both tasks.

These problems of conventional expert systems result from their lack of more fundamental knowledge of the domain. Research in qualitative physics tries to address this problem by reasoning with a detailed domain model, i.e., an explicit representation of the causal mechanisms and first principles of the domain that underlie heuristic knowledge.

Temporal Reasoning.   Another motivation for research on qualitative physics is the need for systems to reason about dynamic aspects
of problems, i.e., reasoning about how situations evolve over time. Many
expert systems reason qualitatively about problems, but most of their
reasoning is static analysis and involves only limited analysis of dynamic
aspects of the problems because they lack a well-developed notion of time
and a sophisticated temporal reasoning mechanism. Numerical simulation programs, on the other hand, can reason about behavior over time,
but they require an extensive amount of numerical computation. One
goal of qualitative physics research is to understand what it takes to
perform qualitative temporal reasoning about behavior and how to represent necessary knowledge in such a way as to enable problem solving.
Allen's temporal logic based on time intervals instead of time points
provides a basis for the representation of temporal states employed by
several qualitative physics systems (Allen, 1984).

Causal Reasoning.   Another important aspect of human reasoning
about the physical world is causal reasoning. There is little doubt that
causality plays an important role in human understanding of the world.
Although a formal treatment of the foundations of science avoids the
notion of causality, in informal explanations of phenomena, statements
of the form "A caused B" are exceedingly common. If an artificial intelligence program is to provide an intuitive causal explanation, it needs
to have an operational concept of causality and knowledge of causal
relations in the world.

Conventional heuristic reasoning systems perform poorly here, too.
The explanatory power of a reasoning system based on compiled heuristic
knowledge tends to be limited by its inability to provide causal accounts.
When a human expert is asked to explain his conclusion, he can do so
in terms of fundamental causal mechanisms of the domain. When a
heuristic program is asked to explain its reasoning, it can only do so in
terms of the heuristics used to draw the conclusion. Such explanations
are usually not sufficient causal explanations because in the process of
compiling heuristic knowledge, knowledge about intermediate causal
steps is left out or combined with other types of knowledge for the sake
of efficiency.

This difficulty of generating intuitive causal explanations exists also
when a problem is solved analytically or numerically. The result of
numerical simulation describes behavior as a set of numerical values of
variables at successive time points, but it does not constitute a causal
explanation of why things behave as they do. When a problem is solved
analytically, a person must interpret the solution so that its intuitive
meaning can be understood. Neither the solution nor the process (problem-solving trace) of obtaining it provides a causal explanation.

By reasoning from knowledge of the structure and physical principles underlying functions in a manner similar to that of humans, qualitative physics programs not only draw conclusions about behavior but also provide intuitive, causal explanation of how the behavior is achieved. Some programs (see Sections E, F, and H) described in this chapter rely on the knowledge of causal relations provided in their knowledge base. Others (see Sections D and G) attempt to infer causal relations in a given model.

What Is Qualitative Physics?

Four tasks underlie describing physical systems. They are listed here in ascending order of the amount of information and efforts required:

1. Identifying the relevant objects, variables, and parameters in the domain.

2. Identifying relations among those variables and parameters, including not only mathematical but also causal relations.

3. Describing behavior of the system in terms of qualitative characteristics (increasing, decreasing, oscillating, melting, boiling, and so on) of the changes over time in the variable values.

4. Predicting the magnitudes of such changes.

Qualitative physics is concerned with tasks 1 through 3. In contrast, physics is concerned with all four tasks. Tasks 1 and 2 are building a model of the domain, and tasks 3 and 4 make use of the model for reasoning purposes.

Consider the following questions and answers about a physical situation:

Question: A few ice cubes are put in a glass. If the glass is left on a table in a room, what will eventually happen to the ice?

Answer: Since ice is at a lower temperature than the surrounding air, heat will flow from the air to the ice, causing the temperature of the ice to rise until it reaches the freezing temperature. At that point, the ice will start to melt, and there will be a mixture of ice and water in the glass for a while, during which time the temperature of the mixture will remain constant at the freezing temperature. When the ice has completely melted, the temperature of the water will start to rise again and will continue to do so until it reaches room temperature. After that point, the temperature of the water will remain constant indefinitely.

Question: What will happen if, instead of leaving the glass on a table, I put it in a refrigerator?

Answer: Provided that you don't put the glass in the freezer, since the air in the refrigerator must be cooler than the room temperature, it will take longer for the temperature of the ice to go up to the freezing temperature and to melt. But it eventually will, and after the ice melts, the temperature of the water will go up to the temperature of the air in the refrigerator and remain constant there.

It is easy for humans to produce and to understand explanations like these. Two important characteristics of the type of inferences demonstrated by these explanations are their qualitativeness and their reliance on the knowledge of fundamental principles (such as physical laws) governing the ways things behave in the domain. The area of research described in this chapter is concerned with building programs that can make these types of inferences about the behavior of physical systems.

Qualitative Inference. As the title of the chapter suggests, the qualitativeness of reasoning is an important characteristics of the research described here, and it distinguishes the field from traditional numerical simulation or automated physics. Inference is qualitative in both the information used and the conclusions drawn; it uses imprecise information about the values of quantities, and nonquantitative information such as causality, stability, and so on.

Imprecise information about a quantity can take different forms, for example, an interval in which the real value lies, whether it is decreasing, steady, or increasing, and so on. Because information about values of quantities is imprecise, the information about functional relations among quantities can be imprecise, also. Functional relations can be described imprecisely as in "x tends to decrease as y increases." Because of this imprecision in the knowledge used, most of the programs perform some type of qualitative simulation of behavior in order to infer possible behavior instead of trying to solve functional relations analytically. Explanations produced by these programs are also qualitative in the sense that they are given in terms of some salient qualitative characteristics of the way things change such as ice melting, the temperature rising, something causing something else, and so on.

For example, in the questions in Section A2, no precise numerical data are given in the description nor are needed to produce the answers. Both the information given explicitly and assumptions made implicitly about quantities are at most ordinal; for example, room temperature is normally higher than the freezing temperature of water and the temperature of ice is probably lower than or at most equal to the freezing temperature. Also, it requires only qualitative knowledge of thermodynamic laws; for instance, the heat flows from a body of a higher temperature to a body of a lower temperature, and the larger the temperature difference, the higher the heat flow rate. It is not necessary to know the exact mathematical form of the laws.

Note, however, that emphasis on qualitative reasoning is certainly not unique to this area of artificial intelligence research. In fact, the reasoning performed by most artificial intelligence programs is more heuristic and qualitative than numerical or analytic. Even before artificial intelligence became an established field, much work had been done in many fields of engineering and science (for example, econometrics, ecology, applied mathematics, control theory, and so on) on qualitative analysis of system behavior.

Reasoning from Domain Principles.   Another important characteristic of this research area is having an explicit domain model. A model in domains of physical systems consists of the knowledge of the physical structure of the system as well as physical principles governing behavior in the domain. The former includes knowledge of the objects involved, their physical relations to each other, and their general behavioral characteristics. The latter include physical laws governing the ways various aspects of the objects change or the ways they interact. Qualitative physics programs infer and explain the behavior of a system as the consequence of objects changing states and interacting with each other according to physical principles.

Moreover, efforts are made to make the representation of the domain knowledge as independent as possible of specific application goals such as diagnosis, prediction, or teaching. In most expert systems that use heuristic knowledge, the knowledge is encoded in a format that is particularly efficient for its application goal. However, a format that is convenient for some specific application, such as diagnosing faults, may obscure the underlying domain principles to which knowledge used in diagnosis must ultimately be reducible. For example, a rule in a diagnostic program for automobile engines may state, "If the engine temperature is abnormally high but the fan is working, stop the engine and check the oil." The basic domain knowledge about the structure of a car engine and how it works is nowhere explicit. However, rules like this one, in which intermediate causal steps are compiled out, linking their antecedent and conclusion directly, are efficient for some purposes. The terms "shallow knowledge" and "deep knowledge" are sometimes used to distinguish compiled knowledge and more basic knowledge about the domain. *Shallow knowledge* refers to compiled knowledge, and *deep knowledge* refers to more fundamental knowledge of the domain. Obviously the *depth* of knowledge is a relative matter. In troubleshooting computer hardware, a knowledge of input/output behavior of individual chip and their interconnections that together produce the overall behavior of the computer can be considered deep knowledge as compared to empirical knowledge such as "when this symptom is observed, replace the board A." However, such knowledge of behavior in terms of input/ output behavior of chip may be considered shallow when we are concerned with how such I/O behavior is achieved by actual electric circuits on the chip.

What makes the domain model explicit or implicit is not the absolute "depth" of knowledge but whether or not a distinction is made between different types of knowledge. Heuristic knowledge arises from different sources, including structural knowledge, laws of nature, knowledge of the functions of subcomponents, empirical or statistical knowledge about what faults are more likely to occur than others, and so on. (Examples of several different types of knowledge underlying the rules in MYCIN knowledge base are discussed by Clancey (1983).) Expert systems relying on heuristic rules make no distinctions between these different types of knowledge because pieces of different types are compiled into one unit of knowledge such as a rule. The domain model is made explicit when distinctions between different types of knowledge and the roles that each of them play in the problem-solving process is made clear. The programs described in this chapter all attempt explicit representation of the domain model in this sense.

In relation to explicit representations of the domain model, physical systems must be explained. The requirement of an explicit domain model makes domains like the physical world, in which we have knowledge of fundamental principles, more suitable for studying qualitative reasoning than other domains in which these principles are not well understood. In medicine, for example, most of the knowledge used for diagnosing and treating diseases is empirical, not based on a model of the relevant biological and chemical mechanisms. The domains dealing with man-made physical devices are particularly suitable because both the physical structure of the device and the physical laws governing the functioning of the device are well understood. In fact, most of the programs discussed in this chapter work in such domains. However, qualitative reasoning techniques that are developed should be, in principle, applicable to a wider range of domains, including natural and social sciences, as long as some theories exist about causal mechanisms in the domain, based on which the user can build a model to explain and predict behavior.

Physics, Naive Physics, and Expert Qualitative Reasoning. The desire to understand people's commonsense physical reasoning provided much initial motivation for qualitative physics research. It still is an important goal for many researchers. However, a clear distinction must be made between this and the goal of reasoning qualitatively about complex situations, which is what most qualitative physics programs are currently pursuing.

In complex domains, human experts with much knowledge of underlying physical principles can set up equations and attempt to solve them numerically or analytically to answer a given question about the domain. However, before attempting a detailed solution, experts often reason qualitatively in a way that is beyond the scope of commonsense physical reasoning. Even though both are qualitative, such expert reasoning appears to be very different from commonsense physical reasoning.

Besides qualitativeness of inference, there is yet another feature common to naive reasoning and expert qualitative reasoning that distinguishes the two from formal physics. It is the emphasis in qualitative physics on *interpretation* of the solution. The formal physics approach to reasoning about a physical situation involves setting up equations that describe the situation. Solving them gives a mathematical answer, which still needs to be interpreted by a human being for it to "make sense" and be useful. "Making sense" in this case involves describing the actual implications of the formal answer in the physical world. For example, an answer that the height of a ball is given by $x(t) = x_0 - gt^2/2$ can be obtained by a formal physics approach, but to interpret the answer, to provide an explanation such as "the ball will keep falling at an ever-increasing speed because of the gravitational force pulling the ball constantly toward the earth" is a different matter. The mathematical approach of formal physics does not help us produce such an interpretation, but a qualitative physics answer will look more like the interpretation than the mathematical expression. Producing this type of explanation (or interpretation) is in fact a very crucial step in the entire endeavor of physical reasoning, and it is hoped that the research in qualitative physics will complement the formal physics approach by shedding light on this interpretation process.

Basic Issues

Many issues must be investigated to build a system to reason qualitatively about behavior based on an explicit domain model. These include representation of the model of the domain, principles along which such models are to be built, representation and reasoning with causality, and complexity of the reasoning process. There are also different tasks that qualitative physics systems perform. This section briefly discusses each of these topics.

Representation. An important characteristic of programs discussed in this chapter is the way a domain model is represented in the knowledge base. Two main types of knowledge need to be represented, structural knowledge and behavioral knowledge. Since the method of representation of the domain knowledge depends very much on the choice of ontological primitives, we discuss them first.

Ontological primitives. All the work to be discussed is concerned in some way with explaining how behavior is brought about. Such explanations are given in terms of basic facts about the domain and their interactions. The choice of which types of facts will be the primitives of the domain representation is an important characteristic of qualitative physics programs. de Kleer and Brown's ENVISION program (see Section D) takes the topological structure of a device, in terms of components and their interconnections, to be the primitives. In Forbus's Qualitative Process Theory (see Section E), the notion of physical processes is primitive. In causal action–based approaches such as those by Chandrasekaran and his colleagues (see Section H2), actions, events, and states, and the causal links to connect them are the primitives.

Structural knowledge. Structural knowledge is about objects in the domain and their physical configurations. In most programs described in this chapter, the structure of a device is represented in terms of its components and physical connections among components.

Behavioral knowledge. Behavioral knowledge includes knowledge about the laws of physics and functions of subcomponents. Behavioral knowledge in the Commonsense Algorithm (see Section H) is represented by various types of causal links connecting events. Similarly, in work by Chandrasekaran and his colleagues, behavioral knowledge is represented by a sequence of states connected by causal links denoting behaviors or functions of subcomponents. Other programs represent behavioral knowledge as qualitative mathematical relations among variables pertaining to various aspects of the objects in the domain. Such mathematical relations must come from various sources, for example, intrinsic characteristics of objects in the domain or influences of active physical processes.

In ENVISION, such mathematical relations must come from the knowledge of physical structure of the domain. In Iwasaki and Simon's work (see Section G), they come from the notion of *mechanisms* in the domain. In the Qualitative Process Theory, behavioral knowledge takes the form of definitions of various types of physical processes that are possible in the domain as well as behavioral characteristics of various types of objects in the domain.

Modeling Principles.

Modeling refers to the process of building a model of a domain. The quality of any inferences made about the domain depends very much on the model as well as on the reasoning scheme employed. If a scheme for reasoning about physical situations is to demonstrate a wide range of applicability, its model of the domain must be constructed according to some general principles to guarantee a high level of objectivity of the model.

de Kleer and Brown's Locality Principle (see Section D) states that effects must propagate locally through specified connections. In qualitative physics, the locality of two locations is defined by whether or not there is some direct physical connection between the two. For example, in the domain of electric circuits, locality is determined by whether or not two points are represented in the structural representation as being directly connected by wire. However, this definition of locality is obviously too narrow for general application as can be seen from the fact that in a domain dealing with forces that act over a distance, such as electro-magnetic force or gravity, propagation of effects does not require any physical connections. In general, whether or not direct propagation of effects is allowed depends on what types of interactions are relevant for bringing about behavior.

de Kleer and Brown's No-Function-in-Structure Principle states that a description of a part of a device should not presume the functioning of the whole. This principle has the same kind of difficulty as the Locality Principle. Since it is not possible to describe the behavior of a part in all possible ways, we must decide what particular aspect of the behavior to represent. In other words, behavior can only be described in some reasoning context. And the particular aspect chosen for description must be the one relevant to the expected behavior of the whole if the knowledge is to be useful at all.

Simon's causal ordering analysis (see Section G) requires that the system of equations comprising a model be self-contained i.e., the same number of equations as variables, and that each equation constituting a model represent a conceptually distinct mechanism in the situation. These requirements force all internal and external mechanisms influencing variables to be clearly identified. However, a model builder is still left with the problem of how to identify conceptually distinct mechanisms or that of how to determine whether a given equation represents such a mechanism.

Although clearly these principles cannot be achieved in their strict sense and they can only be approximated to a degree, they still provide good guidelines for building a model that is as free as possible of hidden assumptions about what its behavior should be. When building a model, it is essential to explicitly state the underlying assumptions to clarify the limitation of its applicability.

Causality. Explanations of behavior must show how a structure and physical laws ultimately give rise to observed or predicted behavior through a series of causal interactions. Effects in one part of a model can be propagated to other parts to cause further effects. The programs described in this chapter have several different ways of handling causality. Some (see Section H) have a predefined knowledge of causal relations between events, and causal relations are considered primitives for these programs. In the Qualitative Process Theory, knowledge of causal relations is given in the definitions of physical processes, which are considered to be the medium to transmit causality. ENVISION defines

causality based on the way effects of a disturbance are propagated to
other parts of the model of a device during the process of predicting its
behavior. Iwasaki and Simon determine causal relations among the variables of a system based on the notion of causal ordering in a system of
equations.

Qualitative Reasoning and Complexities. We have emphasized
qualitativeness of reasoning as one of the defining characteristics of this
field. In actually building a program, this is accomplished by reasoning
about changes not with actual values of quantities but with their qualitative features such as the signs of the values and the direction (increasing, decreasing, or steady) in which they are changing, ordinal relations
among them, and so on. It was hoped that by using only qualitative
information, we could predict most of the important aspects of the behavior with much less computational effort than would otherwise be
required.

However, using qualitative information almost always means that
inferences are highly ambiguous. For example, the initial behavior of a
ball thrown straight up into the air is that its vertical position is positive
and increasing, zero being defined as ground level and positive being
above the ground. This description alone does not even allow us to
determine whether or not it will stop rising eventually. Even if the
information that the upward speed is decreasing is added, we cannot
answer this question because the possibility is not ruled out that the
upward speed approaches zero asymptotically. A prediction based on this
type of qualitative information is highly ambiguous as it predicts many
possible courses of behavior without the means to select the correct or
the most likely ones. In fact, the process of predicting qualitative behavior is combinatorially explosive.

Therefore, it becomes important both to control combinatorial explosion and to eliminate spurious behaviors as much as possible by adding
information, for example, additional assumptions, domain specific heuristics, teleological knowledge of components, and information on higher
order derivatives. Exploiting abstraction hierarchies is also important
in reducing complexity.

Tasks Performed. Most qualitative physics systems perform some
type of prediction or simulation. Several different types of tasks fall into
this category. One is prediction of the device behavior over time; determining a likely course of future behavior, given a representation of a
device and some initial conditions. The word "envisioning" is often used
to refer to this activity. There are several ways to represent behavior
over time when this type of prediction is carried out. In ENVISION and
QSIM (see Section F), behavior over time is represented as a sequence of
qualitative states, defined by a set of qualitative value assignments to
variables. In the Qualitative Process Theory, on the other hand, behavior

is represented by instances of physical objects and processes coming into existence or disappearing during some time interval, as a result of changes in the world, and causing more changes in turn. An advantage of the latter representation is that parts of the world that do not interact may be reasoned about separately.

Other related types of prediction involve the prediction of effects of some external disturbance or of some change in a system parameter. They are called disturbance analysis or comparative analysis. For example, what will happen to the behavior of a mass-spring system if the block is replaced by a heavier one? Or, what will happen to the efficiency of the coal-burning boiler if the atmospheric pressure increases? If the system is assumed to be in equilibrium when the disturbance happens, will it return to equilibrium after some time?

Another task, similar to prediction, is *consolidation*, studied by Bylander (see Section H3). Consolidation is a process of generating behavior descriptions of a device by combining behavior descriptions of its components. The output is not a prediction of an actual behavior but behavioral knowledge of the device that can be used, for example, by a simulation program.

In this Chapter

The remainder of this chapter is organized as follows. Section B gives the basics of the qualitative calculus used by many qualitative physics programs to represent and reason about quantities and the functional relations among them. Section C goes on to describe how this calculus can be used to reason about behavior over time. The rest of the chapter describes various qualitative physics programs. Section D describes de Kleer and Brown's work on the program called ENVISION. Section E discusses Forbus's Qualitative Process Theory. Section F discusses Kuipers's qualitative simulation program, QSIM. Section G describes Iwasaki and Simon's work on Causal Ordering and their program called CAOS. All these approaches use qualitative functional relations among variables to describe behavior. In contrast, the work described in Section H, including the Commonsense Algorithm of Rieger and Grinberg, the functional representation of Chandrasekaran, and consolidation of Bylander, employs representation in terms of causal states and links.

References

See Bobrow (1984) for a brief summary of issues in qualitative physics research. Hayes' work on naive physics is described in Hayes (1978 and 1979). Fishwick (1988) and Rajagopaian (1986) survey qualitative reasoning and modeling from the standpoint of computer simulation.

Clancey (1983) discusses different types of knowledge in MYCIN knowledge base.

References in qualitative spatial reasoning include Forbus (1981), Faltings (1987a and 1987b), Davis (1986), Nielsen (1988), and Joskowicz (1987). Forbus (1987) discusses the difficulties in establishing a general framework for qualitative spatial reasoning and proposes mixed quantitative and qualitative approach.

B. QUALITATIVE CALCULUS

THE PROGRAMS discussed in this chapter reason qualitatively as people do about physical phenomena. In this section, we describe what it means to reason qualitatively. In particular, we describe qualitative calculi that many programs use to reason qualitatively about quantities.

To reason qualitatively is to reason with information that is less precise than actual numerical data such as the signs, relative magnitudes, and the directions of change in variable values. Since these data are imprecise, our conclusions will be imprecise also. However in many situations, imprecise conclusions are sufficient or they are the best we can hope for. Consider the following examples:

Question: If a rabbit and a turtle run a race of the distance of one block, who will win the race?

Answer: The rabbit will probably win because a rabbit can run faster than a turtle.

Question: If an ice cube is left at the room temperature, what will eventually happen to the ice cube?

Answer: The temperature of ice is 0°C or less, and the normal room temperature is above 0°C. Since the heat flows from an object at a higher temperature to one at a lower temperature, heat will flow into the ice cube from the surrounding atmosphere. As a result, the ice will eventually melt.

We do not need to know the absolute speeds of the rabbit and the turtle, or the length of the block, or the temperatures of the ice cube and the ambient air, to solve these problems. The values of these variables can be imprecise. Signs and ordinal relations will suffice. Observe, though, that our answers are themselves necessarily qualitative: "The rabbit will reach the goal *before* the turtle." "The ice cube will melt *eventually*."

Imprecise knowledge of quantities and relations between quantities are expressed in terms of qualitative variables, qualitative equations, and qualitative inequalities. The value of a usual (quantitative) variable specifies only one element in the set of possible values. If the set is the entire real number line, a value represents a specific point. On the other hand, the value of a qualitative variable can represent an element as well as a set of elements.

Functional relations also can be described qualitatively. Take, for instance, Hooke's law of ideal springs, which is expressed as

$$F = kX$$

where F is the force on the spring, k is the spring constant, and X is the distance from the equilibrium point. This relation can be described qualitatively as: "The stronger the force on the spring, the larger the displacement from the equilibrium position."

Qualitative variables are constructed as follows. For a variable with a continuous domain, the entire domain is subdivided into a finite number of nonoverlapping subintervals, and all values in the same interval are treated as equivalent. The qualitative value of a variable, then, is the name of the interval in which its actual numerical value lies.

Subdividing the continuous domain of a variable is counterproductive if we lose important information about the behavior of physical systems by doing so. Ideally the values at the boundaries between subintervals should reflect significant changes in behavior, whereas behavior within a subinterval should be qualitatively uniform. One such significant value is 0°C for the temperature of water because the behavior of water changes significantly as water changes between solid and liquid phases at that temperature. The behaviors of cool water and cold water are not noticeably different, but behavior of water and ice are so qualitatively different that our language gives them different names.

Boundary values used to subdivide a continuous domain are called *landmark values* or *distinguished values*. A variable can have any number of landmark values at which behavior changes significantly, but qualitative reasoning programs usually assume their number to be finite. The most common subdivision of continuous domains is into three intervals: negative, zero, and positive. We will use this subdivision in the following description of the qualitative calculus, but the discussion can obviously be extended to cases where different quantizations are used. One significant aspect of this particular subdivision into negative numbers, zero, and positive numbers is that when a variable represents the rate of change in the value of some quantity, the value of the qualitative variable indicates whether the quantity is decreasing, constant, or increasing.

Qualitative Arithmetic Rules

Qualitative calculus is calculus of intervals instead of real numbers. In this section, we subdivide real numbers into three intervals: $(-\infty, 0)$, $[0, 0]$, and $(0, +\infty)$. We denote these three intervals by $-$, 0, and $+$. Qualitative variables take these values only. In addition, we assume that all the variables are continuous and differentiable everywhere. The notation $[x]$ denotes the qualitative variable corresponding to the quantitative variable x. The relation between x and $[x]$ is defined as follows:

$$[x] = + \text{ iff } x > 0$$
$$[x] = 0 \text{ iff } x = 0$$
$$[x] = - \text{ iff } x < 0$$

The value of $[x]$ is thus the sign of the value of x. The brackets $[\ \cdot\ ]$ can be thought of as the operator that generates a qualitative variable given a quantitative variable.

Qualitative equations and inequalities involve only qualitative variables. Because they are relations among signs of variables, the conditions on the actual values of variables represented by these relations are weaker than those represented by their quantitative counterparts. For example, the following quantitative equation represents a relation between the variables x and y:

$$c_1 x + c_2 y = 0$$

where c_1 and c_2 are positive constants. The qualitative version of this equation is as follows:

$$[x] + [y] = 0.$$

The qualitative equation correctly expresses that y must be 0 if x is 0, and if not, that x and y are of opposite signs, as implied by the original equation. However, the information, also implied by the original equation, that

$$\frac{x}{y} = -\frac{c_2}{c_1}$$

is lost in the qualitative equation.

The meaning of some qualitative calculus operators and qualitative equality and inequality are defined as follows. (Note that some values are undefined and denoted by "?".)

Addition: $[x] + [y]$

[y] \ [x]	+	0	-
+	+	+	?
0	+	0	-
-	?	-	-

Subtraction: $[x] - [y]$

[y] \ [x]	+	0	-
+	?	-	-
0	+	0	-
-	+	+	?

Multiplication: $[x] \times [y]$

$[y]$ \ $[x]$	$+$	0	$-$
$+$	$+$	0	$-$
0	0	0	0
$-$	$-$	0	$+$

Unary Minus: $-[x]$ ... unary minus x

$[x]$	$-[x]$
$+$	$-$
0	0
$-$	$+$

Qualitative Equality: $[x] = [y]$

$[y]$ \ $[x]$	$+$	0	$-$
$+$	T	F	F
0	F	T	F
$-$	F	F	T

Qualitative Inequality: $[x] > [y]$

$[y]$ \ $[x]$	$+$	0	$-$
$+$	F	F	F
0	T	F	F
$-$	T	T	F

With these definitions, quantitative equations can be converted to qualitative equations. Consider the following examples, where x and y are variables, and c is a constant.

Quantitative Equation	Qualitative Equation
1. $x + y = z$	$[x] + [y] = [z]$
2. $x - y = z$	$[x] - [y] = [z]$
3. $x \times y = z$	$[x] \times [y] = [z]$
4. $x + cy = z$	
Case 1 $c = 0$	$[x] \quad\quad = [z]$
Case 2 $c > 0$	$[x] + [y] = [z]$
Case 3 $c < 0$	$[x] - [y] = [z]$

Observe that in examples 3 and 4, both multiplication and division in quantitative equations become multiplication in the qualitative equations: No division operator is needed in this qualitative calculus of signs. Also, constant coefficients in qualitative equations are dropped but their signs are maintained in the qualitative equations.

Qualitative Derivatives

Qualitative physics is concerned with the dynamic behavior of the physical world, but knowing whether quantities are negative, zero, or positive only tells us about the state of the world, not about its behavior. However, qualitative variables can describe behavior when they stand for time derivatives of quantities. The qualitative derivative of x is defined as $[dx/dt]$, the qualitative variable of the derivative of x. We will write $[dx]$ instead of $[dx/dt]$ to designate the qualitative derivative of x to simplify the notation. Qualitative derivatives are important for describing behavior because the value of a qualitative derivative indicates how the value of the variable is changing, as follows:

$[dx]$	Direction of Change in x
+	Increasing
0	Steady
−	Decreasing

With equations of qualitative variables and derivatives, we can formulate qualitative rules that govern how quantities change. For example, the following qualitative equation tells us that a quantity x increases monotonically as another quantity y increases, but not the actual functional relation between x and y or between dx/dt and dy/dt:

$$[dx] = [dy]$$

Many qualitative reasoning systems, including those discussed in Sections D through F, use equations with qualitative derivatives to represent their knowledge about behavior.

Sources of Equations of Qualitative Derivatives

Before we describe the procedure for predicting the qualitative behavior of a system from qualitative equations, we discuss where the knowledge of qualitative functional relations may come from.

Differential equations.   If the differential equation describing the dynamic behavior of the system is known, it can be converted to a qualitative equation. A differential equation

$$\frac{dx}{dt} c(y + x),$$

where $c > 0$, is converted into the qualitative form

$$[dx] = [y] + [x].$$

Qualitative knowledge of how variable values depend on others.   We may notice that the viscosity of a liquid decreases as its temperature increases, although we may not know the precise functional relationship between viscosity and temperature. The relation is expressed qualitatively as

$$[dv] = -[dk],$$

where v and k represent viscosity and temperature, respectively.

Differentiating an equation with respect to time. Differentiating the equation

$$x + y = z \tag{1}$$

yields

$$\frac{dx}{dt} + \frac{dy}{dt} = \frac{dz}{dt}, \tag{2}$$

which can be converted into a qualitative equation

$$[dx] + [dy] = [dz]. \tag{3}$$

We must be careful about interpreting qualitative equations such as equation (3). If the original equation expresses an equilibrium condition of a physical system, it gives no information about how the variables will change when the equilibrium is disturbed. Thus equations produced by time-differentiating equilibrium equations do not necessarily describe how variables change when the system is out of equilibrium.

If equation (1) is an equilibrium condition, to assume equations (1) and (2) is to assume that an equilibrium relation between x, y, and z is instantly restored when disturbed, and therefore equilibrium between x and y holds practically all the time. Imagine that x in equation (1) is increased suddenly while y is held constant. Then since equation (2) is always true, z must increase by the same amount at the same time as x is increased, restoring equilibrium instantly. Since in reality it takes some time for any signal to propagate from one place to another, equation (2) will not strictly hold if equation (1) represents a physical phenomenon. Only if equation (1) represents a purely mathematical relation (e.g., a definition of z in terms of x and y) will equation (2) be strictly true. Nevertheless equation (2) is often a reasonable assumption when the signal propagation time among variables is negligible with respect to the time scale of the behavior of interest. For example, de Kleer and Brown make this (*quasi-static*) assumption that disturbances propagate instantaneously through a network of qualitative equations, and equilibrium is restored in no time. (See Section D.)

Solving Systems of Qualitative Equations

Solving systems of qualitative equations means finding qualitative values of variables that satisfy the equations. Unlike quantitative equations, a set of n qualitative equations in n variables can have more than one solution. The problem of finding a set of qualitative variables consistent with the given set of qualitative equations is a constraint-satisfaction problem, where the equations are the constraints to be satisfied. Techniques for solving constraint satisfaction problems can be applied to solving systems of qualitative equations.

Value propagation is a common technique for determining the values of variables in systems of qualitative equations. Given the values of all but one of the variables in an equation, the value of the unknown variable can be determined by substituting in the values of the known variables and simplifying the expression. This can be regarded as propagating values through networks of equations. In fact, when the equations model a physical device and variables in an equation represent physically connected components of the device, value propagation can be interpreted as the propagation of causal effects within the device. (Section D discusses this causal interpretation of value propagation in more detail.)

The following system is an example of qualitative equations and the determination of unknown variable values by value propagation.

$$[a] + [b] = [c] \tag{4}$$
$$[d] = [a] \tag{5}$$
$$[e] + [f] = [b] \tag{6}$$

Given the following values for $[d]$, $[e]$, and $[f]$, we can determine the values of the rest of the variables.

$$[d] = 0 \tag{7}$$
$$[e] = + \tag{8}$$
$$[f] = 0 \tag{9}$$

Substituting equations (8) and (9) in equation (6) gives

$$+ \, + \, 0 = [b],$$

which simplifies to

$$[b] = +. \tag{10}$$

Substituting equation (7) in equation (5) gives

$$[a] = 0. \tag{11}$$

Substituting equations (10) and (11) in equation (4) gives

$$0 + + = [c],$$

which simplifies to

$$[c] = +. \tag{12}$$

Ambiguities in Qualitative Calculi

Although the values of variables are uniquely determined in the previous example, in general a set of qualitative equations cannot be solved to obtain a unique solution. There are several reasons for this. One is that the qualitative calculus is inherently ambiguous, as indicated by the many ?'s in the definitions of qualitative calculus operators.

Observe what happens if equation (9) is now changed to

$$[f] = -. \tag{13}$$

From equations (6), (8), and (13), we obtain

$$+ + - = [b].$$

According to the addition table on page 341, the value of $[b]$ is undetermined. Any value, $+$, $-$, or 0 for $[b]$ is consistent with the rest of the equations and value assignments. If we wish to determine the values of remaining variables, we must consider three possible cases, depending on the value assumed for $[b]$, and continue to propagate for each case.

Case 1 $[b] = +$, $[a] = 0$, $[c] = +$
Case 2 $[b] = 0$, $[a] = 0$, $[c] = 0$
Case 3 $[b] = -$, $[a] = 0$, $[c] = -$

This is an inevitable consequence of using only qualitative information of variable values. This ambiguity leads to a very large number of possible courses of behavior being predicted as the size of the system becomes large. The only means to reduce this type of ambiguity is to use more quantitative information.

Limitations of the Value Propagation Method

Due to its sequential nature, the value propagation method alone is weaker than the more general method for solving systems of linear equations.

Consider the following equations and the value given for $[x]$:

$$[x] + [y] + [z] = 0 \tag{14}$$
$$[y] - [z] = 0 \tag{15}$$
$$[x] \qquad\qquad = 0 \tag{16}$$

This system of equations cannot be solved by value propagation. After substituting the value of $[x]$ into the first equation, we are left with

$$[y] + [z] = 0 \tag{17}$$
$$[y] - [z] = 0 \tag{18}$$

with no means to reduce the equations further.

In cases like this we can try different value assignments exhaustively. We can assume the value of a variable and continue propagating values to other variables unless we encounter a contradiction. This amounts to a depth-first search in the space of value assignments to variables.

For example, to solve equations (17) and (18), we might first introduce the assumption

$$[y] = +. \tag{19}$$

Then equation (18) becomes

$$+ - [z] = 0,$$

which simplifies to

$$[z] = +. \tag{20}$$

Equations (19) and (20) yield

$$+ + + = 0,$$

which is a contradiction. Therefore, assumption (19) cannot be true. So we introduce a new assumption:

$$[y] = 0. \tag{21}$$

From equations (18) and (21), we obtain

$$0 - [z] = 0,$$

which simplifies to

$$[z] = 0. \tag{22}$$

Since equations (21) and (22) are consistent with the original set of equations, $[x] = [y] = [z] = 0$ is a solution for the equations (14), (15), and (16).

Because of the ambiguity of the qualitative calculus, systems of equations can have multiple solutions. However, the complexity of the search for a solution can grow very rapidly with the number of variables in the system and the number of possible assumptions. In fact, the complexity of the problem of finding consistent variable value assignments in a set of qualitative equations is NP-complete. Considering that one goal of the qualitative calculus is to make reasoning easier, this is a disappointing revelation. The problem of solving a set of normal linear equations is $O(n)$, where n is the number of variables. This seems to suggest that reasoning qualitatively actually makes the problem harder in some sense instead of easier. But this is not surprising because we lose much information by making a problem description qualitative.

Improvements

There have been many suggestions for dealing with the problems of ambiguity and search complexity in qualitative calculus. Some involve using additional knowledge, including quantitative information. Others involve extending the methods for propagating values.

Heuristic Knowledge to Guide Search. Search efficiency can often be improved by ordering and pruning the search with heuristic knowledge. To increase the efficiency of search for a consistent set of variable value assignments, de Kleer and Brown use heuristic rules that restrict the types of assumptions introduced during value propagation. (See Section D.)

Use of More Quantitative Knowledge. This simple qualitative calculus allows only the three values: +, 0, and −. A qualitative calculus that allows more qualitative values is an obvious direction for improvement. QSIM, described in Section F, employs a qualitative calculus where each variable can have any number of landmark values as long as the number is finite.

Some of the ambiguities in qualitative calculus can be resolved by knowing ordinal relations among variables. An arithmetic reasoning system called the Quantity Lattice, developed by Simmons (1986), is capable of representing and reasoning with information of partial ordering relations among variables and calculus expressions. Order of magnitude reasoning by Raiman (1986) extends qualitative calculus to make use of order-of-magnitude information about variables. Karp (1985) developed an abstract mathematical language that is more sophisticated than the simple one introduced in this section for expressing imprecise knowledge of mathematical constraints. MINIMA, developed by Williams (1988), is a more general hybrid algebra that offers a user the flexibility of being able to choose an abstraction level between algebra of signs and that of real values.

Extending the Value Propagation Technique. Dormoy and Raiman (1988) extend the value propagation method by allowing a variable to be eliminated between two qualitative equations in a manner analogous to the Gaussian elimination procedure that is used to solve sets of normal linear equations. It can greatly improve the efficiency of the search by reducing the number of times assumptions must be made during value propagation. However, the use of qualitative resolution must be controlled because the number of its possible applications can grow exponentially, resulting in increased complexity (Dormoy, 1988).

References.   The qualitative calculus introduced in this section is largely based on that described in de Kleer and Brown (1984). The complexity of the search for a solution of a set of qualitative equations is discussed in Davis (1987) and Struss (1987).

The technique of qualitative constraint propagation is used to reason about the behavior of electrical circuits in EL by Stallman and Sussman (1977), in EQUAL by de Kleer (1984), and in TQ (temporal qualitative) analysis by Williams (1984), to name some of the most notable work.

C. REASONING ABOUT BEHAVIOR USING QUALITATIVE CALCULUS

THE PREVIOUS SECTION described qualitative arithmetic and explained how the technique of value propagation can determine the values of variables given qualitative equations. We now turn to a discussion of how to predict behavior with qualitative equations.

C1. Qualitative Behavior and Qualitative States

LET'S DEFINE system X to be a finite set of variables,

$$X = \{x_1, x_2, x_3, ..., x_n\},$$

where n is the number of variables in X. A qualitative behavior of system X is represented as a sequence of qualitative states that the system goes through over time. A qualitative state is defined as a set of qualitative values of the system variables. The number of different combinations of qualitative value assignments to a set of n variables is

$$\prod_{i=1}^{n} q(x_i),$$

where $q(x_i)$ is the number of distinct qualitative values the variable $[x_i]$ can take. This is also the total number of qualitative states that can be defined by the set of variables. We will continue to use the simple qualitative arithmetic of $+$, $-$, and 0 defined in the previous section. Therefore, $q(x) = 3$ for all x. We will use $[x(s)]$ to denote the value of $[x]$ in state s, $[x(t)]$ to denote the value of $[x]$ at some time t, and $x(t)$ to denote the actual value of x at time t. Note the difference between $[x(s)]$ and $[x(t)]$. The former is the value of $[x]$ that is part of the definition of s, whereas the latter simply denotes a value. This difference is due to the fact that a state s represents a certain condition, whereas t represents a time instance.

A system is said to be in state s at time t if the value of every qualitative variable at time t is equal to the value of the same variable in the definition of the state. In other words, a device is in the qualitative state s at time t if and only if $[x(s)] = [x(t)]$ for all x. There are states in

350

which the device can stay only for an instant, and states in which the device must stay for a nonzero interval of time.

The rules governing the behavior of a system are given as a set of qualitative equations representing constraints on variables. A system behavior may be described by several different sets of constraints, each of which describes a behavior under different conditions. For example, different *phases* of substances (and different *operating regions* of devices) warrant different sets of behavior equations. The behavior of water depends on whether it is vapor, liquid, or ice. Consequently, a different set of equations must be given for each of the three possible phases.

Among all possible combinations of qualitative values of variables, only the states satisfying the given set of qualitative equations are physically realizable by the device. These are the *legal* states of the device. Here, a *legal* state does not mean that it is a normal state for the device to be in. When a set of qualitative equations describes the normal behavior of a system, modeling its faulty behavior may require a different set of qualitative equations. States that are legal in the normal behavior model may be illegal in a model of the faulty device, or vice versa. Predicting how faults change qualitative equations is an important question for programs performing fault diagnosis based on qualitative physics techniques.

C2.   State Transitions

GIVEN THE SET of all legal states, predicting the behavior of a device over time involves determining the order in which the device will go through these states. Such ordering is not necessarily a total ordering if the device can move into several states from a given state. Predicting a sequence of qualitative states and state transitions is called *envisioning*, and the prediction produced is an *envisionment*.

In practice, there are two ways to generate an envisionment for a device. One is to start from one state and to generate the sequence of all states that can follow. Such a prediction is called *possible envisionment*, and it amounts to searching all the states reachable from the initial state. Another is to generate all legal states and all state transitions. Such a prediction is called *total envisionment* and requires a complete search of the space. Possible envisionment consists of the future states that can follow the given initial state, whereas total envisionment consists of all the states that the device can be in and all the possible transitions between states.

Note that, since the information used to generate an envisionment is qualitative and the predictive power of the information is weaker than that of more precise information, both a total and possible envisionment can contain states and transitions that are not possible in reality. This problem and others in envisionment are discussed in Section C3.

Generating an Envisionment

We will illustrate how an envisionment can be generated for the ideal mass-spring system shown in Figure C–1. A block is attached to an ideal spring resting on a frictionless table top. The system consists of four variables, x, a, f, and v, where x represents the position of the block, v is its velocity ($v = dx/dt$), a is acceleration ($a = dv/dt$), and f is the force acting on the block. $x = 0$ is defined to be the rest position of the block when the spring is relaxed. $x > 0$ when the block is to the right of the rest position, and $x < 0$ when it is to the left.

The block is pulled to the right and released. Two rules govern the behavior of the system. Newton's second law states that the force equals mass times acceleration, that is,

$$f = ma,$$

where m (> 0) is a constant representing the mass of the block. A qualitative statement of this law is

$$[f] = [a]. \tag{23}$$

Hooke's law of ideal springs states that a spring applies a force proportional to the displacement in the opposite direction. In other words,

$$f = -(k \times x),$$

where k (> 0) is the spring constant. Again, this equation is converted to a qualitative equation as

$$[f] = -[x]. \tag{24}$$

Given the qualitative constraints (23) and (24), we can produce all combinations of variable values that satisfy them, using the technique

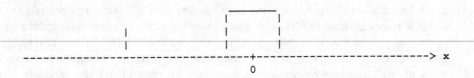

Figure C–1.   A mass-spring system.

described in the previous section. Table C–1 shows all the possible states for the mass-spring system.

Determining State Transitions

The value of qualitative derivative in a state indicates whether the variable is increasing, decreasing, or stable. Based on this information, we can determine what other states the device may move into from each state. For example, if we know that x is negative and increasing in state s, we can infer that x may eventually become 0, making the system transition into a new state.

Recall that we assumed earlier that all the variables were continuous and differentiable. The following rules governing transitions between states follow from these assumptions and the mean value theorem of calculus.

Continuity Rule. Since the actual values of variables are assumed to be continuous, their qualitative counterparts must also vary continuously in the space of qualitative values, $-$, 0, and $+$. This means that the value of a qualitative variable cannot jump from $+$ to $-$ or from $-$ to $+$ without passing through 0. For instance, if $[x(s1)] = +$ and $[x(s3)] = -$, $s3$ cannot immediately follow $s1$ (or vice versa); the system must pass through another state $s2$ where $[x(s2)] = 0$ before reaching $s3$.

Derivative Rule. The value of the qualitative derivative of a variable indicates whether the variable value is increasing, decreasing, or constant. The value of a variable cannot change unless its derivative is nonzero. This is stated more precisely as follows:

$$[dx(s0)] = 0 \equiv [x(s0)] \text{ implies } [x(s1)] \tag{25}$$
$$[x(s0)] < [x(s1)] \text{ implies } [dx(s0)] = + \tag{26}$$
$$[x(s0)] > [x(s1)] \text{ implies } [dx(s0)] = - \tag{27}$$

where we assume $s1$ is a state immediately following state $[s0]$.

TABLE C–1
All States for the Mass-Spring System

State	s1	s2	s3	s4	s5	s6	s7	s8	s9
$[x]$	+	+	+	0	0	0	−	−	−
$[v]$	+	0	−	+	0	−	+	0	−
$[a]$	−	−	−	0	0	0	+	+	+
$[f]$	−	−	−	0	0	0	+	+	+

Observe that the converse is not true for implications (25) through (27). That is,

$$[dx(s0)] = + \text{ or } -$$

does not imply

$$[x(s0)] < [x(s1)] \text{ or } [x(s0)] > [x(s1)])$$

because $[x]$ can remain positive or negative in both $s0$ and $s1$ even if it is changing.

Change-from-zero Rule (or Change-from-equality Rule). If in a state s a variable is equal to 0 and changing, the system must immediately transition out of s into another state where the variable is not equal to 0. More precisely,

If $s1$ is an immediate successor of $s0$, then

$$[x(s0)] = 0, [dx(s0)] = +,$$

and

that $+$ is one of the possible values for $[x]$,
implies $[x(s1)] = +$

and

$$[x(s0)] = 0, [dx(s0)] = -,$$

and

that $-$ is one of the possible values for $[x]$,
implies $[x(s1)] = -.$

Moreover, the system can stay in state $s0$ only for an instant because when a quantity is changing continuously, its value can equal any particular value only for an instant.

This rule easily generalizes to qualitative calculi with different ways to subdivide the domains of continuous variables. The generalized version of this rule is called the *Change-from-equality rule*. For example, if the domain of a variable y is $(-\infty, +\infty)$, the set of distinguished values is $\{d1, d2\}$ such that $d1 < d2$, and the corresponding set of qualitative values for y is $\{q0, d1, q1, d2, q2\}$, where $q0$ represents the interval $(-\infty, d1)$, $q1$ represents $(d1, d2)$, and so on, then the Change-from-equality rule in the vicinity of $d1$ will state:

If $s1$ is an immediate successor of $s0$, then

$$[y(s0)] = d1 \text{ and } [dy(s0)] = + \text{ implies } [y(s1)] = q1$$

and

$$[y(s0)] = d1 \text{ and } [dy(s0)] = - \text{ implies } [y(s1)] = q0$$

Change-to-zero Rule (or Change-to-equality Rule). A change-to-zero is a transition from a state where x is moving toward 0 (but is not zero) into a state where x is 0. Unlike a change-from-zero, a change-to-zero is not a necessary transition, because x can approach 0 asymptotically, never actually becoming equal to 0. As in the case of Change-from-zero rule, this rule can be generalized to other qualitative calculi, where it is known as Change-to-equality rule.

Moreover, if a change-to-zero does occur, it does not happen instantaneously. Let $s1$ and $s0$ be states such that $s0$ can immediately follow $s1$, x is positive and decreasing in $s1$, and x is 0 in $s0$. While the system is in state $s1$, there is a nonzero difference between the value of x and 0. Since x is continuous, it takes a nonzero amount of time for the value of x to change from its current value to zero. Therefore, transition from $s1$ to $s0$ cannot happen instantaneously, and it follows that the state $s1$ must last for a nonzero time interval. These facts have further implications on the ordering of states, summarized in the following Instantaneous-change rule.

Instantaneous Change Rule. If, in a given state s, x is equal to 0 and changing, and y is not equal to 0 but changing toward 0, the device must transition into a new state where $x <> 0$ and $y <> 0$ before it can transition into a state where $y = 0$.

Consider a system with two variables, x and y, and three legal states shown in the Table C–2. Since x is 0 and increasing in state $s1$, it must be positive in the state immediately following $s1$. Also, y is positive and decreasing in $s1$, which means that it may become 0 in the following state. However, as noted earlier, a change-from-zero happens instantaneously, whereas a change-to-zero takes time. Therefore the transition to state $s3$ must happen first. This rule can be generalized as could the previous two rules. Note that in the generalized version, the distinguished value that x is equal to and the one that y is approaching need not be the same.

These rules enable us to determine transitions between states. In general, a state may have more than one successor and more than one predecessor. We can conveniently display the result of a state transition

TABLE C–2

Three States of the System with
Variables x and y

State	$s1$	$s2$	$s3$
$[x]$	0	0	+
$[dx]$	+	+	+
$[y]$	+	0	+
$[dy]$	−	−	−

analysis in a directed graph whose vertices represent states. A transition from state s_i to state s_j is represented in a transition graph by an arc from vertex s_i to vertex s_j.

Example: The Mass-spring System

We now show an example of a transition analysis for the mass-spring system in Figure C–1. All the legal states of the system are shown in Table C–1. Given these, we can determine state transitions.

Suppose the current state is $s1$. In $s1$, x is increasing but since x is already positive, $[x]$ cannot change. Since v is positive but decreasing, $[v]$ can become zero in the next state. Therefore, $s2$ is the only state that can immediately follow $s1$.

In $s2$, x is not changing since $[v] = 0$. But since $[v] = 0$, and $[a] = -$, by the Change-from-equality rule, the system must immediately transition into a state where $[v] = -$, which is $s3$.

In $s3$, the only change that can happen is $[x]$ becoming 0. $[x]$ is 0 in states $s4$, $s5$, and $s6$. $s4$ is ruled out because $[v]$ would change from $-$ to $+$ in the transition from $s3$ to $s4$, violating the Continuity rule. $s5$ is also ruled out because $[v]$ cannot become 0 in the next state since v is negative and decreasing in $s3$. The only possible successor of $s3$ is $s6$.

In $s6$, since $x = 0$ and decreasing, the system must immediately transition into a state where x is negative. There are three such states: $s7$, $s8$, and $s9$. $s7$ is ruled out because $[v]$ changing from $-$ to $+$ would violate the Continuity rule. $s8$ is also ruled out because $[a]$ is 0 in $s6$ and thus $[v]$ cannot have a different value in a following state. $s9$ is the only possible successor to $s6$.

Likewise, it can be shown that $s9$ is followed by $s8$, then $s7$, then $s4$. Finally, the only possible successor state of $s4$ is $s1$. Note that the system never enters state $s5$, the quiescent state. Since nothing is changing in $s5$, no other state can be reached from $s5$. Moreover, it is easy to see that $s5$ cannot be reached from any other state.

Figure C–2 shows the total envisionment of the mass-spring system. It is the transition graph showing all the possible qualitative states and transitions among them. The diagram has a loop ($s1 \rightarrow s2 \rightarrow s3 \rightarrow s6 \rightarrow s9 \rightarrow s8 \rightarrow s7 \rightarrow s4 \rightarrow s1$), indicating a cyclic behavior. The loop corresponds to the oscillation of the spring. Keep in mind that the graph indicates that an oscillatory behavior is *possible* but not *necessary* since some of the arcs in the cycle ($[s1, s2]$, $[s3, s6]$, $[s9, s8]$, and $[s7, s4]$), which are indicated by dotted lines in the figure, represent possible transitions, whereas the others, indicated by solid arrows, represent necessary ones. Also, even if oscillation is assumed, we cannot tell from the graph whether it is a harmonic (constant amplitude), damped (decreasing amplitude), or forced (increasing amplitude) oscillation. In reality, if the system starts out in any of the states in the loop, oscillation will neces-

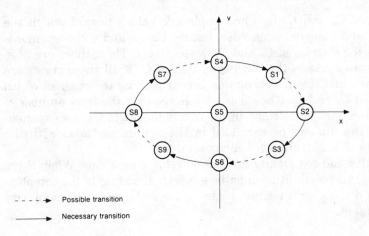

Figure C–2.   Transition graph for the mass-spring system.

sarily happen and it will be harmonic oscillation since we assumed a frictionless surface. However, the initial qualitative formulation of the problem lacks the necessary information to make such distinctions.

C3.   Difficulties in Qualitative Prediction

As THE PREVIOUS example of oscillation attests, envisionments are usually ambiguous in the sense that they indicate several possible behaviors without providing any way to decide which are most likely. Moreover, some predicted behaviors may never happen in reality. These problems arise from the fact that the knowledge used to generate envisionments is qualitative.

Two important issues for qualitative prediction are completeness and soundness. Soundness here refers to whether all the behaviors predicted by a qualitative prediction procedure can in fact be physically realized in the situation. Completeness, on the other hand, refers to whether or not the behaviors predicted by the procedure include all those that can be physically realized. Kuipers has shown the qualitative simulation algorithm used by the QSIM program (see Section F) to be complete. Soundness is not achieved by any qualitative reasoning programs, which cannot avoid producing spurious behaviors because of inherent ambiguities in the information used.

Another serious problem with envisionment is complexity. Envisionments become unmanageable very rapidly as the size of the problem increases. To see how quickly complexity can grow, consider the following situation. Let C_x and C_y be some landmark values toward which the variables x and y are moving. Also assume that x and y change monotonically in the vicinity of C_x and C_y, respectively. Then, there are $3^2 = 9$ possible states just in the vicinity of C_x and C_y if all these states are legal and if no additional information is constraining the order in which x and y reach C_x and C_y. Thus it is easy to see that the total number of possible states and transitions in an envisionment can grow exponentially with the number of variables in the system and also with the number of landmark values for each variable.

Ambiguity and complexity are closely related problems. When there is ambiguity, all possibilities must be generated, adding to the complexity. We next discuss some techniques to reduce ambiguity and complexity in envisionment.

Knowledge About Ordinal Relations

Information about ordinal relations among variable values and landmark values can often help reduce complexity. For example, if x and y are both negative and increasing in a state $s0$, there are three possible states into which the system can move as shown in Table C–3, assuming that x and y keep increasing past 0.

If we have additional information that $x > y$, states $s1$ and $s3$ are no longer permissible and $s2$ is the only possible successor of $s0$.

Partitioning of a Problem

One cause of complexity is the fact that all states are global states. This sometimes forces us to consider relations between variables that we would normally consider unrelated. In the previous example, as x and y move towards 0, we must distinguish the cases in which x reaches 0 first, y reaches 0 first, or they reach 0 simultaneously *even if this distinction is not interesting*. Williams (1986) offers an interesting illustration of this point. Imagine we are studying the activities of a panda bear in China and a polar bear in the Arctic. Though the bears' activities are

TABLE C–3

Possible Transition from State $s0$

Variables \\ State	$s0$	$s1$	$s2$	$s3$
$[x]$	−	−	0	0
$[y]$	−	0	−	0
$[dx]$ and $[dy]$	+	+	+	+

independent for all practical purposes, having only global states to describe their behavior forces us to create an enormous number of states to represent every possible temporal relation between the panda's activities and the polar bear's activities—states that contribute nothing to our understanding of the bears' behaviors.

When the situation to be modeled can be divided into different subparts that do not interact or interact only rarely, modeling each part separately reduces the complexity of envisionment. Obviously the envisionment procedure will be more complex since it must be able to detect and properly treat the interactions between subparts.

Forbus employs Hayes's notion of histories to represent behavior in terms of processes taking place at different times. This representation does not force us to impose temporal orderings between two processes until a possibility of interaction makes it necessary. (See Section E for more discussion of Forbus's representation of history.)

Higher Order Derivatives

Knowledge about higher order derivatives of variables can sometimes resolve ambiguity about the ordering of states (de Kleer, 1979). Imagine a ball is thrown straight up toward the ceiling and it bounces back. Let h be the vertical position of the ball, 0 being the level of ceiling and $h < 0$ being below the ceiling. Thus h is defined on $(-\infty, 0]$. Given the qualitative constraint

$$[dh] <> 0 \quad \text{when } [h] = -,$$

we can generate all the legal states as shown in Table C–4.

The transition graph of this system, shown in Figure C–3, leads us to believe that transitions between states $s2$ and $s4$ and between states $s3$ and $s4$ are possible in both directions. The graph even suggests that the ball can oscillate forever among these states, which is certainly counterintuitive. This ambiguity can be eliminated by adding knowledge about the second derivative of h. We will denote the qualitative value of the kth derivative of variable x as $[d^k x]$. Since the gravitational force

TABLE C–4

All Legal States for the Ball Thrown Against the Ceiling

Variables \ State	s0	s1	s2	s3	s4
$[h]$	−	−	0	0	0
$[dh]$	+	−	−	+	0
$[d^2 h]$	−	−	−	−	−

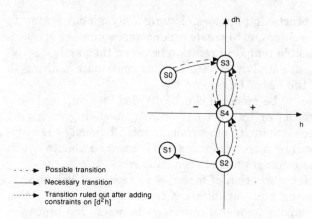

Figure C–3.   Transition graph for the ball.

acting on the ball always accelerates it downwards, this knowledge can produce the following additional constraint:

$$[d^2h] < 0$$

The additional constraint adds a row of $-$'s for $[d^2h]$ in Table C–4 without adding to the number of states. The transitions from $s4$ to $s3$ and from $s2$ to $s4$ in the transition graph of Figure C–3 are ruled out as a result. Thus the addition of the constraint on the second derivative of h reduces ambiguity.

We must be careful with this technique, however. Each new variable v (whether or not it is the derivative of an existing variable) multiplies the total number of states by the number of distinct qualitative values for $[v]$. Unless additional knowledge about higher order derivative constrains the predicted behavior substantially, it will only make envisionment more complex.

Asymptotic Behavior

We noted earlier that due to the possibility of asymptotic behavior, a change-to-zero transition does not happen necessarily, as does a change-from-zero transition. This is why some of the arrows represent necessary transitions, whereas others represent merely possible transitions in the transition graph of the mass-spring system shown in Figure C–2.

Some qualitative reasoning systems that perform envisionment assume no possibility of asymptotic behavior. More formally, if x is positive (or negative) and decreasing in state $s0$ and if a state $s1$ where x is equal to 0 is a possible successor of $s0$, the system will eventually move into $s1$ from $s0$. This assumption makes all the arcs in the transition graph of Figure C–2 necessary transitions, reducing ambiguity in the envisionment. This is a heuristic, and if asymptotic behavior is actually possible, the program will fail to predict it. Nevertheless, in domains where asymptotic behaviors are unlikely or uninteresting, it is a reasonable assumption.

Abstraction

Abstraction is another powerful way to control the complexity of the qualitative prediction process. In order for a reasoning scheme in general to be able to handle a domain of even a moderate complexity, the ability to abstract away unnecessary details is essential if the problem is to remain computationally tractable. In qualitative reasoning about behavior, abstraction can be carried out along several dimensions. Structural descriptions are usually organized in an abstraction hierarchy consisting of subcomponent relations. Functional and behavioral descriptions can be abstracted along the same dimension as subcomponent hierarchies.

It is also possible to abstract functional and behavioral descriptions along the temporal or causal dimensions. Kuipers proposes the use of levels of temporal abstraction and additional mathematical knowledge to control the combinatorial explosion of the qualitative simulation process of QSIM (Kuipers, 1987a, and Kuipers and Chiu, 1987). In a slightly different vein, Weld proposes abstraction by recognizing cycles in a sequence of steps in behavior simulation process, and aggregating the steps in one cycle into a macro-step to be used to speed up the simulation process.

References

The envisioning procedure described in this section is based on those described in de Kleer and Brown (1984) and Kuipers (1986). A similar envisioning procedure is also described in Williams (1984). Kuipers shows that the envisioning procedure of QSIM is complete but not sound (Kuipers, 1986).

Sacks developed a more sophisticated qualitative mathematical reasoner that can generate a qualitative description of the behavior of a wider class of functions by dividing the entire domain of a function into discrete intervals, in each of which the behavior of the function is monotonic (Sacks, 1987a and 1987b).

Weld has studied another, slightly different type of reasoning about behavior, which he calls *comparative analysis* (Weld, 1988). Given a description of a system and its behavior, comparative analysis predicts how the behavior would change if the system were slightly modified.

D. ENVISION

THE RESEARCH of de Kleer and Brown at the Xerox Palo Alto Research Center has been among the most influential work on qualitative reasoning about physical systems. Their work is motivated by the desire to identify the core knowledge that underlies people's physical intuitions. In their research on qualitative physics, they attempt to provide an alternative way to describe physical phenomena that is far simpler than the classical physics but still captures all the important aspects of the physical phenomena. An additional goal is to produce causal accounts of physical mechanisms that are easy to understand.

de Kleer and Brown implemented a program called ENVISION. ENVISION predicts the behavior of an entire device as a sequence of possible future states along with complete causal analysis for the behavior. It is given a description of the physical structure of a device, a set of behavior rules for each component, and an input force applied to the device.

D1. Device Model

ENVISION TAKES a component-oriented view of a device. This means that a device is described in terms of physically disjoint components and conduits connecting the components.

Conduits are defined as physical parts of a device whose only function is to transmit information between components without altering the information. For example, in the domain of electric circuits, pieces of wire connecting the components are conduits; in the domain of fluid flow, conduits are pieces of pipe. Wires and pipes are assumed to have no resistance because conduits are supposed to transmit information without altering it. This is an idealization and cannot be strictly true in reality, but it is a reasonable assumption in many situations.

Components, on the other hand, have more complex behavior. Components are typed, and rules determine the behavior of each type. Behavior rules are encoded in the form of qualitative equations of component variables.

Since the goal of de Kleer and Brown is to predict the behavior of a device from the descriptions of individual components and their connections, the description of a component must be as free as possible from

362

presuppositions about how the component is to be used, such as the function of the entire device or the way the component is supposed to contribute to that function. Otherwise, it would be impossible to know whether the inferences made about the behavior of the device are already implicit in the descriptions of components. Two principles have been formulated to ensure the generality of their approach, by preventing knowledge of the expected behavior of the whole device from being somehow built into the descriptions of individual components. The two principles are as follows:

1. *Locality Principle*. The description of a component should not refer to any other part. For example, if a behavioral rule of a component A specifically referred to a parameter of a neighboring component B, the rule would not be a general description of the behavior of A because it is only valid when A is connected to B.

2. *No-function-in-structure Principle*. The description of a component should not presume the functioning of the whole. For example, a behavior rule of an electrical switch that states "if the switch is closed, current will flow between the two terminals" violates this principle because it presumes that the switch is connected to a power source, that the circuit is closed, and so on.

In reality, it is impossible to adhere strictly to these principles in describing components because all descriptions require some context. Choices among the many ways a physical component can be described must be influenced by the knowledge of the purpose the component is expected to serve in the device. For example, a piece of coil can function as a conduit, as a resistor, as a generator of a electromagnetic field, as a spring, and so on. A component's type cannot be decided without knowing the context in which it will be used.

As for conduits, their behavior descriptions are relatively simple since, by definition, they only transmit information without altering it. In addition, the following two conditions are imposed on qualitative equations for conduits:

1. *Continuity Condition*. Conduits are assumed to be always completely full of incompressible material. Therefore, any increase of flow at one end of a conduit it is reflected by an increase at the other end without delay. In other words, conduits transmits information instantaneously.

2. *Compatibility Condition*. When there are multiple conduits between two components, the sum of the pressure drops along a conduit between the two components must be the same for all the conduits.

Example. We will illustrate de Kleer and Brown's approach with the device shown in Figure D–1, which consists of two tanks connected

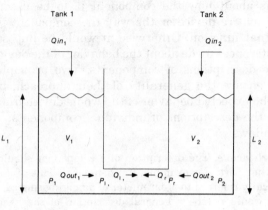

Figure D–1. Two tanks connected by pipe.

by a conduit. First, we present behavioral descriptions of the types of components and the conduit. The behavioral rules for a liquid container with an opening at the bottom are listed here, with the variables defined as follows:

P The pressure at the bottom of the container. $P \geq 0$
L The level of liquid in the container. $L \geq 0$
V The volume of liquid in the container. $V \geq 0$
Q_{in} The flow rate of liquid into the container from the top. $Q \geq 0$.
Q_{out} The flow rate of liquid out of the container through the opening
   in the bottom.

- The pressure is proportional to the level of the water. Therefore, $P = L \times c$, where c is some positive constant. Differentiating both sides with respect to time and converting it to a qualitative equation produces this qualitative equation in terms of time derivatives of the variable, which de Kleer and Brown call a *confluence*.

$$[dP] = [dL]$$

- Likewise, the level of the water is a monotonically increasing function of the volume.

$$[dL] = [dV]$$

- The difference between the flow rate in and the flow rate out is the change in the volume.

$$[Q_{in}] - [Q_{out}] = [dV]$$

The behavioral rules for a conduit are listed next, with the variables defined as follows:

Q_l, Q_r The flow rate into the pipe through the two ends of the conduit.

P_l, P_r The pressure at the two ends of the conduit. $P_r, P_l \geq 0$.

P_d The difference between the pressures at the two ends.

- By conservation of material:

$$Q_l = - Q_r.$$

By differentiating and taking the qualitative form, we have

$$[dQ_l] = - [dQ_r].$$

- The flow rate is proportional to the pressure difference between both ends:

$$[dQ_l] = [dP_d].$$

- From the definition of P_d:

$$[dP_d] = [dP_l] - [dP_r].$$

ENVISION's representation of this device is composed of two components—the containers—and a conduit.

The behavior rules for the device are in Figure D–1. The variable subscripts indicate to which container the variable belongs.

The constraints for container C1.

(1) $[dP_1] = [dL_1]$
(2) $[dL_1] = [dV_1]$
(3) $[Q_{in_1}] - [Q_{out_1}] = [dV_1]$

The constraints for container C2.

(4) $[dP_2] = [dL_2]$
(5) $[dL_2] = [dV_2]$
(6) $[Q_{in_2}] - [Q_{out_2}] = [dV_2]$

The constraints for the conduit.

(7) $Q_l = - Q_r.$
(8) $[dQ_l] = - [dQ_r].$
(9) $[dQ_l] = [dP_d].$
(10) $[dP_d] = [dP_l] - [dP_r].$

The constraints for the connections between the conduit and container C1.

(11) $[Q_{out_1}] = [Q_l]$
(12) $[dQ_{out_1}] = [dQ_l]$
(13) $[dP_1] = [dP_l]$

The constraints for the connections between the conduit and container C2.

$$(14)\ [Q_{out_2}] = [Q_r]$$
$$(15)\ [dQ_{out_2}] = [dQ_r]$$
$$(16)\ [dP_2] = [dP_r]$$

D2.   Predicting Behavior

THE BEHAVIOR of a device is predicted using its qualitative equations. de Kleer and Brown distinguish two types of behavior: *inter-state* behavior and *intra-state* behavior. A state is defined by the qualitative values of all variables of the system. Intra-state behavior determines the qualitative values of variables in one state. Inter-state behavior, on the other hand, is the sequence of qualitative states that the system goes through over time.

Intra-state Behavior

The intra-state behavior, that is, the behavior within one qualitative state, is determined by propagating the values of the parameters whose values are known to other variables through qualitative constraint equations to determine their values. The procedure of value propagation is described in Section B. In the process of propagating values, the program must often make assumptions about the values. ENVISION has some heuristics for this; for example, "if a variable representing an input or output flow rate of a conduit is changing, assume that the corresponding input or output pressure variable of the conduit is changing in the same direction," and "if some but not enough variables in an equation are known to be changing, assume that the ones that are not known to be changing are negligible."

Mythical Causality.   de Kleer and Brown view value propagation as a causal process. If an external disturbance to a system makes a system variable $[a]$ to be $+$, and "$[a] = +$" is propagated through a constraint equation "$[a] + [b] = 0$", to determine $[b] = -$, the value of $[a]$ is considered to "cause" the value of $[b]$. However, unlike the usual notion of causal processes that act over time, value propagation among variables is assumed to take no time. This concept of causality within a state is called *mythical causality* because it acts instantaneously. If the variable values that are initially known are regarded as given by some external disturbances to the system, the intra-state behavior is a description of the way the system reacts instantaneously to the disturbances through mythical causality.

Example: The Two-tank System. The following example demonstrates the procedure for determining the intra-state behavior with the model of the device in Figure D–1. We will determine the intra-state behavior of the device when liquid is added to the container on the left ($Q_{in_1} = +$). We assume that no liquid is added to the container on the right from the top ($Q_{in_2} = 0$), and that there is initially no flow of liquid between the containers ($Q_{out_1} = Q_{out_2} = 0$).

	Variable Value Assignments	Justifications
(17)	$[Q_{in_2}] = 0$	Given
(18)	$[Q_{in_1}] = +$	Given
(19)	$[Q_{out_1}] = 0$	Given initial condition.
(20)	$[dV_1] = +$	(3), (18), (19)
(21)	$[dL_1] = +$	(2), (20)
(22)	$[dP_1] = +$	(1), (21)
(23)	$[dP_l] = +$	(13), (22)
(24)	$[dP_d] = +$	(10), (23), assuming dP_r is negligible.
(25)	$[Q_l] = 0$	(11), (19)
(26)	$[Q_r] = 0$	(7), (24)
(27)	$[Q_{out_2}] = 0$	(14), (25)
(28)	$[dV_2] = 0$	(6), (17), (26)
(29)	$[dL_2] = 0$	(5), (27)
(30)	$[dP_2] = 0$	(4), (28)
(31)	$[dP_r] = 0$	(16), (29)
(32)	$[dQ_l] = +$	(9), (31)
(33)	$[dQ_{out_1}] = +$	(11), (32)
(34)	$[dQ_r] = -$	(8), (32)
(35)	$[dQ_{out_2}] = -$	(15), (34))

Note that the assumption on line (24) in the preceding example is not the only one that could be made. Another alternative would be to assume that dP_d is negligible with the conclusion that $[dP_2] = +$. When an assumption is introduced in the process of propagating values, it may lead to value assignments to the rest of variables that satisfy the equations, or it may lead to a contradiction. If an assumption leads to a contradiction, the assumption is incorrect and must be retracted. Different assumptions may lead to different sets of values for variables, and more than one set may be consistent with the constraint equations. In such a case, each one is a valid mythical causal account of the intra-state behavior. As many assumptions can usually be introduced in a given case, ENVISION has heuristics to restrict the kinds of assumptions made in different situations, thus reducing the number of alternative causal interpretations produced by the system.

Feedback. A variable can be initially assumed negligible, but later a disturbance can be propagated that assigns it a nonzero value. ENVISION interprets this as an indication of a possible feedback loop. If there is a loop in the structural description that corresponds to the feedback path in the network of constraints, ENVISION decides that it is a real feedback loop. For example, on line (31) in the preceding example, a signal propagates back to P_r, which is assumed negligible earlier on line (24), indicating a potential feedback loop. But because there is no loop in the structure of the device, ENVISION decides it is not a real feedback loop.

Inter-state Behavior

Once the intra-state behavior is determined, the future states of the device can be predicted. The procedure for doing this is essentially the one described in Section C. The device in the previous example has five legal qualitative states if one keeps adding liquid to container C1 but not to C2 (in other words, $[Q_{in_1}] = +$ and $[Q_{in_2}] = 0$.) Table D–1 shows these states, and Figure D–2 shows the transition graph.

D3.   Conclusion

GIVEN A description of the physical structure of a device, a set of behavior rules and an input force applied to the device, ENVISION predicts its behavior in terms of a sequence of possible future states along with complete causal analysis for the behavior. The behavior rules are constraint equations that must be satisfied by parameters of components.

TABLE D–1

Five Possible States

Variables \ States	s1	s2	s3	s4	s5
$[Q_{in_1}]$	+	+	+	+	+
$[Q_{in_2}]$	0	0	0	0	0
$[dV_1],[dL_1],[dP_1],[dP_l]$	+	+	+	+	+
$[Q_{out_1}],[Q_l]$	+	−	0	+	+
$[dQ_{out_1}],[dPd],[dQ_l]$	+	+	+	−	0
$[dV_2],[dL_2],[dP_2],[dP_r]$	+	−	0	+	+
$[Q_{out_2}],[Q_r]$	−	+	0	−	−
$[dQ_{out_2}],[dQ_r]$	−	−	−	+	0

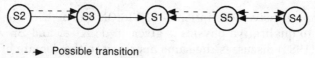

Figure D–2.   Transition graph.

ENVISION distinguishes two types of behavior: inter-state and intra-state behavior. Intra-state behavior is concerned with the assignment of qualitative values to variables and the direction in which they are changing within one state, and it is determined by constraint propagation. Inter-state behavior is concerned with the transition from one state to another. Intra-state behavior within one state determines the subsequent inter-state behavior. Causality within one state, called mythical causality, is determined on the basis of how the initial disturbance produced by the input force applied is propagated through the network of constraints.

de Kleer and Brown require models to adhere to the no-Function-in-structure Principle to prevent the inferences made by the system about the behavior from being implicitly pre-encoded in the structural description. Also, the Locality Principle restricts propagation of disturbances strictly to topological paths so that prior expectations about the device function will not influence the process of inferring its behavior from the structure.

In reality, any description of device topology is likely to have some knowledge of the function built in because deciding what topological paths to represent explicitly in the structural description requires some prior knowledge about the function, especially about the main forces involved in the device function and all the paths through which these forces can act. Paths, which are also the paths through which disturbances propagate, are not always obvious because they may not be visible as physical structures of the device. Radiation and magnetic force provide examples of ways objects can interact without being visibly connected. Therefore, it is not necessarily possible nor desirable to describe any system without assumptions, but it is critical to make underlying assumptions explicit, so that they can be retracted and new ones made as needed. de Kleer and Brown's two principles provide good guidelines about how to build a model and reason about its behavior in such a way that the conclusions of the program will have a high degree of objectivity given the assumptions underlying their approach.

References

A comprehensive description of ENVISION and de Kleer and Brown's approach to qualitative physics is given in de Kleer and Brown (1984). de Kleer (1984) discusses the same approach in the domain of electrical circuit analysis. They discuss the problem of ambiguity in envisioning and some techniques for reducing ambiguity in de Kleer (1979) and de Kleer and Bobrow (1984). Iwasaki and Simon (1986a and b) and de Kleer and Brown (1986) discuss mythical causality in comparison with another approach to causality described in Section G.

E. QUALITATIVE PROCESS THEORY

QUALITATIVE PROCESS THEORY (QPT) was developed by Ken Forbus at Massachusetts Institute of Technology. The goal of research on QPT is to understand commonsense reasoning about physical processes. Forbus's program, Qualitative Process Engine (QPE), uses general knowledge about physical processes and objects in the world to infer which processes will occur, their effects in given physical situations, and when they will stop. The research was directed toward developing a framework for representing commonsense knowledge about various types of physical processes and objects and an inference procedure to use the representation to perform everyday physical reasoning. The Qualitative Reasoning Group, led by Forbus at the University of Illinois, Urbana-Champaign, is continuing this research.

In QPT, physical situations are modeled as collections of objects, their relationships and processes. Objects have variables to represent their properties, and processes act through time to influence properties of objects. The notion of physical processes plays the central role in QPT. They are the sole agents of change. A description of behavior over time is given in terms of processes and their effects on the world.

Examples of processes in QPT include heat flow, fluid flow, boiling, motion, and so on. QPT itself does not define any particular theory about how such processes occur, but it provides a language for stating such theories. The language allows us to define processes in terms of their preconditions and effects. QPT also provides an inference procedure to predict what will happen, given a theory about the physical world. We can encode in QPT any theory of physics such as the Newtonian and impetus theories of motion, and QPE will make predictions about physical situations according to the theory.

The overall operation of QPE is divided into four phases:

1. Given a collection of objects and general knowledge of processes (i.e., a theory of processes), decide which instances of processes can exist in the given situation.

2. Determine which process instances are active by examining whether their conditions are satisfied.

3. Determine which changes will be caused by active processes. When several processes affect one variable, try to determine the net effect on the variable.

4. Predict behavior over time. Changes brought about by active processes may eventually cause conditions for other inactive processes to become true, or those for currently active processes to become false, thereby making formerly inactive processes active, or active ones inactive. QPE produces an account of the activity of processes over time.

We will describe the QPT representations of objects and processes, and then QPE's envisionment procedure is illustrated with an example of reasoning about boiling water.

E1. Representation of Objects

A PHYSICAL SITUATION is described as a collection of objects and their relations. Objects in the physical world can exhibit dramatically different characteristics depending on conditions—even if they are made of the same substance. For example, water looks and behaves very differently depending on whether it is frozen, liquid, or vaporized. Even liquid water is viewed very differently depending on, for example, whether it is completely contained or is part of a larger body of liquid and is free to move around in any direction. Views of objects that focus on the enabling conditions of their behavioral characteristics are called *individual views* in QPT.

There can be individual views for generic types of objects, objects under specific conditions (compressed, evaporated, and so on), and combinations of objects in particular relations to each other (e.g., liquid and its container). Some examples of individual views are solid, liquid, gas, elastic object, plastic object, compressed object, contained liquid, and so on. Individual views are organized in a general-to-specific hierarchy in QPE's knowledge base.

Figure E–1 shows a definition of a contained liquid as an example of an individual view.

An individual view is defined in four parts, as follows:

1. *Individuals.* The objects involved. This part specifies the set of objects that must exist for the individual view to hold. For example, for the individual view of an elastic object to hold, an object must exist. Likewise, the individual views of compressed, relaxed, and stretched object all require the existence of an elastic object. The preceding example of the contained-liquid individual view requires a set of objects, a liquid, and a container.

2. *Quantity Conditions.* Statements of inequalities between quantities belonging to the individuals, and statements about whether other

Individual view: Contained-Liquid
Individuals:
　con: a container
　sub: a liquid
Preconditions:
　con can contain sub.
Quantity Conditions:
　The amount of sub in con is greater than zero.
Relations:
　There is p such that:
　　p is a piece-of-stuff,
　　the substance of p is sub,
　　p is in con,
　　the amount of p is equal to the amount of sub in con.

Figure E–1.　Example of an individual view definition.

individual views and processes hold. For example, for the individual views of compressed, relaxed, or stretched object to hold, the length of the object must be less than, equal to, or greater than the rest length of the object, respectively. For the liquid to be contained in a container, nonzero quantity of the liquid must exist.

3. *Preconditions*. Further conditions that do not pertain to quantities. For example, for the individual view of elastic object to hold, the object must be made out of elastic substance. For the liquid to be contained in a container, the container must be capable of holding the liquid.

4. *Relations*. Statements of further relations among attributes of individuals that hold whenever the individual law holds. For example, when the individual view of gas holds, certain relations hold among its temperature, pressure, and volume such as $PV = nRT$

Individuals, preconditions, and quantity conditions together specify the sufficient conditions for the view to hold. Relations give further consequences and properties of the individuals.

E2.　Process Representation

PROCESSES ACTING on objects are the sole agents of change. Some examples of processes are heat flow, liquid flow, boiling, and motion. The representation of a process is similar to that of an individual view except that it must describe the effects of the processes. The definition of a process must include what objects must exist in the world for the process to happen, in what circumstances the process will happen, and what changes are caused by the process. Figure E–2 shows examples of process definitions for boiling and heat flow processes.

Process: heat-flow
Individuals:
   src: an object with a quantity, $heat_{src}$
   dst: an object with a quantity, $heat_{dst}$.
   path: a path through which heat can travel between src and dst.
Preconditions:
   path is not obstructed.
Quantity Conditions:
   $temperature_{src} > temperature_{dst}$.
Relations:
   Let flow-rate be a quantity.
   Flow-rate > 0.
   Flow-rate $\propto_{Q+}$ ($temperature_{src} - temperature_{dst}$)
Influences:
   $I-(heat_{src}$, flow-rate)
   $I+(heat_{dst}$, flow-rate)

Process: boiling
Individuals:
   w : a contained-liquid. The boiling temperature of w is $temperature_b$
   hf: an instance of the heat-flow process, such that the destination of hf is w.
Quantity Conditions:
   hf is active.
   $\sim(temperature_w < temperature_b)$.
Relations:
   There is g such that:
      g is a piece-of-stuff,
      g is gas,
      g is of the same substance as w,
      $temperature_b = temperature_g$.
   Let generation-rate be a quantity.
      generation-rate > 0.
      generation-rate $\propto_{Q+}$ flow-rate$_{hf}$
Influences:
   $I-(heat_w$, flow-rate$_{hf}$) ; counteracting the heat flow's
                         ; influence
   $I-(amount_w$, generation-rate),
   $I+(amount_g$, generation-rate),
   $I-(heat_w$, generation-rate),
   $I+(heat_g$. generation-rate)

Figure E–2.　Examples of process definition.

In these process definitions, src, dest, path, w, and hf are variables that are bound to specific instances of individual views or other processes when an instance of the process is created.

Here, we must introduce the QPT notation for describing mathematical relations among quantities qualitatively, which is different from the notation introduced in Section B. In QPT,

$$[I+(a, b)] \text{ and } [I-(a, b)] \tag{28}$$

denote a direct positive or negative influence of b on a. (See the following explanation of Influences and Relations for the distinction between direct and indirect influences.) The notation of equation (28) means that a is increased (or decreased) by b. In the notation of Section B, the qualitative functional relations implied by equation (28) can be written respectively as

$$[da] = [b] \quad \text{and} \quad [da] = -[b] \tag{29}$$

However, the QPT expressions of equation (28) not only imply the relations of equation (29) but also imply that a causally depends on b. In other words, while the relations of equation (29) are symmetric and acausal, those of equation (28) are antisymmetric and causal.

Likewise,

$$a \propto_{Q+} b \quad \text{and} \quad a \propto_{Q-} b \tag{30}$$

denote a qualitative proportionality relation between a and b. The expressions of 30 mean that a increases (or decreases) as b increases. In the notation of Section B, they imply

$$[da] = [db] \quad \text{and} \quad [da] = -[db]. \tag{31}$$

In addition, they imply that a is causally dependent on b.

A process definition consists of five parts:

1. *Individuals*. The individuals involved; objects or instances of individual views. For example, in the heat flow process of Figure E–2 there must exist some objects to act as heat source and sink and also a heat path between them. For the stretching and compressing process to take place, there needs to be an elastic object.

2. *Preconditions*. Nonquantitative conditions that must hold for the process to be active. For example, for a flow process to take place, the passage of flow between the source and the destination must not be blocked. For an object to be able to move, the position of the object must not be constrained.

3. *Quantity Conditions*. Conditions on quantities that must hold among the individuals. Also, requirements about presence or absence of other processes and individual views. For example, for the heat flow

process to take place, the temperature of the source must be higher than that of the sink. For the stretching process to take place, the elastic object must not be compressed. If it is compressed, the process of it lengthening is called relaxing and not stretching.

4. *Relations*. The set of relations that the process imposes on individuals, along with any new entities that are created. For example, in the heat flow process, the rate of heat flow is proportional to the temperature difference. In the boiling process, a new entity, vapor, is created as a consequence of the process.

5. *Influences*. The direct influences caused by the process on the variables of individuals. The distinction between relations and influences is as follows: Since processes cause changes, influences are the primary changes caused by the process, whereas relations are further conditions that hold among quantities whenever the process takes place. For example, we usually mean by *heat flow* a transfer of thermal energy from one body to another. Therefore, the direct effects (i.e., influences) of heat flow is that the total thermal energy of the source decreases and that of the destination increases.

E3. Predicting Behavior

GIVEN A DESCRIPTION of the world as a collection of objects and their relationships, QPE first looks for individual views that are valid in the situation. If objects in the scene satisfy the conditions (individuals, preconditions, and quantity conditions) of the definition of an individual view, an instance of that individual view is created. Likewise, instances of processes are created. Process instances are determined active if their conditions are satisfied.

Individual views and processes impose qualitative functional relations on variables of objects in the situation. Also, active processes specify what and how variables are changing. Given these relations and changes, QPT predicts the future course of events in terms of processes happening and stopping, causing changes in the situation.

Representation of Behavior Over Time

QPT employs Allen's (1984) representation of time. Time is composed of intervals, which are related by various relations such as before, after, and during. The QPT representation of behavior over time uses Hayes's notion of *history*. Behavior is represented as a collection of fragments, each of which describes a particular condition of one part of the situation in some time interval. Such fragments can be about a variable taking on a particular qualitative value, a process being active, or a valid individual view. The two types of fragments are called *episodes* and *events* of individual views and processes. The difference between episodes and events is that the former last for nonzero periods of time while the latter are instantaneous.

Here are some examples of episodes and events:

- The temperature t of an object A is increasing—an episode of the variable t.

- The instance hf_1 of heat-flow process is active—an episode of the process instance hf_1.

- The position x of the object A is location l—an episode or an event of x depending on whether x stays at l only for an instant or longer.

- An object A is a compressed, elastic object—an episode of an individual view about A.

A sequence of episodes and events describing the possible evolution of the situation is called a *history*. Histories describe behavior in terms of variable values changing, processes happening and stopping, and individual views becoming valid or invalid over time. A predicted history is not necessarily a linear sequence of events and episodes since in many situations several possible courses of behavior can be predicted.

Quantity Space of QPT

The space of values of each variable is specified by a finite number of distinguished values and ordinal relations among them. Qualitative values of a variable are either a distinguished value or a range of values between two distinguished values such that there is no other distinguished value between the two. Therefore, the number of qualitative values of a variable is finite. The quantity space of QPT has a more complex structure than the space of +, 0, and − used in the qualitative calculus (Section B). Since the distinguished values of a variable need not be totally ordered, every possible total ordering of distinguished values that do not contradict known ordinal relations give a set of totally ordered qualitative values. The quantity space of QPT must include all of them.

For example, consider the variable x defined on $(-\infty, \infty)$ with three distinguished values, v_0, v_1, and v_2, such that $v_0 > v_1$ and $v_0 > v_2$. Since the ordinal relation between v_1 and v_2 is unknown, there are three possibilities: $v_1 > v_2$, $v_1 = v_2$, and $v_2 > v_1$. In each case, there is a set of totally ordered qualitative values for x as follows:

$$v_1 > v_2 \ : \ (-\infty, v_2), \ v_2, \ (v_2, v_1), \ v_1, \ (v_1, v_0), \ v_0, \ (v_0, \infty)$$
$$v_1 = v_2 \ : \ (-\infty, v_2), \ v_2, \ (v_2, v_0), \ v_0, \ (v_0, \infty)$$
$$v_1 < v_2 \ : \ (-\infty, v_1), \ v_1, \ (v_1, v_2), \ v_2, \ (v_2, v_0), \ v_0, \ (v_0, \infty)$$

And the quantity space of the qualitative values of x includes all of these possible qualitative values.

Limit Analysis

Since processes are the only causes of changes, identifying active processes enables QPT to predict changes. If the value of a variable p is increasing due to an active process, the episode EP1, defined as

$$\text{EP1: } [dp] = +,$$

is created. Moreover, if the initial value, p_0, of p is known to be less than a distinguished value p_d, and if there is no other distinguished value between p_0 and p_d, the episode EP1 may be followed by the event (or an episode, depending on whether p continues to change afterwards) of p being equal to p_d. This may trigger other processes to become active or may terminate active processes.

This process of looking for distinguished values toward (or away from) which variables are moving is called *limit analysis* in QPT. If a limit analysis shows that the value of a variable is moving toward a nearest distinguished value, a new event defined by the variable taking on the value is created to follow the current episode. If a variable has a distinguished value currently and is changing, a new episode is created for the variable value being greater (or less, depending on the direction of change) than the current value.

Example: Boiling Water

We demonstrate the procedure for behavior prediction using the example of boiling water. In the initial situation, pictured in Figure E–3, a container filled with water is placed over a heat source. To simplify the example, all properties of the container are ignored except that it holds water and heat flows through it. Also, we ignore the vapor generated by boiling, and we assume that the temperature of the heat source stays constant.

The quantity space for the temperature t_w of the water consists of the following distinguished values and inequalities:

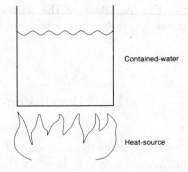

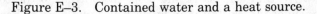

Figure E–3.   Contained water and a heat source.

t_{init} The initial temperature of the water.
t_{src} The temperature of the heat source.
t_{boil} The boiling temperature of the water.

$$t_{\text{init}} < t_{\text{boil}}$$
$$t_{\text{src}} > t_{\text{init}}$$

Since the individual view of contained liquid, shown in Figure E–1, is valid here, an instance of it is is created. Also, an instance of the heat flow process, whose definition is shown in Figure E–2, is created and is made active. The variables src and dst in the definitions are bound to the heat source and the water.

Initially heat flow is the only active process. The heat flow process causes the temperature of the water to increase, creating an episode

$$\text{EPO: } [dt_w] = +.$$

Limit analysis shows that t_w may reach either t_{src} or t_{boil}. There are three possibilities depending on the ordinal relation between t_{src} and t_{boil}.

$t_{\text{src}} < t_{\text{boil}}$ In this case, t_{src} is reached first. t_w becoming equal to t_{src} will invalidate the quantity condition of the heat flow process, deactivating the process.

$t_{\text{src}} > t_{\text{boil}}$ In this case, t_{boil} is reached first. When t_w becomes equal to t_{boil}, an instance of boiling process becomes active. While the boiling process is active, the temperature remains at t_{boil}, but the amount of water decreases. A limit analysis shows that the amount of water will eventually become 0, at which point the individual view instance of contained liquid ceases to be valid and both the processes, boiling and heat flow from the heat source to water, terminate.

$t_{\text{src}} = t_{\text{boil}}$ In this case, t_w reaches t_{boil}, at which point the heat flow process terminates. Since a boiling process requires an active heat flow process, it will not become active, and there will be no further change.

Figure E–4 shows the evolution of the water temperature along with the episodes and events, individual views, and processes for the second case.

E4. Conclusion

QPT WAS DEVELOPED by Forbus to understand how physical processes can be reasoned about, namely, how to identify their causes and effects and to detect when they will start and stop. In contrast to the component-oriented view of the world taken by de Kleer and Brown, Forbus takes a process-oriented view. Different types of physical processes are defined in terms of objects that must be present, the preconditions that must be satisfied by the objects for the process to take place, and the qualitative relations that hold between parameters when it does occur. Given this knowledge of processes, Forbus's program, Qualitative Process Engine,

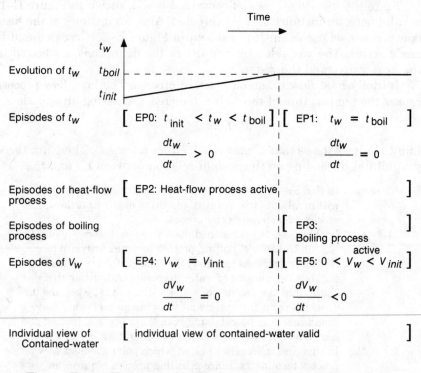

Figure E–4.   Histories of boiling and evolution of some of the variables.

detects the processes that must take place in a given situation and predicts their course. QPT provides a way of formalizing a given interpretation of causal actions. It is an attempt to model people's commonsense reasoning about physical processes.

QPT has been applied to many different physical domains. It provides a language for describing a wide variety of processes. By defining an appropriate set of individual views and processes, QPT can be also applied to domains outside physics where it is natural to think of changes as manifestations of underlying processes taking place.

References

A good source of information about QPT is Forbus (1984). Forbus (1983) discusses using QPT for interpreting measurements. Falkenhainer and Forbus (1988) discusses using a layer of QPT models at different abstraction levels in order to manage the complexity of modeling a large system.

F. QSIM

THE QSIM PROGRAM, developed by Kuipers, simulates the behavior of physical systems described as systems of qualitative equations. It takes a set of qualitative functions describing the behavior of a device and an initial state description, and it produces a sequence of future states, possibly with branching. Although the basic ideas of using qualitative mathematics to predict possible future courses of behavior are similar to those explained in Sections B and C, the quantity spaces of QSIM can be much more complicated than the simple space of +, 0, and − described in Section B.

The procedure for generating future states is different from that described in Section C. Given an initial qualitative state for each function, QSIM first generates all possible successor states for each function. Then, it uses qualitative constraints among functions and also global consistency rules to rule out inconsistent or redundant combinations of states.

Quantity Space of QSIM

In QSIM, all variables are functions of time. QSIM assumes that all functions are *reasonable* functions defined on a subset of the extended real number line $R^* = (-\infty, +\infty)$. A reasonable function is a function $f:[a, b] \longrightarrow R^*$, where $[a, b] \subseteq R^*$, such that f is continuous and differentiable, has only finitely many critical points in any bounded interval, and the limits of $df(t)/dt$ as t approaches a from above and b from below exist in R^*. A *system* in QSIM is defined as a finite set of reasonable functions.

The qualitative calculus employed by QSIM is a generalization of the simple qualitative calculus introduced in Section B. Variables in the simple qualitative calculus have only one landmark value, namely, 0, and three qualitative values, +, 0, and −. The functions in QSIM can have any number of landmark values as long as the number is finite. Each function $f(t)$ defined on $[a, b]$ has its own set of landmark values, which must include at least 0 and the values of $f(t)$ at all its critical points. If $a > -\infty$ or $b < -\infty$, the set of landmark values must also include the values of f at the end points, $f(a)$ and $f(b)$. These landmark values divide the entire range of a function into a finite number of intervals. If function f has n landmark values, $\{l_0, l_1, l_2, ..., l_{n-1}\}$, and the range of the function is R^*, the range is divided up into the following nonoverlapping intervals and points: $\{(-\infty, l_0), l_0, (l_0, l_1), l_1, ..., l_{n-1}, (l_{n-1}, +\infty)\}$. These $2n + 1$ intervals and points are the qualitative values of function f. A time point t such that $f(t)$ equals a landmark value of f is called a *distinguished time point* of f.

Qualitative States

A qualitative state of a function is defined as a pair of a qualitative value for the function and its direction of change, determined by the sign of its time derivative. A qualitative state can last for either an instant or for a nonzero period of time. The qualitative state of the function f at time t (or during a period of time (t_i, t_j)), denoted $QS(f, t)$ or $QS(f, t_i, t_j)$, is a pair $<\text{qval}, \text{qdir}>$, where qval is a qualitative value of f and qdir is one of decreasing (*dec*), increasing (*inc*) or steady (*std*) at time t (or during (t_i, t_j)).

The behavior of a function over time is represented as an alternating sequence of instantaneous states and states that last for a nonzero period of time. For example, consider the function $f(t)$ whose behavior is shown in Figure F–1. Assume that $f(t)$ is a reasonable function, that l_0, l_1, and l_2 are among the landmark values of $f(t)$, and that t_0, t_1, and t_2 are distinguished time points of f such that $f(t_0) = l_0$, $f(t_1) = l_1$, and $f(t_2) = l_2$. Furthermore, $f(t)$ is strictly increasing over $[t_0, t_2]$. Then the qualita-

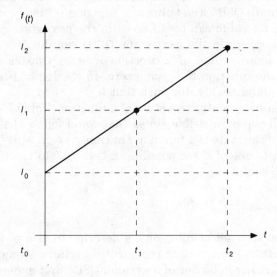

Figure F–1.   Behavior of function $f(t)$ over $[t_0, t_2]$.

tive behavior of $f(t)$ over the period $[t_0, t_2]$ is described by the following sequence of qualitative states of f:

1. $Q(f, t_0) = <l_0, \text{inc}>$

2. $Q(f, (t_0, t_1)) = <(l_0, l_1), \text{inc}>$

3. $Q(f, t_1) = <l_1, \text{inc}>$

4. $Q(f, (t_1, t_2)) = <(l_1, l_2), \text{inc}>$

5. $Q(f, t_2) = <l_2, \text{inc}>$

Since a system is defined as a set of functions, a qualitative state of a system at time t (or during (t_i, t_{i+1})) is the set of qualitative states of the functions in the system at t, or during (t_i, t_{i+1}). Likewise, a behavior of a system is an alternating sequence of instantaneous and noninstantaneous qualitative states of the system.

State Transitions

A transition from an instantaneous state to a noninstantaneous state is called a *P-transition*, and a transition from a noninstantaneous state to an instantaneous state is called an *I-transition*. Table F–1 shows all the permissible state transitions. Note a slight difference between transitions from a value permitted in the qualitative simulation procedure described in Section C and QSIM. In the procedure described in Section C, if the value of a variable v is l_j at time t, its derivative must be nonzero at the same time in order for its qualitative value to be different in the following state. In QSIM, the value of a function is steady in one instantaneous state, its value can be different in the next state as long as the derivative is nonzero in the next state. QSIM can discover a previously unknown landmark value of a function if other constraints force the derivative of the function to become zero. In the list of I-transitions, l^* denotes a new landmark value such that $l_j < l^* < l_{j+1}$.

Given an initial qualitative state of a function, Table F–1 enables us to generate all the permissible states that could follow the initial state. For example, if the state of a function f at time t_i is $<l_j, \text{std}>$, the function can transition to one of three possible states: $<l_j, \text{std}>$, $<(l_j, l_{j+1}), \text{inc}>$, and $<(l_{j-1}, l_j), \text{dec}>$.

Qualitative Constraints

In addition to a set of functions, a description of a physical system includes qualitative constraints representing relations among the functions. To predict the behavior of a system, QSIM first generates for each function all the qualitative states that could succeed the current quali-

TABLE F–1

State Transition Table

P-transitions	$QS(f, t_i)$	=>	$QS(f, t_i, t_{i+1})$
P1	$<l_j, \text{std}>$		$<l_j, \text{std}>$
P2	$<l_j, \text{std}>$		$<(l_j, l_{j+1}), \text{inc}>$
P3	$<l_j, \text{std}>$		$<(l_{j-1}, l_j), \text{dec}>$
P4	$<l_j, \text{inc}>$		$<(l_j, l_{j+1}), \text{inc}>$
P5	$<(l_j, l_{j+1}), \text{inc}>$		$<(l_j, l_{j+1}), \text{inc}>$
P6	$<l_j, \text{dec}>$		$<(l_{j+1}, l_j), \text{dec}>$
P7	$<(l_j, l_{j+1}), \text{dec}>$		$<(l_j, l_{j+1}), \text{dec}>$

I-transitions	$QS(f, t_i, t_{i+1})$	=>	$QS(f, t_{i+1})$
I1	$<l_j, \text{std}>$		$<l_j, \text{std}>$
I2	$<(l_j, l_{j+1}), \text{inc}>$		$<l_{j+1}, \text{std}>$
I3	$<(l_j, l_{j+1}), \text{inc}>$		$<l_{j+1}, \text{inc}>$
I4	$<(l_j, l_{j+1}), \text{inc}>$		$<(l_j, l_{j+1}), \text{inc}>$
I5	$<(l_j, l_{j+1}), \text{dec}>$		$<l_j, \text{std}>$
I6	$<(l_j, l_{j+1}), \text{dec}>$		$<l_j, \text{dec}>$
I7	$<(l_j, l_{j+1}), \text{dec}>$		$<(l_j, l_{j+1}), \text{dec}>$
I8	$<(l_j, l_{j+1}), \text{inc}>$		$<l^*, \text{std}>$
I9	$<(l_j, l_{j+1}), \text{dec}>$		$<l^*, \text{std}>$

TABLE F–2

QSIM Predicates and their Meanings

QSIM Predicate	Meaning
ADD(f, g, h)	$f(t) + g(t) = h(t)$
MULTI(f, g, h)	$ft(t) * g(t) = h(t)$
MINUS(f, g, h)	$f(t) - g(t) = h(t)$
$M^+(f, g)$	f is some monotonically increasing function of g.
$M^-(f, g)$	f is some monotonically decreasing function of g.
DERIV(f, g)	$f(t) = dg(t)/dt$

tative state of the function using the list of possible transitions in Table F–2. Each combination of such qualitative states for the functions defines a possible successor state of the system. Once all successor states for each function are generated, qualitative constraints among functions are used to rule out system states that are inconsistent with the given constraints.

The constraints are represented as two-place or three-place predicates of functions, expressing qualitative mathematical relations among functions. The predicates used in QSIM are explained next. Assume f, g, and h are reasonable functions.

The predicates M^+ and M^- enable us to represent monotonic relations between functions without specifying exact functional forms of the relations. For example, if $f(t) = 2t$ and $g(t) = e^t$, the relation between f and g can be represented as $M^+(f, g)$.

QSIM has many rules to exclude combinations of functional states based on qualitative constraints. Since a qualitative state of a function is defined as a pair—a qualitative value and a direction of change—a qualitative constraint among functions can rule out combinations of states in two ways: by constraining qualitative values of functions and by restricting the directions of changes.

Constraining Qualitative Values. Qualitative constraints on functions restrict the qualitative values of functions. For example, consider a system S consisting of three functions f, g, and h. If $ADD(f, g, h)$ holds, and if the qualitative values of f and g over the time interval (t_1, t_2) are as follows:

qualitative value of f is (l_1, l_2)
qualitative value of g is (m_1, m_2),

then the qualitative value (n_1, n_2) of h over the same time interval must be such that the following holds:

$$(n_1, n_2) \subseteq (l_1 + m_1, l_2 + m_2).$$

Furthermore, suppose that all the functions are decreasing over (t_1, t_2) and also that $l_1 + m_1 = n_1$. In other words, the qualitative states of the functions are as follows:

$$QS(f, t_1, t_2) = \ <(l_1, l_2), \text{dec}>$$
$$QS(g, t_1, t_2) = \ <(m_1, m_2), \text{dec}>$$
$$QS(h, t_1, t_2) = \ <(n_1, n_2), \text{dec}>$$

Given the state of f, g, and h during the period (t_1, t_2), Table F–1 shows that I-transitions I5, I6, I7, and I9 are possible for each function. Therefore there are $4^3 = 64$ possible states for the system consisting of these three functions.

Since all the functions are decreasing toward landmark values l_1, m_1, and n_1, respectively, zero, one, two, or all of the functions could reach their respective landmark value in the next instantaneous state to follow if there were no constraints. However, the constraint $ADD(f, g, h)$ and the fact that $l_1 + m_1 = n_1$ imply that it is not possible for two of the functions to reach their landmark values in the next state while the remaining one does not. Given the states for f, g, and h and the constraint

ADD(f, g, h), the only possible states of the system at time t_2 are those in which one of the following conditions hold:

1. $f(t_2) = l_1$, $g(t_2) = m_1$, $h(t_2) = n_1$

2. $f(t_2) = l_1$, $g(t_2) > m_1$, $h(t_2) > n_1$

3. $f(t_2) > l_1$, $g(t_2) = m_1$, $h(t_2) > n_1$

4. $f(t_2) > l_1$, $g(t_2) > m_1$, $h(t_2) > n_1$

For example,

$$QS(f, t_2) = <l_1, \text{dec}>,$$
$$QS(g, t_2) = <(m_1, m_2), \text{dec}>,$$
$$QS(h, t_2) = <(n_1, n_2), \text{dec}>$$

is a possible state of S at time t_2, but not

$$QS(f, t_2) = <l_1, \text{dec}>,$$
$$QS(g, t_2) = <m_1, \text{dec}>,$$
$$QS(h, t_2) = <(n_1, n_2), \text{dec}>.$$

Among the original 64 possible successor states for system S, 32 of them are ruled out by this constraint on the qualitative values of functions.

Constraining Directions of Changes. Qualitative constraints can also represent constraints on the directions of changes of functions. For example if ADD(f, g, h) holds, and if f and g are increasing in a given state, h cannot be decreasing or steady in the same state. Table F–3 shows the rules for determining the direction of change of h from those of f and g in the same state if ADD(f, g, h) holds. Similar tables can also be produced for other predicates, MINUS, MULTI, M^+, and M^-.

Table F–3 is essentially identical to the table of qualitative addition given in Section B if inc, dec, std, and any are replaced by $+$, $-$, 0, and ?, respectively. This is because predicates of QSIM in general represents the same constraints expressed by qualitative equations of derivatives involving analogous qualitative operators. For example, the constraint implied by ADD(f, g, h) on the direction of changes can be expressed as $[df] + [dg] = [dh]$ in the qualitative arithmetic language presented in Section B.

TABLE F–3

Directions of Changes Satisfying ADD(f, g, h)

g \ f	inc	std	dec
inc	inc	inc	any
std	inc	std	dec
dec	any	dec	dec

Going back to our sample system S, in any possible state of system S at time t_2, f and g can be either decreasing or steady. In such a case, Table F–3 shows that the direction of change of h is determined uniquely from those of f and g. For example,

$$QS(f, t_2) = <l_1, \text{dec}>,$$
$$QS(g, t_2) = <m_1, \text{dec}>,$$
$$QS(h, t_2) = <n_1, \text{dec}>$$

is a possible state of S at time t_2, but not

$$QS(f, t_2) = <l_1, \text{dec}>,$$
$$QS(g, t_2) = <m_1, \text{dec}>,$$
$$QS(h, t_2) = <n_1, \text{std}>.$$

This constraint on the directions of changes further reduces the total number of possible states of S at time t_2 to 16.

The Qualitative Simulation Algorithm

This section describes what the algorithm QSIM employs to generate an envisionment. The system used as an example is a system consisting of a ball thrown upward. The example used to illustrate the algorithm is the one given by Kuipers (1986). The system involves the following three variables:

Y   The vertical position of the ball.
V   The vertical speed of the ball.
A   The vertical acceleration of the ball.

The constraints are as follows:

DERIV(Y, V)   V is the derivative of Y.
DERIV(V, A)   A is the derivative of V.
$A = g < 0$ There is constant downward acceleration due to gravitational force.

Assume that the current state is where the ball is moving upward with a decreasing speed. In other words, if (t_0, t_1) is the current state, then

$$QS(A, t0, t1) = <g, \text{std}>$$
$$QS(V, t0, t1) = <(0, \infty), \text{dec}>$$
$$QS(Y, t0, t1) = <(0, \infty), \text{inc}>$$

Given the current state and the set of constraints, the steps QSIM goes through to generate the list of possible successor states are as follows:

Step 1. *For each function, generate the list of possible transitions from the current state.* For the ball system, given the current state, which is an interval, the set of possible transitions for each function according to Table F–4 is shown below. L^* and M^* denote new landmark values for V and Y, respectively, such that $L^* < 0$ and $M^* > 0$. For simplicity, we disregard the possibility of the next state being at $t = \infty$, thereby excluding I2 and I3 for Y from further consideration.

Step 2. *For each constraint, generate the set of tuples of transitions of its arguments, and filter out the ones that are inconsistent with the constraint.* For each constraint of the ball system, there are the following pairs of transitions of the arguments:

DERIV(Y, V): (I4, I5), (I4, I6), **(I4, I7)**, **(I4, I9)**, **(I8, I5)**, **(I8, I6)**, (I8, I7), (I8, I9)

DERIV(V, A): (I5, I1), **(I6, I1)**, **(I7, I1)**, (I9, I1)

Among these pairs, those that are not in bold letters are filtered out because they violate the constraint. For example, <I4, I5> and <I4, I6> both violate the constraint DERIV(Y, V) because I4 indicate that Y is increasing, whereas I5 and I6 each indicate that V, the derivative of Y, is 0.

Step 3: *Perform pairwise consistency filtering on the sets of tuples associated with the constraints in the system. This is essentially the same as Waltz filtering used in vision (Waltz, 1975). If two constraints have some variables in common, they must agree on the transition assigned to the common variables.* Among the remaining pairs of transitions for the ball system, (I4, I9) and (I8, I5) for the pair (Y, V) are eliminated by this step because neither I9 nor I5 is allowed for V according to the constraint DERIV(V, A).

TABLE F–4
Transactions and States for the Ball System

Function	Transition	Next State
A	I1	$<g, std>$
V	I5	$<0, std>$
	I6	$<0, dec>$
	I7	$<(0, \infty), dec>$
	I9	$<L^*, std>$
Y	I4	$<(0, \infty), inc>$
	I8	$<M^*, std>$

Step 4: *Generate all possible global interpretations from the remaining tuples. Create new qualitative states resulting from each interpretation, and filter them for global consistency. The remaining global states are the possible successor states.* The remaining pairs for the ball system can be formed into the following two global transitions:

Y	V	A
I4	I7	I1
I8	I6	I1

Since the first one of these will result in a state that is identical to the current state, it is not necessary to pursue it any further. Therefore, the only global transition leading to a new state is the second one.

Even though in the case of this particular example there is only one successor state, in general there can be several. To produce an envisionment, successors to each of the possible successor states must be generated in turn. The number of states in the envisionment can grow exponentially as QSIM carries out one cycle of the simulation algorithm. This problem of complexity plagues all envisionment programs, and how to control the complexity is a topic actively investigated in qualitative physics.

Conclusion

Kuipers studies how a qualitative description of the behavior of a system is derived from a qualitative description of its mathematical relations between variables. QSIM is Kuipers's qualitative simulation program. His "causal structural" description consists of a set of constraints holding among time-varying parameters. The envisioning process consists of a constraint propagation part and a prediction part corresponding to the determination of intra-state and inter-state behavior in ENVISION. As in the case of ENVISION, Kuipers's concept of causality is based on mathematical constraints among variables. However, unlike ENVISION, QSIM does not determine the causal structure in a model but is given a causal structural description as an input in the form of a network of constraints. Kuipers does not address the problem of how directions of causality in a network of constraint relations are determined in order to construct a causal structure. A causal account in QSIM is an account of how variable values change over time according to these constraints.

References

Good sources of information on QSIM are Kuipers (1986) and Kuipers (1987b). Kuipers (1985) discusses the limitations of QSIM algorithm. The problem of controlling the complexity of qualitative simulation is discussed in Kuipers (1987a), Kuipers and Chiu (1987), and Berleant and Kuipers (1988).

G. CAUSAL ORDERING

CAUSALITY is the central issue in Iwasaki and Simon's research in qualitative reasoning. A number of artificial intelligence systems have been built to perform reasoning with causal knowledge, but all but a few of them have knowledge of the domain in which directions of causality are prespecified. Such knowledge is less general than the acausal functional description usually employed in formal description of a phenomenon. Iwasaki and Simon focus on the problem of inferring causal relations in a model consisting of acausal mathematical relations.

Their approach is based on the theory of causal ordering first presented by Simon (1952 and 1953). They have explored the theory and its extension in reasoning about the behavior of physical systems. Their approach has been implemented in a program named CAOS. The program consists of a collection of modules for generation of an equation model, causal analysis of the model, dynamic stability analysis, and qualitative prediction of the effects of external disturbance on the model. The causal analysis module takes a description of a system in terms of a set of equations and determines the causal relations among the variables. In this section, we mainly focus on the causal analysis module.

Theory of Causal Ordering

The theory of causal ordering provides a technique for inferring the causal relations among variables in a set of functional relations. The theory of causal ordering defines *causal ordering* as an asymmetric relation among the variables in a set of simultaneous equations. Causal ordering reflects people's intuitive notion of causal dependency relations among variables in a system. Establishing a causal ordering involves finding subsets of variables whose values can be computed independently of the remaining variables and then using those values to reduce the structure to a smaller set of equations containing only the remaining variables. The approach offers a computational mechanism for defining a causal dependency structure.

Causal Ordering in an Equilibrium Structure. Causal ordering was initially defined by Simon for an equilibrium structure consisting of equilibrium equations (Simon, 1952). First we need to define an equilibrium structure.

Definition 1: Self-contained equilibrium structure.

A self-contained equilibrium structure is a system of n equilibrium equations in n variables that possesses the following special properties:

1. That in any subset of k equations taken from the structure at least k different variables appear with nonzero coefficients in one or more of the equations of the subset.

2. That in any subset of k equations in which $m \geq k$ variables appear with nonzero coefficients, if the values of any $m - k$ variables are chosen arbitrarily, the equations can be solved for unique values of the remaining k variables.

Condition 1 ensures that no part of the structure is over-determined. Condition 2 ensures that the equations are not mutually dependent; if they are, the equations cannot be solved for unique values of the variables.

The idea of causal ordering in a self-contained equilibrium structure can be described roughly as follows. A system of n equations is called self-contained if it has exactly n unknowns. Given a self-contained system S, if there is a proper subset s of S that is also self-contained and that does not contain a proper self-contained subset, s is called a minimal complete subset. Let S_0 be the union of all such minimal complete subsets of S; then S_0 is called the set of minimal complete subsets of zero order. Since S_0 is self-contained, the values of all the variables in S_0 can, in general, be obtained by solving the equations in S_0. By substituting these values for all the occurrences of these variables in the equations of the set $(S - S_0)$, we obtain a new self-contained structure, which is called the derived structure of first order. Let S_1 be the set of minimal complete subsets of this derived structure. It is called the set of complete subsets of first order.

Repeat the preceding procedure until the derived structure of the highest order contains no proper subset that is self-contained. For each equation e_i in S, let V_i denote the set of variables appearing in e_i, and let W_i denote the subset of V_i containing the variables belonging to the complete subsets of the highest order among those in V_i. Then, the variables in W_i are said to be *directly causally dependent* on the elements in $(V_i - W_i)$.

Since the preceding definition is very syntactic, the notion of causal ordering depends critically on the choice of equations included in the model. For the preceding procedure to produce causal relations in the model that agree with our intuitive understanding of the causal relations in the real situation, the equations comprising a model must come from an understanding of mechanisms. The term "mechanism" is used here in a general sense to refer to distinct conceptual parts in terms of whose functions the working of the whole system is to be explained. Mechanisms are such things as laws describing physical processes or local components that can be described as operating according to such laws. An equation representing such a mechanism is called a *structural equation*, and every equation in the model should be a structural equation standing for a mechanism through which variables influence other variables. This requirement is crucial for the correct application of the method of causal ordering.

According to the theory of causal ordering, the notion of causal dependency relationship is context-dependent. Knowledge of one mechanism alone does not imply a causal relation among the variables in the mechanism. It is only after all the other mechanisms influencing the variables are known and assumptions about the exogenous mechanisms, including external mechanisms controlling the system variables, that we can discover asymmetric relations among them. Requiring that the equations be structural and that the structure be complete for causal analysis forces all such mechanisms to be taken into consideration and the context of causal analysis to be clearly identified. What causal ordering analysis accomplishes after these requirements are met is to make explicit the asymmetric relations among variables implied by the model and assumptions.

In general, given a device, we can write down a large number of correct equations about its behavior, and we must choose from these equations the ones that reflect our understanding of mechanisms to produce a correct causal structure. Unfortunately there is no simple formal answer to the question of how to know that an equation is structural. Iwasaki and Simon's solution to this problem is to have an explicit representation of mechanisms from which equations can be systematically derived in such a way that only structural equations are produced. They use a network representation of processes for the purpose of explicitly representing our understanding of mechanisms underlying an equation model (Iwasaki, 1988a).

Another thing to note about the method of causal ordering is that it does not require knowledge about the precise functional forms of equations. The only information that the method makes use of is what variables appear with a nonzero coefficient in what equations, which in terms of mechanisms translates to what variables are causally linked by each mechanism.

Causal Ordering in a Dynamic Structure. Although the causal ordering just introduced provides a means to determine causal dependency relations in a model describing an equilibrium state, the word "behavior" usually implies changes over time. This section introduces causal ordering in a dynamic system, in particular, causal relations in a system of first-order differential equations. Differential equations of higher order can be converted into a set of first-order equations by introducing new variables to stand for derivatives. The definition of a self-contained dynamic structure (Simon and Rescher, 1966) is as follows:

Definition 2: A self-contained dynamic structure.
A self-contained dynamic structure is a set of n first-order differential equations involving n variables such that:

1. In any subset of k functions of the structure, the first derivative of at least k different variables appear.

2. In any subset of k functions in which r $(r \geq k)$ first derivatives appear, if the values of any $(r - k)$ first derivatives are chosen arbitrarily, the remaining k are determined uniquely as functions of the n variables.

The preceding definition of self-containment for a dynamic structure is analogous to that for an equilibrium structure. As in the case of an equilibrium structure, condition (1) ensures that no part of the structure is over-determined, whereas condition (2) ensures that the structure is not under-constrained.

Given a self-contained dynamic structure, we can perform elementary row operations to the equations to solve them for the n derivatives. This operation produces an equivalent system of equations in canonical form. A differential equation is said to be in *canonical form* if and only if there is only one derivative in the equation, and the derivative is the only expression that appears on the left-hand side of the equation. A self-contained dynamic structure in n variables, x_1, ..., x_n, in canonical form consists of n equations of the following form:

$$x_i^{'} = f_i(x_1, x_2, ..., x_n),$$

where f_i's $(1 \leq i \leq n)$ are functions of their arguments.

The equations in this form in a dynamic structure are interpreted to be *mechanisms* of the system. Therefore, ith equation, the only one containing $x_i^{'}$, is regarded as the mechanism determining the time path of x_i. Furthermore, variable x_i, whose derivative appears in the ith equation, is said to be directly causally dependent on the variables that appear with a nonzero coefficient in the equation.

Causal Ordering in a Mixed Structure. When the behavior of a system is described in terms of equations, the description very often consists of a mixture of dynamic and static equations. Iwasaki and Simon extended the concepts of self-contained structures and of causal ordering to apply to such mixed systems. First, they define self-containment for mixed systems. Causal ordering in such a mixed system is a natural extension of the ones for equilibrium and dynamic structures. Dynamic structures can be regarded as extreme cases of mixed structures.

Before defining self-containment for mixed structures, we must introduce some notation. Let M be a system of n equations in n variables such that some of the equations are equilibrium equations and others are dynamic equations of the type defined in the previous section. Then, let $Dynamic(M)$ be the subset of M consisting of all the differential equations in M, and let $Static(M)$ be the set consisting of all the equilibrium equations in M and one constant equation for every variable v whose derivative appears in $Dynamic(M)$. A constant equation of a variable is an equation of the form $v = c$, where c is a constant.

The intuitive meaning of the set $Static(M)$ may be understood as follows. The set of equilibrium equations in a mixed set represent mechanisms that restore equilibrium so quickly that they can be considered to hold in 0 units of time within some time frame (e.g., days if the time frame is centuries). On the other hand, the dynamic equations represent slower mechanisms that require nonzero units of time for the variables on their right-hand sides to affect appreciably the variable on their left-hand sides. Therefore, in a very short period of time—shorter than is required for the variables on the right-hand sides of d_1 and d_2 to appreciably affect x_1 and x_2 on the left-hand sides—x_1 and x_2 can be considered unchanging. Thus, set $Static(M)$ represents a snap-shot picture (i.e., a very short-term equilibrium description) of the dynamic behavior of mixed structure M.

Definition 3. The set M of n equations in n variables is a self-contained mixed structure if:

1. One or more of the n equations are first-order differential equations, and the rest are equilibrium equations.

2. In any subset of size k of $Dynamic(M)$, the first derivative of at least k different variables appear.

3. In any subset of size k of $Dynamic(M)$ in which r ($r \geq k$) first derivatives appear, if the values of any $(r - k)$ first derivatives are chosen arbitrarily, the remaining k are determined uniquely as function of the n variables.

4. The first derivatives of exactly d different variables appear in $Dynamic(M)$, where d is the size of the set $Dynamic(M)$.

5. $Static(M)$ is a self-contained static structure.

Conditions 2 through 4 in the preceding definition ensure that the dynamic part of the model is neither over-constrained nor under-constrained. Condition 5 ensures that its short-term, snap-shot picture is also self-contained.

Given a self-contained mixed structure, as defined earlier, the causal ordering among its variables and derivatives follows the definitions of causal ordering in dynamic and static structures. In other words, the causal ordering in a mixed structure can be determined as follows:

1. The ordering among n variables and m derivative in subset $Dynamic(M)$ is given by the definition of causal ordering in a dynamic structure.

2. The ordering among variables (but not their derivatives) in $Static(M)$ is given by the definition of causal ordering in a static structure.

A mixed structure can be viewed as an approximation of a dynamic structure. When a mechanism in a dynamic structure acts very quickly to restore relative equilibrium, we can regard it as acting instantaneously. Or, when a mechanism acts much more slowly than other mechanisms in the system so that its effect on the variable it controls is negligible, the variable may be considered constant. In the first case, the description of a system behavior as a dynamic structure may be simplified by replacing the differential equation representing the fast mechanism by the corresponding equilibrium equation, an operation called *equilibrating*. In the second case, the model can be simplified by replacing the equation representing the slow mechanism with a constant equation, which is called *exogenizing*. In contrast to numerical model abstraction techniques (Simon and Ando, 1961), equilibrating and exogenizing are qualitative techniques.

No precise numerical information is necessary to produce a mixed structure from a dynamic structure. The equations comprising the original dynamic structure may be qualitative, and the decision as to which equations among them to equilibrate or to exogenize is made based on qualitative knowledge about relative speeds at which different mechanisms restore equilibrium.

Example: A Mixed Model of an Evaporator

This section presents a detailed example of an application of the concepts defined in Section G1 to a mixed model of the evaporator.

We describe this representation using the example of an evaporator, a component of a refrigerator, in which the refrigerant evaporates, absorbing heat from the surrounding medium. Figure G–1 shows an evaporator. Liquid refrigerant flows through an expansion valve from the receiver into the evaporator. When it goes through the valve, it starts to vaporize because of the sudden pressure drop, which causes the refrigerant's boiling temperature to fall below its current temperature. At first, the vaporization takes place without any heat flowing from the surrounding medium into the refrigerant because the thermal energy in

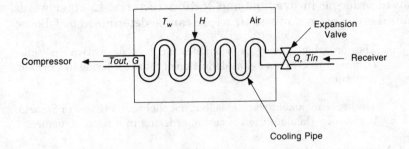

Figure G–1. Evaporator.

the liquid supplies the requisite latent heat to convert it into vapor, sharply decreasing the temperature of the liquid refrigerant.

The refrigerant temperature continues to drop sharply until it becomes equal to the temperature, T_w, of the medium surrounding the cooling pipe. It continues to decrease, but more slowly, because T_w's is now higher than the refrigerant temperature, which causes heat to start flowing into the refrigerant from the surrounding medium. Eventually the refrigerant temperature falls to the condensing temperature at the ambient pressure and stabilizes, but the refrigerant continues to boil, the latent heat now being entirely supplied by the heat absorbed through the cooling-pipe wall from the surrounding medium. The refrigerant that passes through the expansion valve is in liquid phase. The refrigerant that leaves the chamber is at the condensing temperature, and is vapor, liquid, or a mixture of both.

The variables and brief descriptions for the model of the evaporator are as follows:

Variables	Description
Q_{in}, Q_{out}	Input and output refrigerant flow rates (mass/second)
T_{in}, T_{out}	Temperatures of incoming and outgoing refrigerant
G	Ratio of vapor to total mass of outgoing refrigerant
H	Heat gained by the refrigerant
P	Pressure within cooling pipe
T_c	Condensing temperature of refrigerant
T_w	Temperature of the surrounding medium

The following equations describe the steady state of the evaporator. In these equations, spl, l, and k are constants denoting the specific heat of the refrigerant in liquid phase, the latent heat of the refrigerant, and the heat conduction coefficient of the cooling pipe wall, respectively.

$$H = k\,(T_w - T_c) \tag{32}$$

Characteristics of the heat flow process: The rate of heat flow from the surrounding medium to the refrigerant is proportional to the temperature difference.

$$H + T_{in} Q_{in} \, spl = G \, Q_{out} \, l + T_{out} \, Q_{out} \, spl \tag{33}$$

Energy flow equation for the output refrigerant.

$$T_c = f(P) \tag{34}$$

Characteristics of the refrigerant: The condensing temperature is a function of the pressure.

$$T_{out} = T_c \tag{35}$$

Characteristics of the evaporator: The output temperature of the refrigerant is equal to the condensing temperature.

$$Q_{in} = Q_{out} \tag{36}$$

The flow equation for the refrigerant flow process.

$$T_{in} = c_1 \tag{37}$$
$$Q_{in} = c_2 \tag{38}$$
$$P \;\;\, = c_3 \tag{39}$$
$$T_w = c_4 \tag{40}$$

Equations (37) through (40) represent the assumptions that the variables, T_{in}, Q_{in}, P, and T_w are externally controlled.

Let M be the mixed structure of the evaporator consisting of equations (32) to (40) with equations (33), (35), and (36) replaced with the following differential equations. The reason these equations are replaced by dynamic ones is that relations represented by equations (32) and (34) are restored to equilibrium very quickly when disturbed, whereas those represented by equations (33), (35), and (36) are restored relatively slowly. Therefore, in an analysis of medium temporal grain-size, it is reasonable to regard the former equilibrium relations as always holding and the latter as taking time.

$$\frac{dG}{dt} = c_5 \left\{ \frac{H + spl(T_{in} Q_{in} - T_{out} Q_{out})}{Q_{out} \, l} - G \right\} \tag{41}$$

$$\frac{dT_{out}}{dt} = c_6 \, (T_c - T_{out}) \tag{42}$$

$$\frac{dQ_{out}}{dt} = c_7 \, (Q_{in} - Q_{out}) \tag{43}$$

M clearly satisfies conditions 1 through 4 of the definition of a self-contained mixed structure. $Static(M)$ consists of equations (32), (34), and (37) through (40) as well as the following constant equations of G, T_{out}, and Q_{out}.

$$G = c_8 \tag{44}$$
$$T_{out} = c_9 \tag{45}$$
$$Q_{out} = c_{10} \tag{46}$$

The equilibrium structure $Static(M)$ is self-contained. Each one of equations (37) through (40) and (44) through (46) forms a minimal complete subset of zero order. Removing these equations and variables from $Static(M)$ produces the following derived structure of first order:

Derived structure of first order: $Static(M_1)$

$$H = k(c_4 - T_c) \tag{47}$$
$$T_c = f(c_3) \tag{48}$$

Equation (48) forms a minimal complete subset of first order. Removing the equation and variable T_c from $Static(M_1)$ produces the following derived structure of second order:

Derived structure of second order: $Static(M_2)$

$$H = k\,(c_4 - f(c_3)) \tag{49}$$

Since $Static(M_2)$ is its own minimal complete subset, the process stops. The causal ordering in M thus derived is shown in Figure G–2. Causal links in the dynamic part of the model, consisting of equations (41) through (43), are indicated by arrows drawn with broken lines. Integration links are indicated by the arrows marked with i. An integration link simply links the derivative of a variable to the variable itself.

The causal structure in Figure G–2 can be explained informally in English as follows: The condensing temperature depends (instantaneously) on the pressure, and the heat flow rate from the surrounding medium to the refrigerator depends (instantaneously) on the condensing temperature and the temperature of the medium. The output refrigerant

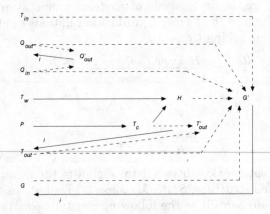

Figure G–2.   Causal ordering in the evaporator.

flow rate changes more slowly depending on its current value and the input flow rate. Likewise, the output refrigerant temperature changes more slowly depending on its current value and the condensing temperature. The percentage of vapor in the outgoing refrigerant changes depending on the condensing temperature, heat absorbed, and input and output flow rates and temperatures. The pressure inside the evaporator, the input flow rate of the refrigerant, the input temperature, and the temperature of the surrounding medium are determined externally.

Reasoning About Behavior

CAOS uses the causal ordering of variables in an equilibrium structure to predict the effects of a disturbance on the variables. A disturbance is given to the system as the direction (up or down) in which one of the variable values is changed, and this information is propagated to the variables that are causally dependent on the first variable to determine how they are affected. This propagation procedure makes use of the information about the signs of coefficients in the equations and is similar to that described in the propagation technique described in Section B. One major difference is that the directions in which CAOS propagates disturbances is determined by the causal ordering relations, whereas the technique described in Section B can propagate a disturbance in any direction.

However, one critical requirement that must be satisfied for such prediction to be meaningful is that the equilibrium be stable. Although an equilibrium system describes the behavior of the device in equilibrium, it does not describe the behavior when it is disturbed out of equilibrium. If the equilibrium is dynamically stable, meaning that the system will eventually go back to equilibrium after a disturbance, the procedure of propagating disturbances in an equilibrium structure is a prediction of how the new equilibrium values of the variables will compare to the old values.

The stability of a system must be determined by examining its dynamic behavior. Given a dynamic structure describing the behavior of a device when it is out of equilibrium, the stability analysis module of CAOS applies various qualitative techniques to determine stability of the system.

Conclusion

This section discussed the application of the method of causal ordering to models of physical devices. The theory of causal ordering provides an operational definition of causal dependency relations among variables in a wide range of models, from entirely equilibrium models to entirely dynamic ones, and from qualitative models to quantitative models. It provides an alternative to approaches used by other researchers in qualitative reasoning. It does not require that knowledge of causal relations be explicitly prespecified in the knowledge base. The approach clearly separates the task of determining causal relations from the task of determining effects of a disturbance on the system.

References

The original accounts of the theory of causal ordering are presented in Simon (1952 and 1953). Iwasaki (1988b) discusses the extension to mixed systems and also the relation with the theory of aggregation of dynamic systems. Iwasaki and Simon (1986a and 1986b) and de Kleer and Brown (1986) compare ENVISION's approach to causality and causal ordering theory.

H. CAUSAL ACTION/
EVENT-BASED APPROACHES

THIS SECTION discusses three other approaches to qualitative reasoning.
They represent knowledge about behavior in terms of causal actions. In
contrast to the work discussed so far, in which knowledge about device
behavior is represented in the form of qualitative mathematical relations
governing the behavior, the work described in this section represents
knowledge about how a device achieves its function in terms of sequences
of events or actions connected by causal links.

The first project described in this section, the Commonsense Algorithm by Rieger and Grinberg (1977), is one of the earliest attempts at
declarative representation of mechanisms. It represents mechanisms as
events, actions, and states, connected by various types of links, which
describe the way states, actions, and events trigger each other. The
second project, by Chandrasekaran and his colleagues, is similar to the
Commonsense Algorithm in that it also represents the way the function
of a device is achieved by a chain of states connected by causal links.
The last work, by Bylander and Chandrasekaran, employs a small number of generic behavior types to describe the behavior of components,
and infers the behavior of a composite device from behavior descriptions
of its components.

H1.   Commonsense Algorithm

THE WORK on Commonsense Algorithm (henceforth CSA) by Rieger and
Grinberg is an attempt to represent causal relations in knowledge about
how devices function and also to use the representation to simulate the
mechanisms in a way that approximates human reasoning.

Representation

CSA represents mechanisms as a graph whose nodes represent events
and whose links represent relations between events, including but not
limited to causal relations. CSA categorizes events, into four types:

Action	An action performed by an external agent such as a human operator.
Tendency	An event that is similar to an action but that happens without someone intending to make it happen. For example, gravity acting on a balloon is a tendency, whereas a person's pulling down on a string attached to the balloon is an action.
State	Any piece of description of a state of anything involved in the mechanisms being described.
Statechange	An event of something undergoing a transition from one state to another. For example, "A being at a location l1" and "A being at l2," where A is some object, and l1 and l2 are distinct locations, are states whereas "A changing locations from l1 to l2" is a statechange.

These four type of events are connected by the following types of relations. For causal, enablement, and state coupling relations, there are one-shot and continuous links. For a one-shot causal link, the causing action only has to happen once, whereas for a continuous causal link, the causing action must be sustained while the effect is happening. Causal, state coupling, and state equivalence links can be qualified by a set of conditions that must be satisfied for the link to be effective.

Causal link	A causal connection from action or tendency to a state or statechange.
Enablement	A link from a state to an action or tendency such that the latter cannot take place without the former. The state "enables" the action or tendency.
State coupling	A link from a state or statechange to another state or statechange that the former indirectly produces. This link makes it possible to abstract out detailed causal steps that link the two events.
State equivalence	State equivalence links two states or statechanges that are equivalent in the sense that they describe the same event in two different ways. For example, "the light is not on" and "the light is off" are two equivalent states.
State antagonism	This links two states or statechanges that are mutually exclusive such as "the light is on" and "the light is off."
Rate confluence	When multiple statechanges are taking place at the same time resulting in some net statechange, the former statechanges are linked by a rate-confluence link to the latter.
Threshold	When there is a state representing some threshold of interest in the mechanisms, and if there is a statechange representing a move toward the threshold, the statechange is linked to the state by a threshold link.

Figure H–1 shows an example of CSA representation of the functioning of a thermostat.

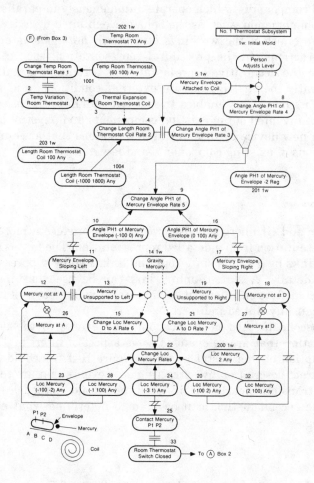

Figure H–1.   CSA representation of a thermostat function.
(Rieger and Grinberg, 1977)

Simulation

When simulating a mechanism, CSA does not directly use the graph representation presented in the preceding section. Instead, the graph representation is first converted into a procedural representation in the form of a collection of small independent computing units. A computing unit is a demon that fires when the attached conditions become true and simulates one event in the declarative representation. Thus, the functioning of the entire mechanism is simulated by a chain of many demons firing, causing changes in the state of the world.

There is a reason for converting the declarative representation to a procedural representation. Any physical system consists of physical principles and components, which operate autonomously in parallel. A gross physical phenomenon, such as the behavior exhibited by a device, is the cumulative effect of the workings of all such autonomous agents and their interactions. In the procedural representation, each cause-effect relation in the declarative representation is a computing unit existing independently, being triggered by external conditions, and producing effects on its own. This enables the user to simulate the behavior of a new device invented out of existing components and physical laws helps debug the new device by discovering interactions that arise from novel combinations of existing components and laws.

Abstraction

Rieger and Grinberg propose two ways to produce a more abstract CSA representation from a detailed representation. The first is to replace multiple links by a single state-coupling link thereby suppressing uninteresting details. A state-coupling link can be used for this purpose because its definition allows it to link any two states or statechanges that are causally linked indirectly.

The second method is to pick out only events in the declarative representation that are relevant to some aspect of interest. Thus, from the description of thermostat given in Figure H–1, we could produce a more abstract description by extracting only events that are relevant to, say, heat transfer. Clearly the first and the second methods can be combined. The second method can be used to determine what events are interesting.

H2.   Functional Representation of Devices

CHANDRASEKARAN and his colleagues' research on functional representation of devices is motivated by the questions of what it means to understand the relation between a function of a device and its structure and of how to represent such understanding so as to enable problem solving. They represent knowledge about how a device achieves its function by a causal chain of states in a fashion similar to CSA representation. Their main interests are in representing such knowledge and using it efficiently to solve problems. In particular, diagnosis of device behavior is one of their goals. The declarative representation of device function is automatically converted into a set of hierarchically organized diagnostic rules. In this discussion, we focus on the representation of mechanisms.

Representation

A device is represented in terms of its structure, function, and behavior. The structural representation consists of a component-subcomponent hierarchy together with interconnections between components.

A function is defined as the intended response of a device to an external or internal stimulus, whereas behavior is a description of how such a response is produced. A behavior is represented as a causal chain of states, where a state is any assertion about the state of some object in the world.

Figure H–2 shows the representation of one of the functions of a buzzer, namely, to buzz. In the figure, pressed(manual-switch) denotes the state where the manual switch of the buzzer is pressed. In the figure, assumption1 is an assumption, represented separately from the function itself, that relies on the assumption being true. It includes such assumptions as the existence of electrical connections between appropriate points in the structure.

A function is achieved by a behavior or set of behaviors. A behavior is a sequence of causally related states, in which each causal link can in turn be explained by the function or the behavior of a component. Thus behaviors and functions form a hierarchy of more and more detailed causal descriptions. Since the distinction between function and behavior is only a matter of relative levels of abstraction, we will drop the distinction in the remainder of this section and use the terms behavior and function interchangeably.

A causal link, besides being explained further by a more detailed functional or behavioral account, can be qualified by a set of conditions, called *assumptions*, that must be satisfied for the causal link to hold. Figure H–3 shows a representation of the behavior behavior1 that enables a buzzer to achieve its function.

In addition to knowledge specific to devices, namely structures, func-

```
FUNCTIONS:
  buzz: TOMAKE buzzing(buzzer)
  IF pressed(manual-switch)
  PROVIDED assumption1
  BY behavior1
END FUNCTIONS
```

Figure H–2. Function: buzz.

```
BEHAVIOR
  behavior1
  state-1 pressed(manual-switch)
     BY behavior2
  state-2  (elect-connected(t7,  t8),  elect-connected(t7,
t8))*
     USING FUNCTION mechanical
     OF clapper(t7, t8, space2)
  state-3 repeated-hit(clapper)
     USING FUNCTION acoustic
     OF clapper(t7, t8, space2)
  state-4 buzzing(clapper)
  state-5 buzzing(buzzer)
```

   s1 ≡ s2 means the states s1 and s2 are equivalent.

   (s1, s2)* means the sequence of states s1 followed by s2 is repeated many times.

   clapper is a component of the buzzer specified in its structural representation.

   Likewise, t7, t8, and space2 are parts specified in the structural representation.

Figure H–3.   Behavior representation.

tions, and behavior, a causal description of how a function is achieved can refer to generic knowledge. Generic knowledge is knowledge about general physical principles, for example, Kirchoff's law of electric currents. Generic knowledge is used in Chandrasekaran's representation as an element in a behavior description, which needs no further explanation.

Knowledge Compilation

The knowledge representation is used to generate a system for diagnosing malfunctions of a device by converting the functional representation into a hierarchy of diagnostic rules. Rules confirm or reject hypotheses about a cause of a malfunction. These rules are called *specialists*. The difference between simple rules and specialists is that the latter not only reject or confirm hypotheses but also include domain specific knowledge about how the antecedent part of the rule can be tested. Conditions in the antecedent of a rule may be very easy to test; for example, the conditions "the switch is pressed" and "the buzzer is buzzing" can be easily tested by simple observation. Others may require taking measurements or even conducting an experiment, e.g., "the terminals t1 and t2 are electrically connected".

Chandrasekaran calls the process of generating diagnostic specialists from functional representations *knowledge compilation*. It is a process of representation transformation from a form that is more descriptive of the way devices function to a form that is more efficient to use for diagnostic problem solving.

H3. Consolidation

THE WORK on *consolidation* by Bylander and Chandrasekaran focuses on the problem of composing the behavior description of components into a behavior description of the whole. Their task is not prediction or simulation, but it is one of aggregation of descriptions. They have a vocabulary of a few generic types of behavior, in terms of which behavior of individual components are described. They also have rules, called *causal patterns*, for combining behavior to generate behavioral descriptions of composite devices. Given information about the structure of a device in terms of the connections among components and descriptions of the behaviors of the components, their system attempts to combine behavior descriptions of more and more components to generate a description of the behavior of the device as a whole.

Representation of Components

In Bylander and Chandrasekaran's representation, a device has *components* and *substances*. Components have behavior and interact with other components through physical connections. Components can also contain substances. Substances are the "stuff" that moves within and between components and affects their behavior. Substances include real physical substances such as fluid as well as other physical phenomena such as heat, which could be thought of as something that moves around. Substances can contain other substances in turn; for example, water can contain heat.

Figure H–4 shows part of an electrical circuit involving a switch and a battery, together with descriptions of some of their behaviors.

One of the central claims in the work on consolidation is that a small set of primitives, describing different generic types of behavior, can be used to describe actions of devices. In this respect, their work is reminiscent of Schank's work on conceptual dependency (Schank, 1975). Schank's goal was understanding of natural language sentences, and he defined eleven primitive actions such that all verbs of a natural language can be given classified as a special case of one of the primitives. In the

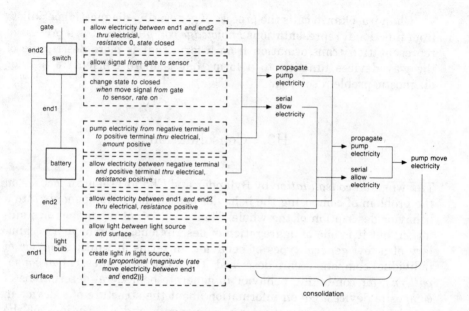

Figure H–4.   Behavioral description of a light bulb.
(From Nishida, T. 1987. Qualitative Reasoning—Formal models of commonsense reasoning. *Journal of Japanese Society for Artificial Intelligence*, Vol. 2(1). Modified from Bylander and Chandresekaran. 1985.)

work on consolidation, the goal is composition of descriptions of component behavior, and the set of primitive behavior types are the following:

Allow	An *allow* behavior indicates that a substance is permitted to move through a specified path. It can be unidirectional or bidirectional.
Expel	An *expel* behavior is an attempt to move a substance from or to a container. It does not specify a path but only a single place from which the behavior happens.
Pump	A *pump* behavior is an attempt to move a substance through a path.
Move	A *move* behavior states that a substance is actually moving from one place to another.
Create	A *create* behavior states that a substance is being created. Includes such behavior as emission of light as well as generation of physical substances.
Destroy	A *destroy* behavior states that a substance is being destroyed. Includes such behavior as obstruction of light and sound as well as disappearance of physical substances.
change modes	A component can have operational modes, in each of which it may behave differently. A *change mode* behavior is changing from one such mode to another.

Composing Behavioral Descriptions

Given descriptions of individual components and the physical connections among components, Bylander and Chandrasekaran's program generates the behavior description of composite components by combining the descriptions of individual components. The program has rules about how to combine individual behaviors for a number of different situations, called *causal patterns*. They combine component behaviors that are physically connected in some fashion: connected in parallel or serial, sharing the same end point, on the same path, and so on. Consider the following causal patterns:

Serial/parallel *allow*, Serial/parallel *pump*, Serial/parallel *move*	An *allow*, a *pump*, or a *move* behavior can be caused by two behaviors of the same type in serial or parallel.
Propagate *expel*	An *allow* and an *expel* located at the end point of the *allow* make an *expel*.
Include *expel*	A *pump* and an *expel* located at the end point of the *pump* make a *pump*.
Propagate *pump*	A *pump* and an *allow* in serial make a *pump*.
Pump move	A *pump* and an *allow* on the same path can cause a *move*.
Carry *move*	A *move* behavior of a substance containing another substance causes a *move* of the latter substance.

The behaviors of the switch and the battery in Figure H–4 can be combined using these causal patterns to generate behavior description of the composite device comprised of the two. The right half of Figure H–4 shows the consolidation process. For example, the "allow electricity" behavior of the switch and the "*pump* electricity" behavior of the battery is combined by the "propagate *pump*" causal pattern to form an aggregate "*pump* electricity" behavior.

H4.   Conclusion

CSA's CAUSE-EFFECT graph consists of various types of nodes representing events, and links representing causal interactions connecting events. With these nodes and links, we can represent our perception of how a device works as a network of causally related events. The purpose of CSA is to represent our common sense understanding of how a device works and not to represent an accurate design model of a device.

The CSA representation suffers from lack of clear definitions for the representation primitives, namely, various types of events and links. Some of the distinctions between different types of events, such as the distinction between tendency and action and that between statechange and tendency, seem arbitrary or irrelevant to the working of a mechanism. The relationship between a mathematical or structural model of a given device and its CSA representation is not obvious, and it would be difficult to define the notions of completeness or soundness for CSA representations of any given device.

Chandrasekaran and his colleagues' research on functional representation of devices is motivated by the questions of what it means to understand the relation between a function of a device and its structure and of how to represent such understanding so as to enable problem solving. They represent knowledge about how a device achieves its function by a causal chain of states, similar to CSA representation. Their main interests are in representing such knowledge and using it efficiently to solve diagnostic problems. The declarative representation of a device function is automatically converted into a set of hierarchically organized diagnostic rules. A device is represented in terms of its structure, function, and its behavior.

As in the case of CSA, Chandrasekaran's functional representation has no obvious relation to the physical structure or the mathematical model of the device. Since no guiding principles are offered about how a given device should be modeled, a functional representation model of any device may be highly subjective, and it will not be easy to assess its predictive power or limitations.

A weakness common to all three systems described in this section is the lack of temporal reasoning. In all cases, a causal link implies only a weak temporal relation between connected states. That state A causes state B implies only that the beginning of B does not precede that of A. The lack of a clear notion of time is not a major difficulty to Chandrasekaran and Bylander's work because the descriptions their systems produce, diagnostic rules or aggregate behaviors, are essentially static, requiring no sophisticated temporal reasoning capability. However simulation performed by CSA does require temporal reasoning. CSA converts a declarative representation to a procedural one in order to simulate a situation with many small demon-like computing units run in parallel. However, without much more information about temporal relations between events connected by causal links, it is difficult to coordinate firing of demons to simulate behavior correctly.

References

CSA is described in Rieger and Grinberg (1977). Use of CSA for simulation is discussed in Rieger and Grinberg (1978). Chandrasekaran's functional representation is described in Sembugamoorthy and Chandrasekaran (1986). Consolidation is described in Bylander (1987).

Chapter XXII

Knowledge-based Simulation

Alfred Round—Intelligent Interfaces

CHAPTER XXII: KNOWLEDGE-BASED SIMULATION

A. OVERVIEW

THE POST-INDUSTRIAL ERA has forced decision makers in all sectors of society to face problems whose scope and complexity are beyond the grasp of any single individual or committee. The manufacturer who wishes to increase productivity, the medical researcher who tries to develop better cancer treatments, and the government bureaucrat who formulates policy all must confront an overwhelming number of potential courses of action that have uncertain outcomes. Since it is generally impractical or unethical to try out even a small fraction of these plans, a decision-maker needs some means of predicting their outcomes in order to make the best choice.

Two of the principal methods for predicting the behavior of complex systems are *simulation* and *knowledge-based programming*. Both of these methods use digital computers to construct models of a system and to execute these models in order to obtain information on the system's behavior. The two methods differ in the way the system is modeled and in how the model is used to make predictions. The behavior of a system is usually represented by mathematical equations or probability distributions in a simulation model, and by rules in a knowledge-based program. Simulators predict the future state of a system by propagating the values of system variables through time, whereas knowledge-based programs infer facts about the state of the system or show how to achieve a predefined state, usually without explicitly considering time. Simulators generally function as black boxes that take numerical data as input and produce numerical data as output, whereas knowledge-based programs are often able to explain the reasoning process that led to a given result.

The choice of technique depends on the application; simulation is suited toward problems that can be modeled analytically, whereas knowledge-based programming is amenable to problems that are better expressed in the form of heuristics. Since the accumulated knowledge about most complex domains has both analytical and heuristic components, it is of great interest to investigate the potential of integrating knowledge-based techniques with simulation for the purpose of predicting complex system behavior.

This chapter surveys the current state of the art in knowledge-based simulation. The field is so new that no attempt shall be made to precisely define the term "knowledge-based simulation." Instead, the programs

417

described in the following sections will illustrate a variety of applications, techniques, and issues in making simulation more "intelligent." Section B presents some background on simulation in general and the motivation for incorporating knowledge-based paradigms into simulation modeling. Section C illustrates the variety of problems that knowledge-based simulation is uniquely qualified to solve. Many simulation applications combine both numerical and rule-based components; the integration of these components is the subject of Section D. Most interesting problems occur in domains where knowledge is incomplete and is represented with varying degrees of precision; Section E discusses simulation techniques that deal with such situations. Section F describes several applications and tools that have been tested in the real world. Section G discusses development issues such as validation, verification, and the use of time. Section H concludes the chapter by emphasizing the importance of proper validation to knowledge-based simulation applications.

B. THE EVOLUTION OF KNOWLEDGE-BASED SIMULATION

THIS SECTION TRACES the roots of knowledge-based simulation in methodologies first developed in the 1950s: discrete-event and continuous simulation. A simple example of discrete-event simulation is presented to give an intuitive feeling for the kind of problems for which simulation is useful. The limitations inherent in the most frequently used simulation techniques are then discussed. Object-oriented programming techniques were originally developed to address these limitations and expanded the range of problems amenable to simulation. We will describe two object-oriented languages, SIMULA and Smalltalk, that were designed specifically for simulation applications; these two languages were influential in the subsequent development of knowledge-based simulation.

B1. An Overview of Simulation

TO ILLUSTRATE discrete-event simulation, we will consider a factory that makes orange juice. A conveyor belt carries each orange to a processing station that slices and squeezes the orange. We would like to know the average amount of time that an orange spends in the system since this knowledge will help us devise ways to increase the rate of juice production. If the processing station is busy when an orange arrives at it, the orange must enter a queue and wait until all the oranges in front of it have been processed; otherwise, the orange gets processed right away. The delay of an orange is equal to the time it spends in queue plus the time it takes to be processed. Only one orange can be processed at a time, and the orange at the front of the queue starts being processed at the instant that the preceding orange departs from the processing station. The time that orange n spends in queue is therefore the departure time of orange $n - 1$ minus the arrival time of orange n.

If the processing rate is much faster than the arrival rate, there will never be a queue, and the average delay of an orange will simply be the average processing time. At the other extreme, if oranges arrive at a rate much faster than the processing rate, the conveyor belt will always be full of oranges. In this case, the average time that an orange spends in queue will be the number of oranges that fit on the conveyor belt times the average processing time. As an example, suppose that the conveyor belt has a capacity of 10 oranges and is always full, and that the average processing time for an orange is 2 seconds. An orange that has just entered the system will have to wait about 20 seconds in queue since each of the 10 oranges in front of it requires about 2 seconds of processing time. The total delay for this orange is about 22 seconds since it requires about 2 seconds of processing time after having waited 20 seconds in queue. If the arrival and processing rates are relatively close, however, there is no simple way to compute the average delay directly. We now show how the average delay can be calculated using simulation.

Simulation of the Orange Juice Manufacturing Facility

We will simulate 5 oranges as they pass through the system. We are given two pieces of data for orange n: the time interval between the arrival of orange $n - 1$ and the arrival of orange n (called the inter-arrival time), and the time it takes to process orange n (called the processing time). These times (in arbitrary units) are shown in Table B–1. Note that the inter-arrival time for orange 1 is 0 since there is no orange preceding it.

These times are not constant because most real-world processes do not occur at a constant rate—oranges sometimes fall off the line, the processing station occasionally breaks down, and so on. These variations are accounted for by *probability distributions*. The input data to a simulation is usually generated by random sampling from the probability distributions for each input parameter. For example, the inter-arrival and processing times in Table B–1 might have been generated by sampling five times from an exponential distribution and a normal distribution, respectively.

TABLE B–1
Inter-arrival and Processing Times for the
Orange Juice Simulation

Orange	Inter-arrival time	Processing time
1	0	5
2	4	9
3	3	7
4	6	9
5	5	5

At time 0, orange 1 arrives at the processing station. Since the processing station is idle, the processing of orange 1 begins right away. We know from the table that the processing time orange 1 is 5, so we calculate that orange 1 will depart from the system at $(0 + 5) = 5$. We also see from the table that orange 2 arrived at time 4. Since orange 1 is undergoing processing until time 5, orange 2 is delayed in the queue $(5 - 4) = 1$. At time 5, orange 2 begins processing. Since the processing time of orange 2 is 9, it will depart the system at time $(5 + 9) = 14$.

In the meantime, orange 3 will have arrived at time $(4 + 3) = 7$, and orange 4 will have arrived at time $(7 + 6) = 13$. Orange 3 arrived at 7 but cannot begin processing until orange 2 departs at 14. The delay in the queue for orange 3 is therefore $(14 - 7) = 7$. Orange 3 has processing time of 7, so it departs the system at $(14 + 7) = 21$. Orange 4 must wait until time 21 to begin processing, so it experiences a delay in the queue of $(21 - 13) = 8$. It has a processing time of 9, and so it departs the system at $(21 + 9) = 30$. Orange 5, which arrived at time $(13 + 5) = 18$, must wait until time 30 to begin processing, giving it a delay in queue of $(30 - 18) = 12$. With a processing time of 5, orange 5 departs the system at $(30 + 5) = 35$.

At this point, all 5 oranges have been processed. We can now calculate the total delay for each orange as the sum of its delay in the queue and its processing time. These statistics are presented in Table B–2. The average delay of an orange is therefore the sum of the total delays divided by 5 (the total number of processed oranges), which turns out to be 12.6.

The moral of the story is that we were able to calculate the average delay of the 5 oranges given their inter-arrival and processing times by using simulation to *predict* the delay in queue for each one. The hallmark of simulation is its ability to predict the future state of a system given a model of the system and its current state. Another way to put it is that simulation predicts the *behavior* of a system, if we use the term "behavior" to mean the set of values that describes a system over a time period of interest.

TABLE B–2

Statistics Derived from the Orange Juice Simulation

Orange	Arrival	Delay in queue	Departure	Total delay
1	0	0	5	5
2	4	1	14	10
3	7	7	21	14
4	13	8	30	17
5	18	12	35	17

Discrete-event and Continuous Simulation

The orange juice facility exemplifies a wide range of systems in which a finite number of entities (such as oranges) arrive at the system, form queues, undergo processing, and depart the system. Since each of these events occurs at a single point in time for each entity, the simulation of such systems is called *discrete-event simulation*. There are 10 events in the orange juice simulation—the arrival of each of the 5 oranges and the departure of each orange after it has been processed. From the data in Table B–2, we can construct a time-ordered list of these 10 events, as shown in Table B–3.

Systems such as a chemical processing plant, a bacterial cell, or an airplane in flight are characterized by variables that change continuously (e.g., the rate of a chemical reaction, the concentration of a molecule, or the velocity of an airplane). The behavior of these systems is usually modeled as a set of differential equations that express how the system variables change with time. Once the initial state of the system is specified, the techniques of *continuous simulation* generate values for the system variables at future times by solving these equations. A combination of discrete and continuous simulation is appropriate for systems such as a chemical reaction that undergoes abrupt changes in temperature or pH. Because of its analytical nature, continuous simulation is sometimes called *mathematical simulation*. We will use the term *numerical simulation* to refer to either discrete-event or continuous simulation

TABLE B–3

Listing of Events in the Orange
Juice Simulation

Event	Type	Time
1	A1	0
2	A2	4
3	D1	5
4	A3	7
5	A4	13
6	D2	14
7	A5	18
8	D3	21
9	D4	30
10	D5	35

A = Arrival, D = Departure
(e.g., A1 is the arrival of orange 1)

since both take an initial set of numerical values and predict a new set of numerical values at a future time.

Computer Implementation of a Discrete-event Simulation

We were able to perform the orange juice simulation by hand since the system is very simple and the number of oranges is very small. Since most real-world systems are much more complex, we will want to simulate them on a digital computer. For the sake of simplicity, we will stick to the orange juice example in order to illustrate the computer implementation of simulation.

Figure B–1 shows the flowchart for the program that implements the orange juice simulation. The program makes use of a *simulation clock*, which always gives the time of the next event. Since nothing happens between events, we can move the simulation clock to the time of event n immediately after event $n - 1$ has been processed.

The INIT routine initializes the simulation by setting the simulation clock and all statistics to 0, and it generates the random variables for the inter-arrival and processing times. The routine for processing arrivals increments the number of oranges in queue and schedules the

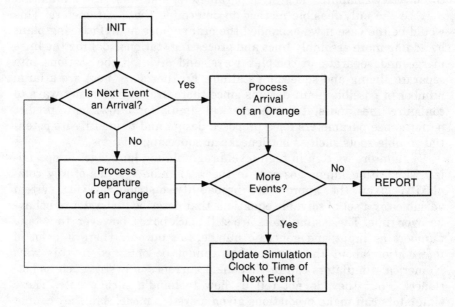

Figure B–1. Flowchart for Orange Juice Simulation.

next arrival, if any. The routine for processing departures decrements the number of oranges in queue, computes the total delay of the orange that just departed, computes the delay in queue of the orange that just started processing, and schedules the departure of the latter orange.

Prior to 1965, almost all simulations were implemented as programs written in a high-level programming language such as FORTRAN. The introduction in the 1960s of specialized simulation languages such as GASP, SimScript, and GPSS helped reduce development time by including routines to automatically process arrival and departure events, generate input data, and collect and report results (Law and Kelton, 1982). Some of these languages also facilitate the coding of continuous simulation models. All numerical simulations have inherent limitations, however; these will be discussed in the next section.

B2. The Limitations of Numerical Simulation

THE AVERAGE DELAY of an orange in the preceding example could have been computed directly using mathematical techniques such as queueing theory; simulation was used for the purpose of illustration. For a more complex system, however, there may be no mathematical technique that can directly compute the system parameters, and numerical simulation may be the only feasible method to determine these parameters. This would be the case if we expanded the orange juice manufacturing plant by adding more assembly lines and processing stations, making the lines merge and separate in complex ways, and dividing the stations into separate slicing and squeezing stations. Furthermore there are a large number of possible plant designs since there are a great many ways to configure lines and stations. Numerical simulation allows us to predict performance parameters for a proposed design and to identify its potential trouble spots such as bottlenecks at squeezing stations.

Simulators written in high-level programming languages or specialized simulation languages can, in theory, handle systems of any complexity, given the appropriate probability distributions for system variables or a set of solvable equations that describe the system's behavior over time. These simulators are still black boxes, however; they take numbers as input and generate numbers as output. There is a lot of information about the system that cannot be obtained in this way. Numerical simulators can predict the occurrence of events such as bottlenecks, but they do not tell us how to handle such events. These simulators can make predictions given a system model, but they cannot decide *which* model is likely to provide the best solution to a problem. This is a serious consideration when there are so many potential models (e.g., the designs of our expanded orange juice plant) that it is not feasible to simulate them all. We may sometimes want to simulate a particular part of the system in detail, perhaps to trouble-shoot a squeezing machine, whereas at other times we are interested only in the overall performance of the whole system and don't need to simulate each component in detail. A separate numerical simulator would have to be run for each component and subcomponent in the system in order to meet this requirement. The user cannot stop the simulation in the middle to inspect the state of the system or to pose "what-if" questions (e.g., "what would happen if I eliminated line 2 and speeded up line 4?"). From a development point of view, a numerical simulation program must be recompiled every time a change is made to the system model. Perhaps most importantly, a numerical simulator provides no *interpretation* or *explanation* of its output; it just generates numbers and leaves their interpretation up to the user.

The theme of this chapter is the incorporation of *knowledge* into simulation in order to overcome these limitations. The next section shows how object-oriented programming languages such as SIMULA and Small-talk took the first steps toward achieving knowledge-based simulation.

B3. Object-oriented Languages for Simulation

SIMULA

SIMULA is an ALGOL-based language that was created to facilitate the development of discrete-event simulation models (Birtwistle et al., 1968). We will first describe the SIMULA language by using it to model a post office (Birtwistle et al., 1968), and then we discuss how to implement a simulation of this model.

The SIMULA Language

All objects can be classified by their *characteristics* and their *behaviors*. For example, all oranges have certain characteristics in common such as size, tartness, juice content, and place of origin. Individual oranges have different sizes, origins, and so on, but the characteristics themselves are shared among all oranges. Likewise, all oranges share certain behaviors such as "growth on trees," even though the time and rate of growth might vary among individual oranges. The common characteristics and behaviors of a set of objects are described in SIMULA by a *class*. Each individual member of the class in called an *instance* of the class.

A class consists of three parts: a *heading*, a *data declaration* part, and an *action* part. A class that represents all the customers that enter the post office can be defined as follows:

```
Heading              CLASS CUSTOMER(NROFTASKS,URGENT);
                     INTEGER NROFTASKS;
                     BOOLEAN URGENT;
                     BEGIN
Data Declaration       Declared list of tasks;
                       REF(CUSTOMER) NEXT;
Action                 WHILE NROFTASKS>0 DO
                       BEGIN
                         Select a task;
                         Select a counter;
                         IF URGENT THEN enter front of
                           counter queue
                         ELSE enter tail of counter queue;
                         Interrupt or wait;
                         Participate in transactions;
                         Leave counter;
                         NROFTASKS:=NROFTASKS-1;
                       END;
                     END;
```

The heading declares a class named CUSTOMER with integer argument NROFTASKS, the number of tasks on the customer's list, and Boolean argument URGENT, which is false unless the customer's needs are urgent. The data declaration part declares the variables that are used by the action part to describe the behavior of a customer. The syntax REF(CUSTOMER) NEXT means that NEXT is a *pointer* to a CUSTOMER instance. As we shall see, such a pointer is used to determine the order of customers in a queue. The data declaration part also contains the list of tasks that a customer will execute while in the post office. The action part describes the behavior of the customer in the post office. For illustrative purposes, the action part is written mostly in English; it would actually be coded as a set of statements in SIMULA. The action part of the CUSTOMER class is a loop that executes once for each item on the list of tasks.

Each customer in the post office is represented by a separate *instance* of the CUSTOMER class. Each instance *inherits* the data declaration and action parts of the class, although the actual contents of these parts will likely be different between different instances. For example, all CUSTOMER instances have a set of tasks, but the tasks may differ between them: Customer1 may have to send a registered letter, pay rent on a box, and apply for a passport, whereas Customer2 just wants to buy a roll of stamps. Similarly, all customers go through the statements in the action part loop once for each task, although the particular action corresponding to each statement differs between customers. The statement "Participate in transactions" is executed for each task by all customers, but the particular transaction may be "apply for passport" for Customer1 and "buy a roll of stamps" for Customer2. As soon as a new CUSTOMER instance is created, it immediately begins to execute the code in its action part, so that different CUSTOMER instances can be engaged in entirely different activities at the same time.

Since there is usually a *queue* at each counter in a post office, it is natural to define a class that represents queues:

```
CLASS QUEUE;
BEGIN
   REF(CUSTOMER)FIRST,LAST;
END;
```

The definition of class QUEUE is unique in our post office example in that it contains no action part. Its data declaration part declares FIRST and LAST as pointers to the first and last customers in the queue, respectively. Figure B–2 shows Queue1, an instance of QUEUE with three customers.

Each arrow in Figure B–2 represents a pointer to a CUSTOMER instance: Queue1.FIRST points to Customer1, Customer1.NEXT points to Customer2, Customer2.NEXT and Queue1.LAST both point to Customer3, and Customer3.NEXT is NIL. In this way, the order of the customers in queue is established.

There must be a *clerk* to handle the customers in each queue. The CLERK class in SIMULA is defined as

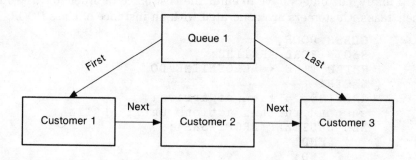

Figure B–2.   The SIMULA implementation of a post office queue.

```
CLASS CLERK(Q); REF(QUEUE)Q;
BEGIN REF(CUSTOMER)PERSON;
SERVICING:
  WHILE Q.FIRST =/= NONE DO
  BEGIN
    PERSON :- Q.FIRST;
    take PERSON out of the queue
  and engage with him in transactions;
  END;
    do other work until interrupted by the
    arrival of a customer in the queue
    GOTO SERVICING;
  END;
```

The Q in the CLERK heading is a pointer to the queue that a clerk
is attending. The PERSON defined in the data declaration part points to
the current customer being served by a clerk. The WHILE loop of the
action part is executed as long as there is a first person in the queue
(i.e., the queue is not empty).

A *counter* is associated with a clerk and a queue. The class
COUNTER is defined as:

```
CLASS COUNTER;
BEGIN REF(QUEUE)Q; REF(CLERK)POSTOFFICER;
  Q :- NEW QUEUE;
  POSTOFFICER :- NEW CLERK(Q);
END;
```

The data declaration part of COUNTER declares pointers to a queue
called Q and to a clerk called POSTOFFICER. The two pointer assignment
statements of the action part *create* a new queue and a new clerk to
service that queue.

Finally, customers have to enter the post office in order to carry out
their tasks. Customers are generated with an instance of class DOOR:

```
CLASS DOOR;
BEGIN REAL ARRTIME;
WHILE TIME <= CLOSETIME DO
BEGIN
ARRTIME := time of arrival;
suspend further actions until ARRTIME;
NEW CUSTOMER(NROFTASKS);
      END;
      END;
END;
```

CLOSETIME is the time that the post office closes. We assume that
the times of customer arrivals are generated by a probability distribu-

tion. The WHILE loop therefore creates a new CUSTOMER instance at each ARRTIME and waits until the next ARRTIME.

The entire post office consists of four counters and a door, as shown in Figure B–3.

We have seen that the clerks and queues are generated from COUNTER instances and that customers are generated from a DOOR instance. What generates the counter and door instances? The *system object* serves the purpose of generating the first objects, from which all other objects will be generated. The action part of the system object can be coded as:

```
BEGIN
    OPENTIME:=8.00;
    CLOSETIME:=17.00;
    wait until OPENTIME;
    SERVICE1:-NEW COUNTER;
    SERVICE2:-NEW COUNTER;
    SERVICE3:-NEW COUNTER;
    SERVICE4:-NEW COUNTER;
    NEW DOOR;
    wait until CLOSETIME;
    close down the post office;
END;
```

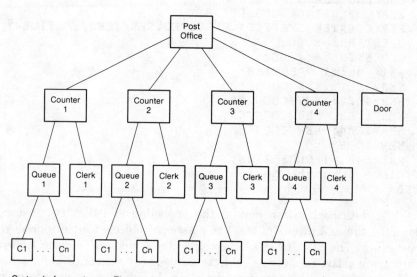

C stands for customer. The number of customers in each queue at a given time is 0 or a positive integer.

Figure B–3. The SIMULA implementation of a post office.

Note.that the pointer to the DOOR instance is not assigned, since it is never referred to by any of the other objects.

The Implementation of Simulation Models with SIMULA

The post office system that we have described consists of a collection of objects (customers, queues, clerks, counters, and a door), each of which executes its action pattern independently of the others. The objects of the collection must *coordinate* their activities in some way, however, if the post office is to operate as we expect. For example, the participation of a customer in a transaction and the service of that customer by a clerk must occur at the same time. The SIMULA language contains a predefined class called **SIMULATION**, which contains procedures for coordinating the actions of objects with respect to time. The class *SIMULATION* is part of SIMULA; it is not defined by a programmer. The entire post office can be represented as an instance of class SIMULATION:

```
SIMULATION CLASS POSTOFFICE;
BEGIN
   PROCESS CLASS COUNTER . . .;
   PROCESS CLASS DOOR . . . . ;
   PROCESS CLASS CLERK . . . .;
   PROCESS CLASS QUEUE . . . .;
   PROCESS CLASS CUSTOMER . . ;
   REAL OPENTIME, CLOSETIME;
   REF(COUNTER)SERVICE1,SERVICE2,SERVICE3,SERVICE4;
   OPENTIME:=8.00;
   CLOSETIME:=17.00;
   wait until OPENTIME;
   SERVICE1:-NEW COUNTER;
   SERVICE2:-NEW COUNTER;
   SERVICE3:-NEW COUNTER;
   SERVICE4:-NEW COUNTER;
   NEW DOOR;
   wait until CLOSETIME;
   close down the post office;
END
```

The data declaration part of the preceding SIMULATION instance contains the definitions of the five classes of objects that comprise the post office. The SIMULATION class provides a *simulation clock* for synchronizing activities between objects. It also provides routines for scheduling activities with respect to the clock. In addition, it maintains an *event queue* of all events that are scheduled to occur in the future, like the one in Table B–3 for the orange juice simulation. The three principal routines for scheduling activities are **HOLD**, **PASSIVATE**, and **ACTI-**

VATE. Figure B–4 shows an initial event queue and how each of these routines affects the queue.

There are three fates that an object can have with respect to time:

1. It can be scheduled for activation at a specific time in the future.

2. It can be suspended for an unknown amount of time until something causes it to resume activity.

3. It can cease to exist as far as the simulation is concerned.

The last occurs when the object has completed executing its action part; for example, when a customer's number of tasks becomes 0. With these definitions, we can rewrite the action parts of the CUSTOMER, CLERK, and DOOR classes as follows:

Action part of CUSTOMER:

```
WHILE NROFTASKS>0 DO
  BEGIN
    select a task;
    select a counter;
    IF URGENT THEN enter front of queue
    ELSE enter tail of queue;
    IF CLERK is free THEN ACTIVATE CLERK
    ELSE PASSIVATE;
    participate in transactions;
    leave counter;
    NROFTASKS:=NROFTASKS-1;
  END;
```

Action part of CLERK:

```
SERVICING:
WHILE Q.FIRST =/= NONE DO
  BEGIN
    PERSON:-Q.FIRST;
    ACTIVATE PERSON;
    engage in transaction with PERSON;
  END;
PASSIVATE;
GOTO SERVICING;
```

Action part of DOOR:

```
WHILE TIME<=CLOSETIME DO
  BEGIN
    ARRTIME:=time of arrival;
    HOLD(ARRTIME-CURTIME);
    NEW CUSTOMER(NROFTASKS,URGENT);
END;
```

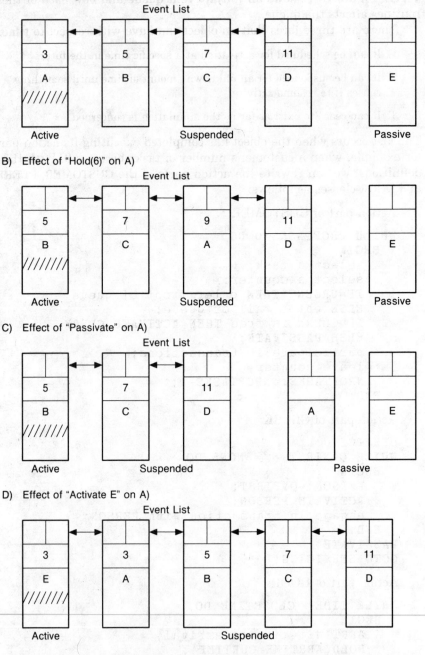

Figure B–4. The effect of messages HOLD, PASSIVATE, and
           ACTIVATE on a SIMULA event queue.
           (Birtwistle et al., 1968, p. 282.)

When the clerk becomes free, the **ACTIVATE** CLERK statement in the CUSTOMER class will cause the clerk to resume executing its action part immediately after **PASSIVATE** (thus executing the GOTO SERVICING statement). If the clerk is not free, the **PASSIVATE** statement will cause the Customer instance to be suspended until it is reactivated by the **ACTIVATE** PERSON statement in the CLERK instance. The **PASSIVATE** statement causes an object to be suspended for an unknown length of time until reactivated by a statement from another object. In contrast, the **HOLD** statement schedules an event for a specific time in the future. The **HOLD** statement in the DOOR class causes an event (the creation of a new CUSTOMER instance) to occur at time ARRTIME by scheduling it ARRTIME − CURTIME time units in the future, where CURTIME is the current time on the simulation clock.

The **HOLD, ACTIVATE,** and **PASSIVATE** statements are called *messages* in object-oriented programming terminology. A message is a statement that tells a particular object to perform a particular action. "**ACTIVATE** CLERK" is a message from a CUSTOMER instance to a CLERK instance; it tells the clerk to resume activity. **HOLD** and **PASSIVATE** are messages an object sends to itself: **HOLD** tells the object to reschedule its activation at a specific future time, and **PASSIVATE** tells the object to suspend itself without scheduling a future reactivation.

By encoding a simulation in terms of its objects, we can describe the characteristics and behaviors of the object. We know, for example, that a customer is in a particular queue and that its position in the queue depends on the urgency of its tasks. We can describe the overall characteristics and behavior of an object by its class definition, which can be specialized for each particular instance. In addition, the class **SIMULATION** implements synchronization between objects. The combination of knowledge about individual objects plus a means of synchronizing their activities gives the SIMULA programmer the ability to *control* the behavior of the model. By writing the appropriate code in the data declaration and action parts of CUSTOMER, for example, the programmer can give very specific directions about how to choose a queue (e.g., based on length of all current queues), what order to perform the tasks on the list (e.g., according to priority), how to handle special cases (e.g., the customer's tasks are urgent), etc. This type of control is impossible with the pure numerical simulation illustrated by the orange juice model.

Smalltalk.   The class concept introduced by SIMULA was adopted and generalized in Smalltalk. We will discuss a version called Smalltalk-80 (Goldberg and Robson, 1983, and Xerox Learning Research Group, 1981).

The Smalltalk-80 Language.   A Smalltalk-80 class consists of a *class name, instance variables,* and *methods,* corresponding to the name,

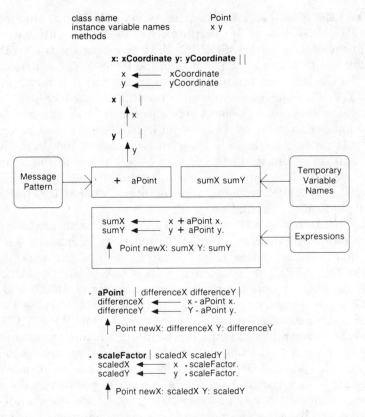

Figure B–5. The definition of the Smalltalk-80 class **Point**.

data part, and action part of a SIMULA class. Figure B–5 shows the definition of the Smalltalk-80 class **Point** that represents points in the Cartesian plane (Xerox Learning Research Group, 1981).

All procedural and behavioral information is implemented in the form of *methods*. A method is analogous to the action pattern of a SIMULA object in that it consists of code that describes the behavior of an object. The difference is that there is only one action part to a SIMULA object, whereas there can be any number of methods for a Smalltalk-80 object. A method consists of a *message pattern*, temporary variable names, and expressions (statements in Smalltalk-80 that implement behavior). Every time a message is sent to an object, the message is compared to the message patterns of the object until a match is found; the corresponding code is then executed. In this way, the object that receives a messages knows which one of its methods it should execute.

For example, consider the class Point in Figure B–5, and two instances called `origin` and `offset`. This class describes operations on points in the Cartesian plane. The expression origin + offset sends the message + offset to the object origin. The receiving object origin searches its message patterns for a match to + offset, and finds it with the message pattern + aPoint. The variable aPoint in the message takes on the value offset. In the first two expressions of the method whose message pattern is + aPoint, x and y refer to the *x*- and *y*-coordinates of **origin**, and aPoint x and aPoint y refer to the *x*- and *y*-coordinates of offset. The variable sumX is assigned the sum of the x-coordinates of origin and sumY is assigned the analogous sum of the y-coordinates. The third expression creates a new instance of class **Point**, with instance variables x and y having the values sumX and sumY, respectively. Two other methods are given for class Point: one has message pattern − aPoint for subtracting two points, and the other has message pattern * scaleFactor for multiplying two poionts.

The Implementation of Simulation Models with Smalltalk-80

The entire Smalltalk-80 environment is implemented using classes that are defined in the Smalltalk-80 language. Two classes are provided specifically for performing simulations.

A simulation is implemented in Smalltalk-80 as an instance of the class **Simulation**. As in SIMULA, each Simulation instance maintains a simulation clock and a queue of events, and can use any of a predefined set of messages that schedule and synchronize the objects that take part in a simulation. A simulation is started by sending the message initialize to a Simulation instance. The message defineArrival-Schedule causes an initial set of simulation objects to be added to the event queue. An object proceeds through the simulation by receiving the messages startUp, tasks, and finishUp, in sequence.

The startUp message is sent to an object at the time that the object is scheduled to enter the simulation. When a simulation object enters the simulation at its scheduled time, it begins executing its associated tasks. The tasks message then causes the object to send a series of messages in sequence. For example, the message holdFor:aTimeDelay is sent by an object to itself in order to suspend execution of its remaining tasks for the amount of time specified by aTimeDelay. Another task might be the scheduling of a different object in the form of the message scheduleArrivalOf: aSimulationObjectClass accordingTo: aProbabilityDistribution to the Simulation instance.

As an example, consider a simulation in which visitors enter a room, remain in the room anywhere from 4 to 10 time units, and leave the room. Visitor is created as a subclass of SimulationObject, and it sends the following message as one of its tasks: self holdFor: (Uniform from: 4 to 10) next. The term self refers to a particular Visitor instance, and `Uniform` indicates a probability distribution in which any value between 4 and 10 is equally likely to occur. The Simulation instance schedules the arrival of each visitor with the message `self scheduleArrivalOf: Visitor accordingTo: (Uniform from: 4 to 8) startingAt: 3`. According to these specifications, a visitor will arrive every 4 to 8 units of simulated time starting at time 3, and stay between 4 and 10 simulated time units.

Smalltalk-80 extended the capabilities of SIMULA by allowing an instance to have any number of actions, each implemented as a method that responds to a specific message. This capability is enhanced by the fact that subclasses and their instances can add their own methods and override the method definitions of their superclasses. In addition, Smalltalk-80 provides classes that implement tools for browsing, editing, window manipulation, command menus, and other features that facilitate program development. The combination of message-passing capabilities, built-in classes for simulation, and a large set of development tools all implemented in classes defined by the Smalltalk-80 language, made Smalltalk-80 the first truly integrated environment for developing and executing simulations.

C. APPLICATIONS OF KNOWLEDGE-BASED SIMULATION

PROBLEMS IN COMPLEX DOMAINS are often solved by combining precise analysis with less precise rules of thumb. A car mechanic may reach a diagnosis by considering both measurements from electronic instruments and heuristic judgments acquired from long experience ("sounds like the timing is off"). The first three systems described in this section solve problems in manufacturing systems design, cancer therapy, and business planning by applying heuristic knowledge to predictions generated through numeric simulation. The fourth system solves a problem in molecular biology by directly using heuristics to make predictions.

C1. The Design of Flexible Manufacturing Systems

MOST MANUFACTURING FACILITIES produce large quantities of a particular type of unit because it is not practical to constantly retool the facility to produce many variations on the unit for different specialized applications. However, economic considerations sometimes make it cost-effective to implement *flexible manufacturing systems* (FMS) that can produce small quantities of customized units in a timely manner. An FMS consists of ". . . machine tools, other workstations (washing, measuring, palletizing for example), a storage system for parts and for tools, a handling system which may consist of robots and/or automated guided vehicles, and a computerized control system" (Wolper, 1987). A layout for an FMS that manufactures engine components is shown in Figure C–1.

The design of an FMS requires the specification of system parameters such as the number and configuration of machine tools and workstations as well as the paths for routing parts through the system. An FMS is also designed with one or more *goals* in mind; such a goal might be the overall maximization of production or profits, or it might be the more modest goal of minimizing inventory or increasing the throughput of a particular part. Simulation is a useful tool for predicting the dynamic behavior of any *given* FMS design. However, the number of potential designs is so large that it is impractical to simulate all of them in order to determine which one optimally satisfies the stated goals.

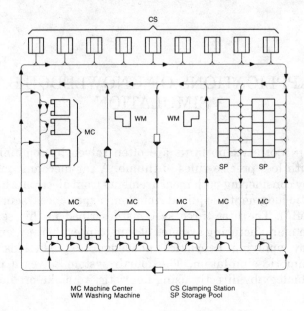

Figure C–1.   The layout of a flexible manufacturing system.
(Seliger et al., 1987, p. 67)

MOSYS is a computer program developed at the Fraunhofer Institute
of Berlin that helps manufacturing systems designers with little simulation experience to design FMSs that optimally meet a set of performance goals (Seliger et al., 1987). The basic idea behind MOSYS is to
take a model of an FMS and refine it until it meets the performance
goals. The refinement of a model consists of three steps:

1. Determine its behavior using analytical techniques such as discrete-
   event simulation.

2. Propose model refinements using a knowledge base that interprets
   the analytical results.

3. Refine the model using the proposals as guidelines.

The cycle of analysis, interpretation, and model refinement is repeated
until the human systems designer is satisfied that the performance goals
have been optimally achieved.

The first step in the design process is to build an initial model by
specifying *functional* and *topological* descriptions of the system (see Figure C–2). The functional description is carried out by specializing the
five functional building blocks—manufacture, assemble, transport, test,
and store—to meet specific system requirements. Interactive graphical

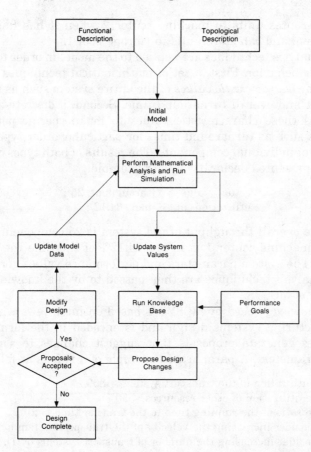

Figure C–2.   Overall MOSYS design process.

tools are available to support this process. The topological description represents the physical layout of system parts as a network of nodes and paths. The building blocks of the functional description are explicitly attached to the nodes of the topological description. The model is represented as a set of declarative statements in PROLOG. For the FMS layout of Figure C–1, these statements include:

```
type_of_function  (mc1,manufacture);
capacity          (mc1,1);
can_substitute    (mc1, mc2);
route             (mc1, mc2);
storage           (mc1, pool1);
```

In other words, machine center 1 serves a manufacturing function, is capable of processing one unit, can be replaced by machine center 2 if necessary, routes units to machine center 2 when it has finished processing them, and can store units in storage pool 1.

Two analysis techniques are applied to the model in order to generate its dynamic behavior. First, a set of mathematical techniques is used to estimate the *characteristic values* of the entire system such as maximum throughput and overall turnaround time. Second, a discrete-event simulator uses these characteristic values to make specific performance predictions such as turnaround times for particular order types and the utilization of individual components. The results of both types of analysis are also represented declaratively, for example,

actual_value (throughput, 25);
utilization_in_% (mc1, 64.12);

That is, the overall throughput of the system is 25 components per unit time, and machine center 1 is in use 64.12% of the time the system is operating. The system parameters and performance values generated by the two analysis techniques are then passed to by the knowledge-based component of MOSYS.

The knowledge used by MOSYS is based on interviews with experts in manufacturing systems design and is encoded in the form of rules. These rules generate proposals that suggest changes to some of the model's parameters. A paraphrased example of a rule is as follows:

If ((the utilization of the transport system > 80%)
and (the utilization of other resources < 50%)
and (the ratio of the running time to the transfer time > 2)
then (consider increasing the velocity of the transport system by 10%)
else (consider increasing the number of transport systems by 1).

The proposals are generated by reasoning about the current model data, the current system values, and the performance goals. The inferencing mechanism inherent in PROLOG is used for this process. The human systems designer then decides whether to accept or reject the proposals. If a proposal is accepted, the model is modified accordingly, and the cycle of analysis, interpretation, and model refinement is repeated until the systems designer is satisfied with the design (see Figure C–2).

MOSYS has been used to design a system that manufactures an engine block and an engine head, each in 3 to 6 different variants, using a variable number of clampings, pallets, and processing times. The following (paraphrased) piece of dialog was generated during the design process:

Goal: maximize throughput
Message: mc_3 is a bottleneck whose utilization is 87%.
Message: 7 out of 7 pallets for clamping_6 are in use.
Proposal: consider increasing the number of pallets for clamping_6 by 1.

The knowledge-based component of MOSYS generates proposals for refining a model based on the results of simulating the model and on a set of performance goals. MOSYS users can rapidly converge on an optimal design by incorporating these proposals on each cycle of model refinement until they decide that the goals have been satisfied. The knowledge-based component does not impact the simulation directly; rather, its value lies in greatly reducing the number of designs that need to be simulated in the first place.

C2.   Planning Therapies for Cancer Treatment

ONYX IS A PROGRAM developed at Stanford University to assist physicians in planning therapies for cancer patients (Langlotz et al., 1985; Langlotz et al., 1986; and Langlotz et al., 1987). A therapy plan consists of a series of treatment decisions based on the patient's test results at each visit. For example, consider a patient who has been taking the anti-cancer drug combination POCC and whose white blood cell count is low on the current visit. The physician has three overall options at this point: reduce the dosage of POCC, delay administration of POCC until the next visit, or administer a different drug combination. Suppose that the decision is to reduce the dosage of POCC. On the next visit, the white blood cell count and tumor size will be measured again, and a new decision will be made based on these results. The therapy plan is the sequence of such decisions made over the entire course of therapy. These plans are created by ONYX in a three-stage process, as illustrated in Figure C–3:

1. *Plan Generation.* Use general treatment strategies to generate a small set of reasonable plans by selecting combinations of treatment components appropriate for the current patient state.

2. *Plan Simulation.* Use knowledge about the structure and behavior of the human body to design simulations that predict the future states of the patient after the execution of each proposed plan.

3. *Plan Ranking.* Use decision analysis (Langlotz et al., 1987) to rank the plans according to how well the predictions for each plan meet the therapeutic goals for the patient.

An enormous number of plans is possible because there are a great many ways to select drug combinations, their dosages, and the timing of their administration. A major goal of ONYX is to reduce the number of possible plans to the few that are most likely to achieve the treatment goals. This reduction is performed during the plan generation step.

We will focus on the second step, plan simulation. The physiological

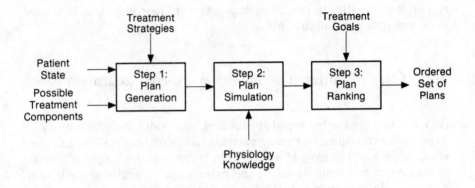

Figure C–3.   The three-step planning process in ONYX.

model to be simulated is represented symbolically as shown in the screen display of Figure C–4. The model on the left side of the figure represents the body in terms of its parts. The parts communicate with each other through *ports*, the small boxes containing an x. Each of these parts can itself be modeled in terms of its component parts, as shown in the case of bone marrow on the right side of the figure. Associated with each part is a mathematical equation that describes its time-dependent behavior. Each such equation contains numerical constants that represent the size, growth, and maturation rate of the cells comprising the part.

ONYX simulates the model shown in Figure C–4 in order to predict the effects of administering a hypothetical anti-cancer drug on bone marrow. The passage of the drug from one part of the body to another is simulated in the form of messages sent between ports. When the port for a body part receives a message (i.e., the drug has just arrived at the part), rules associated with that part are fired. These rules predict the effect of the drug on the numerical constants in the mathematical equation that represents the behavior of the part. The equation is then solved to predict the change in the variables that describe the part. For example, the arrival of a toxic drug at the bone marrow may invoke rules that change the growth rate parameters in the equation that models the

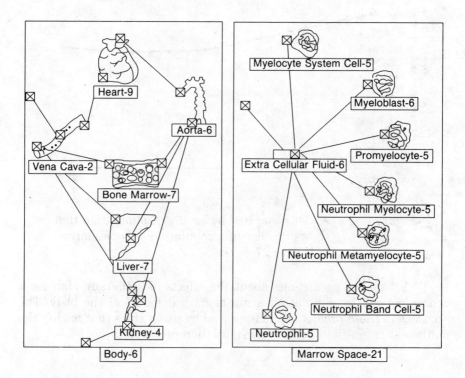

Figure C–4.   ONYX model of the bone marrow and its context
within the body. Each of the two large
rectangular boxes signifies a model. Solid lines
represent connections between models. (Langlotz
et al., 1987, p. 291.)

number of marrow precursor cells over time. When the equation is solved,
the values of the variables describing bone marrow may change. These
updated values then trigger rules that cause new messages to be transmitted to all body parts connected to the bone marrow.

Both intermediate and final results of a simulation can be visually
depicted. For example, the movement of a drug through the parts of the
physiological model is graphically displayed during simulation. Once a
simulation is complete, plots of the state variables over time can be
displayed, as shown in Figure C–5. Such information can be useful in
determining how well the simulated plan will meet actual treatment
goals. Once all plans proposed by the plan generation step have been
simulated, the plan ranking step is performed in order to rank the plans
according to the treatment goals.

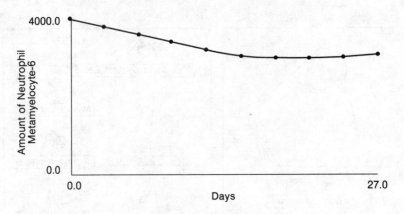

Figure C–5. A plot generated by an ONYX simulation that
shows the size of a population of bone marrow
cells over 27 days.

ONYX makes predictions about the effects of a therapy plan for a
cancer patient by simulating a mathematical model of the body. The
accuracy of these predictions is improved by using rules that modify the
mathematical model itself as the simulation proceeds.

C3.   Evaluating Business Proposals

IN THE PREVIOUS TWO EXAMPLES, the simulation component of the program was developed in conjunction with a knowledge-based component.
As we saw in Section B, however, most existing simulators operate
without a knowledge-based component; they perform discrete-event or
mathematical simulation on a set of input data to generate a set of
output data. Can knowledge be used to interpret the mass of numbers
that come out of an already existing discrete-event or mathematical
simulator, without having to modify the simulator? A program called
EXSYS (Moser, 1986), developed at James Madison University for the
purpose of evaluating business proposals, does just that.

EXSYS models a business situation as a set of variables whose values
describe the situation and a set of mathematical equations that express
the relationships between the variables. These variables might include
the price of raw materials, transportation costs, advertising budgets, and
tax rates. Simulation is performed by solving the set of equations for a
given time period in order to compute the values of the relevant variables
for the next time period. The values of the variables can be computed
for any number of consecutive future time periods during which the

model is considered to be valid. The following simulation model is for a proposed business project in which the time interval between simulation runs is one year (only 6 out of 15 equations are shown):

```
TOTMKT  = 1.10 * TOTMKT (total market)
SALES   = 1.13 * SALES (total sales)
UNITS   = SALES / PRICE (units produced)
LABCOST = 650000 / UNITS (labor costs)
MATCOST = 590000 / UNITS (cost of materials)
MARGIN  = PRICE − LABCOST − MATCOST (profit margin per
          unit)
```

The variables on the left-hand sides of the equations are computed from the values of the same variables from the previous year and from external variables such as tax rates. For example, the first equation predicts a 10% annual market growth rate for a product, and the second equation predicts a 13% annual sales growth rate for the company if it goes ahead with the project. By running the simulator (i.e., solving the set of 15 equations) for each of the years 1986 to 1991, the table of values in Figure C–6 is generated:

EXSYS uses a knowledge base of 240 rules to interpret simulation data such as that of Figure C–6. Two paraphrase rules from this knowledge base are as follows:

```
If (Net Present Value <= 0.0)
then (Profitability := 'very low')

If ((Profitability = 'low')
   and (risk = 'high')
   and (market = 'normal')
   and (tech = 'normal))
then (reject project)
```

The first rule states that if the "net present value" (the difference between the cash inflows and the cash outflows of a project) is zero or negative, then the profitability should be rated as "very low." The second rule states that if the profitability of the project is low, the risk is high, the market is not particularly interesting, and there are no special technological advantages, then the project should be rejected. The knowledge base also contains a library of functions for computing values of interest such as net present value. An inference engine applies the rules to data generated by the simulation. The inference engine can run in either forward-chaining or backward-chaining mode according to the user's wishes; the default is backward-chaining mode. Any conclusion inferred by running the knowledge base can be justified by the *explanation component* of the system.

A sample session illustrating the operation of EXSYS is shown in Figure C–7. After running the simulation, the user selects the goal

```
EXSYS-SIMULATOR
```

	1986	1987	1988	1990	1991
TOTMKT	45000004.00	49500004.00	54450004.00	59895004.00	65884504.00
SALES	4520000.00	5107600.00	5771588.00	6521894.50	7369741.00
MKTSHARE	0.10	0.10	0.11	0.11	0.11
SGADMEX	542400.00	612912.00	692590.56	782627.31	884368.88
UNITS	18080.00	20430.40	23086.35	26087.58	29478.96
LABCOST	35.95	31.82	28.16	24.92	22.05
MATCOST	32.63	28.88	25.56	22.62	20.01
FIXCOST	600000.06	672000.06	752640.06	842956.88	944111.69
DEPREC	560000.00	560000.00	560000.00	560000.00	560000.00
MARGIN	181.42	189.31	196.29	202.47	207.94
CONTMARG	3280000.25	3867599.75	4531587.50	5281894.50	6129741.50
NETOPINC	1577600.25	2022687.75	2526357.00	3096310.25	3741261.00
TAXES	709920.06	910209.44	1136860.63	1393339.63	1683567.38
INTEREST	336000.00	336000.00	336000.00	336000.00	336000.00
NETINCOME	682880.13	927678.31	1204696.38	1518170.63	1872893.63

```
GLOBAL INDICATORS
```

NET PRESENT VALUE (NPV)	=	109665.50
INTERNAL RATE OF RETURN (IRR)	=	13.51%
PAYBACK PERIOD (PBP)	=	3.6 YEARS

Figure C–6.   Sample results of an EXSYS simulation.

EXSYS - main commands
```
------------------------------------------------------------
          function                command        abbrev.
------------------------------------------------------------
    create knowledge base         CBASE            CB
    delete knowledge base         DBASE            DB
    review library                LIB              LI
    run a consultation            CONS             CO
    print results                 PRES             PR
    explain reasoning             EXPLAIN          EX
    load knowledge base           LBASE            LB
    enter goals                   GOALS            GO
    enter additional data         DATA             DA
    show a knowledge base         SBASE            SB
    print a knowledge base        PBASE            PB
    edit a knowledge base         ZBASE            ZB
------------------------------------------------------------
```
For other possibilities and commands see the EXSYS manual

* PLEASE ENTER A COMMAND :   CONS
* NAME OF THE KNOWLEDGE BASE :   PROJ86
* KNOWLEDGE BASE CONNECTED. WARNING: THE KNOWLEDGE BASE
  CONTAINS GLOBAL INDICATORS THAT REQUIRE A SIMULATION.
* NAME OF THE SIMULATION MODEL: MODEL 86
* SIMULATION MODEL CONNECTED.

DO YOU WANT TO START THE SIMULATION NOW (Y/N) ? : Y.
* Please wait.

* Simulation completed. Consultation session resumes.
* WOULD YOU LIKE TO EXPLORE A PARTICULAR GOAL (Y/N)? : Y
* NAME OF THE GOAL OR CONCLUSION : REJECT PROJECT
* Please wait

* CONCLUSION: NOT SUFFICIENT EVIDENCE TO   REJECT PROJECT.
* WOULD YOU LIKE TO TRY ANOTHER GOAL (Y/N)? :   Y
* NAME OF THE GOAL OR CONCLUSION : ACCEPT PROJECT
* Please wait

* CONCLUSION: SUFFICIENT EVIDENCE TO   ACCEPT PROJECT.
* RECOMMENDATION: ACCEPT PROJECT
* PLEASE ENTER A COMMAND :   EXPLAIN

Figure C–7.   Partial transcript of an EXSYS consultation session.
              (Moser, 1986, p. 228)

"reject project" and invokes backward chaining in order to see if there is any chain of inferences that would cause the project to be rejected. In the present example, there is not. The user then selects the goal "accept project," and again the backward-chaining mechanism tries to come up with a chain of inferences, this time leading to the conclusion that the project should be approved. Such a chain is indeed found, and the user invokes the explanation component in order to display the line of reasoning that led to this conclusion.

The simulation models used by EXSYS, as illustrated by the preceding subset of equations, were developed and used completely independently of EXSYS. Like all other numerical models, these equations are only capable of generating numbers such as those of Figure C–6. EXSYS has shown that a knowledge-based component can be applied to the output of a numerical simulation in order to help evaluate a business proposal.

C4.   Solving Problems in Molecular Genetics

THE MOSYS, ONYX, AND EXSYS examples have shown how discrete-event or mathematical simulation models can be integrated with knowledge-based components in order to solve design and planning problems that could not be solved by these simulation techniques alone. In the next example, the behavior of a virus is predicted solely by inferencing on a knowledge base of facts and rules without the use of numerical simulation.

The virus called *bacteriophage lambda* can inject its DNA into a bacterial cell with two possible outcomes: the DNA can incorporate itself directly into the chromosome of the bacterium (*lysogenic growth*) or it can exist apart from the chromosome (*lytic growth*). In either case, the genes on the viral DNA direct the synthesis of viral proteins through a process called *transcription*. These proteins have finite lifetimes and must therefore be continuously synthesized by the cell if the virus is to survive.

Molecular biologists are interested in understanding what causes lambda to choose between lytic and lysogenic growth. To investigate this problem, biologists perform experiments that introduce mutations into the genes of lambda. The combinations of mutations that lead to each mode of growth are noted. Researchers hope that this information will be useful in formulating a theory that explains the choice of growth mode. Since each experiment is costly and time consuming, a knowledge-based simulator was developed (as part of the MOLGEN project at Stanford University (Meyers and Friedland, 1984)) (see also, Article XV.02, Vol. 3) to predict whether the DNA of lambda will undergo lysogenic or lytic growth given a set of mutations on the lambda genes. The simulator was developed with the *Unit System* (Stefik, 1979) for the acquisition, representation, and manipulation of hierarchically organized knowledge.

The overall structure of the knowledge base used by the simulator is shown in Figure C–8. The knowledge base consists of two parts: rules that are completely general to regulatory genetics, and facts that are specific to the regulation of lambda. The rules are contained in the box labeled SIM-RULES in Figure C–8. These rules predict the activity of each DNA regulatory unit (active or inactive), the state of each gene (undergoing transcription or not), and the remaining lifetime of each protein (a non-negative integer). An example of a rule that determines the lifetime of a viral protein is:

```
If BEING-TRANSCRIBED GENE is false, then set
NEWLIFE to NEWLIFE-1, else set NEWLIFE to LIFESPAN.
```

This means that if a gene is not being transcribed during the current simulation cycle, no new protein will be produced during this cycle, so the remaining lifetime of the currently existing protein will be decremented by one unit of simulation time. If the gene is being transcribed, new protein is being created during this cycle, so the remaining time for the existence of this protein equals the intrinsic lifespan of the protein.

The facts specific to lambda are divided into three classes: genes, proteins, and DNA loci (the regulatory units on the DNA, such as *promoters*), corresponding to the similarly named boxes in Figure C–8. Each class is represented by a *prototypical unit* in the Units System. A *unit* describes an object class or instance with *slots*, each of which contains a name, data type, and value. The value of a slot in a prototypical unit can be a particular instance (such as the name of the creator of the unit),

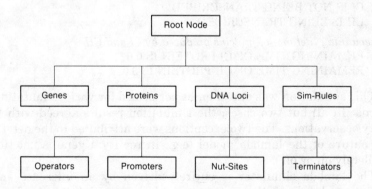

Figure C–8.   Structure of the lambda knowledge base. (Meyers and Friedland, 1984, p. 5)

or it can be the set of permissible values (such as TRUE or FALSE). The prototypical unit GENES is partially encoded as follows:

Name	Datatype	Value
DESCR:	<DESCR>	"This node is the root of all genes"
CREATOR:	<CREATOR>	"CSD.MEYERS"
ORGANISM:	<STRING>	One of: ["LAMBDA" "E-COLI"]
PROMOTERS:	<LIST>	Units:
MUTATED:	<STRING>	One of: ["TRUE" "FALSE"]
BEING-TRANSCRIBED	<STRING>	One of: ["TRUE" "FALSE"]

The specific genes that will be used in the simulation are created as *children* units of the prototypical GENES unit; the slot values of these units are either inherited from the prototypical unit or directly assigned as specific instances (e.g, a particular set of promoters for the PROMOTERS slot).

The input to a simulation run is a set of mutations to the genes of a lambda virus. The simulation proceeds in *cycles*. During each cycle, forward chaining is invoked on all applicable rules in order to update the states of all genes, the activities of all DNA loci, and the lifetimes of all proteins. At the end of each cycle, the current state of all genes, DNA loci, and proteins is used to determine whether a choice between lytic and lysogenic growth can be deduced. The cycles continue until such a choice has been asserted, at which point the simulation ends. The following example shows part of the output for a simulation cycle on a lambda virus with mutations in the *n* and *trl* genes:

states of promoters E and L
   P-E IS INACTIVE
   P-L IS ACTIVE

states of genes CI and CII
   CI IS NOT BEING TRANSCRIBED
   CII IS BEING TRANSCRIBED

remaining lifetimes of proteins produced by CI and CII
   REMAINING TIME OF CI-PROTEIN IS 0.0
   REMAINING TIME OF CII-PROTEIN IS 3.0

This simulation was one of eight performed for various mutations of lambda. In all but two cases, the simulation results agreed with laboratory observations. The two exceptions were attributed to the deterministic nature of the lambda model (e.g., in reality a gene is not turned completely on or off).

The lambda simulator is entirely driven by an inference engine acting on rules. Once the system variables are initialized, the forward-chaining mechanism keeps deducing facts until a conclusion about the viral growth mode is reached.

The lambda simulator has uses beyond the prediction of growth mode. A molecular biologist can confirm theories by encoding them in a model with UNITS, running simulations with a variety of inputs, and comparing the simulation results with laboratory results. If there are discrepancies between the two types of results, and if the model can be verified as correctly representing the theory being tested, the molecular biologist must revise the theory. This incremental approach to theory formation and testing could greatly facilitate research since it is much faster and cheaper to simulate experiments on a computer than to actually perform them. For this reason, a major emphasis of the MOLGEN project has been to provide a user interface that assists the molecular biologist in constructing and modifying the knowledge base rules and data.

D. THE DESIGN OF KNOWLEDGE-BASED SIMULATION SYSTEMS

WE HAVE SEEN that many knowledge-based simulation applications use numerical simulation models. The overall design of a knowledge-based simulation system can be described by the way in which information is transferred between the numerical and knowledge-based components. This section explores several ways in which numerical and knowledge-based components can be integrated (see O'Keefe (1986) for a comparable classification scheme):

1. The information flow is one-way in *sequential integrated systems*. A knowledge-based component generates results that are then used by the simulation component, or vice versa. In either case, the two components are run one after the other in sequence.

2. Information in a *parallel integrated system* is continuously passed back and forth between the knowledge-based and simulation components during run-time.

3. A knowledge-based component can serve as a *front-end* for defining a numerical simulation model, which is subsequently used on its own.

4. Some systems (including MOLGEN, (Section C4) are entirely *rule-driven*.

D1. Sequential Integrated Systems

THE MOST COMMON type of sequential integrated system runs a knowledge-based component to generate scenarios for achieving a set of goals and then calls a numerical simulator to predict the results of implementing each of the competing scenarios. The simulation results are then evaluated in order to choose the scenario that best satisfies the set of goals.

A sequential integrated system was developed at the University of

Florida to select the best insecticide for controlling velvetbean caterpillar infestation of Florida soybean fields (this system will subsequently be referred to as VBC) (Jones et al., 1986). The knowledge-based component of the system is used to generate a set of candidate insecticides. A numerical simulator called the Soybean Integrated Crop Management Model (SICM) (Wilkerson et al., 1983) is then used to predict the results of using the candidate insecticides. Finally, these results are evaluated according to their cost-effectiveness. The sequence of candidate selection, prediction, and evaluation is analogous to the ONYX scheme of plan generation, simulation, and ranking (see Section C2).

The heuristics used in the knowledge-based component come from two sources:

1. General rules of thumb obtained from agricultural extension publications, including knowledge about critical insect population thresholds, relative effectiveness of various spray materials, and insecticide application rates.

2. Interviews with two expert entomologists.

A set of candidate insecticides is obtained by applying these heuristics to information such as the current VBC density, the date that the soybean crop was planted, the current growth stage of the crop, and facts about the proposed insecticides.

The SICM simulation model is then run for each of the candidate insecticides as well as for various combinations of insecticides. SICM predicts both the relative increase in crop yield that would be gained by using the insecticide (denoted as dy) and the number of applications that would be necessary to achieve a given level of pest control (denoted as Napp). SICM also computes the threshold of insect density below which it is not cost-effective to apply insecticide.

As shown in Figure D–1, there is a tradeoff between dy and Napp since maintaining a lower insect density threshold will result in a correspondingly higher crop yield but will require more insecticide applications (hence a higher cost). The situation is complicated by the fact that this threshold is not constant but depends on the date of crop planting and the stage of growth since the crop is more susceptible to VBC infestation at certain times of the year and at certain growth stages. Another tradeoff that SICM must consider occurs when insecticide A is cheaper than insecticide B, but B requires fewer applications than A.

For each choice of insecticides, SICM produces a value for dy and for Napp. These two values are plugged into the following formula:

$$Z = (P * dy) - (Napp * (Ci + Ca))$$

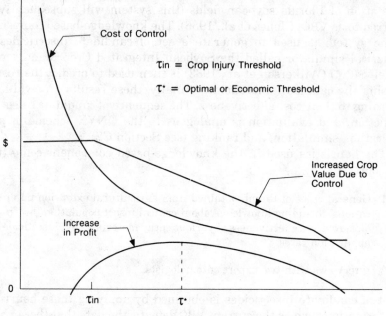

Figure D–1. Schematic of the components in the simple VBC economic model: cost of control for the remainder of the season, increased crop value due to maintaining the threshold at different levels for the rest of the season, and increase in profit. (Jones et al., 1986, p. 17.)

where

Z = net dollar return on the crop
P = value of crop per kilogram
Ci = cost of insecticide per application
Ca = cost of applying insecticide per application

The last three variables are assumed to be constant, and dy and Napp are predicted by SICM for each insecticide choice. The first term in the equation, P * dy, represents the gain from saving dy kilograms of crop whose value is P dollars per kilogram. The second term, Napp * (Ci + Ca), represents the expense of Napp applications, each of whose total cost is Ci + Ca. The equation thus simply represents the net economic gain of applying an insecticide choice. When SICM has been run for all choices and the results plugged into the equation, the results can be evaluated simply by ordering them from highest to lowest Z.

We have seen that the VBC insecticide program runs a knowledge-based component and a numerical simulator in sequence. A sequential integrated system can also run in the other direction; a numerical simulator can generate data that is then acted upon by the knowledge-based component. We saw an example of the latter design in Section C3; the EXSYS system first runs a simulator to generate values of system variables for a number of time periods, and then the knowledge-based component applies its rules to these values in order to evaluate business proposals.

D2. Parallel Integrated Systems

PARALLEL SYSTEMS consist of a knowledge-based component and a numerical simulation component, each of which functions as an independent entity. The two components pass data back and forth to each other as needed in order to assert facts or calculate numerical results.

Most modern manufacturing processes use a large number of machines. Since machine failures are inevitable, it is desirable to anticipate or detect them as soon as possible in order to minimize the time and expense of repairs. Researchers at the University of Louisville have demonstrated the potential of a parallel integrated system to automate the early detection of failures in manufacturing processes (Brown et al., 1985). The drilling of holes in a pipe was used as a test application.

The Louisville program simulates the drilling of two pipe parts having similar dimensions but different tolerance requirements. The required tolerance of the hole in pipe type A is 0.1 inch, whereas that of pipe type B is 0.001 inch. Each pipe is fed to the drill and held in place by a hydraulic clamp. After being drilled, the pipe is passed to an inspection station, which checks whether the hole meets the tolerance requirement for the type of pipe.

Two kinds of system variables are simulated: signals from the drilling station and the tolerance fits of the drilled holes. The signals from the drilling station are the temperature of the main drill spindle bearing and the vibration at the fixture clamp. Variations in these signals can cause three fault conditions to occur:

1. When both temperature and vibration increase, there is a *tool wear condition*. An exponential distribution is used to predict the next time that both temperature and vibration will increase.

2. When only the vibration increases, there is a *fixture fault*. An exponential distribution is also used to predict the next time that only vibration will increase.

3. When the vibration sharply decreases, there is *tool breakage*. A fixed probability that a sharp decrease in vibration will occur at any time is assumed.

The tolerance fits of the holes are modeled by normal distributions. A tool wear condition or fixture fault in either pipe causes a change in the parameters of the normal distribution for the diameter of the corresponding hole since the tolerance requirements are less likely to be met in this case.

A flowchart of the entire system is shown in Figure D–2. The times at which the next fault conditions will occur are generated from the probability distributions for the temperature and vibration at the drilling station. The system is simulated by advancing a simulation clock from event to event, where an "event" is the occurrence of a fault. On each event, two types of facts can be asserted:

1. *Process facts* (e.g., the temperature and vibration are increasing).

2. *Product facts* (e.g., the diameter of the hole is within a standard deviation).

For example, suppose that the next event generated from the distributions is an increase in vibration 6 minutes from the current time. If no events are scheduled during the next 6 minutes, the simulation clock is advanced 6 minutes and the process fact (vibration increases) is asserted. On each event, the process and product facts are passed to the knowledge-based component, which determines the appropriate action to take, if any. Note that the time of an event is a multiple of a basic time unit (e.g., one minute), and that this unit represents simulated time, not computer processing time (this issue is discussed further in Section G1).

The knowledge-based component uses forward chaining on three types of rules: part, process, and link rules. *Part rules* take the product facts and infer conclusions about whether the process is out of control. Consider the following part rules:

(Rule 1 (If (No unnatural states detected)) (Then (Natural)))
(Rule 2 (If (x is beyond 3 Sigma Limit)) (Then (Unnatural)))
(Rule 3 (If (2 of 3 points beyond 2 Sigma Limit)) (Then (Unnatural)))
(Rule 6 (If (Control Limit less than specs)) (Then (Can Proceed)))

where x refers to the hole diameter, *Sigma Limit* refers to the standard deviation of the normal distribution that models the diameter, and *Unnatural* means that the process is out of control.

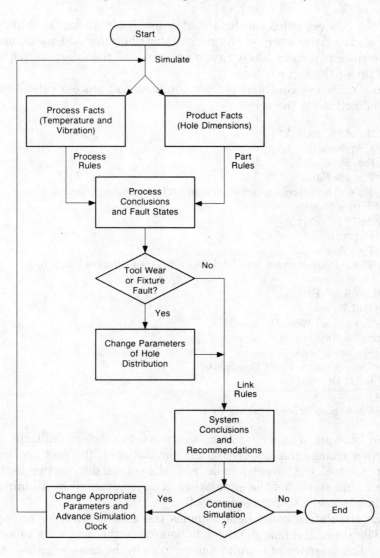

Figure D–2. Flowchart for the drilling simulation.

Process rules take the process facts and make conclusions about possible faults. Examples of process rules include:

(Rule 8 (If (Temperature and Vibration Increase)) (Then (Tool Wear)))
(Rule 9 (If (Vibration Increases)) (Then (Fixture Fault)))
(Rule 10 (If (Vibration Decreases)) (Then (Tool Breakage)))
(Rule 11 (If (Tool Breakage)) (Then (Stop Process)))
(Rule 12 (If (Nothing Happens)) (Then (Steady Process)))

If the process rules conclude that a tool wear or fixture fault has occurred, the parameters of the normal distributions for hole diameter change since it is more likely that a hole will fail the tolerance requirements under these conditions.

Link rules use conclusions from the part and process rules to recommend actions to the user:

(Rule 14 (If (Part A)
  (Unnatural)
  (Can Proceed)
  (Fixture Fault)
  (Then (The process is out of control, but can continue to run. Cause:
  Fixture Fault)))
(Rule 18 (If (Part A)
  (Natural)
  (Tool Wear)
  (Then (Process in control. Tool Wear detected. Process likely to go
  out of control.)))
(Rule 19 (If (Part A)
  (Tool Wear)
  (Then (Tool Wear Detected)))
(Rule 20 (If (Part A)
  (Fixture Fault)
  (Then (Fixture Fault Detected)))
(Rule 21 (If (Part B)
  (Tool Wear)
  (Then (Stop Process – Tool Wear)))

For example, if rule 20 is fired in response to a fixture fault, the user can either change the tool or stop the simulation. If the user decides to change the tool, the parameters defining the normal distribution for hole diameter are reset and the simulation clock is advanced by 10 minutes (the time required to change the tool).

The simulation component samples the distributions for temperature, vibration, and hole diameter to determine the next time to assert a fault. The assertion of a fault triggers rules in the knowledge base that forward chain on the current system state to infer a recommended action. If the user takes the action, the hole dimension distribution parameters are modified, which affects the next value of hole dimension that is sampled during simulation. The hole dimension, in turn, triggers rules to determine whether the process is going out of control (see Figure D–2). The simulation and knowledge-based components thus continuously pass information back and forth to each other in order to assert a fault as soon as possible. These two components are independent of each other as well; the probability distributions could be used by themselves to drive a discrete-event simulation, and the rules are generally valid for the drilling system, independent of the way that the process and product facts are generated. The drilling system is analogous to the plan simulation component of ONYX (Section C2); the rules in ONYX modify constants in mathematical equations that are then solved, whereas the drilling system rules modify the parameters of probability distributions that are then sampled.

D3.   Intelligent Front Ends for Building Numerical Simulation Models

BOTH EXSYS (Section C3) and VBC (Section D1) integrate a knowledge-based component with an existing numerical simulation model that had been used independently of the integrated system. In both cases, the user interacts with the knowledge-based component, which either interprets the output from a simulation (as in EXSYS) or generates scenarios to be simulated (as in VBC). The user can enter, delete, or modify information in the knowledge-based component and can ask it to explain the line of reasoning that led to an assertion. The simulation component, on the other hand, is a black box in both systems. There is no way to modify, query, or interact in any way with the simulation model. This presents two problems. First, an end user or domain expert is unlikely to be proficient in the mathematical, simulation, and programming skills that are required to develop a numerical simulation model. Second, there is no assurance that an off-the-shelf simulation model accurately reflects the particular circumstances of the problem to be solved. For example, is SICM (Section D1) valid for a slightly different type of soybean, or for farms in Georgia as well as in Florida, or for a different strain of velvetbean caterpillar? In general, the only way to know how variations in the model's original assumptions affect its predictions is through experience in applying the model. Both of these problems could be largely overcome through tools that assist end users and domain experts in building numerical simulation models without having to acquire the requisite programming and simulation skills.

ECO is a program developed at the University of Edinburgh as an intelligent front end "designed to help ecologists with little mathematical modeling experience to construct dynamic simulation models of ecological systems" (Meutzelfeldt, 1986). ECO captures the facts and relations about a particular ecological domain through dialog with an ecologist. These facts and relations are then converted into a FORTRAN program that performs numerical simulation on that domain.

The overall structure of ECO is shown in Figure D–3. The central

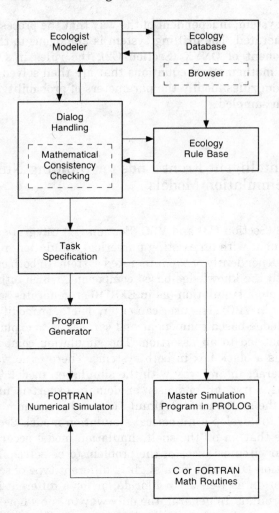

Figure D–3.   Overall structure of ECO.

component of ECO is the *task specification*, which encodes the user's ecological description as a well-defined mathematical model that eventually is converted into a FORTRAN numerical simulator. The encoding of the task specification is supported by three components:

1. A set of dialog systems that allow the user to describe a model.

2. A database of domain-specific facts and relations.

3. A rule base that checks the consistency of the growing model.

Three dialog systems—free-form, menu-based, and question-and-answer—are available to the user for describing a model. A *free-form dialog system* allows the user to enter a description using a small set of standard sentence forms, for example:

component action
e.g. `GRASS RESPIRES`

component action component
e.g. `SHEEP EATS GRASS`

variable USES module-name
e.g. `GRAZING USES DONREC`

SET variable value
e.g. `SET RADIN 53`

A *menu-based dialog system* presents the user with a set of dialog options relevant to the current context, for example,

Do you want to:
1. Specify a component.
2. Specify a process.

A *question-and-answer dialog system* prompts the user with a specific question at each point in the dialog; the answer to one question provides the context for the next, for example,

1. What components do you wish to include?
   deer, trees
2. What attribute(s) characterize deer?
   population density
3. What are the units for population density?
   numbers per hectare
   .
   .
   .
9. What attribute(s) characterize trees?
   volume per hectare

Domain-specific knowledge for ECO is provided by a database. The database stores facts (e.g., statistics on the fecundity of deer in Scotland), relationships (e.g., equations relating the rate of photosynthesis to light intensity), and loosely structured information based on observation. All of the knowledge in the database is readily accessible during model construction through the *browser*, which can search the database for any desired piece of information at any time.

As it grows, the model is continuously checked for mathematical correctness and for "ecological sense." The checks for mathematical correctness include detecting loops among functional relationships, ensuring the consistency of substructure specifications among different model components, and verifying that the time scales of different processes are consistent. These checks are part of the code that implements dialog handling and construction of the task specification. In contrast, the checks for ecological sense are made by a rule base that monitors the dialog and attempts to detect inconsistencies in the developing model. For example, this rule base would detect an inconsistency if the user asserts that "grass eats sheep," since the rule base knows that grass is a plant, a sheep is a herbivore, and herbivores can eat plants, but not vice versa.

The final task specification is represented in the form of PROLOG predicates that assert the properties of model elements and their relationships. Once complete, the task specification can be converted into an executable numerical simulation in two ways. A program generator can create a FORTRAN program from the task specification and from a set of FORTRAN subroutines that implement the mathematical relationships encoded by the task specification. Alternatively the task specification itself can be used to directly control a master simulation program written in PROLOG, whereas the mathematical relationships are implemented in FORTRAN or C. The latter approach allows a more detailed specification of model substructure as well as the ability to switch between model development and model simulation at any point since no program generation or compilation is involved.

The result is a standalone mathematical simulator that executes independently of any knowledge-based component. The simulator is a direct implementation of the ecologist's conceptual model of a particular ecological system. The model is captured in the form of a task specification that is independent of the particular language into which it is ultimately converted, so the ecologist is spared the necessity of learning a programming language. The model can be altered at will; the changes are captured in the task specification, so it is guaranteed that they will also be implemented in the revised simulation program.

D4. Rule-driven Simulation

THE MOLGEN program (Section C4) determines the lifestyle of a lambda virus by forward chaining on sets of rules. Predictions about the future state of the viral system are therefore made by inferencing on the current system state, rather than by running a numerical simulator. Time is measured in simulation cycles instead of clock time (see Section G1); for example, the remaining lifetime of each protein is decremented by one unit on each simulation cycle until reaching zero.

The choice between rule-based and numerical simulation depends on what is known about the problem domain and on the type of results that are sought (see Section G2). If there is considerable detailed knowledge in the domain and precise predictions are required, numerical simulation is likely to be the most appropriate technique. If the knowledge in the problem domain is heuristic, vague, or incomplete, and the desired results can be expressed as overall trends or approximate classifications, rule-based simulation is probably the technique of choice.

E. QUALITATIVE ASPECTS OF KNOWLEDGE-BASED SIMULATION

THE KNOWLEDGE that we possess about most interesting domains is a mixture of precise numerical measurements, general heuristics, and educated guesses. This knowledge is necessarily incomplete, and at present there is no methodology for representing "what we know we don't know" (Modjeski, 1987). The fact that there are so many different types of knowledge in a given domain presents a paradox. On the one hand, the amount of detailed quantitative information may overwhelm our (or the computer's) ability to make sense out of it. On the other hand, the generality and vagueness of heuristic information may preclude the prediction of concrete results. This section describes several methodologies that have been developed for making predictions using knowledge with different degrees of precision.

E1. Simplification of Processes

THE GENETIC REGULATORY SYSTEM of the amino acid tryptophan has been modeled by researchers as a set of 15 partial differential equations. However, this set of equations is not solvable! To be of practical use to molecular biologists, we need a representation of the tryptophan system's behavior that is both solvable and accurate. There are many other real-world systems whose precise description is extremely complicated, but whose behavior can be represented in a relatively simple and tractable way that is sufficient for making good predictions.

A program called QSOPS (Round, 1987; another part of the MOLGEN project is described in Section C4) provides molecular biologists with a graphical simulation environment for making predictions about the behavior of the tryptophan (trp) system under a variety of experimental conditions. QSOPS uses a very simple representation of the processes that make up this system, and its predictions are consistent with known experimental and theoretical results. QSOPS is implemented in KEE 2.1 (see Section F2) and INTERLISP on a Xerox 1186 workstation. Before discussing how QSOPS represents processes, we describe the trp system.

Trp is synthesized by proteins called *trp-proteins*. These proteins are coded by five genes on a piece of DNA called the *trp-operon* (see Figure E–1; the five genes are labeled E through A, and the components to the left of the genes regulate the trp-operon). The trp-operon undergoes *transcription* when a molecule of *RNA polymerase* binds to the promoter (pro in Figure E–1) and slides down the genes; the result is an RNA copy of the trp-operon genes called mRNA. The mRNA then undergoes *translation* into the trp-synthesizing proteins when a ribosome binds to it and slides down its length. The other processes regulate the rate of transcription in order to maintain a steady-state concentration of trp in the cell. This cycle of processes, pictured in Figure E–2, constitutes a negative feedback loop: an increased concentration of trp increases the rate of trp repression (process 5) and vice versa.

The QSOPS view of simulation is that a process creates new objects and/or destroys old objects at a certain frequency. Each object also has a finite lifetime. For example, the process of trp synthesis (process 3 in Figure E–2) converts a trp-precursor molecule into a trp molecule. If the frequency of trp synthesis is 50 reactions per second and the simulation clock ticks once per second, 50 trp-precursor molecules will be destroyed and 50 trp molecules will be created on the current tick. If 40 trp molecules have reached the end of their lifetime on this tick, there will be a net gain of 10 trp molecules. An object is thus created by a process and is either destroyed by another process or expires at the end of its lifetime.

A process is simulated by recomputing the concentration of its product molecule on each clock tick, using the process frequency and product lifetime. The frequency of each process is computed once per tick using a simple rule. These frequency rules model a process as a reaction between two molecules to form a product molecule. One of the reactant

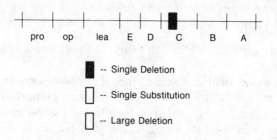

Figure E–1.   Decomposition of the trp-operon. The promoter, operator, and leader constitute the control region. The five genes, labeled E through A comprise the structural region. Mutations such as the single deletion mutation in gene C can be placed anywhere on the trp-operon.

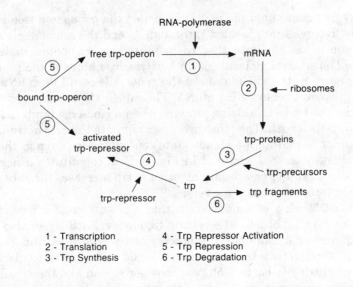

1 - Transcription   4 - Trp Repressor Activation
2 - Translation   5 - Trp Repression
3 - Trp Synthesis   6 - Trp Degradation

Figure E–2.   The trp-operon process cycle. (Round, 1987,
              p. 214)

molecules is present in great excess relative to the other. The frequency
of the process is directly in proportion to the concentration of the molecule that is not in excess. For example, the rule that determines the
frequency of translation is as follows:

```
If [ribosome] is in excess,
then frequency = k*[mRNA]
else if [mRNA] is in excess,
then frequency = k*[ribosome]
else frequency = 0.5 * k * ([mRNA] + [ribosome])
```

where [x] means the concentration of molecule x, and k is a proportionality constant.

This rule makes intuitive sense since if ribosomes are in great excess
over mRNA, the rate of the reaction will change proportionately to the
concentration of mRNA but will not be affected by the concentration of
ribosomes (and vice versa). The frequency of translation computed by
this rule gives the number of trp-protein molecules created on the current
tick. To obtain the actual trp-protein concentration on this tick, the
number of trp-protein molecules that have expired on this tick are subtracted from the number created. The lifetimes of molecules are given
as constants. Therefore, if trp-proteins have a lifetime of 5 ticks, the trp-
proteins that expire on the current tick are those that were created 5
ticks previously.

The process frequencies and molecule lifetimes are initialized before starting the simulation. At each tick of the clock, a new round of simulation begins. The frequency rule of process 1 (transcription in Figure E–2) computes a new value for [mRNA], and this new value causes the frequency of process 2 to be recomputed. The frequency rule of process 2 then computes a new value for [trp-proteins], which causes the frequency of process 3 to be recomputed, and so on. The current round of simulation ends when a new value for [free trp-operon] is computed by process 5 and the frequency of process 1 is recomputed. At the end of a simulation round, new concentrations for all molecules have been obtained.

The QSOPS user can choose to automatically graph the concentrations of any of the molecules as the simulation proceeds. In addition, the user can interrupt simulation at any point and change any quantity in the system (such as temperature, pH, or concentrations of molecules). This facility enables users to ask what-if questions, for example, "What would happen if I double the concentration of trp?". The user can also enter mutations on the trp-operon before or during simulation. Figure E–1 shows a single deletion mutation placed on gene C of the trp-operon. The placement of a mutation triggers a rule that recomputes the proportionality constant k for the relevant process. For example, a mutation rule for process 1 is:

If there is a single deletion mutation on a gene, then $k = 0.1 * k$.

The rule for process 1 will then use the new value of k for as long as the single deletion mutation holds.

The simulation technique used by QSOPS is "qualitative" in the sense that it represents a great simplification of actual behavior, but "quantitative" in that values of the simulated concentrations are real numbers. QSOPS has been used to predict the concentration of trp over time with a variety of mutations, and in all cases the results have been consistent with known experimental results.

E2. Aggregation of Processes

QSOPS (Section E1) accurately predicts the behavior of the trp system by modeling it as a cycle of five discrete processes, each of whose behavior is represented by a simple linear equation. Since this cycle of five processes repeats continuously, it is reasonable to ask if even greater simplification could be achieved by modeling the entire cycle as a single continuous process.

A simulator called PEPTIDE, developed at the Artificial Intelligence Laboratory of the Massachusetts Institute of Technology, integrates both discrete and continuous process models for the purpose of predicting the behavior of molecular genetic systems (Weld, 1984 and 1985). PEPTIDE defines continuous processes by a set of *preconditions* and a set of *influences*. For example, the process of discharging a battery has the two preconditions "switch closed" and "battery voltage greater than 0," and the two influences "decrease in battery charge" and "increase in resistor temperature." PEPTIDE predicts the outcome of a continuous process through *limit analysis*, a technique that determines when the preconditions of a process are violated or satisfy the preconditions of another process. Limit analysis predicts that a battery will continuously discharge until its voltage drops to zero since one of the preconditions of the process ("battery voltage greater than 0") is then violated.

PEPTIDE has used these concepts to predict the effects of reacting a molecule of DNA with an enzyme E that cleaves a fragment from the end of the DNA molecule (Figure E–3):

Two discrete processes are defined:

1. *BIND*. If there is an E whose cleft is empty and there is a DNA with nothing bound to its right end, then the E will bind the right end of the DNA.

2. *SNARF*. If there is an E bound to the right of a DNA, then the E will digest the end segment of the DNA. The result will have E floating free, and the length of DNA one segment shorter than before.

For each of these discrete process definitions, the preconditions are given in the "if" part, and the influences are given in the "then" part. For example, the two preconditions of BIND are "there is an E whose cleft is empty" and "there is a DNA with nothing bound to its end," and the single influence is "E binds to the end of the DNA."

When the simulation begins, only the preconditions of BIND are satisfied. PEPTIDE therefore simulates the BIND process. The result is depicted as (Figure E–4):

Now the preconditions for SNARF are satisfied, whereas those for BIND are not. Therefore, the SNARF process is simulated, with the result shown in Figure E–5):

The piece of DNA is now shorter than the original piece, but the preconditions for BIND are again satisfied. At this point, a PEPTIDE

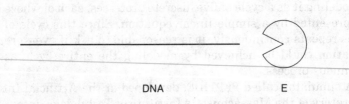

DNA   E

Figure E–3.   Initial situation. (Weld, 1985, p. 141)

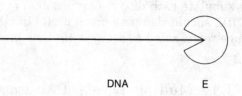

DNA   E

Figure E–4.   Situation after E binds DNA. (Weld, 1985, p. 141)

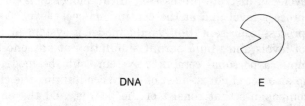

DNA   E

Figure E–5.   Situation after E digests a section of DNA. (Weld, 1985, p. 141)

component called the *aggregator* recognizes that BIND has been active before, and searches through a history of the processes that have already been simulated in order to detect a cycle. In this case, the cycle recognized is (BIND SNARF). The aggregator then generates a single continuous process that represents multiple iterations of the cycle. This continuous process is defined in terms of the preconditions and influences of the cycle. In the present example, the aggregator determines that the preconditions of the cycle are "there must be at least one free DNA" and "there must be at least one free E," and that the single influence is "decrease in length of DNA." Finally, PEPTIDE uses limit analysis to determine the eventual outcome of the continuous process. When the length of DNA becomes 0, the cycle precondition "there must be at least one free DNA" is violated. The outcome is therefore that E remains, but there is no more DNA.

The aggregator can also detect cycles within cycles. For example, if there are many molecules of DNA and one molecule of E, the continuous process generated by multiple iterations of (BIND SNARF) repeats for each molecule of DNA until no molecules of DNA remain. If the continuous process for a single DNA molecule is called CP1, the continuous process for many DNA molecules can be modeled as (CP1).

PEPTIDE's "knowledge" lies in its ability to detect cycles and to predict the outcome of executing those cycles continuously over time. The efficiency of simulation is greatly increased by eliminating the need to repeatedly simulate each discrete process in a cycle. The techniques used by PEPTIDE should therefore prove useful in other domains whose processes can be represented as cycles of discrete processes.

E3.   Multiple Levels of Abstraction

QSOPS (Section E1) models the behavior of a cyclic set of discrete processes at one level of abstraction. PEPTIDE (Section E2) recognizes continuous cycles of discrete processes and can model behavior at both the discrete process level and at the continuous cycle level. An even more general process representation would model a system at an arbitrary number of levels and would permit simulation at any one these levels. For example, a personal computer system could be modeled from the bottom up as a set of chips, a set of boards containing the chips, a set of system components that consist of the boards, and the entire system, which is built up from the system components. To understand the behavior of the CPU, we do not need to simulate the overall system. Conversely, it should not be necessary to simulate the behavior of every subcomponent in order to predict overall system power consumption.

MARS (Singh, 1983; Brown, Tong, and Foyster, 1983) is an experimental program, developed at the Knowledge Systems Laboratory of Stanford University, that hierarchically models the structure and behavior of an integrated circuit and permits the simulation of its components at any level in the hierarchy. As an example, the device D74 shown in Figure E–6 has three inputs and two outputs. The substructure consists of three multipliers and two adders; the adders, in turn, are made up of four full-adders (Figure E–7), each of which is composed of a collection of gates (Figure E–8). All statements about the structure and behavior of a device are coded as propositions in the declarative language MRS (Genesereth, 1980). For example, the first input port of adder A1 in D74 is represented in MRS as (port in1 a1). A partial description of D74 is:

```
(type m1 multiplier)
(type a2 adder)
(conn (port out m1) (port in1 a1))
(conn* (port out m2) (port in2 a1) (port in1 a2))
```

The first two propositions state that m1 is a multiplier and a2 is an adder. The third proposition states that the output port of m1 is connected to the input port of a1. The conn* relation describes multiple connections; the fourth proposition uses it to state that the output port of m2 is connected to both the second input of a1 and to the first input of a2. The entire hierarchical structure of D74 is as follows:

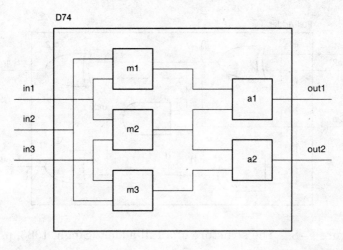

Figure E–6.   The top-level structure of device D74. (Singh, 1983, p. 5)

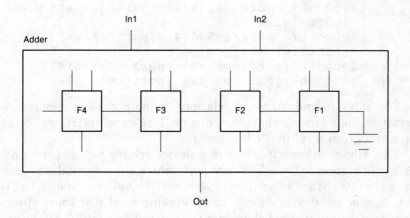

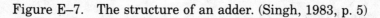

Figure E–7.   The structure of an adder. (Singh, 1983, p. 5)

```
(prototype d74
  ((subpart* d74 m1 m2 m3 a1 a2)
    (type m1 multiplier) (type m2 multiplier)
    (type m3 multiplier)
    (type a1 adder) (type a2 adder)
    (conn (port out m1) (port in1 a1))
    (conn* (port out m2) (port in2 a1)
      (port in1 a2))
    (conn (port out m3) (port in2 a2))
```

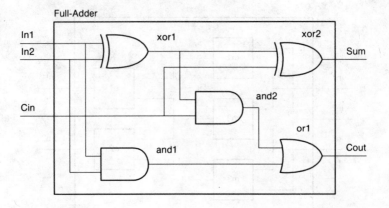

Figure E–8.   The structure of a full-adder. (Singh, 1983, p. 5)

```
(subconn* (port in1 d74) (port in2 m1)
    (port in1 m2))
(subconn* (port in2 d74) (port in1 m1)
    (port in2 m3))
(subconn* (port in3 d74) (port in2 m2)
    (port in1 m3))
(subconn (port out a1) (port out1 d74))
(subconn (port out a2) (port out2 d74))))
```

The subconn and subconn* relations define port connections across hierarchy boundaries, whereas the conn and conn* relations connect ports at a given level in the hierarchy.

The behavioral specification of a device relates values between its ports with respect to time. To relate port values, the *true* relation is used; it has the form (true (value (port <p> <dev>) <val>) <time>), i.e., the port <p> of the device <dev> has the value <val> at time <time>. Given this definition, the behavior of D74 can is defined in MRS as follows:

```
(protobehavior d74
((if (and (true (value (port in1 d74) $a $t)
        (true (value (port in2 d74) $b $t)
        (true (value (port in3 d74) $c $t)
        (= $d (+ (* $a $b) (* $a $c)))
        (= $e (+ (* $a $c) (* $b $c)))
    (and (true (value (port out1 d74) $d $t)
        (true (value (port out2 d74) $e $t))))))
```

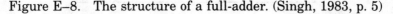

where $t is the variable representing time.

The description of D74 is completed by creating similar definitions for the structure and behavior of all the lower level components (adders, multipliers, full adders, and so on). The set of operations that can be performed on values may depend on the level at which they occur in the hierarchy. For example, a proposition in the prototype behavior of an adder (see Figure E–7) is:

```
(if (and (true (value (port in1 adder) $v) $t)
         (= $b (bit $j $v)))
    (true (value (port in1 fa1) $b $t)))
```

The preceding proposition states that if the value at port 1 of the adder is $v at time $t, then the value at port 1 of full adder 1 is the *j*th bit of $v at time $t. The variable $v represents an integer, whereas the variable $b represents a Boolean value. The operations at the adder level consist of arithmetic on integers, whereas those at the full adder level are Boolean operations on bits.

The MARS simulator propagates an initial set of signals through the structural and behavioral description of the device in order to predict its behavior. Values are propagated through device components via a forward-chaining inference mechanism. For example, consider the following propositions:

```
(if (and (type $x multiplier)
         (true (value (port in1 $x) $a) $t)
         (true (value (port in2 $x) $b) $t))
    (true (value (port out $x) (* $a $b)) $t))

(type foo multiplier)

(true (value (port in2 foo) 3) 4).
```

The rule describes the behavior of multipliers. It states that if $x is a multiplier, the value of input port 1 of $x is $a at time $t, and the value of input port 2 of $x is $b at time t, then the value of the output port of $x is a*b at time $t. The two facts assert the foo is a multiplier whose second input port has value 3 at time 4. If the fact (true (value (port in1 foo) 2) 4) is also asserted, then all the preconditions in the rule will be satisfied, and the fact (true (value (port out foo) 6) 4) will be asserted (since 2*3 = 6).

In the examples so far, all the values have been propagated instantaneously. However, rules can schedule an event for a future time and can refer to past events. The MARS simulator maintains an event queue, and the simulation clock moves from event to event. On simulating a given event, only the values of ports affected by the event are recomputed; the effect of propagating a change is usually local, so it would be wasteful to recompute the state of every port on every event. The way MARS handles time will be further discussed in Section G1.

The simulation of a full adder is depicted in Figure E–9 and is

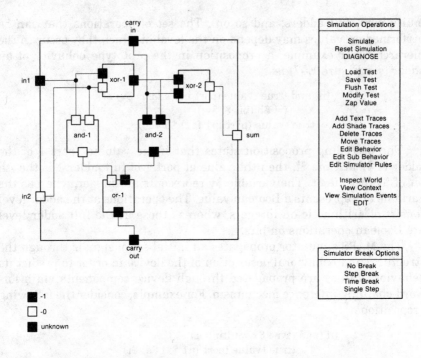

Figure E–9.   Simulation of a full-adder. (Singh, 1983, p. 30)

controlled through the menus shown in the figure. The first step is to build a simulation model of the full adder by describing its structure and behavior. The structure is described graphically by selecting and connecting symbols representing the inputs and outputs of the full adder and the gates that make up its subcomponents. The behavior of the full adder is entered textually in the form of MRS propositions. The behavior of the subcomponents can also be entered or modified if necessary.

The initial inputs to the simulation are specified by assigning values to the three input ports of the full adder; for example,

```
(true (value (port cin foo) 1) 0)
(true (value (port in1 foo) 1) 0)
(true (value (port in2 foo) 0) 0).
```

That is, at time 0, the carry-in and the first input of the full adder are 1 and the second input is 0. The user can select the Add Shade Traces option to specify the nodes to be monitored during simulation; in the present example, these nodes can be any subset of the subcomponents, including the entire full adder.

By interrupting the simulation with a break, the user can inspect the state of the full adder and its subcomponents at that point, and make changes to the design if desired before resuming. Break conditions can be specified on the port values, the number of event occurrences, and the number of simulation cycles. As signals are propagated during simulation, ports whose value is *true* are displayed in black, and those whose value is *false* are displayed in white. As shown in the lower right menu of Figure E–9, the simulator can be single-stepped, set to stop on a break, or run continuously.

MARS can automatically select the hierarchical level at which to simulate. This level depends on which components in the hierarchy have a behavioral description and which nodes are being monitored by the user. It is not required that every node have a behavioral description associated with it. If a node does not have a behavioral description, it must be simulated at the highest subcomponent level at which the behavior is completely specified. For example, if there is no behavioral description of the full adder in Figure E–9, the full adder must be simulated at the level of its subcomponent gates. If the gates are at the most primitive level in the hierarchical structure and one or more gates lack a behavioral description, the full adder cannot be simulated. If the full adder does have a behavioral description, then that description is sufficient for simulation, and no reference need be made to the behavioral descriptions (if any) of the gates. The simulation level is also affected by the nodes selected for monitoring since simulation cannot be performed at a level higher than the lowest level containing a selected node.

The user can also select the simulation level manually via the *simsub* and *simtop* relations. The simsub relation declares that a part is to be simulated in terms of its subcomponents, and the simtop relation indicates that the top-level behavior is to be used. For example, (simsub (part $x d74)) indicates that all subparts of d74 are to be simulated in terms of their substructure.

MARS provides justifications for the state of any component of the simulated device. For example, to inquire why the carry output bit of the full adder has value 1 at time 0, the user can select the *why* command and enter the query

            (true (value (port co fa) 1) 0).

The system responds with

        P542: (true (value (port co fa) 1) 0) by:
        P658: (if (true (value (port out o1) 1) 0)
                 (true (value (port co fa) 1) 0))
        P541: (true (value (port out o1) 1) 0)

That is, the carry output of the full adder is 1 because the output of the *or* gate is 1. The *why* command can be applied to the propositions in the justification to obtain further explanation; for example, the user can query (why 'P541).

MARS generalizes the process abstraction abilities of QSOPS and PEPTIDE by defining and simulating a design in terms of its hierarchy of structure and behavior. MARS resembles the MOLGEN system of Section C4 in that both perform simulation by forward inferencing. The MARS simulator is more powerful and general, however, due to its ability to specify hierarchy, to automatically select the simulation level, to schedule events in the future, and to reason about events in the past.

E4.   Multiple Levels of Precision

THE THREE SYSTEMS described so far in this section have abstracted processes in the form of linear equations (QSOPS), continuous cycles (PEPTIDE), and hierarchically specified device behaviors (MARS). Even though the processes are modeled abstractly, the simulated values that are propagated through a process model are precise: concentrations are real numbers in QSOPS, DNA lengths are integers in PEPTIDE, and signals are integers or Booleans in MARS. There are many situations in which we would like to predict the future state of a system, but our knowledge of its current state is vague. As an example, consider the problem of predicting the time it takes to drive a car from point A to point B. We might know that the gas tank is almost full, that our speed is 60 mph and increasing, that we are probably somewhat over the speed limit, that the oil light is not on, and that traffic looks pretty heavy up ahead. How can values such as "almost full," "60," "increasing," "somewhat over," "not on," and "pretty heavy" be simultaneously propagated through a traffic model in order to predict the time of arrival at point B?

In the domain of molecular biology, there is quite a bit of quantitative information about genetic regulation, but the values and interrelationships of some state variables are known imprecisely or not at all. Recent work in the MOLGEN project (see Sections C4 and E1) has attempted to create a framework for simulating genetic regulatory systems whose variables take on values with a wide range of precision (Karp and Friedland, 1987). The techniques used by MOLGEN for representing variables, their interactions, and their propagation will be presented after describing the research domain.

The domain of this research is the same as that of the QSOPS system described in Section E1—the regulation of the set of genes responsible for synthesizing the amino acid tryptophan (trp). These genes lie on a piece of DNA called the *trp-operon*, depicted in Figure E–1. The enzyme RNA-polymerase can bind to a site on the trp-operon called the *promoter* (labeled *pro* in Figure E–1). After binding to the promoter, RNA-polymerase synthesizes *mRNA* as it zips down the trp-operon in a process called *transcription*. The mRNA then undergoes processing to yield the enzymes that synthesize trp. The whole process of trp synthesis is therefore regulated by the rate of transcription. Regulation of transcription is achieved by a molecule called *activated trp-repressor* that binds to the *operator* (labeled *op* in Figure E–1), directly adjacent to **pro**. When activated trp-repressor is bound to **op**, it blocks transcription since RNA-polymerase cannot simultaneously bind to **pro**. Activated trp-repressor has a molecule of trp attached to it; it is no longer active if it loses its trp. When the concentration of trp increases, the fraction of the trp-repressor that is bound by trp also increases. Activated trp-repressor binds to the promoter, preventing RNA-polymerase from initiating transcription, so the concentration of trp decreases. The reduced trp concentration decreases the fraction of trp-repressor that is bound by trp, allowing more RNA polymerase to bind to the operator, and resulting in an increased rate of transcription and an increased concentration of trp. This negative feedback mechanism is the principal form of regulation of trp synthesis.

The state variables of the system and their interrelationships are depicted in Figure E–10. The arrows indicate *influences*; for example, the amount of Activated.trp-R (activated trp repressor) is influenced by the amounts of trp and Total.trp-R (total trp repressor). Assertions about the values of variables can be made with respect to quantitative values (e.g., trp = .001, trp < .005) or relative to other values (e.g., trp < trp.maximum, trp = 2 * trp.equilibrium). Three types of representations are provided for describing the interactions among variables: *pairwise interactions*, *functions*, and *mappings*. Each of these representation schemes is implemented as a data structure called a *frame* in the expert system development tool KEE (see Section F2).

A *pairwise interaction* describes whatever is known about how one variable influences another. The information associated with a pairwise interaction might include the sign of the interaction, whether the interaction is monotonic, and the form of the functional relationship (e.g., linear, higher polynomial, exponential, unknown). The following pairwise interaction describes the influence of Free-Promoter.Lifetime on Transcription.Initiation.Rate (see Figure E–10):

Input.Variable:	Free-Promoter.Lifetime
Output.Variable:	Transcription.Initiation.Rate
Monotonic:	T
Functional.Form:	LINEAR
Slope:	INCREASING

The second way of representing relationships among variables is called a *function*, which describes how a *combination* of input variables

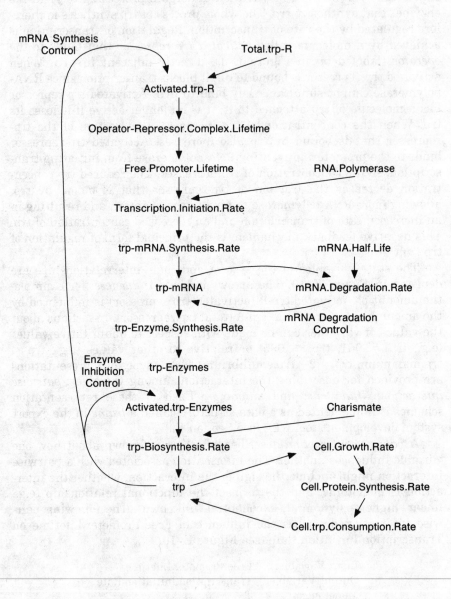

Figure E–10. The network of state variables in the trp system used in simulations. (Karp and Friedland, 1987, p. 17)

influences an output variable. All combinations are additive, multiplicative, or unknown. A function that describes how RNA-Polymerase and Free-Promoter.Lifetime combine to influence Transcription.Initiation. Rate (see Figure E–10) is encoded as:

> Input Variables: (RNA-Polymerase Free-Promoter.Lifetime)
> Output.Variable: Transcription.Initiation.Rate
> Combined.Influence: Additive

The third type of representation, called a *mapping*, is a list of corresponding values between two sets of variables. Mappings are useful when the complete functional relationship between two sets of variables is unknown, but a few points have been experimentally determined. The following mapping describes how the amount of activated trp-repressor varies with trp for three points:

```
Clamped.Influences:  (Total.trp-R Total.trp-R.
                        normal)
Input.Variable:      trp
Output.Variable:     Activated.trp-R
Points:              ((0 0)
                     (equilibrium-trp-concentration
                       (Total.trp-R * .5))
                     (trp-excess-
                     threshold  Total.trp-R))
Monotonic:           T
Functional.Form:     UNKNOWN
Slope:               INCREASING
```

For example, when trp is at its equilibrium concentration, activated trp-repressor will be one half of total trp-repressor. If a mapping is monotonic and linear, additional points can be obtained by interpolation. Also, the definition of a function can include one or more mappings.

Pairwise interactions, functions, and mappings provide a context for representing process behavior over a wide range of precision. A precise mathematical formulation of a process is achieved by assigning numbers to all the slots in the frames that represent the process relationships. The omission of numeric values from the frames results in qualitative constraints on the relationships. Minimal information will result in minimally precise relationships.

Since interactions can be modeled over any range of precision, there must be a means of propagating values of varying degrees of precision during simulation. Six methods are available for dealing with this problem. All six methods are considered when propagating a value since each method may provide unique information. The following six methods are listed in order from most quantitative to least quantitative:

1. *Numerical calculations.* The interaction is represented by an analytical expression, and exact quantitative values are known for all the variables to be propagated. If A = 2*B + C is a relationship among integers, and if integer values have been assigned to B and C, then the propagation step assigns an integer value to A by performing the arithmetic.

2. *Using mappings.* Mappings can be used to directly evaluate functions if a value in the domain of the mapping is represented. For example, if trp = equilibrium.trp.concentration and the mapping just described is valid, then the propagation step asserts that Activated.trp-R = Total.trp-R * 0.5.

3. *Interpolating mappings.* If the value of a variable is not in the range of a mapping, but some information about the nature of the relationship is available (e.g., that it is monotonic and linear), then the range and domain values can be interpolated. If we know that the preceding mapping is monotonic and linear with a y-intercept of 0, and that trp = 4 * equilibrium.trp.concentration, then we can infer that Activated.trp-R = 2 * equilibrium.trp.concentration.

4. *Relative calculations.* Interpolations can also be performed in the absence of mappings. If the behavior of the system is known at tryptophan concentration **trp1**, its behavior at **(trp2 = trp1 * 2)** can be predicted by interpolation if the relevant interactions are known to be linear with y-intercepts of 0.

5. **Qualitative calculations**. If nothing is known about a pair of interacting variables except their relative values, the propagation step asserts a constraint between the variables by applying inference rules. Several examples of such rules are as follows:

   (X rel Y) implies (X-Y rel 0)
   (Y rel 0) implies (X+Y rel X)
   ((X rel 0) and (Y > 1)) implies (X*Y rel X)
   ((X rel 0) and (Y > 0) and (Y < 1)) implies (X rel X*Y)

   where rel stands for one of the relations (<,<=,=,<>,>=,>).

6. *Monotonicity calculations.* If a function is known to be monotonic, its inputs can be analyzed to deduce whether it increases, decreases, or remains constant with respect to its value at a previous point in time. For example, if the current value of trp is greater than its previous value while Free.trp-R has remained the same, the value of Total.trp-R has increased from the previous to the current time.

These techniques for representing and simulating systems whose variables and functional relationships are known with varying degrees of precision have been used to make predictions about the behavior of the trp-operon system. Table E–1 shows the values associated with the state variables in the network of Figure E–10 after the first and second rounds of simulation. These values are expressed relative to a constant (e.g., Transcription.Initiation.Rate.1 = Transcription.Initiation.Rate. maximal) or relative to a value from a previous simulation cycle (e.g., trp-Enzymes.2 > trp-Enzymes.1) The simulation was started by assigning initial values to the external variables (such as Total.trp-R, RNA-Polymerase, and trp, which is assigned an initial value of 0).

Sometimes the rate of a process and the amount of its product change in opposite directions. For example, trp-mRNA.Synthesis.Rate.2 has value (< trp-mRNA.Synthesis.Rate.1), whereas trp-mRNA.2 has value (> trp-mRNA.1). This is because the rate of mRNA degradation has increased on the second cycle but is still less than the rate of mRNA synthesis. Results of the type shown in Table E–1 are consistent with molecular genetic theory.

TABLE E–1

Qualitative Simulation of the trp-operon System

	Initial Values	Values at End of Cycle 1	Values at End of Cycle 2
Total.trp-R Activated.trp-R	= Total.trp-R.normal 0	= Total.trp-R.normal 0	= Total.trp-R.1 < (0.5 * Total.trp-R.2)
Free.Promoter.Lifetime	= Free.Promoter.Lifetime. Maximal	= Free.Promoter.Lifetime. Maximal	< Free.Promoter.Lifetime.1 > Free.Promoter.Lifetime. minimal
RNA-Polymerase	= RNA.Polymerase. normal	= RNA.Polymerase.normal	= RNA.Polymerase.1
Transcription.Initiation. Rate	0	= Transcription.Initiation. Rate. maximal	< Transcription.Initiation. Rate.1 > Transcription.Initiation. Rate.Minimal
trp-mRNA.Synthesis. Rate	0	= trp-mRNA.Synthesis. Rate. maximal	< trp-mRNA.Synthesis. Rate.1
trp-mRNA	0	< trp-mRNA.equilibrium	< trp-mRNA.equilibrium > trp-mRNA.1
trp-Enzyme.Synthesis. Rate	0	< trp-Enzyme.Synthesis. Rate. equilibrium	< trp.Enzyme.Synthesis. Rate. maximal
trp-Enzymes	0	< trp-Enzymes.equilibrium	< trp.Enzymes.equilibrium > trp.Enzyme.1
trp-Biosynthesis.Rate	0	< trp.Biosynthesis.Rate. equilibrium	< trp.Biosynthesis.Rate. Maximal > trp.Biosynthesis.Rate.1
trp	0	< trp.equilibrium	< trp.equilibrium > trp.1

F. REAL-WORLD APPLICATIONS OF KNOWLEDGE-BASED SIMULATION

MOST OF THE PROGRAMS described so far have not been extensively applied to solve problems "in the field." This section describes two applications and two tools that have proven beneficial in solving real-world applications. Cotton farmers in Mississippi have reported greatly increased yields using COMAX. SimKit has facilitated the development of simulation models for a number of manufacturing systems. Physicists have reduced the start-up times of particle accelerators by two orders of magnitude with ABLE. Finally, Forecast Pro is a low-cost, off-the-shelf PC product that has been used to predict business trends.

F1. COMAX — Knowledge-based Simulation for Cotton Crop Management

COMAX (Lemmon, 1986, and Comis, 1986) assists cotton farmers by predicting the dates for irrigation, fertilizer application, and harvesting that will maximize crop yield.

The fruit of the cotton plant, called a cotton boll, contains the lint that is of commercial value. The yield of bolls is affected by the amount of nitrogen applied to the crop through fertilizer, the amount of water applied to the crop through irrigation and rainfall, and the date of harvesting. Insufficient nitrogen or water (as indicated by the conditions known as nitrogen stress and water stress) will stunt plant growth. Too much nitrogen is economically wasteful and causes excessive plant growth, making the crop difficult to harvest. Yield will be low if the crop is harvested before enough bolls have sufficiently matured. On the other hand, if the cotton is not harvested before the rainy season, yield will also suffer since rain can knock the bolls off the plant, lower cotton weight, and cause discoloring fungus growth. These factors must be considered in combination as well as separately. For example, increased irrigation can induce plant growth, thereby increasing the demand for nitrogen. The problem that COMAX must solve is how to schedule irrigation, fertilizer application, and harvesting to achieve optimum yield, taking into account the particular conditions of each individual farm.

The overall structure of COMAX is indicated in Figure F–1. COMAX works by running the GOSSYM numerical simulation model (Baker et al., 1983) and interpreting its results. GOSSYM is a program that simulates the growth of a cotton plant for an entire growing season, given a set of soil conditions and the daily weather data (real or predicted) throughout the season. In particular, it predicts the dates that the plant will next go into nitrogen and water stress.

The COMAX knowledge base consists of facts about the present conditions on a particular farm and rules that apply to all cotton farms in the same geographic area. The facts include the prior history of nitrogen applications, irrigation, and daily weather conditions on that farm for the current growing season. The rules determine the next dates for nitrogen application, irrigation, and harvesting. These dates depend on the weather for the remainder of the growing season. Since the future weather is unknown, COMAX predicts these dates by running GOSSYM for each of three future weather scenarios (hot and dry, normal, and cold and wet) and applying its rules to the resulting dates of nitrogen and water stress.

COMAX is run once a day throughout the growing season. On each new day, the actual weather for the previous day is used by GOSSYM, so

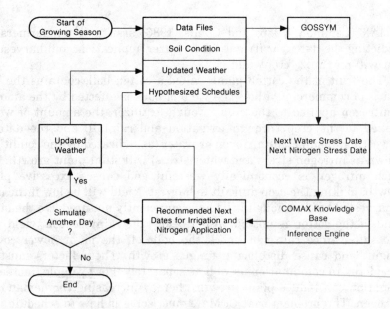

Figure F–1.   The overall structure of COMAX.

that the predicted dates become more accurate as the growing season progresses. To determine the next irrigation date, COMAX calls GOSSYM for each of the three weather scenarios. For each scenario, GOSSYM predicts the next water stress date, which in turn triggers rules that determine the best irrigation date. Running COMAX with the hot-dry scenario gives the earliest date by which irrigation would be needed, whereas the normal scenario gives the most likely date. These dates can change as the actual weather for the current day is used in the next day's run. For example, if the current day turns out to be cold and rainy, the predicted irrigation date under the hot-dry scenario will be later on the next day's run than on the current day's run. The rules that determine the next irrigation date also take into account such factors as the type of irrigation system used on the farm and the number of days required for an application.

Nitrogen applications are determined in a similar manner. For each of the three weather scenarios, GOSSYM predicts the next date of nitrogen stress, and this date is used by rules to predict the best date and amount for nitrogen application. Each predicted nitrogen application is then fed into GOSSYM again to determine whether the application will cause nitrogen stress or undesired plant growth; the amount of nitrogen is adjusted by the rules and GOSSYM is rerun until the amount of nitrogen causes neither nitrogen stress nor excessive growth.

An entire growing season can be run with simulated weather data in 20 to 30 minutes on an IBM PC-AT. The results can be displayed graphically as in Figure F–2. Each row in Figure F–2 gives the results of a growing season with a particular set of nitrogen and water applications. The first graph in each row shows the date and amount of nitrogen applications, and the degree of nitrogen stress. The second graph in each row shows the timing of water applications and the water stress. The third graph in each row shows the development of the plant throughout the growing season in terms of its height and the number of bolls and squares. The fourth graph in each row shows overall yield at harvest time.

The first two rows in Figure F–2 were generated by COMAX immediately after the third application of nitrogen. Comparison of the first two rows shows that additional water applications in row 2 relieved water stress but aggravated nitrogen stress; the overall yield was the same as in row 1. In the third row, COMAX hypothesized a fourth nitrogen application of 30 pounds per acre, which relieved the nitrogen stress relative to that of the second row. In the fourth row, 60 pounds per acre was hypothesized for the fourth nitrogen application. Doubling the nitrogen eliminated nitrogen stress entirely and increased the final yield, but it also induced a spurt of new growth at the end of the season (see third graph), which would make the cotton difficult to harvest. In the fifth row,

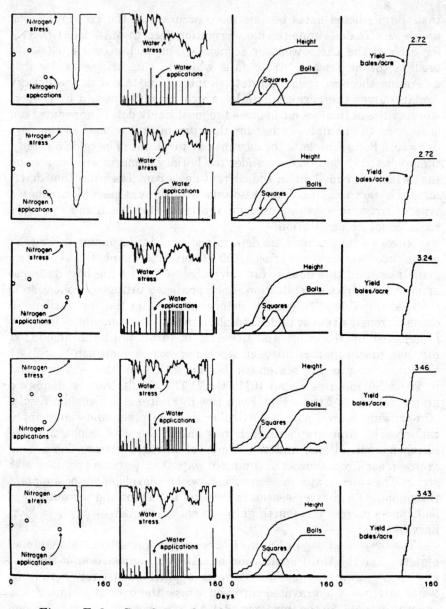

Figure F–2.   Graphs produced by COMAX from the results of
GOSSYM simulations, showing the process
whereby COMAX reduces the water stress and
then the nitrogen stress. (Lemmon, 1986, p. 32)

a compromise of 50 pounds per acre was hypothesized. This amount gave almost the same yield as would be obtained by applying 60 pounds, without the growth spurt. The fifth row therefore represents the nitrogen and irrigation schedules predicted by COMAX for maximum cotton yield.

COMAX has actually been tested on cotton farms in Mississippi. Weather conditions are automatically entered into the farmer's PC every day from a weather station, and COMAX is run with the updated weather. The last row of Figure F–2 was COMAX's prediction for an actual 6,000-acre farm. The farmer had not intended to make a fourth nitrogen application, so he cautiously tested COMAX by applying 20 pounds per acre on a 6–acre test plot (COMAX recommended 50 pounds). At harvest time, the test plot gave a net increase of at least 115 pounds per acre, representing a net gain of at least $60 per acre. The gain from this small plot is comparable to the cost of all the hardware needed to run COMAX, including the computer, the printer, and the weather station.

F2.   SimKit: An Integrated, Knowledge-based Environment for Simulation

SimKit comprises a set of general-purpose modeling and simulation tools built on top of KEE, a frame-based programming environment written in CommonLISP. Both SimKit and KEE are commercial products sold by Intellicorp. A discrete-event simulation model is built in SimKit using knowledge bases called *libraries*. We will discuss the development of libraries, the development of models using these libraries, and the simulation of the resulting models.

The Development of Libraries

A SimKit library is a KEE knowledge base that contains definitions of object classes and the relationships between them. A library representing a factory might contain object classes for drills, lathes, conveyor belts, and storage bins, for example. Each class is implemented as a *frame* in KEE. A frame contains slots, which are like the fields of a record in structured programming languages, except that slots can contain LISP functions as well as data. The frames that implement object classes therefore give both the structure and the behavior of the objects they describe.

To model a system, we need to know the relationships between objects as well as their internal structure and behavior. For example, if a manufacturing process requires that a part is first assembled and then drilled, we can say that the assembling machine is *upstream* of the drill, or that the drill is *downstream* of the assembling machine. Interobject relations such as "upstream" and "downstream" can be defined with SimKit.

Libraries are created and modified with the SimKit *Library Editor*, which is used to define the object classes and relations in a library. Each object class and relation is graphically depicted with an *icon*. An icon is either provided by SimKit or created as a bitmap by the library developer. Icons associated with each class and relation are displayed in the editor *viewports*, as shown by the simple model of a factory in Figure F–3. The object classes viewport on the left contains one icon to represent each of the object classes defined for the library. The relations viewport on the right contains icons that represent the relations between classes. The design viewport in the center is used to construct, display, modify, and run a model.

Object classes are created for a library by creating their frames, defining slots for the frames, and giving values to the slots. The process of object class creation is facilitated by using pop-up menus, interactive dialog, and other tools provided by KEE for knowledge base construction (Intellicorp, 1986).

A new relation is defined with the *Relations Editor* by giving its name, the name of its inverse relation, and its domain and range. The classes of domain and range objects must be specified. For example, machine set A (the domain) can be upstream of machine set B (the range);

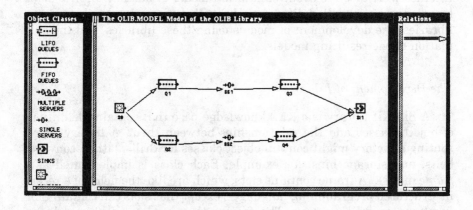

Figure F–3.   The SimKit Library and Model Editors with a
small queueing model. The design viewport is
in the center. The object class viewport is on the
left, and the relation viewport is on the right.
(Stelzner et al., 1987, p. 9)

this specification automatically causes set B to be the domain and set A to be the range of the downstream relation, if downstream is defined as the inverse of upstream. The frame representing an object class has a slot for a relation if the object class is in the domain or range of the relation. The instances of the object class will also contain the relation slot. For example, the frames representing objects in the machine sets A and B have both upstream and downstream slots whose values are the machines at the other end of the relation. As with object classes, relations are created with simple mouse and menu operations.

Sublibraries are specializations of parent libraries to narrower domains. For example, a library that describes a general manufacturing system can be specialized for an airplane factory or an automobile assembly plant. Each sublibrary automatically *inherits* the classes and relations of its parent library using the KEE inheritance mechanism. A sublibrary can add new object classes and relations and can override or delete those inherited from the parent library.

The Development of Models

A major goal of SimKit is to allow nonprogrammers to easily and rapidly construct simulation models of a system. This goal is achieved with the SimKit *Model Editor*, a user interface that helps the modeler create simulation models from libraries of object classes and relations. The particular objects that comprise a model are selected with a mouse from the object class viewport and moved into the design viewport (see Figure F–3). The relations between objects are selected with a mouse from the relations viewport and moved between the objects they connect. In Figure F–3, the downstream relation, represented by the arrow in the relations viewport, connects Q1 (queue 1)and SS1 (single server 1) to show that SS1 is downstream of Q1. In this way, the user creates a model on the screen that intuitively reflects his concept of the objects and relations that comprise the system to be simulated.

The underlying computer representation of the model is encoded as a knowledge base that contains a frame for each object in the model. The frame for each object is an *instance* of the object class to which it belongs (see the discussion of classes and instances in Section B3). The close correspondence between the graphical depiction of objects on the screen and the underlying representation of those objects as frames in a knowledge base permits easy modification of the model. For example, to add single server SS3 between Q3 and SI1, the user simply selects "SINGLE SERVERS" from the object class viewport, moves the single server icon between Q3 and SI1, names the single server SS3, and invokes a pop-up menu to select "splice." Figure F–4 shows the result of applying these actions to the model of Figure F–3. A frame for SS3 is created, and the

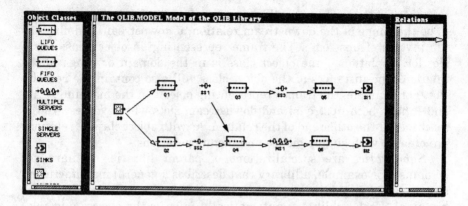

Figure F–4.   The queueing model after several modifications.
(Stelzner et al., 1987, p. 9)

splice operation converts the downstream relation between Q3 and SI1
into two downstream relations: one from Q3 to SS3, and the other from
SS3 to SI1. The values of the upstream and downstream slots of Q1, SS3,
and SI1 are automatically updated to reflect the splice operation.

Another useful modeling feature provided by SimKit is the *Composite
Object Editor*. This editor allows the grouping of several object classes
into a single composite class within a library. The modeler can then use
the model editor to create instances of a composite class, just as it creates
instances of single classes.

To summarize, a *library* is a set of object classes and relations that
are created by programmers proficient in KEE and LISP; a *model* is a
representation of a system that nonprogrammers can create by selecting
instances of object classes and relations that are defined in a library.
Both libraries and models are implemented as knowledge bases in KEE.
The implementation of a model as a knowledge base is transparent to
the model developer.

The Simulation of Models

As in Smalltalk, the objects in a SimKit simulation model contain
methods that are invoked by messages. The frames that represent object
classes have special slots for methods, so the objects in simulation models
automatically inherit these slots and methods. A method can contain
either functions coded in LISP or rules coded in the declarative rule
language of KEE. The behavior of a system is modeled by defining the
messages that objects can send to each other and the way that objects

respond to them through their methods. The name of the slot that contains a method is explicitly included as part of a message. This contrasts with the Smalltalk approach, which requires pattern matching between the message and the method that it invokes.

There is also a way to invoke methods in SimKit without receiving any message. This technique is useful in situations where an action should automatically be taken whenever some change in the state of the model occurs. For example, whenever a part arrives at the queue for a drill, the queue object might invoke a method that determines whether to divert that part to another drill queue. This method is implemented as an *active value*, which is attached to the slot in the drill queue that contains the number of parts in the queue. This active value is a method that is automatically executed whenever the number of parts in the drill's queue increases. Active values are another example of a KEE facility that is available to SimKit library developers.

To perform discrete-event simulation, SimKit must have a means to *schedule* the transmission of messages. Every model created with SimKit automatically includes instances of the object classes *CALENDER*, *CLOCK*, and *SIMULATOR*. These object classes are part of SimKit, just as similar classes are defined as part of SIMULA and Smalltalk (Section C3). A model can also include objects that generate random variables from probability distributions to drive the simulation and objects that collect statistics on the simulation results.

The CALENDAR object for a model maintains an event queue in its FUTURE.EVENTS slot. When it is time for an event to occur, that event is deleted from the FUTURE.EVENTS slot and placed in the CURRENT.EVENT slot. The CALENDAR then formulates and sends a message to the appropriate object. The method invoked within the receiving object might in turn generate another message that causes a new event to be added to the FUTURE.EVENTS queue. The CLOCK object of a model is always updated to the time of the current event. The simulation continues until one of the following occurs: there are no more events, a pre-specified amount of time has elapsed, or the simulation is interrupted.

A model's SIMULATOR object controls the simulation by initializing the model and by starting and stopping simulation runs. The SIMULATOR object contains a slot with the message INITIALIZE! that causes all objects in the simulation model to return to a standard starting point or to a default state. The SIMULATOR object also provides a menu that allows the user to control the simulation. The *run* option on this menu permits specification of the terminating conditions for a simulation run (e.g., when there are no more events). The user may step through a simulation, event by event, in order to debug the model or to better understand how the model works. The simulation can always be interrupted regardless of whether it is running one step at a time or continuously.

Some messages sent between objects in the model pictured in Figure F–3 might include:

An ITEM.ARRIVES! message that is received by an object when an item arrives at the object.

A START.ACTIVITY! message that is sent to an object so that it can begin processing the item that arrived.

A COMPLETE.ACTIVITY! message that is sent to an object when it has finished processing an item.

An ITEM.DEPARTS! message that is sent to an object when an item departs it so that it can prepare for the next one.

For example, when the COMPLETE.ACTIVITY! message is sent to an object that has just finished processing an item, it invokes a LISP function in that object that determines the next downstream object of the item and whether the downstream object can accept the item. If the downstream object can accept the item, an ITEM.DEPARTS! message is scheduled for the upstream object and an ITEM.ARRIVES! message is scheduled for the downstream object. Otherwise, the upstream object puts itself into a waiting state until the downstream object becomes available.

SimKit and Smalltalk take very similar approaches to simulation. SimKit goes beyond Smalltalk in both the range of systems it can model and the ease of developing models due to:

Its ability to express object behaviors in a variety of ways: procedural code, rules, active values, or some combination thereof. This ability is important since object behaviors differ in the way they are most naturally expressed. Smalltalk offers only procedural code for implementing behaviors.

Its distinction between libraries and models. Libraries are created by programmers for subsequent use by model builders who need know nothing about the underlying implementation of the models they are developing. A Smalltalk model builder must know the Smalltalk language in order to develop a model.

Its interface to the modeler. The model editor allows simple and rapid construction of simulation models that directly reflect the modeler's intuition about the structure and behavior of a system.

Finally, SimKit provides automatic *verification* of simulation models to ensure their correct implementation. This important subject is considered further in Section G2.

F3.   ABLE—Knowledge-based Control for Particle Accelerators

To SUCCESSFULLY PERFORM experiments in elementary particle physics, an accelerator must provide an extremely well-focused and well-positioned beam to a target that can be kilometers away from the source. The beam travels through a pipe and is focused by many magnets that surround the pipe at various positions along its length. Beam particle monitors (BPMs) are interspersed throughout the beam line to measure the deviation of the beam trajectory from the ideal trajectory (see Figure F–5).

When an accelerator is brought up for the first time, or resumes operation after a long shutdown, calibration and alignment errors in the magnets cause the beam to deviate from its desired trajectory. The diagnostic problem is to figure out which magnets are the sources of these deviations. The strengths and alignments of the offending magnets can then be adjusted to deliver the beam along its proper path.

For most of the 30-year history of accelerator operation, physicists have had only their intuition to aid in the search for the error-causing magnets. More recently, interactive simulators have been developed which predict the beam trajectory that corresponds to a given set of magnet strengths and alignments. These simulators use a mathematical model of particle beams to generate the trajectory for a set of magnets. The physicist can "twiddle the knobs" to adjust magnet settings and then run the simulator. The resulting simulated trajectory is then compared to the actual trajectory by computing a statistical fit between the simulated and actual BPM measurements. If the fit is very close, it is reasonable to suppose that the "twiddled" magnets are causing the problem.

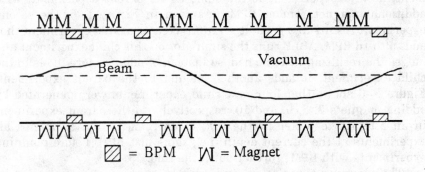

Figure F–5.   Segment of a beam line. (Selig, 1987, p. 1.)

An optimization program was subsequently developed to partially automate this process by eliminating the "knob twiddling." With the optimizer, the physicist needs only to specify the particular magnets and BPMs to simulate. The optimizer then computes the magnet settings that will result in the best possible fit between the simulated and real trajectories. If this fit is close enough, the simulation and optimization are repeated using the same magnets and additional BPMs further down the beam line. Otherwise, a magnet might be added to or subtracted from the current set of magnets in order to improve the fit. This process is repeated until the measurements from all BPMs in the beam line have been included.

The overall strategy taken by the physicist using these techniques is to plan an experiment (a set of magnets and BPMs), simulate the experiment with optimized magnet settings, and evaluate the closeness of fit between the simulated and actual BPM data. The cycle of experiment planning, simulation, and evaluation continues until all BPM readings in the beam line of interest have been fit. This approach saves time and money by solving the problem on a computer instead of using the actual accelerator, but it doesn't tell the physicist which magnets should be experimented with in the first place. As a result, the start-up procedure can still take weeks to complete. A program called ABLE (Selig, 1987, p. 1), developed at Stanford University in conjunction with the Stanford Linear Accelerator Center, uses the same overall strategy, but greatly decreases the start-up time by automating the planning and evaluation stages of the experiment cycle.

As its first experiment, ABLE fits the first BPM (relative to the particle beam source) with the first magnet. It then tries to fit the first and second BPMs with the first magnet (this experiment is called plan1#1&1–2 in Figure F–6, meaning plan1 is using magnet 1 to fit BPMs 1 through 2). This experiment is called a *child* of the first experiment; a child experiment is the same as its parent experiment, with additional magnets and/or BPMs. As seen in Figure F–6, the second experiment results in a good fit, so ABLE creates a child experiment that adds a third BPM. ABLE runs the simulator on this child experiment and judges the resulting fit to be bad, so instead of adding more BPMs to the child experiment, it adds another magnet to the parent experiment. Figure F–6 shows that four new child experiments were generated by adding magnets 7, 8, 9, and 10, respectively, to the parent experiment in an attempt to better fit the first three BPMs. ABLE completes all experiments at the current depth (i.e., same last BPM) before planning experiments with BPMs further down the line.

The planning, simulation, and evaluation stages are controlled by rules in ABLE's knowledge base. Figure F–7 shows the structure of these

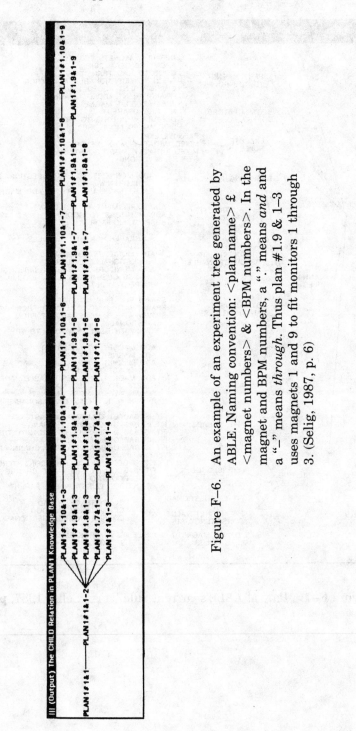

Figure F–6.   An example of an experiment tree generated by ABLE. Naming convention: <plan name> £ <magnet numbers> & <BPM numbers>. In the magnet and BPM numbers, a "." means *and* and a "–" means *through*. Thus plan #1.9 & 1–3 uses magnets 1 and 9 to fit monitors 1 through 3. (Selig, 1987, p. 6)

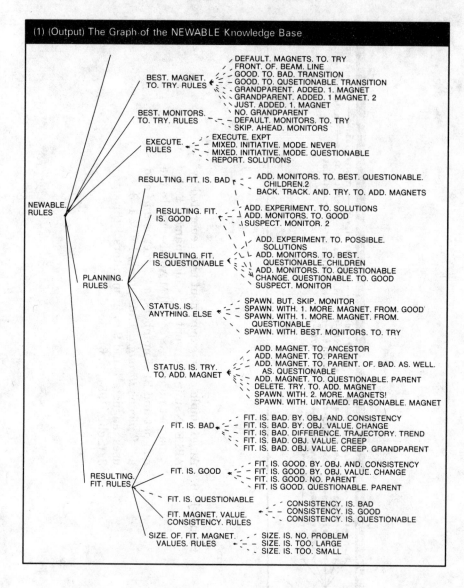

Figure F–7.   Part of ABLE's current rule base. (Selig, 1987, p. 5)

rules in their implementation as part of a KEE knowledge base (see Section F2). The overall flow of control in ABLE is shown in Figure F–8. The first planned experiment is always the same: fit the first BPM with the first magnet. All subsequently generated planned experiments are kept in an *experiment queue*. The Execute.Rules (see Figure F–7) of ABLE take the first experiment off the experiment queue and run it through the optimizing simulator. These rules are also able to recognize and report solutions to the fitting problem for the entire segment.

The Resulting.Fit rules take the results of a simulation and judge them to be "good", "questionable", or "bad." Two principal criteria are used to make this decision. One, called the *objective value*, is the statistical measure of how well the simulated trajectory fits the actual trajectory. The other criterion is a measure of the change in each magnet's strength between the current and parent experiments since an abrupt change in magnet strength may require backtracking to the experiment where this magnet was added. An example of a Resulting.Fit rule is:

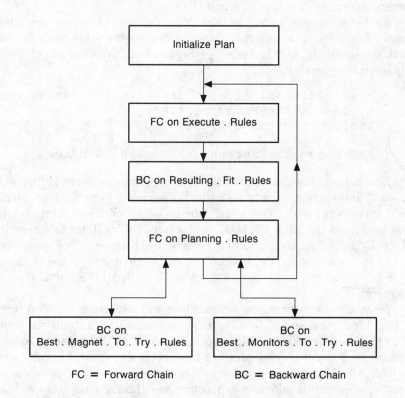

Figure F–8.   The flow of control between ABLE's rule clusters.
(Selig, 1987, p. 8)

```
if ((> (the objective.value.change of ?exp)
       (* 0.75 (the
        max.allowable.objective.value.change of
        controller))
    and
      (the fit.value.consistency fo ?exp is bad))
then
      (change.to (the resulting.fit of ?exp is bad)
      using planning.rules)
```

The maximum allowable objective value change referred to in the first premise of the rule is a threshold value for distinguishing between questionable and bad fits. This premise is true if the change in objective value from the parent experiment to the current experiment is greater than 75% of this maximum value. If this premise is true, backward chaining is performed on the second premise to determine whether the magnet strengths are sufficiently consistent between the current and parent experiments. If both premises are true, the resulting fit of the current experiment is asserted to be bad.

An assertion made by the Resulting.Fit rules triggers the Planning.Rules. The planning rules contain rule subsets for dealing with good, questionable, and bad fits (see Figure F–7). An example of a rule triggered by a good fit is:

```
if ((the resulting.fit of ?current.exp is good) and
    (< (last.monitor ?current.exp)
       (last.monitor of segment))
then
      (the status of ?current.exp is add.monitors)
```

This rule means that if the fit of the current experiment is judged to be good, and there are more BPMs in the segment to be fit, then plan a child experiment with more BPMs. The assertion of this conclusion triggers backward chaining on the Best.Monitors.To.Try.Rules to determine which BPMs should be added to the current experiment. The result is a child experiment that is placed on the experiment queue and that will later be simulated to fit the new set of BPMs with the current set of magnets.

There are two strategies for handling a questionable fit. The "optimistic" strategy assumes that the current path will eventually turn out to be good, so it creates a child experiment just as if the parent experiment were good. If a descendant of the parent experiment turns out to be bad, ABLE backtracks to the parent experiment. The "pessimistic" strategy waits until all other experiments at the same depth have been completed, and then compares the results of these experiments with each other to determine which ones should be extended.

The basic strategy for handling a bad experiment is to backtrack to the parent experiment and generate new child experiments by adding another magnet. The Planning.Rules that fire on bad experiments assert a status of *Try.To.Add.Magnet*, which in turn triggers backward chaining on the *Best.Magnet.To.Try.Rules*. An example was shown in Figure F–6, where four child experiments of plan1#1&1–2 were generated when plan1#1&1–3 was judged to be bad.

The cycle of experiment planning, execution, and evaluation continues until all the BPMs have been fit for the beam line segment under consideration. ABLE may conclude that there are many good solutions for the segment. The set of good solutions represents the pruning of the entire search space of solutions down to a few that are worth testing on the real accelerator. All good solutions must be asserted since the actual cause of the physical beam deviation is unknown.

ABLE was first implemented in KEE 3.0 (see Section F2) on a Symbolics 3600 LISP machine. The ABLE control panel, shown in Figure F–9, is used to specify how ABLE should be run. By selecting from the "stop executing when?" menu, the user can single-step through experiments, stop on a break condition, or run without pause until all solutions have been found. The user can change the "resulting fit" of any experiment and can add, delete, or modify any of the rules in the knowledge base. Since a physicist will learn to modify and refine his own heuristics for experiment search and evaluation as he gains experience with ABLE, the ability to easily and rapidly make changes to the knowledge base is essential.

The performance of ABLE has been tested by comparing its diagnoses with those of experts for six sample problems. ABLE achieved comparable results to those obtained by the experts, but in vastly less time. A FORTRAN version of ABLE called GOLD has been used on actual beam

Figure F–9. The ABLE control panel. (Selig, 1987, p. 12)

line data from several accelerators and achieved excellent results that could not have been obtained using any other existing techniques. The validation of ABLE is further discussed in Section G3.

F4.   Forecast Pro—Intelligent Prediction of Business Trends

ALL BUSINESSES make plans based on how they perceive the future. These plans are usually formulated by extrapolating from past experience. A number of statistical techniques have been developed that analyze past data in order to predict future trends. Most business planners, however, are not sufficiently versed in these techniques to decide which one is most appropriate for interpreting a given case. Several recent commercial products combine numerical simulation with an expert system in order to guide the user in running the simulation. For example, the Retail Planning System and Advisor (developed by Jacques LaFrance (1989) and colleagues at MPSI) combines a demographic simulation model with expertise on how to run the model so that retailers can formulate optimal plans for their distribution outlets. Users of this program are guided by suggestions on which parameters to change (e.g., store locations and hours of operation) in order to achieve specified goals given constraints on time and cost.

Another commercial product for assisting business planners in making forecasts based on past data is Forecast Pro (Forecast Pro, 1987; Goodrich, 1987; and Bryan, 1987) from Business Forecast Systems. Its use does not require any knowledge of statistics. The input to a forecasting session is a set of *time series*. A time series is a sequence of values for a variable at equally spaced intervals over a given time range. The example shown in Figure F–10 gives airline passenger data every month over a 12-year period.

A time series can be statistically characterized in a number of ways. Two commonly used characteristics of a time series are its *volatility* (degree of randomness) and its *seasonality* (extent of cyclic trends, such as the yearly patterns shown in Figure F–10). The choice of an appropriate forecasting technique depends on the evaluation of such characteristics for a given time series.

The three forecasting techniques used by Forecast Pro are called *exponential smoothing, Box-Jenkins,* and *dynamic regression.* Exponential smoothing is often used when there are relatively few data points or when the data is highly volatile. Box-Jenkins is used in cases where the data is relatively stable and there are many points, but there are no

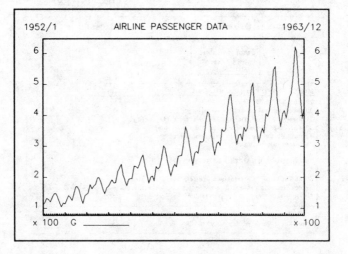

Figure F–10.   A time series for airline passenger data.
(Forecast Pro, 1987)

leading indicators (variables that are considered especially significant in the forecast). Dynamic regression is used when there are one or more leading indicators, or when it is desirable to test the effect that changing certain variables has on the forecast. Note that these methods do not forecast by simply attempting to fit the time series data to a function and then extrapolating the function since more recent data is more highly indicative of future trends than is less recent data.

The first step taken by Forecast Pro in creating a forecast is to analyze the time series data to determine their characteristics. A forward-chaining, rule-based expert system then uses these characteristics to deduce the forecasting technique most appropriate to the data. If exponential smoothing is selected, the expert system recommends one of five variations of this technique. The forecast and all associated statistics are generated automatically when exponential smoothing or Box-Jenkins is used. If dynamic regression is selected, Forecast Pro starts an interactive dialog that guides the user in adding, modifying, or deleting variables that may be relevant to the forecast. A set of diagnostics automatically analyzes and interprets the resulting models, and the expert system then suggests the next step that the user should take. The Forecast Pro graphics module can display multiple time series, error functions, and statistics. All transactions that take place during a forecasting session are stored in an *audit trail*, which can be queried to explain its decisions by selecting "Why?" on the main screen (see Figure F–11).

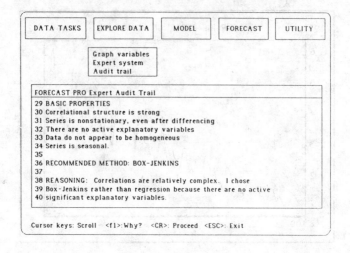

Figure F–11.   The FORECAST PRO main screen and Expert
Audit Trail. (Forecast Pro, 1987, p. 1)

Forecast Pro is a menu-driven program. The menu bar of the main
screen is shown in Figure F–11. The first step in a forecasting session is
to select or enter the time series data by choosing "Define Variables"
from the Data Tasks submenu. This data can be displayed by choosing
"Graph Variables" from the Explore Data submenu (see Figure F–11). If
the user wants to let the program determine the appropriate forecasting
technique, he chooses "Expert System" from the Explore Data submenu.
The statistics and error data for the resulting model can then be
inspected by choosing the "Examine Model" option of the Model submenu. The "Compute Forecasts" and "View Forecasts" options of the
Forecast submenu can then be chosen, with the results displayed as in
Figure F–12. This figure shows upper and lower confidence intervals for
the forecast. Finally, the forecast can be graphed by choosing the "Graph
Variables" option from the Explore Data submenu.

Forecast Pro has made accurate forecasting accessible to a large
number of individuals and organizations because its embedded rule base
can automatically deduce the most appropriate forecasting technique for
a given set of data. It is an off-the-shelf product that runs on IBM personal
computers and compatibles.

As a final note to this section, it is interesting to observe that the
knowledge bases of COMAX, ABLE, and Forecast Pro all contain about
50 rules. Perhaps this indicates that only a small set of well-selected
rules is needed to greatly extend the capabilities of numerical simulation.

DATA TASKS	EXPLORE DATA	MODEL	FORECAST	UTILITY

Compute forecasts
View forecasts
Write forecasts

FORECAST PRO Expert Audit Trail

41	Forecast variable &FORECST		
42	Period	Forecast	Lower (95%)	Upper (95%)
43	1-1986	22.836084	19.589694	26.082475
44	2-1986	25.759111	22.479790	29.038433
45	3-1986	27.667364	24.352913	30.981815
46	4-1986	29.663895	26.312090	33.015699
47	5-1986	34.618729	31.336131	38.118932
48	6-1986	34.545349	31.185475	38.051982
49	7-1986	37.450520	33.927260	38.022721
50	8-1986	36.714371	24.059770	40.286787
51	9-1986	27.683107	25.978360	31.306444
52	10-1986	29.654873	24.026326	33.331386

Cursor keys: Scroll   <f1>:Why?   <CR>: Proceed   <ESC>: Exit

Figure F–12.   A forecast generated by FORECAST PRO.
(Forecast Pro, 1987, p. 3)

G. ISSUES IN THE DEVELOPMENT AND USE OF KNOWLEDGE-BASED SIMULATION

Now THAT WE have described a number of programs that use knowledge-based techniques for simulation, we turn our attention to issues that the developer and end user of all such programs must face. We first consider the role of time since numerical simulators and knowledge-based programs generally handle time in very different ways. We then explore the problems that must be addressed in the development of these programs. Finally, we focus on an aspect of development that is particularly important to the end user: the validation of a knowledge-based simulation model.

G2. Simulation, Inferencing, and Time

THE CONCEPT of simulation is associated with predicting the values of system variables at future points in time, whereas knowledge processing usually refers to making inferences about the state of a system at a given time. Is there a way of handling time that is particular to knowledge-based simulation, or is time simply handled by the simulation component and ignored by the knowledge-based component? Before answering this question, we will try to clarify what is meant by time in a knowledge-based simulation.

Simulation Time vs. Computer Time

Many of the systems discussed in previous sections run a simulation model on each tick of a simulation clock. EXSYS (Section C3), for example, solves a set of simple algebraic equations in sequence to evaluate the variables of a business system for a given year using the values of the variables from the previous year. The clock therefore "ticks" once a year. This does not mean that the computer running EXSYS is idle for each 365-day period between simulation runs! The simulation of a business model over many years takes place on the computer in a matter of microseconds, since the values of the variables for each year are used to calculate those for the next year up to the last year of interest. If the time period of interest is 10 years, the computer will simply solve 150 algebraic equations in succession since there are 15 equations to solve for each of the 10 years. The rate-limiting step in running EXSYS is the interactive dialog with the user; the actual simulation time is negligible by comparison.

ABLE (Section F3), on the other hand, is not directly concerned with time; its goal is to deduce combinations of magnets that may be causing deviations from the actual beam trajectory. Many hours of processing time may be consumed in generating all the solutions for a given beam line due to the large number of computer operations that are executed each time the numerical simulator and optimizer are run for an experiment. If ABLE is run automatically, then almost all of its processing time is taken up by simulation and optimization; that is, simulation time and computer processing time are nearly the same in this case.

The meaning of time in a knowledge-based simulation therefore depends on the context of the system being simulated. In a clock-driven simulation such as EXSYS, simulation time is the total number of clock ticks multiplied by the interval between ticks (which is one year in the case of EXSYS); the amount of computer processing that is performed on each tick may be none or may be enormous, but it is independent of this interval. In a simulation such as ABLE that is not clock-driven, simulation time is equivalent to the amount of computer processing time required to perform simulation. This distinction will now be discussed in more detail.

Clock-Driven Knowledge-based Simulation

The purpose of a clock-driven simulation is to predict the values of system state variables over a specified time period. Two types of clock-driven simulations can be distinguished: those that process actions on each tick of the clock and those that process actions only on the occurrence of an event. EXSYS and the three MOLGEN systems (Sections C4, E1, and E4) are examples of the former: on each tick of the clock EXSYS solves the set of 15 equations that models a business system, and the MOLGEN programs apply rules to deduce the states of the molecular components of the trp system. The interval between ticks is exactly one year in EXSYS since it predicts the values of system variables for each successive year. The interval between ticks in the MOLGEN examples are not directly correlated to any time period in the actual cell, although the remaining lifetimes of proteins in the virus lifestyle predictor (Section C4) are decremented by one unit of simulation time on each tick. The results obtained from simulating the trp system show the overall trends of its behavior over time. For example, running QSOPS (Section E1) over many units of simulated time generates a regular oscillation in the concentration of trp, although the amplitude and frequency of this oscillation do not correspond to any experimentally measured values.

The second type of clock-driven simulation is illustrated by the drilling system of Section D2. This simulation is driven by sampling from probability distributions to predict the times of machine failures. The machine repair times are given as constants. The simulation clock is advanced from event to event, where an event is either a machine failure or completion of a machine repair. Even though the simulation is "event-driven," a clock tick is implicit since every event has to occur at a multiple of some basic time unit (e.g., a second, minute, day, or year). Nothing happens between events, however, so the simulation proceeds from event to event. This is in contrast to EXSYS and MOLGEN, which assume that the state of the system changes on each tick.

COMAX is a hybrid of the clock-tick and event-driven approaches. Each day, the GOSSYM simulator is run with the previous day's weather; the COMAX knowledge base then schedules the dates of irrigation and fertilization "events" by reasoning about the results of the daily GOSSYM run.

Clock-independent Knowledge-based Simulation

The term "clock-independent" is applied to programs that employ knowledge-based simulation to deduce specific results that are meaningful at the present time, as opposed to generating the behavior of system variables over time. An example is provided by VBC (Section D1), which attempts to choose the best insecticide to use on Florida soybean fields. The statement of the problem implicitly assumes that the decision is made once and for all at an early stage in the growing season. For each candidate insecticide selected by the rules, the SICM simulator predicts the relative crop yield and the expected number of insecticide applications for the entire growing season. The insecticides can then be ranked based on the results of the simulation. The SICM simulator itself uses time to make its predictions, but this use of time is transparent to the user, who only sees the listing of insecticides ranked by economic advantage.

Another example is provided by ABLE. The problem here is to determine which combination of magnets is causing the beam to deviate from its desired trajectory. ABLE's numerical simulator does use time in order to generate a beam trajectory, but the only purpose of generating this trajectory in the first place is to allow the rules to solve the beam deviation problem. As with VBC, the purpose of knowledge-based simulation in ABLE is to solve a problem now, and not to predict future states of the system per se.

Reasoning about Time

The previous discussion has classified knowledge-based simulation programs with respect to time. We can also classify these programs according to whether the simulation is performed by inferencing on rules (e.g., the MOLGEN virus lifestyle predictor) or numerically (e.g., EXSYS). We saw that in the MOLGEN examples, each tick of the simulation clock invokes rule-based inferencing in order to make assertions about the current state of the system. This type of inferencing has no explicit notion of time; it cannot make assertions about the future, nor can it reason about past events.

We now directly address the question posed at the beginning of this section: Is there a way of handling time that is unique to knowledge-based simulation? More specifically, can a rule-driven simulator reason about time? Can such a simulator assert facts about the future and reason about events in the past? We again look at MARS (Section E3) to help answer these questions.

The discussion of MARS in Section E3 provided several examples of how the behavior of circuit components was coded in MRS. The premises and conclusions of the MRS rules often contained a time variable; e.g., (true (value (port in1 $x) $a) $t) means that at time $t, the value of input port 1 of device $x is $a. Such rules assume that there is zero delay in propagating values between ports. However, devices can have arbitrary delay. The example of the multiplier in Section E3 can be modified to introduce a delay of 3 time units at the output:

```
(if (and (type $x multiplier)
         (true (value (port in1 $x) $a) $t)
         (true (value (port in2 $x) $b) $t))
    (true (value (port out $x) (* $a $b)) (+ $t 3)))
```

That is, if at time $t the value of input port 1 is $a and that of input port 2 is $b, then at time ($t + 3) the value at the output port will be ($a * $b). Now suppose that, just as in Section E3, we assert the following facts:

```
(type m1 multiplier)
(true (value (port in1 m1) 2) 4)
(true (value (port in2 m1) 3) 4)
```

That is, the values at time 4 on input ports 1 and 2 are 2 and 3, respectively. The forward-chaining inference mechanism will then use the rule and these facts to deduce

```
(true (value (port out m1) 6) 7).
```

Now suppose that the output port of multiplier m1 is connected to the first input port of adder a1, as in Figure E–6. If we are currently at time 4, and we do not know what the value of the second input port of a1 will be at time 7, we cannot assert the value of the first input port at time 7. To handle this situation, MARS implements an *event queue* of facts that are to be asserted in the future. Each fact in the event queue is stored along with the time at which it is to be asserted; all facts that are true for a given time are asserted when that time arrives. The assertion of a fact in MARS can therefore trigger one of two responses: forward chaining on the fact at the current time or placement of the fact on the event queue for future assertion.

MARS also has the capability of reasoning about past events. To illustrate, we consider the behavior rule for the D flip-flop D1, shown in Figure G–1. The device has two input ports (a clock and a data port) and an output port. A rule describing the behavior of D1 is:

> (if (and (true (value (port clock D1) high) $t)
>   (true (value (port clock D1) low) (− $t 1))
>   (true (value (port data D1) $v) $t))
>   (true (value (port output D1) $v) $t))

This rule states that whenever there is a rising edge at the clock input (i.e., the clock changes from low at time ($t − 1) to high at time $t), then the output port at time $t has the same value as the data port at time $t.

More generally, MARS allows the behavior rules to refer to the state of the simulation at any time in the past. To do so, it must have access to the state of the system (i.e., the values at all ports) for all times since the start of the simulation. A great deal of memory would be wasted by storing all port values at all times since most of these values do not change from one simulation time to the next. MARS solves this storage problem by dividing the assertions about port values into *partitions*. Each partition corresponds to a single simulation time and contains only those assertions that became true at that time.

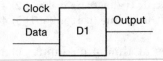

Figure G–1.   The flip-flop D1.

To illustrate, consider the simple circuit of Figure G–2, which consists of an inverter and a buffer. If the values at a and b are both 0 at time 0, their values for simulation times 0 through 3 are:

a	b
0	0
0	1
1	1
0	0

The boxes in Figure G–3 indicate the assertions that were made at times 0, 1, 2, and 3, respectively. Partition 1 does not contain the assertion a = 0 because this assertion was made previously at time 0 and did not change at time 1.

To determine the value of a port at time t, it is then necessary to begin searching the most recent partition less than or equal to t, and to sequentially search the preceding partitions until an assertion about the value of that port is found. The value of inverter port b of Figure G–2 at time 2.5 would be found in partition 1 because no assertion about this port is found in partition 2, which is the most recent partition at time 2.5.

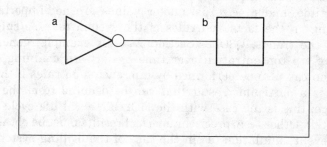

Figure G–2.   A simple circuit consisting of an inverter and a buffer.

```
   0              1              2              3

┌─────────┐   ┌─────────┐   ┌─────────┐   ┌─────────┐
│ a = 0   │   │ b = 1   │   │ a = 1   │   │ b = 0   │
│ b = 0   │   │         │   │         │   │         │
└─────────┘   └─────────┘   └─────────┘   └─────────┘
```

Figure G–3.   Partitioning the simulation time in MARS.

Even though partitioning greatly reduces the amount of information that needs to be stored, the reduction might not be sufficient. MARS has several strategies for handling this case, all of which require user input. For example, the user can specify particular port values to save and keep only the most recent values of the others, or he can specify that information on all ports is to be kept for only the given number of time units in the past.

G2.   The Development of Knowledge-based Simulation Applications

IN THIS SECTION, we briefly discuss some of the issues involved in actually building a knowledge-based simulation program. One of these issues, validation, is important enough to warrant a separate section (Section G3).

Should the simulation be performed by inferencing or by running a numerical simulation model?   One way to answer this question is by considering the type of simulation output that is desired. If the purpose of simulation is to predict overall trends of system variables through time, and precise parameter values are not important, then inferencing on the facts and rules of the system may be sufficient to generate the trends. QSOPS (Section E1), for example, generates the pattern of trp concentration over time by forward chaining on rules. Simulation can also be performed by inferencing on rules if the desired outcome is a particular result that can be deduced from the system's knowledge; this is the case with the MOLGEN viral life cycle predictor (Section C4). Otherwise, precise numerical results must be obtained from discrete-event simulation (as in the case of the drilling system, MARS, and the orange juice plant of Section B) or mathematical simulation (as in the case of VBC, COMAX, and ABLE).

Another way to answer the question is by considering the type and extent of knowledge in the simulated domain. A great deal of precise information is known about the systems modeled by GOSSYM and SICM, so mathematical simulation is appropriate in these cases. If no numerical models are available but there is some heuristic knowledge about a system, rule-based simulation may be the best alternative.

How should knowledge be integrated with numerical simulation?   The knowledge-based component can serve as the "front end" by generating a set of scenarios for the simulation component to evaluate (e.g., VBC, ONYX) or as the "back end" by evaluating the results of a prior simulation (e.g., EXSYS). These two cases are referred to as "sequential integrated systems" in Section D. Alternatively, numerical simulation and inferencing can alternate with each other for many cycles—the results of a simulation run trigger rules that modify the state of the system; this new state is then simulated on the next run, and so on (e.g., the drilling system, COMAX, and ABLE). Such simulators were called "parallel integrated systems" in Section D.

How can existing numerical simulation models be used to develop knowledge-based simulation applications?   It would certainly require much less time to build a knowledge-based application if the numerical simulator were already available. We have seen that EXSYS, VBC, COMAX, and ABLE all run numerical simulators that existed prior to their integration with knowledge-based components. There are two requirements for using an existing numerical simulator with a knowledge-based component. First, the outputs of one component must be compatible with the inputs of the other component. For example, the result of an ABLE simulation is a beam trajectory, which is compared to the experimental trajectory to compute a statistical goodness-of-fit measure. It is this measure that triggers the subset of rules that determines whether the fit is good, questionable, or bad. Second, the numerical simulator and knowledge-based components must be compiled and linked together into an executable form. This is an important consideration since numerical simulators are usually coded in a high-level programming language such as FORTRAN, whereas the knowledge-based components are often coded in LISP or PROLOG.

What tools are available for building the numerical simulator? the knowledge base?   If either or both of these components must be built, it is reasonable to choose tools that will save development time and are appropriate for the application. As discussed in Section B1, most numerical simulations were and still are written in a high-level programming language like FORTRAN or in a simulation language such as GASP. In addition, SIMULA, Smalltalk, and SimKit all facilitate the implementation of discrete-event simulation models by allowing the developer to code or select objects and their methods, messages, and relations. Forecast Pro chooses an appropriate statistical model based on past data, and ECO creates a standalone numerical simulator through interactive dialog with a human modeler.

The knowledge-based components of some of the integrated programs are encoded directly in a high-level declarative language such as PROLOG (MOSYS) or MRS (MARS). Others use tools such as UNITS (MOLGEN in Section C4) or KEE (QSOPS and MOLGEN in Section E4, ABLE, and the SimKit Library Editor) that facilitate the encoding of simulation models as knowledge bases by making techniques such as object-oriented programming, inheritance, and active values available to the programmer. The SimKit Model Editor allows simulation models to be created without programming; the developer need not even be aware that the model is implemented as a knowledge base.

The choice of tools depends on the application. A principal idea of ABLE is that accelerator physicists should be able to modify its knowledge base as they acquire experience using it. It was therefore more appropriate to use a tool such as KEE that has facilities for rapidly adding, deleting, modifying, and verifying knowledge rather than a language like PROLOG that does not have these facilities. On the other hand, if the number of rules is small and a programmer is available, it may be cost- and time-effective to code the rules in a high-level language such as PROLOG, LISP, or MRS.

How is the user to interact with the program? In most of the preceding applications, the user interacts with the program through its knowledge-based components since the simulation components usually appear as black boxes. EXSYS and Forecast Pro use rules to formulate an interactive dialog that guides the user during a simulation session. In contrast, COMAX and ABLE can be run automatically without any user input. Some of the programs (QSOPS and ABLE) can be interrupted in the middle of a simulation run so that the user can pose queries or make changes to the model before resuming. This capability allows the user to obtain a deeper understanding of the behavior of the model.

The role of the user in running the simulation is an important consideration in the choice of development tool. If the ability to interrupt a simulation to query or change the model is a desired feature, it would be appropriate to develop the model in a knowledge-based environment such as KEE that supports this capability.

How is the program verified? Verification is the process of ensuring that the computer model of a system correctly implements the intentions of the model's developer. Usually a number of constraints on the structure and behavior of a system must be reflected in its computer model. If a factory model includes two conveyor belts that head toward each other and collide, there is an error in the model. This might occur, for example, if a SimKit model developer makes a mistake filling in values for the *upstream* and *downstream* slots of the objects on either end of the conveyor belts. This mistake might be difficult to detect and might lead to erroneous simulation results if there is no way to automatically verify the model before it is used. Verification is especially important when the knowledge used by the simulation model is expected to be modified often.

The SimKit library developer has access to the *value class* and *cardinality* verification mechanisms provided by KEE, and to the SimKit *KB Verifier* as well. A value class defines the set of permissible values for a frame slot, similar to a variable type in a procedural programming language. The SimKit developer is immediately warned whenever an attempt is made to assign a value to a slot that is not in the value class defined for that slot. The cardinality of a slot is the number of values that the slot can contain. The "relatives" slot in a "person" object can have any nonnegative number of "person" values, whereas the "pH" slot of a "chemical solution" object must have exactly one numerical value. As with value classes, an attempt to violate the cardinality of a slot immediately generates a warning.

The SimKit KB Verifier is an automatic verification tool that is run on user request to check slots for value class and cardinality violations. The KB Verifier can be run on an entire library or model or on any subset thereof. It also allows the library developer to create and run his own verification tests.

What are the development costs?   The development of any sizable program incurs substantial costs for its design, coding, testing, verification, validation, support, and maintenance. It is hard to make general comparisons between the costs of developing a knowledge-based simulation application and those of other types of programs because these costs depend on the particular application. The scope of some programs may require that they be developed on mainframes, regardless of whether they are knowledge-based simulations. Although software tools such as SimKit may seem to shorten the time required to code, test, and verify an application, this advantage may be offset by the time required to acquire the application knowledge in the first place.

However, the knowledge-based approach offers a clear advantage over its purely numerical counterparts for one aspect of development— the rapid prototyping of simulation models. Facilities such as object-oriented programming, graphical interfaces, active values, rules, and automatic verification that are incorporated into tools such as KEE and SimKit reduce development time from weeks or months to hours or days. An example is provided by FORCEM, "a fully automated theater-level combat simulation model . . . used by the US Army Concepts Analysis Agency as an analytic tool in the study of theater-level issues for the Army" (Modjeski, 1987). A complete working prototype of FORCEM was developed in 36 hours by a programmer using KEE 2.0 on a Symbolics 3670 LISP machine.

G3.   The Validation of Knowledge-based Simulation Applications

IN GENERAL, a system is said to be *valid* if it accomplishes its purpose. More specifically, *validation* is the measurement of how well a system achieves stated performance goals. Does the use of MOSYS achieve "better" designs for flexible manufacturing systems, as proven by increased throughput, less down times, or any other stated goal? Does the use of VBC decrease crop losses due to insects? Does the use of ABLE permit faster start-ups of particle accelerators? In this section, we will see how these questions might be answered. First we, discuss some of the requirements for performing a validation. Next, we consider the qualitative and quantitative techniques that are used to validate a model. Finally, we ask whether there are any considerations or techniques that are unique to the validation of knowledge-based simulations, and which of the programs discussed so far have actually been validated.

Requirements for Performing a Validation

The following set of issues that must be considered before validating a knowledge-based simulation is adapted from O'Keefe et al. (1987), which discusses the same issues for validating expert systems:

What to validate. The results of a knowledge-based simulation program are what ultimately must be validated. These results may consist of designs, plans, recommendations, numbers, or problem solutions. The validation of simulation results is meaningful only in terms of the original performance goals. In the case of the MOLGEN work on viruses (Section C4), the result is a binary choice between two viral lifestyles. It would seem easy to validate such a program since it is easy to tally how many choices were correct and incorrect. The issue is not so simple, however, if we ask how to establish meaningful performance criteria. In the MOLGEN case, is 80% correct performance excellent, fair, or unacceptable? The validation of ABLE in terms of its results is perhaps more straightforward because the fit between a simulated and experimental beam trajectory can be objectively measured. This still leaves the question, however, of determining how good a solution's fit must be to qualify as "good enough."

What to validate against. There are three overall types of criteria against which the results of a knowledge-based simulation are evaluated: known results, expert judgment in the presence of known results, and expert judgment in the absence of known results.

Validating against known results has an obvious advantage—we can directly compare known results with the output of a knowledge-based simulator operating on prior data. For example, we might claim that EXSYS has been validated if it is run on actual business data from 1980 to 1985, and the simulated 1986 results agree with the known 1986 results. If, however, we are given no reason to believe that the program will perform well in cases other than those against which it was validated, we might be begging the question of why we developed the program in the first place. Presumably, we didn't develop the program just to tell us what we already knew. The QSOPS simulator (Section E1) uses knowledge-based simulation to predict that the concentration of trp will oscillate regularly over time, which was already known to be true under most circumstances. Does the use of QSOPS contribute anything to molecular biology besides making this prediction? This is an important question because the same result could have been obtained by simply modeling the concentration of trp with a sine wave.

Expert systems are often validated against the judgments of experts, so it seems reasonable to apply the same approach to knowledge-based simulations. If there are known results as well, is it meaningful to validate against expert judgment for the cases that produced these results? If the answer is yes, we assume that expert judgment is in some way "better" than the actual results. If the answer is no, there is no reason to validate against expert judgment for any cases. If there are no known results, expert prediction may be the only validation criterion available. Validation against expert prediction in the absence of results is a Catch-22 in two ways, however:

1. There is no way to independently validate the expert predictions except by obtaining additional predictions from different experts.

2. Since there are relatively few experts in most domains, it is likely that the expert predictors are the same people who contributed their knowledge to the system in the first place, thereby "guaranteeing" validation.

What to validate with.   To obtain predictions to use in validation, a knowledge-based simulator must be run on a set of test cases. The MOLGEN system for predicting virus lifestyle (Section C4) was tested on 8 combinations of viral mutations whereas ABLE tried to solve 50 combinations of magnet misalignments. The question here is how to know that a sufficient number and variety of test cases has been run in order to conclude that the system has been validated for the stated performance goals. Even if the performance goals are clear, there are still many problems in determining the number and type of test cases:

1. Suppose the three possible outcomes of a situation are A, B, and C, with probabilities .05, .25, and .70, respectively. We then might assume that 5% of the test cases should result in A, 25% in B, and 70% in C (O'Keefe et al., 1987). It may be difficult or impossible to obtain such a "stratified sample" in many situations, however.

2. Even if stratified sampling were possible, it is still not obvious how many tests should be run. Furthermore, the cases that result in B and C may be easy for nonexperts to handle, whereas the A cases may be considerably more complex and require a high level of exper-

tise. The program might be declared "95% valid" if it handles B and C correctly but not A, yet the real proof of performance is in how it handles A since these are the cases where the program's knowledge is really put to use.

3. By definition, a system "works" on the cases used in its development. A knowledge-based simulator could be declared "valid" if it was coded to be valid. This error usually occurs innocently but all too frequently.

4. There may not be any known test cases, so scenarios have to be invented. This is likely to be the case in extremely complex and rapidly changing environments such as might be found in military domains. The meaning of simulation, whether knowledge-based or otherwise, may be questionable in such situations.

When to validate.   Presumably, validation should be an ongoing process, with the knowledge-based simulator becoming "more valid" with time as it is tested in the field and its knowledge-based and/or simulation components are revised based on field experience. A Catch-22 occurs in critical domains where lives or fortunes are at stake, however: the level of performance must be very high from the start, yet it is difficult to achieve a high level of performance unless the system has undergone extensive field testing.

The cost of validation.   The validation of a system may be time consuming and expensive in terms of the human and technical resources required. A tradeoff must be made between the cost of validation, the importance of validation, and the risks of using a system that is not properly validated.

Techniques for Performing Validation

We now consider how a validation might actually be carried out. We very briefly consider both qualitative and quantitative validation techniques that have been applied to both expert systems and numerical simulation models (O'Keefe et al., 1987).

Qualitative techniques for validation.   The following discussion is based on Law and Kelton (1982). Several techniques for qualitatively validating a system include:

1. *Face validation*. The designers, experts, and potential end users can intuitively compare the performance of the simulator with known results or with expert judgments.

2. *Predictive validation*. The simulator runs historical test cases, and the results are compared with known results (if available) or with expert predictions.

3. *Turing tests*. Human experts evaluate the performance of the simulator and domain experts without knowing which results came from which source.

4. *Field tests*. The simulator is tested by its performance in "real" situations. As mentioned earlier, this method of validation is usually not feasible in critical applications.

5. *Subsystem validation*. The modeled system is decomposed into subsystems, which are separately validated. Validation of subsystems does not guarantee validation of the entire system, however.

Quantitative techniques for validation. There are a number of statistical tests for comparing the results of a simulation with either known results or expert judgments. The reader interested in pursuing these statistical methods should consult Law and Kelton (1982). It will simply be noted here that the limitations and appropriateness of a given statistical technique should be thoroughly understood before the technique is used. In the case of numerical simulations, for example, the simulation output is not directly amenable to classical statistical tests because the simulation output is both *nonstationary* (the distribution of the output results changes over time) and *auto-correlated* (the simulation results are not independent of each other).

Validation Techniques for Knowledge-based Simulation

We now return to the questions posed at the end of the first paragraph of this section: Are there validation techniques specific to knowledge-based simulation? Which of the programs discussed so far have actually been validated?

The first question is impossible to answer in a theoretical way. Most of the issues and techniques mentioned earlier apply both to numerical simulators and to expert systems; whether there are issues or techniques uniquely applicable to knowledge-based simulators is difficult to say. We will probably have to acquire a great deal more experience in attempting to validate such systems in order to begin answering this question.

This leads us directly to the second question: What experience has been acquired so far in the validation of knowledge-based simulators? Of the more than 80 knowledge-based simulation programs reviewed for this chapter from published reports, only 2 directly addressed the issue of validation. COMAX was informally "validated" through a few field tests. ABLE is the only reviewed program that directly discusses validation against both field test results (again a very small number) and expert judgment.

H. CONCLUSION

THE MAIN PURPOSE of this chapter has been to describe a variety of knowledge-based simulation programs from the published literature. The only conclusion that can safely be drawn is that knowledge-based paradigms such as object-oriented programming and rule-based inferencing seem to *facilitate* the development of computer simulation models in many domains. It is tempting to make assertions like "the integration of numerical and rule-based components greatly extends the range of systems that can be simulated," but the general lack of validation currently makes such statements true on paper at best.

It is to be hoped that formal validation techniques will be developed and consistently applied for knowledge-based simulation programs. Until then, it is important that such programs are not used in critical applications that affect individual or societal well-being. Formal validation might require years for a program such as COMAX, which can literally be "field tested" only once per year on a given cotton farm. However, the benefits of proper validation will undoubtedly outweigh the risks of prematurely accepting these programs.

Acknowledgements

I would like to thank Marilyn Stelzner and Harold Brown for helpful discussions on the subject of knowledge-based simulation and for reviewing initial drafts of this chapter.

Chapter XXIII

Computer Vision Update

Robert M. Haralick—University of Washington
Alan K. Mackworth—University of British Columbia
Steven L. Tanimoto—University of Washington

CHAPTER XXIII: COMPUTER VISION UPDATE

A. OVERVIEW

COMPUTER VISION is the science and technology of obtaining models, meanings, and control information from visual data. Inputs of a computer vision system typically are scanner outputs (usually in the form of digital images), range finder outputs, or images reconstructed by medical imaging equipment. Vision science and technology have grown more and more varied in recent years. The range of applications has been widening, and it includes many uses in manufacturing, medicine, and remote sensing.

As with artificial intelligence in general, work in vision falls mainly into two camps. The first kind of work seeks a coherent theory of visual perception and understanding (this approach is called *computational vision*), and researchers in this group often develop computational models of biological vision processes. The second camp does research and development directed toward useful applications (this is sometimes called *machine vision*). Their emphasis is on working, economical solutions to industrial, medical, and military problems rather than on the discovery of new theories or knowledge about human perception.

Perhaps the most significant development of the last five years in computational vision has been the emergence of *regularization theory* as a means for making mathematically ill-posed surface-inference problems well posed. This technique has applications in many kinds of vision problems, including reconstructing intensity maps from a limited set of samples, analyzing stereo pairs of images, and computing optical flow in dynamic imagery.

During the same period, the applications side of the field has seen important advances in three-dimensional modeling and model construction, experience with methods like those of "mathematical morphology," (resulting in better methodologies for applying such techniques), and exciting improvements in parallel computer architectures tailored to vision applications.

There has also been an interplay between computational vision and machine vision. The stereo algorithms, developed largely within the computational vision camp, have moved out into the realm of industrial application. Computer architectures, developed with industrial vision in mind, are influencing studies in computational vision, for example, in the development of parallel algorithms for solving reconstruction problems on meshes.

Because of the large amount of activity in these two areas of com-

521

puter vision, and because of page limitations here, the scope of this chapter is necessarily limited. The major advances in low-level vision, computational vision, and vision architectures are emphasized. Relatively little is said about specific software implementations (this is in contrast to the vision coverage in Chapter XIII of the *Handbook*).

B. LOW-LEVEL VISION

UNDERLYING some approaches to computational vision and to machine vision are basic tasks of breaking up an image into component regions. This *segmentation* problem must be tackled before determining 3-D surface characteristics or recognizing objects in the scene. A large variety of methods have been invented and studied for this initial analysis task. The next subsection gives an overview of this subfield, expanding upon the description of *region analysis* in Article XIII.C5 in Volume III.

B1. Segmentation Techniques

IN TRADITIONAL APPROACHES to computer vision, the pixels of an image are grouped into regions in a process called *segmentation*, and this is done prior to any attempt to interpret the regions as objects in the scene. A perceived advantage of computing a segmentation is that one could, relatively easily, achieve a relatively concise representation of the image's essential pictorial aspects, and that this would permit the semantic phase of the analysis to be accomplished painlessly. Except in certain artificial environments, segmentation has proven to be difficult in itself, and it seems that semantic considerations are often needed at the segmentation level. Nonetheless, various segmentation methods make up an important part of the arsenal of techniques that can be employed in computer vision, and they provide a good starting point for a tutorial overview of developments in vision.

What should a good image segmentation be? Although this depends largely on the application, it can be answered in an application-independent way to a certain extent. Let us attempt to do so.

Regions of an image segmentation should be homogeneous—uniform with respect to some characteristic such as gray tone or texture. Region interiors should usually be simple and without many small holes. Adjacent regions of a segmentation should have significantly different values with respect to the characteristic on which they are uniform. Boundaries of each segment should be simple, not ragged, and must be spatially accurate.

Achieving all these desired properties is difficult because strictly uniform and homogeneous regions are typically full of small holes and have ragged boundaries. Insisting that adjacent regions have large differences in values can cause regions that ought to be kept separated to merge and thus the intervening boundaries to be lost.

Just as there is no generally accepted theory of clustering in statistics, there is no well-accepted theory of image segmentation. Image segmentation techniques tend to be ad hoc. They differ in the ways in which they emphasize one or more of the desired properties and in the ways in which they balance and compromise one desired property against another.

Image segmentation techniques can be classified into one of the following groups:

1. Measurement-space–guided spatial clustering

2. Single-linkage region-growing schemes

3. Hybrid-linkage region-growing schemes

4. Centroid-linkage region-growing schemes

5. Spatial clustering schemes

6. Split-and-merge schemes

As this brief typology suggests, image segmentation can be viewed as a clustering process. The difference between image segmentation and clustering is in grouping. In clustering, the grouping is done in measurement space (e.g., the space of gray values rather than the space of pixel coordinate pairs). In image segmentation, the grouping is done on the spatial domain of the image, and there is an interplay in the clustering between the (possibly overlapping) groups in measurement space and the mutually exclusive groups of the image segmentation.

The single-linkage region-growing schemes are the simplest and most prone to the unwanted region-merge errors. The hybrid-linkage and centroid-linkage region-growing schemes are better in this regard. The split-and-merge technique is not as subject to the unwanted region-merge error. However, it suffers from large memory usage and excessively blocky region boundaries. The measurement-space–guided spatial clustering tends to avoid both the region-merge errors and the blocky boundary problems because of its primary reliance on measurement space. But the regions produced are not smoothly bounded, and they often have holes, giving the effect of salt-and-pepper noise. The spatial clustering schemes may be better in this regard, but they have not been tested well enough. The hybrid-linkage schemes appear to offer the best compromise between having smooth boundaries and few unwanted region merges.

The remainder of this section describes the main ideas behind the major image segmentation techniques. Additional image segmentation surveys can be found in Zucker (1976), Riseman and Arbib (1977), Kanade (1980), and Fu and Mui (1981), and Haralick and Shapiro (1985).

Measurement-space–Guided Spatial Clustering

This technique for image segmentation uses the measurement-space clustering process to define a partition in measurement space (e.g., the space of pixel gray values of the image). Then each pixel is assigned the label of the cell in the measurement-space partition to which it belongs. The image segments are defined as the connected components of the pixels having the same label.

The accuracy of image segmentation using the measurement-space clustering process depends directly on how well the objects of interest on the image separate into distinct measurement-space clusters. Typically the process works well in situations where there are a few kinds of distinct objects having widely different gray-tone intensities (or gray-tone intensity vectors, for multiband images) and these objects appear on a nearly uniform background.

Clustering procedures that use the pixel as a unit and compare each pixel value with every other pixel value can require excessively large computation times because of the large number of pixels in an image. Iterative partition-rearrangement schemes such as ISODATA have to go through the image data set many times and if done without sampling can also take excessive computation time. Histogram-mode seeking, because it requires only one pass through the data, probably involves the least computation time of the measurement-space clustering techniques, and it is the one we discuss here.

Histogram-mode seeking is a measurement-space clustering process in which it is assumed that homogeneous objects on the image manifest themselves as the clusters in measurement space. Image segmentation is accomplished by mapping the clusters back to the image domain where the maximal connected components of the mapped back clusters constitute the image segments. For single-band images, calculation of this histogram in an array is direct. The measurement-space clustering can be accomplished by determining the valleys in this histogram and declaring the clusters to be the interval of values between valleys. A pixel whose value is in the ith interval is labeled with index i and the segment it belongs to is one of the connected components of all pixels whose label is i.

Ohlander et al. (1975) refines the clustering idea in a recursive way. He begins by defining a mask selecting all pixels on the image. Given any mask, a histogram of the masked image is computed. Measurement-space clustering enables the separation of one mode of the histogram set from another mode. Pixels on the image are then identified with the cluster to which they belong. If there is only one measurement-space cluster, the mask is terminated. If multiple clusters are present, the process is repeated for each connected component (region) associated with each cluster. Note that one cluster may produce more than one connected component. During successive iterations, the next mask in the stack selects pixels in the histogram-computation process. Clustering is repeated for each new mask until the stack is empty. The process is illustrated in Figure B–1.

Single-linkage Region Growing

Single-linkage region growing schemes regard each pixel as a node in a graph. Neighboring pixels whose properties are "similar enough" are joined by an arc. The image segments are maximal sets of pixels all belonging to the same connected component. Single-linkage image-segmentation schemes are attractive for their simplicity. They do, however, have a problem with chaining, because it takes only one arc leaking from one region to a neighboring one to cause the regions to merge.

The simplest single-linkage scheme defines "similar enough" by pixel difference. Two neighboring pixels are similar enough if the absolute value of the difference between their gray-tone intensity values is small enough. Bryant (1979) defines "similar enough" by normalizing the difference by the quantity $\sqrt{2}$ times the root-mean-square value of neighboring pixel differences taken over the entire image.

For pixels having vector values, the obvious generalization is to use a vector norm of the pixel-difference vector. Instead of using a Euclidean distance, Asano and Yokoya (1981) suggest that two pixels be joined together if the absolute value of their difference is small enough compared to the average absolute value of the center pixel minus neighbor pixel for each of the neighborhoods to which the pixels belong. The ease with which unwanted region chaining can occur with this technique limits its potential on complex or noisy data.

Hybrid-linkage Region Growing

Hybrid single-linkage techniques are more powerful than the simple single-linkage technique. The hybrid techniques seek to assign a property vector to each pixel where the property vector depends on the neighborhood of the pixel. Pixels that are similar are so because their neighborhoods in some special sense are similar. Similarity is thus established as a function of neighboring pixel values, and this makes the technique better behaved on noisy data.

One hybrid single-linkage scheme relies on an edge operator to establish whether two pixels are joined with an arc. Here an edge operator is applied to the image, labeling each pixel as edge or nonedge. Neighboring

pixels, neither of which are edges, are joined by an arc. The initial
segments are the connected components of the nonedge labeled pixels.
The edge pixels can either be left as edges and be considered as background or they can be assigned to the spatially nearest region having a

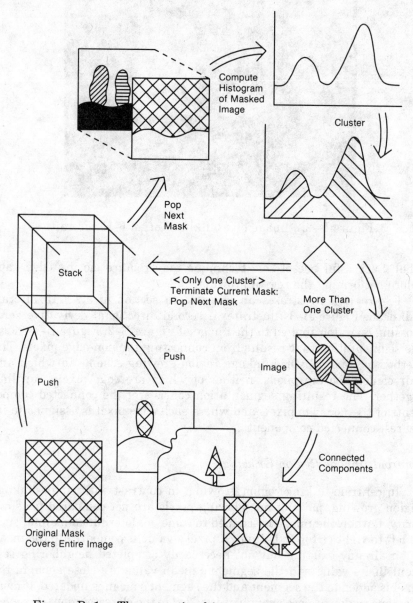

Figure B–1.   The recursive histogram spatial clustering
              method of Ohlander.

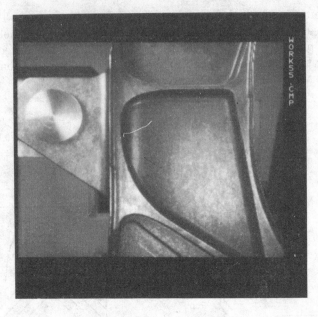

Figure B–2.   Image of a bulkhead of an F-15 aircraft.

label. Successful use of this technique may require closing edge gaps before performing the region growing.

Figure B–2 illustrates an image of a section of an F-15 aircraft bulkhead. Figure B–3 illustrates a second directional derivative zero-crossing operator applied to the image of Figure B–2. Figure B–4 shows the segmentation that results from connecting the non-edge pixels. The method is thus a hybrid-linkage region-growing scheme in which any pair of neighboring pixels, neither of which are edge pixels, can link together. The resulting segmentation consists of the connected components of the nonedge pixels and where each edge pixel is assigned to its nearest connected component.

Centroid-linkage Region Growing

In centroid-linking region growing, in contrast with single-linkage region growing, pairs of neighboring pixels are not compared for similarity. Rather, the image is scanned in some predetermined manner such as left to right or top to bottom. A pixel's value is compared to the mean of an already existing but not necessarily completed neighboring segment. If its value and the segment's mean value are close enough, the pixel is added to the segment and the segment's mean is updated. If more than one region is close enough, it is added to the closest region. However, if the means of the two competing regions are close enough, the two

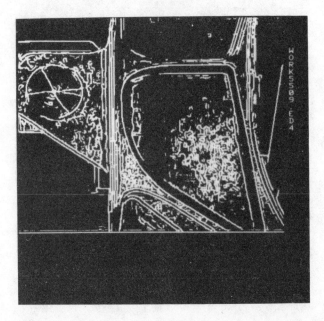

Figure B–3. Directional derivative zero-crossing operator applied to the F-15 image.

regions are merged and the pixel is added to the merged region. If no neighboring region has its mean close enough, a new segment is established having the given pixel's value as its first member. The scan geometry for the centroid-linkage region-growing scheme is shown in Figure B–5.

Keeping track of the means and scatters for all region as they are being determined does not require large amounts of memory space. There cannot be more regions active at one time than the number of pixels in a row of the image. Hence a hash table mechanism with the space of a small multiple of the number of pixels in a row can work well.

One way of performing the region growing is by the use of the T-test. Let R be a segment of N pixels neighboring a pixel with gray-tone intensity y. Define the mean $\overline{X}$ and scatter S^2 by

$$X = \frac{1}{N} \sum_{(r,c)\in R} I(r, c) \tag{1}$$

and

$$S^2 = \sum_{(r,c)\in R} (I(r, c) - X)^2 \tag{2}$$

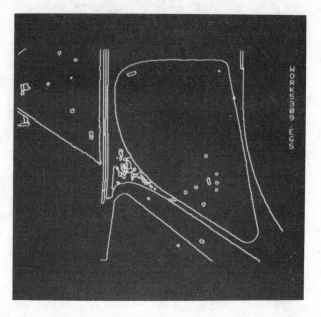

Figure B–4.   Segmentation of the F-15 image.

Under the assumption that all the pixels in R and the test pixel y are independent and identically distributed normals, the statistic

$$T = \left[\frac{(N - 1)N}{(N + 1)} (y - \overline{X})^2 / S^2 \right]^{1/2} \tag{3}$$

has a T_{N-1} distribution. If T is small enough, y is added to region R and the mean and scatter are updated using y. The new mean and scatter are given by

$$\overline{X}_{new} \leftarrow (N\overline{X}_{old} + y)/(N + 1) \tag{4}$$

and

$$S^2_{new} \leftarrow S^2_{old} + (y - \overline{X})^2 + N(\overline{X}_{new} - \overline{X}_{old})^2 \tag{5}$$

If T is too high, the value y is not likely to have arisen from the population of pixels in R. If y is different from all of its neighboring regions, it begins its own region. A slightly stricter linking criterion can require that not only must y be close enough to the mean of the neighboring regions, but also that a neighboring pixel in that region must have a close enough value to y. This combines a centroid linkage and single linkage criterion.

The Levine and Shaheen scheme (1981) is similar. The difference is that Levine and Shaheen attempt to keep regions more homogeneous

2	3	4
1	y	

Figure B–5.   Region-growing geometry for the one-pass scan,
left-right, top-bottom region growing.

and try to keep the region scatter from getting too high. They do this by
requiring the differences to be more significant before a merge takes
place if the region scatter is high. For a user-specified value θ, they
define a test statistic T where

$$T = |y - X_{new}| - (1 - S/\overline{X}_{new})\theta \qquad (6)$$

If $T < 0$ for the neighboring region R in which $|y - \overline{X}|$ is the smallest, y
is added to R. If $T > 0$ for the neighboring region in which $|y - \overline{X}|$ is the
smallest, y begins a new region.

Figure B–6 illustrates the application of the centroid-linkage region-
growing technique to the bulkhead image. This application uses two
successive scans of the image. The first is a left-right top-down scan, and
the second is a right-left bottom-top scan.

Hybrid-linkage Combination Techniques

The centroid-linkage and the hybrid-linkage methods can be combined in a way that takes advantage of their relative strengths. The
strength of the single-linkage method is that boundaries are placed in a
spatially accurate way. Its weakness is that edge gaps result in excessive
merging. The strength of the centroid-linkage method is its ability to
place boundaries in weak-gradient areas. It can do this because it does
not depend on a large difference between the pixel and its neighbor to
declare a boundary. It depends instead on a large difference between the
pixel and the mean of the neighboring region to declare a boundary.

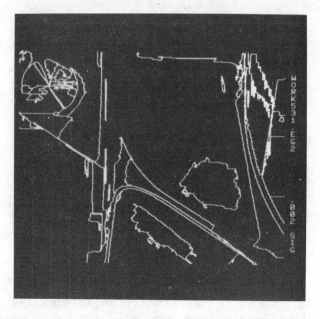

Figure B–6.   The two-pass top-down centroid segmentation of
the bulkhead image.

The combined centroid-hybrid linkage technique does the obvious
thing. Centroid linkage is only done for nonedge pixels; that is, region
growing is not permitted across edge pixels. Saying it another way, edge
pixels are not permitted to be assigned to any region and cannot link to
any region. Thus, if the parameters of centroid linkage were set so that
any difference, however large, between pixel value and region mean was
considered small enough to permit merging, the two-pass hybrid combination technique would produce a connected components of the nonedge
pixels. As the difference criterion is made more strict, the centroid linkage produces boundaries in addition to those produced by the edges.
Figure B–7 illustrates the application of the hybrid-linkage technique
to the bulkhead image.

Split-and-Merge

The split-and-merge method for segmentation begins with the entire
image as the initial segment. Then it successively splits each of its
current segments into quarters if the segment is not homogeneous
enough. Homogeneity can be easily established by determining if the
difference between the largest and smallest gray-tone intensities is small
enough. Algorithms of this type were first suggested by Robertson (1973)

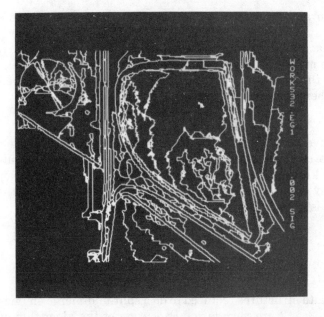

Figure B–7.   Segmentation using the one-pass combined
centroid and hybrid linkage method.

and Klinger (1973). Kettig and Landgrebe (1975) try to split all nonuni-
form 2×2 neighborhoods before beginning the region merging. Fukada
(1980) suggests successively splitting a region into quarters until the
sample variance is small enough. The efficiency of the split-and-merge
method can be increased by arbitrarily partitioning the image into
square regions of a user-selected size and then splitting these further if
they are not homogeneous.

Because segments are successively divided into quarters, the boundaries produced by the split technique tend to be squarish and slightly
artificial. Sometimes adjacent quarters coming from adjacent split segments need to be joined rather than remain separate. Horowitz and
Pavlidis (1976) suggest a split-and-merge strategy to take care of this
problem. Muerle and Allen (1968) suggest merging a pair of adjacent
regions if their gray-tone intensity distributions are similar enough.
They recommend the Kolmogorov-Smirnov test.

Chen and Pavlidis (1980) suggest using statistical tests for uniformity rather than a simple examination of the difference between the
largest and smallest gray-tone intensities in the region under consideration for splitting. The uniformity test requires that there be no significant difference between the mean of the region and each of its quarters.

The Chen and Pavlidis tests assume that the variances are equal and known.

Let each quarter have K pixels, X_{ij} be the jth pixel in the ith region, X_i be the mean of the ith quarter, and $X..$ be the grand mean of all the pixels in the four quarters. Then, for a region to be considered homogeneous, Chen and Pavlidis require that

$$|X_i - X..| \le \epsilon, \qquad i = 1, 2, 3, 4 \tag{7}$$

We give here the F-test for testing the hypothesis that the mean and variances of the quarters are identical. The value of variance is not assumed known. If we assume that the regions are independent and identically distributed normals, the optimal test is given by the statistic F, which is defined by

$$F = \frac{K \sum_{i=1}^{4}(X_{i.} - X..)^2/3}{\sum_{i=1}^{4} \sum_{k=1}^{K}(X_{ik} - X_{i.})^2/4(K - 1)} \tag{8}$$

It has a $F_{3,4(K-1)}$ distribution. If F is too high, the region is declared not uniform.

The data structures required to do a split-and-merge on images larger than 512×512 are very large. Execution of the algorithm on virtual-memory computers results in so much paging that the dominant activity may be paging rather than segmentation. Browning and Tanimoto (1982) describe a split-and-merge scheme where the split-and-merge is first accomplished on mutually exclusive subimage blocks and the resulting segments are then merged between adjacent blocks to take care of the artificial block boundaries.

B2.   Edges

IF AN IMAGE is successfully segmented into regions, the contours of the regions are available for shape analysis. However, it is sometimes more expedient to compute the contours directly from the image, rather than to go through one of the previously described segmentation processes. To compute contours directly from the image, "edge detection" must be performed. This subsection discusses the important characteristics of edges. Edge detection continues to be a subject of intense research. Elementary methods for edge detection, including the Roberts cross operator and the Sobel operator, are described in Article XIII.C4, Vol. III.

The Difficulties of Finding the Contours of Objects in an Image

What is an edge in a digital image? The first intuitive notion is that a digital edge occurs on the boundary between two pixels when the respective brightness values of the two pixels are significantly different. "Significantly different" may depend on the distribution of brightness values around each of the pixels.

We often point to a region on an image and say this region is *brighter* than its surrounding area, meaning that the mean of the brightness values of pixels inside the region is greater than the mean of the brightness values outside the region. Having noticed this, we would then say that an *edge* exists between each pair of neighboring pixels where one pixel is inside the region and the other is outside the region. Such edges are referred to as *step edges*.

Step edges are not the only kind of edge. If we scan through a region left to right observing the brightness values steadily increasing, and then after a certain point we observe that the brightness values are steadily decreasing, we are likely to say that there is an edge at the point of change from increasing to decreasing brightness values. Such edges are called *roof edges*.

Thus, in general, an *edge* is a place in an image where there appears to be a jump in brightness value or a jump in brightness value derivative.

In some sense, this summary statement about edges is quite revealing because in a discrete array of brightness values there are jumps (in the literal sense) between neighboring brightness values if the brightness values are different, even if only slightly different. Perhaps more to the heart of the matter, there exists no definition of derivative for a discrete array of brightness values. The only way to interpret jumps in value and jumps in derivatives when referring to a discrete array of values is to assume that the discrete array of values comes about as some kind of sampling of a real-valued function defined on a bounded and connected subset of the real plane R^2. The jumps in value and jumps in derivative really must refer to points of discontinuity of f and to points of discontinuity in the partial derivatives of f.

Edge finders should then regard the digital picture function as a sampling of the underlying function f, where some kind of random noise has been added to the true function values. To do this, the edge finder must assume some kind of parametric form for the underlying function f, use the sampled brightness values of the digital picture function to estimate the parameters, and finally make decisions regarding the locations of discontinuities of the underlying function and its partial derivatives based on the estimated values of the parameters.

Of course, it is impossible to determine the true locations of discontinuities in value or derivatives based on samplings of the functions. The locations are estimated by function approximation. The location of the estimated discontinuity will be where the first derivative has a relative maximum. This is where the second derivative will have a negatively shaped zero-crossing if the edge is being crossed from low value to high value. Sharp discontinuities will reveal themselves in high values for estimates of first partial derivatives. Sharp discontinuities in derivative will reveal themselves in high values for estimates of the second partial derivatives. This means that the best we can do is to assume that the first and second derivatives of any possible underlying image function have known bounds. Therefore any estimated first- or second-order partials that exceed these known bounds must be due to discontinuities in value of the underlying function. The location of the estimated discontinuity in derivative will be where the second derivative has a relative extremum and this will be where the third derivative has an appropriately shaped zero-crossing.

Recent Developments

Marr and Hildreth (1980) used for the second derivative the isotropic Laplacian. Haralick (1984) and Canny (1986) used, for the second derivative, the second directional derivative taken in a direction that extremizes the first directional derivative. The implementation of each of these zero-crossing edge operators is quite different.

Since the differentiation of a sampled signal is, properly speaking, an ill-posed problem, it has been proposed that edge detection be performed by first filtering the image (or "regularizing" it) and then differentiating it. A mathematical problem is *well-posed* in the sense of Hadamard, provided its solution exists, is unique, and depends continuously on the given data. Regularization refers to the transformation of an ill-posed problem into a well-posed one. Standard methods of regularization have been developed—see, for example, Tikhonov and Arsenin (1977)—and applied in edge detection. Details may be found in Torre and Poggio (1986). A good overview of edge detection, including a discussion of regularization, may be found in Hildreth (1987).

B3.   Stereo

Overview

The objective in many computer vision problems is to reconstruct a three-dimensional surface representation of a scene from the image information output by cameras. Video cameras provide only 2-D images, and stereo methods must be used to obtain depth information. The use of two (or more) images of the same scene, taken from different positions, can permit the determination of depth using *parallax*—the analysis of each triangle formed by some notable surface point in the scene and the two camera viewpoints. With two such images, the method of depth determination is called *binocular stereo*. With three, it is *trinocular stereo*. With more, it is sometimes called *multiple-image stereo*. For an introduction to binocular stereo, see Article XIII.D3, or see Barnard and Fischler (1987). When the scene is static but a sequence of images is taken from a moving viewpoint, *motion stereo* may be used to establish 3-D information.

The usual sequence of steps needed in binocular stereo is as follows:

1. Input images either from two cameras or from one camera at two different times and positions.

2. Determine camera parameters—position, orientation, focal length, and so on.

3. Detect/select feature points in the images that are candidates for matching (e.g., edge points).

4. Match feature points by constructing a correspondence between feature points of the two images.

5. Compute depth values at the locations of the matched feature points.

6. Interpolate depth values at all or many of the points in the image that are not locations of matched feature points.

Feature Point Detection/Selection

With a simple camera geometry we may assume that the two images of a point in the scene have a positional disparity along the x-axis of the image but not along the y-axis. To determine this disparity, using feature-based or edge-based stereo, the points must be detected in each image and then put into correspondence. Generally speaking, only certain points in the image are capable of being matched directly; these are prominent locations in the image that are easily distinguished from neighboring points. In most cases the feature points can be obtained using edge-detection methods.

A popular method for finding feature points for stereo matching requires that the Laplacian operator be applied to the image (see Volume 3, p. 211–212). Then the zero-crossing contours of the resulting image are identified. The points on the zero-crossing contours are taken as the feature points. Since the digital images have a limited number of scan lines, the number of zero-crossing points is generally manageable.

Because the disparities occur in the x direction, it is usually sufficient to perform the differentiation (or apply the Laplacian) in one dimension, along each scan line of the image. This is computationally inexpensive in comparison with two-dimensional Laplacians.

If general camera geometries are used, the feature points must be distinguishable in both the x and y directions. Although the detection of these points is therefore more computationally expensive, the resulting number of points is usually less than for one-dimensional analysis, and this can speed up the matching process. Scene points that generate good feature points with distinction in both dimensions are corners (vertices) of polyhedra and bright spots and corners of 2-D patterns painted on the surfaces of objects in the scene.

It is also possible to match areas rather than features. In area-based matching, correspondences are typically established using cross-correlation. This tends to be computationally more expensive and also less accurate than feature-based or edge-based matching. However, area-based stereo can be more robust in cases of noisy images or images with poorly defined edges.

Matching. Although matching for stereo is similar in spirit to model matching for object recognition, it is also somewhat different. In the case of horizontally constrained displacement, we have a collection of one-dimensional matching problems, one for each scan line. We can expect the disparity function along the scan line to exhibit some coherence as we move to each successive scan line, as well as along the line. Therefore the solutions to each 1-D matching problem are not completely independent.

Some of the approaches to matching are as follows:

1. Coarse-to-fine (see Marr and Poggio, 1977; and Grimson, 1985)

2. Dynamic programming (see Baker and Binford, 1981)

3. Energy minimization (see Direct Matching with Simulated Annealing, described below)

4. Ad hoc correspondence building

Interpolating Depth Values. The problem of obtaining a full set of depth values from the sparse set obtained from feature-based stereo can be solved with interpolation. However, this interpolation should satisfy both smoothness on surfaces and maintain sudden depth changes at surface boundaries. In the case of natural terrain, quadratic surface fitting may be appropriate (see Smith, 1984). For rapid interpolation subject to smoothness constraints, multigrid methods may be used (see Section D).

Direct Matching with Simulated Annealing. A method of matching a stereo pair of images using simulated annealing has been proposed by Barnard (1987). This is an area-based rather than a feature-based approach. An energy measure E is to be minimized through the adjustment of disparity values $D_{i,j}$:

$$I = \sum_{i,j} \left(|\Delta I_{ij}| + \lambda |\nabla D_{ij}| \right)$$

where $\Delta I_{ij} = I_L(i,j) - I_R(i, j + D_{ij})$; I_L and I_R are the left- and right-image intensity values; and D_{ij} is the disparity value for location (i,j). This measures the difference in intensity between each two matched points as well as the unsmoothness of the disparity function. If both of these terms are zero, the two images match perfectly, except for a translation, and the scene must be flat.

Starting from an initial high-energy state, the disparity values are adjusted stochastically according to the Metropolis algorithm (see page 576) or with an alternative method proposed by Barnard.

Nonbinocular Methods. *Trinocular stereo* employs three images of a scene to obtain 3-D surface data. The third image, taken from a viewpoint not colinear with the other two, greatly reduces the number of incorrect matches and it can increase the accuracy of the resulting depth information. A method that permits the three cameras to be in arbitrary positions is described by Ayache and Lustman (1987). One that requires the viewpoints to form a right triangle is given by Ohta et al. (1986). Others are given by Yachida et al. (1986), Ito and Ishii (1986), and Pietikainen and Harwood (1986). The number of viewpoints need not be limited to three. Multiple-image stereo allows additional improvements in accuracy at the expense of higher computational cost (see Yachida, 1985).

In addition to binocular, trinocular, and multiple-image stereo, surface orientation may be computed using two images from the same viewpoint, but taken under illumination by a light source in two different positions. This method is called *photometric stereo* and is described briefly in the Overview to Chapter XIII in Volume III of the *Handbook*. The change in shading at a surface point from one image to the other gives an indication of the surface gradient at that point. Such methods are described in Woodham (1980).

B4.   Mathematical Morphology for Image Analysis

A CLASS OF TECHNIQUES called *mathematical morphology* has found a variety of applications in industrial machine vision. This section presents the primary operations of mathematical morphology: dilation, erosion, opening, and closing. In addition to their definitions, some properties of these operations are also given.

The mathematical morphology approach to the processing of digital images is based on shape. Appropriately used, these techniques can simplify image data, preserving essential shape characteristics and eliminating irrelevancies. Since the identification of objects, features, and manufacturing defects depend closely on shape, this approach is natural for such tasks.

Although the techniques are being used in the industrial world, the basis and theory of binary morphology are not covered in many texts or monographs. Exceptions are the highly mathematical books by Matheron (1975) and Serra (1982).

The language of mathematical morphology is that of set theory. Sets in mathematical morphology represent the shapes that are manifested on binary or gray-tone images. The set of all the black pixels in a black and white image (a binary image) constitutes a complete description of the binary image. Sets in two-dimensional Euclidean space are represented by foreground regions in binary images. Sets in three-dimensional Euclidean space may actually represent time-varying binary imagery or static gray-scale imagery as well as binary solids. Sets in higher dimensional spaces may incorporate additional image information such as color, or multiple perspective imagery. Mathematical morphology transformations apply to sets of any dimensions, including those in Euclidean N-space and its discrete or digitized equivalents, the set of N-tuples of integers, Z^N. For the sake of simplicity we will refer to either of these sets as E^N.

Those points in a set being morphologically transformed are considered as the *selected set* of points, and those in the complement set are considered as not selected. Hence, morphology from this point of view is *binary* morphology. We begin our discussion with the morphological operation of dilation.

Dilation

Dilation is a morphological transformation that combines two sets using vector addition of set elements. If A and B are sets in N-space (E^N) with elements a and b, respectively, $a = (a_1, ..., a_N)$ and $b = (b_1, ..., b_N)$ being N-tuples of element coordinates, then the dilation of A by B is the set of all possible vector sums of pairs of elements, one coming from A and one coming from B. Denoting dilation by $\oplus$,

$$A \oplus B = \{c \in E^N \mid c = a + b \quad \text{for some } a \in A \text{ and } b \in B\}$$

Dilation as a set theoretic operation was proposed by Minkowski (1903) to characterize integral measures of certain open (sparse) sets. Dilation as an image-processing operation was employed by several early investigators in image processing as smoothing operations: Unger (1958), Golay (1969), and Preston (1961, 1973). Dilation as an image operator for shape extraction and estimation of image parameters was explored by Matheron (1975) and Serra (1972).

Mathematically the roles of the sets A and B are symmetric; the dilation operation is commutative because addition is commutative. Hence $A \oplus B = B \oplus A$. In practice, A and B are handled quite differently. The first operand is considered to be the image undergoing analysis, whereas the second operand, referred to as the *structuring element*, is thought of as constituting a single shape parameter of the dilation transformation.

Dilation of a set by a structuring element in the shape of a disk results in an isotropic swelling or expansion of the set. (Approximating the disk by a small square, 3×3, the expansion can be implemented as a neighborhood operation on a mesh architecture or pipelined image-processing architecture.) Some sample dilation transformations are illustrated in Figures B–8 and B–9. In Figure B–8, the upper left is the input image consisting of a cross. The lower right shows an octagonal structuring element. The upper right shows the input image dilated by the octagonal structuring element. In Figure B–9, the upper left contains the input image consisting of two objects. The upper right shows the input image dilated by the structuring element $\{(0, 0), (14, 0)\}$. The lower left shows the input image dilated by the structuring element $\{(0, 0), (0, 14)\}$. The lower right shows the input image dilated by the structuring element $\{(0, 0), (14, 0), (0, 14)\}$. This example illustrates that dilation can be viewed as the replication of a pattern. In actual use, the replicated copies of the pattern usually overlap, as in Figure B–8.

Since addition is associative, the dilation of an image A by a structuring element D, which is itself a dilation $D = B \oplus C$, can be computed as

$$A \oplus D = A \oplus (B \oplus C) = (A \oplus B) \oplus C$$

Figure B–8. Dilation by an octagonal structuring element.

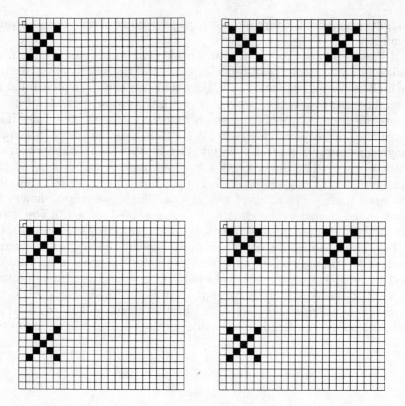

Figure B–9.   Dilation with an additional structuring element.

That is, dilation is associative. The form $(A \oplus B) \oplus C$ gives a considerable savings in number of operations to be performed when A is the image and $B \oplus C$ is the structuring element. The savings come about because a brute force dilation by $B \oplus C$ might take as many as N^2 operations, whereas first dilating A by B and then dilating the result by C could take as few as $2N$ operations, where N is the number of elements in B and in C.

The dilation of A by B can be computed as the union of translations of A by the elements of B. That is,

$$A \oplus B = \bigcup_{b \in B} (A)_b$$

Erosion

Erosion is the morphological dual to dilation. It is normally used to eliminate small protrusions on a shape or islands in an image. It can widen cracks and holes. Erosion combines two sets using vector subtraction of set elements. If A and B are sets in Euclidean N-space, the *erosion* of A by B is the set of all elements x for which $x + b \in A$ for every $b \in B$.

Let us denote the erosion of A by B as $A \ominus B$. Erosion is thus defined by

$$A \ominus B = \{x \in E^N \mid x + b \in A \quad \text{for every } b \in B\}$$

The utility of the erosion transformation is better appreciated when the erosion is expressed in a different form (that given by Matheron, 1975). The erosion of an image A by a structuring element B is the set of all elements x of E^N for which B translated to x is contained in A.

$$A \ominus B = \{x \in E^N \mid (B)_x \subseteq A\}$$

Erosion is illustrated in Figure B–10. The upper left shows the input image consisting of two blobs. The upper right shows the input image eroded by the structuring element

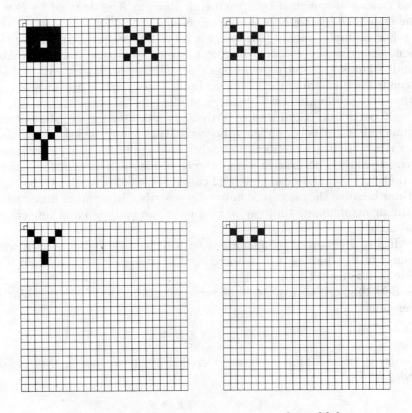

Figure B–10.   Erosion of an image of two blobs.

$$\{(0, 0), (-14, 0)\}$$

The lower left shows the input image eroded by the structuring element

$$\{(0, 0), (0, -14)\}$$

The lower right shows the input image eroded by the structuring element

$$\{(0, 0), (0, -14), (-14, 0)\}$$

Openings and Closings

In practice, dilations and erosions are usually employed in pairs, either dilation of an image followed by the erosion of the dilated result or image erosion followed by dilation. In either case, the result of iteratively applied dilations and erosions is an elimination of specific image detail smaller than the structuring element without the global geometric distortion of unsuppressed features. The *opening* of image B by structuring element K is denoted by $B \circ K$ and is defined as $B \circ K = (B \ominus K) \oplus K$. The *closing* of image B by structuring element K is denoted by $B \bullet K$ and is defined by $B \bullet K = (B \oplus K) \ominus K$.

For example, opening an image with a disk-shaped structuring element smooths the contour, breaks narrow isthmuses, and eliminates small islands and sharp peaks or capes. Closing an image with a disk-structuring element smooths the contours, fuses narrow breaks and long thin gulfs, eliminates small holes, and fills gaps on the contours.

Of particular significance is the fact that image transformations employing iteratively applied dilations and erosions are idempotent, that is, their reapplication effects no further changes to the previously transformed result. The practical importance of idempotent transformations is that they comprise complete and closed stages of image analysis algorithms because shapes can be naturally described in terms of under what structuring elements they can be opened or can be closed and yet remain the same.

If B is unchanged by opening it with K, we say that B is open with respect to K, whereas if B is unchanged by closing it with K, then B is closed with respect to K.

Sets that can be expressed as some set dilated by K are necessarily open under K.

$$A \oplus K = (A \oplus K) \circ K$$

Similarly, images that have been eroded by K are necessarily closed under K.

$$A \ominus K = (A \ominus K) \bullet K$$

From these two facts, the idempotency of opening and closing follows. Openings and closings have other properties. For example, it follows immediately from the increasing property of dilation and the increasing property of erosion that both opening and closing are increasing.

There is a nice geometric characterization to the opening operation. This characterization justifies why mathematical morphology provides material for extracting shape information from image data. The opening of A by B is the union of all translations of B that are contained in A.

Discussion

Dilation, erosion, opening, and closing can be used as the basis of image algebras. These algebras allow the definition of shape transformations that are customized for particular applications. A sequence of these operations, with suitable structuring elements, can be used to identify gear teeth in images of gears, or holes of particular sizes in images of machine parts. These techniques have been successfully applied to the problem of visually detecting shorts and open circuits in the wiring of printed circuit boards. This is illustrated schematically in Figure B–11.

Opening removes small protrusions, isthmuses and islands. Closing removes small cracks, bays, and holes. Taking the exclusive-OR of the resulting image with the original gives an image in which only potential defects remain. The original binary image is shown in the upper left. The result after erosion is in the upper center. After dilating that image, the result in the upper right is obtained. A second step of dilation takes us to the result in the lower left, and then another erosion takes us to the lower center. Exclusive-ORing this with the original produces the image of the isolated defects, shown in the lower right.

These operations can be efficiently computed with appropriate hardware. An entire session of the 1985 IEEE Computer Society Workshop on Computer Architecture for Pattern Analysis and Image Database Management was devoted to computer architecture specialized to perform morphological operations. Papers included those by McCubbrey and Lougheed (1985), Wilson (1985), Kimmel, Jaffe, Manderville, and Lavin (1985), Leonard (1985), Pratt (1985), and Haralick (1985). Gerritsen and Verbeek (1984) show how convolution followed by a table lookup operation can accomplish binary morphology operations.

Mathematical morphology is being extended to encompass more and more general classes of operators. Gray-scale extensions have been studied. Efforts have been made to cast morphology operations into a digital signal processing framework. A tutorial article presenting many more of the details of mathematical morphology is the paper by Haralick, Sternberg, and Zhuang (1987).

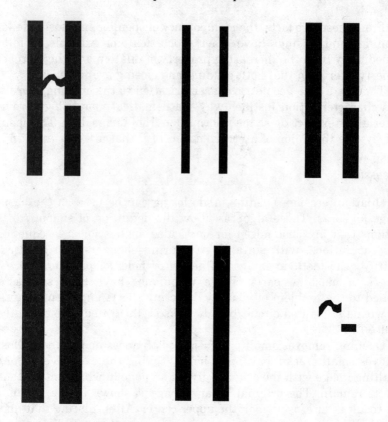

Figure B–11.   Application of opening and closing to PC board inspection.

C. COMPUTATIONAL VISION ADVANCES

C1. Shape Representation and Analysis

THE TASK FACING a computational vision system is to compute descriptions of a 3-D scene given projections of that scene into 2-D images. The current paradigm for computational vision research assumes that a system must be structured into levels or modules with various special-purpose representations at each level and that processes transform descriptions from one representation into another. Each representation serves to make explicit some properties of the image or scene and leave others implicit. The choice of a representation for each particular level constitutes the determining design decisions for a particular vision system. A wide variety of criteria enter into these choices; it is important to discover and explicate these criteria. (See Articles II.C5 and XIII.D5, 6 for discussions of earlier work.)

For vision, we can distinguish four varieties of domains that need explicit shape representation:

1. *Functions of one variable* such as those that occur in, say, examining the intensity profile across a discontinuity in an image.

2. *2-D shapes* such as the contour of an image region.

3. *Functions of two variables* such as the depth map of a visible surface that gives depth as a function of x and y.

4. *3-D shapes* such as the bounding surface of a solid object.

This section will be structured around descriptions of some advances in representation techniques for each of these domains.

C2. Criteria for Shape Representation

GIVEN THAT THE CONCEPT of "shape" is intuitive rather than formal and the fact that for any shape domain there are infinitely many possible representations of the "shape" of an object, many researchers have felt the need to explicate *adequacy criteria* for shape representations. These necessary criteria allow us to make sensible design decisions and trade-offs when choosing a "good" shape representation. Here we shall provide a set of criteria based on the current state of the art (Marr and Nishihara, 1978; Binford, 1982; Brady, 1983; Mokhtarian and Mackworth, 1986a; Mackworth, 1987; Woodham, 1987a, 1987b).

Computable: Given the input data and model assumptions, the representation should be efficiently computable on a suitable serial or parallel architecture; that is, the computational complexity should be a low-order polynomial in time, space, and number of processors.

Local: A useful representation must still be computable for portions of an object. If the parts of the representation depend only on data in a defined neighborhood of the object, it has local support. If only some of the neighborhoods are present in the data, a useful representation can still be computed for occluded or distorted objects. Also the inherent parallelism can be exploited by using special-purpose architectures that process the neighborhoods in parallel.

Stable: A small local change in the object should induce a small local change in the representation. This is required for noise resistance and shape matching.

Unique: A given object must have a unique representation. The mapping from object to representation must be a single-valued function from the object domain to the representation domain. This rules out schemes that make arbitrary choices about the mapping.

Complete: For a large and important domain of objects, the function from object to representation should be "total"; that is, for each and every object there is a corresponding representation.

Invertible: Ideally the mapping from object to representation should be invertible (also called *rich* or *information preserving*). If the object-to-representation mapping is many-to-one, different objects cannot be distinguished on the basis of their representation. Thus the mapping must be one-to-one; that is, a representation specifies a unique object. If the one-to-one mapping is computationally invertible (which it might not be even if the mathematical mapping is one-to-one), then, for example, the visual appearance of an object can be predicted from its representations.

Invariant: If a pair of 2-D or 3-D objects differ only by a rigid translation or rotation or by a magnification (a uniform change in scale), we say they have the same shape. Accordingly we require that the shape representation be *essentially* invariant under these transformations. This requirement is apparently in conflict with the requirement for invertibility; two objects seem to have the same representation. However, if this representation includes translation, rotation, and magnification parameters as components, the conflict with invertibility is resolved.

Scale-sensitive: The representation should incorporate information about the object at varying levels of detail, coarse to fine. This usually corresponds to varying the size of the "neighborhood of local support." It also contributes to the required stability and matching properties of the representation. By suppressing the fine detail in the representation, we can concentrate on the broad, overall shape features and save on storage and processing time at the expense of accuracy and the invertibility criterion.

Composite: 2-D and 3-D objects have a natural recursive part-whole composition structure that should be explicit in the representation.

Matchable: The representation should be designed to support a matching process that compares two shape descriptions (one, for example, from the image; the other, a stored prototype) and returns a description of their difference. This includes computing properties of an object using the representation. For example, we can determine whether or not an object is symmetric by matching its description with that of a generic symmetric object.

Generic: A shape representation should support the description of a generic class of objects as well as specific objects (perhaps through parameterization). Thus if the representation is invertible as well as generic, it can be used in symbolically predicting appearances.

Refinable: If the representation supports generic descriptions, they should be refinable with the acquisition of more constraints (from the image or elsewhere) to characterize a more specific object class.

These dozen criteria serve as useful tools not only for the evaluation of existing shape representations, but also for their elaboration and the discovery of new methods. We now turn to examine their applications to the four levels of object domains found in most vision systems.

Descriptions of Functions of One Variable

Suppose we wish to describe a noisy one-dimensional signal $f(x)$ in order, say, to find intensity changes. A Fourier decomposition of the signal has many desirable properties. It satisfies many of our criteria, but crucially fails to satisfy the criterion of locality: that each of the Fourier basis functions have an infinite neighborhood of support.

Suppose we want to use the description to find edges characterized by abrupt changes of intensity. If the signal has undergone significant degradation due to blurring and noise processes, an edge can be said to exist at location x and scale σ if the slope at point x and scale σ achieves a local maximum with respect to x. To make this precise, the slope at point x and scale σ can be defined to be the result of differentiating the function $F(x, \sigma)$ that arises from convolving $f(x)$ with the Gaussian $G(x, \sigma)$.

$$F(x, \sigma) = G(x, \sigma) \otimes f(x)$$
$$= \int_{-\infty}^{\infty} \frac{1}{\sigma\sqrt{2\pi}} e^{-(x-u)^2/2\sigma^2} f(u) du$$

An "edge" exists at location x and σ wherever $F_x(x, \sigma)$ reaches a maximum or minimum or where

$$F_{xx}(x, \sigma) = 0 \quad \text{and} \quad F_{xxx}(x, \sigma) \neq 0$$

This technique, introduced by Stansfield (1980) and, most effectively, by Witkin (1983), is known as *scale-space filtering*. It plays an important role in many new techniques for shape representation. The (x, σ) space, known as scale space, can be used to represent a binary image, the scale space image of $f(x)$, with a mark wherever $F_{xx}(x, \sigma) = 0$ and $F_{xxx} \neq 0$.

We note the following:

$$F_{xx}(x, \sigma) = \frac{\partial^2}{\partial x^2} [G(x, \sigma) \otimes f(x)]$$
$$= G_{xx}(x, \sigma) \otimes f(x)$$

Thus the scale space image can be computed by precomputing the masks, $G_{xx}(x, \sigma)$.

For an extensive discussion of scale-space methods with good examples, see Witkin (1987). The Gaussian is the only filter that does not create generic zero-crossings as the scale increases, and this is true in any dimension (Babaud et al., 1986, Yuille and Poggio, 1986). This key *monotonic property* means that the scale-space image of a function of one variable is hierarchically structured. In the scale-space image, the contours of $F_{xx}(x, \sigma) = 0$ only have maxima—not minima. This property allowed Witkin (1983) to define the interval tree in scale space. The "edges" whose scales exceed any given value of σ partition the x-axis into intervals. As σ is decreased from a coarse scale, new edges appear in pairs dividing the containing intervals into three subintervals.

This subdivision process continues as σ is decreased down to the finest available scale (Witkin, 1987). This *interval tree* can be used as a representation of the shape of the function that satisfies many of the criteria of Section C2. It is not as stable as one might like—small changes in the function can produce large changes in the topology of the interval tree. Surprisingly, it is invertible.

Yuille and Poggio (1984) show that the scale-space image uniquely characterizes the curve modulo a multiplicative constant and a linear additive component, but the inversion may not be "computationally well conditioned" even if the slope or strength of each zero-crossing is known (Hummel, 1986).

Mokhtarian and Mackworth (1986) show how to match scale-space images using the A* algorithm (cf. Volume I).

Clark (1987) observes that the "edges" marked in the scale-space image can be classified as "authentic edges" and "phantom edges." "Authentic edges" correspond to positive maxima and negative minima of $F_x(x, \sigma)$, whereas "phantom edges" correspond to negative maxima and positive minima of $F_x(x, \sigma)$. These can be simply discriminated based on the sign of $F_x(x, \sigma) \, F_{xxx}(x, \sigma)$. The removal of the phantom edges from the scale-space image produces a reduced scale-space image that is not as well behaved as the scale-space image.

Canny (1986) presents an edge detector that is almost optimum with respect to the tradeoff of detectability in the presence of noise and localization based on similar multiscale techniques. His operator detects local maxima in the convolution with the first derivative of a Gaussian. Deriche (1987) improves on Canny's results.

Descriptions of Two-Dimensional Shapes

An arbitrary curve in 2-D space is the simplest generalization possible beyond a function of one variable. A 2-D connected region in a binary image may be represented by the simple closed curve corresponding to the exterior boundary and zero or more closed curves corresponding to the boundaries of any holes. It is, therefore, important to have shape representations for open and closed curves that satisfy our criteria.

Many current vision systems use global 2-D shape-dependent features such as the number of holes, aspect ratio, the ratio of perimeter squared to the area, moments of inertia, and the like (Brady, 1983). Although such properties can be computed efficiently and can be used in simple industrial inspection jobs (where the lighting can be controlled and the context is narrowly limited), they are not sufficiently local, stable, invertible, scale-sensitive, composite, generic, or refinable to handle more general vision tasks such as interpreting outdoor scenes.

Brady and Asada (1984) proposed smoothed local symmetries as a representation of 2-D shape. Essentially a local symmetry exists for a pair of points A and B on a simple smooth closed curve if and only if the right bisector of the straight line joining A and B serves as an axis of symmetry for the tangents to the curve at A and B.

In Figure C–1 the point O lies on an axis of local symmetry. In theory, for all pairs of points on the curve, we compute the set of all points that lie on axes of local symmetry. Then we compute the maximal smooth loci of those points. Each locus is a candidate axis. A local symmetry constitutes a locally plausible way to describe a portion of the contour and the region it subtends, called the "cover" of that axis. Each axis whose cover is properly contained in the cover of another axis is deleted to give the final representation.

In practice, the algorithm must contend with incomplete and noisy

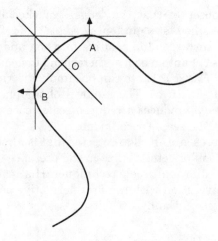

Figure C–1.   Point O lies on an axis of local symmetry.

data and so is more complicated and must be optimized for better efficiency. Brady and Asada (1984) propose placing *knots* at points of high
curvature on the bounding contour, constructing a piecewise smooth
approximation to the curve using straight lines and circles, and then
computing the smoothed local symmetries of the approximation to the
contour. Asada and Brady (1986) propose using the scale-space image of
the curvature as a function of arc length to recognize the existence of
certain primitives that embody orientation and curvature discontinuities.

The smoothed local symmetries representation is a development of
the symmetric axis transform (Blum and Nagel, 1978) and the 3-D generalized cylinder representation (see Section C3). The symmetric axis
transform is the locus of the centers of maximal circles contained within
the region. Such circles must touch the boundary at two points, at least.

Hoffman and Richards (1982) also used curvature, proposing that
knots be placed at negative minima of curvature and that a dictionary
of "codons" be used as primitives between the knots. This has the advantage of nicely explaining figure-ground reversal segmentation phenomena as occur in Rubin's Vase (see Figure C–2), for example, but it does
not satisfy the need for scale-sensitive and stable representations.

In searching for ways to generalize the scale-space transform from
functions of one variable to two-dimensional shape analysis, several
approaches are possible. We have already mentioned smoothing the
boundary curvature as a function of arc length (Asada and Brady, 1986).
Another approach would be to smooth the 2-D image of the region with
a 2-D Gaussian filter and extract the zero-crossings of the Laplacian

Figure C–2.   Rubin's Vase.

operator $(\partial^2/\partial x^2 + \partial^2/\partial y^2)$ (Marr, 1982). Unfortunately, as Yuille and Poggio (1986) show, as the scale of the filter is increased, a zero-crossing contour so obtained can split into two, or two contours can merge into one. Babaud et al. (1986) show a dumb-bell–shaped region that exhibits both these behaviors. The single initial contour splits into two as the scale increases, but as it increases still further, they merge back again into a single contour. Although the monotonic property discussed earlier holds for 2-D smoothing in the sense that no new contour can appear (without splitting off an existing contour), this behavior is nonmonotonic in the sense that the number of regions defined goes from 1 to 2 and back to 1 as σ increases. This is not satisfactory from the point of view of scale-sensitivity.

Accordingly, Mokhtarian and Mackworth (1986) propose a boundary smoothing approach. It is not appropriate to smooth $y = y(x)$ as a function of x for several reasons, one of which is simply that a smoothed version of the curve and the smoothed version of the curve rotated through $\pi/2$ would have radically different shapes, which violates our invariance criterion. They propose smoothing in a natural path-based coordinate frame. The curve is described parametrically as

$$\{(x(t), y(t))|t \in [0, 1]\}$$

where t is a linear function of path length. Then the curve is smoothed by a 1-D Gaussian kernel $G(t, \sigma)$. The resultant smoothed curve represents the original curve at coarser detail. If the original curve is closed, the smoothed curve is closed. The zeros of curvature (the inflection points) on the smoothed curves can be displayed as a map in (t, σ) space as a *generalized scale-space image* of the curve. This hierarchically structured scale-space image is a useful representation of the shape of the curve or the region contained in the curve if it is closed. Mokhtarian and Mackworth (1986) show how to use this representation to match landforms in a map and a LANDSAT satellite image using a coarse-to-fine strategy. The major disadvantage of this representation is that all simple convex curves have the same representation, the empty scale-space image, because they have no points of inflection. Compared with the alternative of smoothing the curvature function (Asada and Brady, 1986), it has the advantage of preserving the closure of closed curves (Horn and Weldon, 1986).

Horn and Weldon (1986) propose a representation called the *extended circular image* for simple, closed convex curves. This is the 2-D analog of the *extended Gaussian image* representation for convex 3-D objects (both discussed later in this article). In the extended circular image, we are given the radius of curvature R as a function of normal direction ψ. For a circle radius R, we have $R(\psi) = R$. In general, $R(\psi) = 1/\kappa(s)$, where $\kappa(s)$ is the curvature as a function of path length. The integral of the extended circular image over a range of angles is the length of the portion of the curve with a normal direction within that range. The extended circular image of a closed convex curve is unique and invertible. One may smooth a closed convex curve by convolving its extended circular image with a smoothing filter (such as the Gaussian) and inverting the result to produce a smoothed, closed convex curve. This representation has most of the properties of a good shape representation. With regard to completeness, its domain is complementary to that of Mokhtarian and Mackworth with respect to the set of all closed curves.

Descriptions of Functions of Two Variables

It is important to have good shape descriptions of single-valued functions of two variables—surfaces in 3-space. Describing the image intensity surface $I(x, y)$ and the visible surface depth map $z(x, y)$ are two examples of where this is needed. The depth map $z(x, y)$ may be an intermediate stage of description of the scene or it may be obtained directly as a *range image* from an active sensor using sonar or structured light from, say, a laser. Besl and Jain (1985) survey some recent work in the description of surfaces.

Haralick et al. (1983) survey several papers on topographical classification of digital surface features and propose a descriptive scheme based on a set of ten labels that include features such as peak, ridge, saddle, planar, and pit. At each pixel in the intensity image, the parameters of an analytical *facet model* are estimated to give the best local fit. Those parameters can then be used to determine slope, the principal directions of curvature, and the two principal curvatures that determine the pixel labels. Nackman (1984) proposes a similar scheme for segmenting surfaces based on critical points (local maxima, local minima, and saddle points).

Scale-sensitive descriptions of functions of two variables may be obtained using the 2-D scale-space approach with the drawbacks discussed in the previous section.

Recovery of the depth map $z(x, y)$ from the image intensity function $I(x, y)$ is in general an ill-posed problem (Tikhonov and Arsenin, 1977) because the solution is not unique—the imaging process is not uniquely invertible. If, however, the imaging model is simple, we can recover the "best" surface that could have produced the given image, under known illumination and imaging geometry and radiometry conditions. Suppose the image intensity at a point on the surface imaged is known to depend only on the surface gradient (p, q) (Mackworth, 1983). Then the image irradiance equation takes the form (Horn, 1986):

$$I(x, y) = R(p, q)$$

Clearly, given $I(x, y)$ on a digital grid as $I_{ij} = I(x_i, y_i)$ and the functional form of $R(p, q)$, we cannot determine $\{p_{ij}\}$ and $\{q_{ij}\}$ because they are underconstrained. The extra constraint necessary can be provided by insisting that the surface found be the one that minimizes a weighted sum of the squared error in the image irradiance equation and a quadratic measure of the smoothness of the surface (Ikeuchi and Horn, 1981). This functional essentially selects a single surface from the set of all possible surfaces. We can determine this surface by setting the partial derivatives of this functional with respect to the orientation parameters equal to zero and solving the large sparse set of linear equations by an iterative relaxation method. Terzopoulos (1986, 1987) has shown that the convergence of this process can be accelerated using multigrid relaxation methods, again demonstrating the importance of scale-sensitive descriptions. (Further details on multigrid methods are given in Section D.) Woodham (1987a) and Horn (1986) provide excellent overviews of the shape-from-shading method and the use of multiple light sources and photometric stereo (Woodham, 1980) to overconstrain the surface gradients.

Another approach to determining shape-from-X is based on fractal modeling of the surface (Pentland, 1983). If we assume that a surface has isotropic fractal characteristics, then under certain imaging assumptions the image intensity surface will also have fractal characteristics. By measuring those characteristics, we can arrive at estimates of the 3-D surface characteristics.

Another class of shape-from-X methods is shape-from-contour. The blocks world scene domain was the development ground for many of these methods as documented in Volume III of the *Handbook*. Despite the fact that most researchers abandoned the blocks world, many important theoretical and practical problems remained unsolved. Sugihara (1986) has continued to attack those problems. His book is an excellent summary of his results. It is organized around the exposition of a four-module procedure for the interpretation of line drawings as polyhedral scenes. The first module is the classical Huffman-Clowes labeling. However, Huffman-Clowes labeling may generate specious labelings that are not realizable as polyhedral scenes (Mackworth, 1977a). Accordingly, the second module determines which of the proposed labelings are realizable. This test of geometric feasibility is carried out by reducing the problem to the determination of a feasible solution to a linear programming problem. The third module allows tolerance in the definition of geometric feasibility by removing redundant constraints and "correcting" the original line drawing (moving vertices and the like). The fourth module allows the use of additional information sources such as 3-D range finding, surface shading, and texture to pick a unique scene interpretation from the infinite number of possible scenes in the equivalence class of interpretations depicted by the image.

There were at least four main open issues at the end of the first decade of blocks world research. First, procedures such as Huffman-Clowes-Waltz labeling and gradient space reasoning applied necessary but not sufficient tests for realizability (see Article XIII.B5, Vol. III). Second, it was not clear how to characterize the degrees of freedom in the scene equivalence class. Third, the computational complexity of the problems and their algorithms was not understood (see Section C4 on constraint satisfaction). Fourth, it was not known how to apply these methods to "real" images, integrating these methods with other shape-from-X methods and coping with noisy data. Sugihara has contributed substantially to the solution of each of these problems.

The old question as to whether this approach will generalize outside the blocks world must be faced. Obviously the techniques will not work on images of tea cups or clouds. But, just as with the gradient space approach, the underlying methodology does apply generally. It is a demonstration of the power of characterizing the equivalence class of scenes in terms of the constraints from the image imposed on the a priori degrees of freedom of the scene (Mackworth, 1983) and furthermore of finding a unique scene by minimizing a functional over the equivalence class. Moreover, Sugihara (1986) contributes to the theme of structure rigidity by developing the analogy between the duality principle behind gradient space structures and the corresponding duality principle behind force diagrams of rod and pin structures. These ideas will generalize far beyond the blocks world as we design and build large space frame structures on earth and beyond. The developments in Sugihara's book depend on recent advances in matroid theory, which makes them somewhat inaccessible to many readers.

Representing Three-Dimensional Shapes

As discussed in Article XIII.D6 of Volume III, three dimensional object shape representations can be vertex and edge-oriented, surface-oriented, or volume-oriented. The volume-oriented representation most commonly mentioned in vision work is the generalized cylinder. As Binford (1982) demonstrates, it satisfies many of our shape representation criteria. But note that it may not be unique—often an arbitrary choice of axis must be made. Shafer and Kanade (1983) provide a very useful categorization of generalized cones and cylinders. Brady and Asada's (1984) smoothed local symmetries can be seen as a 2-D generalized cone representation. It may be useful for accessing stored 3-D representations.

The extended Gaussian image (EGI) is an important 3-D object representation tool that has received attention recently (Horn, 1986, Chapter 16). For a convex solid object, this is an invertible shape representation. It can be derived from the needle map produced by photometric stereo or a depth map produced either by binocular stereo or by a direct depth sensor.

The extended Gaussian image of an object is defined on the unit Gaussian sphere that corresponds to the set of all possible normals on the object. For a polyhedron, the EGI is a set of impulses. Each impulse corresponds to the face with the appropriate normal. The weight of the impulse is the area of the face. Little (1983) shows how to invert the representation; he reports on an iterative algorithm that reconstructs a polyhedron, given the areas and orientations of the faces.

The EGI of a smooth convex object must be approximated by tessellating the Gaussian sphere. The weight of each facet on the sphere equals the surface area on the object for which the normals lie within the facet. Coarse-to-fine EGI representations can be constructed using successively finer tessellations. The extended circular image discussed in Section A4 is the 2-D analog of the EGI.

An interesting proposal for 3-D shape modeling is the superquadratics approach (Barr, 1981) advanced by Pentland (1986). This can be seen as an attractive alternative to the generalized cones approach. The primitives in this approach are chosen from a parameterized family of superquadric 3-D shapes. A simple superquadric is a shape described by the following equations:

$$x(\eta, \omega) = (\cos \eta)^{\epsilon_1} (\cos \omega)^{\epsilon_2}$$
$$y(\eta, \omega) = (\cos \eta)^{\epsilon_1} (\sin \omega)^{\epsilon_2}$$
$$z(\eta, \omega) = (\sin \omega)^{\epsilon_2}$$

where $(x(\eta, \omega), y(\eta, \omega), z(\eta, \omega))$ is a 3-D vector that sweeps out a surface parameterized by latitude η and longitude ω. The shape of the surface is controlled by the parameters ϵ_1, and ϵ_2. For example, if $\epsilon_1 = \epsilon_2 = 1$, the shape is a sphere. But the complete family of superquadrics also includes cubes, diamonds, pyramids, and cylinders. The complete modeling system allows these parts to be stretched, bent, twisted, and tapered, and then combined using Boolean combinations (ANDs, ORs, and NOTs) to form new prototypes that can then, recursively, be again deformed and combined with other prototypes. From the perspective of our adequacy criteria for shape representation, this proposal offers several advantages. The completeness of the domain of coverage is high, though there are still some difficulties with such things as pentagonal solids. Most other proposals such as generalized cones are essentially subsumed by superquadrics.

C3.　Object Recognition

LET US NOW REVIEW developments in the automatic recognition of objects. We refer to several important systems that focus on recognition in a "bin-picking" (factory robotics) environment. Bolles and Cain (1982) present the "local-feature-focus method" for recognizing and located 2-D possibly occluded objects. An object model consists of a graph whose vertices represent features such as corners and holes and whose edges are labeled with the distance and relative orientation of the two features related by the edge. The edge constraints help to control the matching process.

Similarly, Grimson and Lozano-Perez (1984) show how to use local measurements of 3-D positions and surface normals to identify and locate objects in a scene from a set of known objects. The objects are modeled as polyhedra with three degrees of rotational freedom and three degrees of translational freedom. The local measurements could come from a set of tactile sensors or 3-D range sensors. The measurements are assumed to have a small range of possible errors, although the normal measurements are assumed to be less reliable than the position measurements. The problem can easily be formulated as an exhaustive search problem; the trick is to reduce the search space to one of manageable size. For each object in the repertoire, the system searches an *interpretation tree*. If there are s measurements and n faces for the object, the tree has s levels and a branching factor of n at each level. The tree has, potentially, n^s leaves each corresponding to a set of assignments of the s measurements to the n faces. However, the search tree may be cut off above the leaf level using such binary constraints as:

1. *Distance constraint*—The distance between a pair of measurements must be a possible distance between the pair of faces assigned to them.

2. *Angle constraint*—The range of angles between measured normals must include the angle between the pair of faces assigned to them.

These and other constraints are used very effectively to prune the interpretation trees as early as possible. Considerable data is provided to demonstrate the power of using such local constraints to control the global object matching process.

Grimson (1986) provides careful combinatorial analysis of the efficacy of various constraints. Grimson (1987) extends the approach to the recognition of objects that can vary in parameterized ways, with parts that may have rotational, translational, scaling, and stretching degrees of freedom.

Bolles and Horaud (1986) describe 3DPO, a system for determining the 3-D position and location of parts in a jumbled bin of identical parts. It generates hypotheses about part locations using 3-D edge features extracted from range data and then matches distinctive features to confirm or refine the match.

Another successful approach to the bin-picking problem has been reported by Ikeuchi and Horn (1984) (see also Horn (1986), Chapter 18). This approach does not use direct range data, relying instead on photometric stereo (Woodham, 1980, and Article XIII.A, Vol. III). Multiple images are captured, changing the position of the light source but keeping the camera in place. These images, combined with a reflectance map model of the imaging situation and the surface reflectance, provide sufficient constraints to extract an image-registered map of surface gradients (the needle diagram).

The needle diagram can then be mapped onto a tessellated Gaussian sphere, giving an orientation histogram where each facet contains the sum of the object surface areas corresponding to that range of orientations. This is a discrete approximation to the visible half of the extended Gaussian image (Section C2). This shape representation can be matched against a stored histogram obtained from a prototype model of the part. The best match gives the attitude (but not the distance away) of the object to be picked up. The object gripper is moved out along the ray from the camera on which the object is known to lie until a proximity sensor is triggered, at which point the gripper can be oriented for the known attitude of the object. The object is then grasped and removed.

Advances in 3-D object recognition from a single intensity image beyond ACRONYM (Brooks, 1981) (*Handbook*, Article XIII.F3, Vol. III) have been reported by Goad (1983) and Lowe (1985, 1987). Goad presents an interesting view of recognition as special-purpose automatic programming. His assumption is that a program to recognize a particular object can be optimized offline for that object by considering all possible views of the object to minimize actual recognition time. Recognition is seen as a process of searching for the camera viewpoint in an object-centered coordinate system. As with Grimson and Lozano-Perez (1987), this process is seen as a tree search that matches image data to model data. In this case the matched data are lines from the image with edges in the model. The order of matching is precomputed to minimize search times. Recognition times on the order of one second are reported on a 1 MIP machine.

Lowe (1987) has also described a system, SCERPO, that can recognize and locate 3-D objects in single gray-scale images. The system first extracts edge-based features and forms perceptual groups (based on collinearity, parallelism, and proximity) that are likely to be invariant over a wide range of viewpoints. These are then matched against object structures with a probabilistic matching structure used to reduce the size of the search space. Finally, the unknown viewpoint and model parameters are determined by an iterative process of spatial correspondence based on Newton's method. Results on an image of a bin of disposable razors show robustness in the presence of occlusion and poor segmentation data.

Besl and Jain (1985) provide an extensive survey of 3-D object recognition systems and techniques with a particular emphasis on the use of range images.

C4.   Constraint Satisfaction

THE TERM "constraint satisfaction" is used both to describe a class of problems and to name a method of solving these problems. Constraint satisfaction problems have considerable importance in vision and other areas of AI (Mackworth, 1987b). We shall briefly survey the two main approaches, emphasizing some recent results. Boolean constraint satisfaction problems, as typified by Huffman-Clowes-Waltz labeling, are one main class. The other is the class of optimization problems that used to be known as probabilistic relaxation problems.

Boolean Constraint Satisfaction Problems

A Boolean constraint satisfaction problem (CSP) is specified if we have a set of variables

$$V = \{v_1, v_2, ..., v_n\}$$

and a set of Boolean constraints limiting the set of allowed values for specified subsets of the variables. Each variable takes on values in some domain. The set of solutions to the CSP is the largest subset of the Cartesian product of the domains of the n variables such that each n-tuple in the set satisfies all the given constraint relations. We may have to list or describe all the solutions, find one, or just report if the solution set contains any members—the decision problem (Mackworth, 1977b; Haralick and Shapiro, 1979).

For example, deciding if an image can be labeled using the Huffman-Clowes labels is a CSP decision problem. There the variables can correspond to the junctions, the domains to the set of possible corners allowed for each junction type, and the constraint relations to the binary constraint that the corners at each end of an edge must have the same label for the edge. Or, dually, we could set up a CSP with the variables corresponding to the edges, the domains to be the set of possible edge labels allowed, and the constraint relations to the k-ary relations corresponding to the set of possible corners allowed by each junction type.

Determining if a planar map can be colored with three colors is a Boolean CSP that is NP-complete; therefore efficient (polynomial) algorithms are unlikely to be found for the general class. Moreover, it has recently been shown that even the Huffman-Clowes labeling CSP is NP-complete (Kirousis and Papadimitriou, 1985).

Since the general problem may well require exponential time to solve, approaches have concentrated on polynomial *approximation algorithms* that enforce necessary but not sufficient conditions for the existence of a solution.

Waltz's (1975) filtering algorithm is one of the arc consistency approximation algorithms. These algorithms are members of a class of network consistency approximation algorithms (Mackworth, 1977b) further generalized by Freuder (1978). Mackworth and Freuder (1985) settled a longstanding debate by proving that Waltz's arc consistency algorithm requires time linear in the number of constraints, at most.

Although in the past it was felt that CSPs are amenable to parallel solution, Kasif (1986) showed that arc consistency is "inherently" a serial problem. Precisely, he has shown that arc consistency is log-space complete for P. (Log-space complete problems for P are those problems solvable on a single Turing machine in polynomial time.) The implication is that it is very unlikely that arc consistency can be solved in time polynomial in $\log n$ with a polynomial number of processors. This somewhat counterintuitive result can be understood better if we realize that we can set up CSPs with serial data dependencies. A local inconsistency can be discovered by one processor at a vertex, which when removed causes an inconsistency at an adjacent vertex and so on. Since this propagation is serial, all but one of the processes may be idle all the time.

Nudel (1983) has shown some tight results on expected time complexity for classes of CSP on a single processor. Mackworth, Mulder, and Havens (1985) have described a new algorithm, hierarchical arc consistency, that exploits the situation where the values within a domain can be organized hierarchically with common properties. They describe the application of the algorithm in a schema-based recognition system for maps and provide theoretical and experimental complexity results. Malik (1987) describes the application of the hierarchical approach to line labeling.

Optimization Problems

In computational vision one is often not just satisfying a set of Boolean constraints, rather one is optimizing the degree to which the solution satisfies a variety of possibly conflicting constraints: trading one constraint off against another. For example, Zucker, Hummel, and Rosenfeld (1977 and as covered in Article XIII.E4) in a curve enhancement application attach weights or "probabilities" in [0, 1] to each of nine labels (corresponding to eight compass orientations and "no line") and the relation matrices or "compatibilities" have entries in [−1, 1] that measure the extent to which two values from related domains are compatible. This scheme, known as *probabilistic relaxation*, iterates the application of a parallel updating rule, modifying the weights in each domain until a fixed point is reached or some other stopping rule applies. For an excellent overview of applications of this paradigm, see the survey by Davis and Rosenfeld (1981).

The probabilistic interpretation has problems of semantics and convergence—other interpretations are now preferred (Ullman, 1979; Hummel and Zucker, 1983). Algorithms in this class have been called *cooperative algorithms* (Julesz, 1971; Marr, 1982). Compatible values in neighboring domains can cooperatively reinforce each other while incompatible values compete, trying to suppress each other. Each value in a domain is competing against each of the other values in that domain. Cooperative algorithms are attractive because they are inherently parallel, requiring only local neighborhood communication between uniform processors that need only simple arithmetic operations and limited memory such as is available on the Connection Machine (Hillis, 1985; and Article D5 of this Chapter). These features suggest implementations for lower level perception (such as stereo vision) in artificial and biological systems (Marr, 1982; Ikeuchi and Horn, 1981; Zucker, 1983; Ackley et al., 1985; Little et al., 1987).

The design of these algorithms is best based on the minimization of a figure-of-merit. Ikeuchi and Horn (1981), as described in Section C2, carry out shape-from-shading using a figure-of-merit based on a combination of a measure of deviation from the image data and a measure of surface smoothness. The iterative relaxation solution corresponds to using *gradient descent* on the figure-of-merit, searching for the best set of orientation values for the surface elements. Note that the domains do not consist of a finite set of values each with a weight in [0, 1], but rather they consist simply of one value that is the current best estimate of the local value of the solution.

Gradient descent techniques are only guaranteed to find the global minimum of the figure-of-merit or "energy" surface if that surface is everywhere an upward concave function of the state variables of the system. In that case, there is only one local minimum and it is the global minimum. If the surface has local minima that are not the global minimum, techniques such as "simulated annealing" based on the Metropolis algorithm and the Boltzmann distribution can be used to escape local minima (Kirkpatrick et al., 1983, and Ackley et al., 1985).

Earlier, in Section C2, we described the shape-from-shading approach of Ikeuchi and Horn (1981) as an example of using regularization theory to solve an "ill-posed" problem. Regularization theory has been applied to a wide variety of early (low-level) vision problems (Poggio et al., 1985). For example, edge detection is an ill-posed problem because locating zeros of the numerical first derivative of the image is unstable; its solution does not depend continuously on the input intensities. Smoothing the image regularizes the problem, making discontinuity detection well posed (Hildreth, 1987).

Poggio, Voorhees, and Yuille (1984) and Torre and Poggio (1986) derive an optimal smoothing operator as follows. Suppose $I(x)$ is the image intensity function and $S(x)$ is the smoothed intensity function required. $S(x)$ should fit the image intensities closely and be as smooth as possible. In other words, $S(x)$ should minimize

$$\sum_{k=1}^{n} [I(x_k) - S(x_k)]^2 + \lambda \int |S''(x)|^2 dx$$

where λ is a constant controlling the tradeoff between fidelity to the image and smoothness. The solution to this minimization problem is equivalent to convolving the image with a cubic spline, which is similar to the Gaussian.

Hadamard defined a problem to be well posed if its solution exists, is unique, and depends continuously on the initial data. An ill-posed problem, one that is not well posed, fails to satisfy one or more of these conditions. A well-posed problem may, however, still be numerically ill conditioned and oversensitive to noise in the initial data (Poggio et al., 1985).

One general approach to the regularization of an ill-posed problem (Tikhonov and Arsenin, 1977) is as follows. Suppose we wish to solve the inverse problem: given $Az = y$, find z given the data y. This is solved by determining the function z that minimizes

$$\|Az - y\|^2 + \lambda \|Pz\|^2$$

where λ, the regularization parameter, controls the relative importance of the fit to the data and the degree of regularization of the solution. $\|Pz\|^2$ is the regularization criterion—usually some measure of "smoothness." Poggio, Torre, and Koch (1985) discuss the regularization of seven ill-posed problems in early vision: edge detection, optical flow, surface reconstruction, spatiotemporal reconstruction, color, shape-from-shading, and stereo. Difficulties arise when the regularization imposes a smoothness constraint on the world that may be inappropriate. They also discuss how linear analog electrical and chemical neuron-based networks could solve the minimization problems that arise in a regularization approach.

D. VISION ARCHITECTURE

Overview

In the past decade the growth of interest in parallel computing within the computer vision community has been changing the field. More and more studies of machine vision are based on or motivated by a particular computer architecture. This section discusses the most influential architectural directions, along with their relationships with computer vision.

Architecture's Influence on Algorithms. Although much research in computer vision is driven purely by the insights about vision that the research community has accumulated, some research responds directly to the possibilities that new computer architectures offer. Computing with cellular-logic processors, connection machines, and real-time video processors has a flavor sufficiently different from conventional mainframe, mini, and micro computing that it has encouraged lines of research substantially different from those of the more traditional computational vision.

Those who have programmed highly parallel machines such as the CLIP4 and the Connection Machine say that after some experience, one begins to think "in parallel" on a whole new, higher, algorithmic plane than before. There are two reasons for this. First, the highly parallel machines offer relatively high-level instructions as the conceptual building blocks for algorithm design. A typical instruction of such a machine causes two images to be added together, whereas an ordinary computer could only add two individual pixels together in one instruction (or it might even take several instructions). Therefore the programmer is encouraged to work at a higher level of abstraction than otherwise. Second, these machines perform such operations very quickly—in a matter of microseconds, rather than seconds. This means that the programmer/researcher can effectively *interact* with the system at this high level of abstraction, rather than work with it in a batch mode.

Relationship with Data Structures. Some highly parallel computers are designed specifically to support operations on certain kinds of data structures. The CLIP4 operates on images. The Connection Machine can operate on images or pointer maps. Some pipelined systems such as Aspex's PIPE operate on video data streams. Parallel pyramid machines operate on pyramid data structures (see Uhr, 1987, for accounts of several pyramid machines).

By operating on these data structures as units, many of these parallel architectures have an organizing principle built in; the data structure becomes the machine structure.

Parallelism in Vision

Although the computing community generally has been moving toward parallel processing, the case for parallelism in vision has been promoted with even greater strength. This is both because the human visual system seems to be a massively parallel system and because it is fairly obvious how images can be handled in regularly structured parallel systems (e.g., one processor per pixel). Nonetheless, parallelism can be used in vision in a significant variety of ways. A review of these will make the essential architectural alternatives clearer.

Parallel Methodologies

SIMD versus MIMD Systems. As is customary, let us divide the realm of parallel architectures into two broad groups:

1. Those in which a single program is being executed and in which at any one time all processors perform the same instruction on their own data.

2. Those in which processors follow different programs or different copies of the same program more or less independently on their own data.

In the terminology of Floyd, the first class of architectures are single-instruction-stream/multiple-data-stream (SIMD) systems, whereas the latter are multiple-instruction-stream/multiple-data-stream (MIMD) systems.

This distinction is a matter of processor autonomy; SIMD systems use many processing elements with little autonomy—they are permitted their own data but must execute programs in lockstep with one another. On the other hand, MIMD systems have highly autonomous processors that may work independently except when their programs call for communication and synchronization with other processors. In reality, many systems do not fall at one end or the other of this spectrum of processor autonomy; for example, their processors may have conditional instructions based on local conditions or they may have highly autonomous addressing capabilities. However, the SIMD-versus-MIMD distinction is very useful in examining the broad realm of parallel architectures.

In the vision community, there are vocal proponents of both SIMD and MIMD architectures. Consequently it is useful to understand the relative strengths and weaknesses of the two families.

First, we have the matter of cost. If cost were measured in the number of logic gates in a computer, we could provide more processing elements in an SIMD system than in an MIMD system for the same cost because the SIMD system's processing elements do not require program counters and instruction-decoding logic. Proponents of MIMD systems argue that the flexibility of MIMD systems allows them to be manufactured and sold in larger quantities and therefore more cheaply than the more special-purpose SIMD systems.

Second, let us consider the programming problems these architectures present. The SIMD architectures tend to be structured according to some data structure such as a two-dimensional image array, and programming them is relatively easy. Whereas an MIMD system requires the programmer to write synchronization protocols and work out load-balancing arrangements, SIMD systems obviate most synchronization, and the programmer is not normally concerned with load balancing. This is because it is impractical to map computations onto the array in a fashion that does not follow the machine's special (e.g., image) structure.

In some ways, SIMD systems execute parallel computations more efficiently than MIMD systems—there is little communication overhead between processing elements because their interactions are preprogrammed and presynchronized. Depending on the interconnection network that links the processing elements, the overhead of routing data can be very low in SIMD systems. A limitation of SIMD systems, however, is that in computations where only one or a small number of processing elements are doing meaningful work, all the others must either operate on dummy or garbage data or wait idly. In MIMD systems, processors are not constrained by the architecture to idle if other meaningful tasks are ready to execute.

Data Flow. Another way of thinking about parallel processing is in terms of the flow of data through a network of operations where the data get transformed. The nodes of a data-flow network represent points in the process where the data is operated upon. It is not necessary that each node correspond to a processor; however, at some point during the computation, each node must be assigned to some processor so that the operation(s) can actually be performed. Several data objects might flow to the same node; one operation involving several operands might take place there, or a succession of operations might be performed at the node.

Data-flow paradigms have not been used much in machine vision except to the extent that image-stream processing may be thought of as data-flow processing. However, this particular kind of data-flow paradigm is better known as *pipelining*. In the future, general data-flow techniques may be appropriate for higher level (symbolic) processing of visual information.

MIMD Systems: Butterfly, Hypercubes, RP3, Warp. Computer systems that incorporate multiple processors, each executing an instruction sequence that is independent of the others, are of interest because of their ubiquity and flexibility, especially for vision-related computations at the symbolic level (rather than the pixel level). Several prominent MIMD systems are these: the Butterfly developed by Bolt, Beranek, and Newman, Inc., the Cosmic Cube developed at the California Institute of Technology (Seitz, 1984), the RP3 developed by IBM (Pfister et al., 1985), and the Warp at Carnegie-Mellon University. Of these, the two architectures designed principally for AI/vision applications are described here in more detail.

The Butterfly architecture covers a family of MIMD parallel processor systems that can have up to 256 processors in a system (Crowther et al., 1985). Each processor has a local memory with access time of about two microseconds, but the processor can also access the local memories of all the other processors through the network, and such an access takes approximately six microseconds. The Butterfly architecture works well on problems that can be decomposed for large-grain parallel processing with only modest amounts of interprocessor communication.

The Warp computer (Annaratone et al., 1987) is a linear array of programmable processors developed at Carnegie-Mellon University. Intended primarily for computer vision, it can also be applied to signal processing and scientific computation. A ten-processor prototype became operational in 1986. Originally it was conceived of as a "systolic" system in which data would be piped through the line of processors with SIMD control. Later it was decided to make the processors autonomous, and it became an MIMD system. The processors in the linear array operate on 32-bit words, and they are interconnected with 16-bit wide data paths. The linear array is connected through an interface unit to a host (Sun-3 workstation plus additional processors).

Multicomputers with Reconfigurable Interconnections. To avoid the limitations of any particular fixed interconnection structure, "reconfigurable" systems have been proposed. At a cost of slightly more switching hardware, the data and control paths among processing elements and control units can be made programmable. The CHiP computer and the PASM are two specific systems that have been described in the literature.

A CHiP (configurable highly parallel) computer is an array of processing elements interconnected with a system of wires and programmable switches (Snyder, 1982). Because the processing elements and switches are laid out on VLSI chips in an integrated manner, it is possible to achieve SIMD cellular array efficiency (including short data paths and synchronous communication). It is also possible to embed rich nonplanar interconnection graphs in a CHiP system because the switches can also be programmed to produce long, convoluted data paths containing crossovers.

The PASM (partitionable SIMD/MIMD) system permits the set of processing elements to be grouped (under program control) and each group associated with a separate control unit (Siegel et al., 1979 and Chu et al., 1987). The effect of this is to allow PASM to contain a multiplicity of SIMD parallel programs each executing independently of (or communicating asynchronously with) the others. A number of simulations have been reported that give the predicted performance of PASM on image analysis tasks.

Neighborhood Parallelism and Pipelined Systems. Another way to organize the processing of image data for parallel computation is to treat the *neighborhood* as the atomic unit of computation. In a neighborhood-parallel, pipelined image processing system, one neighborhood (generally a 3×3 set of pixels) is processed in a single machine cycle. The image data is shifted through the neighborhood processor so that every neighborhood (of the given size) is processed in a single scan of the image. Examples of neighborhood-parallel pipelined systems include PICAP (Kruse, 1980), the Cytocomputer (Lougheed et al., 1980), and PIPE (Kent et al., 1985), among others. It has also been proposed that such systems be implemented optically (Huang et al., 1987).

Let us describe PIPE (pipelined image processing engine) in more detail. It is a commercially available system that is oriented largely toward the processing of digitized video data in real time (30 frames/ second). A PIPE consists of from three to eight "modular processing stages," each of which consists of a frame buffer, a neighborhood processing unit, and an address generator. In addition to these stages, there are an input stage, output stage, control unit, and control and data paths. Six modular processing stages and their interconnections are diagrammed in Figure D–1.

In typical operation, a stream of digitized video is passed from the input stage to the first processing stage, where a filtering operation is performed on it. By piping the image through the 3×3 neighborhood processor (which computes a single output value with the help of programmable lookup tables), the filtering is accomplished in a frame time. The result is then fed to the second stage where it is averaged with a similarly filtered picture from the video frame preceding the one on which this filtered image is based. This output is then passed to a third modular processing stage where an edge template is applied. The final outputs may be displayed or passed to a host for additional analysis. Because almost all aspects of the computation are programmable (neighborhood operators, data paths, and address generators), the programmer has substantial flexibility in designing algorithms for PIPE.

Although processing the nine points of a neighborhood in parallel can significantly speed up an image processing operation, an architecture that provides a separate processor for each pixel of an image can achieve

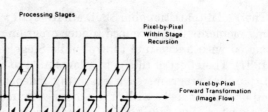

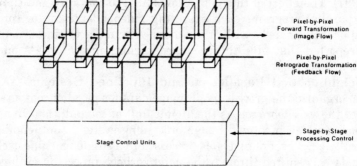

Figure D–1. Modular processing stages and data paths in
             PIPE (from Kent et al., 1985, courtesy of
             E. Kent).

much faster performance, albeit at an increased hardware cost. The
mesh-based architectures of the next section demonstrate this.

Mesh Architectures

The period 1980 to 1987 saw major advances in the realization of
massively parallel mesh-oriented processors. Notable systems in this
group include the CLIP4, MPP, and the Connection Machine.

CLIP4. The first such machine, CLIP4 (Cellular Logic Image Processor, version 4), became operational in early 1980 at the Department
of Physics and Astronomy, University College, London (Duff, 1976). The
CLIP4 consists of a 96×96 array of processing elements controlled by a
single program-interpretation unit. Each processing element (PE) of the
CLIP4 has one bit of input from each of its eight nearest neighbors. These
inputs can be masked under program control and then logically OR'ed
and further combined with Boolean data from the PE's local memory.
Thus each CLIP4 instruction performs a cellular-logic operation on an
entire 96×96 binary image in one cycle. A conventional computer would
have to perform over 10 billion operations per second to keep up with
the CLIP4 (Preston and Duff, 1984).

MPP. The Massively Parallel Processor (MPP) became operational
in 1983. Developed by Goodyear Aerospace under sponsorship of the
NASA Goddard Space Flight Center, the MPP contains a 128×128 array
of processing elements roughly comparable in power to the CLIP4 PEs.

Each PE in the MPP has a reconfigurable shift register that speeds up bit-serial arithmetic by a constant factor over the CLIP4; however, each PE in the MPP can only access a bit of data from one neighbor at a time, rather than eight at a time in CLIP4. The MPP augments the mesh with a "staging memory," which is provided to lessen the effect of the input/output bottleneck from which both the CLIP4 and the MPP suffer (Batcher, 1980). By using later technology than the CLIP4 and a larger array, the MPP achieves approximately the equivalent of one trillion operations per second on a conventional computer (Preston and Duff, 1984).

Multilevel Architectures

Mesh-based architectures are highly efficient for computing transformations of images where the output at a pixel is only a function of the local neighborhood of that pixel. However, many computer vision problems require the computation of more global and symbolic representations of an image. To make the more general kinds of computation efficient, meshes have been augmented in a variety of ways. The CLIP4 and MPP actually include a feature that lets the control unit know whether any PE has a nonzero value in its accumulator. However, this is a very minimal augmentation to a mesh.

Pyramid Machines. A relatively straightforward augmentation to a mesh is some additional meshes. Although it would be possible to build a three-dimensional mesh and thereby increase processing power and efficiency for 3-D spatial problems, such a system would still lack the capability to efficiently gather data globally from an image. An alternative is to let the additional meshes get progressively smaller, tapering to a point, thus forming a "pyramid." By connecting each PE to four "children" in the mesh below and a "parent" in the mesh above, a quadtree of interconnections is added to the mesh interconnections. The pyramid can then perform the computations of a tree machine if and when desired. For example, after some filtering operation has been applied to the image in the largest (bottom-level) mesh, the average value can be obtained by letting each PE compute the average value from its four children, until the global average emerges at the apex; the value is obtained in $O(\log N)$ time, whereas a pure mesh would require $O(N)$ time.

Pyramid machines also efficiently support multiresolution computations (Tanimoto, 1983; Rosenfeld, 1984; and Dyer, 1987) as well as hierarchical extensions to cellular logic (Tanimoto, 1984). These systems can also be thought of as specialized processors for manipulating pyramid data structures (see Article XIII.E1). Prototypes of pyramids have been constructed at the University of Washington (Tanimoto et al., 1987),

George Mason University (Schaefer et al., 1985), and are under development elsewhere (Cantoni et al., 1987). Closely related to the pyramid architecture is the mesh augmented by a tree without auxiliary meshes; an example of such a system is NON-VON, developed at Columbia University (Shaw, 1985).

Darpa Image Understanding Architecture. Another multilevel architecture based on a mesh is one developed at the University of Massachusetts (Levitan et al., 1987). This system was designed specifically for vision applications in which computation is to proceed in real-time at three levels of abstraction: the pixel (or low) level, the feature (or intermediate) level, and the symbolic (or high) level. The architecture calls for three corresponding processor levels: a mesh of 512×512 PEs, another mesh (64×64) of more powerful intermediate-level processors, and a collection of 64 LISP processors. Shared between the lowest two levels is a one-gigabyte dual-ported memory, whereas a 512-megabyte shared memory sits between the upper two levels.

The system is designed to efficiently support the algorithms developed for the VISIONS system (Riseman and Hanson, 1986), among others. A prototype is currently under development with the cooperation of Hughes Aerospace and sponsorship of the Defense Advanced Research Projects Agency.

The Connection Machine. Rather than augment a mesh with a tree or additional meshes, the Connection Machine uses a data-routing network, which is physically arranged as a hypercube. The general architecture of the system is given in Hillis (1985). The first version of the Connection Machine, the CM-1, became operational in 1986. That model allows either a 128×128 or a 256×256 array of processing elements to be installed. Each PE has 4K bits of local memory. The system operates from a 4MHz clock. The CM-2, available since the fall of 1987, uses 64K bits/PE and an 8MHz clock, plus optional floating-point hardware. The hypercube-based router of each model is 12-dimensional, with each router node responible for 16 PEs. However, the user programs data transfers as if each PE were accessible directly from any other. A good account of how the Connection Machine may be programmed for computer vision problems is given in Little et al. (1987).

Part of the inspiration for the Connection Machine was NETL (Fahlman, 1979), which is a model for a large hardware system based on a semantic-network/neural-network paradigm. Neural networks have also inspired research into a more amorphous family of information processing systems that are usually described as "connectionist."

Connectionist Architectures

The various models of computing that fall under the heading of *connectionist architectures* generally have their roots in observations of human and other biological neural systems. In addition to the influence of neurophysiology and experimental psychology, the connectionist approach benefits from a recognition of some inherent limitations of conventional computers.

The "Von Neuman bottleneck" is the principal limitation of a conventional serial computer system. There is only one processing unit, the CPU, and it can perform only one operation at a time. These operations involve only one word-sized data object at a time, and memory can be accessed directly only by using addresses (not by contents, by semantic associations, or by structure). It is true that today's serial computers can perform an operation in 100 nanoseconds. Yet these operations are comparatively simple, and those required for artificial intelligence applications are complex enough to need thousands of the elementary operations. The result is that AI applications (and especially vision applications) run very slowly on Von Neumann–style computers.

Further underscoring the limitations of the traditional serial architecture is the fact that biological systems succeed at complex tasks even though their neural computing elements run several orders of magnitude more slowly than the corresponding electronic elements. The biological "proof" that parallelism works starts with the observation that a neuron requires on the order of one millisecond to fire, whereas computer switching times are on the order of 10^{-8} seconds (10 nanoseconds). To account for the computing power and intelligence of the human brain, we are forced to rule out the speed of the neuron as the key; the speed of human perception must be due to the brain's parallel architecture, not the speed of individual computing elements.

If we could have the same massive parallelism that we have in the brain, but with electronic computing elements instead of neurons, it seems that we should be able to obtain intelligent systems with 1,000 times the power of the brain. With systems of this power, what would take a human three years to learn might take such a computer only one day to learn, if the computer could somehow be provided with an efficient enough learning environment. The hope that man will be able to improve machine intelligence by building highly parallel, highly interconnected computer systems has stimulated considerable activity in connectionist research.

General Structure of a Connectionist System. A connectionist architecture consists of a specification for an elementary processing element, called a "unit" plus a specification of the interconnections among a collection of these units.

A unit may be thought of as a processor: a computing element that takes one or more inputs, maintains a state, and may produce one or more outputs. One of the inputs may be *external*, from outside the system; whereas other inputs to the unit may be the outputs or the states of other units, which are tied to the unit by *connections*. The set of states that a unit can be in may be binary (i.e., the set {0, 1}), or it may be the set of real numbers or some interval of the reals or the integers, or it may be some other set. Many connectionist architectures use units that sum their inputs and then compare the sum with a threshold. Other systems use units that compute other, sometimes more complex, functions.

The connections among units are like the arcs of a graph; units are connected pairwise. Each connection from unit A to unit B is assigned a *weight* (or a *strength*). The weights are usually real numbers that regulate the influence that the state of one unit can have on the state of another. In some architectures, connections are constrained to be symmetric; in a symmetric-weight architecture, the connection from A to B always has the same weight as the connection from B to A.

An important aspect of some connectionist architectures is the manner in which the network changes over time. In addition to units changing state, the weights on the interconnecting arcs may change value.

Knowledge is represented in connectionist systems in different ways. In the "localist" approaches, each unit holds some knowledge. In the "wholistic" approaches, a given item of knowledge is represented as a configuration of several (and possibly all) units.

In the remainder of this section, we present several well-known types of connectionist networks and attempt to describe the manner in which they may solve problems.

The terms "connectionist architecture," "connectionist network," and "neural network" are often used interchangeably. We will often use the abbreviations "network," or "net" to refer to such a system.

Perceptrons. In the late 1950s and 1960s, a class of connectionist networks called *perceptrons* were studied (Rosenblatt, 1962). In the excitement of the day, great expectations were raised about the capabilities of perceptrons. Some negative results by Minsky and Papert (1969) triggered a backlash that subdued attention given to these systems for approximately a decade. Today there is a better understanding of perceptrons that makes it clear that many of the limitations cited by Minsky and Papert can be overcome by generalizing the model. (The introduction of "hidden units" into the networks is the key to increasing their power.)

Perceptrons have been most commonly studied as layered systems in which computations proceed bottom-up. Typically, input signals from sensors are fed up into the first layer, in which combinations of the inputs are weighted, summed, and thresholded to obtain a set of outputs from the first layer. These are subsequently weighted, summed, and thresholded in a second layer, etc., until the desired level of abstraction is reached. At that level, the inputs are classified (e.g., "Grandmother is in the picture").

Hopfield Nets. Whereas a layered perceptron typically produces each classification on a single separate output unit and therefore represents results *locally*, another approach is to represent results as global states of the network. This notion is combined with an iterative relaxation approach in the model of Hopfield (1982). In a Hopfield net, the units are started in a pattern of states that represents the input vector. Each unit then continually examines the units to which it is connected and computes a local energy function. Whenever this energy would be lowered by the unit's changing its state, it does so. Because the overall energy in the network decreases as long as there is activity, a Hopfield net must relax or converge. An analogous convergence criterion for relaxation labeling has been given by Hummel and Zucker (1983). The global state at which it converges represents the output.

Let us describe the Hopfield model more precisely. For a network of units connected symmetrically, the connection between unit i and unit j has a weight w_{ij}, which represents the extent to which the two units should attempt to be in the same state. A fixed threshold θ_i is associated with each unit. Let s_i denote the (current) state of unit i; that is, $s_i = 1$ if unit i is on, and 0 if it is off. Then the energy of the net (for a given state vector) is

$$E = - \sum_{i<j} s_i s_j w_{ij} + \sum_i s_i \theta_i$$

Each unit can compute the effect that its changing state would have on the total energy, using the formula,

$$\Delta E = E_{i_{\text{off}}} - E_{i_{\text{on}}} = \sum_j s_j w_{ij}$$

If the unit is off and ΔE is negative, it should turn on. If the unit is on and ΔE is positive, it should turn off; otherwise, it should maintain its current state.

To use a Hopfield net for pattern recognition, certain units can be designated as input units. After holding the input units in the input state until the rest of the system converges, the global state represents a local minimum configuration consistent with the input. This state may not be a global minimum.

Boltzmann Machines. To overcome the tendency of a pure Hopfield net with hidden units to become trapped in local minima that are not global minima, the transition of each unit from one state to another can be made probabilistic. By starting the relaxation at a high "temperature" in which transitions are almost completely random, and then gradually lowering the temperature so that transitions tend more and more to only reduce the system's energy, the probability of finding the global minimum can be made close to 1. This method, known as *simulated annealing*, was developed by Geman and Geman (1984) and independently with a different emphasis and name—Boltzmann machine—by Fahlman, Hinton, and Sejnowski (1983).

A Boltzmann machine is a computational system consisting of a set of elements called *units*. Each unit may be in either the 0 state or the 1 state, and it changes its state at each iteration (of a system cycle) stochastically according to the probability:

$$p_i = \frac{1}{(1 + e^{-\Delta E_i/T})}$$

where ΔE_i is the difference in energy between the 1 state and the 0 state of the ith unit, and T is a parameter analogous to temperature.

A Boltzmann machine can be thought of as a network of binary processors that use a form of the *Metropolis algorithm* (Metropolis et al., 1953) to update their states (Hinton and Sejnowski, 1987).

The Metropolis Algorithm. The Metropolis algorithm is a general procedure for finding the minimal energy state of a system by stochastically making local adjustments to it. It is a precursor of simulated annealing. The algorithm goes as follows:

Randomly select a state S.
Set $T \leftarrow$ initial temperature (high).
while $T > 0$ do
    Randomly generate an adjustment yielding state S'.
    Compute the energy difference: $\Delta E \leftarrow E(S') - E(S)$.
    If $\Delta E \leq 0$ then accept the state change: $S \leftarrow S'$.
        else accept it anyway with probability P:
        $P \leftarrow e^{-\Delta E/T}$.
        $x \leftarrow$ random number in [0,1].
        If $x < P$ then $S \leftarrow S'$.
    If there has been no significant decrease in E for many iterations
    then lower the temperature T.

An important element of such a procedure is the *temperature schedule*, which controls the gradual lowering of the temperature from one iteration to the next. Geman and Geman (1984) suggest the following schedule, where k is the iteration number and C is an appropriate energy constant:

$$T = C/\log(1 + k)$$

Clearly, in early iterations, when T is large, the system energy is permitted to increase often, thus allowing the system to escape from local minima. As T approaches zero, the system energy decreases almost monotonically; then the system "freezes" at a local minimum that is very likely to be the global minimum.

Application to Figure/Ground Discrimination. To illustrate how a stochastic-relaxation approach (which is based on a neural-network model) can solve problems in machine vision, an example is presented in which a figure/ground discrimination must be made. As demonstrated in Kienker et al. (1986) and in Hinton and Sejnowski (1987), a parallel system can efficiently solve this problem even when the input information is noisy and incomplete.

A classical problem of visual perception is to take a binary (black and white) image and decide whether the black regions are figure and white regions background, or vice versa. The chalice of Rubin (Rubin's vase) is a particularly ambiguous case (see Figure C–2). The problem is just as difficult or more difficult when the black/white information is gone and only edge information is available.

Let us consider an array such as that shown in Figure D–2. Each square or triangle in the figure represents one unit. Each unit is connected to those immediately adjacent to it. The square units may be thought of as small regions, and the triangles represent oriented edges. A triangle that is on (white) corresponds to a strong edge, whereas one that is off indicates the lack of the corresponding edge. If a square is on, it is interpreted as belonging to the figure; otherwise, it is taken to be background.

The connections among units embody constraints about what constitutes a reasonable figure/ground interpretation. The weights are symmetric and isotropic (equivalent under 90-degree rotations). A square is connected to each of its eight nearest neighbors with weight +10. The

Figure D–2.   Cell array for figure/ground resolution, showing (a) excitatory and inhibitory connections to a square (shaded), and (b) excitatory and inhibitory connections to a triangle (also shaded) Diagram after Sejnowski and Hinton (1987).

weight between a triangle and the square A it points to is $+12$, whereas for the one B that it points away from the value is -12. For each of the two squares on either side of A the weight with the triangle is $+10$, whereas for those on either side of B the weight is -10. The weight between an adjacent pair of triangles (facing in opposite directions) is strongly inhibitory (-15).

The input to the algorithm is an initial assignment of values to each unit. The inputs to the triangles represent the strengths of edges in an image, and they are called "bottom-up" inputs since they depend on the image data. On the other hand, the figure units are given initial weights "top-down" from an imaginary process that controls the focus of attention.

In the example shown, the edge elements bordering on a 9×6 rectangle were given initial inputs of 60; since those with values over 41 are shown in Figure D–3, this rectangle is visible. The top-down inputs to the figure units were given values according to a Gaussian distribution centered on the unit just to the right of the rectangle's center. The figure units shown are those with values exceeding 1.

Applying simulated annealing to this network, Kienker et al. (1986) found that it consistently converged on the desired solution. Figure D–4 shows their results. Although the method provides a useful demonstration of cooperative computation with simulated annealing, it breaks down on more complicated shapes such as spirals, unless a very long annealing schedule is adopted. However, figure/ground distinctions are also difficult for humans to make in cases of highly convoluted shapes like spirals.

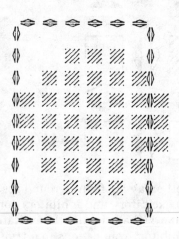

Figure D–3.   Display of initial input values for the figure/ ground problem. (Courtesy of T. Sejnowski.)

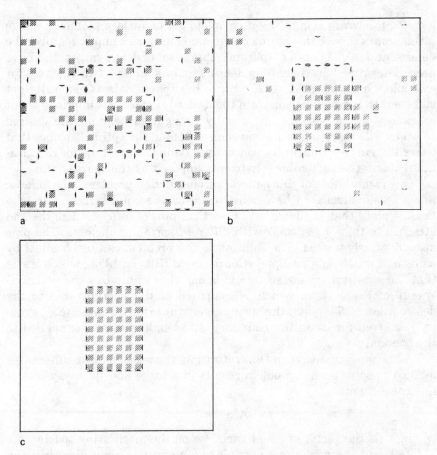

a

b

c

Figure D–4. Stages in the simulated annealing of the figure/ground problem: (*a*) after three iterations and $T = 16.2$, (*b*) after ten iterations and $T = 7.7$, and (*c*) after 28 iterations and $T = 3.3$. (Courtesy of T. Sejnowski.)

Multigrid Algorithms. Over the past decade it has been found that certain vision problems require the solution of two-dimensional numerical constraint satisfaction or optimization problems. Traditional numerical algorithms for these problems are computationally expensive. However, a class of numerical techniques called *multigrid* methods has been brought to the attention of the vision community by Terzopoulos (1984a). These methods make the solution of certain field reconstruction problems computationally much more attractive than they otherwise would be.

As noted in the preceding pages of this chapter, several vision problems boil down to computing a complete set of surface points or image pixels from sparse data. Stereo image analysis, for example, requires the determination of a depth map from a sparse set of depth values that have been determined by matching feature points in the two images (for example, Grimson, 1981, 1985). Since the sparse data is generally not sufficient to completely constrain the desired surface, assumptions about continuity of the surface are usually brought to bear on the desired solution. The resulting problem is one of finding the optimal surface that obeys the surface continuity constraints (which may allow for discontinuities) and the particular constraints imposed by the sparse data.

One formulation of this general reconstruction problem is as follows: imagine the surface to be reconstructed as the equilibrium state of a flexible plate that is supported by vertical pins of different lengths and attached to them by springs with different spring coefficients. The pins are irregularly spaced. The solution to the problem can be obtained by using a "variational principle" (Courant and Hilbert, 1953), which states that the equilibrium surface $u(x,y)$ is one that minimizes the potential energy of the system, which is composed of the energies due to the deformation of the plate, the springs, general external forces (e.g., gravity), external forces on the boundary, and bending moments applied to the boundary.

After approximation and discretization, the use of a finite-differences method to solve such a problem results in a large and sparse system of linear equations,

$$\mathbf{A}^h \mathbf{u}^h = \mathbf{f}^h$$

where $\mathbf{u}^h$ is the vector of nodal variables on the mesh using spacing h.

Although it is sometimes possible to solve such systems directly using Gaussian elimination or other methods to obtain an exact solution (up to machine precision), direct methods are more often than not inapplicable to realistic problems. For these cases, iterative techniques are required. Conventional iterative methods such as the Jacobi and Gauss-Seidel iterations continually update their current approximation, normally converging on the solution. Such convergence, however, is slow. On the other hand, multigrid methods perform their iterations at different levels of resolution in such a way as to accelerate the convergence.

The reason that the Jacobi and Gauss-Seidel methods converge slowly (when they converge) is that each local updating operation works on the neighborhood of a point in the mesh. Consequently excess energy or a deficiency of energy in the current approximation can move only one grid unit per iteration. This means that although high frequency components of the error surface can be damped rapidly, the low frequency portions require many iterations for their attenuation.

Multigrid relaxation achieves its acceleration of convergence by allowing the low frequency components of the error surface to move rapidly across the space at coarse resolution levels. As in a pyramid data structure, a single neighborhood at a coarse level covers a large area in the finest level. Once a coarse level solution has been found, it can be projected into the next finer level as the starting approximation for a relaxation at that level.

Although the most obvious approach to multilevel relaxation (performing a sequence of conventional relaxation operations starting at a coarse level and progressing to the finest level) improves on unilevel relaxation, the best results are obtained by a more complex schedule of relaxation steps at different levels. Such schedules are discussed in Briggs (1987), and Hackbusch and Trottenberg (1982). One schedule is that implicit in the following two procedures adapted from Terzopoulos (1986):

> procedure FullMultiGrid
> $\mathbf{u}^{h_s} \leftarrow$ SOLVE$(s, \mathbf{u}^{h_s}, \mathbf{f}^{h_s})$;
> for $l \leftarrow s + 1$ to L do
> $\mathbf{v}^{h_l} \leftarrow$ EXPAND$(\mathbf{u}^{h_{l-1}})$;
>   MultiGrid$(l, \mathbf{v}^{h_l}, \mathbf{f}^{h_l})$;
>
> procedure MultiGrid
>   if $l = s$ then $\mathbf{u} \leftarrow$ SOLVE$(s, \mathbf{u}, \mathbf{g})$
>   else
>   for $i \leftarrow 1$ to n_1 do
>   RELAX$(l, \mathbf{u}, \mathbf{g})$;
> $\mathbf{v} \leftarrow$ REDUCE$(\mathbf{u})$;
> $\mathbf{d} \leftarrow \mathbf{A}^{h_{l-1}}\mathbf{v} +$ REDUCE$(g - \mathbf{A}^{h_l}\mathbf{u})$;
>   for $i \leftarrow 1$ to n_2 do MultiGrid$(l - 1, \mathbf{v}, \mathbf{d})$;
> $\mathbf{u} \leftarrow \mathbf{u} +$ EXPAND$(\mathbf{v} -$ REDUCE$(\mathbf{u}))$
>   for $i \leftarrow 1$ to n_3 do $\mathbf{u} \leftarrow$ RELAX$(l, \mathbf{u}, \mathbf{g})$

Here SOLVE applies unilevel relaxation long enough to achieve some desired degree of accuracy. RELAX applies a single unilevel iteration of the relaxation. The parameters n_1, n_2, and n_3 are set to obtain the best performance for a given class of problems. The coarsest level (or "starting" level) is indexed by s, and L is the index of the finest level. The vector $\mathbf{u}^{h_s}$ holds the approximation to the solution at the starting level. Vectors $\mathbf{u}$, and $\mathbf{v}$ hold current approximations at any level, with $\mathbf{v}$ one level coarser than $\mathbf{u}$ at any particular time. The matrices $\mathbf{A}^{h_l}$ and $\mathbf{A}^{h_{l-1}}$ represent versions of the original matrix $\mathbf{A}^h$ at resolution levels l and $l - 1$, respectively.

The function EXPAND(u) takes a current approximation at level $l - 1$ and produces an approximation at level l by using bilinear interpolation. Thus it maps data from one grid to the next finer grid.

Similarly, the function REDUCE(u) takes the approximation at level

l and produces a reduced-resolution version of it at level $l - 1$ using simple injection.

Multigrid methods have been applied by Terzopoulos to a variety of visual reconstruction problems including reconstruction of geometric surfaces, depth maps from stereo, lightness, and optical flow fields. The computational savings over unilevel relaxation were found to be quite significant; typically the time required for the multigrid approach was only two percent of that used by the non-multigrid method.

For addition information on multigrid algorithms see Terzopoulos (1986, 1984a), the tutorial by Briggs (1987), the collection of papers edited into a book by Hackbusch and Trottenberg (1982), and the seminal paper of Brandt (1977). For related work on relaxation in computer vision, see Article XIII.E4, and Glazer (1984).

Bibliography

List of Abbreviations

AAAI	American Association for Artificial Intelligence
ACM	Association for Computing Machinery
AFIPS	American Federation of Information Processing Societies
AMS	American Mathematical Society
CACM	Communications of the Association for Computing Machinery
IEEE	Institute for Electrical and Electronic Engineers
IJCAI	International Joint Conferences on AI
IJCPR	International Joint Conferences on Pattern Recognition
IRE WESCON	Western Conference of the Institute for Radio Engineers
SIGART	ACM Special Interest Group on AI
SIGPLAN	ACM Special Interest Group on Programming Languages
SPIE	Society of Photo-Optical Instrumentation Engineers
TINLAP	Workshops on Theoretical Issues in Natural Language Processing

BIBLIOGRAPHY

AALPS. 1985. SRI: AI and the military. *The Artificial Intelligence Report.* 2(1): 6–7.

Ackley, D. H., Hinton, G. E., and Sejnowski, T. J. 1985. A learning algorithm for Boltzmann machines. *Cognitive Science* 9:147–169.

Adelsberger, H. H., Pooch, U. W., Shannon, R. E., and Williams, G. N. 1986. Rule based object-oriented simulation systems. Society for Computer Simulation, Simulation Series 17(1): 107–111.

Adelson, B. and Soloway, E. 1985. The role of domain experience in software design, *IEEE Transactions on Software Engineering*: 11(11)1351–1360.

Agresti, W. W. 1986. *Tutorial on new paradigms for software development.* Washington, D.C.: IEEE Computer Society Press.

Aiello, N. 1983. A comparative study of control strategies for expert systems: AGE implementation of three variations of PUFF. *Proceedings of the National Conference on Artificial Intelligence*, 1–4.

Aiello, N. 1986. *User-directed control of parallelism: The CAGE system.* Technical Report KSL Report 86-31, Knowledge Systems Laboratory, Computer Science Department, Stanford University.

Aiello, N., Bock C., Nii, H. P., and White, W. C. 1981. *AGE reference manual.* Heuristic Programming Project, Stanford University.

Allen, J. F. 1979. *A plan-based approach to speech act recognition.* Ph.D. thesis, University of Toronto.

Allen, J. F. 1984. Towards a general theory of action and time. *Artificial Intelligence* 23(2):123–154.

Allen, J. F. 1987. *Natural language understanding.* Menlo Park, Calif.: Benjamin/ Cummings.

Allen, J. F., and Koomen, J. A. 1983. Planning using a temporal world model. *Proceedings of the Eighth International Joint Conference on Artificial Intelligence,* Karlsruhe, West Germany.

Allen, J. F., and Perrault, C. R. 1980. Analyzing intention in utterances. *Artificial Intelligence* 15 (3):143–178 (reprinted in RNLP).

American Association for Artificial Intelligence. 1989. *Proceedings of the conference on innovative applications of artificial intelligence.* Stanford University, March 28–30, Menlo Park, Calif.

Annaratone, M., Arnould, E., Gross, T., Kung, H. T., Lam, M., Menzilcioglu, O., and Webb, J. A. 1987. The Warp computer: Architecture, implementation, and performance. *IEEE Transactions on Computers* C-36(12):1523–1538.

Appelt, D. E. 1982. *Planning natural language utterances to satisfy multiple goals.* Technical Note 259, SRI International, Menlo Park, Calif.

Aragones, J. K., and Bonisonne, P. P. 1985. LOTTA: An object-based simulator for reasoning in antagonistic situations. General Electric Corporated Research and Development.

Arkin, R. C., Riseman, E. M., and Hanson, A. R. 1987. ArRA: An architecture for vision-based robot navigation. *Proceedings of the DARPA Image Understanding Workshop*, Los Angeles, Calif., 17–431.

Arthur Anderson & Co. Cell design aid. Artificial Intelligence Series.

Arthur, L. J. 1988. *Software evolution: The software maintenance challenge*. New York: Wiley, 1–13.

Asada, H., and Brady, J. M. 1986. The curvature primal sketch. *IEEE Transactions on Pattern Analysis and Machine Intelligence* PAMI–8:2–14.

Asano, T., and Yokoya, N. 1981. Image segmentation schema for low-level computer vision. *Pattern Recognition* 14:267–273.

Ayache, N., and Lustman, F. 1987. Fast and reliable passive trinocular stereovision. *Proceedings of the First International Conference on Computer Vision*, London, England, 422–427.

Babaud, J., Witkin, A. P., Baudin, M., and Duda, R. O. 1986. The uniqueness of the Gaussian kernel for scale-space filtering. *IEEE Transactions on Pattern Analysis and Machine Intelligence* PAMI–8:15–25.

Baker, D. N., Lambert, J. R., and McKinion, J. M. 1983. S.C. Agric. Exp. Stn. Tech. Bull. 1089.

Baker, H., and Binford, T. O. 1981. Depth from edge and intensity based stereo. *Proceedings of the Seventh International Joint Conference on Artificial Intelligence*, Vancouver B.C., 631–636.

Balzer, R. 1985. A 15 Year Perspective on automatic programming. *IEEE Transactions on Software Engineering* (SE-11)11:1257–1267.

Balzer, R. 1985. Automated enhancement of knowledge representations. *Proceedings of the Ninth International Joint Conference on Artificial Intelligence*, Los Angeles, Calif., 203–207.

Balzer, R., Cheatham, T. E., and Green, C. 1983. Software Technology in the 1990s: Using a New Paradigm. *IEEE Computer* 16(11):39–45.

Barnard, S. T. 1987. Stereo matching by hierarchical microcanonical annealing. Technical Note No. 414, SRI International, Menlo Park, Calif.

Barnard, S. T., and Fischler, M. A. 1987. Stereo vision. In S. Shapiro (Ed.), *The encyclopedia of artificial intelligence*. New York: Wiley, 1083–1090.

Barr, A. 1981. Superquadrics and angle-preserving transformations. *IEEE Computer Graphics and Applications* 1:1–20.

Barr, A., Cohen, P. R., and Feigenbaum, E. A. 1981. *Handbook of artificial intelligence, Volumes I–III*. Reading, Mass.: Addison-Wesley.

Barstow, D. 1988. Automatic Programming for Streams II: Transformational Implementation. *Proceedings of the Tenth International Conference on Software Engineering*, Singapore.

Barstow, D. 1984. A perspective on automatic programming. *AI Magazine* 5(1):5–27.

Barstow, D. 1985. Domain-specific automatic programming. *IEEE Transactions on Software Engineering*, SE-11(11): 1321–1336.

Barstow, David R. 1979. An experiment in knowledge-based automatic programming. *Artificial Intelligence Journal* 12(2):73–119.

Barth, P., Gutery, S., and Barstow, D. 1985. The Stream Machine: a data flow architecture for real-time applications. *Proceedings of the Eighth International Conference on Software Engineering*, London, England, 103–110.

Batcher, K. E. 1980. Design of a massively parallel processor. *IEEE Transactions on Computers* C-29:836–840.

Bates, M. 1978. The theory and practice of augmented transition networks. In L. Bloc (Ed.), *Natural language communication with computers*. New York: Springer.

Benda, M., Jagannathan, V., and Dodhiawalla, R. 1985. *On optimal cooperation of knowledge sources*. Technical Report BCS-G2010-28, Boeing AI Center, Boeing Computer Services, Bellevue, Wash.

Berleant, D., and Kuipers, B. 1988. Using incomplete quantitative knowledge in qualitative reasoning. *Proceedings of the Seventh National Conference on Artificial Intelligence*: 324–329.

Besl, P. J., and Jain, R. C. 1985. Three-dimensional object recognition. *ACM Computing Surveys* 17(1):75–145.

Biggerstaff, T. J., and Perlis, A. J. (Eds.) 1989. *Software Reusability, Vol. 1: Concepts and Models*. Reading, MA: Addison-Wesley Publishing Company.

Biggerstaff,T. J., Hoskins, J., and Webster, D. 1989. *Design Recovery for Reuse and Maintenance*. MCC Technical Report, STP-378-88.

Binford, T. O. 1982. Survey of model-based image analysis systems. *International Journal of Robotics Research* 1(1):18–64.

Birnbaum, L., and Selfridge, M. 1981. Conceptual analysis of natural language. In R. Schank and C. Riesbeck (Eds.), *Inside computer understanding*. Hillsdale, N.J.: Lawrence Erlbaum.

Birtwistle, G. M., Dahl, O. J., Myhrhaug, B., and Nygaard, K. 1968. SIMULA BEGIN, Studentliteratur, Lund, Sweden.

Bisiani, R. 1986. A software and hardware environment for developing AI applications on parallel processors. *Proceedings of the National Conference on Artificial Intelligence*, Philadelphia, 742–747.

Blakemore, J. W., Dolins, S. B., and Thrift, P. 1986. A general purpose robotic vehicle simulator. Society for Computer Simulation, Simulation Series 18(1): 151–161.

Bliss, D. R. 1979. Analysis of the dynamic behavior of the tryptophone operon of escherichia coli: The functional significance of feedback inhibition. Ph.D. Thesis, Dept. of Biology, University of California at Riverside.

Blum, H., and Nagel, R. N. 1978. Shape description using weighted symmetric axis transforms. *Pattern Recognition* 10:167–180.

Bobrow, D. G. (Ed.) 1980. *Artificial intelligence (Special Issue on Nonmonotonic Logic)* 13:1–1–2.

Bobrow, D. G. 1984. Qualitative reasoning about physical systems: An introduction. *Artificial Intelligence* 24:1–5.

Bobrow, D. G., and Stefik, M. J. 1986. Perspectives on Artificial Intelligence Programming. *Science* 231:951–957.

Boehm, B. W. 1986. A spiral model of software development and enhancement. *ACM SIGSOFT Software Eng. Notes* 11(4):22–42.

Boehm, B. W. 1981. *Software engineering economics*. Englewood: Prentice Hall.

Bolles, R. C., and Cain, R. A. 1982. Recognizing and locating partially visible objects: The local-feature-focus method. *International Journal of Robotics Research* 1(3):57–82.

Bolles, R. C., and Horaud, P. 1986. 3DPO: A three-dimensional part orientation system. *International Journal of Robotics Research* 5(3):3–26.

Bond, A. H., and Gasser, L. 1988. *Readings in distributed artificial intelligence*. San Mateo, Calif.: Morgan Kaufmann.

Borgida, A., Greenspan, S., and Mylopoulos, J. 1985. Knowledge representation as the basis for requirements specifications. *IEEE Computer*, 18(4):82–90.

Brady, J. M. 1983. Criteria for representations of shape. In J. Beck, B. Hope, and A. Rosenfeld (Eds.), *Human and machine vision*. New York: Academic Press.

Brady, J. M., and Asada, H. 1984. Smoothed local symmetries and their implementation. In *Proceedings of the First International Symposium on Robotics Research*. Cambridge, Mass.: MIT Press, 331–354.

Brandt, A. 1977. Multi-level adaptive solutions to boundary value problems. *Mathematics of Computation* 31:333–390.

Briggs, W. L. 1987. *A multigrid tutorial*. Philadelphia, Penn.: Society for Industrial and Applied Mathematics.

Brinkley, J. F., Buchanan, B. G., Altman, R. B., Duncan, B. S., and Cornelius, C. W. 1987. *A heuristic refinement for spatial constraint satisfaction problems*. Technical Report KSL-87-05, Knowledge Systems Laboratory, Computer Science Department, Stanford University.

Brodie, M. L., Mylopoulos, J., and Schmidt, J. W. (Eds.), 1984. *On conceptual modeling: Perspectives from Artificial Intelligence*. New York: Springer-Verlag.

Brooks, F. P., Jr. 1982. *The mythical man-month*. Reading, Mass.: Addison-Wesley.

Brooks, R. A. 1981. Symbolic reasoning among 3-D models and 2-D images. *Artificial Intelligence* 17:285–348.

Brown, C. M. 1984. Computer vision and natural constraints. *Science* 224(4655):1299–1305.

Brown, H., Buckman, J. et al. 1982. *Final report on HANNIBAL*. Technical Report, ESL, Inc. Internal document.

Brown, H., Tong, C., and Foyster, G. 1983. Palladio: An exploratory environment for circuit design. *IEEE Computer*, 41–56.

Brown, J. S., and Burton, R. R. 1978. A paradigmatic example of an artificially intelligent instructional system, *Int'l. J. of Man-Machine Studies* 10:323–339.

Brown, T., Alexander, S. M., Jagannathan, V., and Kirchner, R. 1985. Demonstration of an expert system for manufacturing process control. In G. Birtwistle (Ed.), *Artificial intelligence, graphics, and simulation*. The Society for Computer Simulation, 110–113.

Browning, J. D., and Tanimoto, S. L. 1982. Segmentation of pictures into regions with a tile-by-tile method. *Pattern Recognition* 15:1–10.

Brownston, L., Farrel, R., Kant, E., and Martin, N. 1985. *Programming expert systems in OPS5*. Reading, Mass.: Addison-Wesley.

Broy, Manfred, and Pepper, P. 1981. Program development as a formal activity. *IEEE Transactions on Software Engineering* SE-7(1):14–22.

Brutlag, D. 1987a. Symbolic simulation of DNA metabolism. Proposal, Department of Biochemistry, Stanford University.

Brutlag, D. 1987b. Expert system simulations as active learning environments. Proposal, Department of Biochemistry, Stanford University.

Bryan, M. 1987. Predicting the future proves easy with forecast pro planner. *PC Week*.

Bryant, J. 1979. On the clustering of multidimensional pictorial data. *Pattern Recognition* 11:115–125.

Buchanan, B. G. 1986. Expert systems: Working systems and the research literature. *Expert Systems* 3(1):32–51.

Buchanan, B. G. 1988. Artificial intelligence as an experimental science. In J. H. Fetzer (Ed.), *Aspects of artificial intelligence*. Amsterdam: D. Reidel.

Buchanan, B. G., and Shortliffe, E. H. 1984. *Rule-based expert systems: The MYCIN experiments of the Stanford heuristic programming project*. Reading, Mass.: Addison-Wesley.

Bundy, A. (Ed.) 1986. *Catalogue of artificial intelligence tools*. New York: Springer-Verlag.

Bundy, A. A., and van Harmelen, A. F. 1988. Experiments with proof plans for induction, Report UK-EDNB-DAI-413, University of Edinburgh.

Burstall, R. M., and Darlington, J. 1977. A transformation system for developing recursive programs. *JACM* 24(1):44–67.

Bylander, T. 1987. *Using consolidation for reasoning about devices*. Technical Report, Laboratory for Artificial Intelligence Research, Department of Computer and Information Science, Ohio State University.

Cammarata, S., McArthur, D., and Steeb, R. 1983. Strategies of cooperation in distributed problem solving. *Proceedings of the Eighth International Joint Conference on Artificial Intelligence*, Karlsruhe, West Germany, 767–770.

Canny, J. F. 1986. Finding edges and lines in images. MIT Artificial Intelligence Lab., Tech. Rep. 720, Cambridge, Mass.

Cantoni, V., and Levialdi, S. 1987. PAPIA: A case history. In L. Uhr (Ed.), *Parallel computer vision*. Orlando, Fla.: Academic Press, 3–13.

Carberry, S. 1983. Tracking user goals in an information-seeking environment. *Proc. AAAI*. Washington, 59–63.

Carbonell, J. G. 1983. Derivational analogy and its role in problem solving. *Proceedings of the National Association for Artificial Intelligence*, 64–69.

Carbonell, J. G. 1986. Derivational analogy: A theory of reconstructive problem solving and expertise acquisition. In R. Michalski, J. Carbonell, T. Mitchell, Eds., *In machine learning: An artificial intelligence approach*, Volume II, Los Altos, Calif.: Morgan Kaufmann, 371–392.

Cellier, F. E., and Zeigler, B. P. 1987. AI's role in control of systems: Structural and behavioral knowledge. *Proceedings of the Second European Simulation Multiconference*, Vienna, Austria, 165–171.

Chandrasekaran, B. 1986. Generic tasks in knowledge-based reasoning: High-level building blocks for expert system design. *IEEE Expert* 1(3):23–30.

Chang, E. 1987. Participant systems. In M. N. Huhns (Ed.), *Distributed artificial intelligence*. New York: Pitman, 311–339.

Cheatham, T. E. 1984. Reusability through program transformations. *IEEE Transactions on Software Engineering* 10:5, 589–594, (reprinted in Readings in Artificial Intelligence and Software Engineering).

Chen, P. C., and Pavlidis, T. 1980. Image segmentation as an estimation problem. *Computer Graphics and Image Processing* 12:153–172.

Chomsky, N. 1956. Three models for the description of language. *IRE Transactions PGIT* 2:113–124.

Chu, H., Delp, E. J., and Siegel, H. J. 1987. Image understanding on PASM: A user's perspective. *Proceedings of the Second International Conference on Supercomputing*, May, 440–449.

Clancey, W. J. 1983. The epistemology of a rule-based expert system—A framework for explanation. *Artificial Intelligence* 20.

Clancey, W. J. 1985. *Heuristic classification*. Technical Report KSL-85-5, Knowledge Systems Laboratory, Computer Science Department, Stanford University.

Clancey, W. J. 1985. Heuristic classification. *Artificial Intelligence* 27(3):289–350.

Clancey, W. J. 1986. From GUIDON to NEOMYCIN and HERACLES in twenty short lessons: ONR final report 1979–1985. *AI Magazine* 7(3)40–60, 187.

Clark, J. J. 1987. Singularities of contrast functions in scale space. *Proceedings of the First International Conference on Computer Vision*, London, England, 491–495.

Clearwater, S. and Engelmore, R. Expert systems in particle beam line analysis. Unpublished manuscript, Knowledge Systems Laboratory, Stanford University.

Cleary, J., Goh, K., and Unger, B. 1985. Discrete event simulation in Prolog. In G. Birtwistle (Ed.), *Artificial intelligence, graphics, and simulation*. The Society for Computer Simulation, 8–13.

Cline, T., Fong, W., and Rosenberg, S. 1985. *An expert advisor for photolithography*. Technical Report, Hewlett-Packard, Palo Alto, Calif.

Clocksin, W. F., and Mellish, C. S. 1981. *Programming in PROLOG*. New York: Springer-Verlag.

Cohen, P. R. 1978. *On knowing what to say: planning speech acts*. Ph.D. thesis, University of Toronto.

Cohen, P. R., and Howe, A. E. 1988. How evaluation guides AI research. *AI Magazine* 9(4):35–43.

Cohen, P. R., and Levesque, H. J. 1987. Intention = choice + commitment. *Proceedings of the National Conference on Artificial Intelligence*, 410–415.

Cohen, P. R., and Perrault, C. R. 1979. Elements of a plan-based theory of speech acts. *Cognitive Science* 3:177–212 (reprinted in RNLP: 423–440).

Cohen, P., and Howe, A. 1988. Toward AI research methodology: Three case studies in evaluation. *COINS Report* 88–31. (To appear in the *IEEE Transactions on Systems, Man, and Cybernetics*, 1989.)

Collins, W. R., and Feyock, S. 1985. Syntax programming, expert systems, and fault diagnosis. Society for Computer Simulation, Simulation Series, 41–46.

Comis, D. 1986. When Comax speaks, farmers listen. *Agricultural Research*, 6–10.

Conry, S. E., Meyer, R. A., and Lesser, V. R. 1988. Multistage negotiation in distributed planning. In A. H. Bond and L. Gasser (Eds.), *Readings in distributed artificial intelligence*. San Mateo, Calif.: Morgan Kaufmann, 367–384.

Conry, S., Meyer, R., and Searlemen, J. 1985. A shared knowledge base for independent problem solving agents. *Proceedings of the IEEE Expert Systems in Government Symposium*, McLean, Va.

Constable, R. 1971. Constructive mathematics and automatic program writers. *IFIP*, Ljubljana, Yugoslavia, 229–233.

Constable, R. L., Allen, S. F., Bromley, H. M. et al. 1986. Implementing mathematics with the Nuprl Proof Development System: New York: ACM Press.

Corkill, D. D. 1979. Hierarchical planning in a distributed environment. *Proceedings of the Sixth International Joint Conference on Artificial Intelligence*, Cambridge, Mass., 168–175. (An extended version was published as Technical Report 79-13, Department of Computer and Information Science, University of Massachusetts, Amherst, Mass., February 1979.)

Corkill, D. D. 1983. *A framework for organizational self-design in distributed problem solving networks*. Ph.D. thesis, University of Massachusetts.

Corkill, D. D., and Lesser, V. R. 1983. The use of meta-level control for coordination in a distributed problem solving network. *Proceedings of the Eighth International Joint Conference on Artificial Intelligence*, Karlsruhe, West Germany, 748–756.

Courant, R., and Hilbert, D. 1953. *Principles of mathematical physics*, Vol. 1. London: Interscience.

Croft, W. B., and Lefkowitz, L. S. 1988. Knowledge-based support of cooperative activities. *Proceedings of the Twenty-first Annual Hawaii International Conference on System Sciences*, 312–318. (Published by IEEE Computer Society Press, Catalog Number 88TH0213-9.)

Crowther, W., Goodhue, J., Gurwitz, R., Rettberg, R., and Thomas, R. 1985. The Butterfly parallel processor. *Newsletter, Computer Architecture Technical Committee*, IEEE Computer Society, Sept./Dec., 18–45.

Curtis, B., Krasner, H., and Iscoe, N. 1988. A field study of the software design process for large systems. *Communications of the ACM*, 31, 1268–1287.

Dahl, O. J., and Nygaard, K. 1966. SIMULA—an Algol Based Simulation Language. *Communications of the ACM* 9, 1268–1287.

Dangelmaier, W., Becker, B. D., and Himmelstoss, P. 1987. Concepts and experiences building a knowledge base for strategy construction in material flow networks. *Proceedings of the Second European Simulation Multiconference*, Vienna, Austria, 83–87.

Darlington, J. 1981. An experimental program transformation and synthesis system. *Artificial Intelligence* 16, North-Holland Publishing Company, 1–46.

Darlington, J., Khoshnevisan, H., McLouughlin, L. M. J., Perry, N., Pull, H. M., Sephton, K. M., and While, R. L. 1989. An introduction to the Flagship Programming Environment. Technical Report, Department of Computing, Imperial College, London, England.

Darlington, J., and Pull, H. M. 1987. A program development methodology based on a unified approach to execution and transformation. IFIP-TC-2 Workshop on Partial Evaluation and Mixed Computation GI, Avernaes, Denmark.

Davis, E. 1986. *A logical framework for solid object physics*. Technical Report 245, Courant Institute of Mathematics, New York University.

Davis, E. 1987. Constraint propagation with internal labels. *Artificial Intelligence* 32(3).

Davis, L. S., and Rosenfeld, A. 1981. Cooperating processes for low-level vision: A survey. *Artificial Intelligence* 17:245–263.

Davis, R. 1982. Expert systems: Where are we? And where do we go from here? *AI Magazine* 3(2):1–22.

Davis, R. 1984. Diagnostic reasoning based on structure and behavior. *Artificial Intelligence* 24:347–410.

Davis, R. 1987. Robustness and transparency in intelligent systems. In *Human Factors in Automated and Robotic Space Systems*. Committee on Human Factors, National Research Council, Washington, D.C., 211–233.

Davis, R. 1989. Expert systems: How far can they go? Part 1. *AI Magazine* 10(1):61–68.

Davis, R., and King, J. 1977. An overview of production systems. In E. W. Elcock and D. Michie (Eds.), *Machine intelligence 8: Machine representative of knowledge*. New York: John Wiley.

Davis, R., and Lenat, D. B. 1982. *Knowledge-based systems in artificial intelligence.* New York: McGraw-Hill.

Davis, R., and Smith, R. G. 1983. Negotiation as a metaphor for distributed problem solving. *Artificial Intelligence*: 20:63–109.

de Kleer, J. 1979. The origin and resolution of ambiguities in causal arguments. *Proceedings of the International Joint Conference on Artificial Intelligence*, Cambridge, Mass.

de Kleer, J. 1984. How circuits work. *Artificial Intelligence* 24:205–280.

de Kleer, J. 1985. An assumption-based TMS. *Artificial Intelligence* 28(2):127–162.

de Kleer, J., and Bobrow, D. G. 1984. Qualitative reasoning with higher order derivatives. *Proceedings of the National Conference on Artificial Intelligence.*

de Kleer, J., and Brown, J. S. 1984. Qualitative physics based on confluences. *Artificial Intelligence* 24:7–83.

de Kleer, J., and Brown, J. S. 1986. Theory of causal ordering. *Artificial Intelligence* 29:31–61.

deKleer, J., and Brown, J. S. 1984. A qualitative physics based on confluences. *Artificial Intelligence* 24:7–83.

Deriche, R. 1987. Optimal edge detection using recursive filtering. *Proceedings of the First International Conference on Computer Vision*, London, England, 501–505.

Dershowitz, Nachum. 1983. *The evolution of programs.* Boston: Birkhauser.

Deutsch, T. 1986. The use of UC-PROLOG for medical simulation. Society for Computer Simulation, Simulation Series 17(1):53–57.

Dewar, R.B.K., Grand, A., Liu, S. C., Schwartz, J. T., and Schonberg, E. 1979. Programming by refinement, as exemplified by the SETL representation sublanguage. *ACM Transactions on Programming Languages and Systems* 1(1):27–49.

Dietzen, S. R., and Scherlis, W. L. 1986. Analogy in program development. *Proceedings of the Second Conference on the Role of Language in Problem Solving*, Amsterdam: North Holland, 95–113.

Dormoy, J. 1988. Controlling qualitative resolution. *Proceedings of the Seventh National Conference on Artificial Intelligence*: 319–323.

Dormoy, J., and Raiman, O. 1988. Assembling a device. *Proceedings of the Seventh National Conference on Artificial Intelligence*: 330–335.

Doukidis, G. I., and Paul, R. J. 1986. Experiences in automating the formulation of discrete event simulation models. Society for Computer Simulation, Simulation Series 18(1):79–90.

Dowty, D. R., Wall, R. E., and Peters, S. 1981. *Introduction to Montague semantics.* Dordrecht, Holland: D. Reidel.

Doyle, J. 1979. A truth maintenance system. *Artificial Intelligence* 24:231–272.

Draper, B. A., Collins, R. T., Brolio, J., Hanson, A. R., and Riseman, E. M. 1988. Issues in the development of a blackboard-based schema system for image understanding. In R. Engelmore and T. Morgan (Eds.), *Blackboard systems.* Wokingham, England: Addison-Wesley.

Dreyfus, H., and Dreyfus, S. 1986. Why expert systems do not exhibit expertise. *IEEE Expert* 1(2):86–90.

Duff, M. J. B. (Ed.) 1986. *Intermediate-level image processing.* London: Academic Press.

Duff, M. J. B. 1976. CLIP4: A large scale integrated circuit array parallel processor. *Proceedings of the Third International Joint Conference on Pattern Recognition*, Coronado, Calif., 728–733.

Dumas, M. B. 1984. Simulation modelling for hospital bed planning. *Simulation*.

Durfee, E. H. 1988. *Coordination of distributed problem solvers*. Norwell, Mass.: Kluwer Academic Publishers.

Durfee, E. H., Lesser, V. R., and Corkill, D. D. 1987. Coherent cooperation among communicating problem solvers. *IEEE Transactions on Computers* C(11):1275–1291.

Durfee, E. H., Lesser, V. R., and Corkill, D. D. 1987. Cooperation through communication in a distributed problem solving network. In M. N. Huhns (Ed.), *Distributed artificial intelligence*. New York: Pitman, 29–58.

Durfee, E. H., and Lesser, V. R. 1987. Using partial global plans to coordinate distributed problem solvers. *Proceedings of the Tenth International Joint Conference on Artificial Intelligence*, Milan, Italy, 875–883.

Durfee, E. H., and Lesser, V. R. 1988. Predictability versus responsiveness: Coordinating problem solvers in dynamic domains. *Proceedings of the National Conference on Artificial Intelligence*, 66–71.

Dyer, C. R. 1987. Multiscale image understanding. In L. Uhr (Ed.), *Parallel computer vision*. Orlando, Fla.: Academic Press, 171–213.

Ebrahimzadeh, M., Barnnon, S., and Sinuani-Stern, Z. 1985. A simulation of a multi-item drug inventory system. *Simulation*.

Elmaghraby, A. S. and Jagannathan, V. 1985. An expert system for simulationists. In G. Birtwistle (Ed.), *Artificial intelligence, graphics, and simulation*. The Society for Computer Simulation, 106–109.

Elmaghraby, A. S., Demeo, R. S., and Berry, J. 1985. Testing an expert system for manufacturing. Artificial Intelligence and Simulation, Society for Computer Simulation, 62–64.

Elmaghraby, A. S., Jagannathan, V., and Ralston, P. 1986. An expert system for chemical process control. Artificial Intelligence and Simulation, Society for Computer Simulation, 1–5.

Elzas, M. S. 1986. The kinship between artificial intelligence, modelling, and simulation: An appraisal. In M. S. Elzas, T. I. Oren, and B. P. Zeigler (Eds.), *Modelling and methodology in the artificial intelligence era*. B.V. (North-Holland): Elsevier Science Publishers, 3–13.

Elzas, M. S. 1986. The applicability of artificial intelligence techniques to knowledge representation in modelling and simulation. In M. S. Elzas, T. I. Oren, and B. P. Zeigler (Eds.), *Modelling and methodology in the artificial intelligence era*. B.V. (North-Holland): Elsevier Science Publishers, 19–40.

Endesfelder, T., and Tempelmeier, H. 1987. The SIMAN module processor—A flexible software tool for the generation of SIMAN simulation models. *Proceedings of the Second European Simulation Multiconference*, Vienna, Austria, 38–43.

Engelmore, R., and Morgan, T. 1988. *Blackboard systems*. Wokingham, England: Addison-Wesley.

Ensor, J. R., and Gabbe, J. D. 1985. Transactional blackboards. *Proceedings of the Ninth International Joint Conference on Artificial Intelligence*, Los Angeles, Calif., 340–344.

Erickson, S. A. Jr. 1986. Fusing AI and simulation in military modeling. Society for Computer Simulation, Simulation Series 18(1):140–150.

Erman, L. D., Hayes-Roth, F., Lesser, V. R., and Reddy, D. R. 1980. The HEAR-SAY-II speech understanding system: Integrating knowledge to resolve uncertainty. *ACM Computing Survey* 12:213–253.

Erman, L. D., London, P. E., and Fickas, S. F. 1981. The design and an example use of HEARSAY-III. *Proceedings of the Seventh International Joint Conference on Artificial Intelligence*, 409–415, Vancouver, B.C., Canada.

Fahlman, S. E. 1979. *NETL: A system for representing and using real-world knowledge*. Cambridge, Mass.: MIT Press.

Fahlman, S. E., Hinton, G. E., and Sejnowski, T. J. 1983. Massively parallel architectures for AI: NETL, THISTLE, and Boltzmann machines. *Proceedings of the National Conference on Artificial Intelligence*, Washington, D.C.

Falkenhainer, B., and Forbus, K. 1988. Setting up large-scale qualitative models. *Proceedings of the Seventh National Conference on Artificial Intelligence*: 301–306.

Faltings, B. 1987a. *Qualitative place vocabularies for mechanisms in configuration space*. Technical Report UIUCDCS-R-87-1360, Department of Computer Science, University of Illinois at Urbana-Champaign.

Faltings, B. 1987b. Qualitative kinematics in mechanisms. *Proceedings of the Tenth International Joint Conference on Artificial Intelligence*, Milan, Italy: 436–442.

Fass, D., and Wilks, Y. 1983. Preference semantics, ill-formedness, and metaphor. *Computational Linguistics* 9:3–4 (Special Issue on Ill-Formed Input), 178–187.

Feather, M. S., and London, P. E. 1982. Implementing specification freedoms. *Science of Computer Programming* 2, Amsterdam, North Holland, 91–131.

Feigenbaum, E. A. 1977. The art of artificial intelligence: I. Themes and case studies of knowledge engineering. *Proceedings of the Fifth International Joint Conference on Artificial Intelligence*, 1014–1029, Cambridge, MA.

Feigenbaum, E. A., Buchanan, B. G., and Lederberg, J. 1971. On generality and problem solving: A case study using the DENDRAL program. In B. Meltzer and D. Michie (Eds.), *Machine intelligence 6*. New York: American Elsevier, 165–190.

Feigenbaum, E. A., McCorduck, P., and Nii, H. P. 1989. The rise of the expert company, forthcoming. New York Times Books.

Feinstein, J. L., and Siems, F. 1985. EDAAS: An expert system at the U.S. Environmental Protection Agency for avoiding disclosure of confidential business information. *Expert Systems* 2(2):72–85.

Fennell, R. D., and Lesser, V. R. 1977. Parallelism in AI problem solving: A case study of HEARSAY-II. *IEEE Transactions on Computers*, 98–111.

Fickas, S. 1987. Automating the software specification process. Technical Report 87-05, Computer Science Department, University of Oregon, Eugene.

Fikes, R. E. and Nilsson, N. J. 1971. STRIPS: A new approach to the application of theorem proving to problem solving. *Artificial Intelligence* 2(3/4):189–208.

Fillmore, C. J. 1968. The case for case. In E. Bach and R. Harms (Eds.), *Universals in linguistic theory*. New York: Holt, Rinehart, and Winston, 1–90.

Findler, N. V., and Lo, R. 1986. An examination of distributed planning in the world of air traffic control. *Journal of Parallel and Distributed Computing* 3:411–431.

Fishwick, P. A. 1988. Qualitative simulation: Fundamental concepts and issues. *Proceedings of the 1988 AI and Simulation Conference*. Society for Computer Simulation.

Fjellheim, R. A. 1986. A knowledge-based interface to process simulation. Society for Computer Simulation, Simulation Series 18(1):97–102.

Floyd, R. W. 1967. Assigning meaning to programs. *Proceedings of the Symposia in Applied Mathematics*, American Mathematical Society, 19:19–32.

Forbus, D. K. 1981. *A study of qualitative and geometric knowledge in reasoning about motion.* Technical Report AI-TR-615, Department of Electrical Engineering and Computer Science, M.I.T.

Forbus, D. K. 1982. *Qualitative process theory.* Ph.D. thesis, M.I.T. Lab Memo 664.

Forbus, D. K. 1983. Measurement interpretation in qualitative process theory. *Proceedings of the Eighth International Joint Conference on Artificial Intelligence*, Karlsruhe, West Germany: 315–320.

Forbus, D. K. 1984. Qualitative process theory. *Artificial Intelligence* 24.

Forbus, D. K., Nielsen, P., and Faltings, B. 1987. Qualitative kinematics: A framework. *Proceedings of the Tenth International Joint Conference on Artificial Intelligence*, Milan, Italy: 430–435.

Forbus, K. D. 1984. Qualitative process theory. *Artificial Intelligence* 24:85–168.

Forecast Pro promotional brochure. 1988. Business Forecast Systems, Belmont, Mass.

Forgy, C. L. 1981. OPS5 User's Manual. Technical Report CMU-CS-81-135, Computer Science Department, Carnegie Mellon University.

Forgy, C. and McDermott, J. 1977. OPS, A domain-independent production system language. *Proceedings of the Fifth International Joint Conference on Artificial Intelligence*, 1:933–939.

Forgy, C., Gupta, A., Newell, A., and Wodig, R. 1984. Initial assessment of architectures for production systems. *Proceedings of the National Joint Conference on Artificial Intelligence*, 16–119.

Fox, M. S. 1979. *Organization Structuring: Designing large complex software.* Technical Report 79-155, Computer Science Department, Carnegie-Mellon University, Pittsburgh.

Fox, M. S. 1981. An organizational view of distributed systems. *IEEE Transactions on Systems, Man, and Cybernetics* 11(1):70–80.

Fox, M. S., and Smith, S. F. 1984. ISIS: A knowledge-based system for factory scheduling. *Expert Systems* 1(1):25–49.

Fox, M., and Reddy, Y. V. Knowledge representation in organization modeling and simulation: Definition and interpretation. Robotics Institute, Carnegie-Mellon University.

Freeman, P., 1987. *Software perspectives: The system is the message.* Addison-Wesley: Reading, Mass.

Freuder, E. C. 1978. Synthesizing constraint expressions. *Communications of the ACM* 21:958–966.

Fried, L. 1987. The dangers of dabbling in expert systems. *Computerworld* 21:6.

Fu, K. S., and Mui, J. K. 1981. A survey on image segmentation. *Pattern Recognition* 13:3–16.

Fujitsu Laboratories, Education Section. 1987. *The application of OS IV ESHELL.* Kawasaki, Japan: Fujitsu Ltd. In Japanese.

Fujiwara, R., and Sakaguchi, T. 1986. An expert system for power system planning. Society for Computer Simulation, Simulation Series 18(1):174–177.

Fukada, Y. 1980. Spatial clustering procedures for region analysis. *Pattern Recognition* 12:395–403.

Futo, I., Gergely, T., and Deutsch, T. 1986. Logic modelling. Society for Computer Simulation, Simulation Series 18(1):117–129.

Futo, I., Papp, I., and Szeredi, J. 1986. The microcomputer version of TC-PROLOG. Society for Computer Simulation, Simulation Series 17(1):123–128.

Gaines, B. R. 1986. Expert systems and simulation in industrial applications. Society for Computer Simulation, Simulation Series 17(1):144–149.

Gaines, B. R. and Shaw, M. L. G. 1985. Expert systems and simulation. In G. Birtwistle (Ed.), *Artificial intelligence, graphics, and simulation*. The Society for Computer Simulation, 95–101.

Galbraith, J. 1973. *Designing complex organizations*. Reading, Mass.: Addison-Wesley.

Galbraith, J. R. 1977. *Organization design*. Reading, Mass.: Addison-Wesley.

Garg, P. K., and Scacchi, W. 1989. The design of an intelligent software hypertext system. *IEEE Expert* 5.

Garzia, R. F., Garzia, M. R., and Ziegler, B. P. 1986. Discrete-event simulation. *IEEE Spectrum*, 32–36.

Gasser, L. 1986. The integration of computing and routine work. *ACM Transactions on Office Information Systems*, New York: ACM Press.

Gasser, L., Braganza, C., and Herman, N. 1987. MACE: A flexible testbed for distributed AI research. In M. N. Huhns (Ed.), *Distributed Artificial Intelligence*. New York: Pitman, 119–152.

Gasser, L., and Rouquette, N. 1988. Representing and using organizational knowledge in distributed AI systems. *Proceedings of the 1988 Distributed AI Workshop*, Lake Arrowhead, CA: May 1988.

Gazdar, G. 1982. Phrase structure grammar. In P. Jacobson and G. K. Pullum (Eds.), *The nature of syntactic representation*. Dordrecht, Holland: D. Reidel, 131–186.

Gazdar, G., Klein, E., Pullum, G. K., and Sag, I. 1985. *Generalized phrase structure grammar*. Oxford: Basil Blackwell.

Geman, S., and Geman, D. 1984. Stochastic relaxation, Gibbs distributions, and the Bayesian restoration of images. *IEEE Transactions on Pattern Analysis and Machine Intelligence* PAMI–6, 6:721–741.

Genesereth, M. 1980. The MRS manual. Heuristic Programming Project Memo HPP-80–24, Stanford University.

Genesereth, M. R., and Nilsson, N. J. 1987. *Logical foundations of artificial intelligence*. San Mateo, Calif.: Morgan Kaufmann.

Georgeff, M. 1983. Communication and interaction in multiagent planning. *Proceedings of the National Conference on Artificial Intelligence*, Washington, D.C., 125–129.

Georgeff, M. 1984. A theory of action for multiagent planning. *Proceedings of the National Conference on Artificial Intelligence*, Austin, Tex., 121–125.

Georgeff, M. 1986. A representation of events in multi-agent domains. *Proceedings of the National Conference on Artificial Intelligence*, Philadelphia, 70–75.

Gerritsen, F. A., and Verbeek, P. W. 1984. Implementation of cellular logic operators using 3×3 convolution and table lookup hardware. *Computer Vision, Graphics, and Image Processing* 27:115–123.

Gevarter, W. B. 1987. The nature and evaluation of commercial expert system building tools. *Computer* 20(5):24–41.

Glazer, F. 1984. Multilevel relaxation in low-level computer vision. In A. Rosen-feld (Ed.), *Multiresolution image processing and analysis*. New York: Springer-Verlag, 312–330.

Glicksman, J. 1986. A simulator environment for an autonomous land vehicle. Society for Computer Simulation, Simulation Series 17(1):53–57.

Goad, C. 1983. Special-purpose automatic programming for 3-D model-based vision. *Proceedings of DARPA Image Understanding Workshop*, Arlington, Va., 94–104.

Goguen, J. A. More thoughts on specification and verification. *ACM SIGSOFT* 6(3): 38–41.

Goguen, J. A., Thatcher, J. W., and Wagner, E. 1978. An initial algebra approach to the specification, correctness, and implementation of abstract data types. In R. Yeh (Ed.), *Current Trends in Programming Methodology*, Vol. IV. Englewood Cliffs, N. J.: Prentice-Hall, 80–149.

Goguen, J. A., and Burstall, R. M. 1985. Institutions: Abstract model theory for computer science. Stanford CSLI-85-30.

Golay, M. J. E. 1969. Hexagonal parallel pattern transformations. *IEEE Transactions on Computers* C-18:733–740.

Goldberg, A., and Robson, D. 1983. *Smalltalk-80. The language and its implementation*. Reading, Mass.: Addison-Wesley.

Golden, D. The use of heuristics in bus route modification. In G. Birtwistle (Ed.), *Artificial intelligence, graphics, and simulation*. The Society for Computer Simulation, 114–118.

Goldman, N., Balzer, R., and Wile, D. 1978. Informality in program specifications. *IEEE Trans. on Software Eng.* 4(2):94–102.

Goodrich, R. L. 1987. Questions and answers on the forecast pro expert system. Seventh International Symposium on Forecasting, Boston.

Gorry, G. A. 1970. Modelling the diagnostic process. *Journal of Medical Education* 45:293–302.

Goyal, S., and Worrest, R. 1988. Expert system applications to network management. In J. Leibowitz (Ed.), *Expert system applications to telecommunications*. New York: Wiley, 3–44.

Green, C., Luckham, D., Balzer, R., Cheatham, T., and Rich, C. 1983. Report on a Knowledge-Based Software Assistant. Technical Report KES.U.83.2, Kestrel Institute, Palo Alto, CA.

Green, Cordell. 1969. Application of theorem proving to problem solving. *Proceedings of the First International Joint Conference on Artificial Intelligence*, Washington D.C., 219–239.

Grimson, W. E. L. 1981. *From images to surfaces*. Cambridge, Mass.: MIT Press.

Grimson, W. E. L. 1985. Computational experiments with a feature-based stereo algorithm. *IEEE Transactions on Pattern Analysis and Machine Intelligence* PAMI-7, 1:17–34.

Grimson, W. E. L. 1986. The combinatorics of local constraints in model-based recognition and localization from sparse data. *Journal of the ACM* 33(4):658–686.

Grimson, W. E. L. 1987. Recognition of object families using parameterized models. *Proceedings of the First International Conference on Computer Vision*, London, England, 93–101.

Grimson, W. E. L., and Lozano-Perez, T. 1987. Localizing overlapping parts by searching the interpretation tree. *IEEE Transactions on Pattern Analysis and Machine Intelligence* PAMI-9:4:469–482.

Grimson, W. E. L., and Lozano-Perez, T. 1984. Model-based recognition and localization from sparse range or tactible data. *International Journal of Robotics Research* 3(3):3–35.

Groen, A., van den Herik, H. J., Hofland, H. G., Kerckhoffs, E. J. H., Stoop, J. C., and Varkevisser, P. R. 1986. The integration of simulation and knowledge-based systems. Society for Computer Simulation, Simulation Series 18(1):189–197.

Grosz, B. J. 1977. The representation and use of focus in a system for understanding dialogs. *Proceedings of IJCAI* 67–76 (reprinted in RNLP: 353–362).

Grosz, B. J., and Sidner, C. L. 1985. Discourse structure and the proper treatment of interruptions. *Proceedings of the Ninth International Joint Conference on Artificial Intelligence*, 832–839.

Grosz, B. J., and Sidner, C. L. 1986. Attention, intention, and the structure of discourse. *Computational Linguistics* 12(3):175–204.

Grosz, B. J., and Sidner, C. L. 1988. Plans for discourse. In Cohen, Morgan, and Pollack, (Eds.), *Intentions in communication*. Cambridge, Mass.: M.I.T. Press.

Gruber, T. R. 1987. Acquiring strategic knowledge from experts. *Proceedings of the Second AAAI Knowledge Acquisition for Knowledge-based Systems Workshop*: 214–219.

Guangleng, X., and Song, A. 1986. An expert system for dynamic system simulation. Society for Computer Simulation, Simulation Series 18(1):106–110.

Haas, A. R. 1986. A syntactic theory of belief and action. *Artificial Intelligence* 28(3):245–292.

Hackbusch, W., and Trottenberg, U. (Eds.) 1982. Multigrid methods, Lecture Notes in Computer Science, Vol. 960. New York: Springer-Verlag.

Halpern, J. Y., and Moses, Y. 1984. *Knowledge and common knowledge in a distributed environment*. IBM Research Report IBM RJ 4421, IBM.

Haralick, R. M. 1984. Digital step edges from zero crossing of second directional derivative. *IEEE Transactions on Pattern Analysis and Machine Intelligence* PAMI-6:58–68.

Haralick, R. M. 1985. A reconfigurable systolic network in computer vision. *IEEE Computer Society Workshop on Computer Architecture for Pattern Analysis and Image Database Management*, Miami Beach, Fla., November 18–20, 507–515.

Haralick, R. M., Laffey, T. J., and Watson, L. T. 1983. The topographic primal sketch. *International Journal of Robotics Research* 2(1):50–72.

Haralick, R. M., Sternberg, S., and Zhuang, X. 1987. Image analysis using mathematical morphology: Part I. *IEEE Transactions on Pattern Analysis and Machine Intelligence* PAMI-9(4):532–550.

Haralick, R. M., and Shapiro, L. 1979. The consistent labeling problem: Part 1. *IEEE Transactions on Pattern Analysis and Machine Intelligence* PAMI-1:173–184.

Haralick, R. M., and Shapiro, L. 1985. Survey: Image segmentation techniques. *Computer Vision, Graphics, and Image Processing* 29:100–132.

Harandi, M. T., and Lubars, M. D. 1986. Knowledge-based software development: A paradigm and a tool. *Proceedings of the 1986 National Computer Conference*, Las Vegas, Nevada, 43–50.

Harmon, P. 1987. Currently available expert systems-building tools. *Expert Systems Strategies* 3(6):11–18.

Harmon, P., and King, D. 1985. *Expert systems: artificial intelligence in business*. New York: Wiley.

Hartman, J. 1989. Automatic control understanding for natural programs. Ph.D. Thesis, Dept. of Computer Sciences, University of Texas at Austin.

Hayes, P. J. 1978. *Naive physics I: Ontology for liquids*. Technical Report 35, Centre pour les Études Semantiques et Cognitives.

Hayes, P. J. 1979. Naive physics manifesto. *Expert Systems in the Microelectronics Age*. Edinburgh: Edinburgh University Press.

Hayes-Roth, B. 1983. *The blackboard architecture: A general framework for problem solving*. Technical Report HPP-83-30, Knowledge Systems Laboratory, Computer Science Department, Stanford University.

Hayes-Roth, B. 1985. Blackboard architecture for control. *Journal of Artificial Intelligence* 26:251–321.

Hayes-Roth, B. 1985. A blackboard architecture for control. *Artificial Intelligence* 26:251–321.

Hayes-Roth, B., Buchanan, B., Lichtarge, O., Hewett, M., Altman, R., Brinkley, J., Cornelius, C., Duncan, B., and Jardetzky, O. 1987. PROTEAN: Deriving protein structure from constraints. *Proceedings of the National Conference on Artificial Intelligence*, 904–909.

Hayes-Roth, B., Hayes-Roth, F., Rosenschein, S., and Cammarata, S. 1979. Modelling planning as an incremental, opportunistic process. *Proceedings of the Sixth International Joint Conference on Artificial Intelligence*, Cambridge, Mass., 375–383.

Hayes-Roth, F., Erman, L. D., Fouse, S., Lark, J. S., and Davidson, J. 1988. ABE: A cooperative operation system and development environment. In M. Richer (Ed.), *AI tools and techniques*. Norwood, N.J.: Ablex Publishing Corporation.

Hayes-Roth, F., Waterman, D. A., and Lenat, D. B. (Eds.) 1983. *Building expert systems*. Reading, Mass.: Addison-Wesley.

Hayes-Roth, F., and Lesser, V. R. 1976. *Focus of attention in a distributed logic speech understanding system*. Technical Report, Computer Science Department, Carnegie-Mellon University.

Hendrix, G. G., Sacerdoti, E., Sagalowicz, D., and Slocum, J. 1978. Developing a natural language interface to complex data. *ACM Trans. on Database Systems* 3(2):105–147.

Hernandez, R. 1987. Big eight firm audits with Mac. *Applied Artificial Intelligence Reporter* 4(7):9.

Hewitt, C. 1977. Viewing control structures as patterns of passing messages. *Artificial Intelligence* 8(3):323–364.

Hewitt, C. 1986. Offices are open systems. *Communications of the ACM* 4(3):271–287.

Hi-Class. 1985. AI brings smarts to PC-board assembly. *Electronics* 58:17–18.

Hickam, D. H., Shortliffe, E. H., Bischoff, M. B., and Jacobs, C. D. 1985. The treatment advice of a computer-based cancer chemotherapy protocol advisor. *Annals of Internal Medicine* 103(6):928–936.

Hildreth, E. 1987. Edge detection. In S. Shapiro (Ed.), *The encyclopedia of artificial intelligence*. New York: Wiley, 257–267.

Hillis, D. 1985. *The connection machine*. Cambridge, Mass.: MIT Press.

Hinton, G. E. and Sejnowski, T. J. 1987. Separating figure from ground with a Boltzmann machine. In M. A. Arbib and A. R. Hanson (Eds.), *Vision, brain and cooperative computation*. Cambridge, Mass.: MIT Press, 703–724.

Hinton, G. E., Sejnowski, T., and Ackley, D. 1985. Boltzmann machines: Constraint satisfaction machines that learn. *Cognitive Science* 9:147–169.

Hirst, G. 1987. *Semantic interpretation against ambiguity.* New York: Cambridge University Press.

Hoff, W., and Ahuja, N. 1987. Extracting surfaces from stereo images: An integrated approach. *Proceedings of the First International Conference on Computer Vision,* London, 284–294.

Hoffman, D. D., and Richards, W. A. 1982. Representing smooth plane curves for recognition: Implications for figure-ground reversal. *Proceedings of the National Conference on Artificial Intelligence,* Pittsburgh, Pa., 5–8.

Hollan, J. D., Hutchins, E. L., and Weitzman, L. 1984. STEAMER: An interactive inspectable simulation-based training system. *AI Magazine* 5(2):15–27.

Hopfield, J. J. 1982. Neural networks and physical systems with emergent collective computational abilities. *Proceedings of the National Academy of Sciences USA 79,* 2554–2558.

Horn, B. K. P. 1986. *Robot vision.* Cambridge, Mass.: MIT Press.

Horn, B. K. P., and Weldon, E. J., Jr. 1986. Filtering closed curves. *IEEE Transactions on Pattern Analysis and Machine Intelligence* PAMI–8:665–668.

Horn, K. A., Compton, P., Lazarus, L., and Quinlan, J. R. 1985. An expert computer system for the interpretation of thyroid assays in a clinical laboratory. *The Australian Computer Journal* 17(1):7–11.

Horowitz, S. L., and Pavlidis, T. 1976. Picture segmentation by a tree traversal algorithm. *Journal of the ACM* 23:368–388.

Huang, K. S., Jenkins, B. K., and Sawchuk, A. A. 1987. Optical cellular logic architectures based in binary image algebra. *Proceedings of the 1987 Workshop on Computer Architecture for Pattern Analysis and Machine Intelligence,* October 5–7, Seattle. Washington D.C.: IEEE Computer Society, 19–26.

Huhns, M. (Ed.), 1987. *Distributed artificial intelligence.* San Mateo, Calif.: Morgan Kaufmann.

Huhns, M. N., and Acosta, R. D. 1987. ARGO: an analogical reasoning system for solving design problems. MCC Technical Report AI/CAD-092-87.

Huhns, M., Mukhopadhyay, U., Stephens, L. M., and Bonnell, R. D. 1987. DAI for document retrieval: The MINDS project. In M. N. Huhns (Ed.), *Distributed artificial intelligence.* New York: Pitman, 249–284.

Hummel, R. A. 1986. Representations based on zero-crossings in scale-space. *Proceedings of IEEE Comp. Soc. Conference on Computer Vision and Pattern Recognition,* 204–209.

Hummel, R. A., and Zucker, S. W. 1983. On the foundations of relaxation labeling processes. *IEEE Transactions on Pattern Analysis and Machine Intelligence* PAMI–5(3):267–287.

Ikeuchi, K., and Horn, B. K. P. 1981. Numerical shape from shading and occluding contour. *Artificial Intelligence* 17:141–184.

Ikeuchi, K., and Horn, B. K. P. 1984. Picking up an object from a pile of objects. In Brady, J. M. and Paul, R. (Eds.), *Robotics Research: The First International Symposium.* Cambridge, Mass.: M.I.T. Press, 139–162.

Intel Corp., 1986. KEE Software Development System, Core Reference Manual, Version 3.0, Doc. #3.0-KCR-1., Mountain View, Calif.

Iscoe, Neil, Browne, J. C., and Werth, John. 1989. Modeling domain knowledge: An object-oriented approach to program specification and generation. Technical Report TR-89-13, Dept. of Computer Sciences, University of Texas at Austin.

Ito, M., and Ishii, A. 1986. Three view stereo analysis. *IEEE Transactions on Pattern Analysis and Machine Intelligence* PAMI–8(4):524–531.

Iwasaki, Y. 1988a. *Model-based reasoning of device behavior with causal ordering.* Ph.D. thesis, Department of Computer Science, Carnegie Mellon University.

Iwasaki, Y. 1988b. Causal ordering in a mixed structure. *Proceedings of the National Conference on Artificial Intelligence:* 313–318.

Iwasaki, Y., and Simon, H. A. 1986a. Theory of causal ordering: Reply to de Kleer and Brown. *Artificial Intelligence* 29:3–32.

Iwasaki, Y., and Simon, H. A. 1986b. Causality in device behavior. *Artificial Intelligence* 29:63–72.

Jackson, M. A. 1978. Information systems: Modeling, sequencing and transformations. *Proceedings of the Third International Conference on Software Engineering,* 72–81.

Johnson, W. L. 1986. *Intention-based diagnosis of novice programming errors.* Los Altos, Calif.: Morgan Kaufmann.

Johnson, W. L. 1988. Deriving specifications from requirements. *Tenth International Conference on Software Engineering,* 428–437.

Jones, J. W., Jones, P., and Everett, P. A. 1986. Applying agricultural models using expert system concepts. *Proceedings of the American Society of Agricultural Engineers,* Chicago.

Joskowicz, L. 1987. Shape and function in mechanical devices. *Proceedings of the Sixth National Conference on Artificial Intelligence:* 611–615.

Julesz, B. 1971. *Foundations of Cyclopean perception.* Chicago, Ill.: University of Chicago Press.

Kahn, G., and McDermott, J. 1986. The mud system. *IEEE Expert* 1(1):23–32.

Kaiser, G. E., Barghouti, N. S., Feiler, P. H., and Schwanke, R. W. 1988. Database Support for Knowledge-Based Engineering Enviorments. *IEEE Expert* 3(2): 18–32.

Kanade, T. 1980. Region segmentation: Signal vs. semantics. *Computer Graphics and Image Processing* 13:279–297.

Kant, E. 1985. Understanding and automating algorithm design. *IEEE Transactions on Software Engineering* SE-11(11):1361–1374.

Kant, E., and Newell, A. 1984. Problem solving techniques for the design of algorithms. *Information Processing and Management* 20(1-2):97–118.

Kaplan, R. M. 1973. A general syntactic processor. In R. Rustin (Ed.), *Natural language processing.* New York: Algorithmics Press: 193–241.

Kaplan, R. M., and Bresnan, J. 1982. Lexical-functional grammar: A formal system for grammatical representation. In J. Bresnan (Ed.), *The mental representation of grammatical relations.* Cambridge, Mass.: MIT Press.

Karp, P. D. 1985. *Thesis proposal: Qualitative simulation and discovery in molecular Biology.* Technical Report KSL-85-36, Knowledge Systems Laboratory, Department of Computer Science, Stanford University.

Karp, P. D., and Friedland, P. 1987. Coordinating the use of qualitative and quantitative knowledge in declarative device modeling. Knowledge Systems Laboratory Report No. KSL 87–09, Stanford University.

Kasif, S. 1986. On the parallel complexity of some constraint satisfaction problems. *Proceedings of the National Conference on Artificial Intelligence,* Philadelphia, Pa., 349–353.

Kelly, Van, and Nonnenmann, Uwe. 1987. Inferring formal software specifications from episodic descriptions. *Proceedings of AAAI-87,* Seattle, Wash.

Kent, E. W., Shneier, M. O., and Lumia, R. 1985. PIPE (pipelined image processing engine). *Journal of Parallel and Distributed Computing* 2(1):50–78.

Kerckhoffs, E. J. H., and Vansteenkiste, G. C. 1986. The impact of advanced information processing on simulation—An illustrative review. *Simulation* 46(1): 17–26.

Kerschberg, L. (Ed.) 1986. *Expert database systems: Proceedings of the first international workshop.* Menlo Park, Calif.: Benjamin Cummings.

Ketcham, M. G. 1987. IBIS: Information-based integrated simulation: The design of a simulation model base for manufacturing. *Proceedings of the Second European Simulation Multiconference*, Vienna, Austria, 26–30.

Kettig, R. S., and Landgrebe, D. A. 1975. Computer classification of multispectral image data by extraction and classification of homogeneous objects. The Laboratory for Application of Remote Sensing, LARS Information Note 050975, Purdue University, West Lafayette, Ind.

Khoshnevis, B., and Chen, A. 1986. An expert simulation model builder. Society for Computer Simulation, Simulation Series 17(1):129–132.

Kienker, P. K., Sejnowski, T. J., Hinton, G. E., and Schumacher, L. E. 1986. Separating figure from ground with a parallel network. *Perception* 15:197–216.

Kimmel, M. J., Jaffe, R. S., Manderville, J. R., and Lavin, M. A. 1985. MITE: Morphic Image Transform Engine, an architecture for reconfigurable pipelines of neighborhood processors. *IEEE Computer Society Workshop on Computer Architecture for Pattern Analysis and Image Database Management*, Miami Beach, Fla., November 18–20, 493–500.

Kirkpatrick, S., Gelcett, C. D., Jr., and Vecchi, M. P. 1983. Optimization by simulated annealing. *Science* 220:671–680.

Kirousis, Papadimitriou, C. H. 1985. The complexity of recognizing polyhedral scenes. *Twenty-sixth Annual Symposium on the Foundations of Computer Science*. Washington, D.C.: IEEE Computer Society, 175–185.

Klahr, P. 1986. Expressibility in Ross: An object-oriented Simulation System. Society for Computer Simulation, Simulation Series 18(1):136–139.

Klahr, P., et al. 1987. The authorizer's assistant: A large financial expert system application. *Proceedings of the Third Australian Conference on Applications of Expert Systems*. New South Wales Institute of Technology, Sydney, 11–32.

Kline, P. J., and Dolins, S. B. 1985. *Choosing architectures for expert systems.* Technical Report RADC-TR-85-192, Texas Instruments Inc.

Klinger, A. 1973. Data structures and pattern recognition. *Proceedings of the First International Joint Conference on Pattern Recognition*, Washington, D.C., October, 497–498.

Kolcum, E. H. 1986. NASA demonstrates use of AI with expert monitoring system. *Aviation Week & Space Technology*, 79–85.

Konolige, K. 1982. Circumscriptive ignorance. *Proceedings of the National Conference on Artificial Intelligence*, Pittsburgh, 202–204.

Konolige, K. 1983. A deductive model of belief. *Proceedings of the Eighth International Joint Conference on Artificial Intelligence*, Karlsruhe, West Germany, 377–381.

Konolige, K. 1985. A computational theory of belief introspection. *Proceedings of the Ninth International Joint Conference on Artificial Intelligence*, Los Angeles, Calif., 502–508.

Kornfeld, W. A. 1979. ETHER: A parallel problem solving system. *Proceedings of the Sixth International Joint Conference on Artificial Intelligence*, Cambridge, Mass., 490–492.

Kornfeld, W. A., and Hewitt, C. E. 1981. The scientific community metaphor. *IEEE Transactions on Systems, Man, and Cybernetics* SMC-11(1):24–33.

Koton, P. H. 1985. Empirical and model-based reasoning in expert systems. *Proceedings of the Ninth International Joint Conference on Artificial Intelligence*, Los Angeles, Calif., 297–299.

Kreiger, H., Bossel, H., Schafer, H., and Trost, N. 1987. Complex models of tree development dynamics and the simulation of tree response to pollution stress. *Proceedings of the Second European Simulation Multiconference*, Vienna, Austria, 197–201.

Kreutzer, W. 1986. *System simulation programming styles and languages*. Reading, Mass.: Addison-Wesley.

Kruse, B. 1980. System architecture for image analysis. In S. L. Tanimoto and A. Klinger (Eds.), *Structured Computer Vision: Machine Perception through Hierarchical Computation Structures*. New York: Academic Press, 189–216.

Kuipers, B. The limits of qualitative simulation. 129–135.

Kuipers, B. 1985. Qualitative simulation of mechanisms. Tech. Rept. TM-274, MIT Laboratory for Computer Science.

Kuipers, B. 1985. The limits of qualitative simulation. *Proceedings of the Ninth International Joint Conference on Artificial Intelligence*, Los Angeles, Calif.: 128–136.

Kuipers, B. 1986. Qualitative simulation. *Artificial Intelligence* 29:289–338.

Kuipers, B. 1987a. Abstraction by time-scale in qualitative simulation. *Proceedings of the Sixth National Conference on Artificial Intelligence*: 621–626.

Kuipers, B. 1987b. Qualitative simulation as causal explanation. *IEEE Transactions on Systems, Man and Cybernetics*.

Kuipers, B., and Chiu, C. 1987. Taming intractible branching in qualitative simulation. *Proceedings of the Tenth International Joint Conference on Artificial Intelligence*, Milan, Italy: 1079–1085.

Kulikowski, C., and Weiss, S. 1982. Representation of expert knowledge for consultation: The CASNET and EXPERT projects. In P. Szolovits (Ed.), *Artificial intelligence in medicine*. Boulder, Colo.: Westview Press, 21–55.

Kunz, J., Fallat, R., McClung, D., Osborn, J., Votteri, B., Nii, H. P., Aikins, J. S., Fagen, L., and Feigenbaum, E. A. 1978. *A physiological rules based system for interpreting pulmonary function test results*. Technical Report HPP-78-19, Knowledge Systems Laboratory, Computer Science Department, Stanford University.

LaFrance, J. 1989. Building an expert system for commercial use. Unpublished Report, MPSI Corporation, Tulsa, Oklahoma.

Laird, J. E., Newell, A., and Rosenbloom, P. S. 1987. SOAR: An architecture for general intelligence. *Artificial Intelligence* 33:1–64.

Lakin, W. L., and Miles, J. A. H. 1984. *A blackboard system for multi-sensor fusion*. Technical Report, ASWE, Portsdown, Portsmouth, England.

Lander, S., and Lesser, V. 1988. Negotiation among cooperating experts. *Proceedings of the 1988 Distributed AI Workshop*, Lake Arrowhead, CA.

Langlotz, C. P., Fagan, L. M., Tu, S. W., Sikic, B. I., and Shortliffe, E. H. 1986. Combining artificial intelligence and decision analysis for automated therapy planning assistance. *MEDINFO 86*, North-Holland, 794–798.

Langlotz, C. P., Fagan, L. M., Tu, S. W., Williams, J., and Sikic, B. 1985. ONYX: An architecture for planning under uncertainty. *Proceedings of the Ninth International Joint Conference on Artificial Intelligence*, Los Angeles, Calif., 1: 447–449.

Langlotz, C. P., Fagan, L. M., Tu, S., Sikic, B. I., and Shortliffe, E. H. 1987. A therapy planning architecture that combines decision theory and artificial intelligence techniques. *Computers and Biomedical Research* 20:279–303.

Lansky, A. L., and Fogelsong, D. 1987. Localized representation and planning methods for parallel domains. *Proceedings of the National Conference on Artificial Intelligence*, Seattle, Wash., 240–245.

Larson, L. G., and Lekteus, I. 1981. Stimulating aircraft in flight: Class basic flying and more. *Proceedings of the Ninth SIMULA Users' Conference*, Geneva, Switzerland, 31–42.

Law, A. M. 1986. Introduction to simulation: A powerful tool for analyzing complex manufacturing systems. *Industrial Engineering*, 46–63.

Law, A. M., and Kelton, W. D. 1982. *Simulation modeling and analysis*. New York: McGraw Hill.

Lee, M., and Clearwater, S. 1987. GOLD: Integration of model-based control systems with artificial intelligence and workstations. Invited talk presented at the Workshop on Model-Based Accelerator Controls, Brookhaven National Laboratory, Upton, New York, August 19, 1987.

Lemmon, H. 1986. COMAX: An expert system for cotton crop management. *Science*.

Lenat, D. B. 1975. Beings: Knowledge as interacting experts. *Proceedings of the Fourth International Joint Conference on Artificial Intelligence*, Stanford, Calif., 126–133.

Lenat, D. B., Davis, R., Doyle, J., Genesereth, M., Goldstein, I., and Schrobe, H. 1983. Reasoning about reasoning. In R. Hayes-Roth, D. A. Waterman, and D. B. Lenat (Eds.), *Building expert systems*. Reading, Mass.: Addison-Wesley.

Lenat, D. B., Prakash, M., and Shepherd, M. 1986. CYC: Using common sense knowledge to overcome brittleness and knowledge acquisition bottlenecks. *AI Magazine* 6(4):65–85.

Leonard, P. F. 1985. Pipeline architectures for real-time machine vision. *IEEE Computer Society Workshop on Computer Architecture for Pattern Analysis and Image Database Management*, Miami Beach, Fla., November 18–20, 502–505.

Lesser, V. R., Fennell, R. D., Erman, L. D., and Reddy, D. R. 1974. Organization of the HEARSAY-II speech understanding system. In *IEEE Symposium on Speech Recognition, Contributed Papers*:11-M2–21-M2. IEEE Group on Acoustics, Speech and Signal Processing, Computer Science Department, Carnegie-Mellon University.

Lesser, V. R., and Corkill, D. D. 1981. Functionally accurate, cooperative distributed systems. *IEEE Transactions on Systems, Man, and Cybernetics* SMC-11(1):81–96.

Lesser, V. R., and Corkill, D. D. 1983. The distributed vehicle monitoring testbed: A tool for investigating distributed problem solving networks. *AI Magazine* 4(3):15–33.

Lesser, V. R., and Corkill, D. D. 1983. The distributed vehicle monitoring testbed: A tool for investigation distributed problem-solving networks. *AI Magazine* 3:2:15–33.

Lesser, V. R., and Erman, L. D. 1977. The Retrospective View of the HEARSAY-II Architecture. *Proceedings of the Fifth International Joint Conference on Artificial Intelligence*, 790–800, Cambridge, MA.

Lesser, V. R., and Erman, L. D. 1980. Distributed interpretation: A model and experiment. *IEEE Transactions on Computers* C-29(12):1144–1163.

Letovsky, S. 1987. Program understanding with the lambda calculus. *Proceedings of the Tenth International Joint Conference on Artificial Intelligence*, Milan, Italy.

Letovsky, S. 1988. Plan analysis of programs. Ph.D. thesis, Yale University CSD Technical Report RR 662, 512–514.

Levine, M. D., and Shaheen, S. I. 1981. A modular computer vision system for picture segmentation and interpretation. *IEEE Transactions on Pattern Analysis and Machine Intelligence* PAMI–3:540–556.

Levitan, S. P., Weems, C. C., Hanson, A. R., and Riseman, E. M. 1987. The UMass image understanding architecture. In L. Uhr (Ed.), *Parallel Computer Vision*. Orlando, Fla.: Academic Press, 215–248.

Lindsay, K. J. 1987. Expert systems in the CIM environment, IntelliCorp.

Lindsay, R. K., Buchanan, B. G., Feigenbaum, E. A., and Lederberg, J. 1980. *Applications of artificial intelligence for organic chemistry: The DENDRAL project*. New York: McGraw-Hill.

Lindsay, R., Buchanan, B. G., Feigenbaum, E. A., and Lederberg, J. 1980. *Applications of artificial intelligence for organic chemistry: The dendral project*. New York: McGraw-Hill.

Liskov, B. H., and Berzins, V. 1986. An appraisal of program specifications. In N. Gehani and A. D. McGettrick (Eds.), *Software specification techniques*. Reading, MA: Addison-Wesley, 3–24.

Little, J. J. 1983. An iterative method for reconstructing convex polyhedra from extended Gaussian images. *Proceedings of the National Conference on Artificial Intelligence*, Washington, D.C., 247–250.

Little, J. J., Belloch, G. and Cass, T. 1987. Parallel algorithms for computer vision on the Connection Machine. *Proceedings of the First International Conference on Computer Vision*, London, England, 587–591.

Little, J. J., Blelloch, G., and Cass, T. 1987. How to program the Connection Machine for computer vision. *Proceedings of the CAPAMI'87*, The 1987 IEEE Computer Society Workshop on Computer Architecture for Pattern Analysis and Machine Intelligence, Seattle, Wash., 11–18.

Lougheed, R. M., McCubbrey, D. L., and Sternberg, S. R. 1980. Cytocomputers: Architectures for parallel image processing. *Proceedings of the IEEE Workshop on Picture Data Description and Management*, Pacific Grove, Calif., 281–286.

Lowe, D. G. 1985. *Perceptual organization and visual recognition*. Boston, Mass.: Kluwer.

Lowe, D. G. 1987. Three-dimensional object recognition from single two-dimensional images. *Artificial Intelligence* 31:355–395.

Lowry, M. R. 1987. Algorithm synthesis through problem reformulation. AAAI-87, Seattle, Wash: 432–436.

Lowry, M. R. 1987. The abstraction/implementation model of problem reformulation. *Proceedings of the Tenth International Conference on Artificial Intelligence*, Milan, Italy, 1004–1010.

Lowry, M. R. 1988. Invariant logic: A calculus for problem reformulation. AAAI-88, St. Paul, Minn.

Lowry, M. R. 1988. The structure and design of local search algorithms. *Proceedings of the AAAI-88 Workshop on Automating Software Design*: 88–97. (Available through AAAI, Menlo Park, Calif.)

Lowry, M. R. 1989. Algorithm synthesis through problem reformulation. Ph.D. thesis, Stanford University.

Lubars, M. D. 1987. Schematic techniques for high-level support of software specification and design. *Fourth International Workshop on Software Specification and Design*, IEEE Computer Society Press, 68–75.

Lubars, M. D. and Harandi, M. T. 1988. The knowledge-based refinement paradigm and IDeA: Concepts, limitations, and future directions. *Proceedings of the 1988 AAAI workshop on Automating Software Design.* (Available through AAAI, Menlo Park, Calif.)

Lubars, M. D., and Harandi, M. T. 1987. Knowledge-based software design using design schemas. *Ninth International Conference on Software Engineering*, IEEE Computer Society Press, 253–262.

Lytinen, S. L. 1986. Dynamically combining syntax and semantics in natural language processing. *Proceedings of AAAI* 574–578.

Mackworth, A. K. 1973. Interpreting pictures of polyhedral scenes. *Artificial Intelligence* 4:121–137.

Mackworth, A. K. 1977a. How to see a simple world: An exegesis of some computer programs for scene analysis. In E. W. Elcock and D. Michie (Eds.), *Machine Intelligence* 8:510–537.

Mackworth, A. K. 1977b. Consistency in networks of relations. *Artificial Intelligence* 8:99–118.

Mackworth, A. K. 1983. Constraints, descriptions and domain mappings in computational vision. In O. J. Braddick and A. C. Sleigh (Eds.), *Physical and Biological Processing of Images*. Berlin: Springer-Verlag, 33–40.

Mackworth, A. K. 1987a. Adequacy criteria for visual knowledge representation. In Z. Pylyshyn (Ed.), *Computational processes in human vision*. Norwood, N.J.: Ablex.

Mackworth, A. K. 1987b. Constraint satisfaction. In S. Shapiro (Ed.), *The encyclopedia of artificial intelligence*. New York: Wiley, 205–211.

Mackworth, A. K., Mulder, J. A. and Havens, W. S. 1985. Hierarchical arc consistency: Exploiting structured domains in constraint satisfaction problems. *Computational Intelligence* 1(3):118–126.

Mackworth, A. K., and Freuder, E. C. 1985. The complexity of some polynomial network consistency algorithms for constraint satisfaction problems. *Artificial Intelligence* 25(1):65–74.

Malik, J. 1987. Interpreting line drawings of curved objects. *International Journal of Computer Vision* 1(1):73–103.

Malone, T. W. 1988. What is coordination theory? *Proceedings of the National Science Foundation Coordination Theory Workshop.*

Malone, T. W., and Smith, S. A. 1984. *Tradeoffs in designing organizations: Implications for new forms of human organizations and computer systems.* Working Paper CISR WP 112 (Sloan WP 1541-84), Center for Information Systems Research, Massachusetts Institute of Technology, Cambridge, Mass.

Manna, Z., and Waldinger, R. 1980. A deductive approach to program synthesis. *ACM Transactions on Programming Languages and Systems* 2(1): 90–121. Reprinted in C. Rich and R. C. Waters (Eds.), *Readings in Artificial Intelligence and Software Engineering*. San Mateo, Calif.: Morgan Kaufmann.

March, J. G., and Simon, H. A. 1958. *Organizations*. New York: Wiley.

Marcus, S. 1987. Taking backtracking with a grain of SALT. *International Journal of Man-Machine Studies* 26(4):383–398.

Marr, D., and Hildreth, E. 1980. Theory of edge detection. *Proceedings of the Royal Society of London B*, 200, 269–294.

Marr, D. 1982. *Vision*. San Francisco, Calif.: Freeman.

Marr, D., and Nishihara, H. K. 1978. Representation and recognition of the spatial organization of three-dimensional structure. *Proceedings of the Royal Society of London* B200, 269–294.

Marr, D., and Poggio, T. 1977. A theory of human stereo vision. Memo 451, Artificial Intelligence Lab., MIT, Cambridge, Mass.

Marsh, C. A. 1985. RBMS—An Expert System for modelling NASA flight control room usage. Artificial Intelligence and Simulation, Society for Computer Simulation, 47–50.

Mason, C., Johnson, R., Searfus, R., Lager, D., and Canales, T. 1988. A seismic event analyzer for nuclear test ban treaty verification. *Proceedings of the Third International Conference on Applications of Artificial Intelligence in Engineering*.

Matheron, G. 1967. *Elements pour une théorie des milieux poreux*. Paris: Masson.

Matheron, G. 1975. *Random sets and integral geometry*. New York: Wiley.

Mazer, M. S. 1987. Exploring the use of distributed problem-solving in office support systems. *Proceedings of the IEEE Computer Society Symposium on Office Automation*, 217–225.

McCarthy, J. 1958. Programs with common sense. *Proceedings of the Symposium on the Mechanisation of Thought Processes*. National Physical Laboratory, 77–84. (Reprinted in 1968 in M. L. Minsky (Ed.), *Semantic Information Processing*. Cambridge, Mass.: MIT Press, 403–409.)

McCarthy, J. 1980. Circumscription: A form of non-monotonic reasoning. *Artificial Intelligence* 13:27–39.

McCarthy, J. 1983. Some expert systems need common sense. *Annals of the New York Academy of Science* 426:129–137. Invited presentation for the New York Academy of Sciences Science Week Symposium on Computer Culture, April 5–8.

McCarthy, J., and Hayes, P. 1969. Some philosophical problems from the standpoint of artificial intelligence. In B. Meltzer and D. Michie (Eds.), *Machine Intelligence 4*. Edinburgh: Edinburgh University Press.

McCartney, R. 1987. Synthesizing algorithms with performance constraints. *Proceedings of AAAI-87*, Seattle, Wash., 155–160.

McCartney, R. 1988. Sibling independence in algorithm synthesis. *Proceedings of the AAAI-88 Workshop on Automating Software Design*. (Available through AAAI, Menlo Park, Calif.)

McClelland, J. L., Rumelhart, D. E., and the PDP Research Group. 1987. *Parallel distributed processing: Explorations in the microstructure of cognition (2 Vols.)*. Cambridge, Mass.: MIT Press.

McClelland, J. L., and Rumelhart, D. E. 1981. An interactive activation model of context effects in letter perception: Part 1, An account of basic findings. *Psychological Review* 88:375–407.

McCord, M. C. 1980. Slot grammars. *AJCL* 6(1):31–43.

McCord, M. C. 1985. Modular logic grammars. *Proceedings of ACL* 104–117.

McCubbrey, D. L., and Lougheed, R. M. 1985. Morpholocial image analysis using a raster pipeline processor. *IEEE Computer Society Workshop on Computer Architecture for Pattern Analysis and Image Database Management*, Miami Beach, Fla., November 18–20, 444–452.

McCune, B. P., and Drazovich, R. J. 1983. Radar with sight and knowledge. *Defense Electronics*, August.

McDermott, J. 1983. Extracting knowledge from expert systems. *Proceedings of the Eighth International Joint Conference on Artificial Intelligence*, Karlsruhe, West Germany, 1:100–107.

McDermott, J., and Newell, A. 1983. *Estimating the computational requirements for future expert systems.* Technical Report, Internal Memo, Computer Science Department, Carnegie-Mellon University.

McKinion, J. K., and Lemmon, H. E. 1986. Symbolic computers and AI tools for a cotton expert system. *Proceedings of the American Society of Agricultural Engineers,* Chicago.

McRoberts, M., Fox, M., and Husain, N. 1985. Generating model abstraction scenarios in KBS. In G. Birtwistle (Ed.), *Artificial intelligence, graphics, and simulation.* The Society for Computer Simulation, 29–33.

Metropolis, N., Rosenbluth, A. W., Rosenbluth, M. N., Teller, A. H., and Teller, E. 1953. Equation of state calculations by fast computing machines. *Journal of Chemical Physics* 21:1087–1091.

Meutzelfeldt, R., Bundy, A., Uschold, M., and Robertson, D. 1986. ECO—An intelligent front end for ecological modelling. Society for Computer Simulation, Simulation Series 18(1):67–70.

Meyer, G. E., and Curry, R. B. 1986. Soybean production decision-making with the real soy model. *Proceedings of the American Society of Agricultural Engineers,* Chicago.

Meyers, S. and Friedland, P. 1984. Knowledge-based simulation of genetic regulation in bacteriophage lambda. *Nucleic Acids Research* 12(1): 1–9.

Michalski, R. S., Mozetic, I., Hong, J., and Lavrac, N. 1986. The multipurpose incremental learning system AQ15 and its testing application to three medical domains. *Proc. AAAI-86.* AAAI, Philadelphia, 1041–1045.

Michie, D., Muggleton, S., Riese, C., and Zubrick, S. 1984. RULEMASTER: A second-generation knowledge-engineering facility. In IEEE, *The first conference on artificial intelligence applications.* Silver Spring, Md.: IEEE Computer Society Press.

Middleton, S., and Zanconato, R. 1986. Blobs: An object-oriented language for simulation and reasoning. Society for Computer Simulation, Simulation Series 18(1):130–135.

Miller, F. D., Copp, D. H., Vesonder, G. T., and Zielinski, J. E. 1985. The ACE Experiment; Initial evaluation of an expert system for preventive maintenance. In J. J. Richardson (Ed.), *Artificial intelligence in maintenance: Proc. joint services workshop.* Air Force Systems Command, Park Ridge, N.J.: Noyes Publications, Publication #AFHRL-TR-84-25, 421–427.

Minkowski, H. 1903. Volumen und Oberfläche. *Mathematical Annals* 57:447–495.

Minsky, M. 1975. A framework for representing knowledge. In P. H. Winston (Ed.), *The psychology of computer vision.* New York: McGraw-Hill, 211–277.

Minsky, M., and Papert, S. 1969. *Perceptrons.* Cambridge, Mass.: MIT Press.

Mishkoff, H. C. 1985. *Understanding artificial intelligence.* Texas Instruments Information Publishing Center, Dallas.

Mitchell, J. M., Carbonell, J. G., and Michalski, R. S. (Eds.) 1986. *Machine learning: A guide to current research.* Boston: Kluwer Academic Publications.

Mittal, S., Dym, C. L., and Morjaria, M. 1985. PRIDE: An expert system for the design of paper handling systems. In C. L. Dym (Ed.), *Applications of knowledge-based systems to engineering analysis and design.* New York: ASME Press.

Modjeski, R. B. 1987. Artificial intelligence study. Research Paper CAA-RP-87–1, Research and Analysis Support Directorate, U.S. Army Concepts Analysis Agency, Bethesda, Maryland.

Mokhtarian, F., and Mackworth, A. K. 1986. Scale-based description and recognition of planar curves and two-dimensional shapes. *IEEE Transactions on Pattern Analysis and Machine Intelligence* PAMI–8:34–43.

Montanari, U. 1974. Networks of constraints: Fundamental properties and applications to picture processing. *Information Science* 7:95–132.

Moore, R. C. 1981. Problems in logical form. *Proceedings of ACL* 117–124, (reprinted in RNLP).

Moser, J. G. 1986. Integration of artificial intelligence and simulation in a comprehensive decision-support system. *Simulation* 47(6):223–229.

Moses, J. 1971. Symbolic integration: The stormy decade. *Communications ACM* 8:548–560.

Mostow, J. 1989. An object-oriented representation for search algorithms. *Proceedings of the Sixth International Workshop on Machine Learning*. Cornell University, Ithaca, N.Y., San Mateo, Calif.: Morgan Kaufmann: 489–491. (Available as Rutgers AI/Design Project Working Paper Number 131.)

Mostow, J. 1989. Exploiting DIOGENES' representations for search algorithms: propagating constraints. 1989 International Joint Conference on Artificial Intelligence Workshop on Automated Software Development. (Available as Rutgers AI/Design Project Working Paper Number 129.)

Mostow, J. 1989. Design by derivational analogy: Issues in the automated replay of design plans. 40:1–3:119–184.

Mostow, J. 1989. Towards automated development of specialized algorithms for design synthesis: Knowledge compilation as an approach to computer-aided design. *Research in Engineering Design* 1:3. (Available as Rutgers AI/Design Project Working Paper Number 141.)

Mostow, J., Barley, M., and Weinrich, T. 1989. Automated reuse of design plans. *International Journal for Artificial Intelligence in Engineering* 4:4.

Mostow, J., and Barley, M. 1987. Automated reuse of design plans. *International Journal on Artificial Intelligence in Engineering* 4:4.

Mostow, J., and Prieditis, A. E. 1989. Discovering admissable heuristics by abstracting and optimizing: A transformational approach. *Proceedings of the Eleventh Joint International Conference on Artifical Intelligence,* Detroit, Mich.: 701–707 (Available as Rutgers AI/Design Project Working Paper Number 114-1.)

Mostow, J., and Tong, C. 1988. Syllabus for graduate seminar in knowledge compilation, September 1988. (Rutgers AI/Design Project Working Paper Number 109.)

Muerle, J., and Allen, D. 1968. Experimental evaluation of techniques for automatic segmentation of objects in a complex scene. In G. Cheng et al. (Eds.), *Pictorial Pattern Recognition*. Washington, D.C.: Thompson, 3–13.

Murray, W. 1988. *Automatic program debugging for intelligent tutoring systems*. Los Altos, Calif.: Morgan Kaufmann.

Nackman, L. R. 1984. Two-dimensional critical point configuration graphs. *IEEE Transactions on Pattern Analysis and Machine Intelligence* PAMI–6(4):442–449.

Nagao, M., and Matsuyama, T. 1980. *A structural analysis of complex aerial photographs*. New York: Plenum Press.

Neches, R., Swartout, W. R., and Moore, J. D. 1985. Enhanced maintenance and explanation of expert systems through explicit models of their development. *IEEE Transactions on Software Engineering* Vol Se-11(11):1337–1351.

Neighbors, J. 1984. The DRACO approach to constructing software from reusable components. *IEEE Transactions on Software Engineering* 10(5):5–27.

Newell, A. 1962. Some problems of basic organization in problem-solving programs. In M. C. Yovits, G. T. Jacobi, and G. D. Goldstein (Eds.), *Conference on Self-Organizing Systems*. Washington, D.C.: Spartan Books, 393–423.

Newell, A. 1969. Heuristic programming: Ill-structured problems. In J. Aronofsky (Ed.), *Progress in operations research*. New York: Wiley, 360–414.

Newell, A., Barnett, J., Green, C., Klatt, D., Licklider, J. C. R., Munson, J., Reddy, R., and Woods, W. 1973. *Speech understanding system: A final report of a study group*. New York: North-Holland.

Newell, A., and Simon, H. A. 1972. *Human problem solving*. Englewood Cliffs, N.J.: Prentice-Hall.

Newell, A., and Simon, H. A. 1976. Computer science as empirical inquiry: Symbols and search. *Communications of the ACM* 19(3):113–126.

Nielsen, N. R. 1985. *Expert systems and simulation*. SRI International.

Nielsen, N. R. 1987. The impact of using AI-based techniques in a control system simulator, IntelliCorp.

Nielsen, P. 1988. A qualitative approach to mechanical constraint. *Proceedings of the Seventh National Conference on Artificial Intelligence*: 270–274.

Nii, H. P., Aiello, N. and Rice, J. 1989. Experiment on cage and poligon: Measuring the performance of parallel blackboard systems. In L. Gasser and M. N. Huhns (Eds.), *Distributed artificial intelligence, Volume II*. San Mateo: Morgan Kaufmann.

Nii, H. P., Feigenbaum, E. A., Anton, J. J., and Rockmore, A. J. 1982. Signal-to-symbol transformation: HASP/SIAP case study. *AI Magazine* 3(2):23–35.

Nii, H. P., Feigenbaum, E. A., Anton, J. J., and Rockmore, A. J. 1982. Signal-to-symbol transformation: HASP/SIAP case study. *AI Magazine* 3:2:23–35.

Nii, H. P., and Aiello, N. 1979. AGE: A knowledge-based program for building knowledge-based programs. *Proceedings of the Sixth International Joint Conference on Artificial Intelligence*, Cambridge, Mass., 645–655.

Nii, H. P., and Feigenbaum, E. A. 1978. Rule-based understanding of signals. In D. A. Waterman and R. Hayes-Roth (Eds.), *Pattern-directed inference systems*, New York: Academic Press, 483–501.

Nilsson, N. J. 1980. *Principles of artificial intelligence*. Palo Alto, Calif.: Tioga.

Nilsson, N. J. 1980. Two heads are better than one. *SIGART Newsletter* (73):43.

Nirenburg, S., and Lesser, V. 1988. Providing intelligent assistance in distributed office environments. In A. H. Bond and L. Gasser (Eds.), *Readings in distributed artificial intelligence*. San Mateo, Calif.: Morgan Kaufmann, 590–598.

Noche, B., Hoppe, U., and Boenke, M. 1987. Integration of CAD and simulation for the planning of material flow systems. *Proceedings of the Second European Simulation Multiconference*, Vienna, Austria, 31–37.

Nolan, P. J. and Fegan, J. M. 1987. An AI-based program generator for discrete event simulation. *Proceedings of the Second European Simulation Multiconference*, Vienna, Austria, XXI–XXVI.

Nudel, B. A. 1983. Consistent-labeling problems and their algorithms: Expected complexities and theory-based heuristics. *Artificial Intelligence* 21:135–178.

O'Keefe, R. 1986. Simulation and expert systems—A taxonomy and some examples. *Simulation* 46(1): 10–16.

O'Keefe, R. M., Balci, O., and Smith, E. P. 1987. Validating expert system performance. *IEEE Expert* 2(4):81–89.

Oddson, J. K., and Aggarwal, S. 1985. Discrete event simulation of agricultural pest management systems. *Simulation*.

Ohlander, R., Price, K., and Reddy, D. R. 1978. Picture segmentation using a recursive region-splitting method. *Computer Graphics and Image Processing,* 8:3, December, 313–333.

Ohta, Y., Watanabe, M., and Ikeda, K. 1986. Improving depth map by right angles trinocular stereo. *Proceedings of the Eighth International Conference on Pattern Recognition,* Paris, 519–521.

Oren, T. I. 1986. Implications of machine learning in simulation. In M. S. Elzas, T. I. Oren, and B. P. Zeigler (Eds.), *Modelling and methodology in the artificial intelligence era.* B.V. (North-Holland): Elsevier Science Publishers, 41–57.

Pan, J. 1984. Qualitative reasoning with deep-level mechanism models for diagnoses of mechanism failures. *IEEE,* 295–301.

Parunak, H. V. D. 1987. Manufacturing experience with the contract net. In M. N. Huhns (Ed.), *Distributed artificial intelligence.* New York: Pitman, 285–310.

Parunak, H. V. D., Irish, B. W., Kindrick, J., and Lozo, P. W. 1985. Fractal actors for distributed manufacturing control. *Proceedings of the Second IEEE Conference on AI Applications,* 653–660.

Pave, A., and Rechenmann, F. 1986. Computer aided modelling in biology: An artificial intelligence approach, AI applied to simulation. Society for Computer Simulation, Simulation Series 18(1):52–66.

Pearl, J. 1986. Fusion, propagation, and structuring in belief networks. *Artificial Intelligence* 29:241–251.

Pearl, J. 1988. *Probabilistic reasoning in intelligent systems: Networks of plausible inference.* San Mateo, Calif.: Morgan Kaufmann.

Pentland, A. P. 1983. Fractal-based description. *Proceedings of the Eighth International Joint Conference on Artificial Intelligence.* Karlsruhe, West Germany, 973–981.

Pentland, A. P. 1986. Perceptual organization and the representation of natural form. *Artificial Intelligence* 28:293–331.

Pereira, F. C. N., and Warren, D. H. D. 1980. Definite clause grammars for language analysis—A survey of the formalism and a comparison with augmented transition networks. *Artificial Intelligence* 13(3):231–278, (reprinted in RNLP: 101–124).

Perrault, C. R., and Allen, J. F. 1980. A plan-based analysis of indirect speech acts. *AJCL* 6(3–4):167–182.

Perry, D. 1987. Version control in the inscape environment. *Ninth International Conference on Software Engineering,* Monterey, Calif., 142–149.

Pfister, G. F., Brantley, W. C., George, D. A., Harvey, S. L., Kleingelder, W. J., McAuliffe, K. P., Melton, E. A., Norton, V. A., and Weiss, J. 1985. The IBM Research parallel processor prototype (RP3): Introduction and architecture. *Proceedings of the 1985 International Conference on Parallel Processing,* 764–771.

Pietikainen, M., and Harwood, D. 1986. Depth from three-camera stereo. *Proceedings of the CVPR '86,* Miami Beach, Fla., 2–8.

Poggio, T., Torre, V. and Koch, C. 1985. Computational vision and regularization theory. *Nature* 317:314–319.

Poggio, T., Voorhees, H. and Yuille, A. L. 1984. A regularized solution to edge detection. MIT Artificial Intelligence Lab. Memo 773, Cambridge, Mass.

Pollard, C., and Sag, I. 1987. Information-based syntax and semantics, *CSLI Lecture Notes 13*, Chicago University Press.

Pollard, C. *Generalized phrase structure grammars, head grammars, and natural languages*. New York: Cambridge University Press, forthcoming.

Pratt, W. K. 1985. A pipeline architecture for image processing and analysis. *IEEE Computer Society Workshop on Computer Architecture for Pattern Analysis and Image Database Management*, Miami Beach, Fla., November 18–20, 516–520.

Preston, K. P., Jr., and Duff, M. J. B. 1984. *Modern cellular automata*. New York: Plenum.

Preston, K., Jr. 1961. Machine techniques for automatic identification of binucleate lymphocyte. *Proceedings of the Fourth International Conference on Medical Electronics*, Washington D.C., July.

Preston, K., Jr. 1973. Application of cellular automata to biomedical image processing. *Computer Techniques in Biomedicine and Medicine*. Philadelphia: Auerbach Publishers.

Raiman, O. 1986. Order of magnitude reasoning. *Proceedings of the Fifth National Conference on Artificial Intelligence*: 100–104.

Rajagopaian, R. 1986. Qualitative modeling and simulation: A survey. *AI Applied to Simulation*: 9–30.

Ramana Reddy, Y. V., Fox, M. S., Husain, N., and McRoberts, M. 1986. The knowledge-based simulation system. *IEEE Software*, 26–37.

Rauch-Hindin, W. B. 1986. *Artificial intelligence in business, science, and industry: Volume I—Fundamentals, Volume II—Applications*. Englewood Cliffs, N.J.: Prentice-Hall.

Raulefs, P., and Thorndyke, P. 1987. An architecture for heuristic control of real-time processes. *Proceedings of the 1987 JPL Workshop on Space Telerobotics*.

Reddy, D. R., Erman, L. D., and Neely, R. B. 1973a. A model and a system for machine recognition of speech. *IEEE Transactions on Audio and Electroacoustics* AU-21:229–238.

Reddy, D. R., Erman, L. D., and Neely, R. B. 1973b. The HEARSAY speech understanding system: An example of the recognition process. *Proceedings of the Third International Joint Conference on Artificial Intelligence*, Stanford University, 185–193.

Reddy, Y. V., Fox, M. S., and Husain, N. 1985. Automating the analysis of simulations in KBS. In G. Birtwistle (Ed.), *Artificial intelligence, graphics, and simulation*. The Society for Computer Simulation, 34–40.

Reed, S., and Lesser, V. R. 1980. *Division of labor in honey bees and distributed focus of attention*. Technical Report 80-17, Department of Computer and Information Science, University of Massachusetts, Amherst, Mass.

Reedy, Y. B., Fox, M. S., and Husain, N. 1984. Automating the analysis of simulations in KBS. Robotics Institute, Carnegie-Mellon University.

Reichman, R. 1985. *Getting computers to talk like you and me*. Cambridge, Mass.: MIT Press.

Reubenstein, H.B., and Waters, R.C. 1989. The requirements apprentice: An initial scenario. *Proceedings of the Fifth International Workshop on Software Specification and Design*, Pittsburgh, Penn.

Rice, J. P. 1986. *Poligon: A system for parallel problem solving.* Technical Report KSL-86-19, Knowledge Systems Laboratory, Computer Science Department, Stanford University.

Rich, C. 1985. The layered architecture of a system for reasoning about programs. *Proceedings of the Ninth International Joint Conference on Artificial Intelligence*, Los Angeles, Calif., 540–546.

Rich, C., Waters, R. C., and Reubenstein, H. B. 1987. Toward a requirements apprentice. *Fourth International Workshop on Software Specification and Design*, IEEE Computer Society Press, 79–86.

Rich, C., and Waters, R. C. 1988. The programmer's apprentice: A research overview. *IEEE Computer* 21(11):10–25.

Rich, R. C. 1981. A formal representation for plans in the programmer's apprentice. *Proceedings of the Seventh International Joint Conference on Artificial Intelligence*, Vancouver, B.C., 1044–1052.

Richer, M. H. 1986. Evaluating the existing tools for developing knowledge-based systems. *Expert Systems* 3(3):166–183.

Richer, M. H., and Clancey, W. J. 1985. Guidon-Watch: A graphic interface for viewing a knowledge-based system. *IEEE Computer Graphics and Applications* 5(11):51–64.

Rieger, C., and Grinberg, M. 1977. The declarative representation and procedural simulation of causality in physical mechanisms. *Proceedings of the Fifth International Joint Conference on Artificial Intelligence*, Cambridge, Mass.: 250–256.

Rieger, C., and Grinberg, M. 1978. A system of cause-effect representation and simulation for computer-aided design. *Artificial Intelligence and Pattern Recognition in Computer Aided Design.* New York: North Holland: 250–257.

Riseman, E. M., and Arbib, M. 1977. Segmentation of static scenes. *Computer Graphics and Image Processing* 6:221–276.

Riseman, E. M., and Hanson, A. R. 1986. A methodology for the development of general knowledge-based vision systems. In M. A. Arbib and A. R. Hanson (Eds.), *Vision, brain, and cooperative computation.* Cambridge, Mass.: MIT Press, 285–328.

Roberston, T. V., Swain, P. H., and Fu, K. S. 1973. Multispectral image partitioning. TR-EE-73-26 (LARS Information Note 071373), August, School of Electrical Engineering, Purdue University.

Robertson, P. 1986. A rule-based expert simulation environment. Intelligent Simulation Environments. Society for Computer Simulation, Simulation Series 17(1):9–15.

Robinson, J. A. 1965. A machine-oriented logic based on the resolution principle. *JACM* 12(1):23–41.

Robinson, J. J. 1982. DIAGRAM: A grammar for dialogues. *Commun. of the ACM* 25(1):27–47, (reprinted in RNLP: 139–160).

Rosenblatt, F. 1962. *Principles of neurodynamics.* New York: Spartan Books.

Rosenfeld, A. (Ed.) 1984. *Multiresolution image processing and analysis.* New York: Springer-Verlag.

Rosenschein, J. S. 1982. Synchronization of multi-agent plans. *Proceedings of the National Conference on Artificial Intelligence*, Pittsburgh, 115–119.

Rosenschein, J. S., and Genesereth, M. R. 1987. Communication and cooperation among logic-based agents. *Proceedings of the Sixth Phoenix Conference on Computers and Communications*, Scottsdale, Ariz., 594–600.

Rosenschein, J. S., and Genesereth, M. R. 1985. Deals among rational agents. *Proceedings of the Ninth International Joint Conference on Artificial Intelligence*, Los Angeles, Calif., 91–99.

Rosenschein, S. 1983. Reasoning about distributed action. *AI Magazine* 84:7.

Rosenschein, S. J., and Shieber, S. M. 1982. Translating English into logical form. *Proc. ACL* 1–8.

Round, A. D. 1987. QSOPS: A workbench environment for the qualitative simulation of physical processes. *Proceedings of the Second European Simulation Multiconference*, Vienna, Austria, 213–217.

Round, A. D. 1989. AI tools for simulation. In M. Richer (Ed.), *Tools and Techniques*. Norwood, N.J.: Ablex, 219–239.

Roussel, P. 1975. Prolog: Manuel de reference et d'utilisation. Groupe d'Intelligence Artificielle, Universite d'Aix-Marseille, Luminy, France.

Royce, W. W. 1970. Managing the development of large software systems: Concepts and techniques. *1970 WESCON Technical Papers* Vol. 14, Los Angeles, Calif.: 328–338.

Rumelhart, D. E., and McClelland, J. L. 1982. An interactive model of context effects in letter perception: Part 2, The enhancement effect and some tests and extensions to the model. *Psychological Review* 89:60–94.

Russell, Stuart. 1985. Unpublished manuscript, Computer Science Department, Stanford University.

Sacerdoti, E. D. 1977. *A structure for plans and behavior*. New York: Elsevier North-Holland.

Sacks, E. P. 1987a. Piecewise linear reasoning. *Proceedings of the Sixth National Conference on Artificial Intelligence*: 655–659.

Sacks, E. P. 1987b. Hierarchical reasoning about inequalities. *Proceedings of the Sixth National Conference on Artificial Intelligence*: 649–654.

Sager, N. 1981. *Natural language information processing: A computer grammar of English and its applications*. Reading, Mass.: Addison-Wesley.

Sathi, A., Morton, T. E., and Roth, S. F. 1986. Callisto: An intelligent project management system. *AI Magazine*, Winter: 34–52.

Schaefer, D. H., Wilcox, G. C., and Harris, V. J. 1985. A pyramid of MPP processing elements — experiences and plans. *Proceedings of the Eighteenth Annual Hawaii International Conference on System Sciences*, 1, 178–184.

Schank, R. C. 1983. The current state of AI: One man's opinion. *AI Magazine* 4(1):3–8.

Schank, R. C. and Abelson, R. 1977. *Scripts, plans, goals and understanding*. Hillsdale, N.J.: Lawrence Erlbaum.

Scherlis, W. L., and Scott, D. S. 1983. First steps towards inferential programming. Tech Report CMU-CS-83-142, Pittsburgh: Carnegie Mellon University.

Schoen, E. 1986. *The CAOS system*. Technical Report STAN-CS-86-1125, Computer Science Department, Stanford University.

Schonberg, E., Schwartz, J. T., and Sharir, M. 1981. An automatic technique for the selection of data representations in SETL programs. *ACM Transactions on Programming Languages and Systems* Vol. 3: 126–143.

Schubert, L. K., and Pelletier, F. J. 1982. From English to logic: Context-free computation of conventional logical translation. *AJCL* 8(1):165–176, (reprinted in RNLP: 293–312).

Scown, S. J. 1985. *The artificial intelligence experience*. Digital Equipment Corp., Maynard, Mass.

Scriber, T. J. 1987. The nature and role of simulation in the design of manufacturing systems. *Proceedings of the Second European Simulation Multiconference*, Vienna, Austria, 5–18.

Searle, J. R. 1969. *Speech acts, An essay in the philosophy of language*. New York: Cambridge University Press.

Searle, J. R. 1975. Indirect speech acts. In P. Cole and J. Morgan (Eds.), *Syntax and semantics 3: Speech Acts*. New York: Academic Press, 59–82.

Seitz, C. L. 1984. The cosmic cube. *Communications of the ACM* 28(1):22–33.

Sejnowski, T. J., and Hinton, G. E. 1987. Separating figure from ground with a Boltzmann machine. In M. A. Arbib and A. R. Hanson (Eds.), *Vision, brain, and cooperative computation*. Cambridge, Mass.: MIT Press, 703–724.

Selfridge, O. G. 1959. Pandamonium: A paradigm for learning. *Proceedings of the Symposium on the Mechanization of Thought Processes*, 511–529.

Selig, L. J. 1987. An expert system using numerical simulation and optimization to find particle beam line errors. Knowledge Systems Laboratory, Report No. KSL 87-36, Stanford University.

Selig, L., Clearwater, S., Lee, M., and Engelmore, R. 1987. Simulation and expert systems for finding particle beam line errors. Second Workshop on AI and Simulation, AAAI Conference, Seattle.

Seliger, G., Viehweger, B., Wieneke-Toutouai, B., and Kommana, S. R. 1987. Knowledge-based simulation of flexible manufacturing systems. *Proceedings of the Second European Simulation Multiconference*, Vienna, Austria, 65–68.

Sembugamoorthy, V., and Chandrasekaran, B. 1986. Functional representation of devices and compilation of diagnostic problem-solving systems. In *Experience, memory, and reasoning*. Hillsdale, NJ: Lawrence Erlbaum Associates.

Serra, S. 1972. Stereology and structuring elements. *Journal of Microscopy*, 93–103.

Serra, S. 1982. *Image analysis and mathematical morphology*. London: Academic Press.

Setliff, D, and Rutenbar, R. 1989. ELF: A tool for automatic synthesis of custom physical CAD software. Design Automation Conference, IEEE: 102–108.

Setliff, D. 1989. Knowledge-based synthesis of custom VLSI router software. Ph.D. dissertation, Carnegie Mellon University.

Setliff, D., and Rutenbar, R. 1988. Knowledge-based synthesis of custom VLSI physical design tools: First steps. *Conference on Artificial Intelligence Applications*, IEEE.

Shafer, G., Shenoy, P. P., and Mellouli, K. 1989. Propagating belief functions in qualitative Markov trees. *International Journal of Approximate Reasoning*, forthcoming.

Shafer, S. A., Stentz, A., and Thorpe, C. 1986. An architecture for sensor fusion in a mobile robot. *Proceedings of the 1986 IEEE International Conference on Robotics and Automation*.

Shafer, S. A., and Kanade, T. 1983. The theory of straight homogeneous generalized cylinders and taxonomy of generalized cylinders. Technical Report CMU-CS-83-105, Carnegie-Mellon Univ., Pittsburgh, Pa.

Shank, R. C. 1975. *Conceptual information processing*. New York: North-Holland.

Shannon, R. E. 1986. Intelligent simulation environments. Society for Computer Simulation, Simulation Series 17(1):150–156.

Shaw, D. E. 1985. NON-VON's applicability to three AI task areas. *Proceedings of the Ninth International Joint Conference on Artificial Intelligence*, Los Angeles, Calif., pp. 61–70.

Sheil, B. 1983. Power tools for programmers. *Datamation*, Feb. 1983, 29(2):131–144.

Sheil, B. 1983. Power tools for programmers. *Datamation* 29(2):131–144.

Sheil, B. A. 1984. Power tools for programmers. In D. R. Barstow, H. E. Shrobe, and E. Sandewall (Eds.), *Interactive programming environments*. New York: McGraw-Hill, 19–30.

Shieber, S. 1984. The design of a computer language for linguistic information. *Proceedings of COLING*, 362–366.

Shirai, Y. 1987. *Three-dimensional computer vision*. New York: Springer-Verlag.

Shortliffe, E. H. 1976. *Computer-based medical consultation: MYCIN*. New York: American Elsevier.

Sidner, C. 1985. Plan parsing for intended response recognition in discourse. *Computational Intelligence* 1(1):1–10.

Siegel, H. J. 1979. PASM: A partitionable multimicrocomputer SIMD/MIMD system for image processing and pattern recognition. *IEEE Computer* C-30(12):934–947.

Siegel, H. J., Siegel, L. J., McMillen, R., Mueller, P., and Smith, S. 1979. An SIMD/MIMD multimicroprocessor system for image processing and pattern recognition. *Proceedings of the 1979 Conference on Pattern Recognition and Image Processing*, Chicago, Ill., 214–224.

The SimKit System User Manual, KEE Version 3.0. 1983. IntelliCorp.

Simmons R. 1986. Commonsense arithmetic reasoning. *Proceedings of the Fifth National Conference on Artificial Intelligence*: 118–124.

Simon, H. A. 1952. On the definition of the causal relation. *Journal of Philosophy* 49:517–28.

Simon, H. A. 1953. Causal ordering and identifiability. In *Studies in Econometric Methods*. New York: Wiley, 49–74.

Simon, H. A. 1957. *Models of man*. New York: Wiley.

Simon, H. A. 1969. *The sciences of the artificial*. Cambridge, Mass.: MIT Press.

Simon, H. A. 1969. *The sciences of the artificial*. Cambridge, Mass.: MIT Press.

Simon, H. A. 1977. Scientific discovery and the psychology of problem solving. In *Models of discovery*. Boston, Mass.: D. Reidel.

Simon, H. A., and Ando, A. 1961. Aggregation of variables in dynamic systems. *Econometrica* 29:111–138.

Simon, H. A., and Rescher, N. 1966. Causes and counterfactual. *Philosophy of Science* 33:323–40.

Singh, N. 1983. MARS: A multiple abstraction rule-based simulator. Stanford Heuristic Programming Project, Memo HPP-83-43, Stanford University.

Smith, D. 1988. KIDS—A knowledge-based software development system. *Proceedings of AAAI-88 Workshop on Automating Software Design*, St. Paul, Minn.

Smith, D. R. 1985. Top down synthesis of divide-and-conquer algorithms. *Artificial Intelligence* 27 (1):43–96.

Smith, D. R., and Lowry, M. R. 1989. Algorithm theories and design tactics. *Proceedings of Mathematics of Program Construction*, Gronigen, The Netherlands, Lecture Notes in Computer Science No. 375, Springer-Verlag.

Smith, D. and Westfold, S. 1987. Application of REFINE to knowledge-based modeling. Application Note 1.3, Reasoning Systems Inc.

Smith, D., and Broadwell, M. 1987. Plan coordination in support of expert systems. *Proceedings of the IDARPA Knowledge-based Planning Workshop*, Austin, Tex.

Smith, G. B. 1984. A fast surface interpolation technique. *Proceedings of the Image Understanding Workshop*, New Orleans, La., October, 211–215.

Smith, R. G. 1978. *A framework for problem solving in a distributed processing environment*. Ph.D. thesis, Stanford University. (A revised version was published by UMI Research Press.)

Smith, R. G. 1979. A framework for distributed problem solving. *Proceedings of the Sixth International Joint Conference on Artificial Intelligence*, Cambridge, Mass., 836–841.

Smith, R. G. 1980. The contract net protocol: High-level communication and control in a distributed problem solver. *IEEE Transactions on Computers* C-29(12):1104–1113.

Smith, R. G. 1984. On the development of commercial expert systems. *AI Magazine* 5(3):61–73.

Smith, R. G., Barth, P. S., and Young, R. L. 1987. A substrate for object-oriented interface design. In B. Shriver and P. Wegner (Eds.), *Research directions in object-oriented programming*. Cambridge, Mass.: MIT Press, 253–315.

Smith, R. G., Winston, H. H., Mitchell, T. M., and Buchanan, B. G. 1985. Representation and use of explicit justifications for knowledge-base refinement. *Proceedings of the Ninth International Joint Conference on Artificial Intelligence*, Los Angeles, Calif., 673–680.

Smith, R. G., and Davis, R. 1981. Frameworks for cooperation in distributed problem solving. *IEEE Transactions on Systems, Man, and Cybernetics*, SMC-11(1):61–70.

Smith, R. G., and Davis, R. 1983. Negotiation as a metaphor for distributed problem solving. *Artificial Intelligence* 20:63–109.

Smith, R. G., and Young, R. L. 1984. The design of the dipmeter advisor system. *Proceedings of the ACM Annual Conference*, 15–23.

Smith, S. F., and Hynynen, J. E. 1987. Integrated decentralization of production management: An approach for factory scheduling. In C. R. Liu, A. Requicha, and S. Chandrasekar (Eds.), *Intelligent and integrated manufacturing analysis and synthesis*. New York: The American Society of Mechanical Engineers, 427–439.

Snyder, L. S. 1982. Introduction to the configurable highly parallel computer. *IEEE Computer* 15(1):47–64.

Spain, D. S. 1983. Application of artificial intelligence to tactical situation assessment. *Proceedings of the Sixteenth EASCON83*:457–464.

Spivey, J. M. 1989. An introduction to Z and formal specifications. *Software Engineers Journal* (UK), vol.4: 40–50. See also J. M. Spivey. 1985. *Understanding Z*. Cambridge University Press.

Stallman, R. M., and Sussman, G. J. 1977. Forward reasoning and dependency-directed backtracking in a system for computer-aided circuit analysis. *Artificial Intelligence* 9:135–196.

Stankovic, J. A., Ramamritham, K., and Cheng, S.-C. 1985. Evaluation of a flexible task scheduling algorithm for distributed hard real-time systems. *IEEE Transactions on Computers* C-34(12):1130–1143.

Stansfield, J. L. 1980. Conclusions from the commodity expert project. MIT Artificial Intelligence Lab. Memo 601, Cambridge, Mass.

Steeb, R., Cammarata, S., Narain, S., Rothenburg, J., and Giarla, W. 1986. *Cooperative intelligence for remotely piloted vehicle fleet control.* Technical Report R-3408-ARPA, Rand Corporation.

Stefik, M. 1979. An examination of a frame-structured representation system. *Proceedings of the Sixth International Joint Conference on Artificial Intelligence,* Cambridge, Mass., 468–476.

Stefik, M. J., and Bobrow, D. G. 1986. Object-oriented programming: themes and variations. *AI Magazine* 6(4):40–62.

Steier, D. M. 1987. Cypress-Soar: A case study in search and learning in algorithm design. *Proceedings of the Tenth International Conference on Artificial Intelligence,* Milan, Italy, 327–330.

Steier, D. M. 1989. Automating algorithm design within a general architecture for intelligence. Ph.D. thesis, Carnegie Mellon University.

Steier, D. M., and Newell, A. 1988. Integrating multiple sources of knowledge into Designer-Soar, an automatic algorithm designer. *AAAI-88,* 8–13.

Steier, D., and Kant, E. 1985. The roles of execution and analysis in algorithm design. *IEEE Transactions on Software Engineering,* Vol. SE-11, 11, 1375–1386.

Steinberg, L. I., and Mitchell, T. M. 1985. The redesign system: A knowledge-based approach to VLSI CAD. *IEEE Design & Test,* 2(1):45–54.

Stelzner, M., Dynis, J., and Cummins, F. 1987. The SimKit system: Knowledge-based simulation and modeling tools in KEE, IntelliCorp.

Stenz, A., and Shafer, S. 1985. *Module programmer's guide to local map builder for ALVan.* Technical Report, Computer Science Department, Carnegie-Mellon University.

Stickel, M. 1983. Theory resolution; building in nonequational theories. *83,* 391–397.

Struss, P. 1987. *Mathematical aspects of qualitative reasoning.* Technical Report, Siemens Corp.

Sugihara, K. 1986. *Machine interpretation of line drawings.* Cambridge, Mass.: MIT Press.

Sweet, L. 1985. Research in progress at General Electric. *AI Magazine* 6(3):220–227.

Sycara, K. 1987. Planning for negotiation: A case-based approach. *IDARPA Knowledge-based Planning Workshop,* 11.1–11.10.

Sycara, K. 1988. Multi-agent compromise via negotiation. *Proceedings of the 1988 Distributed AI Workshop,* Lake Arrowhead, CA.

Sycara, K. 1988. Resolving goal conflicts via negotiation. *Proceedings of the National Conference on Artificial Intelligence,* 245–250.

Sycara-Cyranski, K. 1985. Arguments of persuasion in labour mediation. *Proceedings of the Ninth International Joint Conference on Artificial Intelligence,* Los Angeles, Calif., 294–296.

Szolovits, P., and Pauker, S. G. 1978. Categorical and probabilistic reasoning in medical diagnosis. *Artificial Intelligence* 11:115–144.

Tangen, K., and Wretling, U. Intelligent front ends to numerical simulation programs. Hovik, Norway: Computas Expert Systems.

Tanimoto, S. L. 1983. A pyramidal approach to parallel processing. *Proceedings of the Tenth International Symposium on Computer Architecture*, Stockholm, Sweden, 372–378.

Tanimoto, S. L. 1984. A hierarchical cellular logic for pyramid computers. *Journal of Parallel and Distributed Computing* 1(2):105–132.

Tanimoto, S. L., Ligocki, T. J., and Ling, R. 1987. A prototype pyramid machine for hierarchical cellular logic. In L. Uhr (Ed.), *Parallel computer vision*. Orlando, Fla.: Academic Press, 43–83.

Teknowledge. 1987. *TEKSolutions: Customer success stories*. Teknowledge, Palo Alto, Calif.

Terry, A. 1983. *The CRYSALIS project: Hierarchical control of production systems*. Technical Report HPP-83-19, Heuristic Programming Project, Stanford University.

Terzopoulos, D. 1984a. Multilevel reconstruction of visual surfaces: Variational principles and finite-element representations. In A. Rosenfeld (Ed.), *Multiresolution image processing and analysis*. New York: Springer-Verlag, 237–310.

Terzopoulos, D. 1984b. Multiresolution computation of visible-surface representations. Ph.D. Thesis, MIT.

Terzopoulos, D. 1986. Image analysis using multigrid relaxation methods. *IEEE Transactions on Pattern Analysis and Machine Intelligence* PAMI–8(2):129–139.

Terzopoulos, D. 1987. Visual depth map. In S. Shapiro (Ed.), *Encyclopedia of artificial intelligence*. New York: Wiley, 1152–1160.

Thorndyke, P. W., McArthur, D., and Cammarata, S. 1981. Autopilot: A distributed planner for air fleet control. *Proceedings of the Seventh International Joint Conference on Artificial Intelligence*, 171–177, Vancouver, B.C.

Tikhonov, A. N., and Arsenin, V. Y. 1977. *Solutions of ill-posed problems*. New York: Winston.

Tomita, M., and Carbonell, J. G. 1987. The universal parser architecture for knowledge-based machine translation. *Proceedings of the Tenth International Joint Conference on Artificial Intelligence*, Milan, Italy, 718–721.

Torre, V., and Poggio, T. 1986. On edge detection. *IEEE Transactions on Pattern Analysis and Machine Intelligence* PAMI–8:147–163.

Tracz, W. 1988. Software reuse: Emerging technology. *IEEE Computer Society*, 299–308.

Uhr, L. (Ed.) 1987. *Parallel computer vision*. Orlando, Fla.: Academic Press.

Ulgen, O. M., and Thomasma, T. 1987. A graphical simulation system in Smalltalk-80. *Proceedings of the Second European Simulation Multiconference*, Vienna, Austria, 53–58.

Ullman, S. 1979. Relaxation and constrained optimization by local processes. *Computer Graphics and Image Processing* 10:115–125.

Unger, B., Dewar, A., Cleary, J., and Birtwistle, G. 1986. The jade approach to distributed software development. Society for Computer Simulation, Simulation Series 18(1):178–188.

Unger, S. H. 1958. A computer oriented to spatial problems. *Proceedings of the IRE* 46:1744–1750.

Uyeno, D. H., and Seeberg, C. 1984. A practical methodology for ambulance vocation. *Simulation*.

Vassilacopoulis, G. 1985. A simulation model for bed allocation to hospital inpatient departments. *Simulation.*

Vaucher, J. G. 1985. Views of modelling: Comparing the simulation and AI approaches. In G. Birtwistle (Ed.), *Artificial intelligence, graphics, and simulation.* The Society for Computer Simulation, 3–7.

Wah, B. W. (Ed.) 1987. *Computer (Special issue on computers for AI applications).* IEEE.

Waldinger, R. J., and Lee, R. C. 1969. PROW: A step toward automatic program writing. *Proceedings of the First International Joint Conference on Artificial Intelligence,* Washington D.C., 241–252.

Walker, T. C., and Miller, R. K. 1986. *Expert systems 1986.* Madison, Ga.: SEAI Technical Publications.

Waltz, D. 1975. Understanding line drawings of scenes with shadows. In P. H. Winston (Ed.), *The psychology of computer vision.* New York: McGraw-Hill, 19–91.

Wang, Q., and Sterman, J. D. 1985. A disaggregate population model of China. *Simulation.*

Waterman, D. A. 1986. *A guide to expert systems.* Reading, Mass.: Addison-Wesley.

Waters, R. C. 1985. The programmer's apprentice: A session with KBEmacs. *IEEE Transactions on Software Engineering,* Vol. SE-11(11): 1296–1320.

Webber, B. L. 1988. Tense as discourse anaphor. *Computational Linguistics* 14(2):61–73.

Weischedel, R. M., and Sondheimer, N. K. 1983. Meta-rules as a basis for processing ill-formed output. *Computational Linguistics* 9(3–4) (Special Issue on Ill-Formed Input), 161–177.

Weiss, S., and Kulikowski, C. 1984. *A practical guide to building expert systems.* Totowa, N.J.: Rowman & Allanheld.

Weld, D. S. 1984. Switching between discrete and continuous process models to predict genetic activity. MIT Artificial Intelligence Laboratory, Technical Report 793.

Weld, D. S. 1985. Combining discrete and continuous process models. *Proceedings of the Ninth International Joint Conference on Artificial Intelligence,* Los Angeles, Calif., 141–143.

Weld, D. S. 1988. Exaggeration. *Proceedings of the Seventh National Conference on Artificial Intelligence*: 291–295.

Wesson, R., Hayes-Roth, F., Burge, J. W., Statz, C., and Sunshine, C. A. 1981. Network structures for distributed situation assessment. *IEEE Transactions on Systems, Man, and Cybernetics* SMC-11(1):5–23.

Westfold, S. J., Markosian, L. Z., and Brew, W. A. 1987. Knowledge-based software development. In V. Montanari and A. N. Haberman (Eds.), *Innovative Software Factories and Ada.* Berlin: Springer-Verlag.

Wile, D. S. 1983. Program developments: Formal explanations of implementations. *Communications of the CACM* 26(11): 902–911.

Wilensky, R. 1983. *Planning and understanding.* Reading, Mass.: Addison-Wesley.

Wilkerson, G., Mishoe, J., Jones, J., Stimac, J., Boggess, W., and Swaney, D. 1983. SICM: Soybean integrated crop management model: Model description and user's guide, Version 4.2. Agricultural Engineering Department Research Report AGE-1, Agr. Engr. Department, University of Florida, Gainesville, Fla.

Wilks, Y. 1975. An intelligent analyzer and understander of English. *Communication of the ACM* 18(5):264–274, (reprinted in RNLP: 193–204).

Williams, B. C. 1984. Qualitative analysis of MOS circuits. *Artificial Intelligence* 24:281–346.

Williams, B. C. 1986. Doing time: Putting qualitative reasoning on firmer ground. *Proceedings of the Fifth National Conference on Artificial Intelligence*, Philadelphia, Penn.: 105–113.

Williams, B. C. 1988. MINIMA: A symbolic approach to qualitative algebraic reasoning. *Proceedings of the Seventh National Conference on Artificial Intelligence*, St. Paul, Minn.: 264–269.

Williams, M. A. 1985. Distributed, cooperating expert systems for signal understanding. *Proceedings of Seminar on AI Applications to Battlefield*:3.4-1–3.4-6.

Williams, M., Brown, H., and Barnes, T. 1984. *TRICERO Design Description*. Technical Report ESL-NS539, ESL, Inc.

Wills, L. M. 1986. Automated program recognition. Massachusetts Institute of Technology Technical Report MIT-AI-TR 904.

Wilson, S. 1985. The Pixie-5000—A systolic array processor. *IEEE Computer Society Workshop on Computer Architecture for Pattern Analysis and Image Database Management*, Miami Beach, Fla., November 18–20, 477–483.

Winkelbauer, L., and Fedra, K. 1987. Intelligent decision support for the management of hazardous substances: Symbolic simulation of chemical production processes. *Proceedings of the Second European Simulation Multiconference*, Vienna, Austria, 191–196.

Winograd, T. 1975. Frame representations and the procedural/declarative controversy. In D. G. Bobrow and A. Collins (Eds.), *Representation and understanding: studies in cognitive science*. New York: Academic Press, 185–210.

Winograd, T., and Flores, F. F. 1986. *Understanding computers and cognition*. Norwood, N.J.: Ablex.

Witkin, A. P. 1983. Scale space filtering. *Proceedings of the Eighth International Joint Conference on Artificial Intelligence*, Karlsruhe, West Germany, 1019–1022.

Witkin, A. P. 1987. Scale space methods. In S. Shapiro (Ed.), *Encyclopedia of artificial intelligence*. New York: Wiley, 973–980.

Wolper, J. T. 1987. F.M.S. behaviour and general systems theory. *Proceedings of the Second European Simulation Multiconference,* Vienna, Austria, 111.

Woodham, R. J. 1980. Photometric method for determining surface orientation from multiple images. *Optical Engineering* 19:139–144.

Woodham, R. J. 1987a. Shape analysis. In S. Shapiro (Ed.), *Encyclopedia of artificial intelligence*. New York: Wiley, 1039–1048.

Woodham, R. J. 1987b. Stable representation of shape. In Z. Pylyshyn (Ed.), *Computational processes in human vision*. Norwood, N.J.: Ablex.

Woods, W. A. 1968. Procedural semantics for question answering. *Proceedings of AFIPS Conference 33*, 457–471.

Woods, W. A. 1970. Transition network grammars for natural language analysis. *Communication of the ACM* 13:591–606, (reprinted in RNLP: 71–88).

Woods, W. A. 1973. An experimental parsing system for transition network grammars. In R. Rustin (Ed.), *Natural language processing*. New York: Algorithmics Press.

Woods, W. A. 1975. What's in a link: Foundations for semantic networks. In D. G. Bobrow and A. Collins (Eds.), *Representation and understanding: Studies in cognitive science*. New York: Academic Press.

Woods, W. A. 1977. Lunar rocks in natural English: Explorations in natural language question answering. In A. Zampoli (Ed.), *Linguistic structures processing*. New York: Elsevier North-Holland.

Woods, W. A. 1978. Semantics and quantification in natural language question answering. In M. Yovitz (Ed.), *Advances in computers* (vol. 17). New York: Academic Press, (reprinted in RNLP).

Woods, W. A. 1980. Cascaded ATN grammars. *AJCL* 6(1):1–12.

Wu, S. D., and Wysk, R. A. 1987. MPECS—An intelligent flexible machining cell controller. *Proceedings of the Second European Simulation Multiconference*, Vienna, Austria, 71–76.

Xerox Learning Research Group. 1981. The Smalltalk-80 System. *BYTE Magazine*, 36–47.

Yachida, M. 1985. 3—D data acquisition by multiple views. *Proceedings of the Third International Symposium on Robotics Research*, Gouvieux, France (Cambridge, Mass.: MIT Press).

Yachida, M., Kitamura, Y., and Kimachi, M. 1986. Trinocular vision: New approach for correspondence problem. *Proceedings of the Eighth International Conference on Pattern Recognition*, Paris, 1041–1044.

Yuille, A. L., and Poggio, T. 1984. Fingerprint theorems. *Proceedings of the National Conference on Artificial Intelligence*, Austin, Tex., 362–365.

Yuille, A. L., and Poggio, T. 1986. Scaling theorems for zero crossings. *IEEE Pattern Analysis and Machine Intelligence* PAMI–8(1):15–25.

Zadeh, L. A. 1979. A theory of approximate reasoning. In J. E. Hayes, D. Michie, and L. I. Mikulich (Eds.), *Machine Intelligence 9*. Chichester, England: Ellis Horwood Ltd., 149–195.

Zave, P. 1982. An operational approach to requirements specification for embedded systems. *IEEE Transactions on Software Engineering* SE-9(3): 250–269.

Zave, P. 1984. The operational versus the conventional approach to software development. *Communications of the ACM* 27:2:104–118.

Zave, P., and Yeh, R. T. 1986. Executable requirements for embedded systems. In N. Gehani and A. D. McGettrick (Eds.), *Software specification techniques*. Reading, MA: Addison-Wesley, 341–360.

Zeigler, B. P. 1986. System knowledge: A definition and its implications. In M. S. Elzas, T. I. Oren, and B. P. Zeigler (Eds.), *Modelling and methodology in the artificial intelligence era*. B.V. (North-Holland): Elsevier Science Publishers, 15–17.

Zucker, S. W. 1976. Region growing: Childhood and adolescence. *Computer Graphics and Image Processing* 5:382–399.

Zucker, S. W. 1983. Cooperative grouping and early orientation selection. In O. J. Braddick and A. C. Sleigh (Eds.), *Physical and biological processing of images*. New York: Springer-Verlag, 326–334.

Zucker, S. W., Hummel, R. A., and Rosenfeld, A. 1977. An application of relaxation labeling to line and curve enhancement. *IEEE Transactions on Computers* C-26:4:394–403.

Cumulative Indexes

NAME INDEX FOR VOLUMES I, II, III, AND IV

SUBJECT INDEX FOR VOLUMES I, II, III, AND IV

Propositional knowledge representation.

Frequency domain contrasted with the spatial domain, III:206

FRL-0, I:221

Front end in numerical simulation model ECO, IV:459–462
  user transaction in, IV:459

Full-width search, I:103

FUNARG, II:46

Function, I:165, II:34
  in the Boyer-Moore Theorem Prover, III:104
  in logic, I:165, II:88–89, III:91

Functional Description Compiler, II:317

Functional distribution, IV:86

Functional relationships, II:245–246

Functional representation of devices, IV:406–409
  knowledge compilation in, IV:408–409
  representation in, IV:407–408

Functionally accurate cooperation
  inconsistent/incorrect information and, IV:118–119, 121
  versus negotiation, IV:122
  open systems, IV:120–121
  problem solving structure, IV:117–118

FUZZY, II:13
  control structures in, II:53–55
  data structures in, II:43
  pattern matching in, II:63–64

Fuzzy automata, III:380

Fuzzy logic, and uncertainty, IV:172

Fuzzy set, II:13

G set (of most general hypotheses), III:386, 424, 426

Game tree, I:25, 43–45, 84
  random, I:92
  totally dependent, I:92
  uniform, I:91–93

Game-tree search, I:84–108, III:339–342. See also Search algorithms; AND/OR tree.
  alpha-beta, I:88–93, 94, 101
  backed-up values, I:87
  dead position, I:87, 99
  forward, I:104
  horizon effect, I:99
  killer heuristic, I:102
  live position, I:87
  method of analogies, I:104

minimax, I:84–87, 88, 90, 91, 94, 98, III:339–342, 465

negmax, I:86–87, 89

plausible-move generation, I:104

quiescence, I:99–100, 103

refutation move, I:102

secondary search, I:100

static evaluation function, I:87, 96–97, 100

tapered forward, I:104

Games, I:153. See also Puzzles.
  backgammon, I:103
  in Intelligent computer-assisted instruction II:234, 252, 254, 261–266
  checkers, I:26, 43, 44, 95, 97, III:332–333, 339–344, 457–464
  chess, I:6, 22, 23, 26, 43, 94–108, 205, 334, 351, II:4, 72, III:11
  Eleusis, III:416–419
  Go, I:103
  Hearts, III:351
  poker, III:331, 465–474
  tic-tac-toe, I:43, 94
  voice chess, I:328, 334, 344

Garbage collection, II:4, 18

GASP, IV:424

General Problem Solver (GPS), I:113–118, 129, 135, 169, 196, II:4, 47, 79, III:3, 7, 11–21. See also Means-ends analysis.

General Space Planner, I:202–203

General Syntactic Processor (GSP), I:268–272

General-to-specific ordering, III:385

Generality vs. power, I:335, IV:158–159

Generality of rules for molecular processes, II:120

Generalization
  in ACT, III:54
  in the Boyer-Moore theorem Prover, III:108
  in learning programs, III:360, 365–368, 385
  response, III:28–35
  stimulus, III:28–35

Generalization methods
  by adding options, III:366, 411, 444, 502
  by climbing concept tree, III:395, 487, 491
  by curve-fitting, III:367, 376–380, 401–405, 457
  by dependency analysis, III:480, 492
  by disjunction, III:366–367, 397
  by dropping conditions, III:366, 385, 391,

in line finding, III:168–172
reduction by smoothing, III:213–215
in region segmentation, III:147–154, 225, IV:524
in speech signal, I:343
in student model, II:260
in training instances, III:362–363, 370, 396–397, 429, 432, 490
in vehicle monitoring, IV:55
Nonalgorithmic procedures, II:144
Noncausal resolution rule, IV:278–281
deductive tableau, IV:279
illustration of use of, IV:279–280
and program synthesis, IV:278–279
Nondeterminism. See Parsing.
Nonmonotonic reasoning, II:74–75, III:114–119
Nonresolution theorem proving, III:94–102.
See also Natural deduction.
Nonsense syllables, III:28
Nonterminal symbols of a grammar, I:239, III:495
Nontutorial CAI, II:291–294
Noun phrases, logical form, IV:209–210
NP-complete problems, I:68, 69
Nuclear-magnetic resonance (NMR) spectroscopy, II:122
NUDGE, I:221
Numerical problems, II:143
Numerical simulation, IV:422–423, 424–425
integration of knowledge issue, IV:510–511
limitations of, IV:424–425
tools for, IV:511–512

Object-centered representation, in vision, III:272, in expert systems, IV:162, 163, 165, 167, 191
Object-oriented languages,
in expert systems, IV:162, 163, 165, 167, 191
for simulation, IV:425
for specification, IV:257–258
Object-oriented programming, inferences in, IV:170
Object recognition in computer vision, IV:558–560
bin-picking problem, IV:559
industrial vision systems, III:301–305
interpretation tree in, IV:558–559

three-dimensional object recognition, IV:559
Objects
classes, IV:165
instances, IV:165
Obligatory transformation in a grammar, I:247
Ocean surveillance, HASP, IV:36–49
Oil well drilling, Dipmeter Advisor System, IV:151–152
ONCOCIN, II:180, IV:157
Ontological primitives, IV:334
See also Semantic primitives.
ONYX, IV:441–444
Opacity, III:252
of knowledge, II:82, 89–90
of reasoning, II:230
Open sets, II:240
Open systems, functionally accurate cooperation, IV:120–121
Open world, II:240
Open-ended problems, IV:157
Openings/closings, in mathematical morphology, IV:544–545
Operationalization methods, III:333, 346, 350–359
approximation, III:355
case analysis, III:354
expanding definitions, III:354
expressing in common terms, III:355
finding necessary and sufficient conditions, III:351
generate-and-test, III:351
heuristic search, III:351
intersection search, III:354
partial matching, III:355
pigeonhole principle, III:351
recognizing known concepts, III:355
simplification, III:355
taxonomy of, III:358
Operator schemata, I:33
Operators, in problem solving, I:22, 32, 36, 74, 110, 113, 119, 123, 128, 135
Operators, in vision
Hueckel, III:218–220
interest, III:250
Laplacian, III:211–212, 218, 264
noise immunity of, III:214, 217
Roberts cross, III:216
Sobel, III:217
windows, III:217
OPGEN, IV:157